9th Edition

D1296384

The Definitive Guide for Novice to Expert

The ABCs of RELOADING

Edited by C. Rodney James

Published by

Gun Digest® Books, an imprint of F+W Media, Inc.
Krause Publications • 700 East State Street • Iola, WI 54990-0001
715-445-2214 • 888-457-2873
www.krausebooks.com

To order books or other products call toll-free 1-800-258-0929
or visit us online at www.krausebooks.com, www.gundigeststore.com
or www.Shop.Collect.com

Library of Congress Control Number: 2010924664

ISBN-13: 978-1-4402-1396-0
ISBN-10: 1-4402-1396-8

Cover Design by Tom Nelsen
Designed by Kara Grundman
Edited by Dan Shideler

Printed in the United States of America

About the Author

C. RODNEY JAMES grew up in Columbus, Ohio, in an academic family. He got the gun bug from his mother's father. An example of about everything that goes bang passed through his hands at one time or another.

At age fifteen, an accident with home-made explosives cost Rodney his hands. Nevertheless he received a doctorate in mass communication studies from The Ohio State University. He has written and produced nontheatrical films and taught courses in film and television at Concordia University in Montréal.

In his "other life" Rodney read everything he could about firearms and has been a shooter and reloader for more than forty years. He has published in this field since 1980. Rodney's technical and historical articles have appeared in *Gun Digest, Handloader's Digest, Guns Illustrated, Shooter's Bible, Guns Magazine and AFTE Journal*, the publication of the Association of Firearm and Tool Mark Examiners. He wrote the 6th Edition of this book.

As an independent firearms examiner Rodney is a member of the International Wound Ballistics Association and the Society for the Scientific Detection of Crime. Recent publications include, *The Gun Digest Book of the .22 Rifle* and a forensic novel, *Original Cyn: A Love Story... with Guns.*

Photo: Ron Gregg

Acknowledgments

A NUMBER OF people helped in the preparation of this book and should receive credit for their efforts. At the top of the list is Mary McGavick, editor and critic who read it all; Wanda Rucker for computer services; Allan Jones (retired); engineer Brett Olin from CCI; Dave Davison of CH/4D; Chris Hodgdon, of Hodgdon Powder; Ben Amonette at Alliant; Mike Kinn and Tim Brant at Federal; Paul Szabo from Winchester; Roger Weir; Bob Williams; Terry Paul at SharpShootR; and Jonathan Doege at Shooter Solutions. For others who have helped whose names I have forgotten, my thanks and apologies.

Many thanks to Tim Jensen for his drawings.

About the Cover

MEC'S 600 JR., their most popular model and the world's top-selling shotshell reloader, has been redesigned to include popular features found on their more expensive models. The MEC 600 Jr. Mark 5 can load eight to 10 boxes per hour, and can be upgraded with the 285 CA primer feed, which eliminates the need to handle each primer individually. Best of all, the price won't shoot anyone's budget. The press is adjustable for 3" shells, and is available in 10, 12 16, 20, 28 gauge and .410 bore. Die sets are available in all gauges.

Novice and seasoned gunners will appreciate these new features along with the time-tested excellence this single-stage reloader has provided over the years with quick, simple operation and a minimum of effort.

For more information, contact
Mayville Engineering Co. Inc.
715 South Street
Mayville, WI 53050
920-387-4500 • www.mayvl.com

3

Contents

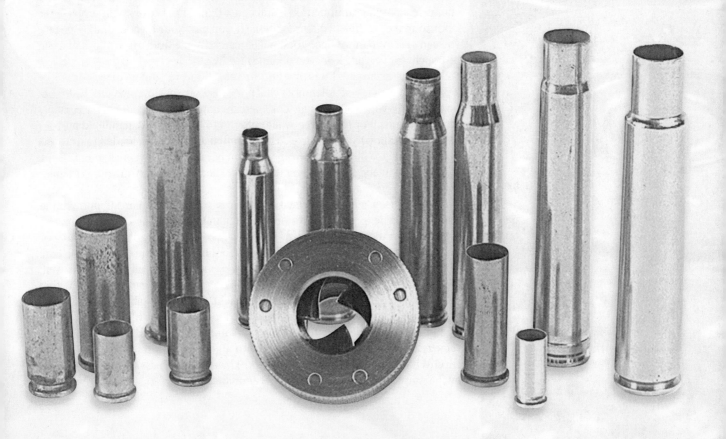

Introduction

THERE ARE AT least five good reasons for reloading. First is economy. Someone who has come to enjoy the sport of shooting soon discovers that the cost of factory ammunition has become almost prohibitive. A pleasant afternoon of target shooting, banging through a half dozen boxes of cartridges or more, can run past the hundred dollar mark if you use anything other than 22 rimfires. By reloading brass centerfire cartridge cases with commercially available bullets, primers and smokeless powder you can reduce this cost by better than 60% over commercial ammunition. Even if empty cases are purchased new, the savings over commercially-made ammunition is still better than 25%, because you supplied the labor to make the finished ammunition. If you cast your own lead-alloy bullets, you can save even more since good bullets can be made from scrap alloys that can be bought for very little or even obtained for free.

Second is accuracy. Firearms and ammunition are standardized– more or less — with a range of tolerances which means that your average gun will function properly with your average commercial ammunition, producing acceptably accurate results. For those who want better than "acceptable," handloading your ammunition allows you to make custom-crafted ammunition, loaded to draw the maximum degree of accuracy from your gun because the powders and bullets are selected by you and tested by you to produce the best accuracy in your particular gun.

A third reason might be termed "usefulness." While commercial ammunition may be available in perhaps two or three loadings, handloaded ammunition can extend this to more than a dozen. Low-power cast-bullet loads can be made for short-range practice, allowing economical shooting with low noise and low recoil. This means not only less wear and tear on your gun, but on yourself as well. Heavy hunting loads can be fabricated for taking the largest game possible within the limits of a particular rifle or handgun. Light, flat-shooting bullets, designed to expand rapidly on small game, can be loaded to turn a "deer rifle" into a varmint rifle offering extended use for spring and summer varmint shooting. Reduced-velocity loads can turn a varmint rifle into a good small game rifle that will kill effectively without destroying edible meat. Thus the usefulness of a gun is doubled by the simple expedient of altering the ammunition.

Necessity, that mother of invention, is a fourth reason to reload. There are any number of older guns, both foreign and domestic, for which commercial ammunition is simply not available. Cartridge cases may be formed by reshaping and trimming from similar cartridge cases that have the same size head and a similar size body. In some instances the cartridge cases you need may be commercially available, but the commercial loadings are not suitable for your gun which, because of its age, may require a lighter load or one of black instead of smokeless powder.

A final reason is added enjoyment. Mastering a craft that will improve your shooting is an extension of the shooting sport. You will gain a better understanding of the dynamics involved in the shooting process. Good shooting is far more than simply good "aiming." Good aim and proper shooting technique are necessary for hitting what you shoot at, but you will score far more hits if you have a clear understanding of the ammunition in your gun and what it is and is not capable of doing and why.

Who should reload? This is a question firearms writers hear fairly often. It's not for everyone. The casual shooter, satisfied with rimfire ammunition performance, the person who targets his gun once or twice a year, the person with no time for hobbies, will find little use for this avocation. Then there are those who may wish to join the reloading clan, but for reasons of safety would be best advised not to. This category includes those persons who persist in drinking or smoking while reloading, the chronically careless, the forgetful and accident prone, and those given to dangerous experimentation. Reloading is far safer than driving a car, but you have to pay attention to what you are doing. Reloading is as safe or as dangerous; as economical or expensive; as simple or complicated as YOU make it.

How do you get started? As an educator facing eager students champing at the bit to get going with the "hands on" part, I began my classes with an apologetic: "Yes, I applaud your enthusiasm, but I really think you should know a little something about what you are you are going to be doing." Those who don't have a bad habit of breaking equipment, getting poor results and having no clue as to why the above happened. You can't learn from your mistakes unless you can figure out what they were and why they happened. To put it another way — some people live and learn, others just live, but never as long or as happily.

What kinds of guns are we loading for? This book is designed basically for shooters of modern guns designed for metallic cartridges using smokeless powder. With the increase in interest the shooting of vintage guns, with light smokeless loads, blackpowder and blackpowder substitutes, a chapter has been added on this subject. The bibliographic material in Chapter 12 will direct the reloader to what is considered advanced reloading. These resources will touch on loading for black powder guns, early smokeless guns which may not be up to modern loads or may have chamber and bore dimensions different from those of current manufacture. This book is not a manual containing loading data, but an overview of the reloading process — to cover those things critical to the craft, but not found in loading manuals.

Before beginning any activity, a solid foundation is needed to build upon, and reloading is no different.

Safety First, Last & Always

WHAT IS A MODERN GUN?

WHEN I WAS GROWING up in the 50's and 60's, cartridge boxes carried the warning that "these loadings are for modern arms in good condition." Contemporary loading manuals did too. But what is a modern gun? Like any other arbitrary definition, it has fuzzy edges. Modern gun designs (such as modern-looking double-action revolvers) came into being in the late 1880's. Modern semiautomatic pistols were on the market by 1900. Bolt-action, 30-caliber rifles intended for high pressure (40,000 to 60,000 psi) smokeless powder ammunition were in general military use by 1895. Roughly speaking, the era of modern gun making begins around 1886-1900.

The real issue is whether the gun for which you wish to reload can take the pressures of modern ammunition. For instance, a solidly-built, tightly-locking Winchester low-wall, single shot or Stevens target rifle from the last century can be safely used with modern, high-velocity 22 Long Rifle ammunition. To use such ammunition in a light revolver or pistol from the same era will soon destroy it. Even guns made as recently as the 1920's

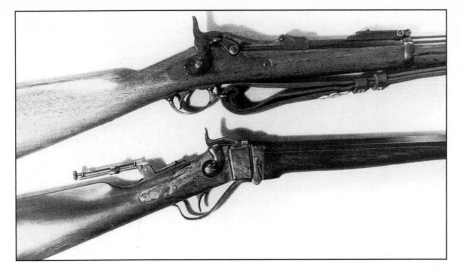

Reproduction 1874 Sharps rifle made of modern steel (4140 for the receiver and 1195 for the barrel). It is capable of handling modern high-pressure 45-70 loadings to 28,000 psi. Allin ("trap door") 45-70 Springfield (top) was made in 1888. The receiver is mild steel, case-hardened. The barrel is mild "decar-bonized" steel. Its maximum pressure rating, at the time of manufacture, was 25,000 psi. It is not a modern gun and must be loaded accordingly.

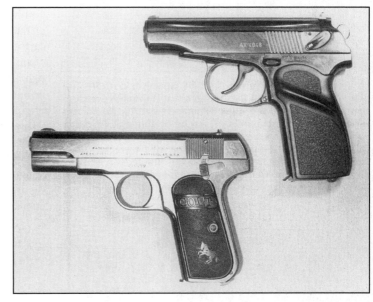

A 94-year-old 32 ACP Colt Model 1903 pocket pistol *(bottom)* and a Cold-War-era 9mm Makarov both qualify as "modern guns."

may not be safe with the high pressures generated by the high velocity loadings. The 22 LR Reising automatic pistol of that period had a breech block with very thin rails which regularly split on the first firing of a high speed round. These guns should not be fired. Early Colt and High Standard semi-auto pistols were intended for standard velocity ammunition only and high speed ammo will batter them into uselessness.

While a modern appearing revolver such as the M-1889 Colt Navy double-action revolver looks very like the 38 Special police models that have been in use for 70 years and counting, the M-89 was made for the 38 Long Colt black-powder cartridge. Some of these early guns will chamber a contemporary smokeless powder 38 Special cartridge. However, to fire such a loading in one of these old Colts is to court disaster.

Some early smokeless powder guns were by no means as strong as later models chambered for the same smokeless-powder cartridge. The soft steel on U.S. Krag rifles — Models 1892-1896 — was not up to the pressure of some heavy smokeless-powder loadings and began to develop cracks

around the locking lug on the bolt after prolonged use. Krag and early 1903 Springfield rifles were inspected "by eye," the proper color indicating proper heat treatment of barrel and receiver steel. When Springfield receivers started failing with higher pressure loadings, the heat treatment process was improved. This occurred at serial number 800,000.

The Colt Single Action Army revolver (Model 1873) is still being made. The original was a black powder gun. The steel was later improved and some internal redesigning was done, making it safe for smokeless loadings. Colt has advised that guns with serial numbers below 160,000 are for black powder only! Except for serial numbers and a few minor details neither the 03 Springfield nor the Colt SAA has changed in external appearance since its introduction.

Early 38 Colt semiautomatic pistols (Models 1900, 1902, 1903) are chambered for the 38 Colt Automatic cartridge, no longer manufactured. The same cartridge, in terms of dimensions, is on the market as the 38 Super Auto. This is the old 38 Auto with a much heavier charge of powder. It is poison for the older guns.

The original Model 1895 Winchester lever-action rifle was

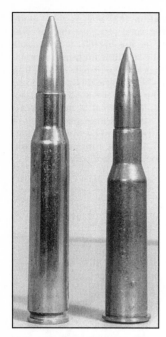

U.S. standard 30-06 Springfield cartridge (left) and Russian 7.62 X 54mm Mosin rifle cartridge are not compatible. Some Russian rifles have had chambers recut to take the 06. The smaller-diameter 30-06 has plenty of room to swell and burst in the oversize Russian chamber.

30-06 Springfield (left) and 8mm Mauser rounds are close enough in size that the Mauser can be fired in a 30-06 chamber. This will happen ONCE! The gun will be wrecked along with the shooter's face by the tremendous pressures generated by an oversize bullet.

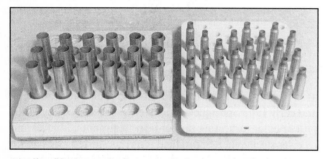

Loading blocks can be home-made from wood as is the one on the left or of moulded plastic, on the right. Loading blocks are not merely a convenience, they are a necessity to keep you from double charging a cartridge case.

chambered for the Springfield 30-06 cartridge. For some reason this rifle got a reputation as having an action that was stronger than the Springfield when in fact it was weaker.

Older guns can be fired quite safely if you are aware of their limitations and don't try for "improved" performance.

Determining what is and is not a "modern" gun in terms of its strength falls under the COIK limitation. COIK is an acronym that stands for Clear Only If Known. Therefore, defining what is a safe "modern" gun at times requires some knowledge beyond the appearance and the date it was introduced. Thus if the gun you are planning on reloading for is questionable in any way regarding the caliber, the cartridge

it is intended for, its age and/or mechanical condition, have it checked by a competent gunsmith – and if you don't like the first answer, a second opinion won't hurt.

Occasionally what might be termed "nightmare guns" turn up on the used market. These are standard rifles, often surplus military weapons, which some amateur gunsmith has attempted to rework into a caliber different from the one it was originally intended to fire. The 6.5mm and 7.7mm Japanese Arisaka and the 7.62mm Russian Mosin Nagant rifles have been converted to take the 30-06 Springfield cartridge. Some were only half converted — the chamber being recut, the barrel left untouched. In the case of the 6.5 rifle, 30 caliber bullets were squeezed down to 25 caliber in the barrel, creating tremendous pressures. Some of these rifles, amazingly, held together for a while. The Russian rifle was never intended to take the pressures of the 30-06 and no reworking of the chamber can replace metal at the rear of the chamber, which is considerably oversize for the 30-06 cartridge. Case swelling and eventual ruptures are a matter of time. There is no way such a butchered rifle can be made right short of rebarreling. Even then the new caliber should be one which will not give pressures greater than that of the original cartridge. If you plan to shoot and reload for a centerfire rifle, know what you have — don't guess! If, on firing some commercial ammunition, there is any sign of trouble, stop right there. What is a trouble sign? The best quick and easy means is to look at the fired cartridge case. If it looks significantly different from an unfired one — swollen or misshapen, with a flattened or pierced primer – take the rifle and case to a good gunsmith for an analysis.

THE LOADING PROCESS

The loading process is not terribly complicated, though it does involve a number of steps. Each step is there for a reason. It may not be apparent to the beginner, at the outset, why those steps are there. This often seems to be a good excuse to take a short cut and eliminate a particular step. This author was once one of those people. He started reloading cases in what he thought was a very safe manner. Each cartridge case was sized and decapped, just as this book tells you to do. Then he inserted a new primer, also according to the manual. He carefully weighed his powder charge on a good scale (he was assembling precision ammunition) and he even weighed his bullets to make sure there was no more than +/- half a grain in weight difference. After weighing the powder charge to an accuracy level of less than one tenth of a grain difference, he put it directly in the case and immediately seated the bullet.

Everything worked fine with this system until the day he was in the process of loading and someone came to the door. He left a cartridge case sitting on the loading bench. It was charged with a small amount of fast burning powder that disappeared in the dark bottom of the cartridge case. After dealing with the visitor, he returned to the bench to continue loading. He picked up where he thought he'd left off. He carefully measured out a charge of powder and fun-

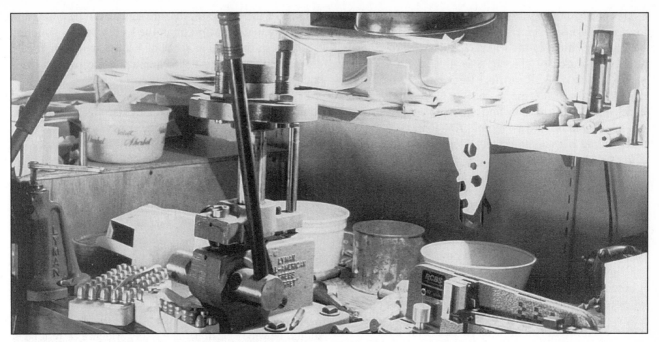

Straight from the chamber of horrors. Before your loading bench looks like this, it's time to clean up and get organized or you will make mistakes and/or waste a lot of time puzzling over what's really in those various bins and boxes.

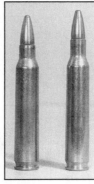

All are ready to shoot, except the one in the middle is a 222 Magnum and the rest are 223. The 223 *(left)* has a shorter neck than the 222 Magnum. If you plan to load similar calibers, extra caution is needed to keep the cases, loaded ammunition and, in some instances, bullets separate.

neled it in the case. He was wary of accidentally getting two charges in one case so he immediately seated a bullet and added the finished cartridge to the box he had been filling.

Two charges is exactly what he loaded! Every instruction manual will warn you not to do this. Use a loading block. Loading block? A small, molded-plastic tray that holds cartridge cases – heads down. They cost a couple of bucks, or you can make your own by boring proper sized holes through a piece of plank and gluing a flat bottom on it. A loading block is a safety device allowing the reloader a second chance to inspect charged cartridges before seating a bullet, because there might be the slight possibility that one of those cartridges got too much powder.

The author discovered his error the following weekend while target shooting. The double-charged case wrecked a nice old Springfield, the purchase price of which would have bought an amazing number of loading blocks. The author was very lucky, because the people who had designed and manufactured that Springfield built in some good safety features. These saved his eyesight. Many reloaders owe a lot to

those who designed and built their guns — people who were smarter than they are.

Everybody who loads will throw double charges. The careful ones won't do it very often and they will catch their mistakes before they are fired. Once is all it takes to ruin a gun. Once is all it takes to ruin your face, eyesight, hearing, and if you are really unlucky, to kill you.

Follow the steps listed in the reloading manuals – all of them in the proper order. They are there for a good reason.

Many reloading accidents stem from simple carelessness – steps avoided, shortcuts taken, not paying attention to your work. Speed, or, more properly, haste can lead to serious mistakes.

One of the more interesting adventures of this sort concerned a reloader who dropped a jacketed bullet he was about to seat. It landed on a deep-pile shag rug. He patted around, found the bullet, slipped it into the case mouth and rammed it home. There followed a violent explosion — pieces of metal sprayed about the room, some of which had to be extracted from him! What happened?!

This one had to be solved by Allen Jones (an experienced forensic firearms examiner). Traces of lead with faint copper plating were found in the seating die. This led to a hands-and-knees search of the rug area around the reloading bench. A second 22 LR cartridge turned up in the shag. The reloader had mistaken the first one for his dropped jacketed bullet. The 22LR was shiny, and about the same size and the rim just caught on the case mouth. Kaboom!

Reloading is a solitary activity. Don't try to watch television or chat with friends while you reload. A radio may be played, but softly. Reloading is a simple task, but one requiring concentration and paying attention to details. Close the door to the room where you reload to keep others out, especially children. If there's an interruption, stop at the completion of an operation and then deal with whatever it is. If this isn't possible back up one step and do it over. Because it is repetitive, reloading can become routine and boring. When it becomes boring is the time to take a break. Never reload when you are tired or ill; this dulls your concentration.

HANDLING MATERIALS SAFELY

My teachers told me — neatness counts. I wasn't very neat and it never bothered me — too much. In reloading it will be your gun that will tell you, not your teacher. A cluttered, messy reloading area leads to more mistakes. Primers not put away get mixed with the next batch that may be different. Cartridge cases that are similar can be mixed and the wrong one can wind up in the loading press, jamming it, or, worse, dropped in a box of loaded ammunition of a different caliber. Mismatched ammunition can wreck guns and shooters.

Primers are perhaps the most potentially dangerous components of the reloading hobby. They come packaged in little packets of one hundred, separated in rows or in individual pockets in a plastic holder. There is a very good reason for this. While modern primers are well sealed there is always the possibility that minute amounts of priming compound can coat an exposed surface of a primer and can flake off as dust. If primers are dumped into a can or bottle this dust can be detonated, followed by all the primers in that can or bottle, in something approaching 25/1000 of a second. That's faster than most people can let go of a can or bottle. Primers should never be dumped more than one hundred at a time and this should be done only in a plastic primer tray. Shaking a can or bottle of primers is not merely tempting fate, but telling fate to go to hell. Primer trays should be wiped clean if there is any evidence of residue in them.

The more advanced loading tools are often equipped with automatic primer feeding devices. The primer tubes will occasionally jam. Dealing with such a jam is a delicate process. All primers that can be removed should be taken out

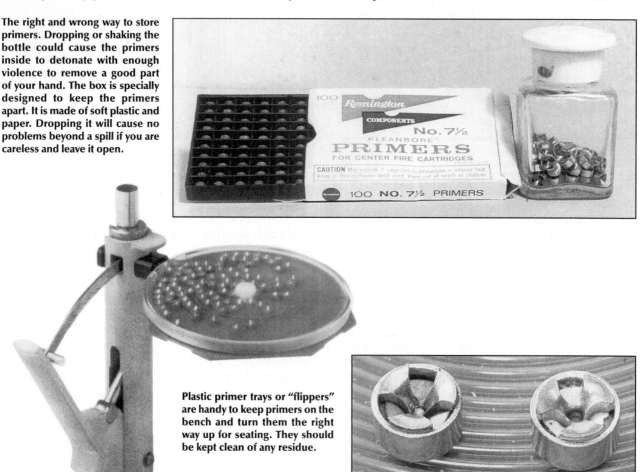

The right and wrong way to store primers. Dropping or shaking the bottle could cause the primers inside to detonate with enough violence to remove a good part of your hand. The box is specially designed to keep the primers apart. It is made of soft plastic and paper. Dropping it will cause no problems beyond a spill if you are careless and leave it open.

Plastic primer trays or "flippers" are handy to keep primers on the bench and turn them the right way up for seating. They should be kept clean of any residue.

Smokeless powder and the newer BP substitutes are safer to store or handle than many common household products that are equally or more inflammable! Smokeless powder is highly inflammable, but less so than gasoline, petroleum-based cleaning fluids and similar household items.

The tall thin tube in the center rear of this progressive reloading press is filled with a stack of primers. If the feeding mechanism jams, the stack can explode if you do not clear it properly. If a jam occurs read the manual and if in doubt, call the manufacturer for assistance.

(Below) **Powder should be stored in the original container. If for some reason this cannot be done, use a similar container and mark it clearly as to the contents. It is a good idea to mark the can with the date of storage.**

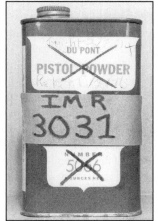

before attempting to clear a jam. You don't want a stack to blow! Problems with feeders are best dealt with via a call or email to the manufacturer.

Safety glasses are a good idea, particularly when loading using an automatic primer feeder. Aeronautical Engineer Edward Murphy came up with a very good set of rules known as "Murphy's Laws" regarding how and why things

fail, concluding that they fail at the worst possible time — airplanes when they are flying, guns when they are being fired, primer feeders when they are packed full of primers.

Modern smokeless powder is far safer to handle than gasoline or other inflammable solvents, acids or caustic substances such as lye-based drain cleaners. Powder can, however, be mishandled and this leads to trouble. Powder left in a measure or unmarked container can lead to guessing regarding what it is and a wrong guess can be disastrous. Powder should always be kept in the original container. If for some reason that container is unusable, the powder should be put into a suitable container — preferably a can or plastic bottle, not a glass jar — and clearly labeled with a label that will not come off, that covers up whatever the original label was, and will not fade or otherwise become unreadable. Powders should never be mixed. This can happen if some is left in a measure or dispensing container and a different powder is poured on top. Such contaminated powder is worthless and should be discarded. Likewise, powders that are in unlabeled containers, from unknown sources, are not worth keeping. Powders that "look like _____" should be considered as "unknown" and discarded. It's not worth risking your gun, let alone your eyesight, hearing and, yes, your life to experiment for the sake of saving a few dollars of material. Every so often someone may decide to try to grind up a coarse military powder to change its structure to one suitable for reloading. This will not work and is VERY dangerous.

Smokeless powder will deteriorate over time; heat and dampness speed this process. If a can of opened powder has a strong vinegar smell and/or appears to contain a rust-colored dust, it has gone by and should be disposed of in a safe manner.

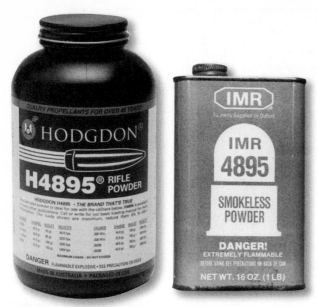

Not the same powder, although the number is identical. Read the reference section for further information and <u>never</u> guess about the burning characteristics of a powder.

Disposing of such powder is easy but should be done sensibly. It can be burned outside, on open ground, in small amounts — no more than a couple of tablespoons at a time. Far easier is to scatter it on your lawn or flower bed (it adds nitrogen). It will break down in the weather rather quickly. Unexploded primers that have been damaged are best buried after soaking in a lye solution. If for some reason you have a large number (we're talking thousands) check with the EPA.

Failure to recognize what sort of powder you are dealing with can have disastrous consequences. Recently, a would-be black powder shooter bought a new-made black powder revolver. The dealer at the gun show didn't have any black powder for sale, advising the buyer to come by his shop the following week where he had plenty. The buyer really wanted to try out his new gun that weekend. A helpful neighbor allowed as how he had some old black powder shotgun shells. These could be broken down, the powder extracted and used. They did that. There was powder in the shells, it was black in color. Two heads may be better than one, so long as the cooperative effort is not simply a pooling of ignorance. When the gun was fired, the charge blew off the top strap, blew out the chamber being fired and the chamber on either side. Fortunately no one was seriously injured. A basic ignorance was the fault. With very few exceptions all gunpowder is colored black by a graphite coating including the fast-burning smokeless shotgun powder that was contained in the neighbor's shells. Never guess about powder.

Related accidents with ignorance at their root have been caused by reloaders loading bullets into blank cartridges. Blanks are loaded with a very fast burning type of powder that will produce a loud report by opening up the crimp on the mouth of a brass cartridge and blowing out a small cardboard wad. If a bullet is loaded on top of such powder, rather than being accelerated down the barrel, the powder burn is so rapid that the bullet has no more than begun to move before the pressure has jumped to a catastrophically high level and the bullet acts in the manner of a plug in a closed container with an explosion inside – a bomb. The author uses steel hooks because he no longer has hands. This is because he was holding a bomb when it exploded. No one wants to be near a bomb when it explodes.

Recognizing powder, as has been pointed out, is easiest when it is in clearly marked containers. There is, however, an additional point to be made here. Powders are identified by manufacturer, trade name and often numbers. There are powders on the market which are very similar but not the same and can be confused, if the reloader does not have a clear understanding of what he is dealing with. The IMR Powder Company (now owned by Hodgdon) makes a powder called IMR 4831 (this was formerly made by DuPont). The Hodgdon Powder Company produces a similar powder called 4831 and is labeled H4831. The IMR powder is much faster burning than the Hodgdon powder and loading data for H4831 would be very dangerous to use with the IMR powder of the corresponding number. To confuse things a little more, there is an IMR powder — IMR 4895 – and a Hodgdon H4895. While these powders are very similar in terms of their burning characteristics, their loading data in not really interchangeable.

LOADING DATA AND LOADING MANUALS

The typical loading manual provides loading data for individual cartridges using a variety of powders and bullets that have been tested and found to be suitable for that particular cartridge. The powder types and charges listed for each cartridge are given as "starting loads" and "maximum loads." Often there will be an "accuracy load" listed that performed particularly well in the firearm that was used for the tests conducted by the publisher of the manual. This data is the result of rigorous testing over long periods of time involving the efforts of a number of engineers and technicians using the latest and most sophisticated test equipment available. This is good for shooters who reload, because it keeps them safe from accidentally making dangerous overloads. This loading data brackets the lowest safe pressure and velocity loads up to the highest. Working within this range, the reloader can work up a loading that performs best in his gun.

The semi-experienced reloader is occasionally tempted to go beyond the bounds of whatever loading guide he is using and try something else. This is fine if the "something else" is to avail himself of more loading books containing tried and proven data and not simply guessing on the basis of, "what if I tried fifty-two grains of _____?" The dangers of exceeding the upper limits of various loadings should, by now, be clear to the reader. There is, though, an appar-

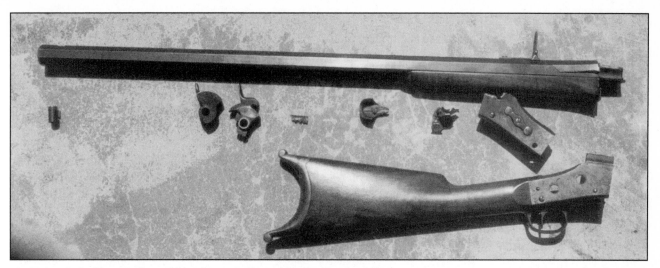

The sad end of a fine old rifle–accidentally overloaded with a double charge. *(Photo courtesy of Tom Trevor)*

ent danger from going in the opposite direction. A certain amount of press has been given to a phenomenon known as "detonation." This involves the generation of excessively high pressures by reduced loads of slow-burning powders – loadings below those recommended in data contained in reloading manuals. There is considerable controversy over whether this phenomenon is in fact "real." Some powder manufacturers have been unable to generate this phenomenon under test conditions. Nevertheless, events of this sort have been reported by reloaders. This author's position is: why take a chance in wrecking your gun and perhaps part of your body? Don't experiment. Never guess at the burning characteristics of a powder or exceed the recommended loadings on either end of the loadings recommended in the manuals.

OLD MANUALS

Books are wonderful things. They contain all sorts of fascinating information. Old gun and ammunition books are among the treasures that fill gun show tables. These provide useful insights into the past. As a firearms writer such books are important tools of my trade. Old loading manuals are there with everything else.

The inexperienced and semi-experienced reloader should be warned of the dangers in attempting to use such data. A vintage Lyman reloading book may list something on the order of: "One of Elmer Keith's favorite loads for the 45-70 was 53 grains of Dupont XYZ smokeless for his elk rifle." And you might think that if it was good enough for the great Elmer it's certainly good enough for me. Here's what the manual doesn't tell you. What (in fact) was the rifle Keith was loading for? A trapdoor Springfield or a M-1886 Winchester with a nickel-steel barrel and a much stronger action?

Another thing the old manual will not tell you is that a particular powder and loading data, while it may have the same name and number as a currently manufactured powder, had different burning characteristics and was (in fact) of a different formulation than the current product. The Laflin & Rand "Unique" powder (mentioned elsewhere in this volume), stored under water in 1899, that is still performing in lab tests as well as it did when it was made, is not quite the same Unique powder marketed today by Alliant.

An experiment on my part with such a Keith load from a 1950's vintage loading manual sounded interesting. What may have been my first mistake was to assume that the loading data was contemporary with the publication of that manual and not simply carried forward from the 1940's, 1930's or even the 1920's editions. Keith generally favored heavy loads that were flat shooters. This particular one for a 45-70 with a 500-grain cast bullet would have almost certainly taken apart a "Trapdoor" Springfield or Remington Rolling Block. I did have the wit to test it in a new-made Shiloh Sharps rifle. According to Wolfgang Droege (who manufactured the gun at that time) proof-load tests to 50,000 psi had been run and the Shiloh had passed with flying colors.

As I recall, I fired two shots. Both produced a cracking report and a recoil I can only describe as "vicious." The buttstock slipped a little on the second shot. It produced a saucer-size bruise on my shoulder that turned a variety of colors over the next two months. The pain was bad enough to curtail my shooting for the remainder of the summer.

On the subject of published loading data there are a couple of final caveats. Old manuals dating from the early 1950's or before were created without the benefits of today's modern pressure-test equipment. Often the weaknesses of particular guns were not known at the time of manufacture or, if they were known, those guns were not being used to an extent great enough to justify their inclusion in the creation of the later loading data. Circumstances alter cases and those weak guns may now be in a larger supply, meeting a larger demand.

Loading data in manuals from the early 1950's and before that, if used with low-strength rifles from the 1870's and '80's, could likely damage those old rifles if not take them apart. There is currently a lot of interest in shooting old cartridge rifles and the new manuals reflect this interest with data developed especially for these older guns.

Then there is the matter of data published in magazines. This is often the work of an individual who has cooked up some handloads he thinks are pretty good. This is an amateur working without the benefits of pressure testing equipment. Magazines publish disclaimers to the effect that any loading data published therein is used at the shooters' own risk. It is indeed.

The weight, composition and fit of the bullet in the barrel are additional factors in the pressure equation. Heavier bullets boost pressures as do those made of harder material. The size of the bullet also plays a role. The tighter the fit of the bullet in the barrel, the greater the force needed to drive it through.

When using modern components, loading problems are usually simple and straightforward, if the reloader keeps in mind that the changing of any component can affect pressure. These include the type of case (military vs. commercial), the type of primer, (pistol vs. rifle vs. the magnum version of either) the make of primer or case and the lengthening and thickening of the mouth of the case, in firing and reloading. This makes for a tighter fit and raises pressures. A final consideration is the capacity of the case. The larger it, is the lower the pressure, all other things being equal.

All these factors must be carefully weighed in the loading game, particularly when working toward maximum pressure/velocity loadings. At this point, particularly with guns of less than the best design and strongest materials, the gap between a safe maximum loading and a destroyed gun can be very close and a slight variation in one of the above-mentioned pressure factors can lead to a case rupture and disaster. The danger is greatest in what might best be termed the area of "advanced reloading." This takes in the obsolete, the foreign and the wildcat or experimental cartridge. In loading these cartridges, the reloader often finds himself in a *terra incognita*, faced with guns whose internal dimensions may vary considerably from book descriptions and with cartridges that are old or of otherwise doubtful quality. Often a gun may not be clearly marked as to the exact caliber. The 11mm Beaumont black powder military cartridge, for instance, can be found in three different lengths and diameters! Rifles chambered for the German 8.15x46 R cartridge were a popular "bring-back" following WW II. This cartridge came in many case shapes and the rifles had bore diameters ranging from .313" to .326", with .318" and .323" being the most common. Guns do turn up that have been rechambered for some cartridge other than the one listed in the books or on the barrel. When in doubt make a chamber cast. The most common problem is that there is often little or no data on loading these cartridges. In such instances even the experienced reloader must proceed with extreme caution.

Firearms/ammunition expert and author Philip Sharpe received many letters during his career as a technical editor and advisor for the *American Rifleman* magazine. By his assessment one of the most dangerous types of reloaders was the "instant expert." This is the person who has read one or perhaps two books on reloading. He has been doing it for a few years and has grown a towering intellect (make that ego) in the process. He has become imbued with an innate savvy of all things firearms related and wants not only to chart new courses in the reloading business, but to share his "discoveries".

This is the person who without the aid of pressure-testing equipment or any form of metallurgical analyses has decided to start experimenting with improved-performance loads – higher velocities, heavier bullets, more pressure. How does he know his gun can take these higher pressures? Because it's a Remington, Winchester, Mauser, whatever. More correctly he has a kind of simple faith that his guns possess hidden powers because those companies make their guns tough enough that they can't be destroyed. This is nonsense. There has yet to be a small arm built that can't be wrecked. Firearms and reloading equipment manufacturers are improving their products to make them safer and easier to use. Nevertheless I will share the recollection of a talented and inventive engineer who made hand-crafted, custom-designed motion picture cameras. When I talked with him, forty years ago, he was in the process of repairing one of his creations after it had suffered abuse at the hands of a supposedly trained cameraman.

"You know," he said, "you can develop and improve upon a product to the point where it is pretty much foolproof. But you can't make it damn-foolproof."

ESSENTIAL RULES

To summarize, here is a list of basic rules drawn from the National Reloading Manufacturers Association.

1. Modern ammunition uses smokeless powder which is more powerful than black powder or any of the black powder substitutes such as Pyrodex.

2. Use a current reloading manual. Follow recommendations exactly; don't substitute components; start with a minimum recommended load.

3. NEVER exceed maximum loads.

4. Understand the basics of what you are doing and why steps are in a particular order.

5. Set up a loading procedure and follow it. Don't vary the sequence of steps.

6. Keep your bench organized and uncluttered; clearly label all components.

7. Stay alert. Don't reload when disturbed, tired or not feeling well.

8. NEVER leave powder in a dispenser without labeling it. Do not leave powder in a dispenser for long periods. Store powder and primers in original containers, in a cool, dry place.

9. NEVER smoke while reloading or expose components to heat, flame or sparks.

10. NEVER eat while handling lead components or cases fouled with lead ammunition residue.

Lead Hazards In the Shooting Sports

by Robert D. Williams, Ph.D.
Director, Division of Toxicology, The Ohio State University Medical Center

LEAD IS AN integral component in the manufacture of ammunition, ranging from a relatively low amount to nearly 100 percent in shot. Lead is also present during bullet casting, reloading, and gun cleaning. Lead interacts with organic matter to produce stable complexes. Specifically, human tissues possess prominent lead-binding characteristics. Thus, with a high degree of accumulation and relatively low turnover in man, concerns over the hazards of lead exposure become apparent in the shooting sports.

Exposure to lead can occur through ingestion, inhalation, and dermal contact. In the general population, the primary route of administration of lead is through ingestion: children eating lead-based paint or drinking water contaminated by lead piping. Individuals involved in shooting sports are exposed to high lead levels through dust inhalation, particularly at indoor and covered outdoor firing ranges, or during bullet casting where inadequate ventilation exists. Although firearm instructors constitute an occupational group at higher risk, studies have demonstrated that even recreational use of small-bore rifles can produce elevated red blood cell lead concentrations and symptomatic toxicity, following a 6-month indoor-shooting season averaging only 70 minutes per week.

Higher air-lead levels have been measured in firing ranges where powder charges were employed relative to ranges where only air guns were used, which in turn were higher than archery ranges. The use of totally-copper-jacketed or solid-copper ammunition has been proposed to decrease shooting range air-lead levels, since most of the airborne lead is vaporized from bullet surfaces.

Natural sources of lead in the atmosphere represent an insignificant risk: providing lead chiefly in its sulfide form, estimated to be half a billionth of one gram per cubic meter of air. Airborne dust from the environment and gases from the earth's crust contribute to the low "background" atmospheric level. Certain areas of the world contain substantially higher than background levels of lead, e.g. cities in industrialized regions where about 98 percent of airborne lead can be traced to the combustion of leaded gasoline. Air-lead levels averaging 660 micrograms/m3, which are over one hundred million times greater than normal environmental levels, have been measured at some indoor firing ranges. One analysis of firing range dust samples revealed it was composed of 24 to 36 percent lead. Soil lead is also enriched during shooting.

Acute lead poisoning is rare and usually occurs from ingestion of lead in soluble form, not sucking or swallowing a bullet–which could lead to chronic poisoning if done long enough. The symptoms of acute poisoning include a sweet metallic taste, salivation, vomiting, and intestinal colic. A large quantity ingested may produce death from cardiovascular collapse. Survivors of acute poisoning frequently develop signs associated with chronic toxicity.

Chronic lead poisoning, or plumbism, is manifest with a variety of symptoms. Initially, the individual is tired and weak due to anemia. Subsequent neurologic problems can

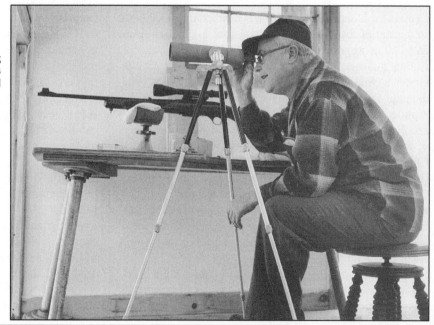

Exposure to lead can occur when shooting in indoor ranges. Airborne lead particles are inhaled into the lungs and absorbed into the blood.

develop which encompass irritability, restlessness, convulsions and, in severe cases, coma. Associated gastrointestinal disorders are constipation and a metallic taste. Neuromuscular symptoms include fatigue and muscle weakness. The most serious effect of lead poisoning, which occurs more often in children than adults, is encephalopathy. The early signs of encephalopathy involve clumsiness, irritability, and insomnia, which develop because of necrosis of brain tissue. Lead sulfide may appear in the gums and gingiva of toxic individuals as a blue-to-black line of discoloration termed the Burtonian line.

Toxicity from lead absorbed by the lungs and gastrointestinal tract is cumulative. In circulation, it is primarily bound to the red blood cells. Lead accumulates in soft tissues such as liver, kidney and brain. It can remain in the kidneys for 7 years and in bone for 32 years. During steady state, blood tests are considered the best indicator of relatively recent exposure. Urine tests are also employed, although urine lead concentrations tend to fluctuate more over time. Furthermore, hair may be tested to determine long-term exposure. Chelating agents are used as a treatment to assist in the removal of lead from the body. In the event lead poisoning is suspected, it is recommended that a primary care or occupational physician be contacted.

Assistance can also be obtained through state health and environmental agencies or local poison control centers. The National Lead Information Center (NLIC) may be contacted for general information regarding household lead at (800) 424-LEAD (5323).

Precautions that reduce lead exposure while involved in shooting sports will result in significantly improved health and a more enjoyable sport. Foremost attention should be given to the presence of children. The same exposure to a child relative to an adult results in a much higher total body burden of lead due to the reduced size of the child. In 1991, as a result of a large volume of epidemiological data, the Centers for Disease Control revised the recommended concentration of lead it considers dangerous in children from 25 to 10 micrograms per deciliter of blood. A number of studies indicate that high blood-lead concentrations can hinder a child's bone growth and can induce neurological damage. Since most young children place objects in their mouths, most lead poisonings in children occur between 1 and 5 years of age. There also tends to be a higher incidence of child-related lead poisonings during the summer months. Children should be kept at a safe distance from any enclosed shooting to avoid breathing airborne lead contaminated dust or soil. Dual cartridge respirators or masks are also advisable. Furthermore, materials which may be laced with lead residue–including cartridge cases, bullets, wads, primers, shot, cleaning patches, and cloths–should be kept out of reach of children.

While cleaning any firearm, avoid contact with bore-fouling residue from oily cloths or patches, which increase the absorption of lead through the skin. Solvents such as

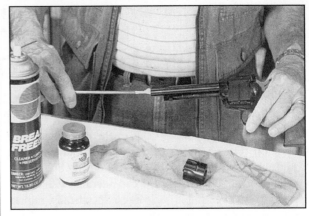

(Above and below) **When cleaning firearms, avoid the fouling left on patches. The residue can be absorbed into the skin, so gloves are recommended. Also, be sure to thoroughly wash your hands and the work area when finished.**

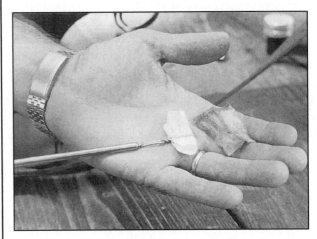

Shooter's Choice Lead Remover effectively removes lead from gun bores. Gloves are recommended as a barrier to absorption during cleanup using this or other products. A detergent containing trisodium phosphate, available at most hardware stores, is effective at solubilizing the lead for proper removal from lead-contaminated areas. Measures should be taken to ensure that all areas—as well as tools and accessories of the loading bench, including presses, dies, scales, gauges, measurers, and funnels—are properly cleaned of lead residues. During bullet casting, an adequate amount of ventilation is required. Outside is best since vaporized lead coming off a melting pot will condense on walls and rafters and can be inhaled directly or as dust in cleaning. Smoking and eating is dangerous when handling any lead-based material because of accidental transfer from hands to mouth. After handling equipment and cleaning the area, hands should be washed.

With adequate precautions, the presence of lead while shooting, reloading or cleaning can be adequately controlled to minimize potential exposure, improving the quality of the sport and the health of each participant. Since toxicity is cumulative, periodic blood tests can provide added assurance for safety.

When reloading, only one component in the load chain is reused over and over.

The Cartridge Case

PURPOSE AND EVOLUTION

THE ORIGINAL PURPOSE of a cartridge was to facilitate quick reloading and serve as a means to keep those loads consistent. The first cartridges contained a bullet and powder charge wrapped in a piece of heavy paper twisted at the ends. These appeared in about 1550. It became apparent fairly early in the shooting game that breech-loading firearms were a lot more convenient than muzzle-loaders. Soldiers especially liked the idea of not having to stand up to load while being shot at, since this interfered with their concentration. Sometimes they would forget where they were in the process, and would load a second powder charge and bullet on top of the first. At least one such soldier tamped more than a dozen loads into his rifle at the Battle of Gettysburg before tossing it away to look for something better to do than try to extract them. Several thousand such multiply loaded rifles were picked up after that battle. This fact finally drilled into the heads of even the most hidebound bureaucrats that the muzzle-loader needed replacing.

Photo courtesy of Starline Brass

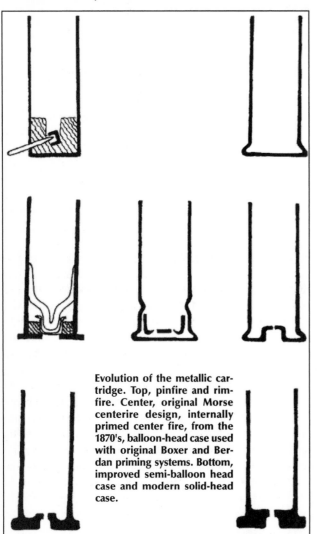

Evolution of the metallic cartridge. Top, pinfire and rimfire. Center, original Morse centerire design, internally primed center fire, from the 1870's, balloon-head case used with original Boxer and Berdan priming systems. Bottom, improved semi-balloon head case and modern solid-head case.

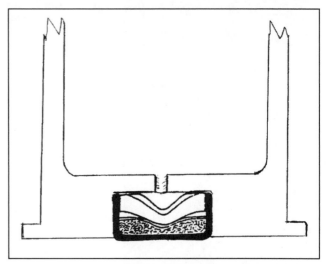

Boxer (above) and Berdan (below) systems are the ones used today.

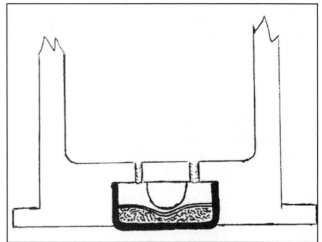

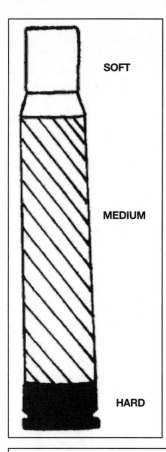

SOFT

MEDIUM

HARD

(Left) **The modern brass cartridge is made hard and thick where the greatest amount of support is needed, springy in the body for easy extraction and soft at the mouth to ensure a good gas-tight seal when fired.**

(Right) **Parts of the cartridge case.**

(Below) **The loaded cartridge fits closely, but not tightly in the chamber. The case swells on firing to make a gas-tight seal in the chamber. After firing, the pressure returns to normal and the case springs back to close to its unfired size for easy extraction.**

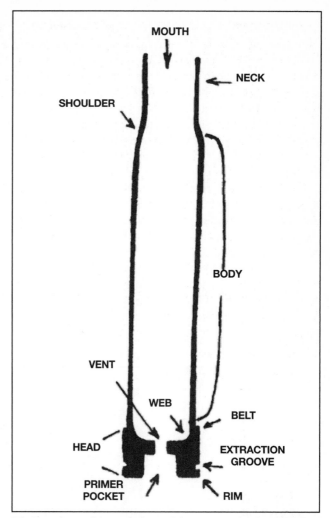

MOUTH

NECK

SHOULDER

BODY

VENT

WEB

BELT

HEAD

EXTRACTION GROOVE

PRIMER POCKET

RIM

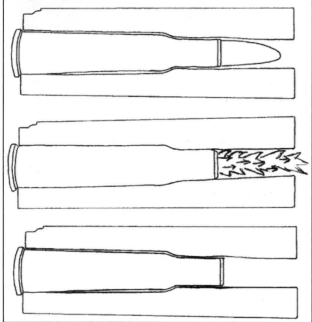

Early self-contained cartridge cases were made of paper, cardboard, linen, rubber, collodion, even sausage skin. All were fired by a separate percussion cap. While they were more or less easy to load, those that went into breech-loading guns still faced the breech-loader's basic problem — gas leaks. Many attempts were made to deal with the nasty habit of breech loaders' spewing fire and smoke out of the joint between breech block and barrel into the face of the shooter.

Their actions also tended to stick and eventually jam when they became encrusted with black-powder fouling. It was these problems that the metallic cartridge really solved, by closing the breech with a gas-tight seal and containing much of the fouling that wasn't in the barrel. At this point the cartridge became not merely a convenient package-form of ammunition, but an integral part of the firearm. By containing all the gas generated in the firing cycle it made the firearm more efficient. It also made possible the use of heavier charges generating higher pressures than could be used in a non-sealed gun. Finally, it served as a safety device containing gases that could otherwise escape into the action of a gun and blow it apart.

Metal cartridges came into being in the 1830's. The first commercially successful, completely self-contained cartridge — primer, powder and bullet, in one package — was invented in 1836 by Casimir Lefaucheux in France. The original style had a metal head and cardboard body, much like a shot shell. The primer was fired by a metal pin protruding above the head. The pinfire cartridge, however, had problems. It was not waterproof, and there was some gas leakage where the pin entered the case. The cartridge had to be properly oriented or "indexed" to enter the breech. If dropped it could accidentally discharge. It was fairly expensive to produce, though it could be reloaded.

The second advance in cartridge design was the rimfire, developed in 1857 by Daniel Wesson of Smith & Wesson based on the tiny "cap" cartridges patented around 1845, in France, by Louis Flobert. The Flobert, known here as the BB cap, consisted of a copper tube closed at one end. The closed end was flattened to create a hollow rim which contained the priming material — the only propellent — held in place by a paper disc. The open end or mouth was crimped to hold a bullet. The cartridge discharged when the rim was crushed at any point by a firing pin. No indexing was necessary. The rim also stopped the cartridge from sliding into the barrel. The rimfire was cheaper to manufacture than the pinfire, was less susceptible to accidental discharge and could be made weather- and water-tight.

The first American rimfire was the Smith & Wesson Number 1 pistol cartridge, now known as the 22 Short. It was longer than the BB cap and filled with black powder. Wesson's major advancement was the creation of machinery to prime the case rim with a wet mixture, spun into the rim. This kept the dried primer in place, allowing an additional powder charge to be loaded without fear of the primer mixture falling out of the hollow rim, rendering the cartridge useless. It also paved the way for larger more powerful cartridges.

Rimfire cartridge cases could not be reloaded. During and shortly after the American Civil War, rimfires for rifles were made in sizes up to 58, even 69 caliber.

Good small designs, when made large, often don't work. This was the case with the rimfire. The larger sizes had the habit of swelling in the head area when fired if this head was not fully supported by the breech of the gun. Bulged heads jammed revolver cylinders, preventing rotation. Solving this problem by making the cartridge head thicker or harder required a very heavy hammer spring to fire it, which made the gun difficult to cock and resulted in an unacceptably heavy trigger pull. The additional amount of powerful priming material in the larger rims of the big cartridges would sometimes blow them off, leaving the tubular body of the case stuck in the chamber.

Non-reloadables. L. To R. 12mm pinfire could be theoretically reloaded, but no components are available. Tiny 230 Morris used a smaller than standard primer, but new cases can be formed from cut-down 22 Hornet cases. Aluminum and steel cases are for one-time use. Posts in aluminum CCI Berdan primer pockets are battered in the first firing. Some steel cases can be reloaded if you find boxer-primed WWII 45 or 30 Carbine cartridges in good shape, but why bother with good brass ones readily available? The 7.62 X 39mm and 7.62 X 54mm Russian, steel military cases are Berdan primed and difficult to decap. The two dark cases are lacquer coated to make them function through autoloaders. This coating will likely come off in your reloading dies. In short, not worth the effort with boxer brass cases becoming commonly available.

Old copper and soft-brass cases from the last century and the early part of this one are a bad bet for reloading. They are often corroded by the black powder they contained or by deterioration through exposure to pollutants or are simply made of poor metal and are too weak for modern smokeless pressures. L. To R. 22 WCF, 25-20 SS, new-made 25-20 case, 38 Long, 44 S&W, two 45-70s.

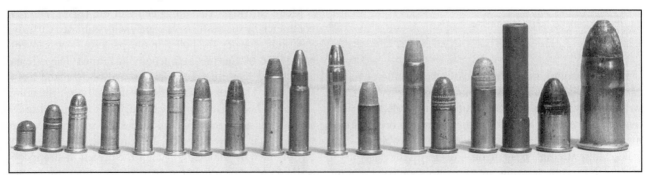

Rimfires are not reloadable. They range from the minuscule 22 BB cap the 52-caliber Spencer from the Civil War Era.

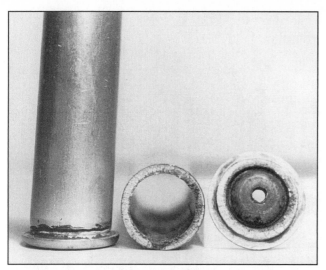

The REM-UMC case on the left suffered a 98% separation caused by mercury contamination. This same factor caused the one on the right to pull apart in the resizing die.

Blanks are made of substandard brass and often contain flaws as does the 223 case with the rose crimp. This crimp as with the flutes on the sides of the 30-06 dummy round weaken the metal. These cases would likely split in the reloading die or on the next firing. In short, don't try to use brass from blanks, grenade-launching or dummy rounds.

During and after the American Civil War, dozens if not hundreds of patents were submitted for all sorts of cartridges – ones with firing pins inside, a spinoff of the rimfire with the entire inside of the base coated with priming compound held in place by a perforated washer. There were others with heads shaped like champagne bottle bottoms in attempts to overcome the shortcomings of the pin and rimfire designs. The basis of the solution came from George W. Morse, who designed a cartridge in 1858 having a solid base with a

small, separate primer in the center of the head. The primer fired when crushed against a wire anvil soldered inside the case. Mass manufacture was impractical, but Morse had overcome the above problems by creating a cartridge that was strong in the head where strength was needed, did not require a heavy firing pin blow to discharge it, did not need to be indexed, was not susceptible to accidental discharge and could be made durable and waterproof.

In the 1870's the first really powerful cartridges were produced, based on the Morse design, with center priming and a reinforced head. The problem to be solved at this point in time was to come up with a design that was rugged, dependable, and lent itself to ease of manufacture. Various folded and composite head systems were tried with limited success. The heart of the problem was to create a reliable, simple-to-manufacture primer. The problem was solved twice — by Hiram Berdan in America, in 1866, and Edward M. Boxer in England a year later. Berdan reduced the Morse wire to a tiny knob in the primer pocket with the priming material in a simple inverted cup above it. The flame entered the cartridge case through two or three vent holes. Boxer crimped a tiny anvil in the primer cup itself with a space on either side to permit the flame to reach the powder charge through a single vent hole in the center of the cartridge case head. These are the two systems in use today. Oddly enough, the Boxer system became the American standard while the Berdan system found favor in Europe. The Boxer priming system with a single vent hole lends itself to easy removal by a simple punch pin, while the Berdan primer must be levered out with a chisel-type of extraction tool.

BRASS VERSUS COPPER CARTRIDGE CASES

Early cartridges were made of copper and soft copper alloys known as gilding metal (95% copper, 5% zinc) because it was easily worked. Soft copper alloys could be formed into complex shapes in punch dies without becoming too brittle and splitting or cracking in the process. This made it suitable for mass produced cartridges. It had a high degree of plasticity. It resisted the corrosion of black powder and early corrosive primers. It was strong enough not to crack under the pressure of firing if well supported and formed a good gas-tight seal in a gun chamber. Gilding metal, however, had one major failing: low elasticity. When fired with a heavy charge, the case had a tendency to stick in the chamber of a gun, particularly if that chamber had became hot and dirty with powder fouling.

Yellow Brass (generally 70% copper 30% zinc for cartridge use) possesses strengths and qualities neither element has separately. Most notable are hardness and elasticity. Modern cartridge brass is the ideal metal for cartridges, being capable of being hardened and softened by the application of pressure and heat respectively. Thus the head can be hardened, the body made semi-elastic and the mouth left relatively soft for a good gas seal. Such a cartridge case swells on firing to make a good gas seal in the chamber.

(Above) **Basic cartridge case forms include the following variations L. To R. Straight-walled rimmed (45-70); straight-tapered (38-55); rimmed-bottleneck (30-40 Krag); straight semi-rimmed (351 Winchester SL, now obsolete); straight rimless (30 Carbine); semi-rimmed bottleneck (220 Swift); rimless bottleneck (30-06); rebated head (.284 Winchester); straight belted (458 Mag); and bottleneck belted (Weatherby 7mm Mag).**

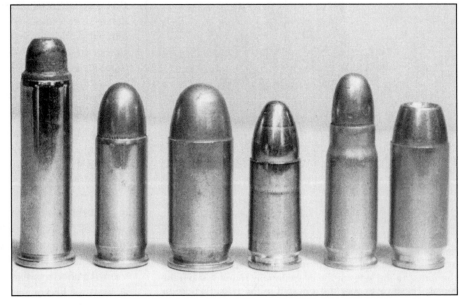

Basic cartridge forms for handguns. L. to R. Straight-rimmed (357 Magnum); straight semi-rimmed (38 ACP); straight rimless (45 ACP); semi-rimmed tapered (9mm Luger); rimless bottleneck (30 Mauser); and rebated head (41 Action Express).

After firing, the case springs back close to its original size, allowing easy extraction from the chamber. By the simple expedient of squeezing a fired cartridge case to its original size in a die and replacing the fired primer with a new one, it can be re-used. A brass case may be used dozens, sometimes over a hundred times. It is the most expensive component in the cartridge.

Because brass is relatively expensive, compared to other alloys, engineers have been at work to find cheaper materials that will do as well. Steel and aluminum-alloy cases have been experimented with since the World War I period. In the last twenty years advances in metallurgy and coatings have resulted in acceptable quality. Acceptable (for one-time shooting) steel and aluminum cases are more economical to make. Neither, however, is very suitable for reloading.

In spite of advanced heat-treating techniques, steel cases cannot be made as selectively elastic as those of brass. Steel cases tend to be rather hard and brittle. After a few resizings, the necks split, rendering them useless. To make steel cartridges feed through various autoloading rifle and pistol actions, they are often coated with a varnish type of lubri-

Case failures are not common, but they happen. The nearer to the case head the rupture is, the more serious the problem.

This 45 ACP has been so badly battered that it will probably not go in the resizing die. The split in the body of the 22 Hornet probably resulted from too many reloadings. The tiny split in the mouth of the 44 Winchester could be easily overlooked. All are rejects.

cant to keep them from sticking in the chamber when fired. In resizing these cases, this coating will tend to slough off in the resizing die and thus lose its effectiveness. Steel cases are most often encountered in military ammunition, the most common being the 7.62 X 39mm rifle cartridge for the SKS and AK-47 Russian and Chinese rifles. These cartridges, in addition to being made of steel, are Berdan-primed and are thus more difficult to reload. Occasionally some steel cased ammunition from WWII will turn up in 45 ACP and 30 M-1 carbine. It is Boxer primed and can be reloaded, but with good-quality, American brass cartridges in the above calibers now in plentiful supply, attempting to reload such cases isn't worth the effort. Some steel-case cartridges loaded with steel-jacketed bullets have been known to rust together — boosting pressures considerably when fired.

Aluminum cases in handgun calibers are manufactured by Cascade Cartridge Inc. These use a special Berdan primer and are specifically marked "non-reloadable." Aluminum suffers some of the same problems as copper in its lack of spring-back though it can be alloyed and heat treated to make good cases for low-powered cartridges. Aluminum does not hold up well under resizing and crimping and the cases frequently split on the first attempt to reload them. It's not worth the effort when good brass cases are available.

The shortcomings of various early types of cases have already been mentioned. But a few points should be added. Pinfire guns and ammunition are obsolete; few were made in this country and those were produced during and shortly after the Civil War. There are a few gunsmiths that offer ammunition and reloading tools on the internet. This is very advanced reloading. Rimfire cases are primed with a

wet mixture spun into the hollow rim. Owners of obsolete rimfire guns have the following options:

1) Searching for ammunition through dealers such as The Old Western Scrounger, or large local dealers who may have some in stock.

2) Conversion. A very few rimfire guns have been converted to centerfire by using custom made bolts and firing pins. The conversion cost is usually more than the original cost of the gun and often two or three times that.

3) Polish them up and hang them on the wall.

Early centerfire cartridges are usually far too valuable as collectibles to shoot. Old cases, however, are still around and are often the only source of ammunition for some obsolete and foreign rifles and handguns. Some of these cases are available from specialty suppliers and manufacturers. If vintage cases have been fired with black powder they are nearly always badly corroded and not safe. Copper and soft brass cases, of the old balloon and semi-balloon-head construction, from the last century, are too weak for use with modern smokeless loadings. Centerfire cases from the 1920's-1940's which have been contaminated by mercuric primers are very dangerous and should not be reloaded. This problem will be addressed in the chapter on primers.

A final word about blank cases: Even with the powder removed, these are not fit for reloading. Blanks are made from substandard cases not capable of meeting pressure and dimension standards for live ammunition. Attempting to remove the crimp in such a case usually splits the mouth and it's finished. The same is true for dummy cases which contain a bullet and no powder or primer and have flutes in the case body.

THE MODERN BRASS CASE

As firearms technology has advanced, guns have become more powerful and sophisticated. Cartridge case design has had to keep pace with this evolution. In reality, cartridges are often designed first and then guns are designed or adapted to fit them.

The basic design of contemporary centerfire cartridge cases include some of the following variations:

1) *Straight walled rimmed.* These date from the 19th century. They include the 32 and 38 S&W revolver cartridges, the 45 Long Colt and the 45-70 rifle. They also include modern cartridges such as the 38 Special, 357 Magnum and 44 Magnum revolver cartridges.

2) *Straight-tapered.* An effort to improve extraction led to this design. It is now nearly obsolete, the 38-55 being the only current survivor.

3) *Rimmed bottleneck.* These include late 19th century smokeless powder cartridges such as the 30-30 and 30-40 , 303 British, and .22 Hornet.

4) *Semi-rimmed straight.* These include currently made 32 Auto and 38 Super Automatic cartridges. The semi-rimmed design was to facilitate feeding through box magazines, with a slight rim to keep the cartridge from entering the chamber.

5) *Semi-rimless bottleneck.* Now rare, the 220 Swift is an example.

6) *Rimless-straight.* A common example is the 45 Colt automatic.

7) *Rimless-tapered.* These incude the 9mm Luger and 30 M-1 carbine.

8) *Rimless-bottleneck.* This is an improved smokeless design from the 1890's. Most modern rifle cartridges use this design.

9) *Rimless belted.* This design is used only on high-pressure magnum rifle cartridges such as the 458 Winchester Magnum.

10) *Rebated head.* This case features a rimless head smaller than the body permitting a slightly increased case capacity. Examples include the 284 Winchester rifle and 41 and 50 Action Express cartridges.

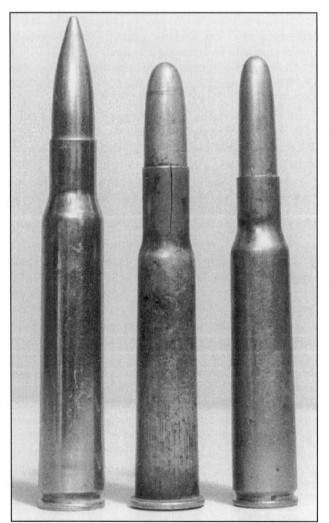

(Above) **Manufacturing defects, in this instance what appears to be poor brass, resulted in split necks in these 223 military cartridges.**

Season cracking – deterioration through exposure to pollutants in the air – caused this 30-40 Krag case (center), made in 1904, to split at the neck. The 7mm Winchester round (right) contains hairline cracks in the deep tarnish at the shoulder. The 30-06 (left) made at the Frankford Arsenal a year after the Krag benefited from the advantages of good storage and is in near-perfect condition.

What headstamps tell you. Commercial ammunition is marked with the caliber and name of the manufacturer, at least in this country. Military ammunition is stamped with the code of the arsenal or manufacturer and the date of manufacture. Top, L. To R. 45-70 current head stamp; pre WWII commercial Winchester and Remington head stamps – good candidates for being mercuric primed; inside-primed military centerfire from the 1870's and 80's. "R" indicates a rifle load, "F" is the code of the Frankford Arsenal, "2 82" indicates it was loaded in February 1882. Bottom, (left) a Frankford Arsenal round loaded February, 1904. Right, Spencer 52 cal rimfire was made by the Sage Ammunition Works.

CASE SELECTION

When buying cartridge cases for reloading, the first thing you want to be sure of is that you have the right one for your gun. Most civilian guns are marked on the barrel regarding the ammunition to be used in it. Military arms, however, are not, or at least not very often. When in doubt, check it out with a good gunsmith. If there is no question about caliber, you want to get new or once-fired cases from a reputable source — marked with the headstamp of a known manufacturer and not from the "Royal Elbonian Arsenal." Military cases referred to collectively as "brass" are often sold at bargain prices. Sometimes they are a bargain if they are fired only once and are not battered up by being run through a machine gun. The best military ammunition bargains are loaded ammunition. That way you get to shoot it first. Military cases do, however, have a few drawbacks. Assuming they are not Berdan primed, they may have been fired with corrosive primers. A wash in hot water and detergent will remove corrosive primer salts after firing.

The main problem with military cases is the crimp holding in the primer. Removing this crimp means a heavy-duty decapping pin and either chamfering the primer pocket or removing the crimp with a primer-pocket swage die, as explained in the chapter "Reloading Rifle Cartridges."

With the exception of new unfired cases in the box, all cases should be given an initial inspection. Bulk, once-fired, military and commercial cases may have loose debris including primers (live and dead) rattling around inside them that should be removed. Cases should be sorted by manufacturer and kept in separate containers. Although the dimensions for all cases of a particular caliber are basically the same, internal dimensions (caused by varying wall thickness and head thickness) and the size of the vent in the primer pocket will vary. This will yield different pressures and velocities. Mixed cases will thus give less accurate shooting. Varying pressures can be dangerous if the load you are using is a maximum one. If for instance this load is worked up using one type of case with a fairly thin wall and thus a comparatively large internal capacity, in combination with a small vent, the internal pressure will be significantly lower than one with a thicker wall, smaller capacity and larger vent.

Beyond separation by manufacturer, cases should be checked for splits in the neck, heavy corrosion and any anomalies indicating pressure or headspace problems or serious battering in the firing process, such as seriously damaged necks, that would render them unreloadable. Oil, grease, grit and dirt should be removed before reloading.

READING HEADSTAMPS

The headstamp markings of cartridge cases contain valuable information that will prove useful in buying ammunition and brass cases. Commercial manufacturers mark their cases with their name or trade mark, the caliber of the cartridge and the name of the cartridge, e.g., WW 45-70 Govt. This tells you it was made by Winchester/Western and it is the 45-70 Government cartridge originally made for the 45 caliber Springfield army rifle.

Markings on cartridge cases made for the military contain similar information, plus a two-digit date of manufacture.

L C is the Lake City Ordnance Plant. W R A is Winchester Repeating Arms Company. R A is Remington Arms Company. A stamp of R A 79 indicates the cartridge was made by Remington in 1979. American military cases are not marked by caliber. Early cartridges made in the Frankford Arsenal in Philadelphia were marked F or FA 3 05. This indicates the source and the month of manufacture (March) and the year 1905. This is not ammunition you would want to shoot, especially if it shows any sign of corrosion. American-made military ammunition used corrosive priming into the early 1950's. Different arsenals switched to non-corrosive priming at different times with all being changed over by 1954. Non-corrosive priming will require less cleaning of your gun.

Liquid case cleaners contain a mild acid and require no more equipment than a stainless steel, plastic or glass pan to soak them in. Cases should be decapped before cleaning and either air-dried or oven-dried at no more than 150 degrees F.

CASE CLEANING

Most shooters like to keep their cases shiny and bright. They look better and are easier to find on the ground. Shined cases are less likely to collect dirt and grit and can be easily checked for damage caused by corrosion. Dark cases hide flaws that may run deep.

There are two basic methods of case cleaning. The first is wet cleaning. This uses a concentrated, acid-based cleaner that is mixed with water. This must be done in a glass, plastic or stainless-steel pan. Warming the pan, with the cases in the mixture, on the stove speeds the process. The cleaned cases must be rinsed to remove all residue and oven dried on "warm." Too much heat can ruin the heat treatment of the cases. Cases should be decapped before wet cleaning.

Dry cleaning is tumbling the cases in an abrasive cleaning media made of ground corn cobs or ground walnut shells. This requires a motor-driven tumbler or spinner-type tool into which the cases and media are put for cleaning. The cleaned cases must be wiped free of dust, and any media trapped inside must be removed.

Vibrator/tumbler case cleaners use ground corn cobs or ground walnut shells to clean cases through abrasive action. This is probably the best system for cleaning large numbers of cases.

Freezer boxes are good for case storage and do a good job of keeping damp and pollutants out if closed on a dry day and kept closed. The cases should always be identified by maker, caliber and number of times fired.

CARTRIDGE CASE and AMMUNITION STORAGE

"Store in a cool dry place" is good advice for keeping about anything, but this isn't always possible. Depending on one's paranoia and/or notion of thrift, the decision may be made to buy a large quantity of cases. Sometimes quantity simply accumulates in the form of various loadings, always expanding with the addition of new guns to a shooting battery. Ultimately the questions arise: how long will this stuff last (both cases and finished ammunition) and how do I take care of it?

In answer to question one, the shelf life of modern ammunition (both commercial and good handloads) is virtually indefinite if kept under ideal conditions — sealed, cool and dry. Most of us don't have this kind of storage. Experts have preached since time immemorial the avoidance of heat and damp when storing. Actually, heat and damp by themselves don't do all that much damage to quality ammunition. Heat does drive off volatiles in lubricants and exposed propellent-powders and to a degree accelerates decomposition in smokeless powders. Heat and damp together are most injurious because water absorbs pollutants and heat accelerates chemical reactions between these pollutants and ammunition. The triple threat in airborne pollution consists of acids, ammonia, and sulfur compounds. All occur naturally in the atmosphere in addition to being man-made pollutants. They are also found in a variety of household products. Salts, through direct contamination, are a fourth hazard. Pinpointing the exact reason why a particular batch of ammunition went bad is a mystery to be solved by an expert metallurgist-detective through chemical analysis and examination of cartridge surfaces with a scanning electron microscope.

I have often heard it said that certain metals "crystalize" and become brittle with age. I put this question to Professor Bryan Wilde — a metallurgist and director of the Fontana Corrosion Center at The Ohio State University. He assured me this was not the case. Cartridge brass has a crystalline structure. When exposed to pollutants in the atmosphere, notably ammonia, a breakdown of the alloy begins as ammonia dissolves the copper. Acids in the atmosphere dissolve the zinc in a process known as "dezincification." In areas where the metal is stressed — case necks, shoulders and crimps – the crystal edges are farther apart, thus speeding the breakdown in a process known as "season cracking."

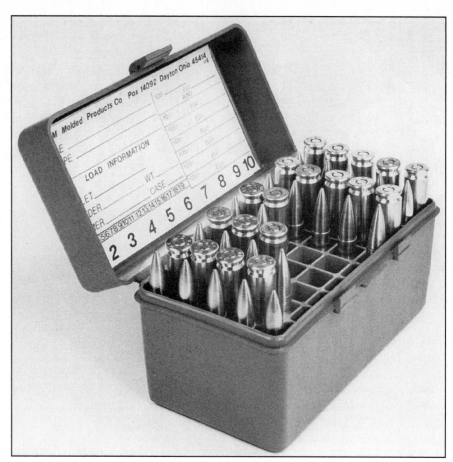

Plastic boxes are best for ammunition storage and come complete with information cards.

Season cracking begins as tarnish, gradually turning into deep corrosion which often follows the edges of the crystals, giving the surface a frosted appearance, leading to the impression the metal is changing its structure. This phenomenon was first recorded in nineteenth-century ammunition used by the British in India, where it was exposed to the ammonia-rich fumes of cow dung and urine in a hot, humid climate.

Salts occur in perspiration and are a problem mainly because they are hygroscopic — they draw and hold water which combines with the salt to corrode metals the wet salt mixture contacts. Sulfur, notably sulfur dioxide (SO_2), causes a tarnish when it combines with lead and copper to form sulfides. When SO_2 combines with water (H_2O) the result is sulfurous acid (H_2SO_3). Lead and lead alloy bullets are subject to damage mainly from acids. These attack lead, causing a hard white crust to form. If the bullet can be hand-turned in the case there is not a hermetically tight seal and sooner or later moisture will enter.

Manufacturers continue to come up with better priming, powder, lubricants, case materials, sealants, and packaging. What you buy represents the manufacturer's state of the art combined with his sense of economy at the time the product was made.

Plating cases with nickel and plating or jacketing bullets with copper inhibits corrosion by acid. Non-hygroscopic bullet lubricants keep moisture away from bullets and out of case interiors. Paper boxes absorb moisture but are no problem if kept dry. Those that contain high levels of acid residues should be disposed of and the cartridges repacked in plastic boxes which are chemically inert and if sealed, keep most moisture out. Therefore, if the cases/ammunition are in good shape when stored, and if kept dry and cool, they will remain in good condition for decades.

A second problem that still crops up is brittle brass. After cartridge brass is formed it gets a final heat treatment called "stress relief." This process involves less heat than annealing and is done to bring the brass to the optimum degree of springiness. Occasionally a batch will get through that is improperly treated. It will perform fine when new, but after ten or more years, the brass will have returned to its original brittle state. This is exacerbated by the process of firing and resizing. Cases will split and sometimes burst. Any corrosion taking place will hasten this process. One advantage of the old gilding-metal cases is that they were less subject to corrosion and stress changes because they were softer.

Beyond cool and dry there isn't much to be added regarding shelf-storage. For the longest run, the best means is a military ammunition can with a rubber gasket along with a fresh packet of desiccant, closed on a dry day and opened as infrequently as possible. If ammunition is stored in a can or tightly sealed cardboard container, don't break the seals (letting in pollutants) to have a look. Second-floor rooms are perhaps the best for shelf-stored ammunition, avoiding attic heat and basement damp. Cartridges should be stored away from cleaning products containing ammonia, bleaches, or acids. If it must be stored in a basement, run a dehumidifier and keep ammunition off the floor. It is a good idea to make timely checks of shelf-stored cartridges in non-sealed boxes — twice a year is fine – to inspect for case tarnish or a haze of white corrosion forming on lead bullets.

To the above might be added a list of dumb things not to do. Slathering a gun with Hoppe's No. 9 may do well to keep it from rust, but if this is the one kept for home defense the ammonia in No. 9 spreading onto the cartridges therein will eat right into them. The same is true for any ammonia-bearing solvent cleaner. A rust inhibitor such as WD-40 spray may work preservative magic, but WD-40 is designed to penetrate and will do so in the seams between primers and cases, eventually working into the priming compound and neutralizing it. Leaving cartridges in leather belt loops may look nifty, but if the leather has residual salts or acids in it these will eat into the metal, etching a ring which adds nothing to the looks or strength of the cartridge case.

Lastly, it should not be forgotten that cartridges are interesting. People can't keep their sweaty hands off them. Ask any collector how often he wipes down his collection after "showing" it to friends. Two suggestions passed to me by collectors are treating specimens with a light coat of rust inhibiting grease or liquid car wax of the Rain-Dance variety as the best defense against repeated attacks of finger-borne corrosion. Like the guy at the gas station used to say: "Rust never sleeps."

CASE FAILURES

In the 19th and early 20th century, case failures were an expected hazard. The "headless" or "broken" shell extractor, once found in every shooting kit, has gone the way of the stereoscope and flatiron. Yet failures still happen; they have to me and they will to you if you do enough shooting.

The quality of today's American-made metallic cartridge ammunition is superb. Nearly three generations of shooters have grown up since the last corrosive-primed, mercuric-primed, centerfires vanished into the mists of erosive smokeless powder, and not a moment too soon. Case failures with new commercially-made, centerfire ammunition is virtually nonexistent.

It is in the business of reloading ammunition that most problems occur. Here the reloader (you) becomes the manufacturer and must become your own quality control expert. In this role you must learn to recognize all the signs that may lead to an accident — in this respect you must become an expert at "reading cartridge cases." This is by no means as easy as it might appear, since similar failures may come from a variety of causes. Flattened, cratered and punctured primers, and gas leaks around primers are generally signs of excessive pressure. Soft primers, stretched primer pockets caused by multiple reloading and a poor fit of the primer, however, can produce results similar to high pressures. Swelling of the case head, often accompanied by the brass flowing back into the extractor port, is a sign of high pressures, but can be caused by soft, poorly-annealed brass. Splits in cases around the head can indicate excessive headspace – a gun problem. Similar splits can also indicate inferior quality brass that contains oxides and impurities — sometimes recognizable by its scaly appearance. Internal corrosion from black powder loads or corrosively primed smokeless loads can also produce such splits, as will improperly annealed brass, in this instance too hard and brittle, or brass made brittle by mercuric primers, or damaged by exposure to external corrosive elements, or stressed by excessive resizing. That's a lot to consider. So we will take it one element at a time.

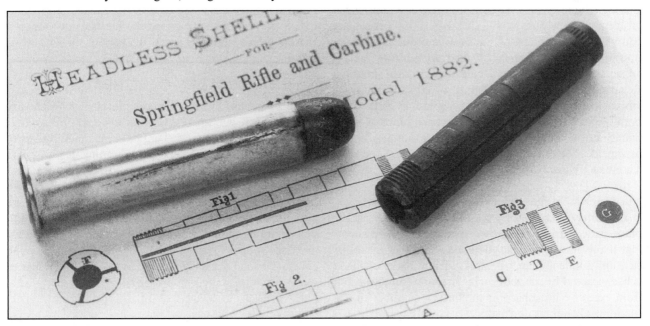

In the last century, the headless shell extractor was a necessary part of the shooter's kit given the poor quality of the cartridge cases.

The old saying that lightning doesn't strike twice in the same place is just as false in cartridge case failures as it is in meteorology. The low overall incidence of case failures might lead to the belief that the one that failed was simply one bad case. Sometimes it is. In my experience, if the problem rests with a defective component, given the consistency in today's ammunition, that problem may run through a case-sized quantity, possibly an entire production lot, or at least until someone in quality control realizes there is a problem and does something about it.

SPLIT NECKS

By the same token, if one case from a particular box or purchase-lot that you have been reloading develops a split in the neck, it has become brittle from resizing and the rest of the lot can sometimes be given a longer life by annealing with a propane torch. This is not recommended since this practice will do nothing to correct other problems of wear and tear brought on by long use. About the only instance where this makes economic sense is with very expensive cases of the custom-made variety. A split neck is a common failure and not dangerous.

BODY SPLITS

Splits in the body of a case are far more dangerous, with the degree of danger increasing in relation to the closeness of these splits to the head of the case. The worst instance is a separation at the case head. This allows high-pressure gas to come rushing back into the action of the gun and into your face, often damaging both. Since eyeballs and ear drums are less robust than a rifle receiver, it is a good idea to wear eye and ear protection when shooting.

LONGITUDINAL SPLITS

Longitudinal splits in the case body can be a gun-related problem — namely an oversize chamber. If this is the cause, you will notice swelling of the cases and difficult extraction with normal "commercial" loads long before you get an actual split. If your gun is bulging cases, stop shooting! Rebarreling is the only solution. If a case suddenly splits with a load you have been using successfully with other brands of cartridge cases, this is likely an instance of poor-quality, brittle brass. If there is visible corrosion inside and/or outside, corrosion may have helped weaken the case. Throw such cases away.

CIRCUMFERENTIAL SPLITS

These may be caused by poor quality, brittle brass, or brass made brittle by mercury contamination. Stop shooting! If this has not happened before with other makes of case and suddenly happens on a different make or lot, it is likely caused by the above. This situation can also result from excessive headspace — in effect, a chamber that is too long. Chambers don't suddenly grow longer. If this is a headspace problem in a gun there will be warnings before such a separation occurs, namely stretch marks on the case as it gradually pulls apart over the course of several firings. These will often appear as bright rings and will be found on all the cases you fire in that particular gun. They will be most apparent on higher pressure loads.

HEAD SEPARATIONS

Head separations can be more or less disastrous depending on how well your gun is engineered for safety — gas-escape ports allowing gases flowing from the chamber, back into the action, to be directed sideways and not in your face. Mercury contamination from mercuric primers is the most likely cause of this since most of the mercury will contaminate the cartridge case nearest the primer. Stop shooting! This batch of cases, from that box or purchase lot, identified by the head stamp markings, is not fit to shoot. Mercury contamination is invisible — the cases look fine until fired. Since mercuric priming was limited to non-military ammunition made from about 1928-1945 there is not that much around, but it can still turn up. At times these contaminated cases will pull apart in the resizing die. This is a definite warning.

STRETCHED PRIMER POCKETS

This condition occurs after many reloadings. The problem is identified by gas leaks (smoke stains) around primers and by primers seating very easily — by thumb pressure. Time to junk those cases when these signs appear. These can also occur when excessively high pressure loadings are fired. This is why maximum loads should only be worked up with new or once-fired cases. With a new case and a heavy load, such leaks tell you — stop shooting!

Primers flattened on firing also indicate high pressure as do ones that are cratered around the firing pin mark or pierced. If these signs appear with a max load – stop shooting! If they appear with a loading that has not produced these signs with other primers, the reason is most likely a soft primer.

SWOLLEN CASE HEADS

Bulges in case heads are nearly always a sign of very high pressures, but can be caused by a too-soft head, poorly annealed. If you are working up a max load, excessive pressure is the likely problem. Stop shooting! If this occurs with a load that has given no such indications and you have changed to a different make or lot of case, it may be a case problem. Excessive pressures are the main culprit and are additionally identified by cases stretching lengthwise and picking up machining impressions from the chamber walls and breech or bolt face. Such cases will stick tight to the chamber wall and give hard extraction — a definite sign of excess pressure.

ABC's of Reloading

Too much of either of these could be a serious problem, possibly leading to serious injury -or worse.

Understanding Pressure and Headspace

PRESSURE MAKES A GUN WORK

GUNS FUNCTION BECAUSE less, burns rapidly, generating a tremendous pressure as the gunpowder is converted from a solid into a gas in a process called deflagration. Gunpowder burned in the air burns far more slowly than in the chamber of a gun. Inside the chamber, increasing pressure accelerates burning. As pressure increases, the powder forms a churning mass accelerating the burn.

The firing sequence begins as the primer ignites the powder. The primer contains a tiny amount of very high explosive that burns with a rapidity that far exceeds that of gunpowder. While smokeless gunpowder burned in the air produces a faint whoosh as the gas dissipates into the atmosphere, priming compound burns so rapidly that when ignited in the air it will explode with great violence. This is why explosives such as priming compound, TNT, PETN, etc., are unsuitable for use as propellants. They burn so rapidly that before a bullet can begin to move down a gun barrel these explosives have burned entirely, generating so much gas that for all intents the bullet is simply a plug in a closed container and the gun barrel has become a bomb.

The priming compound thus serves to get the powder burning. It functions much like burning balls of paper thrown into a pile of dry leaves to get the pile blazing. By throwing a greater number of fire balls into the leaf pile it will be set alight faster and more evenly than if only a few are tossed on. A magnum primer represents a high saturation of fire balls by comparison to a standard primer. By starting the fire

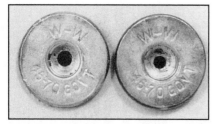

The primer is the sparkplug that starts the powder burning. Magnum primers contain more burning compound and additives such as aluminum which become white-hot sparks blown into the powder to give the charge even ignition. *(Courtesy Speer)*

The vent hole on the case at the left was deliberately enlarged to burn a compressed, black-powder load. If this case were loaded with smokeless powder significantly, possibly dangerously high pressures would be generated.

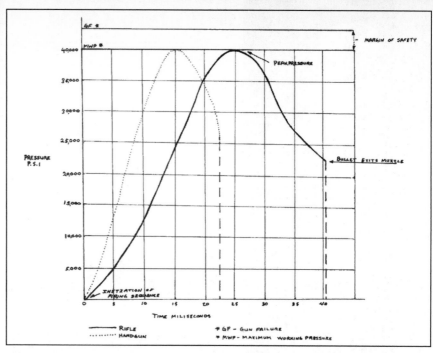

The time-pressure curve. The curve starts at the point of ignition. In a few milliseconds the event is over. The peak pressure is reached as the bullet is an inch or so forward of the chamber. After it has been swaged into the rifling, pressure declines and drops to zero as the bullet exits the barrel. A fast-burning pistol powder in a short barrel develops a sharp curve (broken line) while a slower rifle powder in a long barrel is flatter. The peak of the curve touches the maximum working pressure (MWP) line on a maximum load. Above this is a margin of safety area and above that is the point of gun failure (GF). (After Naramore)

in more places at once, the mass of powder is burned more rapidly and completely. More rapid and complete burning will generate more gas and higher pressure.

To continue the bonfire analogy, a fast burning powder could be likened to dry leaves while a slow burning powder is more like a pile of twigs or wood shavings. The twigs take more/hotter fire balls to get them burning, but they will burn longer than the leaves and generate more hot gas more slowly. The fast burning powder is ideal for a short barreled gun. The rapid burn releases gas quickly, generating a high-speed movement of the bullet quickly. This sudden release of gas produces a relatively high pressure in the chamber. Therefore only a limited amount of such a powder can be used without generating dangerously high pressures.

A slow burning powder (sometimes referred to as a "progressive" burning powder) can be loaded in greater amount. By virtue of releasing more gas at a slower rate, it works well in long barrels where the burn time is extended by the length of time it takes the bullet to travel to the end of the barrel. The slow burning powder keeps on generating gas throughout the length of time it takes the bullet to exit. The long burn thus generates lower peak pressure and keeps the average pressure up for a longer time. Once the bullet has passed out the muzzle, further burning is pointless.

This burning process is best illustrated in what is called the "time pressure curve." A fast burning powder such as Alliant Bullseye is intended for handguns and produces a typically short sharp curve. A slower burning rifle powder such as IMR 4320 produces a longer, flatter curve in a rifle-length barrel.

Of most critical interest to the reloader is the peak pres-

sure generated by a particular load, for it is this peak pressure that will act as a hammer blow to your gun and wreck it if the peak pressure exceeds the elastic limit of the barrel. This will cause it to swell and eventually burst. To keep both guns and shooters from harm, arms and ammunition manufacturers design their products for a "maximum working pressure." This is below the failure point by a margin of safety. Loading above this maximum working pressure will drastically shorten the life of a gun and place the shooter at significantly higher risk of a catastrophic failure every time such a load is fired.

Beyond the strength of the barrel and action, "working pressure" is limited by the strength of the cartridge case. The modern alloy steel in today's rifles make them capable of withstanding peak pressures of well over 100,000 pounds per square inch (psi). Even the strongest brass cartridge cases are not capable of withstanding more than 50,000 to 60,000 psi and at pressures above that will swell, distort even flow until an unsupported point gives way and gas escapes, often wrecking the gun. Most cartridge cases are intended for pressures well below these figures.

The most obvious means of raising pressure in a barrel is to put more powder in the cartridge. This is also the most obvious means of generating higher velocity. Higher velocity means flatter shooting with less rise and fall in a bullet's trajectory and thus hitting a target at an unknown distance is made easier, ask any varmint shooter. The downside to such high velocity loadings is the generation of very high pressures. An interesting phenomenon some shooters may not be familiar with is that as loadings are increased for greater velocity, pressures begin to go up at an increasingly

The balloon-head case on the 38 Special (left) offers more powder capacity, and thus lower pressure, but is a weaker design than the solid head .357 Magnum case on the right.

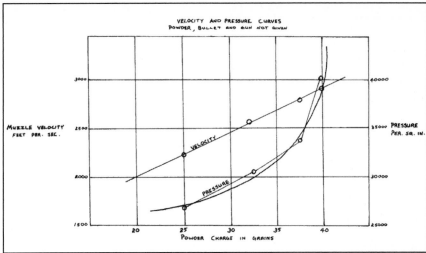

(Above) **The pressure-velocity curve illustrates the relationship between velocity and the pressure generated by adding more powder. As powder is added more of the energy of the expanding gas is worked against the chamber walls and of the gas against itself. Additional powder added at the top end of a load generates little additional velocity and considerable pressure. (After Naramore)**

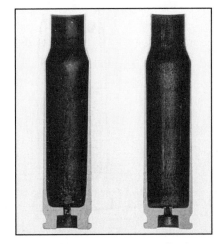

The same cartridge but with different internal dimensions. The smaller capacity case will generate higher pressures with the same load. Some brands have thicker (or thinner) walls, meaning different capacities. Sort your brass by maker.

higher rate. This can be most clearly expressed in what is known as the "pressure-velocity curve." In conventional firearms – ones that use gunpowder – there is a ceiling on the velocity that can be achieved. This is because at a certain point, as the bullet is made smaller and lighter to achieve higher velocity, the base of that bullet has less surface area to be worked upon and the gas in the chamber is working against the chamber walls and the molecules of gas against one another. This velocity ceiling is in the range of 11,000 feet per second (fps). This is achieved with a steel ball blown out of a smooth-bore barrel – hardly practical. The pressure and heat generated at velocities of 5000-6000 fps will "wash" the rifling out of a barrel in a very few shots. A little over 4000 fps is the maximum practical velocity that can be expected to produce a reasonable barrel life — over a thousand shots. Thus the quest for high velocity is at the cost of shortened barrel life and greatly increased pressures as the top end of the maximum working pressure is reached — where the last few additions of powder produce far more pressure than they add in velocity.

OTHER FACTORS AFFECTING PRESSURE

Reduced loads of certain slow-burning powders, loads well below those recommended in loading manuals, have apparently generated some very high pressures. This phenomenon has been given the term "detonation." Detonation may be caused by what has been termed the "log jam" effect caused by the position of the powder in the case wherein the powder charge is forward in the case. Powder ignited in the rear slams the rest of the charge into the base of the bullet

and the shoulder of a bottleneck case resulting in a solid plug. As burning continues, pressures jump and a bomb effect is created.

The problem with this theory is that it has been very difficult to duplicate such events in the laboratory. Undoubtedly, a certain number of supposed detonations were instances of bullets fired from such reduced loadings sticking in rifle, or more likely, revolver barrels. The unwary shooter fires a second shot and this bullet slams into the one stuck in the barrel with unhappy results. Whatever the reason, there have been a significant number of accidents involving reduced loads of slow-burning powders. Therefore, it is prudent not to experiment below the starting loads listed in the manuals.

With faster burning powders, it has been noted that the position of the powder charge in the cartridge case in less than full-case loads will affect pressures. If the charge is at the rear near the vent, pressures will be higher since a greater amount of powder will be ignited and is not blown out the barrel. With the charge forward as in an instance where the gun is fired almost straight down, pressures may be lower by more than 50% since less of that charge is actually burned.

PRIMERS

Primers, as has been mentioned earlier, are the fire starters that get powder burning. The more efficient ones — magnum primers that burn longer and hotter, throwing more sparks into the powder charge – will burn that charge more completely and more efficiently. This will generate more gas and, naturally, more pressure.

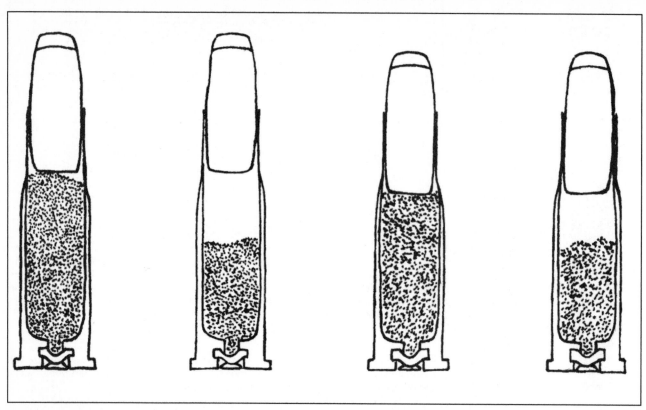

The "loading density" – the amount of powder and empty space – in a cartridge will affect the pressures therein, all other things being equal. The greater the density of the powder and the less space there is, the higher the pressure will be. On the right is a maximum, high density load. Cartridge #2 is a low-density load with the bullet seated far out. The pressure generated would not be particularly high. Cartridge #3 contains the same load as #1 compressed by a deep-seated bullet. This would likely generate dangerously high pressure. Cartridge #4 contains the same charge as #2, but will generate higher pressures. Case-wall thickness affects loading density by increasing or decreasing the internal capacity: very critical when a maximum load is used.

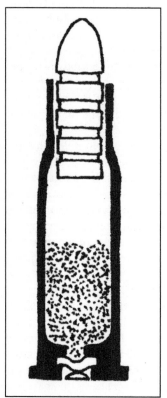

Never seat a cast bullet below the bottom of the neck into the shoulder area of a bottleneck case. The base will be melted and expanded, ruining accuracy and raising pressure.

VENT HOLE SIZE

A larger vent hole will affect powder burning rate by letting more of the primer flash pass into the case more quickly. A large vent, by increasing the rapidity of the burn, will raise pressures. Vent hole size has been determined by ammunition manufacturers for optimum performance with smokeless powders. Altering vent hole size should not be done.

CASE CAPACITY

Cartridge case capacity is critical in the pressure equation. All other things being equal, if the same amount of the same type of powder is loaded into a small capacity case such as a 223 Remington and a large capacity one such as a 45-70, much higher pressures will be generated in the smaller case. This is because there is less volume in the smaller case, thus less surface area for the pressure to work against. According to published data in the *Accurate Smokeless Powder Loading Guide Number One*, a load for the 223 of 23.5 grains of Accurate arms 2495 BR powder behind an 80 grain jacketed bullet generates an average of 51,600 psi of chamber pressure, while 66.0 grains of the same powder behind a 300 grain jacketed bullet in the 45-70 generates about 22,100 psi. As was mentioned in the last chapter, some cases have

(Above and right) **Slugging the bore consists of carefully driving a small, soft pure lead slug down the barrel. If done from both ends, the two slugs can be compared for tight and loose spots in the barrel.**

(Right) The slug is measured from one land on the slug to the land on the opposite side to find the groove diameter of the barrel.

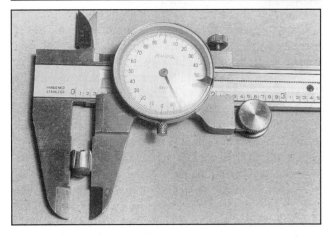

slightly thicker walls and larger vents than others. Military cases are generally thicker than those made for the civilian market. This slight reduction in internal capacity can raise pressures.

OVERALL CARTRIDGE LENGTH

By making a finished cartridge longer than a manufacturer's specification, the bullet may rest against or even be forced part way into the rifling. This will raise pressures. If a case is not trimmed to the proper length and the case mouth extends into the rifling, the case mouth cannot expand properly and the bullet will be forced through what amounts to an undersize mouth in a swaging action that will increase pressures while degrading accuracy.

CHAMBER AND BORE SIZE

All American-made guns are standardized according to specifications set forth by the Sporting Arms and Ammunition Manufacturers Institute (SAAMI). Customized, foreign, and obsolete arms however may have dimensions different from this standard. Smaller, tight chambers and undersize bores can increase pressures with "normal" ammunition. When there is a reason for doubt, slugging the

bore with a piece of soft lead to find the dimension, possibly making a chamber cast with Wood's Metal or sulfur may be necessary to find the exact dimension.

BULLETS

Bullets affect pressure, with the weight of the bullet having the most influence. The heavier they are, the greater the pressure needed to get them moving. Beyond this is the hardness of the bullet. Hardened lead alloys, bronze or copper jacketed bullets require more energy to swage them into the rifling than does a soft lead bullet which is more easily engraved. Finally there is the fit of the bullet in the bore. A

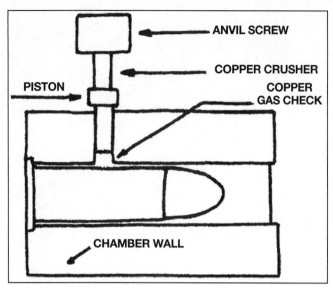

Crusher-type pressure gun for measuring pressure. Pure copper and lead slugs are compressed to determine peak pressures on firing.

tight fit offers more resistance than a loose fit where gas may blow by an undersize bullet which will not obturate the bore properly. A bullet seated too deeply — below the shoulder of a bottlenecked case – particularly a lead-alloy bullet, will often expand in the case and be swaged down as it passes into the neck. This will raise pressures and degrade accuracy.

INSTRUMENTAL MEASUREMENT OF PRESSURE

Until the middle of the 19th century the only way to test for maximum pressures was to keep increasing powder charges until the test gun blew up. It was thus assumed, at times erroneously, that similar guns would blow up with the same charge. The artillery designer Thomas Rodman developed one of the first pressure testing devices used in the U.S. in 1861. It consisted of boring a hole in a gun chamber and inserting a rod with a chisel point on the other end. A copper plate was affixed to the barrel above the chisel blade. After the gun was fired the plate was compared to similar plates marked with chisel indentations made by known amounts of force. A year earlier, in England, Sir Andrew Noble developed a more refined device that featured a piston that fit tightly in a hole drilled in a chamber wall. A frame secured to the barrel held an anvil above the opposite end of the piston. Between the piston and the anvil, a small copper cylinder was placed. When the gun was fired the cylinder was compressed and later compared to similar cylinders compressed by known degrees of force. The accuracy of this system depends on keeping the purity and hardness of the copper cylinders, called "crushers," consistent. Calculations are affected by whether the cartridge case is first drilled or the force needed to blow a hole in the case is factored in. Sharp pressure rises are more easily registered than more gradual ones. For shotgun ammunition, some handgun ammunition and rimfire ammunition which gener-

ate relatively low pressures a lead cylinder is used instead of copper. Measurements t,aken in this manner are expressed as copper units of pressure (c.u.p.) or lead units of pressure (l.u.p.). These have been interpreted as pounds per square inch (psi), This isn't really the case, but until more efficient means of measurement came along the l.u.p./c.u.p. designation was regarded as an acceptable means of pressure calculation.

More sophisticated systems of pressure measurement developed in the 20th century consist of electronic transducer systems. These are of two types – piezoelectric and strain gage (yes that's how it's spelled). The piezoelectric system, perfected in the mid 1930's, uses a quartz crystal in place of the copper cylinder, which is in a sealed tube with a diaphragm in the interior of the chamber wall. The crystal, when subjected to pressure, generates electrical current in direct proportion to the amount of pressure applied. The advantage of such a system is a quick and relatively easy electronic readout and the reusability of the crystal. Disadvantages are calibration of equipment and crystals changing their value or varying in value.

The strain gage system derives pressure readings from implied information rather than direct. The device consists of a thin wire placed on the exterior surface of the barrel at the chamber point or around it. When the gun is fired the chamber swells to a degree before returning to its original size thus stretching the wire. The increased resistance in electrical conductivity of the stretched (thinner) wire during the firing sequence indicates pressure through the amount of stretch. Calibration is determined by measurement of inside and outside chamber diameters. Of the three systems, this one is of most interest to handloaders, since it is the only one that is non-destructive, in terms of not having to bore a hole in a gun barrel at the chamber and is available for home use. The first such device marketed is the "Personal Ballistics Laboratory - Model 43" available from Oehler Research. This method, as with the piezoelectric system. allows measurement over the time of the shooting event (the entire pressure curve) rather than simply recording the maximum pressure spike.

VISIBLE SIGNS OF PRESSURE

For most handloaders these are the most critical indicators of something being wrong. They are also by far the most unreliable and imprecise. There is no way to estimate pressure from observation or even physical measurement of cartridge cases or primers. Nevertheless, these components can warn of pressures that are in the danger zone.

As was indicated in the previous chapter, case failures may have a number of causes. Sorting out what the cause might be is often difficult. The only sensible way to determine whether the loadings you are assembling may be too hot for the particular gun you are using is to eliminate as many variables as possible thus leaving only those cartridge anomalies caused by excessive pressure or excessive headspace. These two problems produce similar appearing, but different effects. What makes these difficult to differentiate is that any problems of excessive headspace are exacerbated by high pressure!

Hard case extractions are a definite sign of high pressure unless you are dealing with an oversize or very rough chamber, something you can determine by looking into it. If your handloaded case is more difficult to extract than a factory load of the same make, this tells you that you have exceeded the elastic limit of the case and you are generating significantly higher pressures. A second means to check this is to take a micrometer measurement of the case body diameter

Three 44 Magnum cartridges fired under the same conditions with the pressure measured by a copper crusher in each case. L. To R. 31,800 C.U.P., 39,000 C.U.P. and 47,700 C.U.P. As can be seen, there is no discernable difference! *(Courtesy Speer)*

Cratered primer (center) appears at first glance to be evidence of excessive pressure. The actual cause was an oversize firing pin hole and a soft primer.

Was the flat primer on the left a result of high pressure or being too soft? The answer is likely high pressure since the case head also flowed into the extractor groove *(circled)*.

A pierced or "blown" primer can be caused by excessive pressure or a firing pin that is too long or too sharp. *(Courtesy Speer.)*

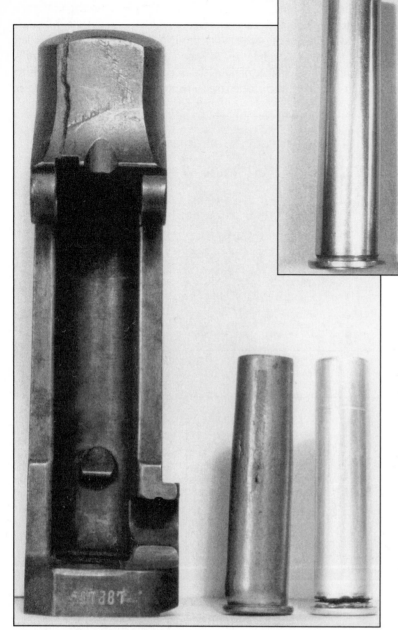

Above) **Definite signs of high pressure are obvious on these 45-70 cases. On the left is an unfired case. The center case was fired with a charge of 68 grains of IMR SR4759 powder – a 174% overload of the maximum loading (39 grains) for this powder with a 405 grain bullet. The barrel was bulged by this event and the case had to be driven out with a rod. The case on the right was fired with 40 grains of Unique behind a 500 grain cast bullet. The maximum load for this bullet is 14.8 grains. This represents better than a 270% overload. The barrel of the same gun was bulged to the point the receiver cracked. The case required considerable pounding with a hammer and a metal rod to remove it. Note the expansion in front of the solid head and the stretching of the case. The case picked up machining marks from the chamber. A stiff extraction and any sign of case swelling are definite signs you are in the danger zone.**

A case-head separation is the worst event, with high pressure gas blowing back into the action and often into the face of the shooter. This is why you always wear shooting glasses. The old balloon-head case on the left combined with a double charge cracked the rifle receiver. Case on right suffered a nearly complete separation because of mercuric priming – no damage to gun or shooter (fortunately).

of a factory loaded case after firing and a handload using the same make of case after firing it for the first time. A larger diameter will tell you you have higher pressure than the factory load.

The flattening of primers is a sign of high pressure. However, many high pressure rifle cartridges will show a good deal of flattening as a matter of course. Again the critical factor is the difference between the flattening of a factory loading and a handload using the same components fired for the first time. If the flattening is greater, you have a higher pressure than the factory loading and are in the upper limit of the margin of safety for your particular gun. Most factory loads are near the maximum. This information is based on an "all other things being equal" basis. Whenever you suspect something is wrong, make sure all other things

are equal and you are not introducing some factor that will alter your results. Getting oil or other lubricants on cartridge cases is part of the reloading process. This should be removed before firing. Oil in a chamber or on a cartridge case will cause that case to slide in the chamber instead of expanding and sticking to the chamber wall during firing. This causes excessive back thrust of the case against the bolt. Back thrust batters the case head, often transferring impressions of machining on the bolt face to the case head. These appear, to the untrained eye, to be caused by high pressure. Battering the bolt face will also increase the headspace in the gun, which is a serious problem.

The puncturing of primers – a so called "blown primer" where a hole is blown through the primer where the firing pin hits it is a definite sign of very high pressure, unless you

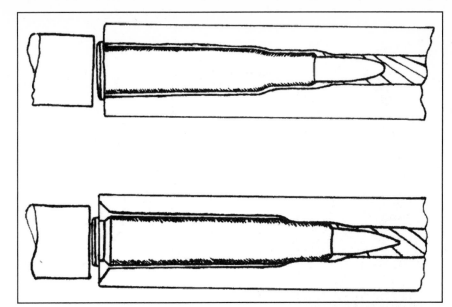

Headspace is measured between the face of the bolt and the front edge of the rim where it touches the breech on any rimmed case (Top). Headspace on a rimless case is measured between the bolt face and the point where the case shoulder or the case mouth contacts the chamber.

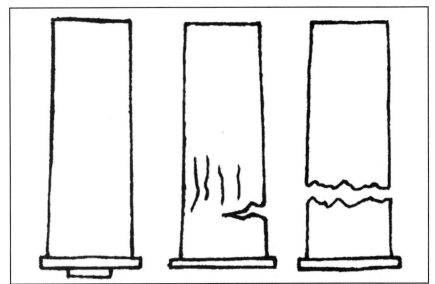

Excessive headspace begins as a backed-out primer. Stage two is the appearance of stretching and cracks. Stage three is separation. If excessive headspace is combined with an overload, stage three may be reached on the first loading.

Stretch marks and crack on this case are indicative of excessive headspace.
(Courtesy Speer)

have a firing pin that is too long. Firing pins do not suddenly grow longer. Stop shooting! Before a primer blows, under pressure, there will be evidence of "cratering." This is where the metal in the primer flows back around the tip of the firing pin and into the hole where the pin comes through the bolt or breech block. Cratering can also be caused by a soft primer and an oversize firing-pin hole. Here again, a comparison with a fired factory round with the same components is the best way to judge differences.

Gas leaks around primers make a black soot smudge at their edges. This is evidence of a gas leak between the primer and the primer pocket. Primer pocket stretching in a case will occur after a number of loadings, particularly high pressure ones. This tells you the case is finished for reloading. If a leak occurs after long use this can be assumed to be normal. When such a leak happens the first time, with a new case, look for other high pressure signs. The above mentioned signs most often come together — hard extraction, flat primer, blown or leaky primer.

Soot-streaking of cases when they are fired, particularly staining near the case mouth, is a sign not of high pressure but of its opposite – low pressure. If a loading is not generating enough pressure to obturate the chamber — i.e., make a complete gas seal between the cartridge case and the chamber wall – a certain amount of gas will leak back into the action and smudge the case. Other than being a minor nuisance this causes no danger. It is an indication that combustion is at too low a level owing to not enough powder or poor ignition of the powder. Such under-powered loads will tend to be inaccurate since the amount of gas that escapes will vary from shot to shot depending on the elasticity of the individual case.

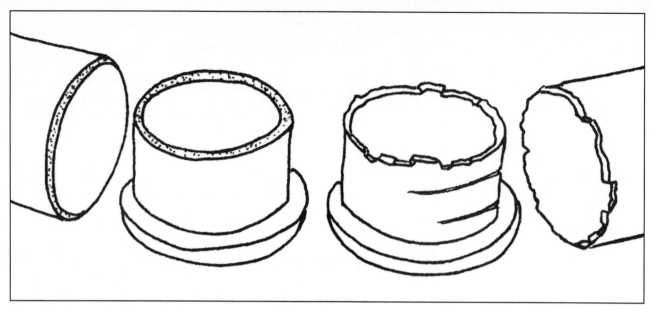

A case-head separation has two basic causes. Type one is brass failure, often caused by mercuric-priming contamination or brass that is otherwise weak and brittle. Type two is excessive headspace in the gun. These result in different types of fractures. Type one (left)is a clean break with a crystalline surface. Type two is characterized by tearing of the metal and stretch marks on the case.

UNDERSTANDING HEADSPACE

In order for a cartridge to enter and exit a gun chamber it has to be made a little smaller than the chamber, with enough room for easy extraction after it is fired. To work properly, however, the case must be firmly supported by the bolt or breech block to keep it from rupturing under pressure. The amount of acceptable tolerance between the head of the case and the face of the bolt or breech block is less than five thousandths of an inch in a good modern gun. Zero tolerance would be best, but guns and ammunition are mass produced products and a certain amount of tolerance must be permitted for variations that are part of the manufacturing process. A tolerance of several thousandths of an inch represents the elastic limits of the cartridge case, allowing the fired case to return to close to its original size for extraction. If the tolerance is greater, the elastic limits of the case are exceeded and it will begin to deform. This situation is known as "excessive headspace."

Tolerances for headspace are set at the factory and remain in place for the life of a gun. That life is shortened by shooting high-pressure loads which batter the bolt or breech block, gradually increasing the headspace. This problem can be corrected by a skilled gunsmith, depending on the type of gun and how bad the situation has become.

CALCULATING HEADSPACE

Headspace is measured with gauges to a thousandth of an inch. In a rimmed or semi-rimmed case the headspace measurement is between the surface of the bolt or breech block and the point where the front of the cartridge rim makes contact with the face of the breech. With rimless cases, the measurement is between the bolt face and the point where the shoulder of the case makes contact with the counterbore in the chamber. In straight rimless cases such as the 45 ACP the measurement is to the point where the case mouth makes contact with the front of the chamber.

EXCESSIVE HEADSPACE

This is when the tolerances become too great. When this situation occurs, the cartridge case is held tightly against the chamber walls in the firing cycle. With the case head unsupported by the bolt or breech block, the case stretches backward under the force of the pressure inside it, until it makes contact with the bolt face and stops. Usually before this happens, the primer is pushed out of its pocket until it meets the bolt face. As pressure drops in the chamber, the case springs back and creeps back over the primer, often jamming the now expanded primer back into the pocket. On examination the flattened primer, at times with gas leaks around it, having expanded the pocket, will appear for all the world like an example of high pressure. The reloader should make sure he has not loaded a maximum load. If this was a max load, he should try a factory cartridge for comparison. If the problem is excessive headspace the signs should be there under normal loads, and they may appear even under reduced loads although somewhat less obvious. Often, the only sign will be a primer backed out of the case.

After a case, stretched in a chamber that is too long, is resized, reloaded and fired, the stretching process is repeated with the next firing. Stretch marks, in the form of shiny rings, begin to appear around the circumference of the case body forward of the head. After a number of reloadings, depending on how much stretching and resizing occurs, the case will become fatigued and rupture, blowing high pressure gas back into the action, often destroying the gun, and into the face of the shooter with similar results. A combination of poor brass, a heavy load and a lot of extra headspace can bring on this condition in a single shot.

Headspace problems can be created in the reloading process! This occurs with rimless cases such as the 30-06 and

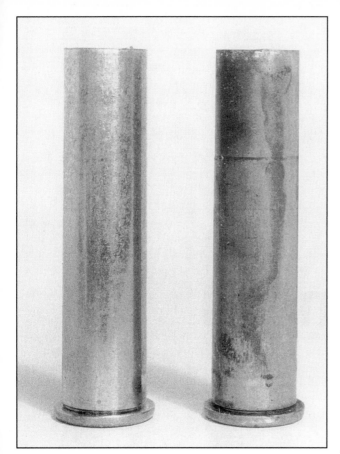

Low pressure is evidenced by the soot stains on the case on the right, which failed to make a complete gas seal when fired.

Primer pockets will stretch, as did the one on the left, after a number of heavy loads have been run through a case. If the leak or stretch appears, suddenly, on a new or nearly new case, you are in the very high pressure range and should reduce your loads.

A leak around a primer indicates an expanded primer pocket. Time to discard the case.

Soft-alloy bullets of lead and tin (the shiny ones on the ends) will yield lower pressures than harder-alloy bullets (numbers 3, 4, and 6 from the left). Jacketed bullets (fifth from the left) create significantly higher pressures as do heavier bullets.

223 where improper use of the sizing die forces the shoulder back on the case body, allowing the case to go further into the chamber than it should. The extractor hook will hold the case in the proper position for firing, but the case has now become too short and has to stretch back to meet the bolt face. If this practice is continued, it is only a matter of time until a rupture occurs with all the grief that goes with it. Any gun showing signs of excessive headspace should not be fired. Examination by a skilled gunsmith will tell you if the situation can be corrected.

Over the years,
ignition of the
powder charge
has been
accomplished in
a number of
ways. Today, big
things come from
small packages.

Primers

THE PURPOSE OF the primer is to ignite the main powder charge. This was originally done with a burning splinter or hot wire jammed into a small "touch hole" at the breech of the gun. Later, sparks from iron pyrites and flint striking steel were employed to set off a small charge of powder in a funnel or "pan" that connected with the propelling charge in the gun barrel. These systems worked, but they didn't work well, which prompted a search for an ignition system that fulfilled the four criteria of today's modern primers: speed, reliability, uniformity and cleanliness.

PRIMER EVOLUTION

Early ignition systems failed in all the above criteria. Match locks, equipped with a slow-smoldering fuse made of chemically treated rope called a "match," would burn out in damp weather and could be blown out by wind. Wind and damp were the enemies of flintlocks that could blow the priming charge out of the funnel-shaped pan or saturate it with moisture to the point where it would not catch fire. Rust and powder fouling in the tiny tube that connected the charge in the pan to the propelling charge in the barrel often prevented a successful firing with only the priming charge burning. The expression "a flash in the pan" is still used to describe a person or enterprise that shows promise, but fails to get past a good beginning. Under the best of circumstances, the flintlock system gave only reasonable reliability. A small piece of cut flint held in the jaws of the hammer struck a steel cover on the pan called a frizzen, knocking it open and scraping the inner side to throw sparks into the powder charge in the pan. In terms of speed it was slow. Anyone who has seen a flintlock fired is familiar with the puff-boom! sound of the report as the priming charge burns with a one-beat pause before the propelling charge fires. History is filled with untold numbers of targets, animal and human, who have ducked to safety during that beat, which was sometimes

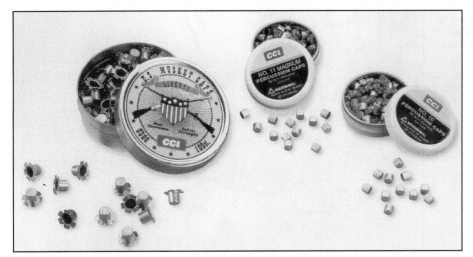

Modern percussion caps are essentially a primer without an anvil inside it, that part being provided by the nipple on the gun.

(Below) **Berdan** (left) **and Boxer primer pockets show the differences in the systems. The ease of reloading made the Boxer primer standard in the U.S.** (Photo courtesy CCI.)

two beats if the day was damp and the tube to the barrel a bit clogged.

Explosives such as fulminate of mercury and mixtures including potassium chlorate that detonated when crushed or struck, were discovered late in the 18th century. After attempts to use them as substitutes for gunpowder failed, they received little attention until the early 19th.

The breakthrough to improved ignition was made by a Scottish Presbyterian minister, hunter, shooter and gun buff — Reverend Alexander Forsythe — who was the first to come up with the idea of using these detonating explosives to ignite propelling charges in firearms. He received a patent in 1807 for a system that did away with the priming pan on the flintlock and filled the tube leading to the barrel with a percussion explosive made of sulphur, potassium chlorate and charcoal. A metal pin was inserted on top of the explosive which caused it to detonate when struck by the gun's hammer. The ignition was far faster and more certain than the flintlock. Forsythe improved his design by attaching a small iron bottle containing a supply of percussion explosive to the side of the lock. The bottle could be tipped or turned to deposit a small pellet of explosive on a touch hole which would be struck by the hammer. The system worked effectively. However, it involved having a small iron bottle filled with explosive very close to the firing point and to the face of the shooter. I have never encountered a report of an accident with a Forsythe lock, but if one happened, it would almost certainly have been fatal.

The superiority of the Forsythe system was soon recognized and dozens of priming systems were introduced including percussion wafers, tubes and strips of paper caps, much like those used in toy cap pistols. The most successful was the percussion cap invented in about 1814 by Joshua Shaw — a British subject who emigrated to America. Shaw's system featured a small steel cup, about the size of a modern large pistol or large rifle primer. The closed end contained the explosive held in place by a tinfoil cover then sealed with a drop of lacquer. This made it waterproof as well as damp proof. The cap was fitted on a short iron nipple, hollow in the center, screwed into the breech of the barrel.

This allowed the fire to enter the chamber of the gun. Shaw came to America in 1814 and began perfecting a lock to work with his invention. Shaw caps were on the market by 1821 and were soon adapted to sporting guns. Improvements were made by changing the cap metal to pewter and later copper. Similar caps were in use about the same time over most of Europe. The percussion cap was not adopted by the U.S. military until after the Mexican War. The military thinking at the time was that the percussion cap was yet another component the soldier had to carry and not reusable in the manner of a gun flint.

Percussion caps made the Colt revolver a practical reality, but the shortcomings of this system became apparent when repeating rifles were made using this system. A "flash over" from one chamber to the next would occasionally send a bullet coasting by the side of the gun. With a handgun this was of little consequence since it was a one-hand weapon. With the rifle or shotgun such an event often amputated the fingers or thumb of the hand supporting the fore-end of the weapon. Revolving rifles, not surprisingly, did not gain much popularity.

Breechloading arms, other than revolvers, using percussion ignition did not fare much better mainly because no one was able to come up with an effective means of engineering a gas-tight seal at the breech closure.

Not surprisingly the first really successful breechloaders and successful repeating arms, other than revolvers, required a self-contained, self-primed cartridge. The step to the rimfire cartridge from the percussion cap was a small but logical evolution. George Morse placed a percussion

Early "tong" reloading tools could be carried in the pocket. These from the old Ideal Company cast bullets, decapped, primed and seated bullets in black-powder calibers.

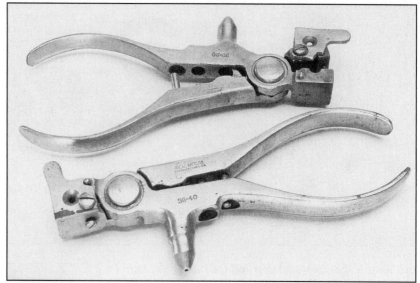

(Below) **Lee Hand Press Kit is a modern version of the old "tong tool." This kit includes dies, case lube, powder dipper, etc., for a little over $65.**

cap in the head of a metal cartridge using a hairpin-shaped anvil inside the case to fire it. Hiram Berdan shortened the hairpin to a tiny knob, while Edward Boxer placed a tiny anvil inside the cap.

CENTER PRIMED

Centerfire ammunition soon pushed all the other non-reloadable types out of the market because it was reloadable. Rimfires were gradually reduced to those types that were small and efficient in calibers that would not lend themselves to reloading.

The military had great influence in ammunition development stipulating that any ammunition developed for a military small arm had to be reloadable. Spent cases were collected and returned to a government arsenal for reloading during peacetime. Professional hunters in the American west needed cartridges they could reload themselves with simple tools. It was this type of equipment that first appeared in the 1870's.

Early priming mixtures used fulminate of mercury or potassium chlorate, eventually, a combination of both. These fulfilled most of the criteria for good ignition — speed, reliability, uniformity and cleanliness, with the possible exception of cleanliness. While the chlorate-based primers did not leave an appreciable residue, they did leave a highly corrosive deposit — potassium chloride — that would eat away a percussion nipple or the web of a cartridge unless neutralized by cleaning with water that removed the salt deposit. The mercury-based compounds were both clean and non-corrosive. Their drawback came when used in combination with brass or copper primer cups and brass or gilding-metal cartridge cases. When fired, the mercury would amalgamate with the copper or brass, making it extremely brittle. The heavy fouling of blackpowder had a mitigating effect on mercury contamination, keeping it in the fouling allowing removal. With smokeless powder, reloading and firing such a contaminated cartridge case can lead to a case-head rupture. In a high pressure loading this can wreck a gun and possibly your face. Mercuric priming was gone from commercial ammunition by about 1945, but mercuric primers made prior to this time were used by commercial reloaders after that and some of them may still be on shelves somewhere.

Because fulminate of mercury contains free, liquid mercury, this mercury will actually migrate through the priming mixture and into the metal of the primer cup or cartridge head after a certain number of years. Ammunition primed with mercuric mixtures made in the early 1930's will probably not fire today while ammunition loaded with chlorate priming made during the Civil War is often still viable, so long as neither the powder or priming compound has been exposed to moisture. Thus a fifth criterion should be added to a successful ignition system — long life.

From 1928 through 1935 American manufacturers worked to perfect a priming mixture akin to the one developed in Germany that was non-corrosive and did not contain mercury. The basis of such priming is in compounds of lead, barium and antimony.

Early non-corrosive, non-mercuric primers did not work very well, giving uneven ignition. Priming material often

Pistol and rifle primers come in two sizes, while shotshell primers are of one size.

(Below) **Pistol primers should not be used in rifle cases since they will seat too deeply as in the case on the left. Center case shows proper seating depth while high primer on the right will give poor ignition and possible slam-fire in an autoloader.**

Check primers to see they are properly oriented before loading. Case on the right exploded in the bullet seating die because the primer was not fully seated. NEVER seat primers in loaded cartridges.

fell out of the rim in rimfire cartridges as the binding material — a vegetable-based glue — deteriorated.

THE MODERN PRIMER

Modern primers of the lead, barium and antimony type fulfill all the necessary criteria for good ignition. The binders are now stable and remain stable for long periods under normal "house" storage conditions where temperatures are under 125 degrees Fahrenheit and moisture is kept at a reasonable level. The newest are the "lead free" primers of tetracene. These, however, are not presently sold as reloading components since the production demand is for finished ammunition. The primary use of such primers is in handgun ammunition to be fired in indoor ranges where airborne lead could present a health hazard.

Because of the difficulty of reloading them, cartridges using Berdan primers and the Berdan primers themselves have virtually disappeared from the U.S. Foreign cartridges often still use this type of priming and can only be reloaded with Berdan primers. Any attempt at "converting" Berdan cases to Boxer priming by drilling them in some manner will

not work and such attempts are very dangerous since they will greatly enlarge the flash hole and may damage the web. At best such conversions give uneven ignition; at worst they can raise pressures to dangerous levels by causing too rapid a burn of the powder charge. The only current source for Berdan primers and Berdan decapping equipment is The Old Western Scrounger.

A modern Boxer primer differs little in structure from those made over a century ago. It is a brass cup containing the priming compound. A paper seal keeps the compound in the cup and is held in place by the metal anvil made of harder brass. A better understanding of metallurgy and chemistry has resulted in a more uniform primer as well as ones which are specifically tailored to a particular type of cartridge.

Primers for pistols and rifles come in two basic sizes: "small" (.175" diameter) and "large" (.210" diameter). There is a .317" primer manufactured by CCI used only in the .50 Browning machine gun cartridge – loaded by a few shooters using extra heavy bench-rest rifles in this caliber. Small pistol primers are used in such calibers as 25 and 32 caliber handgun ammunition while the large size are used in 41, 44 and 45 caliber handguns. Large pistol primers are also made in a "magnum" variant. These are for large capacity cases using slow-burning powders that are harder to ignite and

(Left and above) **Primers are sold in strips which can be refilled with the RCBS strip-loading tool. You have to buy the system.** *(Photo courtesy RCBS.)*

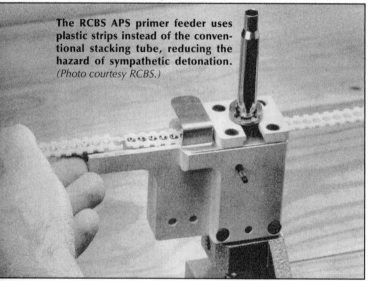

The RCBS APS primer feeder uses plastic strips instead of the conventional stacking tube, reducing the hazard of sympathetic detonation. *(Photo courtesy RCBS.)*

require a longer-burning, hotter primer to draw the most uniform and complete burning from these powders.

Rifle primers are made in the same two diameters as pistol primers and are designated "small" and "large" although they are slightly higher to fit the deeper pocket in the rifle cartridge case. For this reason pistol primers should not be seated in rifle cases since they will seat too deeply and will thus often give uneven ignition. Rifle primers contain more priming compound than pistol primers since they have to ignite more powder in larger capacity cases. If you are loading both handgun and rifle ammunition, care must be taken not to mix rifle and handgun primers. If rifle primers are seated in pistol cases they will not fit properly. They can also raise pressures to the danger point. Pistol primers tend to burn cooler, and produce more of a flame type of explosion — good for igniting fast-burning pistol powders. Rifle primers burn longer and hotter. They often contain metallic elements such as aluminum which create burning sparks that

are blown forward into a charge of slower-burning powder. This separates, the grains thus setting the charge on fire in a number of places at once to achieve an even burning of the charge. This explosive quality is known as "brisance." Magnum rifle primers have still more compound, burn longer and hotter and are used in very large-capacity cases such as the 458 Winchester Magnum. Companies such as CCI also market a "bench rest" rifle primer. This is simply a standard rifle primer, but made to very strict tolerances assuring the reloader that each primer in a given lot will have a very precisely measured amount of compound and that the diameter and hardness of all components are within very strict tolerances. These premium-quality primers give very even ignition needed for the exacting demands of the expert, competition target shooter.

Shotshell primers have special characteristics needed to work properly in modern, plastic shotshells. Early shotshells were made of brass and were generally of a rifle-type of construction. They used rifle-style primers. Modern shells are of a composite construction with a metal head surrounding a paper, now primarily a plastic body. Inside is a base wad made of plastic or compressed paper.

Shotshells have unique ignition problems. As the mouth of the shell becomes worn and softened with repeated reloading the opening of the crimp becomes progressively easier. Modern shotgun powders require a certain amount of pressure and confinement to function properly. This decreases as the crimp softens. For proper ignition, the powder requires a very high temperature over a longer than usual burn time but without the brisant quality of the magnum rifle powder which would tend to blow the crimp open before much of the powder was ignited. A shotshell primer produces what is often referred to as a "soft ignition."

Because of the design of modern shotshells, the primer is held in a large, longer than normal housing called a "battery cup" which extends well into the base wad so the flame

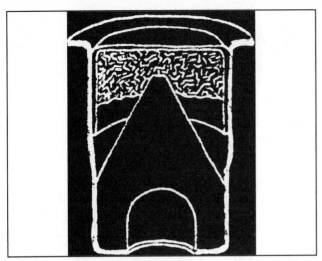

Shotshell "battery cup" primer comes with the primer pocket and vent as part of the unit, all of which is replaced at reloading time.

issuing from the primer mouth will not be inhibited by any part of the wad and can direct its full blast into the powder charge.

HANDLING AND STORAGE

As has been mentioned in the safety section, primers are the most dangerous component in the reloading operation. They are subject to shock and explode with a violence that belies their small size. Children often have a penchant for playing with small shiny objects and primers should definitely be kept out of their hands. Primers are packaged to keep them from shock and from striking one another. Julian Hatcher in his *Notebook* tells of a young worker in an ammunition plant carrying a metal bucket of primers, casually bouncing it as he walked. There was a sudden, violent explosion. As I recall a part of a foot was the largest piece recovered.

Primers should only be stored in the packaging they come in, never in a can or bottle where they can rattle around. Automatic primer feeding devices of a tube design should be loaded with great care because this brings a considerable number together in a way that if one accidentally explodes, the remainder will go too. The explosive force of a primer is many, many times that of the most powerful smokeless powder.

Properly stored, primers do not present a particularly dangerous hazard. They will explode quite loudly if thrown in a fire and come flying with enough force to penetrate a cardboard carton a foot or more away. People have lost eyesight from such injuries, so this is not the way to dispose of damaged, though unexploded primers. The best way to dispose of unfired primers is to load them in an empty cartridge case and snap them. If this is not practical they can be deactivated by soaking in a strong lye solution for a week. The liquid may be flushed away with a large quantity of water. The potassium chlorate in the old corrosive primers is very water soluble and water soaking works well with this type.

We are talking here about small numbers of primers — not more than two dozen. If for some reason you should have to dispose of a large number of primers, call the local, gun shop, fire department or police department for assistance. Counties that have "hazmat" recycling may take material of that sort. Always check first.

Shelf storage should be in a cool dry place, away from containers of gunpowder and away from children's reach. To avoid an explosion hazard in case of fire they should not be stored in a closed heavy metal container such as a military ammunition can. Primers can stand a fair amount of heat before they will "cook off." An account by Julian Hatcher of a fire in a gun shop noted that cardboard boxes of primers on shelves were scorched, but none of the primers inside exploded.

The lacquer seals used in modern primers keeps them free of deterioration from dampness. Basement storage is not recommended for any ammunition component unless that basement is kept dry with a dehumidifier. About the only uniquely vulnerable feature about primers is the paper seal which could be attacked by mold under extremely damp conditions.

Three questions frequently asked by shooters of military foreign, and obsolete guns are: (1) How can you determine if military ammunition you are planning to shoot and reload is Berdan primed? (2) How can you determine which ammunition is corrosively primed? and (3) How can you tell if a case has been contaminated by mercuric primers?

The answer to the first is fairly simple — usually. Berdan primers are almost always of a larger diameter than the equivalent Boxer primers, although the CCI non-reloadable primer currently manufactured is virtually the same size. Most foreign military primers are the Berdan type and are larger although some are not. The surest way to know is to examine a fired cartridge case and look into the case for the small twin vents that are the trademark of this system. This is not possible when buying ammunition. About the best you can do is ask the dealer if the stuff is Boxer primed or not and get a guarantee that if it isn't, he will take the unfired portion back.

Question two — corrosive priming is a little more complicated. Corrosive priming was a serious problem in the early days of smokeless powder ammunition, since corrosive salts were deposited in large quantities in the barrels of guns that fired it. Black powder fouling, while corrosive to a degree, helped to hold these salts and the fouling was relatively easy to clean with a soap and warm water mixture. After cleaning, the bore was wiped dry and then oiled to protect it. With the introduction of smokeless powder there was very little powder fouling in the bore. Jacketed bullets moving at high velocities left a hard metallic fouling in rifle bores composed of copper and nickel from the jackets. This metal fouling was difficult to remove and trapped the corrosive salt (potassium chloride) in a layer between the barrel surface and the metal coating. A barrel could appear perfectly clean, but days later even though the bore was saturated with oil or grease, it would rust heavily under this protective coating.

To combat this problem, cleaning solvents were developed that would dissolve this metal fouling and remove the salts from the corrosive priming. Most of these solvents contained ammonia which readily dissolves copper and nickel. A water-based solution of ammonia does a very good job of removing both metal fouling and primer salts. Years ago, this author cleaned up after firing a lot of corrosive-priming/copper-jacket fouling by corking the chamber of his 303 Enfield with a rubber stopper and carefully filling the bore with household ammonia, then letting it stand for an hour or so. The dissolved salts and copper fouling were removed when the barrel was tipped. The fouling was obvious in the blue-green tint it gave to the ammonia solution. After dumping the liquid, a couple of wet patches were run through the bore then a couple of dry patches and the bore was swabbed with Hoppe's Number 9 or similar solvent until everything came clean. Care had to be taken not to spill ammonia on any blued surface since it will remove the blue. Care also had to be taken not to leave the solution too long or, worse, let it dry on any exposed steel surface since it will readily rust that surface.

Commercial solvents with ammonia, bearing names like "Chlor oil" "Fiend oil" and "Crystal Cleaner" were once marketed for cleaning up corrosive priming. They have been

Crystal Cleaner was an ammonia-based metal-solvent from Winchester in the early days of corrosive priming. U.S. Military bore cleaner in the old dark-green can combined ammonia and powder solvent in a brown, evil-smelling combination that did a good job of removing corrosive primer residue and metal fouling.

(Above and below) **Military ammunition generally has the primer swaged in the case with a "military" primer crimp that makes initial removal and repriming difficult.**

CORROSIVE/NON-CORROSIVE PRIMING: U.S. MILITARY AMMUNITION (U.S.- and Canadian-manufactured ammunition)			
Headstamp	Mfr.	Changeover Date	Non-Corr. Headstamp
FA	Frankford	Oct 1951 (30)	FA 52-
		July 1954 (45)	FA 55-
DEN	Denver	All corrosive during WWII	
DM	Des Moines	All corrosive during WWII	
EC	Eau Claire	All corrosive during WWII	
LC	Lake City	June 1951 (30)	LC 52
		April 1952 (30 AP)	LC 53
SL	St. Louis	May 1952 (30)	SL 53
		July 1952 (30 AP)	SL 53
TW	Twin Cities	Dec 1950 (30)	TW 51
		Feb 1952 (30 AP)	TW 53
U and UT	Utah	All corrosive during WWII	
DAQ	Dominion (Canada)	All noncorrosive	
VC	Verdun (Canada)	All noncorrosive	
FCC	Federal	Nov 1953 (45)	FC 54-
RA	Remington	Nov 1951 (30)	RA 52-
		Sept 1952 (45)	RA 53-
WCC	Western	June 1951 (30)	WCC 52-
		Nov 1952 (45)	WCC 53-
WRA	Winchester	Aug 1951 (30)	WRA 52-
		June 1954 (30 AP)	WRA 55-
		Nov 1951 (45)	WRA 52-

All 223 (5.56mm), 30 Carbine, 308 (7.62mm), 9mm Luger and 38 Special military ammunition is non-corrosive. Exceptions are the 1956 NATO 308 Match ammunition made at the Frankford Arsenal and 30-06 Match ammunition made at the Frankford Arsenal in 1953, 1954 and 1956. All are stamped FA with the two-digit date. (This information was adapted from the NRA *Handloader's Guide*.)

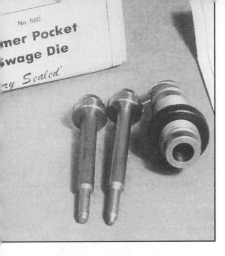

No. 500
mer Pocket
wage Die
ny Sealed

Primer crimps are removed with this handy tool that returns the primer pocket back to its original size.

gone from the scene so long that few people remember their names. The U.S. military came up with its own preparation called simply "Bore Cleaner" — a dark brown concoction with a smell you will never forget (although you wish you could) that combined ammonia with water-soluble oil and powder solvents. This worked quite well.

Corrosive priming was gone from commercial ammunition by the 1930's. In the early 1950's noncorrosive priming gradually replaced the corrosive type in U.S. military ammunition and a decade or so later, the Army switched to a newer type of cleaner which is sold commercially under the name "Breakfree." By this time most shooters had forgotten about corrosive primed ammunition. Cleaners of the "Break Free" type do a reasonable job of removing powder fouling and preventing rust from external causes, such as exposure to damp conditions. Currently the Army favors one such named "Clenzoil." These do not, however, remove corrosive potassium salt which must be removed with a water-based cleaner since salt does not dissolve in oil.

With the importation of Russian and Chinese Tokarev, Moisin, SKS and AKM rifles and ammunition, corrosive priming is back on the American scene and many of the current powder solvents were ineffective in removing the corrosive salt. The old Army bore cleaner still does a good job. It is still available at many gun shops and military-surplus outlets. After cleaning with that, run several dry patches until the bore is clean; then oil with a good protective oil or grease with rust inhibitors. Another option is to use one of the solvents that remove copper fouling. There are a number of new products of this type available. Check any solvent/cleaner you buy for clear information that it will remove corrosive fouling. Never guess about implied promises.

Identifying corrosive-primed American military ammunition is an easy matter of consulting the accompanying list that was compiled by the NRA several years ago. When it comes to foreign ammunition, unless it is in the original box from a commercial manufacturer and clearly marked "Non-corrosive" assume it is corrosive, particularly if it is military ammunition, especially that from any former East-Bloc country. If you wish to experiment, collect some fired cases and place them outdoors for a week or two in warm humid weather or stand them on their heads, with a drop or two of water in the case and let it stand over night. If corrosive salt is present, there will usually be evidence of corrosion inside the case particularly near the vent. Moisture, and a black/green color will be clearly evident.

The question of mercuric priming is best dealt with on the basis of: if the ammunition or cases are pre-WWII and not corrosive primed, they are likely mercuric primed. If the ammunition is in the original box and the box declares it to be "non-corrosive, non-mercuric," and it's in good (appearing) condition, it's probably good to shoot or, if the old non-mercuric primers are no good, the bullets can be pulled and the cartridges can be reloaded, if you think it's worth the effort.

Oftentimes batches of old fired cases turn up and the shooter has no idea whether they are usable. If the caliber is something currently available, don't bother. The knotty problem is when such a batch turns up in some obsolete caliber like 351 or 401 Winchester and you have one of those rifles and nothing to shoot in it. Converting some other cartridge to these is very difficult. Loaded new ammunition in these calibers is available from The Old Western Scrounger as well as new brass, but the price may make you gasp. A batch of old cases might be a bargain, if they are in good condition and all the same make. If there is heavy tarnish and season cracking, forget it. If they have a scaly appearance or are stretched, bulged or otherwise evidence damage or distortion, forget it. This leaves the possibility of mercury contamination, which leaves no visible evidence. The only test I could find to make the determination of mercury contamination comes from *Handloader's Manual* by Earl Naramore. It was published in 1937. Naramore states that you must sacrifice a case for testing. It must be carefully sectioned with a fine hacksaw. After sectioning, the cut surface should be filed with a fine metal file to remove the saw marks and then polished on a piece of fine emery paper or crocus cloth. The polished case is then submerged for a few seconds in a 20% solution of nitric acid until the polished surface takes on a dull or slightly-roughened appearance. Leaving the case in the bath too long will pit the surface.

After the case is properly etched, the walls can be examined with a magnifying glass for flaws in the metal. The case should be removed from the etching bath with a pair of tweezers and washed in clear water.

States Naramore: "The action of the nitric acid will clean the fouling from the inside of the case thoroughly and if the surface has a silvery appearance, it is a sure indication that the case has been fired with a mercuric primer. This silver-looking coating, which is really mercury, will disappear into the brass after the specimen has stood a little while, so the condition should be looked for immediately after taking the case out of the etching solution. Unfortunately, the failure of the mercury to appear does not offer assurance that the case has never been fired with a mercuric primer, but the mercury will usually show up." Naramore goes on to urge the reloader to examine the etched case for cracks or splits in the head, which can usually be seen with the unaided eye or with a magnifying glass.

Blackpowder
has some modern
competition that's
cleaner and safer

Blackpowder and Its Variants

GUNPOWDER IS THE driving force that makes a gun shoot. It does this by changing from a solid to a large volume of hot gas in a very short time in what is best termed a low-velocity explosion. This works very well for propelling bullets down gun barrels without raising the pressure too suddenly, which would cause the barrel to burst before the bullet gets moving. High velocity or "high" explosives are unsuitable for use in guns for this reason.

BLACKPOWDER

The original "gunpowder" is what is now referred to as "blackpowder" (BP) and is actually a dark gray in color, but the commercial form is coated with graphite. Its origin dates back about a thousand years. All sorts of ingredients have been added at various times, but the basic mixture is composed of potassium nitrate (75%), charcoal (15%), and sulphur (10%). Many people have made blackpowder at home. This practice is NOT recommended for the following reasons:

It is dangerous. One mistake can prove disastrous. Such a mistake cost this author both hands at the age of fifteen. He considers himself lucky he still has everything else intact. For those not impressed by danger, it may be added that home-made powder is never up to the standards of purity and consistency of the manufactured product.

Blackpowder and BP replacements continue to proliferate as new products come on the market and old ones disappear.

Blackpowder was the only practical propellent for use in guns until the first successful nitrocellulose powders came on the scene in about 1866. The coming of "smokeless" powders, which produce smoke, but less than blackpowder, brought an end to the general use of BP and the muzzle-loading guns in which it was used.

LOADING BLACKPOWDER

Blackpowder guns were intended for ONLY blackpowder. With the invention of the metallic cartridge some of the later, stronger ones will function well with reduced charges of smokeless powder. No traditional muzzle-loader, however, should ever be loaded with any smokeless powder.

The burning rate of blackpowder is determined by the size of the granulation. Very fine powder burns very rapidly and can raise pressures into the danger zone if the improper granulation is used in an otherwise safe load. Some people say you cannot overload a gun with blackpowder. YES YOU CAN!

Commercial BP is mixed then ground in a wet state to prevent an explosion. It is pressed into a cake and then granulated and sifted through screens to determine grain size. The grains are coated with graphite for ease in pouring. It is sold in four granulations: FFFFG for priming flintlocks, FFFG for handguns and rifles to 40 caliber, FFG for rifles above 40 caliber to 58 caliber and FG for rifles over 58 caliber and large bore shotguns. GOEX is the only U.S. manufacturer of blackpowder. Imports from Europe, South America, and China come and go.

Cleanup of BP fouling is best accomplished with one of the blackpowder solvents on the market or with patches saturated with warm water with a little detergent in it, followed by dry patches and then a good oil to protect the clean bore.

HANDLING AND STORAGE

Blackpowder and its modern variants do not present any unusual problems in storage. They should be kept cool and dry since they are hygroscopic (absorb moisture) to varying degrees. Never leave powder containers open for any length of time since this will allow moisture to enter. Never shake any can of powder. This tends to break down the granules and alter the burning characteristics. NEVER have any powder near an open flame or burning cigarette, cigar, or pipe. One spark in the can and you have a very sudden very hot fire or an explosion if it is in a heavy container.

Always keep powder in the original container. Since blackpowder is a mixture of basic elements its life span is indefinite. Unexploded shells filled with blackpowder fired during the siege of Québec in 1759-60 detonated with considerable vigor in the early 1970's after they were discovered during construction.

FFg blackpowder is a fairly coarse-grained propellant. The scale above is 1 inch divided into hundredths.

Hodgdon's Pyrodex is an improved form of blackpowder with cleaner burning characteristics.

PROBLEMS WITH BLACKPOWDER

The corrosive and hard, crusty fouling caused by BP became evident with its use in the earliest guns. It produces a thick, white smoke obscuring targets and marking the position of a shooter. As guns were refined, in terms of accuracy, particularly with the introduction of the rifled barrel, these problems were of a serious enough magnitude to preclude adoption of the rifle as the main-line infantry weapon until the fouling problem was addressed. Early efforts included the Minié bullet (undersize for easy loading) with an expanding skirt and the Williams bullet with an expanding zinc washer attached to the base to scrape out fouling. Both were used during the Civil War.

Blackpowder formulation was refined and improved throughout the 19th century. Strategies such as compressing the powder into a nearly solid cake and using a longer burning, hotter primer — an innovation developed by the Frankford Arsenal for loading the 45-70 rifle cartridge — resulted in cleaner-burning ammunition than that with loose-loaded charges.

Nevertheless, blackpowder (potassium nitrate, sulfur, charcoal) leaves a residue in the form of sulfur dioxide (SO_2) that combines with water in the atmosphere (H_2O) to form sulfurous acid (H_2SO_3) that readily attacks many metals including steel and brass. Combined with this corrosive property, black powder residue is 56% solids which soon build up in rifle barrels and must be removed in a timely manner for accurate shooting.

BLACKPOWDER PERFORMANCE

Believe it or not, all black powders are not equal. The better ones use laboratory-quality chemicals while others use agricultural quality chemicals and substitute ammonium nitrate for potassium nitrate. The purity affects burning rate and seems to also alter the amount of fouling produced. Variations in performance vary not only from one maker to another, but from one production lot to another from the same source.

BLACKPOWDER CARTRIDGES

Blackpowder cartridges were still made for older guns, but by the 1930's these were gone. Guns from the 19th century in calibers that could handle smokeless were used with reduced loads or BP handloads. Those that couldn't entered the "wall-hanger" class.

A few hard-core enthusiasts hung on to blackpowder shooting and eventually formed the National Muzzle Loading Rifle Association (NMLRA). With the American bicentennial an increasing number of people became more history conscious, which for some included an interest in those "wall hanger" guns and how they might shoot. Along came The American Single Shot Rifle Association (ASSRA), The International Blackpowder Hunting Association (IBHA), and The Single Action Shooting Society (SASS) among other national organizations.

GOEX BLACKPOWDER

GOEX is the only U.S. maker of blackpowder and is the standard for comparison. GOEX is part of Hodgdon Powder, which distributes GOEX.

EARLY BLACKPOWDER SUBSTITUTES

Experiments to develop a propellent superior to blackpowder predate the Civil War. Early attempts to use guncotton (a crude form of nitrocellulose) and nitroglycerine regularly destroyed guns. Experimentation with these compounds eventually led to the development of successful smokeless powders in the late 1870's and early 80's.

Various mixtures of so-called "white" gunpowders were created during the Civil War period with the idea of alleviating the fouling problem. These contained potassium chlorate, ammonium nitrate, potassium ferricyanide, combined with such materials as sawdust, sugar, coal dust, mercuric fulminate, even talcum powder. The success of these concoctions is evident in the fact they are unknown today. The chlorate, while cleaner burning, became potassium chloride – a salt extremely corrosive to steel. Ammonium nitrate was hygroscopic and highly destructive to brass cartridges.

Both chlorate and mercury fulminate were sensitive to shock. As a result, virtually all the factories producing these products blew up sooner or later (mostly sooner) with considerable loss of life, bringing an end to their production.

HYBRID POWDERS

Not to be confused with the Hodgdon smokeless powder of this name, experimentation began immediately after the Civil War, in the creation of hybrid powders that combined elements of both black and smokeless powder that could be used in BP guns. They are known as semi-smokeless powders. These included nitrated wood or cotton – created by dissolving these materials in nitric acid, then washing out the acid residue with water. Failure to remove all the acid resulted in a highly unstable nitrocellulose compound, sensitive to shock, friction, and extremely dangerous. The usual number of explosions occurred, but successful propellants made of various forms of nitrocellulose, some combined with potassium nitrate, charcoal and sulfur were marketing successes under such names as "American Wood Powder," "Brackett's Sporting Powder," "King's Semi-Smokeless" and "Lesmok."

These powders had the advantage of producing consistent burning qualities and excellent accuracy. The fouling they produced was considerable, and corrosive, but relatively soft and thus (marginally) easier to remove than that of black

powder. "Lesmok" powder was loaded in 22 Long Rifle match ammunition until 1946. Semi-smokeless was used in both rimfire and centerfire ammunition into the 1930's.

The performance of "Lesmok" and semi-smokeless made them useful to the handloader and they were sold for this purpose. Both, however, were extremely dangerous to handle. They were very sensitive to friction, shock and ignition by electrical discharge of the sort generated by a person's scuffing across a wool rug on a cool, dry day. If a can of either turns up on a collector's table, you might want to buy the can, but get rid of the powder!

The evolution of nitrocellulose into smokeless powder created the viable product we use today. Thus, development of an improved blackpowder ceased before 1900, there being neither a need for nor interest in such a product.

DUPLEX LOADING

Reloaders for blackpowder guns have made their own "version" of improved blackpowder ammunition by loading a small ignition charge of smokeless powder and then filling the rest of the case with blackpowder. Known as "duplex loading" or "duplexing," this system produces less fouling since the smokeless powder burns up much of the BP fouling. The legendary barrel maker, Harry Pope, may have been the originator of this idea. Sometime before 1900 he developed a powder dispenser that would drop measured charges of smokeless and black powder (in that order) into a case. It sounds great, but...

All of the loading data on duplex loads is anecdotal – not tested in any laboratory, never produced by any ammunition company. Substitutions of one type of smokeless powder for another in the ignition charge can have unknown effects. If the charges are not packed firmly in a case the powders can mix and mingle resulting in wide variations in pressure and velocity — enough to blow up your gun! Added to this is the little known fact that the smokeless ignition charge causes a scouring effect by the blackpowder granules, weakening the case walls near the base. Plenty of blackpowder guns have been blown up with duplex loads, or what the shooter thought was a safe duplex load. Perhaps he reversed the proportions of black and smokeless, or forgot to put in any black at all and filled the case with smokeless, who knows? The list of duplex victims includes some very experienced reloaders. This author considers duplex loading to be the Devil's own invention.

NEW SUBSTITUTES FOR BLACKPOWDER

After 1900, an interest in blackpowder shooting with historic arms continued at a low, but consistent level throughout the twentieth century. It was after WWII, however, that interest began to grow, at a modest rate, mainly as a by-product of an increased interest in gun collecting. This led to the establishment of organizations of serious competi-

The chore of blackpowder cleanup is now easier with better cleaners and treated patches.

tive shooters such as the NMLRA and ASSRA. The U.S. bicentennial elevated interest in history including military reenactments and beyond.

Many collectors now wanted to shoot their guns. The NRA lent support to competitive events using historic arms and interest grew. The phenomenon of "Cowboy Action Shooting" – spawned by baby-boomers raised on matinee westerns – led to the establishment of the Single Action Shooters Society which sets rules and holds competitions. States sanctioned muzzle-loading hunting and both muzzle-loading and blackpowder cartridge rifles were brought out of retirement for competitive use. When the supply of vintage guns became scarce and expensive, the demand was met with replica arms. Blackpowder was back!

Shooters new to the blackpowder game, used to the quick and painless clean-up of smokeless-powder fouling, began to express a desire for something better than blackpowder. They wanted powder that they could load in the same manner, that left fouling that was easy to remove, and that was non-corrosive, while avoiding the pressure hazards of smokeless in old guns.

PYRODEX

By the 1970's, demand was great enough to generate a series of new substitutes for blackpowder. First out of the gate was Pyrodex, the creation of Dan Pawlak at Hodgdon Powder. At first blush (1976) this powder impressed this author as a reincarnation of the old Lesmok or semi-smokeless, particularly after it killed its creator in an explosion. Pyrodex, however, does not contain any form of nitrocellulose, being composed of potassium nitrate, charcoal, sulfur, potassium perchlorate, sodium benzoate, dicyandiamide dextrine, wax and graphite. The latter ingredients make it look like BP and flow smoothly through powder measures. The original formulation has been tweaked and the granulation size varied for use in different types of guns.

A later addition was pellets of compressed Pyrodex listed as "50 caliber 30 GR volume equivalent" and "50 caliber 50 GR equivalent." These feature a shiny end which contains an igniter layer and are intended for quick loading of .50 caliber muzzle-loaders. The actual pellets are about .456" diameter and will just slip into a .45-70 case.

Pyrodex, unlike Lesmok, is far safer to handle with a higher ignition threshold and is not particularly sensitive to shock or friction. This product has achieved considerable popularity and has proven itself capable of holding its own in competition. While Pyrodex "smokes like, smells like blackpowder," it also produces acid in the residue and will corrode steel and brass. Clean-up is easier, since the fouling is soft in comparison to BP and permits a greater number of accurate shots before bore cleaning is needed. Hodgdon once sold a cleaner (EZ Clean) which neutralizes both black and Pyrodex residue and is easier and neater than the old hot water and suds method. Versions of this product are available from a number of cleaning-product manufacturers.

This small sample is all I have of "Golden Powder." It appears unchanged by time – still terrible.

TRIPLE SEVEN

Hodgdon recently released an improved muzzle-loader and cartridge propellent: Triple seven. The name is derived from the story that the formula was the 777th combination tried. Triple Seven is also available in pellet form. The formulation contains charcoal, potassium nitrate and potassium perchlorate. It seems to be designed in part as a non-fouling, non-corrosive propellent for modern in-line muzzle-loaders. Feedback from two advanced shooters/reloaders of my acquaintance include cracking reports and heavy recoil. A .44 Magnum Ruger Redhawk with a full case load and cast bullet produced a violent recoil though no case swelling or extraction problems. I would strongly caution against use in a vintage BP gun. Triple Seven (among others) carries the warning in the loading manual cautioning against compressed loads.

WHITEHOTS

This is currently available from the IMR Co., now part of Hodgdon. Whitehots are of a similar formulation to 777, minus the charcoal. It is currently available only in pellet form for use in in-line muzzle-loaders.

GOLDEN POWDER

The idea of a non-corrosive BP substitute had enough appeal that various entrepreneurs ballyhooed products with this claim. In the late 1980's the first of these was "Golden Powder." It was of a fine, even granulation and looked very like instant coffee. My small sample still does. I recall seeing it for sale at a gun show at a (then) hefty price of $18 a pound. I did not succumb. I later heard from a local dealer who did, that it took "a three-inch column in a .45 caliber muzzle-loading rifle to generate "any velocity at all." Another story was of two pounds failing to blow a stump. "Golden Powder" soon exited the scene.

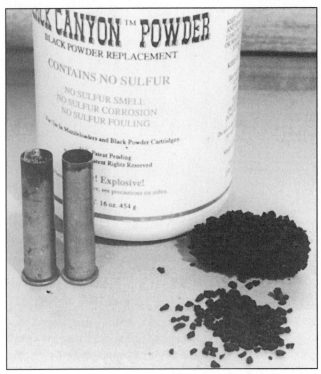

"Black Canyon" powder congealed into this evil-smelling lump. The heavy tarnish on the cases appears in a matter of hours if the ascorbic-acid-powder residues are not removed.

and M-1888 Springfield rifles gave poor accuracy and very uneven velocities — even with charges weighed to .1 grain. The supposed secret to getting accuracy from this powder was to have proper and consistent compression of the charge. I was never able to achieve this and my shots strung up and down the paper as the rifle alternately "popped" and "boomed." I never encountered anyone who had better results.

Experiments burning Black Canyon on scrubbed steel sheets demonstrated its non-corrosive qualities, in that there was no rusting for a couple weeks, in a dry environment. Truth in advertising, however, goes only so far, so I found, when I examined fired brass cases the morning after, during humid summer weather. The new case was now black around the mouth and the formerly shiny inside was black and green. When tipped, water, tinted greenish black dribbled out. Black Canyon was very hygroscopic. A tightly closed plastic container of Black Canyon, examined a year later, gave off a strong "burnt sugar" odor and had congealed into a solid chunk.

Golden Powder and Black Canyon were of a very similar formulation – potassium nitrate, charcoal and ascorbic acid (vitamin C). The ascorbic acid was harmless to steel. There was little visible fouling. Black Canyon soon followed the path of Golden Powder.

BLACK CANYON POWDER

Next up was Black Canyon Powder — a 1990's "miracle" from Legend Products Corp. Black Canyon featured dark irregular granules and the same promise of non-corrosiveness as Golden Powder. Tests I made in .45-70 M-1884

BLACK MAG

The next contender was from a company called Arco Powder, labeled "Black Mag." Black Mag contained the same basic ingredients as its two "non-corrosive" predecessors. A couple of articles heaped superlatives on this latest marvel, but nobody ever seemed to have any for sale. I finally called

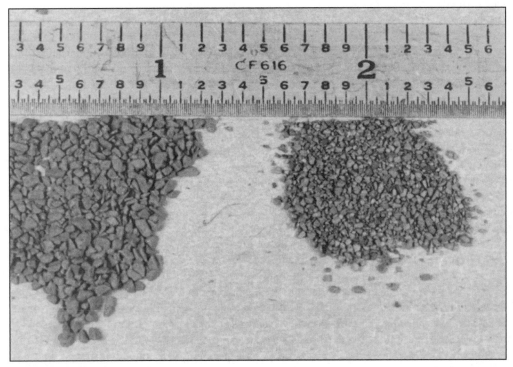

The Arco Black Mag (left) was about an FG granulation. The new formulation is finer and darker. The Arco Black Mag was one of the best shooting products of its type and is still in good condition after 15 years storage.

Black Mag XP now Black Dot (as marketed by Alliant) has a (purportedly) improved formulation featuring higher velocities at lower pressures.

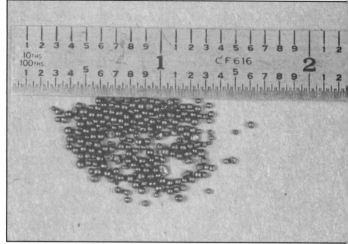

Clear Shot powder was a departure from previous formulations and grain shape, looking very much like smokeless ball powder. It shot well, but GOEX has no current plan to revive it.

the inventor/maker, Anthony Cioffe, who described himself as "a seat-of-the-pants-chemist" and went on to explain that his garage-shop operation was only the beginning of something big. He had purchased the Golden Powder formula and "tweaked" it to produce even, constant, ignition properties plus an indefinite shelf life. The product would soon be made by one of the big manufacturers — VihtaVuori was mentioned — as was a deal with NASA for a variant to serve as solid propellant for rockets.

I received a single, pound can of "Black Mag II" powder. It was light brown – resembling percolator-grind coffee. Like Black Canyon, it produced a cloud of gray smoke that was practically odorless, and little fouling — about like smokeless. In terms of accuracy, the results were two-inch hundred-yard groups out of my Springfield M-1884 rifle and only slightly larger from a M-1877 Springfield carbine – equalling the best I ever shot with black powder and very close to my best smokeless groups. I went as far as leaving a Springfield uncleaned for over a week – carefully monitoring it several times a day. Eventually, a soft, gray coating appeared on the bore surface but no obvious corrosion. That was in 1995. Alas, Mr. Cioffe died about a year after our conversation. The deals never came to pass owing to the inability of anyone to make Black Mag in larger than "garage-size" batches. It would seem the stuff of legends.

As of this writing (2010), Black Mag, however, is back in production from newly formed Black Mag Industries. It is slated to be sold as "Black Dot" powder through the Alliant Powder Co.

The new product is of a finer granulation than the original Black Mag and darker in color. On May 14, 2010, the Black Mag plant in Vermont blew up. So it will be a while before this product will become available in quantity.

CLEAN SHOT/ AMERICAN PIONEER POWDER

One of the people I talked with on the phone from Clean Shot Technologies, Inc. mentioned that he had worked with Arco and sold Black Mag Powder. "Clean Shot" powder appears very like Black Mag in its granulation, but is a darker brown, nearly black, and is of the same general formulation. It is sold in black powder grades using the "FG" system. After a year-plus, the burnt-sugar smell is detectable and there is some caking of the product. Clean Shot performed less well than Black Mag, with five-shot groups running around 2" to 3" at a hundred yards. It produced a gray odorless smoke and practically no fouling.

Clean Shot was offered in pellet form for quick loading in the manner of the "Pyrodex" pellets and were close enough to the Hodgdon product that Hodgdon filed suit against Clean Shot and won. American Pioneer's successor to Clean shot is simply called American Pioneer Powder. A pelletized form of this product is currently sold as "Jim Shockey's Gold."

CLEAR SHOT

Shortly after, "Clean Shot" came "Clear Shot" powder from GOEX. It uses the "FG" grading system, but looks nothing like black powder. The FFG sample I have is shiny-black, fine spheres and appears almost identical to smokeless "ball" powders such as Hodgdon's "Ball C." Clear Shot differs from the previously discussed four powders in that it contains no ascorbic acid. The formulation features potassium nitrate and iron ascorbate, the latter being a product acquired by dissolving iron in an ascorbic-acid solution. It leaves slight fouling, but does produce a black discoloration on brass which eventually becomes corrosion. The smoke is odorless. It shoots about as well as Black Mag.

Unfortunately, the GOEX Clear Shot plant blew up in 2001 (Employee negligence, not a product problem.) Plans to rebuild, however, were scrapped.

PINNACLE

"Pinnacle" was created when GOEX teamed with American Pioneer Powder. The result was a product looking much like Black Canyon, but without the problems of moisture absorption and clumping. The faint burnt sugar odor is there. Performance was about on a par with Clear Shot. It did not do well in the marketplace.

I discussed the shooting qualities of BP replacements with Bill Bagwell, who tests for GOEX and is a competitive black-powder silhouette shooter. Bagwell usually places in the top twenty in NRA events and often in the top ten. His experience is that none of the above deliver accuracy as good as the best lots of GOEX blackpowder. The best black delivers inch (or less) five-shot 100 yard groups in his Pedersoli Sharps — Clean Shot 1.25" to 1.8". "Cowboy action shooters love it," he said, in a phone interview. "But for silhouette shooting, those fractions add up at 800 yards."

In conclusion, it can be said that the quality of BP substitutes runs the gamut from good to terrible in the accuracy department, though with easier clean-up. More of these will undoubtedly appear. Beware claims of non-corrosive properties!

Before shooting any of this stuff, get a piece of soft steel. Sand or grind the surface to the bare metal. removing any coatings or treatments. Clean with a degreaser. Burn about half a teaspoon of your "non-corrosive" BP substitute on this cleaned spot (about one inch square) and let stand in a humid environment two days at least. A week or two is better. Monitor your experiment at least twice a day. If beads of moisture appear, the same will happen in your barrel and rust will follow. If rust appears in a day or so, you have a corrosive product. Despite what the manufacturer may claim for cleanup, use a water-base cleaner that will neutralize acid and dissolve salts. Don't be stingy with it, either. The cost of a replaced barrel will buy an awful lot of cleaner.

One of my SASS shooting friends mixes 4 oz. "Lestoil" to a quart of water. This low-suds mix is good for cleaning both brass and gun barrels fouled with BP, Pyrodex or whatever.

The mess of black-powder cleanup has been reduced with the introduction of new cleaners. Wipe Out comes in both a blackpowder and a smokeless version. Patch Out Wipe Out is stronger than the aerosol version and is good for both blackpowder and corrosive primer fouling and removes copper.

A different
animal entirely.

Smokeless Powder

DEVELOPMENT OF SMOKELESS powder began in the mid-19th century with the first really successful type being that developed by an Austrian chemist, Frederick Volkmann, in about 1871. It was made by dissolving wood fiber in nitric acid which was later washed in water to remove the acid, then gelatinized in an ether-alcohol mixture to form a plastic colloid, now known as nitrocellulose. The powder was marketed locally and the Austrian Government (in its wisdom) stuck with blackpowder and shut the operation down for not paying proper license fees.

The defining moment in the evolution of smokeless powder came some fifteen years later (in 1886) when the French government switched from a black-powder single-shot rifle to a high-velocity, 8mm repeater, the Lebel, which used a smokeless-powder cartridge powered by a similar powder developed by the French chemist Paul Vieille. Within two years all of Europe had abandoned blackpowder for military rifles and every government armed its troops with repeaters using jacketed bullets and smokeless powder. The United States was the last major power to switch to a smokeless-powder repeater, when it (reluctantly) gave up the 45-70 Springfield in 1892.

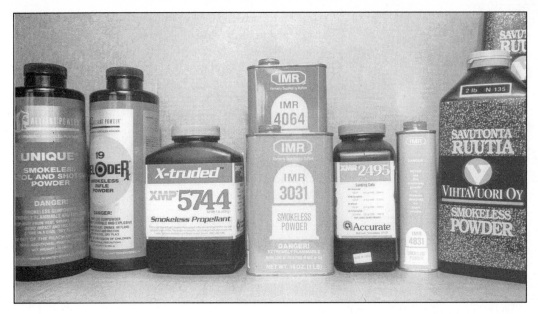

American manufacturers and importers offer a wide variety of smokeless powder for reloaders.

Early smokeless powders were hygroscopic and if the acid were not completely washed out would deteriorate in a short time. Coatings were later added to make the powder more water resistant and to control burning. The power of smokeless powder was further enhanced by the addition of nitroglycerine. These two types of powder – nitrocellulose and nitrocellulose plus nitroglycerine – are the two basic types manufactured today. They are known respectively as single-base and double-base powders. Nearly all smokeless powders are coated with graphite to keep them from caking so they will flow smoothly through powder measures, dippers and funnels.

The outstanding characteristic of smokeless powder is that while it is of two basic types, by changing the size and shape of the granulation the burning characteristics can be varied considerably and controlled to a high degree. This gives smokeless a tremendous advantage over blackpowder, the burning characteristics of which could be only roughly controlled and in a more limited range in terms of power.

Smokeless powder varies in granule size from flakes as fine as ground pepper – used in fast-burning pistol powders – to finger-size cylinders nearly two inches long for huge naval guns. The burning can be further altered by extruding powder into macaroni-like tubes allowing them to burn on both the outside and inside at the same time. Spherical forms can be varied to exact size, while adding chemical coatings can control the burn rate.

SELECTING THE RIGHT POWDER

Modern powders are divided into three basic types on the basis of their use. These are pistol powders, shotgun powders and rifle powders. Pistol powders are generally of the fast-burning double base type for use in short-barreled guns. Shotgun powders are also fast burning and double base, designed to burn completely under low pressures. Rifle powders are generally slower burning to accelerate a rifle bullet down a long barrel with maximum velocity while producing minimum pressures.

In point of fact many powders for pistol use are quite suitable for shotguns and vice versa. Some slower-burning pistol and shotgun powders will also work well for reduced-velocity rifle loadings where a light bullet and light powder charge are used.

Before buying a quantity of powder, it is a good idea to consult one or more reloading guides to see what is offered and what looks to be the best selection for your particular gun or guns.

STORAGE AND HANDLING

Modern powders are almost completely gelatinized, making them less affected by damp. A sample of Laflin & Rand, (later Hercules, now

Placed under water in 1899, this sample of Laflin & Rand Unique smokeless powder has been tested periodically since then and is still performing quite well after better than 100 years. Modern powders now contain stabilizers (unknown at that time) to keep them viable for a long shelf life.

The Old Western Scrounger, now joined by Navy Arms, is one of the few sources of new, factory-made blackpowder ammunition. This lets the history buffs replicate original loads in original guns.

Alliant) Unique powder was placed in storage under water in 1899 to test its viability. It was last tested in this century and performed as well as when it was made. Testing will continue, perpetuating one of this country's longest ongoing experiments.

Depending on their storage condition, smokeless powders will deteriorate, as they generate small amounts of nitric acid. Stabilizers are added to these powders to absorb acid byproduct. Most powders have fifty or more years of life before the stabilizers are used up and nitric acid begins to leach out of the nitrocellulose, leaving plain cellulose and reducing the efficiency of the powder. Occasionally powder will deteriorate owing to acid residue that was not properly washed out in the manufacturing process. Such powder will take on an unpleasant acidic (vinegar) smell and a brown dust looking very like rust will appear in the powder. Powder in this condition will not shoot well, giving poor ignition and low power. It should be disposed of.

Metal cans containing powder will sometimes rust on the interior producing a very similar appearing dust, but without the characteristic odor. This does not harm the powder and can be removed by dumping the powder on a flat piece of bed sheet, spreading it evenly, and gently blowing off the dust. The powder should then be placed in another container — an empty plastic powder bottle is good so long as it is clearly marked as to what it is. It is a good idea to mark containers of powder with the date of purchase and use the oldest first. Opened containers of powder should be checked at least every year for signs of rust or deterioration if they are not being used. Sealed containers should be left sealed until they are to be used.

Alcohols and occasionally camphor are added to stabilize burning characteristics. Powder containers should be kept tightly closed to keep these volatile additives from evaporating into the air. Smokeless powder is quite safe to handle, as it is not sensitive to shock. The main caution that must be taken is to keep it from open flame or heat. It will ignite above 400 degrees F. Shelf storage is suitable, preferably on a second floor where temperatures remain most stable. Powder should never be stored in heavy closed metal containers which could act as bombs in case of a fire. Never have more than one container of powder open at a time. If there is a fire this practice hopefully limits it to one can.

Smokeless powder is toxic if ingested; the nitro-glycerine component causing heart irregularity. British soldiers in WWI chewed smokeless powder from rifle cartridges to cause a brief though severe illness to get off the line, until medical authorities discovered this practice. Children have a tendency to taste things; smokeless powder should not be one of them.

LOADING DENSITY

As mentioned earlier, various combinations of bullets and powder charges can be assembled to achieve the same velocity. Some are going to be more accurate than others. Various manuals will often indicate loads that gave the best accuracy in particular guns. This is usually the best place to start, although such a combination will not necessarily be the best performer in your gun. Generally speaking, when selecting a powder, there are a few rules of thumb worth following. Larger-capacity rifle cartridges with heavy bullets generally perform best with slow-burning powders. For best accuracy, a powder charge that fills the case with little or no air space tends to give better accuracy than a small charge that can shift position in the case. Shooters of reduced loads, particularly in rifles, get better results by tipping the barrel skyward before each shot to position the powder to the rear of the case. This can also be achieved by using wads or wads plus fillers to fill up the space, but the results are usually not as good. A filler wad should NEVER be placed over the powder with an air space between it and the bullet. The space must be filled entirely. If there is a space, the wad will come slamming against the base of the bullet with enough force to make a bulged ring in the case and often in the chamber of the gun!

COMPRESSED LOADS

Never compress powder in a cartridge case unless such a load is recommended in a reloading manual. Compressed loads should never be more than 10% above the case capacity. A compression of more than this often leads to lower than desired velocities. If the compression is excessive it can actually bulge the case or cause the case to stretch in the loading process, resulting in a cartridge that is oversize or too long and will jam the gun.

AVAILABLE POWDERS

As of this writing smokeless powders are available from the following manufacturers or importers. These include the IMR Powder Co. (Formerly DuPont), now owned by Hodgdon; Winchester Powder, also part of Hodgdon; Alliant Powder Co. (formerly Hercules); Alliant Tech Systems New River Energetics; Hodgdon Powder Co.; Ramshot Powder/ Accurate Powder Co., both owned by Western Powders Inc.;

VhitaVuori Oy (Finland), imported by Kaltron-Pettibone, distributed by Hodgdon Powder Co.; and Norma Powder, distributed through Black Hills Shooters Supply, Inc.

IMR POWDERS

IMR makes both single and double-base powders of the flake type and the cylinder type for a wide variety of uses.

Hi-SKOR 700-X. This is a double-base flake powder primarily ,designed for shotshells, but works well in many target and light handgun loadings.

HI-SKOR 800-X. This is a double-base shotgun powder for heavy shotgun loads. It is also applicable to some handgun loadings.

TRAIL BOSS. This was designed for low-velocity lead-bullet loads keyed for Cowboy Action shooting. This is primarily a pistol powder, but of a high density nature allowing full-case loads for best accuracy with relatively low pressures suitable for guns of older manufacture and design.

PB. PB is a porous base, flake powder of the single-base type. It is used for many shotgun loads as well as in a number of handgun cartridges. PB works well in cast-bullet loads.

SR 7625. Although it carries the sporting rifle designation, its main use is for shotshell and handgun cartridges. It works well with a number of cast-bullet rifle loadings. It is the fastest burning of the SR series of powders.

SR 4756. A slightly slower burning single-base powder. It works well in some rifle cartridges, with cast bullets. The main use of this powder is in shotgun loadings and a number of handgun loads.

SR 4759. This is the slowest-burning powder in this series. It is a cylinder powder rather than a flake type as are the other SR powders. SR 4759 has a very good reputation with cast-bullet shooters, working well in cases as large as the 45-70. Once withdrawn, it is back by popular demand and will hopefully stay with us.

IMR 4227. IMR stands for improved military rifle. This the fastest burning in the series. It, like all the IMR series is a single-base powder of a cylinder type. It works well in small rifle cases such as the 22 Hornet, the 223 Remington, even the 458 Winchester. It works well in heavy handgun loads and can be used in the 410 shotgun.

IMR 4198. This powder is slightly slower burning, but works very well in small to medium-capacity cases such as the 22 Hornet and 222 and 223 where it is prized for varmint and bench-rest shooting. The burn rate may make it less than reliable in some autoloading actions. It works well in large cases including the 444 Marlin and even the 45-70.

IMR 3031. A favorite for the 30-30 and similar medium capacity cases with jacketed bullets, 3031 is one of the most versatile on the market, giving good results in cartridges as small as the 17 Remington and as large as the 458 Winchester.

IMR 8208 XBR. Newest in the line. This short-grained rifle powder is designed for match/varmint shooting in cartridges such as the 223, 6mm PPC, and 308. It combines maximum velocities with high accuracy. It works very well in AR-based autoloading actions.

IMR 4064. Very similar to IMR 3031, 4064 has great ver-

Powder in a powder measure should not be left open for volatiles to escape and dirt to enter. Never leave powder in a measure after loading or you may find yourself guessing about what kind it is.

Compressed loads should be approached with extreme caution.

satility in the 30 caliber range, performing well in the 30-06 and 308. It also works well in many of the larger rifle calibers.

IMR 4895. This medium-slow burning powder is very similar to the Hodgdon powder of the same number. It is an excellent performer in the 30-06, but works well in slightly reduced loads with cast bullets in rifles such as the 45-70. Excellent accuracy is produced in the 223 with this powder in bolt-action rifles as well as the 17 Remington, 243 winchester and many others.

IMR 4064. A medium burn rate powder with a wide range of uses from 223 on up to magnums. It is on of the most versatile in the IMR line of rifle powders.

IMR 4320. Originally used as a propellent for military match ammunition, it is relatively slow burning and will produce good velocities with less recoil than the faster-burning types. It is applicable to cartridges from 22 to 458 caliber.

IMR 4007 SSC. This is a short-grain powder with a burning rate between 4320 and 4350. The medium burn rate of this powder makes it an excellent choice for 22 through 25 caliber cartridges. It works well in short magnum cartridges such as the 243 and 25 WSM as well as in the 30-06.

IMR 4350. This is a slow burning powder intended for large capacity cases. Its bulk fills these cases well. A favorite for the 7X57 Mauser, 30-06, 243 and 270 Winchester, 4350 is an excellent maximum load for long range work.

IMR 4831. Introduced in 1971 this powder carries the same number as the Hodgdon H4831, but it is not an equivalent . IMR 4831 is faster burning than the Hodgdon product! IMR 4831 is intended for magnum rifle cartridges although it works very well in the 270 Winchester.

IMR 7828. This is the slowest burning in the IMR series. It is designed for the 50 Browning and large magnum rifle cartridges including the 300 and 338 Magnums. It will work well in a number of African big game cartridges. IMR 7828 is intended for pushing large heavy bullets at high velocities, without raising chamber pressures into the danger zone.

IMR 7828 SSC. The burn rate of this powder is the same as 7828, but is of a short cut design. This makes it run through charging meters more smoothly for precision dispensing of the powder charge. The granules fit well in cases, allowing 4% additional space with an increase in velocity. Loads are marked with an asterisk for this powder where 7828 will not fit.

WINCHESTER POWDERS

Winchester makes double-base powders in a spherical configuration. This "ball" powder achieves controlled burning and cooler temperatures by the use of additives. The ball shape makes it flow easily through mechanical powder measures.

WAAlite. This is a ball powder for shotgun use. Excellent results with light loads where low recoil and minimal muzzle blast are desired.

WST. This shotgun propellent is for skeet and trap shooting. Its burning characteristics allow reloaders to duplicate AA trap loads. WST is useful for 38 Special and 45 ACP loading as well.

231. The fastest burning of the Winchester powders, it is for handguns and is best used for light to medium target loads in which it produces excellent accuracy in 9mm, 38 Special and 45 ACP loadings.

Super Handicap. Another shotgun powder duplicating that used in the Winchester Super Handicap commercial load. High velocity provides long-range potential for sporting clays.

AutoComp. As is implied in the name, this powder is designed for semi-auto pistols. A top contender for competitive shooting in 9mm Luger, 38 Super, 40 S&W and 45 ACP. AutoComp offers clean burning with less flash and smoke.

WSF. This versatile powder works well in 20 and 12 gauge target loads as well as in 9mm, 38 Super and 40 S&W semi-autos.

296. This is a pistol powder with a fine granulation. It is most useful in magnum handguns such as the 357 and 44 Magnums; it will also work well in 410 shotgun loadings.

748. Used in military loadings for the 223 (5.56mm) rifle, this powder offers low flame temperature for increased barrel life. It is suitable for a great variety of centerfire rife loadings in 22 through 30 caliber on up to the 458.

760. This powder duplicates factory ballistics for Winchester loadings for the 30-06. It works well in the 22-250 and many 30 caliber rifle loadings on up to the 300 Win Mag.

Supreme 780. This is a magnum ball powder used in a considerable number of factory loaded cartridges. 780 delivers top velocities in the Winchester 243, 270, and 300 Magnum with excellent accuracy in medium to maximum loads.

ALLIANT POWDERS

These were formerly made under the trade mark of Hercules and before that Laflin and Rand. Alliant currently offers double-base powders.

Bullseye. A longtime favorite of pistol shooters this flake powder works well in cases as small as the 25 ACP and as large as the 44 Magnum and 45 Long Colt. It is a very fast burning powder.

Power Pistol. A fairly recent arrival designed for high-performance semi-autos for maximum velocity loads in the 9mm and 10mm class.

2400. A finely granulated powder, 2400 works well in small rifle cases such as the 22 Hornet and similar varmint cartridges. One of the older powders in the line, it is still popular for magnum pistol loads in the 357, 41 and 44 Magnums. It produces good accuracy in reduced cast rifle-bullet loadings. Care, however, must be taken not to overload, since this is a powerful powder that takes up very little space in large cases.

Newest in the line are the Power Pro series of canister powder sincluding *Power Pro Varmint, Power Pro 4000MR, 2000MR,* and *3000LR.* These duplicate many factory loadings for popular rifle calibers.

Winchester, like most manufacturers, has replaced metal cans with plastic packaging which keeps volatiles in and moisture out of the powder inside.

300MP. This powder is for magnum pistol loads, but is versatile enough for light varmint loads in the smaller 22 centerfires. It performs well in light to medium to magnum rifles.

Pro Reach. Pro Reach Is the latest product for long-range 12 ga shotgun use in clay target shooting. It works equally for long-range hunting as well.

Reloder 7. This is the fastest burning of the reloader series of rifle powders. It works well in medium capacity rifle cases of the varmint class on up to the 458 Magnum in which it delivers excellent accuracy with heavy bullets. Reloder 7 has been a favorite with bench-rest shooters for its accuracy in the 222.

Reloder 10X. This recent arrival is an excellent propellent for many benchrest cartridges where it delivers fine accuracy. This quality makes it a good choice for varmint loads in the .223 and 22-250 with lighter bullets.

Reloder 15. Reloder 15 is slightly slower burning. It works well in a wide range of rifle cases from the 223 to magnums of the 458 and 416 Rigby size. It is generally used for heavy loadings.

Reloader 17. This works well in medium rifle cartridges and is a good choice for use in the short magnum calibers where it delivers high velocities.

Reloader 19. A slow-burning powder, Reloder 19 works in heavy varmint cases such as the 22-250 where it yields the highest velocities. It does well in thirty-caliber cases including the magnums.

Reloder 22. This is the slower burning powder in the Reloder series. It is intended for large-capacity, magnum-rifle cases although some shooters have obtained good results in the 220 Swift with this powder.

Reloder 25. Slower burning than Reloder 22, 25 is an excellent choice for maximum velocities in heavy and overbore magnum cartridges.

Reloader 50. As the name implies this one is formulated for long-range 50 caliber rifle shooting. It 's noted for very clean burning and velocities that are both high and consistent.

20/28. Newest in the shotgun line, 20/28 is dedicated to the 20 and 28 gauge guns for skeet and sporting clays competition.

410. As is implied this powder is one for the small bore gun for maximum accuracy and performance. It meters well and is very clean burning.

American Select. Designed for target loads in the 12 ga. It offers good performance with lower recoil. Select is also a good performer in handguns.

Blue Dot. This is a very slow burning shotgun powder that also works well in magnum handgun cartridges.

Clay Dot. Considered optimum for light and standard 12 ga. target loads it duplicates the performance of Hodgdon's Clays.

e3. A shotgun target powder, this one is for target loads. Low charges yield high efficiency.

Extra-Lite. This powder is designed for 12 gauge shooters looking to reduce loads to 1-1/8 oz to 7/8 oz. The lower charge allows for the use of standard components with lower recoil.

Green Dot. This flake, shotgun powder burns slightly slower than Red Dot and has an equal variety of applications for field and target use.

Herco. This is a moderately slow-burning shotgun powder with application to handgun loads. The granulation is coarse and it is best for magnum loads.

Promo. A good choice for target loads at an economy price.

Red Dot. A flake shotgun powder, Red Dot will also work well in light and medium pressure handgun loads. Some shooters have gained good results with light cast-bullet rifle loadings as well.

Steel. This one is crafted especially for use with steel-shot loadings. It works well at all temperatures and offers maximum velocity.

Alliant (formerly Hercules) Unique – a powerful, fast-burning double-base powder used in pistol and light rifle loads. It is a fine, flake powder which has been made for over a century.

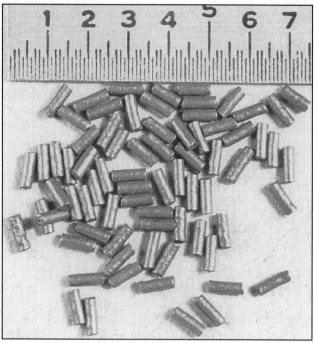

IMR 3031 powder is an extruded single-base powder made of nitrocellulose. IMR 3031 has a fairly slow burning rate and has long been a standard for military rifle cartridges.

Unique. This is a flake powder with a great number of uses. It works well in shotgun loads from 28 to 12. Unique is suitable for many handgun loads and is considered one of the most accurate in the Colt 45 and 44 Magnum and 40 S&W. It will make good medium velocity loads for the 380, 38 Special and the 45 ACP. It is well adapted to cartridges as small as the 25 ACP.

HODGDON POWDERS

Hodgdon originally packaged surplus military powder and some of this may still be around. If a load is developed with one of the surplus types, if the newly manufactured type is later substituted, the loading should redeveloped as burning characteristics may be altered. Check the container for identification regarding new and surplus powder. All Hodgdon powders are of the double-base type unless otherwise indicated.

Titewad. This fastest burning powder is designed for 12 gauge only. As the name implies, this flattened ball powder is for light loads for trap and field use where light recoil and minimum report are desired.

Clays. This shotgun powder, introduced in 1992, is mainly used for light target loads. Clays can also be used in the 38 Special and 45 ACP where it delivers excellent accuracy.

International. This is an improved form of the Clays formula. It yields reduced recoil in 12 and 20 gauge target loads and works well in light, medium and heavy loads.

Universal. This is a flake shotgun powder with burning characteristics similar to Unique. The granulation is slightly finer. Good performance is found in the 28 gauge. Universal works very well in a variety of handgun cartridges from 25 ACP to 44 Magnum.

HP-38. This a spherical powder. It is fast burning and is similar to Winchester 231, but loading data should not be substituted. As the name indicates, it was developed as a propellent for the 38 Special. It works well in a variety of medium-size pistol cartridges, producing fine accuracy.

HS-6. This spherical powder is good for heavy shotshell loads and works well in handgun loads in medium and large calibers when high velocities are desired.

Longshot. A new spherical powder for shotgun use, Longshot is for heavy field use in 28 gauge through 10 gauge guns producing magnum velocities and excellent patterns

H110. This spherical powder was developed for the 30 M-1 carbine cartridge. It works very well in medium and large handgun cartridges. It is particularly well suited to magnum handgun cartridges where it will duplicate factory performance in these calibers. Good results have been produced in the 410 with both 2 ½" and 3" shells.

Lil Gun. This powder was designed for the 410 for precise measuring and easy loading. Clean burning characteristics are its outstanding feature making it a good performer in magnum handguns and 22 centerfires such as the Hornet.

H4198. This extruded powder is a short-cut design for easy and precise loading. It has similar burning characteristics to the IMR product of the same number. It produces

IMR 4320 is a slow-burning single-base rifle powder for use in large bore and high powered rifles. The extruded grains are of a "short cut" design.

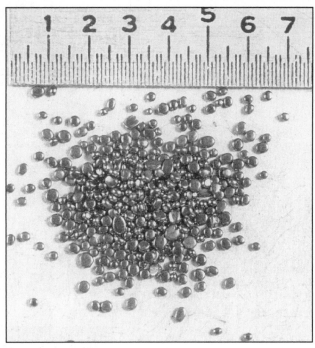

Hodgdon's Ball C #2 is a spherical powder. This fast burning double-base powder has a well-deserved reputation for flowing very smoothly through powder measures.

fine accuracy in the 222, 223 7.62x39 and similar small to medium rifle cases.

H322. This single base powder has found favor with bench-rest shooters in the 222 and 6mm Remington BR. It works well in a variety of 30 calibers and even in straight-walled cases as large as the 45-70.

Benchmark. As implied by the name, Benchmark was developed for competitive shooting. Its small grain size allows for precise metering. Excellent results are produced in 222, 223, 22PPC, 22BR and 6mm BR cartridges. Good results with lighter bullets are produced in the 308.

H335. This double based ball powder was developed for the 5.56 military round (223) and it also works well in the 222.

H4895. Hodgdon's version of the IMR powder. Single-base, 4895 is one of the most versatile rifle powders around. It produces fine performance in calibers from the 17 Remington to the 458 Winchester Magnum. It works very well in reduced loadings, burning evenly for charges as light as 3/5 of the maximum.

Varget. Varget is one of Hodgdon's "extreme" powders, so called for its ability to function well in a wide range of temperatures. Known for easy ignition and clean burning, Varget works in calibers from 223 up to 375 H&H. An excellent load for cast bullets in the 45-70.

BL-C(2). This spherical powder known as "ball C lot 2" gives excellent accuracy in the 222 and 223 and was often used for bench-rest and competition shooting. It began as a

surplus powder but is now newly manufactured. Fine results and reliable functioning is produced in autoloaders.

H380. This is a double-base powder, but slow burning — in the class of IMR 4320. It performs well in 30 caliber cases, but also does well in large capacity varmint rounds such as the 22-250.

H414. This works well in the 30-06 and similar 30's particularly with lighter bullets where higher velocities are desired.

H4350. This single-base powder carries the same designation as the IMR powder, although the Hodgdon version is slightly slower burning. Like the IMR powder, it is intended for large-capacity, magnum-rifle cartridges where it does well with light and medium weight bullets.

Hybrid 100V. A recent arrival with a burning rate between H4350 and H4831. Excellent results are achieved in cartridges such as the 270 Winchester, 243 Winchester Short Magnum, 280 Remington, and 25-06 Remington.

H4831. This was originally a military surplus powder, but is now newly manufactured. It is single-base, extruded powder and gives the best accuracy with heavy bullets in 30 calibers and larger, though it is excellent in the 270. It carries the same number designation as the IMR powder 4831, but the burning characteristics are not the same.

H4831SC. This is the same powder as H4831, but with a shorter grain — the SC stands for "short cut." The finer granulation makes this powder flow more evenly through powder measures.

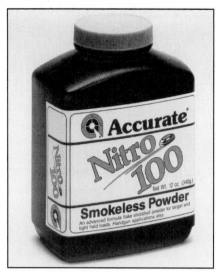

Accurate Arms' Nitro 100 is a double-base flake powder best used in shotgun target shooting. It has pistol applications as well.

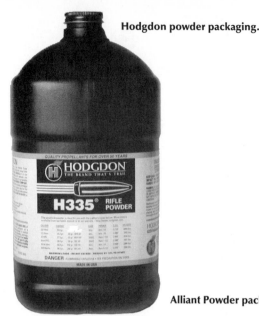

Hodgdon powder packaging.

Alliant Powder packaging.

H1000. This is a very slow-burning single-base powder. It works well with heavy-bullet loads in large-capacity cases like the 300 Winchester Magnum. Fine results are obtained in the 257 Weatherby, 270 Winchester and 7mm Remington Magnum. H1000 has found favor with long-range match shooters.

Retumbo. This magnum powder for very large "over-bore" magnum cartridges to deliver maximum velocities. It's proper fodder for such cartridges as the 7mm Remington Ultra Mag, 300 Remington Ultra Mag and the 30-378 Weatherby.

US869. A spherical powder for use with heavy bullets this one delivers accurate, high-velocity performance in the "overbore" magnums and the 50 BMG where it is suitable for 1000-yard shooting.

H50BMG. As the name implies, this is for loading the 50 Browning machinegun cartridge. The burn rate is very stable in a wide range of temperatures. This keeps velocities consistent – a must for long-range competitive shooting.

H870. This is the slowest-burning powder made by Hodgdon. Its use is limited to very large capacity cases such as the 50 BMG and a few of the large magnums for African big-game use.

IMR Originally stood for "Improved Military Rifle" powder. Originally a DuPont Trademark, IMR became an independent brand, but is now part of Hodgdon.

ACCURATE POWDERS

Accurate powders come from abroad with some domestic manufacture. The line is primarily for rifle and handgun use. They are marketed through Western Powder.

Nitro 100. This is a double-base flake powder for 12 gauge target loads. It works well in the 45 Colt and other medium to large handgun cartridges.

No.2. This is a fast-burning double-base ball powder for use in the 38 Special and similar medium capacity handguns. It does well in light and target loadings. It is similar to Bullseye.

No.5. This is another double-base ball powder, slightly slower burning and comparable to Unique. It gives good results in a wide variety of medium to large handgun cases.

No.7. This double-base powder is intended for 9mm Luger and similar medium to large capacity pistol rounds. It is clean burning and gives good accuracy at target velocities.

No.9. A double-base ball powder and considered one of the best for the 44 Magnum. It works very well in the 41 and 357 Magnums as well. Good results have been obtained in the 22 Hornet and the 30 Carbine. It will work well in the 410 shotshell.

1680. This double-base ball powder was designed specifically for the 7.62 X39mm Russian cartridge. It is fast burning and delivers high velocities in the 22 Hornet. Beyond these two, its use is rather limited.

2015. A small-grain extruded powder of the single-base type, it has many uses. It performs very well in small to medium rifle cases producing excellent accuracy in many 22 centerfires. The 6mm PPC and 7mm Remington have produced excellent groups with this powder. It also does well in straight-walled rifle cases such as the 45-70 and 458 Magnum.

2230. A double-base ball powder, with a fairly rapid burn, 2230 does well in the 223 and similar medium-capacity cases.

2460. This double-base ball powder is slower burning than 2230, which extends its use from medium capacity 22 centerfire calibers to the 308 and 30-06.

5744. This double-base powder has a burn rate between that of No.9 and 1680. Versatility is a hallmark of 5744, it works well in pistol cases such as the 6mm TCU, 357 Magnum, 38-40, 41 Magnum, 44 SPL, 44-40, 44 Magnum and 45 Colt. In rifles it performs well in the 22 Hornet, 222, 25-20, 30 Carbine, 30-30, 308 and 30-06. It has produced good groups in the 45-70 with cast bullets.

2495. This powder has very similar burning characteristics to IMR 4895 and H4895. It is a single-base extruded powder with great flexibility giving excellent accuracy in 22 centerfires through the 30 caliber class. Accurate's 2495 works well with cast bullets.

2520. A ball powder with a medium-slow burning rate, 2520 gives excellent results in many medium-capacity rifle cases. Fine accuracy is obtained in the 308. Its pressure curve makes it suitable for use in autoloaders.

4064. This single-base rifle powder is short-cut for better metering and fits cases in the 30 caliber range such as the 30-30. It has found favor with service-rifle competitors, in particular the 30-06.

Magpro. This propellent is designed especially for the recently developed short magnum rifle cartridges. Magpro produces optimum velocities with close to full-case loads. Uniformity of shape is ideal for progressive loading machines where it works well in many standard magnums.

2700. Accurate's latest ball powder, 2700 is designed for use with heavy bullets in the belted-magnum class of rifle cartridge. It works well in the 17 Remington, 220 Swift and 22-250 — notable exceptions to the rule.

4350. This powder is equivalent to the IMR 4350 and H4350. It has the same applications doing well in the 375 Magnum class.

3100. This is a single-base extruded powder for use in medium capacity cases. It delivers fine performance in the 243 and 7mm Remington Magnum. Its burning rate is between that of IMR 4831 and H483. It works well with heavy bullet loadings.

Solo 1000. A fast-burning, double-base flake powder for shotgun use, it is similar to Bullseye and has handgun applications for light loads such as cast bullets in the 45 ACP.

4100. This powder is very similar to Accurate No. 9. It is slightly slower burning and is designed especially for the 410 2-1/2 inch, half-ounce skeet load. It can be used for handguns such as the 357 and larger magnums using both cast and jacketed bullets.

RAMSHOT POWDERS

Ramshot is imported and distributed by Western Powder. Ramshot powders are mainly for rifle use, but do well in handguns and shotguns.

Competition. A double-base powder for 12 gauge target work offering clean burning with low recoil. These qualities make it useful for pistol loads for the cowboy action shooter.

Magnum. Formerly known as "Big Boy" Magnum for the 25-06, 7mm Remington Magnum and cartridges in the 300 Weatherby/Winchester Magnum class.

Hunter. This ball powder is excellent for the short-magnum calibers including the 223 WSM, 7mm WSM, 270 WSM, and 300 WSM.

Big Game. As the name implies, this powder is for the 270 to 30-06 class. It works well, however, in the 22-250, 6mm and 7mm-08.

TAC. This versatile powder does well in a number of calibers. Good results are obtained with bullets as heavy as 80 grains in the 223. TAC works well in the 308.

X-Terminator. A double-base ball powder that is designed for 22 centerfires. Excellent results are produced in 222, 223 and a number of benchrest cartridges.

Enforcer. Similar to X-terminator, this powder does well in the 22 Hornet but also works well in magnum pistol car-

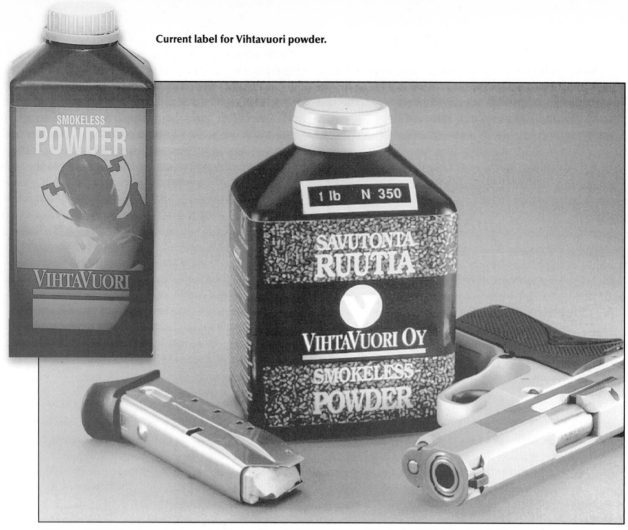

Current label for Vihtavuori powder.

Vihtavuori N350 is a slow pistol powder for medium to large calibers. It is also suitable for shotshells.

tridges such as the 357, 41 and 44 Magnums, 454 Casull and 480 Ruger.

True Blue. This handgun powder is well suited to medium pistol calibers on up to the 454 Casull.

Silhouette. An excellent choice for target work, this powder offers low flash, high velocity and clean burning. It is well suited to the 9mm, 38 Super, 357 SIG, and 10 mm.

Zip. This flattened ball powder is useful in small to medium handgun calibers. Low charge weights perform well in 9mm, 38 Spl, 40 S&W and 45 ACP.

VIHTAVUORI POWDERS

VihtaVuori powder is produced in Finland and imported by Kaltron Pettibone. It is distributed through Hodgdon. As of this writing VihtaVuori makes twenty-six powders, both single and double base, for rifle and pistol use.

N110. This is a fast-burning rifle powder in the class of Alliant 2400, Winchester 296 and Hodgdon H110. It works well in the 22 Hornet and other small to medium case 22 centerfires. It serves well in the 357 Magnum 44 and 45 Magnums.

N120. Similar to IMR 4227, N120 is designed to work well in the 22 centerfire class of rifle cartridges. Its application beyond this, however, is limited, though good results have been obtained in the 7.62x39mm.

N130. This powder burns faster than N120. It has applications in 22 centerfires such as the 223 and medium capacity cases in the 25 to 27 caliber range, but works well in 45-70 and 458. It is similar to Hodgdon 335.

N133. The burning rate of this powder is close to that of IMR 4198. It works well in the 222 and 223 and good results have been obtained in the 45-70. It is a favorite with benchrest shooters.

N135. This powder burns with moderate speed, similar to IMR and Hodgdon 4895. It is a versatile powder with applications from the 17 Remington to the 458 Winchester. Fine results have been achieved in the 308.

N140. A relatively slow-burning powder, N140 can be used in place of IMR 4320 and Alliant Reloder 15 and Hodgdon H380. Best results are in 30 to 35 caliber rifle cases. This is a powder with a wide range of uses.

N150. This powder has a slow burn rate similar to IMR 4350. It works well in 30 caliber and up. A good choice for heavier hunting bullets.

N160. This is another slow-burning powder designed mainly for magnum rifles. It works well with light-bullet loads and with heavy bullets in the 30-06. Good results have been obtained in the 220 Swift, 243, 25-06, 264 and 7mm Remington Magnum, 300 Win Mag and the Winchester short magnums.

N165. Slightly slower than N160, this powder is for heavy bullet loads in the 30-06 and magnums in the 30 caliber range and up to the 416 Rigby.

N170. This slowest burning of the N100 series powders is suitable for large capacity cases only such as the 300 Weatherby Magnum, 300 Remington Ultra Magnum and 338 Lapua Magnum.

N530. This double-base powder is the fastest burning in the N500 series and is similar to Hodgdon BL-C(2). Originally developed for NATO cartridges, it gives fine results in the 5.56 (223), and 308 with 155 grain bullets.

N540. This is a double-base powder with a burning rate much like N140. It is designed for the 308 Winchester, but produces good results in the 30-06 and 223.

N550. Another double-base powder with a burning rate like N150, and close to the IMR 4350. N550 gives good results in the 308, 30-06, and 6.5x55 Swedish Mauser.

N560. The burning rate of this powder is very like N160, but it is designed for the 270 Winchester and the 6.5X55 Swedish Mauser. Fine results have been produced in 7mm and 300 magnums on up to the 338 Lapua.

N570. This most recent in the series features a large grain size for slow burning and high energy in very large capacity cases. Use is limited to the larger magnums: 6.5-284 Norma, 300 Remington Ultra Mag, 300 Win Mag and the 338 Lapua.

24N41. This powder is especially designed for the 50 BMG. A single-base powder like the N100 series, but the grain size is larger and burning rate slower.

20N29. Another 50 BMG powder. This one burns slightly slower than 24N41.

N310. This pistol powder is comparable to Bullseye. Its fast burning rate lends itself to use in the 25 ACP on up to the 44 Magnum, in which it produces excellent accuracy for light target loads.

N320. Suitable for shotshells (about like Red Dot) and mid-range handgun loads, N320 works well in cartridges in the 38 to 45 caliber class.

Tin Star. (N32C) This is a recent arrival designed for the Cowboy Action market. Clean burning makes it popular with those who shoot a lot between cleanings. Fine for lead-bullet revolver loads and for handgun caliber rifles.

N330. The burning rate of this powder is similar to Green Dot. It performs well in pistol cartridges from the 38 to 45 range.

N340. This powder has a slightly slower burning rate and is similar to Winchester 540 or Blue Dot. Good results are obtained in medium to large handgun calibers.

N350. This is the slowest pistol powder in the N300 series,

which lends it to use in shotshells. In this regard, it is about like Blue Dot. Use in handguns is limited to medium to large calibers — 9mm to 45 ACP – where it lends itself to more high powered loads.

3N37. This is not really an N300 series powder. It is used in high velocity rimfire loads and shotshells. The burning rate is between N340 and N350. Good results have been obtained in 9mm, 38 Super Auto, 38 Special and the 45 ACP. Similar results have been achieved with the 357 and 44 Magnums.

3N38. Developed primarily for competitive handgun shooting, 3N38 is preferred by those who want high-velocity loads in 9mm, 38 Super and 40 S&W.

N105 Super Magnum. This is a special powder with a burning rate between N350 and N110. It was developed for heavy-bullet loads and large-capacity cases. Best results have been in magnums in the 357 to 454 Casull class.

NORMA POWDERS

Norma powders are produced in Sweden and distributed in the U.S. through Black Hills Shooters Supply, Inc. They are packaged in 500-gram canisters.

Norma 200. This is their fastest burning powder for rifle use. 200 is suitable for smaller 22 centerfires such as the Hornet, 222 and 223. Norma 200 works well for light bullets at lower velocities in 30 calibers such as the 308.

Norma 201. Slightly slower burning, 201 works well in various 30-calibers and can be used for light-bullet loads in the 45-70.

Norma 202. This powder was developed specifically for use in the 308 for maximum power loadings. It produces good results in calibers in the 30-35 range such as the 8x57 Mauser, 9.3x63 and 9.3x74R.

Norma 203-B. This powder is a variant of 202, but more versatile. Norma 203-B works well in the 22-250 through 6mm and 308 on up to the 358 Norma Magnum.

Norma 204. This is a slower burning powder providing both power and accuracy in the 6.5x55, 308 and 30-06.

Norma URP. A good choice for mid-size 25 through 30 caliber cartridges. It works well in 7x64, 308 and 30-06.

Norma MRP. This is a "magnum powder" designed for calibers with large case capacity and heavy bullets. As a progressive burning type, it produces higher velocities within safe pressure limits.

Norma MRP-2. This is a slightly slower burning version of MRP for use in for "over bore" calibers such as 6.5-284, 6.5-06 and the Weatherby large magnums.

AN IMPORTANT NOTE AT THE END

The above listed powders are listed on the websites of their distributors. In addition to being an excellent source for the latest and best loading data, these sites provide the first/best warnings on recalled lots of powder! A timely check of the websites of the powder manufacturers is a recommended practice.

With so many
projectiles
available in so
many shapes and
sizes, how do you
find the one
that's best? It
depends what
you're looking for.

Bullets

THE BEST BULLET FOR YOUR GUN

BUYING BULLETS FOR reloading is a fairly simple process. Most guns of today are standardized in terms of bore diameter and rifling characteristics. If you are dealing with a knowledgeable dealer, a simple request for "some hunting bullets for my 30-30" will probably get you what you want. Unfortunately there are dealers who are not very knowledgeable and a few who are mainly interested in unloading what they have in stock. "Caveat emptor" is still the safest position to take. This section refers to getting the "best" bullet. The first thing you should have in mind when you go to buy bullets is a clear idea of what "best" means for your intended use. For any gun the first consideration for any use should be accuracy. Whether it's for target or game, an inaccurate bullet is worthless. The quickest and easiest rule of thumb when it comes to buying bullets is to get what duplicates the factory loading. If you want ammunition for special purposes, which most handloaders eventually will, then you will have to do a little research like reading this book. Old guns and those of foreign extraction can often be confusing in regard to what their bore and groove size actually is. The best information collected over the past century indicates that the most accurate bullet is the

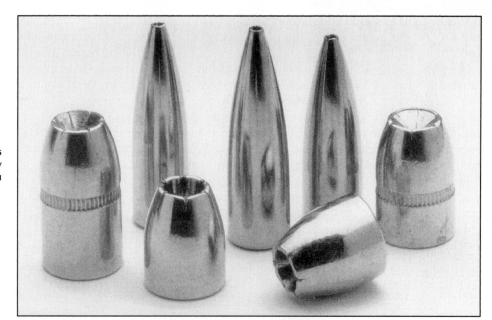

The "best" bullet for your gun is the one that shoots accurately and otherwise does what you want it to do.

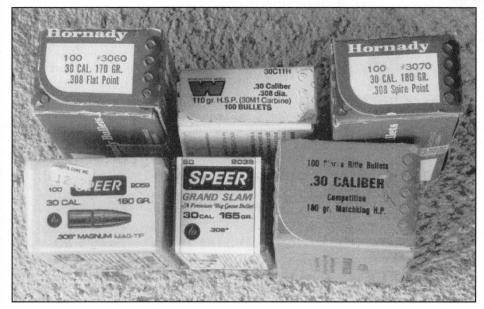

Bullets are packed 100 to a sturdy box marked with the diameter, weight and style of bullet – flat point, hollow point, etc., marked on the box.

one that fits the groove diameter of the barrel exactly. In the final analysis this is determined by slugging the bore of your gun and measuring the slug with a micrometer or vernier caliper and getting bullets that fit.

Proper diameter bullets can most easily be determined by reading the information on the box they come in or by measurement, if you are buying bullets in a plastic bag from someone you don't know. This can be a little confusing. For instance, 22 caliber bullets for the early 22 Hornet rifles were properly .223" diameter. The modern ones are .224". And the 223 Remington (5.56mm) is .224" diameter, not .223"! Good loading manuals usually give warnings regarding groove diameters in the data they provide for foreign and early rifles if there is a considerable variation in these within a particular type of rifle. My Lyman manual indicates that groove diameters on the 303 British military rifles vary from .309" to .317"! Put too fat a bullet in one of the tight ones

along with plenty of powder and you can create a dangerous pressure situation in addition to inaccurate shooting. The 303 Enfield, if loaded properly, is a fine, accurate rifle, capable of turning in some excellent groups.

BULLET LENGTH AND RIFLING CHARACTERISTICS

Beyond the question of bullet diameter there is the matter of bullet length and the relationship of bullet length to the rifling twist in the barrel and how this affects accuracy. Bullets aren't identified by length, but by weight when they are sold. All other things being equal, heavier bullets of a given diameter are longer. One way to find out which bullets will work best in your gun is trial and error. Another way is to limit yourself to the recommendations in loading manuals. These are basically guidelines and performance for the caliber of your gun and may or may not be satisfactory to you. Beyond this there are some basic calculations which may save you a lot of time and expense on bullets that don't work.

Therefore, a second thing you should know about the barrel of the gun you will be loading for, beyond its groove diameter, is the rate of the rifling twist. This can be found in loading manuals for a great many standard guns, certainly for the test guns used to prepare the data. This figure will be expressed, for example, as "Twist 1-10"." This indicates that the rifling spiral makes one complete turn in ten inches. Different lengths of bullets require different rifling twists to shoot to their best advantage. If the match between bullet length and rifling is too far off, bullets may fail to stabilize and tumble in flight on the one hand or be so over stabilized they will actually break apart in flight on the other.

Good shooting comes only when you have the correct diameter and weight.

If there is any doubt in your mind about the twist rate of your gun, determining this is simplicity itself, at least with a rifle length barrel. With handguns, you will have to interpolate as best you can. Stand the rifle against a plain vertical surface such as a wall or door. Place a good tight patch on your cleaning rod — one that does not have a ball bearing in the handle. Once the patch is started, mark the handle and beside it make a mark on the vertical surface. Push the rod down the barrel, allowing the handle to turn freely. Make a second mark at the point where the handle has made one complete rotation. Measure the distance between the top and bottom marks and you know the twist rate to a very close degree, although there will always be a slight amount of slippage.

As a rule of thumb, longer bullets of a given caliber require a faster twist to stabilize them to the point where they shoot accurately than shorter bullets. This is true without regard to weight or velocity. The familiar 22 Long Rifle shoots best in a 1-16" twist barrel. This holds true for 40 grain target loadings as well as 30 grain hyper-velocity hollow point hunting bullets. These are always made to be close to the 40 grain LR bullet's length. The stubby, 30 grain 22 Short does best in a 1-20" twist barrel. It will stabilize in a 1-16" barrel, but accuracy is not good. Rifles marked "22 Short, Long, or Long Rifle" are actually bored for the Long Rifle or occasionally with a compromise twist of 1-17", which may slightly improve the accuracy of the Short, without adversely affecting the accuracy of the Long Rifle.

Once you know the twist of your gun you can calculate which bullets will likely perform best and save money by not buying those that won't.

THE GREENHILL FORMULA

There are some elaborate computer programs to calculate bullet length to rifling twist, but there is a very simple method that works with a pocket calculator or even paper and pencil — The Greenhill Formula. The Greenhill for-

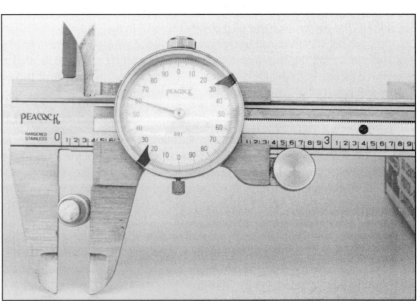

If you have any doubt about the caliber of bullets you are buying, check them with an accurate caliper or micrometer.

mula for determining twist rates was the work of Sir Alfred George Greenhill, a mathematics professor at Cambridge University who later served as an instructor at the Woolrich Military Academy from 1876 to 1906. Greenhill discovered that the optimum twist rate for a bullet is determined by dividing 150 by the length of the bullet in calibers (100ths of an inch). The number 150 is a good choice since it allows a useful margin in the calculations. Most twist rates that are close to the formulated ideal will usually work well. The beauty of this formula is that it works very well for lead or jacketed bullets. Weight does not appear to be a critical factor. Shape and design do not seem to have that much effect either up to velocities of 2200 fps and to a degree, above this. To compensate for increased rotational speed at velocities over 3000 fps some authorities recommend a slightly reduced twist rate. Although velocity does not appear to be considered within this formula, it is included in the rotation segment in a concealed form.

Assume a 1-12" barrel firing a bullet at 1000 fps. This equals 1000 rotations per second. At 2000 fps the rotations per second double. Higher velocity yields a faster spin and is thus considered in the calculations, although it is not specifically mentioned. The most recent interpretations of Greenhill opt for a slightly faster twist with the higher velocity cartridges in the belief that erring on the side of over-stabilization is better than under-stabilization that may result in a tumbling bullet.

The popular 223 Remington is a good candidate for study. Rifles for this cartridge are currently available with the following twist rates — 1-7", 1-8.5", 1-9", 1-10", 1-12" and 1-14". To apply the Greenhill Formula using the original 55 grain bullet yields the following, for one brand of full metal jacket (FMJ) military type bullet measuring .647" in length. The bullet diameter is .224", which divided into the length of .647" gives 2.89 calibers long. Dividing 2.89 into 150 yields a figure of 51.90 or an ideal twist rate of one turn in 51.90 calibers. Multiply 51.90 by the bullet diameter (.224") equals one turn in 11.63" for this particular bullet.

The original twist for the 223 caliber M-16 rifle is 1-12". In its wisdom (?) the Army decided a heavier (longer) bullet was necessary and the M-16A1 is bored with a 1-10" twist. The new military bullet will not stabilize in the 1-12" barrels. Bullets as heavy as 70 grains are available for the .223 Remington. For a 70 grain bullet measuring .785" in length, .785 ÷ .224 = 3.50. 150 ÷ 3.50 = 42.86 or one turn in 42.86 calibers. 42.86 X .224 (i.e., the bullet caliber) = 9.60. Thus a twist of 1-9" or 1-10" is required to shoot this bullet accurately, while a 1-12" will not stabilize it and as for a 1-14", forget it. There are other factors involved, such as the amount of bearing surface on the bullet, velocity and barrel length. In some cases bullets that are not well matched to twist rate can be made to function. For example, a short, 40 or 45 grain bullet, in a 223 with a fast twist of 1-9" or 1-10", will perform, if the powder charge is cut back. By decreas-

Rifling twist is important when matching bullets to a particular gun especially with the popular 223 Remington (5.56mm). This Olympic Arms PCR-1 223 rifle comes in either a 1-8.5" twist or a 1-10" twist. Other models come in a choice of 1-7", 1-9", 1-12" or 1-14".

Ruger's Mini-14/5R 223 features a 1:9-inch twist.

Eagle Arms' M15A2 Post-Ban Heavy Barrel Rifle in 223 has a 1:9-inch twist.

Remington's 40-X target rifle in 223 has a 1:14-inch twist.

ing the velocity, you can keep the bullet from tearing itself apart. This might be called a limited success, since in the manner of the .22 Short in the 22 Long Rifle barrel, accuracy will likely suffer.

Applying the Greenhill formula can save time and money not spent on ammunition that won't shoot well. It can serve as a useful guide when it comes to buying a gun or having one custom barreled if you know in advance what kind of shooting you will be doing and thus what kind of bullets you will use.

RIFLE BULLETS

Military surplus and military overrun bullets may be a terrific bargain if all you want is some cheap practice ammunition. Military bullets suitable for practice are of the full metal jacketed variety. They feature a solid lead alloy core with a copper, bronze or soft steel jacket and are referred to as "ball" ammunition. These bullets are made to military specifications and will produce reasonably good accuracy for preliminary sighting in and practice. The full metal jacket prevents nose expansion and is not good for hunting. Occasionally shooters have tried to make hunting ammunition out of FMJ bullets by filing the points off of the spitzer (pointed) military bullets, exposing the lead cores. This is a dangerous practice since the bullet already has the lead core exposed at the base. Opening the point often results in the core being blown right through the jacket leaving the jacket stuck in the barrel. When the next shot hits the jacket, the barrel is bulged and ruined. Don't try to modify FMJ bullets! Because of bullet-to-bullet weight variation, military ammunition will never produce fine accuracy.

In a worst-case scenario, such a "bargain" could turn out to be tracer, incendiary, explosive or armor piercing bullets. Most military ammunition is identified by the color of the lacquer on the tip and in the case of the tracer, by exposed burning material at the base of the bullet. There are various books on military ammunition that will tell you how to interpret these colored-lacquer codes on a country-by-country basis.

Surplus armor piercing ammunition has been used for years as cheap practice fodder, mainly in military rifles. Philip Sharpe in his book *The Complete Guide to Handloading* responded to the question of whether this did any harm to rifle barrels by conducting an experiment wherein he took a "gilt-edged" match rifle barrel, targeted it with match target ammunition, then fired a few rounds of armor piercing then targeted it again with the same match ammunition, carefully cleaning between groups. His finding was that after the AP rounds, the match group had opened considerably and in spite of further cleaning did not repeat its former performance. This was with the AP ammunition of WWII, not the so called "light armor" piercing, steel-core ammunition sold today which has a far softer steel center. Would I put this newer kind through the barrel of a fine match rifle I owned? I don't think so, at least not until someone else tests

it in his match barrel first. Would I use it in a $150 AK or SKS? Sure.

Match ammunition is full-metal jacketed and of a reduced-base "boattail" design. This type of bullet has good aerodynamic qualities producing a flat trajectory which is very desirable for hitting targets at long range. Often these match bullets have a small hollow point to shift the center of gravity slightly back and improve stabilization. Match bullets often have very thin jackets and are "soft swaged" to keep these jackets smooth, flawless and of the exact same thickness. Great care is taken to ensure that these bullets are of the exact same weight and diameter. Since this type of bullet is used for punching paper targets or knocking down metal silhouettes, expansion is not needed. Even though these bullets have hollow points they are not intended to expand on game and they do not. They are very prone to ricochet and are not suitable for hunting.

Bullets for varmint hunting are either flat-base or boattail and feature a tapered or spire point with the lead core exposed and swaged into a point. The jackets are thin, allowing these bullets to expand rapidly with an explosive force on woodchucks, prairie dogs and similar-sized, thin-skinned animals. This design also keeps these bullets from ricocheting when they strike the ground at velocities near 2000 fps. Because of their frangibility, varmint bullets are not suitable for large game.

Bullets for medium to large game require thicker jackets to keep them together while they penetrate deep into vital areas. They are designed for controlled expansion allowing the bullet to upset or "mushroom" as it goes deeper, making a larger hole which renders it far more lethal than a non-expanding type or a frangible one that breaks into fragments shortly after it strikes a body.

In medical terms, "lethality" is the effect of a particular bullet on a body. According to Dr. Martin Fackler — the leading wound ballistics expert in the country — bullet lethality is an easily understood concept. Lethality is determined by answering two questions: How big is the hole it produces? How deep is this hole? Bigger and deeper holes are more likely to intersect with vital organs, cause greater loss of blood, and result in death.

Game bullets are generally of a pointed-soft-point design — known as spitzer or semi-spitzer. These hold their velocity much better than less aerodynamic designs. Also available are large-hollow-point, flat-nose or round-nose designs with the lead core exposed. Attempts at improving expansion have been tried by varying the thickness of the jacket and by making cuts or skives in the jacket at the bullet nose to enable the jacket to split open and peel back in an even pattern as the core upsets. Other modifications are hollow points filled with hollow copper tubes, metal or nylon plugs which are driven back on impact, expanding the bullet.

Bullets for very large, dangerous game are subject to special requirements, since they often have to penetrate a considerable amount of muscle tissue and often heavy bone to

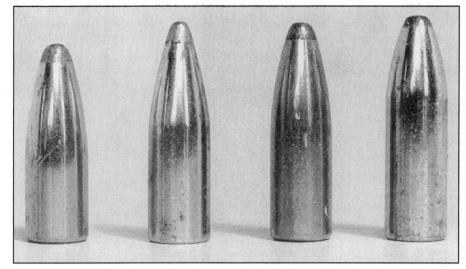

Bullets for the 22 centerfire *(from left)*: 55-, 60-, 63- and 70-grain. They look very alike and can be easily mixed up, which is why unloaded bullets should always be returned to the original container after you are through loading ammunition. The 70-grain bullet will not work well in slow-twist (1:14-inch) barrels.

Match ammunition usually features a hollowpoint design and often a boat-tail. While these are very accurate, they are unreliable when it comes to expanding on game or varmint animals and often ricochet rather than break up when they hit the ground.

reach a vital spot. Bullets for this type of hunting feature very thick jackets. Some like the old RWS and contemporary Nosler have two cores with a solid web of bronze running through the center of the bullet so that in section it looks like the letter "H". The top half expands, but only to the center web which insures that the base portion will stay together. Barnes Bullets offers what they call a "monolithic solid" which is simply a solid bronze bullet. Since these are made in large calibers such as 416 they are in effect pre-expanded. Speer offers a copper alloy bullet called "African Grand Slam" with a tungsten carbide dowel in the center for use on such extremely dangerous and hard-to-kill game as cape buffalo.

HANDGUN BULLETS

Handgun bullets for target use are often swaged from lead alloy and deliver good accuracy when properly lubricated. Their design ranges from a cylinder, called a "wadcutter," because it punches clean holes in paper targets, to round nose and truncated cone styles. Use in indoor ranges of such ammunition has raised fears of lead poisoning, since a certain amount of lead is vaporized from the bullet's surface upon firing. To counter this hazard, the "total metal jacket" or TMJ bullet was developed. The full metal jacket leaves an exposed lead base, while the TMJ covers the entire surface of the bullet. This jacket is applied by electroplating the bullet core with copper. After the plating process is completed, the bullets are "bumped" up to bring them into proper size and roundness. They don't expand as well as soft-lead alloy bullets and are thus a poor choice for hunting, but do keep lead levels down in indoor ranges.

For indoor use we are seeing more "green" bullets made of compressed copper and other non-lead metals which are designed to disintegrate on impact with a steel backstop. This virtually eliminates ricochets and (except for lead primer residue) eliminates lead contamination in indoor ranges.

Such bullets are available as reloading components. These must be handled with more care than a lead or jacketed bul-

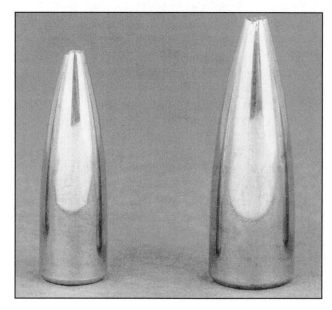

let as they are prone to break apart in the loading process if they are seated roughly or there is inadequate "belling" of the case mouth.

Hunting bullets for handguns are modifications of rifle designs, with some major engineering differences. Early attempts to improve handgun-bullet lethality led to softpoint and hollow-point designs based on rifle bullets. Results were unsatisfactory when it was discovered that these generally failed to expand and behaved no differently than FMJ types. In the last few years new designs have emerged that will expand reliably at handgun velocities — 900-1600 fps. The secret to bringing this about was to design bullets with nearly pure lead cores, large hollow points and thin, relatively soft jackets of pure copper, copper alloys or aluminum. Skives or cuts through the jacket and into the core improve expansion, increasing the lethality of these relatively low-velocity bullets. Since most handgun hunting is done at ranges of under 100 yards, this expansion is still reli-

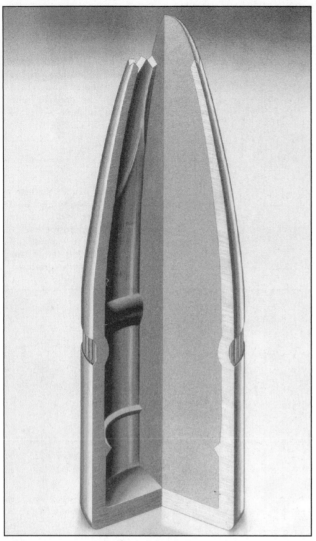

This Hornady hunting bullet features an exposed lead point and a lead core. The core is held in place by knurled cannelures in the jacket. (Courtesy Hornady)

Winchester's Silvertip hunting bullet features a thin aluminum jacket over the lead point. This allows good expansion but prevents the bullet from getting nicked and dented as the cartridge is fed through the magazine.

able on most game animals of deer size or smaller, assuming that the handgun is a powerful one in the 357 Magnum to 50 Magnum class. Handguns of less than this performance level simply cannot be loaded heavily enough to do any serious hunting and to try to "load them up" for this purpose is a foolish risk to both the gun and its shooter. Shooting any jacketed handgun bullet at low velocities is not recommended, particularly in revolvers. The greater resistance of the jacketed bullet to swaging in the barrel requires higher pressures than with lead bullets. Underpowered loads, particularly in revolvers with a generous gap between the cylinder and barrel, may result in a stuck bullet waiting to be slammed by the next one fired.

HANDLING AND STORAGE

The care and storage of bullets is much the same as for cartridge cases or loaded ammunition. Commercially made bullets are packed in boxes of 100 and the boxes they come in are about the best containers to keep them in. These are generally of plastic or reinforced cardboard and will last a long time. Bullets should not be dropped or shaken since this will impart nicks and dents which do nothing to improve their accuracy. Lead bullets are the most susceptible to this kind of damage.

The early experiments of Franklin Mann, recounted in his book *The Bullet's Flight From Powder to Target* demonstrated the frailty of bullets when it comes to having their accuracy severely affected by even minor damage. Bullet bases are the most vulnerable. A lead or soft lead alloy bullet dropped on a wood floor and receiving a ding on the edge of the base has just been converted into scrap. They can be used for warming and fouling shots, but their former accuracy is gone.

Perhaps the one caution with bullet storage is to be careful that bullets are not mixed up. If you are loading two very similar calibers there is a possibility of accidentally getting

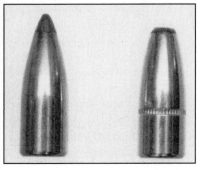

Pointed softpoint and flat-point bullets are both good hunting bullets. The pointed bullet is more susceptible to damage in feeding; the flatpoint loses velocity slightly faster.

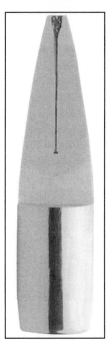

Barnes X-Bullet is a solid copper projectile designed for deep penetration, no fragmentation and good accuracy. This cutaway shows construction.

Good handgun bullet designs are the wadcutter *(left)*, so named for the neat holes it makes in paper targets, the round-nose *(center)*, and semi-wadcutter *(right)*.

Handgun bullets designed for hunting must offer rapid expansion at relatively low velocities. To this end, they feature large hollowpoints, serrated jackets and pure lead cores.

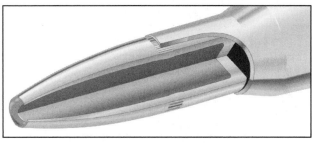

Norma's Oryx hunting bullet is a flat-based, semi-spitzer design with a thick jacket and bonded core for maximum game-stopping ability.

Nosler Ballistic tip polymer tip bullets like those of Combined technology Ballistic Silver Tip provide controlled expansion for varmint and medium-size game.

Nosler Accubond hunting bullets feature a tapering jacket for controlled expansion. The core bond features a proprietary process to eliminate core separation.

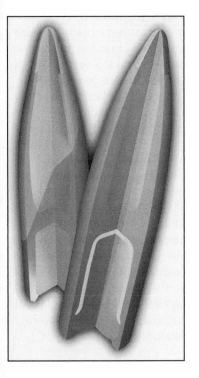

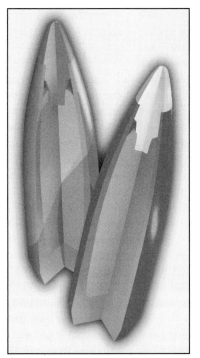

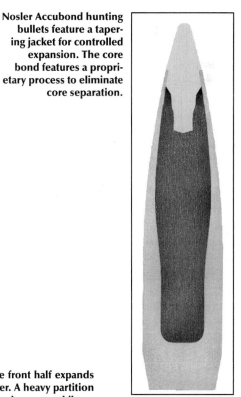

Nosler's Partition bullets are designed so the front half expands in conventional manner, but only to the center. A heavy partition keeps the back half intact, retaining weight and energy, while an ordinary bullet might fragment.

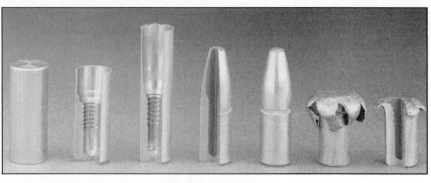

These are the steps in making one version of the Speer "Grand Slam" hunting bullet. Solid copper slug is punched to form the jacket. The jacket is then drawn and trimmed before the lead core is inserted. The jacket is very thick at the base to keep the bullet from fragmenting. Internal grooves and a thick base insure the jacket does not shed the core, yet thinning the jacket in the forward portion insures good expansion. Such bullets are for large dangerous game where deep penetration is needed. *(Courtesy Speer)*

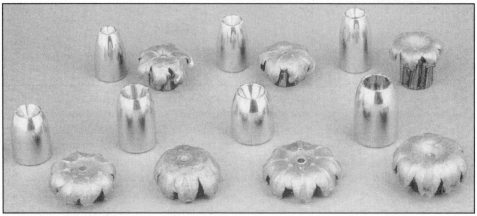

These Speer "Gold Dot" handgun bullets in 38, 40 and 45 caliber, after being fired into ballistic gelatin, show considerable expansion. *(Courtesy Speer)*

a 40 caliber or 10mm bullet in a box of 9mm bullets of the same style and approximate weight. You would likely catch this in the loading process at the time of seating this bullet, but there are some people who might persist in attempting to jam such a bullet in a 9mm case. Perhaps more likely is the confusing of bullets of the same caliber, but different weights. These will seat perfectly well, but the heavier ones are going to have a higher trajectory and will land in a different place. A heavier bullet will, of course, raise pressures. If you are using a maximum load this can have serious consequences. It is a good idea never to have two boxes of similar bullets open on your loading bench at the same time. Using boxes with snap tops or putting a bit of tape on the lid to keep it from opening accidentally is a good idea. I think most people will agree, particularly after having spilled a box of 22 caliber bullets and having to pick them all up.

BUYING BULLETS

Most gun stores carry a good selection of bullets for most shooter's needs. The directory in the back of this book lists about 200 suppliers of bullets of about every description. Bullets can be bought by mail. Most of the large bullet manufacturers such as Sierra, Nosler, Hornady and Speer offer reloading guides for their products. The smaller companies offer catalogs and sometimes limited amounts of loading data.

Custom bullets are supplied by small manufacturers and are often geared to special types of guns or for special types shooting such as metallic silhouette competition. At times these manufacturers or their jobbers will sell their bullets at gun shows where they can be bought at a lower cost and

without the shipping and handling. I always enjoy attending these affairs and chatting with the dealers. It is a good place to pick up information and misinformation. Buying bullets in a plastic bag is a pig in a poke, but I don't recall getting burned too badly except for some cast bullets that either had a bad alloy or too little or a poor quality lubricant since they deposited generous amounts of lead in one of my rifle barrels.

BULLET FOULING AND BORE CLEANING

The subject of cleaning has been touched upon in the powder and primer sections. The main fouling problem affecting accuracy is caused by bullets. To reiterate, the problem of primer deposits is one of corrosive salts. It is very similar, in effect, to the corrosive deposits left by back powder or Pyrodex. A water-based cleaner does a good job of getting these out of your barrel since salt and acid are readily dissolved in water and can be flushed away. The deposit left by smokeless powder is mainly soot, graphite, from the coating on the powder grains, small amounts of unburned powder and bullet lubricant. Often this is deposited in a varnish-like layer in the gun bore. It is not corrosive and does not draw water nor does it tend to build up in thick deposits in the manner of black-powder fouling. After a lot of shooting this fouling will begin to affect accuracy. It is easily removed by the many "nitro" powder solvents on today's market. These are petroleum based and do an excellent job of dissolving lubricant and the sooty deposits of smokeless powder. As mentioned earlier unless it has a water component it will prove ineffective on corrosive primer and black powder deposits.

Bullets deposit metallic fouling. This is basically of two

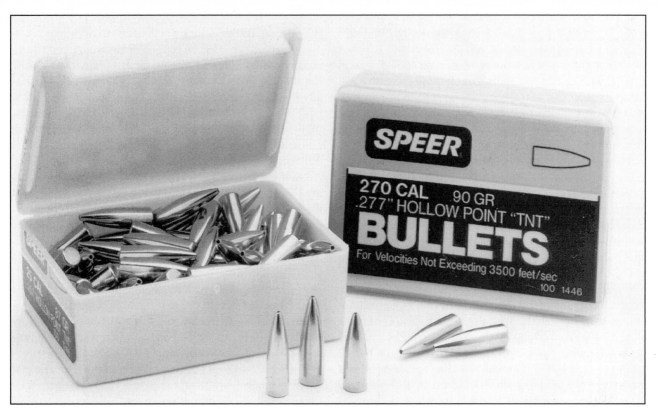

Speer's all-plastic snap-lock boxes keep out moisture and pollutants and prevent corrosion from getting a start on the bullets inside.
(Courtesy Speer)

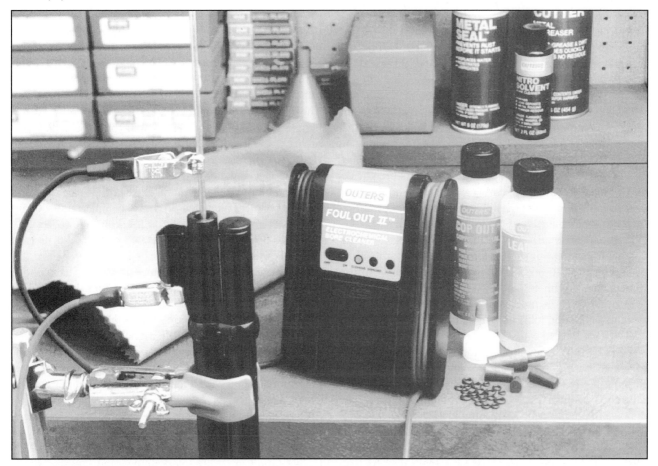

Outer's Foul Out III electrochemical system is the easiest method of dealing with serious metal fouling problems.

types, lead and copper. Lead fouling, known as "leading," will ruin accuracy very quickly. A poorly lubricated bullet or an over or under-size lead bullet can deposit enough lead in a barrel with one or two shots that all those thereafter will fail to stabilize and go tumbling down range to the extreme consternation of the shooter. Exactly what causes leading is not really known and the phenomenon may have more than one cause. The original theory was that lead bullets that were too large or were inadequately lubricated stripped as they passed down the barrel and that the following bullets encountered this lead and plastered it to the bore and in the process stripped off more lead. Gradually rough clumps of lead piled up in the barrel to the point to where the rifling was so clogged that it failed to stabilize the bullets. This certainly seems possible.

This theory however fails to explain how undersize bullets with plenty of lubricant on them can do the same thing. The second theory holds that an undersized lead bullet will not obturate the bore fully, especially if made of too hard an alloy. Hot gasses rushing by this undersize bullet melt the surface, blowing particles of melted lead down the barrel. These cool and solidify gradually building up a layer of lead forward of the chamber which is added to and plastered down by successive bullets to the point where accuracy is ruined.

I am a believer in both theories since they seem logical. I have had oversize and under-lubricated bullets do this. The surface of the recovered bullet has a scraped, stripped surface with the rifling striae poorly defined. In the case of undersize bullets, the recovered bullet evidences little or no rifling marks whatsoever. The surface has a semi-melted appearance and there is often evidence of gas cutting — melted channels extending forward from the base of the bullet. Furthermore, the leading in each case is of a distinctive type. Stripping generally happens at about the mid point of a rifle barrel, or where the bullet runs out of lubricant, and continues out to the muzzle. The deposits are streaks and clumps usually in the corner where the land joins the groove. For some reason the heaviest concentration seems to be about three-quarters of the way down the barrel.

Heat soldering, caused by gas blow-by, deposits a smooth coating of lead beginning just forward of the chamber and extending eight to ten inches. Subsequent bullets burnish this coating, making it shine and it is thus difficult to see.

In either case, the problem is: getting the lead out. Nitro solvents with good lubricating qualities can flow under the lead and lift it to an extent, but the process takes days. The usual practice is to use a phosphor-bronze cleaning brush, saturated with solvent, and working it back and forth through the barrel, making sure not to change directions until the brush has cleared each end. Failure to do so can damage the bore surface. An overnight soak, heavily coating or filling the barrel with solvent, helps speed things on a badly-leaded bore. Outers, among others, sells high-powered solvents containing ingredients which actually dissolve metal fouling to the point of cutting the job by half, but there is still, at least, half an hour's worth of brush work to do.

Copper fouling is left by copper, brass, bronze and cupro-nickel bullet jackets and by steel jackets plated with any of the above. Copper fouling is usually a thin wash that gradually builds into a thicker layer. Occasionally copper alloy jackets will leave clumps of fouling which will degrade accuracy markedly and suddenly, much like strip-leading. Brush and solvent removal is the same process as for lead, the main difference being the process takes about three times as long. Ammonia-based solvents work well to dissolve copper fouling. The usual thin build-up is barely noticeable, but after it reaches a certain point, groups begin to open up — a timely reminder it's high time for a cleaning. *Gun Tests* magazine tested a number of copper fouling cleaners. Montana X-treme 50 BMG Copper Remover was their pick; the old standard, "Sweet's" received a "Buy it" rating.

At present, Outers, with its "Foul Out" system, offers the most advanced cleaning system. Though somewhat complicated and expensive (compared to a rod, brush and solvent combination) this is the best/easiest when it comes to dealing with a really bad case of fouling.

Foul Out works on the electroplating principle. The gun barrel is plugged at the breech with a rubber stopper, then filled with a solution containing lead or copper, depending on the type of fouling to be removed. A stainless-steel rod is inserted in the barrel and held in the center by rubber washers. Electrical contacts are attached to the barrel and the rod. A weak current passing through the solution causes the lead or copper fouling to detach itself molecule by molecule to be deposited on the rod in the center. Every so often the rod must be removed and the lead or copper scrubbed off. When the solution gets weak it too must be replaced. The process takes a couple of hours, but it works. Everything is removed down to the steel of the barrel. Old layers of rust and burned-on powder varnish are loosened as well. Best of all there is no elbow-work — nothing more than a periodic checking. For barrels that haven't been cleaned in a long time or those that are a bit on the rough side it doesn't get much better. When the process is complete a few damp patches to remove traces of the solution followed by dry patches followed by a preservative oil and your barrel is as clean as the day you bought it.

New products are coming out all the time. Sharp Shoot R Precision Products offers a line developed by chemist Terry Paul which includes "Wipe-Out – a foam cleaner that removes all the above fouling plus molybdenum. "Wipe-Out" foam is squirted into the barrel which penetrates below metallic fouling allowing it to be removed with a patch. "Wipe out" can be left in a bore overnight. Cleaning of really bad fouling may take a day or two, but is not powered by elbow grease.

Good quality nitro powder solvents and some for black-powder are available from a plethora of makers — Hoppe's, Tetra Gun Care, Clenzoil Corp, Gunslick, Outers, Shooter's Choice Gun Care, Flitz International, and Pro-Shot Products to name a few.

Homemade
projectiles have
been used
for centuries,
but recent
generations have
enjoyed many
advancements in
the art.

Casting Bullets

PEOPLE HAVE BEEN casting bullets out of lead for hundreds of years. In the 19th century, bullet casting came into its own as a craft verging on a science. Experimenters assembled composite bullets with hard bodies and soft/heavy noses, even going as far as pouring mercury into the mixture. (Horrors!) Those who did that died sooner or later (more likely sooner) from the poisonous vapor. Bullets used with black powder were made of lead and lead alloyed with tin. The latter gave much better results because the tin improved the quality of the cast bullet, causing it to fill the mould more completely.

It was found that the velocity of lead alloy bullets could only be raised to a certain point — about 1500-1600 fps. At that point lead begins coming off the bullet and being deposited in the barrel, ruining accuracy until the lead is removed. Flintlock shooters had solved this problem by wrapping their lead ball in a greased leather or cloth patch. Higher velocities with conical bullets were obtained by wrapping a slightly-undersize lead bullet in a thin, tough, paper jacket (much like banknote paper) which was applied wet and shrunk to a tight fit as the cloth fibers contracted on drying. "Paper patch" bullets, as they were known, produced fine accuracy in addition to achieving velocities close to 2000 fps. Expansion was good since the bullet alloy could be kept

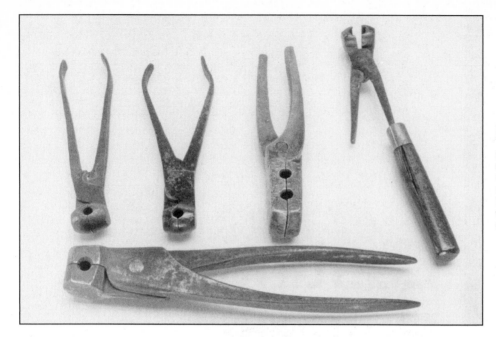

Bullet moulds from the late 18th/early 19th century cast round balls and roughly shaped conical bullets. The metal handles heated up right along with the mould blocks. The finished bullet was trimmed up with a pocket knife.

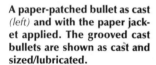

A paper-patched bullet as cast *(left)* and with the paper jacket applied. The grooved cast bullets are shown as cast and sized/lubricated.

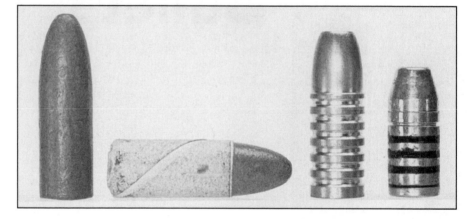

soft – unlike a grooved, lubricated bullet which had to be hardened to keep it from deforming from the heat, friction and pressure of high-velocity loads. When metal-jacketed bullets supplanted lead bullets for rifle use, about the time smokeless powder appeared on the scene, paper-patched bullets all but vanished, and cast lead bullets were relegated to handguns and old, blackpowder rifles.

The new jacketed bullets, however, were discovered to have their drawbacks — a considerably shorter gun-barrel life, caused by erosion and wear, and a hard copper fouling. This fouling was not only difficult to remove, but often covered up the corrosive salts left by primers which ate up the barrel very quickly.

Shooters began to have second thoughts about abandoning lead alloy bullets. Unfortunately, soft lead bullets and smokeless powder are not always happy together. The higher flame temperature of the smokeless powder had a tendency to melt the bases of lead bullets. Around the turn of the century, John Barlow of the Ideal Manufacturing Company — makers of bullet moulds — came up with the idea of placing a small copper cup known as

a "gas check" on the bases of cast bullets to prevent this from happening. After Barlow's death, the Ideal Company was taken over by the Lyman Gun Sight Company and began publishing some of the first good manuals on reloading. It was not until the 1930's, however, that the basics of making good cast bullets for smokeless loadings were clearly understood.

BULLET ALLOY

Hardening lead bullets with tin improved their casting quality, but tin is expensive and adding one part to twenty parts lead, by weight, did not achieve much additional hardening. In fact, as the tin content is increased much above this point it becomes more like solder, since the addition of tin lowers the melting point and metal fouling begins to build up in the barrel.

Antimony, while it does not truly alloy with lead, will combine in crystalline form and harden it to a great degree. The best hard lead alloys are composed of lead, tin and antimony. The tin serves to coat the antimony crystals and bond them to the lead. The antimony adds a great deal of hardness in proportion to the amount added, by weight. Tin is about twelve times as expensive as lead, while antimony is about three times as much. The addition of both metals to lead increases its fluidity in the molten state which makes it ideal for casting type metal or bullets, both of which require hardness, toughness, and precise dimensions.

When preparing or buying bullet-alloy material, it is best to first consider what purpose you wish to use these bullets for, since there is no point in spending the money to produce "gold plated" ammunition for plinking. Harder bullets, particularly those hardened with antimony, tend also to become brittle. Hard alloys are a poor choice for making hunting bullets since they will either drill straight through or shatter rather than expand evenly. Harder bullets are a good choice for long-range target use or metallic silhouette shooting where velocity and flat trajectory is important and there is no need for expansion.

Bullets made of lead, tin, antimony alloy will become harder as they age. After a month or so they have reached their maximum hardness. If harder bullets are desired, one way to achieve this without adding additional antimony is to harden them at the time of casting by dropping the bullet (hot out of the mould) into a pan of cold water rather than letting it cool slowly. A bullet of wheel-weight metal with a normal hardness of 12.4 BHN can be hardened to better than twice that by the above method. Similar hardening can be done by placing cast bullets in a pan, heating them in an oven to about 500 degrees F, then quenching them in cold water. Hot bullets must be handed very carefully since they are soft to the point of being in a near-melted state and are easily damaged.

Bullet alloys can be bought pre-mixed from various sources, or you can buy lead, tin and antimony and mix your own. Since antimony has a melting point almost twice that of lead, it cannot be melted over an ordinary gas stove or electric melting pot. Good bullet alloys can be made from a variety of scrap materials that can be obtained at a lower cost than pre-mixed alloys or pure metals. The main thing is to know what you are getting, at least as far as possible, and to avoid bad materials that will ruin your metal for further use. Zinc is poison to lead alloys because it will not mix properly and ruins the casting qualities. Bullets have been made of nearly pure zinc under such trade names as "Zamak" and "Kirksite." Zinc alloys are generally too light weight for shooting at long range. They tend to gas-cut rather badly because they cannot be gas-checked.

Battery plates were at one time salvaged for bullet making. That was before they were made of lead and calcium which, like zinc, ruins the casting quality of your alloy. Babbitt, bearing metal with high amounts of tin and antimony, is of use mainly to harden other lead alloys. Babbitt contains slight amounts of copper, but this floats to the surface and generally does not cause serious problems when the metal is melted down.

Bullet alloys can roughly be classed as soft, medium, hard and extra hard. Soft alloys are lead with about 3% to 4% tin or about 1% antimony. They are suitable for most handgun loads and low velocity rifle loads — to about 1300 fps. Medium alloys need to be about 90% lead 5% tin and 5% antimony and are good to about 1700fps. Hard alloys are about 84% lead, 12% antimony and 4% tin. This is the alloy used in linotype and will shoot well at close to or above 2000 fps. Extra hard alloys can be anything up to 72% lead 19% antimony and 9% tin. Beyond this, bullets begin to become too light in proportion to their size and efficiency is lowered.

The cast/lubricated bullet will give equal or better accuracy than the jacketed hunting bullet, while producing less barrel wear, and can be made at a fraction of the cost. At ranges of 100-150 yards, it will kill just as effectively.

Copper gas checks applied to bullets designed for them allow increased velocities and keep hot gas from melting the bullet bases.

Block lead and tin, as well as pre-mixed alloys, ensure purity in the metal alloy. Many scrap alloys, however, may be used to make good bullets, including wheelweights, lead plumbing pipe and lead cable sheathing. Scrap 22 rimfire bullets recovered from indoor shooting ranges can also be a viable source.

MIXING ALLOYS

Alloying and bullet casting should be done in a well-ventilated place or, better still, outdoors. The equipment needed for mixing alloy is an iron melting pot and a lead thermometer or electric melting furnace with a thermostat, a steel spoon or skimmer to stir the metal and skim off dross. A can to hold the dross and an ingot mould complete the list of basics. A lead pot is about $20 - $40, a thermometer about $40. An electric melting pot with a thermostat is about $250-$350. An ingot mould runs about $13 and a dross and clip skimmer (a spoon with holes) is $20 — a useful item. Small ingots — 2" X 1" or less – melt faster than large ones.

This electric melting pot with bottom-pour spigot holds about 10 pounds of alloy.

BULLET METALS AND THEIR RELATIVE HARDNESS

Alloy	Tin	Lead	Antimony	Copper	BHN
		----% By Weight----			
Monotype	9	72	19	—	28
Stereotype	6	80	14	—	23
Linotype	4	84	12	—	22
Electrotype	3	94.5	2.5	—	12
Tin Babbit	83	—	11	6	23
Lead Babbit	—	83	11	6	22
Tire weights	1	96	3	—	12.4
Antimony	—	—	100	—	50
Tin	100	—	—	—	7
Lead	—	100	—	—	5

Note: Lead, tin and antimony alloys harden with age. The maximum hardness is reached in about two weeks. Heat treating and quenching in cold water will harden bullets. If they are worked through a sizer, this will soften the worked surface. Tire or wheel weights, as they are often called, are now being made with slightly more lead and less antimony and are softer, though the alloy will vary. This alloy should be tested for hardness if hardness is critical.

It is a good idea to keep the alloying operations and bullet casting separate. Alloy should be made up in two-pound lots if you are experimenting. Once an alloy is found that suits your needs and shoots well, you can make up as much as you like — the more the better to maintain bullet-weight consistency.

Cleaning scrap involves removing dirt, oxides, and such extraneous items as the steel clips on wheel weights by melting it. To keep the metal fluid and separate the unwanted material, it needs to be fluxed with a piece of

Small ingot moulds are the best way to store bullet alloy. To avoid mixups, ingots should be marked to identify them if different alloys are being used to avoid mixups.

This lead and debris skimmer from Bill Ferguson easily removes clips from tire weights and similar unwanted material from the lead alloy.

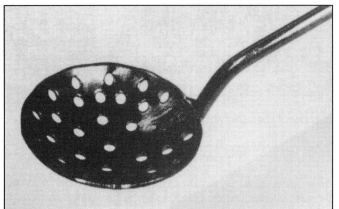

A large plumber's lead pot is best for mixing lead alloys and cleaning scrap alloy. This one can be used for casting as well.

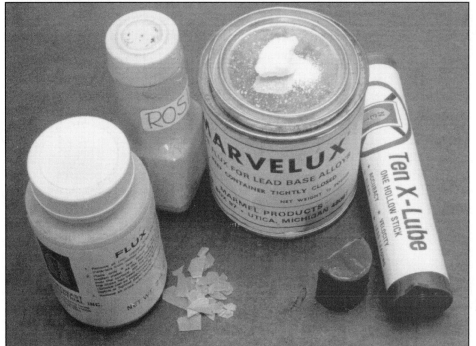

Molten metal needs to be fluxed to remove impurities and to keep tin and antimony mixed evenly throughout the alloy instead of floating on the surface. Commercial fluxes or a piece of bullet lubricant will do the job.

Casting Bullets   **87**

beeswax or paraffin the size of the first joint of your finger. This creates smoke which can be burned off by lighting it. The metal should be stirred with a spoon or lead dipper to work the flux into the metal and bring impurities to the top. While this stirring should be fairly rapid, it should not be so vigorous as to flip or spill hot metal on yourself. Impurities will collect on top be and should be skimmed after stirring and fluxing. Fluxing will work tin and antimony into the lead which would otherwise float to the top.

Do not skim off your tin, which forms a silvery gray coating on the surface. When you reach this stage, flux and stir again to blend it all together and pour the cleaned

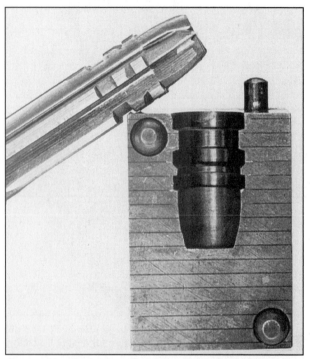

The mould cavity is given final form with a "cherry," a reaming tool in the form of the bullet.

scrap alloy into moulds for use as is, if it is suitable for bullet casting, or for blending with tin or lead or a harder alloy, if it needs to be hardened or softened for your ultimate bullet mix. This final fluxing and stirring assures a consistent mixture which should be mirror bright with a few brown spots of burned beeswax on it when in the molten state. The alloy can then be poured into a mould for small ingots about 1"X 2" for bullet making. These should be remelted in a clean pot for bullet casting. Use a scriber or magic marker to mark your finished ingots so you will know what the alloy is, since they all look pretty much alike.

The hardness of lead alloys is determined by the Brinell scale (BHN) and is tested by dropping a known weight with a point a known distance and measuring the impact hole. Lead testers, at $70-$90, are useful tools when making up precise alloys that will yield bullets of an exact hardness and weight. Scrap alloys are not always precise in their makeup, so they must be considered "approximate" in their composition. A quick easy test for pure lead is to see if you can scratch it with your fingernail. Pure lead sources from scrap include plumbing pipe, block lead and cable sheathing. Scrap 22 rimfire bullets contain less than 1% antimony and by the time they are melted, fluxed and skimmed can be considered nearly pure lead. Tin is a component of lead-tin solder and can be bought in ingots, but it is expensive. Automobile, wheel weights are a good source of alloy and can be used as-is for low to medium-velocity pistol and rifle bullets.

THE BULLET MOULD

The bullet mould has two metal blocks with a cavity between them where the bullet is cast. These are aligned by pins and held together by handles much like pliers. On top of the blocks is a plate with a funnel-shaped hole, through which metal is poured. When the pouring is complete, this "sprue plate" is given a rap with a wood rod to

The modern bullet mould is a precision tool and a far cry from the old "nut cracker" moulds of the past. Moulds are damaged by rough treatment and should be kept free of rust and never battered with a metal tool.

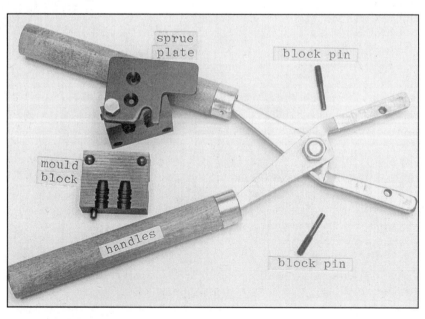

Aluminum moulds do not require as much breaking-in as iron or steel moulds. The cavity must often either be coated with carbon "smoke" or a special compound to get good bullets.

This nose-pour mould from Colorado Shooter's Supply delivers a bullet with a perfect base since the cut-off is at the bullet nose.

pivot it to one side, cutting off the excess metal or "sprue" left on top.

Bullet moulds can be made from a variety of materials and each mould maker has his preferences for his own reasons. There is no such thing as the perfect material. Custom mould-maker James Andela prefers 11L17 — a leaded steel of low-carbon content that machines easily to a bright smooth surface. This is the same basic type used in Lyman moulds. The material cost is low and a cold rolled bar is virtually free of inclusions and holes and possesses a dense grain structure. Oil retention is low and thus the break-in time is faster than with iron moulds.

Moulds are generally made by roughing out the cavity with a drill, then cutting the impression for the bullet with a fluted cutting tool called a "cherry." The cherry makes an exact negative impression of the bullet as the mould blocks are slowly pushed together on the cherry as it rotates.

Fine-grain cast iron is a common mould material with the advantages of low shrinkage and easy machinability, producing a fine powder as opposed to the larger chips from steel which are more difficult to control in the machining process and may damage the mould if not carefully removed. Iron is very stable with less inclination to warp or shrink in manufacture or with heating and cooling. When an iron block is used in conjunction with a steel sprue plate, these dissimilar metals work well together to form a polishing action rather than a galling action where alike metals may tend to tear pieces from one another.

Brass and various bronzes (all alloys of copper) have been used for moulds with great success. They generally machine well and take a good finish. Copper alloys of all sorts have the added advantage of being highly corrosion

This hollowpoint plug fits into the nose end of a base-pour mould.

Bullet moulds can be warmed by placing them (carefully) on the edge of the melting pot. A pre-warmed mould will start producing good bullets before a cold one.

The author has had best results by holding the mould about an inch below the spigot rather than having it in direct contact.

resistant and they heat quickly and evenly. The main disadvantages of brass and bronze is the cost of the material which may be three times that of iron or steel. Brass and bronze are softer than steel or iron and such moulds must be handled more carefully to avoid damage. Any copper alloy (both brass and bronze) has an affinity for lead and tin and must be kept free of any acidic or similar material that could act as a flux and solder the blocks together in the casting process. Such an event usually finishes the mould. Nickel has been used to a limited extent in mould making and might very well be the perfect material, pos-

sessing the qualities of hardness, smooth finish, corrosion resistance and non-solderability, giving it an edge over iron, steel and copper alloys. The main problem is that it is very expensive and for this reason no one uses nickel any more.

Aluminum and various aluminum alloys are widely used in mould making. Aluminum moulds require no break-in period. Aluminum's resistance to soldering, corrosion and its ability to heat to proper casting temperature quickly when combined with light weight and low cost of material make it nearly ideal. The major problem with aluminum alloy is its proneness to galling. The melting point of aluminum (1200 -1600 degrees F) is near enough to that of the lead alloys used in bullet making that the casting process has a tendency to anneal aluminum blocks and thus soften them to the point where the sprue cutter will gall the blocks. Aluminum blocks are also subject to cutting and denting. Alignment pins, usually of steel, will tend to wear aluminum blocks, unless the mould is used with greater care than an iron or steel mould. The overall useful life of an aluminum mould will be less than one of iron or steel.

TYPES OF MOULDS

The most common mould is a simple, single cavity mould that casts one bullet at a time. These cost about $50-$60 and run to about $200 for a custom mould. The next size up is the double cavity at about the same price as a single, for small bullets. Moulds that cast up to ten bullets at a time are known as "gang moulds" and are used mainly by custom bullet-makers because of their speed of production. They are expensive ($500). Moulds are also available with special inserts that will cast hollow-base and hollow-point bullets in single-cavity blocks for an additional $10 or so. Most moulds are of the "base-pour" variety with the bullet base at the top below the sprue plate. A few are "nose pour" moulds with the sprue cut off made at the nose. The theory behind these is that they give a more perfect base since base regularity is the most important factor in accuracy with cast bullets. Nose-pour moulds are generally custom-made and intended for long range, heavy target bullets.

While a bullet mould may look like a nutcracker, it is in reality a precision tool that can be easily damaged by rough handling. Dropping a mould can knock the blocks out of alignment as can whacking it with any kind of tool. Bullets will, at times, tend to stick in one of the mould blocks when they are opened. To get the bullet to drop free, it may be necessary to give the mould a rap to do this, with a wooden rod or mallet. This should only be done by tapping the joint between the handles. Never strike the mould blocks themselves! This will ruin their alignment. By the same token, the sprue cutter plate on top of the mould should never be hit with anything but a wood rod or mallet. A metal tool will damage the sprue cutter.

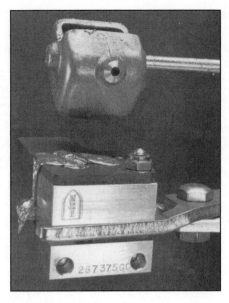

A good puddle of metal on the sprue plate helps force alloy into the mould and keep it hot so all bands in the bullet are filled out.

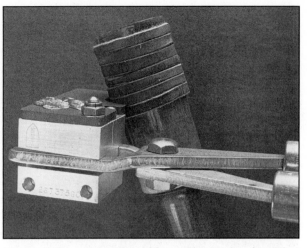

Never hit the sprue cutter with anything made of metal. A wooden dowel, in this case wrapped with rawhide, makes an effective cut without damage to the mould.

Moulds generally require a break-in period before they will cast proper bullets. The first step in preparing a mould for casting is to remove all traces of oil or grease from the blocks, particularly the inner surfaces. A solvent such as Outers "Crud Cutter" is good for this purpose. Once the blocks are clean and the metal in the melting pot is free-flowing (650 -750 degrees F) you can start casting. It may take a couple hundred bullets before the good ones start coming. Patience is required. Aluminum blocks do not require a break-in, but often need to be coated with carbon (smoke from a candle flame) or a special mould prep before they behave properly.

In a properly made mould, the blocks should make an almost seamless fit, with only a faint line where the blocks join. Operation should be smooth without the alignment pins binding or holding the blocks apart. The setting of these pins is done at the factory so usually they are in proper adjustment. Occasionally, it may be necessary to adjust these pins into the blocks if they bind or the blocks do not close completely, or if the fit is not complete and the blocks move across one another in the closed position. Adjustment should never be more than a couple thousandths of an inch at a time. It should be done with the handle and sprue plate removed. Occasionally a mould will be made where the two blocks are made of steel or iron from different lots that have a different coefficient of expansion. This will result in bullets with a larger side and a smaller side and a seam in the middle. Such a mould along with a sample bullet should be returned to the manufacturer for replacement.

After casting is finished, if the mould will not be used for weeks or months, and if it is made of iron or steel, the inside should be coated with a good rust-resistant oil or rust resistant powder solvent containing oil. A rusted mould is ruined if roughened or pitted. A solvent spray removes the oil when you are ready for the next casting session.

BULLET CASTING

Bullet casting is best done outdoors or in a place where there is cross ventilation or a hood with an exhaust fan to remove lead fumes. Beyond the bullet mould the following items are necessary for bullet casting. A lead melting pot capable of holding about 10 pounds of metal is the center of your activity. The best methods of keeping the metal the proper temperature are to use an electric melting furnace equipped with a thermostat or to use a lead thermometer in a plain iron pot with a gas fire under it. The alloy temperature can vary from about 650 to 750 degrees F for the alloy to flow properly. Too much heat will oxidize the tin in the alloy. The metal should be stirred frequently and fluxed every ten minutes or so to keep the mixture constant. Failure to do this will result in bullets of uneven weight. Electric pots have a bottom-pour feature with a handle that releases the metal through a spigot in the bottom. This has the advantage of getting hotter metal and fewer impurities that may be floating on the top into the mould.

Bullet casting, like reloading, is a solitary activity. Children and pets should be kept out of the area because of exposure to lead fumes and possible spilled hot metal. A countertop or tabletop operation is a good set up as is one on the floor. Comfortable seating is necessary because the activity will usually go on for two or more hours. The melting pot must have a steady base. There is nothing like a lap full of molten lead to drive this point home. The pot is the center of activity and all other components should be laid out in neat order near the pot, all within convenient reach. These include your bullet mould; a lead-dipper with a pouring spout, if you are using an open pot; a supply of alloy ingots to be added when the metal gets low; lumps of beeswax or a container of flux powder and a spoon; matches or lighter to burn off the flux vapor; a spoon or skimmer for stirring the metal and skimming off dross; a can for dross collection; an ingot mould to

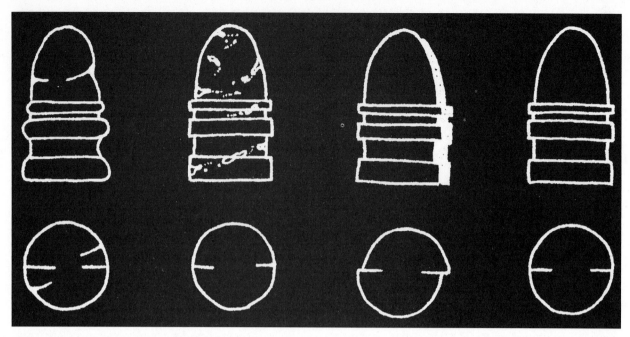

Some examples of bullet-casting problems include, left to right: mould or alloy too cold, alloy has impurities; misaligned mould blocks. A good cast bullet has all bands equally filled out with a shiny surface.

recover leftover alloy; a wood mallet or rod to rap the sprue cutter and the mould joint; a tray or box lid to catch sprue trimmings; and a folded blanket or soft rug to catch the cast bullets.

Moulds should be warmed up for casting. This can be done by placing them on the top edge of the electric pot or by holding them briefly in the gas flame if you are using a stove. Overheating a mould can warp the blocks and ruin it! Never dip an iron, steel or brass mould into the pot of molten metal to warm it. To do so can result in soldering the blocks together and ruining the mould. Aluminum moulds, however, can be dipped to bring them to the proper temperature.

The actual casting process should be done in a smooth, rhythmical manner. If you try for quality, speed will follow. Begin by stirring the pot; this should be done frequently to keep the alloy from separating. Lead from the dipper or from the spigot should be poured smoothly into the mould. Some people advocate placing the spout of the dipper or spigot of the electric pot directly into the sprue funnel. In my experience this is a bad idea, because it traps air in the cast bullet and the resultant bubbles produce bullets of varying weights with different centers of gravity. My best results have been achieved by running a fairly rapid stream into the mould and allowing the metal to puddle out over the sprue plate to about the size of a quarter. This helps keep both the mould and the metal inside hot so the bullets fill out all the grooves properly. Once the cast is made, the sprue should be cooled by blowing on it for two to five seconds. The sprue cutter should then be given a sharp rap with a wood rod to make a clean cut. The sprue plate should turn easily on its

pivot, but fit flush to the top of the mould blocks to give an even base to the bullet. If lead begins to smear over the blocks, or if the cutting of the sprue tears a chunk out of the bullet base, the bullet is still too hot for cutting. Slow down and blow a little longer. The sprue plate may tend to come loose with heating and need to be tightened. Do not over-tighten. A drop of melted bullet lubricant or beeswax should occasionally be applied to the hinge on the sprue plate to keep it moving freely. Be sure not to get lubricant into the bullet cavity.

Once the sprue is removed, the handles should be pulled apart quickly. If everything is working properly, the bullet will drop free of the mould. A soft rug or towel (cotton, not a meltable synthetic) should be used to catch the finished bullets. These should be spread apart every so often to keep from dropping one bullet on another and damaging them. Hot bullets are very soft and should be treated very gently. If you wish to harden your bullets, drop them from the mould into a pot of cold water.

When the alloy level in the pot gets about two thirds to three-quarters of the way down, it may be a good time for a break to inspect your products. The first bullets will have seams on the noses and the drive bands between the grooves will not be fully filled out, with clean, square corners on the drive bands. This is because either the metal or the mould or both were too cold for good casting. A mould that hasn't been broken in will produce similar results, often with one half being better filled out than the other. These bullets, along with the sprues are returned to the melt pot. Expect quite a few of these in the beginning. A good bullet will be evenly filled out everywhere. Corners on drive bands will be square and the bands will be of even width all round. By rolling a bullet across a flat surface irregularities in band width may be easily seen. Discard all those that are noticeably uneven.

Irregularities, including drive bands not completely filled out, especially in a limited area, may be caused by oil or grease having not been fully removed from that spot in the mould. Until this is completely clean you will not get good bullets. The burned-on oil or grease should be removed with a strong solvent and a cleaning brush or wood stick such as an orange stick (available at the nail-care area of your drugstore). Occasionally lead will become stuck on the inside surfaces of the blocks, preventing them from closing properly. Any lead smear of this sort will tend to build up unless completely removed. An orange stick, and on a bad case, solvent, will remove this. Never use a metal tool, acid or an abrasive to clean the interior of a bullet mould.

Just as the temperature of the mould or the alloy can be too cool for good results, it can also be too hot. Overheating oxidizes the tin and antimony, thus changing the quality of the alloy. Bullets cast at too high a temperature or from a mould that has become too hot exhibit a dull, frosted appearance rather like the surface of a piece of galvanized sheet metal. Sometimes they will contain undersize drive bands as well. When such bullets appear, reduce the alloy temperature and give your mould some time to cool off. A lightly frosted bullet generally causes no problems, but it is an indication you are operating on the hot side.

Since bullet casting is a fairly messy operation and one that requires a certain amount of preparation and clean up, it is best to set aside an afternoon for the project. Once you get into the swing of pouring, sprue-cutting and popping the bullets out of the mould, speed will come and production can be expected to rise to 200 or more per hour for plain-base bullets. Casting hollow-point or hollow-base bullets is more complicated, since an additional pin or post in required to make the cavity. The hollow point attachment goes into the bottom of the mould and turns to lock into position. Once in place, the metal is poured. After cooling, the pin is turned for removal and the bullet is then dropped from the mould in the normal manner. The extra step takes a bit more time. The secret of good production is consistency. Fluxing and stirring of the metal often is the best way to maintain a consistent alloy mixture throughout the pot. Failure to do this will start yielding bullets of varying weights, depending where you dip from the pot. Dipping serves to stir the mixture. Bottom-pour electric pots have to be stirred or the lighter metals will float to the top.

Like any other task involving hazardous material, casting should be done with a clear head, not when you are tired. At the end of the casting session an inspection of the finished bullets should be made and the obvious duds along with sprue cuttings should be returned to the melt pot. When melted, this should be poured into an ingot mould for storage. If you are using different alloys, mark your ingots with some sort of scriber to identify the alloy so you don't mix them up.

Cast bullets are far more easily damaged than the jacketed variety and must be carefully stored. Never dump or pour a batch of bullets into a bucket or box. This will cut and nick the bases and accuracy will suffer accordingly. Good methods of storage include small boxes where the bullets can be stood on their bases packed closely together so they don't tip over. Plastic or paper boxes are far less likely to cause damage than metal containers. Storage bins with small sliding drawers, made of plastic, used to store screws, nuts and similar small parts are a handy means of keeping cast bullets for ready use. Proper labeling, whether a card or "post it" note in the drawer or a description written on the box, is necessary to keep things straight. The same bullet cast of different alloys will have different weights and should be kept separate. If they become mixed it's too bad, because they all look alike and the only way to re-sort them is by weighing each one.

Now that you've cast a projectile to load, you can't just seat it and shoot it. There's much more to it than that.

Bullet Sizing and Lubricating

BULLET SELECTION

AS WITH JACKETED bullets, cast bullets and the moulds for them should be selected with consideration to the twist of the rifling of the gun you plan to shoot them in. Shorter bullets will do best in a relatively slow twist, while longer ones will require a faster twist. Beyond this is the matter of bullet design.

Cast, boattail bullets will simply not work well since the unprotected, tapered base will be surrounded by hot gases and melted, with this lead then deposited on the bore of the gun. Cast bullets work best that have a flat or slightly dished base. Hollow-base bullets, in the style of Civil War Minié ball, were designed to be undersize to fit muzzle-loaders and expand to bore size when fired at velocities under 1000 fps. Use of this type in cartridge guns other than handguns, is not a good idea. At velocities over 1000 fps the skirt tends to be blown out too far and often unevenly as it exits the muzzle. The skirt may actually separate from the rest of the bullet if loaded too heavily. This can cause serious problems if the skirt remains lodged in the barrel. Accuracy in cartridge rifles is not good.

Excellent accuracy may be obtained from cast bullets. Left and center are plain-base designs; the bullet on the right is designed to take a gas check (note rebated base).

With cast bullets, the best accuracy is generally obtained with bullets that have a relatively short ogive and the greater part of their surface bearing on the rifling. The ogive is that part of the bullet that tapers from the point where the bullet's surface is in contact with the bore to a point or meplat (a flat point) at the front of the bullet. The greatest degree of stability is achieved with a cast bullet that has nearly all of its length in contact with the groove portion of the bore. The downside of this is increased drag and lowered velocities. Cast bullets of this design, however, are sometimes the only ones that will perform well in shallow-groove or multi-groove barrels.

The aerodynamic shape of a bullet with a long ogive makes it a good one for long-range shooting, but such bullets are difficult to seat absolutely straight and accuracy with cast bullets of this design is generally very poor. Much has been said in favor of "bore-riding" bullets which offer the best compromise between the two extremes. Bullets of this design feature a relatively short drive-band area with a long nose of smaller diameter which has a short taper to a point. The front portion is designed to coast along the surface of the lands – the bore – without being more than lightly engraved by them if at all. This design provides stability without the drag encountered by a bullet with a long bearing surface which is engraved by the rifling nearly its entire length.

PROPER BULLET SIZE

The importance of slugging the barrel (as described in Chapter 1) to obtain the correct groove diameter and thus best accuracy cannot be overemphasized. If a barrel is worn or of a type known to have a wide variations, this is a must. While under-size jacketed bullets will give good performance in a barrel of larger diameter, undersize cast bullets will often fail to expand or "upset" properly, filling the grooves, particularly if these bullets are made of hard alloy. The result is considerable lead fouling and terrible accuracy, especially with deep-groove barrels. Cast bullets shoot best that are groove size.

With every rule it seems there is an exception. In this regard there is one that I know of, and possibly others of which I am unaware. This exception is the 45 Allin "trapdoor" Springfield. This rifle was designed for black-powder ammunition. It features deep-groove (.005") rifling and the groove diameter may be as deep as .463". A .457" or even a .460" diameter bullet is clearly undersize. If groove-diameter bullets are used in this rifle, the cartridge case will be enlarged to the point the round will not chamber! Some frustrated shooters have gone to the extreme of having their chambers reamed out to accommodate these larger bullets. The bullets worked in the sense that they didn't foul the barrels, but they developed fins of lead on the rear and were not very accurate. Springfield 45 barrels were engineered to use a very soft lead-tin alloy bullet about .549" diameter that would upset as it left the cartridge case. The purpose was to design a black powder rifle that would shoot accurately with a dirty barrel. Each bullet would thus expand to fill whatever groove space was available. These rifles and carbines will shoot very well using lead-tin bullets of a 20-1 to 30-1 alloy. Bullets with any serious amount of antimony in them lack the necessary malleability to expand properly and will pile up lead in the bore. If you own an old rifle with a very deep-groove barrel and find that a groove-diameter bullet expands the case to the point where it will not chamber, a soft-alloy, lead-tin bullet may be the only cast bullet you can shoot in it. As far as I know this was a unique system, but some of the old Bullard rifles used this type of rifling, and there may be others.

BULLET LUBRICANTS

Nobody actually knows how bullet lubricants work since there is no known way to observe a bullet as it is fired through the barrel of a gun. Lead-alloy bullets can be fired at very low-velocity — 600 to 800 fps without lubricant – and they do not cause leading, assuming the barrel is a very slick one. Revolvers, however, are something of an exception to this rule, probably because of their bullets tipping slightly or by having some gas blown by the bullets as they jump the

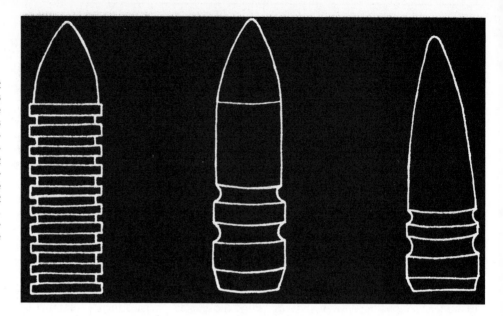

The best rifle accuracy with a cast alloy bullet is with one that has a short ogive. The bullet on the left has many lubricant grooves and will shoot well in multi-groove and shallow-groove barrels owing to good bore contact over most of its length. The center bullet is a "bore-riding" type also with a short ogive. The right bullet is of a long-ogive design. Difficulty in getting such a bullet properly seated in the case makes it a poor shooter.

gap from cylinder to the forcing cone in the barrel.

Lubricants prevent leading by reducing friction in the barrel, but they also have a considerable effect on accuracy. There are any number of lubricants that will prevent leading, but their accuracy record is often poor. Through the years any number of lubricant formulas have been tried with success rates ranging from excellent to terrible. Heavy grease of various sorts works well, as can be attested to by anyone who has shot some of the 22 Long Rifle ammunition made in the 1940's and early 50's. The problem, however, was that it would melt in warm weather and when shot it combined readily with powder fouling to form a black greasy coating that wound up all over your hands, face, clothing — anything it touched. The use of such grease-lubricant in inside-lubricated cartridges ruined them in short order as the grease soaked into the powder and even into the primer, killing both.

Grease/petroleum jelly in small amounts can be combined with various waxes with reasonable success to make a good bullet lubricant, but under warm conditions it has a tendency to "sweat" out of the mixture and get into the powder. Some greases will oxidize and harden over time or evaporate to a degree. These are poor candidates for long term storage if that is desired. Lithium based grease appears not to sweat out since it has a very high melting point.

Some early formulas for bullet lubricants included resin. Since resin is an abrasive and not a lubricant, this is a bad idea. Tests conducted by Philip Sharpe among others demonstrated that resin in the mixture actually shortened barrel life.

Japan wax is obtained from an oriental sumac berry and is similar to bayberry wax. It was used in many early lubricant formulas. It has a tendency to dry over time and become brittle, at which point it loses much of its lubricating

Bullets must be of the proper size and alloy to shoot well. On the left is a 45-70 rifle bullet cast of 20-1 lead tin alloy, sized .459 – the proper diameter for the original 45 Springfield rifle. Next to it is the same bullet after firing. On the right is a very similar bullet sized .459, but made of an alloy containing too much antimony. This hard bullet has failed to expand to fill the grooves. The rifling mark is barely visible where hot gas blew by and melted the bullet surface. The results: good accuracy from the left, a leaded bore and terrible accuracy on the right. Soft bullets tend to give better accuracy with deep-groove barrels, particularly where the bullets are deliberately made undersize as was the original 45-70.

qualities. It is to a degree hygroscopic, not good if your bullets may be exposed to moisture. Sharpe found that Japan wax when combined with copper-plated lead bullets caused them to corrode to the point they were unshootable in a rather short time. Bullet lubricants which are hygroscopic or evaporate through time allowing bullets to corrode are for short term use only. About the only thing that can be done is to keep such ammunition away from heat and damp.

Carnauba wax is a tree wax from Brazil and is the main ingredient in shoe polish. It is a hard wax that needs softening to make a good bullet lubricant.

Paraffin is often included in lubricant mixtures, mainly as a stiffener. Paraffin has rather poor lubricating qualities unless heated. Paraffin when subjected to pressure crumbles as it forms layers. It can be used in lubricants, but only sparingly.

Beeswax is hard and must be softened for bullet lubricant. In the pure form it can be used for outside lubricated bullets, like the 22 Long Rifle, since it remains hard and will not readily pick up dirt and grit in the manner of softer lubricants.

Ozocerite/ceresine wax are the same, but ceresine is the refined form, often sold as a beeswax substitute. Ozocerite is a mineral wax with many industrial uses since it is cheaper than beeswax. Candles are made of this material, often with coloring matter added. It is too hard to use as is and must be softened with some form of oil to make it useable for bullet lubricant.

Tallow is animal fat. In refined form it is called lard and was an early lubricant for patched bullets in muzzle loaders. The vegetable equivalent – Crisco — has long been a favorite for muzzle-loader fans because it keeps black-powder

Liquid Alox is available from Lee and Lyman. This product goes on wet and dries to a waxy finish. It works well on handgun bullets, particularly those shot as cast.

After lubrication there should be no evidence of distortion or pieces of lead in the lube grooves. The accurate bullet is one that leaves the barrel evenly rifled with no asymmetrical distortion.

fouling soft. Tallow gets rancid and melts in warm temperatures as does Crisco. These preclude their use in cartridge ammunition except as an additive.

Graphite is a mineral which is neither a wax or a lubricant, but a very fine abrasive. Colloidal graphite is the finest granulation available and when mixed with waxes and oils remains in suspension. It will not burn off and has a fine polishing action and (so it has been claimed) will improve a barrel by filling pores in the metal. A little goes a long way in a lubricant, but the results have been good.

COMMERCIAL AND HOMEMADE LUBRICANTS

Commercial lubricants are available in sticks or blocks, with the sticks being molded to fit in sizing-lubricating machines. The ingredients in commercial lubricants can best be described as: some combination of the above in varying amounts. Prices vary though claims of effectiveness are always high. Most are tested and give good results. These formulas are proprietary and the ingredients are sometimes referred to or at least hinted at in their various trade names – Bore Butter, Alox, Lithi Bee and so on.

When it comes to getting a good bullet lubricant there is no magic formula. Most of the commercial products will do the job. They have the advantage of being cast into small cakes or sticks designed to fit into sizer-lubricator machines or come in liquid form which can be applied by gently tumbling bullets in it, then setting them on wax paper to dry. They are clean and easy to handle.

Lyman Orange Magic is a stick lubricant intended for hard-alloy cast bullets to be shot at maximum cast bullet velocities and high temperatures.

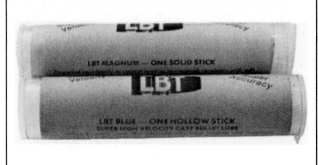

LBT Blue Soft Lube is intended for shooting cast bullets at slower velocities and low temperatures.

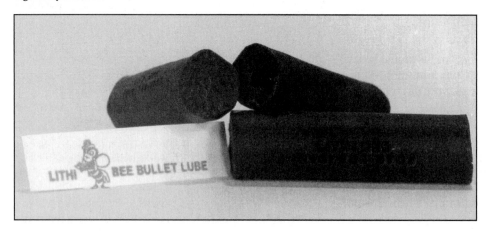

Lithi Bee is a stick lubricant made of lithium-based grease combined with beeswax. The mixture is an old favorite.

Taurak bullet lube is a hard grease with a high melting temperature, available in sticks from NECO.

The advantage of making up your own lubricant is two-fold – economy and versatility. Home-made lubricant is about half as expensive as the commercial product – less than that if you make it in quantity. Versatility is probably more important since as is the case with bullet alloys one formula is not suitable for all uses. Lubricant for low-velocity handgun bullets does not have to stand up to a lot of heat and pressure and can be fairly soft. A soft, sticky-type of lubricant is an absolute must for use with black powder or Pyrodex since the lubricant must keep the fouling soft and easy to remove. A very good lubricant of this type was developed by Spencer Wolf in his research on reproducing original ammunition for the 45 Springfield and Colt SAA revolver. The lubricant consists of beeswax and olive oil mixed in equal parts by volume. Beeswax must be melted in a double boiler to avoid oxidizing it. Beeswax heated to too high a temperature will turn dark brown and lose some of its lubricating properties. When I questioned Wolf if there was something special about olive oil Wolf replied that it was on sale and was thus the least expensive vegetable oil around at the time. Presumably any vegetable oil would do. These oils blend a little better with beeswax than petroleum based oils and show no tendency to sweat out even under warm conditions. Interestingly the beeswax-olive oil mixture does well under fairly high temperatures. The Wolf mixture is very similar in texture to the commercial SPG lubricant and a little softer than Bore Butter.

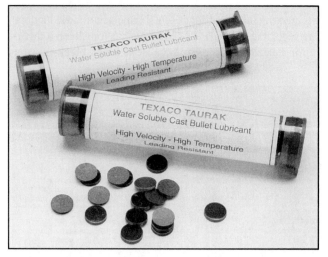

Soft lubricants are the best for cold weather shooting. Hard lubricants become harder when chilled and often fail to work causing bores to lead. Harder formulas, however, are best for shooting high pressure, high velocity loads. Harder lubricants generally stand up under warm summer conditions where ammunition may be heated to well over 100 degrees F as it sits in a box or loading block in the sun.

When trying your hand at making bullet lubricant always remember to keep records of your experiments. It doesn't get much sadder than when you stumble onto a perfect formula and can't remember what went into it.

A "cake cutter," which is more of a cookie cutter, can be made by drilling out or cutting off the head of a fired cartridge for the bullets you wish to lubricate. The bullets are placed in a shallow pan of melted lubricant and removed when it has cooled. The pan can be filled to lubricate all or only some of the grooves.

Lee Lube sizer kit fits on their press. This sizing die and integral container is designed for bullets coated with liquid Alox. The pre-lubed bullets are pushed through the sizer and held in the container.

BULLET LUBRICATION TECHNIQUE

Some bullets shoot best "as cast" and should be used that way if they are the proper diameter as they come from the mould. This is often the case with old guns and others that have larger groove diameters. The diameter as well as the roundness of your bullets should be checked by measuring with a vernier caliper or micrometer.

Lubricating bullets as cast is easily done by placing them base-down in a flat, shallow pan of melted lubricant, making sure that the level of the liquid covers all of the lubricating grooves on the bullets. When the lubricant hardens, the bullets are removed using a home-made tool fashioned from a fired cartridge case, of the same caliber, with the head cut off. A short case may have to be soldered or otherwise attached to a larger diameter case or metal tube to provide a suitable handle. Bullets are removed from the hardened lubricant by simply slipping the case mouth over the bullet and cutting it free. This is known as the "cake cutter," more aptly "cookie cutter" method. As the tube handle fills with bullets, they are removed from the top and collected. Finished bullets should have their bases wiped free of lubricant. This is best accomplished by wiping them across a piece of cloth lightly dampened with powder solvent. They should then be placed in clean plastic boxes for storage pending reloading. As bullets are run through the mixture, lubricant must be added, with each subsequent batch, to keep the level at the proper height. It is best to do a full pan load each time.

USE OF A SIZER-LUBRICATOR

Sizer-lubricators are machines that perform three functions; first is to lightly swage the cast bullet into perfect roundness and second to fill the grooves with lubricant. The optional third is to attach a gas check. They cost about $150 and up.

Bullets as they come from the mould are generally larger than is required and it is necessary to bring them to the pre-

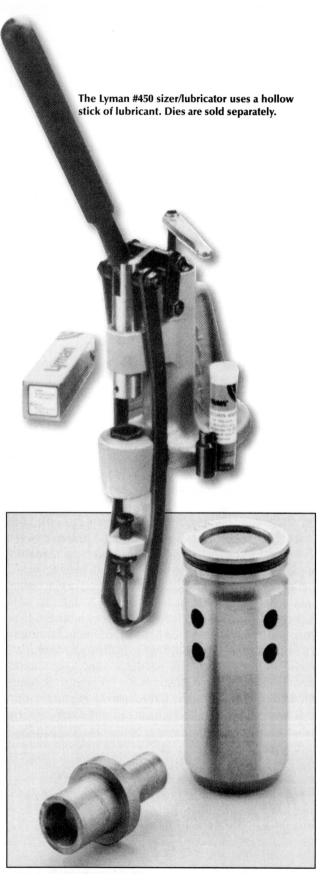

The Lyman #450 sizer/lubricator uses a hollow stick of lubricant. Dies are sold separately.

Lube/sizer dies and top punches are interchangeable between Lyman and RCBS.

cise size for best accuracy. This is done by forcing the cast bullet through a die, swaging it to exact diameter. When purchasing a bullet mould and a sizing die it is a good idea to get moulds that will produce bullets very close to the proper final size. There will always be a certain amount of shrinkage of the bullet as it cools in the mould. If this did not happen, extracting this bullet would be nearly impossible. Moulds are sold with an indication of the cast bullet size, but this will vary depending on the composition of the alloy that is being cast. Bullets should not be sized down much over .003". Excess sizing tends to distort the bullet and adversely affect accuracy. While sizing gives a bullet a shiny mirror-like surface, it also reduces the hardness of the surface by working the metal – another reason to avoid excess sizing.

Sizer lubricators are made by several manufacturers. They all combine the same basic features – a frame to hold the die, a handle that drives the top punch that forces the bullet through the die and a lubricating pump that holds a stick of bullet lubricant and forces it through holes in the sizing die and into the grooves of the bullet. One nice feature of the machines made by Lyman and RCBS is that the dies, top punches and lubricating sticks are all interchangeable. Top punches are about $20; dies are about $55 and include a top punch.

The sizer-lubricator is a bench-mounted tool for it must have solid support, otherwise the force delivered to the operating handle would lift it off the bench or take the top off a flimsy table. The tool should be bolted to the loading bench or bolted to a solid plank and held on a sturdy table with C-clamps. Soft-alloy bullets size rather easily, while those of linotype metal require far more force. Using these machines takes a bit of skill, much like bullet casting, but mastering it is not very difficult and speedy production will follow, once you master the basics. The first step is to be sure you have the proper top punch. A flat point top punch will mash the nose on a round-nose bullet and too large or too small a punch will produce their own distortions, including inaccurate alignment in the sizing die. Top punches should be matched to particular bullets. Loading manuals, particularly those dealing with cast-bullet shooting include data on the proper top punch for various bullets.

Sometimes the exact form of punch is not available. Two solutions are to get the nearest larger size then putting epoxy in the punch and matching the contour of a cast bullet by inserting one with a little grease on the nose to release it from the epoxy. The other method, if the top punch is only slightly undersize, is to chuck it in a drill or metal lathe and re-contour it with a file, cutting tool or emery cloth. This may be necessary if you are using an obsolete or custom bullet mould. Such an alteration, however, is permanent.

Once the proper top punch is selected, the reservoir of the lubrication pump should be filled. Most take a solid or hollow stick of lubricant. If you are making your own, you can either cast your own sticks in home-made moulds fabricated from the proper size of pipe or you can try pouring melted lubricant directly into the reservoir itself. This must be done

A bullet pops up after having been lubricated on a SAECO machine. A solid mounting is needed to keep the machine from lifting off the bench top. Proper die adjustment is necessary to keep lubricant from squirting over the bullet nose. The small amount seen here can easily be wiped off.

with the sizing die in the up (closed) position, otherwise melted lubricant will come welling up through the die to run all over the place. Pouring into the reservoir is difficult, particularly if it is of a type that uses a hollow lubricant stick and has a metal pin in the center. A pouring pot with a long spout is the only kind to use to avoid spilling lubricant all over. Solid lubricant is very difficult to remove – a putty knife will lift it off a flat surface. It is nearly impossible to remove from a rug. I make sticks.

With the reservoir filled with the die in the down position, at room temperature, the lubricator pump handle is pushed two or three times to force lubricant into the die chamber. A bullet is seated in the center of the die and the operating handle is pulled firmly down forcing the bullet into the sizing die. Once sized the handle is pushed back and the bullet pops up – the proper size and with the grooves filled with lubricant. The die must be adjusted, however, for the length of the bullet you are lubricating. This is done by means of an adjustment screw on the base of the lug that holds the die. If a short bullet is pushed too far into the die, lubricant will squirt up over the nose. If a long bullet is not seated deep enough it will not get far enough below the level of the lubricating holes in the sizing die and some of the grooves will not be filled with lubricant. With pistol bullets, to be loaded at target velocities, it may not be necessary to fill all the grooves to obtain good accuracy without leading.

The up stroke on the operating handle should be faster than the down stroke. This avoids having the bullet in the down position too long. Quick operation avoids lubricant building up on the base of the bullet and the face of the bottom punch where it has to be wiped off. The lubricator pump handle has to be given a couple of turns about every other bullet to keep the pressure high enough to fill all of the grooves completely. Oftentimes the bullet has to be run through the die a second time to fill all the grooves. One advantage of the Redding/SAECO tool is that the lubricant reservoir has a spring-fed top on it which keeps constant pressure on the lubricant allowing the operator to lube several bullets before having to run the pump handle. This is basically all there is to it. The trick to not smearing lube all over the bottom punch and bullet base is not to have too much pressure on the lubricant and to bring the bullet up out of the die as quickly as possible. Always keep pressure on the handle after completing the down stroke. Failure to do so will allow lubricant to work in under the bullet. It is a matter of practice and developing a "feel" for this operation.

SEATING GAS CHECKS

Gas checks are intended for use on specially designed gas-check bullets. They are of two basic types: the Lyman type that are intended to drop off the base of the bullet shortly after it leaves the muzzle of the gun and the Hornady crimp-on variety that are intended to remain attached until the bullet reaches the target. I prefer the Hornady-type since I feel they do a better job of keeping hot gas from getting around

The SAECO Lubri-Sizer is a quality tool that will last a lifetime.

the base of the bullet. High velocities with gas-checked bullets are obtainable only with hard, tough alloys and lubricants that will stand up to high temperatures and pressures. Applying gas checks to hard-alloy bullets takes more muscle than for softer ones, but can be done so long as those alloys are no harder than linotype (BHN22).

Seating gas checks is simplicity itself. They are placed on the face of the die punch and the bullet is seated in it. It is then pushed through the sizing die, and the bullet lubricated in the normal manner. Make sure that when the bullet bottoms in the die that it does so firmly in order to get a good fit with the crimp-on type of gas checks. When applying gas checks to soft alloy bullets, care must be taken not to apply too much pressure and flatten the nose of the bullet. The leverage on these machines is very good, allowing you to apply a great deal of pressure with minimal effort.

BULLET INSPECTION AND STORAGE

Bullets should be inspected after they come out of the sizer to see that the grooves are well filled with lubricant. Sizing will not make out-of-round bullets perfect. If the grooves are wider on one side than they are on the other, this bullet was not completely filled out in the mould. These and ones with irregular drive bands should be scrapped if they are really bad or separated for use as warming and fouling shots. Finished bullets should be loaded immediately, or stored in closed containers where they will not gather grit, lint and similar foreign matter that will not make them shoot better and can actually damage your barrel.

Bullets that have been dropped on the floor and dented on the base will no longer shoot straight. Bullets that have rolled through primer ash, metal filings and the like should be wiped clean with a soft cloth moistened with solvent or light oil and relubricated.

Finished bullets should be weighed on your powder scale. The finest consistent accuracy is from those that are within a tolerance of +/- .05 grain in weight. Changes in alloy and temperature or lack of stirring and fluxing can affect weight by varying the content of the alloy in that particular bullet. By the same token, pouring technique can trap air bubbles in bullets and alter their weight. Bullets should be sorted by weight and stored and marked accordingly for best accuracy. It is best to handle finished, cast-lubricated bullets as little as possible. This keeps them clean and your fingers won't wipe lubricant out of the grooves.

the base of the bulletand melting channels in the bearing surface — what is known as "gas cutting." Sometimes the drop-off gas checks do not drop off and remain on the bullet all the way to the target, making that bullet several grains heavier than the others in the series of shots and, particularly at long ranges, causing it to hit low.

Gas checks permit cast bullets to be driven almost as fast as jacketed bullets – 2200 fps, by acting as a hard gasket at

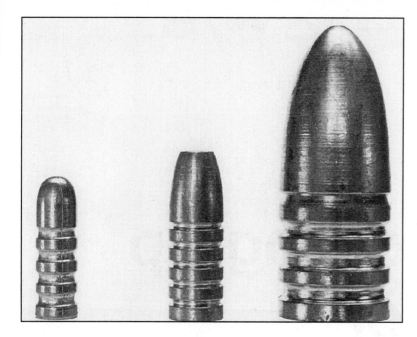

Bullets should be inspected before sizing and lubricating. Good cast bullets should have square edges and even grooves.

WADS AND FILLERS

Distortion of the base of a cast bullet, particularly a rifle bullet is a constant problem. Smokeless powder of the coarser granulations will be forced into the base of soft-alloy bullets peppering them with small dents and often gas-cutting the sides to a degree.

Various strategies to overcome this problem have been tried with varying degrees of success. One thing seems absolutely clear, however. NEVER have an airspace between any kind of wad and the base of the bullet! This will cause that wad to come slamming forward to strike the base of the bullet and expand there. This will make a ring in the case and in many instances in the chamber of a rifle and ruin the barrel. I have had light tufts of kapok weighing about a grain, used to keep a light charge of powder in the base of a 45-70 case, make a ring in this case. These were propelled by 9 grains of Unique when they hit the base of a 150 grain bullet. Wads of felt, cork and cardboard have been used with success. A lubricated felt wad such as the Ox Yoke Wonder Wad does an excellent job of acting as a gas seal if you have a snug fit. All wads, however, must completely fill the void between the powder and the bullet base. Fillers between wads such as Cream of Wheat have also been tried and the results are bad. Wads punched from corrugated cardboard can be placed between a felt wad and bullet base to fill the void.

From time to time there is a resurgence of interest in various types of lubricating wads for use with both cast and jacketed bullets. Wax wads and "grease wads" have demonstrated effectiveness in improving accuracy and lengthening barrel life. These consist of a thin disc of bullet lubricant cut to exact case-mouth diameter. The lubricant is generally harder than that used in a lubricating pump. The discs are punched out of a flat sheet about the thickness of the cardboard on the back of a writing tablet. One of the better known formulas was the development of Edward A. Leop-

old and was sold as "Leopold's Oleo Wads." They consisted of (by weight) 5 oz. each of Japan wax and beeswax, 2 oz. ozocerite, and 3-4 teaspoons Acheson Unctious graphite #1340. According to the developers of the 220 Swift – G.L. Wotkyns and J.B. Sweany – grease wads behind the jacketed bullets decreased erosion and improved accuracy.

Lubricated cardboard wads were at one time loaded in rifle ammunition by UMC and Winchester for the 40-70 and 40-90 black-powder cartridges. Bearing the above warnings in mind, those who wish to experiment with making their own wax wads will find that about the only way to get an even sheet of lubricant is to take a very clean straight-sided glass bottle, fill it with cold water and dip it straight down into a pot of melted lubricant. A deep narrow pot and a bottle that nearly fills it will be most practical. The thickness of the layer is controlled by the number of dips. When the lubricant layer on the bottle is well cooled, a straight cut is made down one side and the sheet is gently peeled off. Wads may be cut by using the mouth of a fired case from which the head has been cut to facilitate removal.

As can be deduced, the easiest and safest kind of loading for use with a wax wad is one in which the case is nearly filled with powder and the wad and bullet base gently compact the charge. Sharpe makes the point that with a bottle-neck case the wad should "stay in the neck of the case." Amen to that! For reduced charge loadings you could try sticking the wad to the bullet base by either warming the bullet base and pressing the wad in place or wetting the wad surface with a volatile solvent and "gluing" it in place with the melted lubricant. This system is not tried or recommended.

Before loading any such ammunition, see how tight the bond is and if the wad drops off or can be easily removed by slipping it or tapping the bullet, don't load it unless it is supported by a charge of powder or a solid wad column of felt, cardboard or cork.

Reloading can
be accomplished
in any number
of ways, from
simple inexpensive
hand tools to
costly progressive
equipment. By
defining your
goals, you'll find
which is best
for you.

Tooling Up For Reloading

RELOADING BEGAN WITH relatively simple tools that could be carried in the pocket or saddlebag. They were shaped in the manner of pliers and leather punches and were referred to as "tong tools." Manufacture of this type of equipment more or less ceased about thirty years ago, with Lyman and Lee being about the only major manufacturers of this type of tool today. They are portable, cheap and capable of turning out rather good ammunition. The disadvantages are that they are slow and require more muscle power to use than bench tools. As "campfire" ammunition making became more a thing of the past, these tools have all but disappeared. They are, however, a useful item if they can be picked up on either the new or the used market, since you can't take a reloading bench into the woods and there may be some instances where you might have need of producing some quick loads in the field.

Today's reloader generally does not have all that much spare time and usually prefers speed in production over the option of taking tools to the field. The beginning reloader is faced with some basic issues that must be determined when it comes time to purchase equipment. These include economy vs. speed in production; speed vs. precision; and, finally, precision vs. economy. These

Plain or fancy, the bench should have enough space for efficient tool mounting.

three issues will be discussed in detail in the hope that you can reach decisions that will match your temperament and shooting habits. The beginning reloader can find himself stunned by information overload as he drifts in indecision while perusing catalogs, absolutely brimming with gadgets and gizmos, all promising more/better/faster.

BASIC EQUIPMENT: GETTING WHAT YOU NEED

One way to enter the water, as it were, is to get acquainted with other reloaders and see what they use and don't use and quiz them on the why's and wherefore's of their equipment. If you are nice, they will generally let you try their equipment. This way you can get a feel for the tools, how they work, and begin to come to some decisions regarding what you might like and what you find difficult or unnecessary.

The reloading bench is the basis of your work area. There is no standardized design and it may well serve a dual purpose as a kitchen counter on which reloading tools are temporarily mounted. If you must use a temporary surface of this type, your reloading press and sizer/lubricator should be permanently mounted on a solid 2" X 6" or heavier plank that can be securely attached to the countertop with "C" clamps. The counter must have a solid top since the levering force exerted on the bullet sizer and the loading press in the process of resizing cartridge cases and sizing bullets, can pull the countertop loose. If you have the space, a solid desk

A basic reloading bench should be sturdy and have plenty of storage space. The individual design is up to the maker. *(Courtesy Speer)*

or work bench arrangement is best. General requirements are that it have enough weight or be attached to the floor so that it will not rock back and forth under use. It should be solid enough that the top will not pry loose under the stress of cartridge and bullet sizing. Whether or not it is to be a

 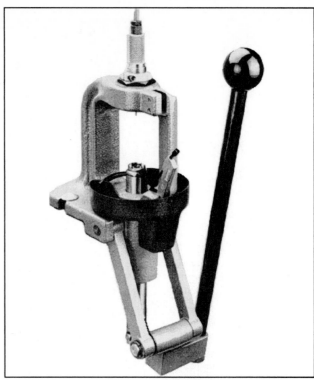

Basic "O" frame presses are reliable, rugged and easy to use. The Redding and RCBS are typical examples.

thing of beauty depends on how much of the public will view it, in a dining room or corner of an apartment, or if it will stay in a garage or basement area. If ammunition and powder are to be stored in the same area — for convenience — I recommend placement of the bench be in an area that is climate controlled. It should have at least one generous-size drawer and be close to shelving or cabinets where bullets, primers, powder, cases, loading manuals, etc., can be located within easy reach. The top should be smooth and free of cracks, holes and splinters.

The bench I built was assembled entirely from scrap lumber. It is a heavy table with a massive top and a single large drawer. The top measures 25" X 47", it stands 33" high and features a single 18"X 20" drawer. The legs are made of doubled 2" X 4" pine blocked so the top sits in them. Single 2" X 4" support rails connect the side and back legs 4" above the floor. These dimensions are not necessarily ideal, but were determined by the most efficient use of a large plywood packing crate and various two by fours I could scrounge around the neighborhood where there was a lot of overpass construction going on. Everything was held together with wood screws and contact cement. Solidity and weight were achieved by making the top a solid lamination of plywood, 5" thick. This allowed mounting of the sizer/lubricator and loading press with lag screws. Movers do not like this bench as it must weigh close to 200 lbs — heavier than is needed. Hey, I had the plywood. If I were to build another, I would have more drawer space and make it a bit lighter. I attached the top, so it could be separated from the frame, by running screws through heavy prefabricated steel angle pieces, punched with a number of holes.

In Canada, where I built the bench, this product was sold under the name of "Dexion." By putting two angled pieces of "Dexion" inside the top of the drawer and hooking them over two similar pieces mounted on wood 2" X 4" rails attached to the bottom of the bench top, I made a suspended drawer without having to frame it in the standard manner.

In addition to weight, the biggest mistake I made was failing to consider the location. The dirty, rough wood looked bad in the corner of the dining room. Thus I spent an inordinant amount of time sanding, staining and finishing it to make it look (more or less) like furniture. If your bench must look like furniture, start with good quality, finished wood.

Once you have your bench, the next step is to choose the basic reloading tool, the heart of your operation — the press. Before parting with any money, it is best to start with the maximum amount of experience and knowledge. This returns to the above mentioned issues of speed, economy and precision. Your first question should be: Am I going to load for pistol, rifle or both? Shotshell reloading requires its own special loading equipment and will be dealt with later. If the answer is to reload both handgun and rifle cartridges, then you will want to purchase a press that is intended for rifle cartridges that will do handgun ammunition as well.

ECONOMY VERSUS SPEED

A bench-mounted loading press of the most basic type starts at about $70-90. And goes up from there for special heavy models, loading very large cartridges on the order

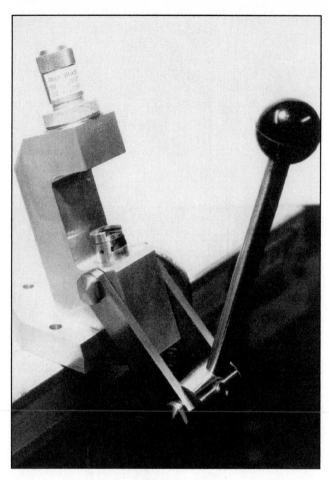

The Ross & Webb Benchrest Press is an extremely strong C-frame design for the serious reloader.

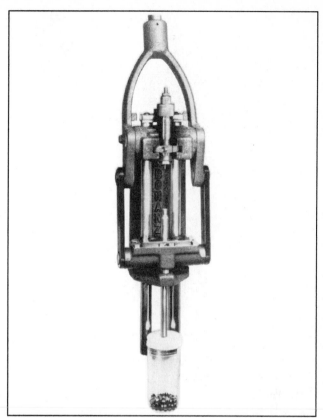

Forster's Co-Ax Press B-2 is a different wrinkle on the "C" and "O" frame designs. Dual guide rods offer precision alignment. Dies snap in and out for quick, easy changing.

of the 50 BMG. This is the basic "O" frame or "C" frame press, so called because the frames are shaped like these letters. Both are rugged and simple. They are sometimes referred to as single-stage presses since they mount a single loading die in the top, so each operation — decapping and sizing, neck expanding and bullet seating – requires that the die be unscrewed and the next die screwed in place for each operation. The manufacturers promise a production rate of 100 finished rounds per hour.

Similar to these are the arbor presses, which mount a single die in the bottom. Arbor presses require a special straight-line type of die that is not compatible with the top-mounted variety used in "C", "O" and turret presses. The price range and speed are about the same. Arbor presses are small and compact and have the advantage of being on a flat base and not requiring permanent bench mounting. This makes them handy to take to the range where ammunition can be fabricated while you shoot. In addition to instant gratification, this avoids time and material put into long runs of test ammunition.

More expensive and faster are the turret and "H" frame machines that allow a full three die set to be mounted along with a powder measure. All dies are in place and the cartridge is moved from one station to the next or the turret is

The Jones arbor press is typical of the type. Arbor presses are compact and do not need to be bench-mounted, making them convenient to take to the range to assemble ammunition on the spot.

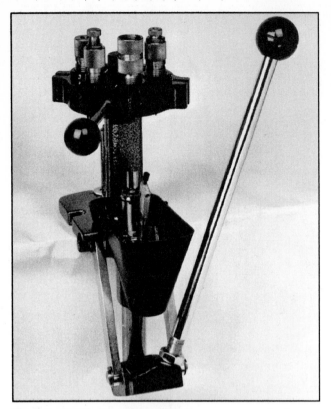

The Lyman T-Mag II is a turret press from a company that has been making this basic design for over forty years. A full set of dies and a powder measure can be screwed into the turret, and each one is then rotated into position for the next step.

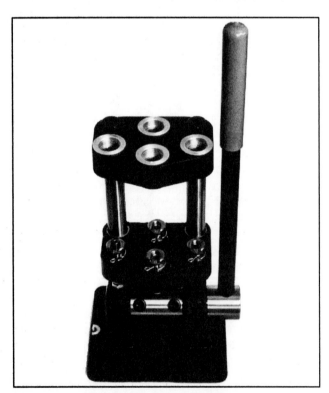

The H-frame press, as typified by the CH/4D No. 444, has many followers since it holds a full set of dies and powder measure. In this system, the "turret" is fixed, thus no rotation between steps is required. The case is simply moved from station to station.

The Dillon RL 1050 will load 1000 to 1200 rounds per hour. A progressive loader of this sort represents a sizable investment and is definitely not for beginners.

rotated to bring the next die into position. Production is estimated at 200 rounds per hour, but the price is up to between $300 and up.

Near the top end, short of buying an ammunition factory, are the "progressive loaders." These are semi-automated machines with feed tubes and hoppers that are filled with cartridges, bullets, primers and powder. Once the various feeding devices are filled, the operator simply pulls a handle and manually feeds one component, usually bullets or cartridges, inserting them into a slot on a revolving plate and the machine does the rest — moving the case from station to station, decapping, primer-pocket cleaning, powder charging and bullet seating. The finished cartridges come popping out at the end of a full plate-rotation cycle and are collected in a convenient bin. The cheapest of these is about $700, the top of the line closing in on $2000. Produc-

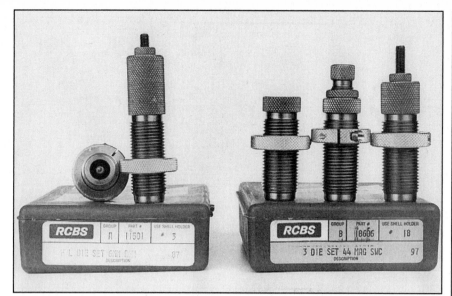

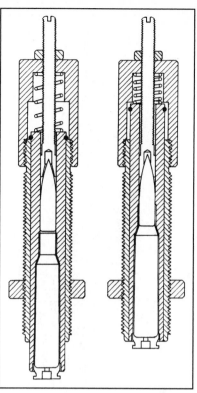

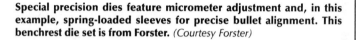

Reloading dies come in two basic formats—a two-die set for rifle cartridges and a three-die set for pistol and cast-bullet rifle loading.

Special precision dies feature micrometer adjustment and, in this example, spring-loaded sleeves for precise bullet alignment. This benchrest die set is from Forster. *(Courtesy Forster)*

tion rates are from about 500 rounds per hour to 1200. Plan to do a lot of shooting if you invest in one of these. You should also plan to have plenty of space since a progressive stands better than two feet high and weighs up to 50 lbs. The top end? Automated machines, motor-driven, equipped with computer technology within, that will crank out up to 5000 rounds per hour. Camdex and Auto Load make these starting around $30,000. They are bought mainly by professional reloading companies.

SPEED VERSUS PRECISION

The basic "C", "O", "H" frame, arbor and turret machines will all produce high quality, precision ammunition, or at least as precise as you make it since quality control is up to the operator. Careful adjustment, precise measurement, locking dies in tightly, and inspecting every step in production are your job and if you do them well, the results will show in the finished product. Some of the older model Lyman turret machines had a tendency to loosen up over time and wear. This allowed the dies to rock out of position and not seat bullets absolutely straight. This problem has been ironed out in the new machines, so the only real difference between the turret and multi-station machines and the single die units is the price and speed of operation.

Progressive loaders are designed more for speed than precision. In the case of handgun ammunition where benchrest/varmint shooting accuracy is not expected, they are the best investment for a shooter who really burns a lot of ammunition, although these are generally purchased in varying grades by clubs, police departments and professional reloaders who sell their ammunition.

While progressives churn out tremendous quantities of ammunition they require a fairly long set-up period and if there is a change of caliber of ammunition, this means a different set of feed tubes and plates as well as dies. Because they are complicated, progressives require more tinkering and cleaning to keep them running smoothly. Automation of the process means you depend on the machine to do it right every time. That doesn't always happen.

PRECISION VERSUS ECONOMY

As has been mentioned above, precision and economy lie mainly with the single-die and turret/H-frame (multi-station) machines. Progressives pay only when there is a demand for high-volume production of one caliber at a time. For my money, the price differential between the single-die and turret/multi-station machines is close enough that it is probably worth the extra money to invest in the latter if you are going to do more than a very modest amount of reloading. They have the advantage of holding a full die set and a powder measure. This means the dies are seated and adjusted once, for the most part, unless you are reloading a number of calibers. The production edge will be noticed as the amount of ammunition you make increases. For a shooter reloading a single caliber, mainly for hunting — someone who does not do a lot of practice and may assemble no more than 200 to 2000 rounds a year – the best buy would be the simple, reliable "O" frame machine. It will do the job.

RELOADING DIES

Once a press is purchased, it must be equipped with one set of dies for each different cartridge you reload. The dies

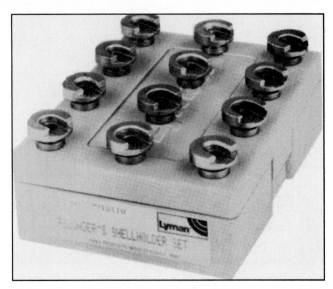

Shellholders must be purchased to fit the cartridge you are reloading. Some accept more than one cartridge, and they can be had in sets.

The primer seater, as shown on this RCBS Rock Chucker, is usually included as part of the press, but if you get used equipment, be sure it's there.

Problems such as crimped-in primers and stuck cases, like this one with the head torn off, require special tools such as a stuck-case removal kit.

screw into the press. The first die decaps the cartridge and resizes it to unfired dimensions. The second expands the case mouth while the third seats the bullet. Rifle dies for jacketed bullets do not expand the case mouth since this is not necessary for hard, jacketed bullets. Cast bullets require this expansion, to keep them from being accidentally cut by a sharp case mouth. Dies come in all grades from plain to fancy. Basic die sets of steel range around $60. They will last for many years and many thousands of rounds of ammunition. Tungsten carbide or titanium nitride dies require little or no lubrication of the cases which speeds the loading process a bit and last longer than steel. Add about $30 for this feature. Forster, Redding and Jones offer micrometer-adjustable bullet-seating dies while Harrell's Precision makes a variable base for reforming bench-rest cases to near chamber dimensions. Specialty dies of this sort start around $125 apiece but they're worth the price if you are getting into competition target shooting. There are special neck sizing dies for use with bottleneck cases that will only be fired in one particular rifle, thus there is no need to put cases through the wear and tear of full-length resizing. There are custom dies for obso-

lete calibers and loading cartridges as large as 20mm. About anything your heart desires will cheerfully be made up by the 4-D Custom Die company of Mount Vernon, Ohio.

PRIMER SEATERS AND CASE HOLDERS

Primer seaters fit in the front bottom of your press and you will need one for large diameter primers and another for small primers. It's probably a good idea to buy both since a pair is generally around $20. Case or shell holders are needed to hold the case as it inserted into the die. One size does not fit all, but Lyman offers a set of 12 that covers most popular rifle and pistol cartridges. A real headache is getting the crimp out of a military case. 4-D, among others, offers a useful die to remove this crimp with a stroke of your loading press handle without removing metal as with the hand-method using a chamfering tool.

SIZER/LUBRICATORS

The second large bench tool you will need is a sizer/lubricator if you are planning on shooting your own cast bullets. In addition to applying lubricant in the grooves of the bullet, the sizer puts them in exact round with mirror-smooth sides, and of a dimension determined by the sizing die. By the use of various dies you can control bullet diameters to .001". These cost about $40 for a rock-bottom priced Lee and go up from there for the Lyman, RCBS, and SAECO machines. Sizing dies are around $40 each, while top punches, needed to push the bullet through the die, are about $12 and, here again, one size does not fit all. Flat-point or round-point punches should not be used on pointed bullets.

SMALL BENCH TOOLS

These are either mounted on the bench or on the press or are free standing on the bench. The list that follows is a basic list, intended for safe, precision loading. Beyond this lies the land of wonderful gadgets that save time and energy, increase production and in general do, or at least promise, all those things that helped put men on the moon and otherwise made America great.

Powder scales are absolutely essential in working up loads and checking those that are measured with a hand dipper or metered by a powder measure. Basic balance scales start at about $60 and top at about $200. Electronic scales with LCD readout start around $160 and go on up to over $450. The speed advantage goes to the electronic models.

The ultimate in precision and speed is the RCBS Charge Master combo which combines an electronic scale accurate to 0.10 grain and an automatic dispenser. You can weight powder, bullets and loaded cartridges on this one.

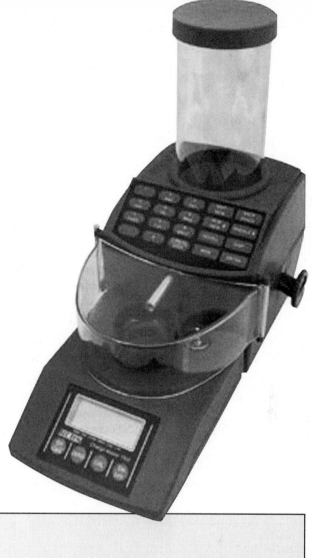

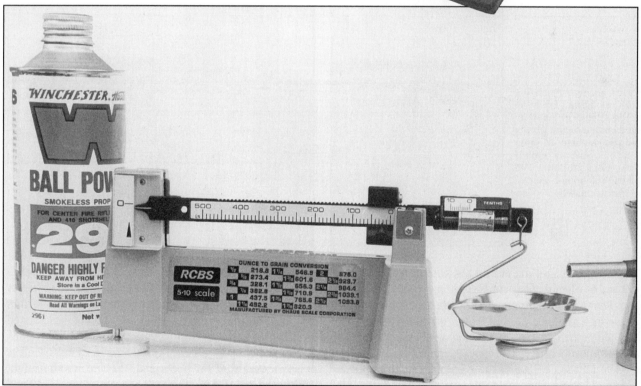

An accurate powder scale is an absolute must for working up loads. Beam-type scales such as this are rapidly giving way to digital scales.

A powder measure speeds production and can throw accurate loads. Precision, however, depends on the consistency of operation.

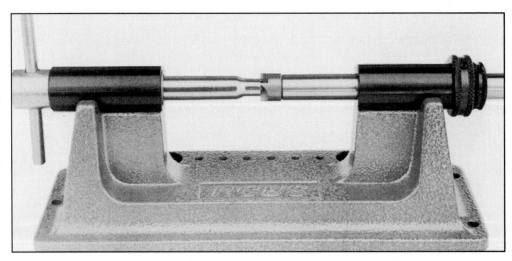

Cases stretch in firing and reloading. Every so often they will need to be trimmed to the proper length. A case trimmer requires various collets (case-head holders) and pilots (case-mouth guides) to trim accurately.

Powder measures are not an absolute necessity but are invaluable when it comes time to get into production loading. They can be mounted on a loading press or a stand. These start at a little over $100 and run on up to well over $200 for models with many bells and whistles. The precision of the adjustment is not all that different. More expensive models adjust faster, a little more precisely, hold their accuracy more consistently, hold more powder and so on. The accuracy of their metering is mainly dependent on the con-

sistency of the operator as he pulls and returns the handle.

Case trimmers are essential in keeping cartridge length consistent. Cases stretch on firing and in reloading dies and must be trimmed back every so often. Hand-cranked models start at a little over $125 as a kit with a selection of collets and pilots to handle most common calibers. Collets grasp the case head and pilots guide the case mouth straight against the cutter. Motorized models run around $150 and up.

HAND TOOLS

Case deburring or chamfering tools come with a bench mount and in the case of the RCBS trimmer can be purchased as an add-on feature. They are also made in hand-held versions. These are necessary to take burrs off the outside of the mouth of a case that has been trimmed and chamfer (bevel) the inside of the case mouth to remove burrs that will otherwise scratch and gall cast and even jacketed bullets. Prices range from $12 to $20.

Primer-pocket cleaners can be simply a flat-blade screwdriver, inserted into the primer pocket and turned several times to get the fouling out. Getting the primer-ash deposit out of the pocket is necessary or the fresh primer will not seat properly. The ash build up will either result in a high primer or one that may give poor ignition as the firing-pin blow is cushioned and the vent blocked by ash. A steel straight-edge ruler will check that your primers are seated deeply enough.

Lyman, Redding and RCBS among others offer case-care kits containing primer-pocket cleaners and an assortment of case brushes to remove interior fouling– a good investment if you are loading black powder or Pyrodex ammunition. If you need power, RCBS offers the Trim Mate at $155 which throws in case chamfering and deburring tools as well.

Loading blocks are the best way to keep from double charging your cases. They come in moulded plastic from several manufacturers and cost about $8. You can make your own by drilling holes in a flat piece of 1" plank the size of the heads of your cartridges and gluing on a flat bottom. A loading block is the best way to inspect your cases after they have been charged with powder, before you seat a bullet. Double-charging is very easy to do especially when using a powder measure and if you shoot one of these loads your gun will never forgive you.

Powder funnels are about $6 and their use is only way to avoid spilling powder when you are working up loads by weighing each one. A charge drawn from a powder measure and dumped into the pan of your scale for checking is the way to maintain accuracy in your measure. If everything is working as it should, the charge in the pan is then funneled into the case. These are available with a long "drop tube" for loading nearly-compressed charges.

Micrometer/calipers are the best means of making all sorts of precision measurements – case length, inside and outside diameters, case neck wall-thickness, checks for bullet roundness and diameter case swelling, etc. My favorite version of this tool is the dial caliper, now available with

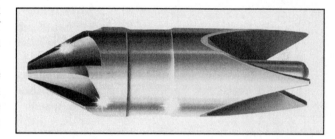

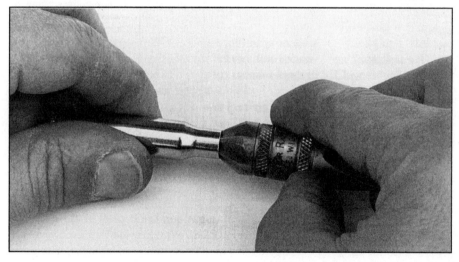

(Above and left) **A deburring tool makes bullet seating easier and lessens damage to the bullet base.**

A primer pocket cleaner removes primer residue for ease in primer seating.

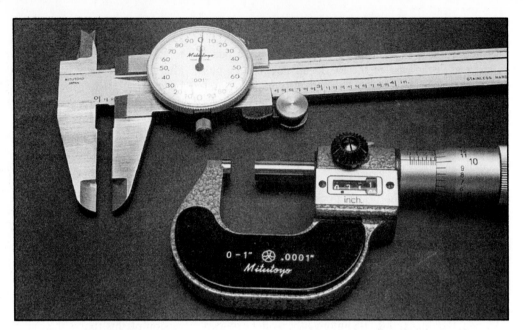

A micrometer and precision caliper capable of accurate measurement to .001" are necessary tools. Those made of plastic are not that reliable.

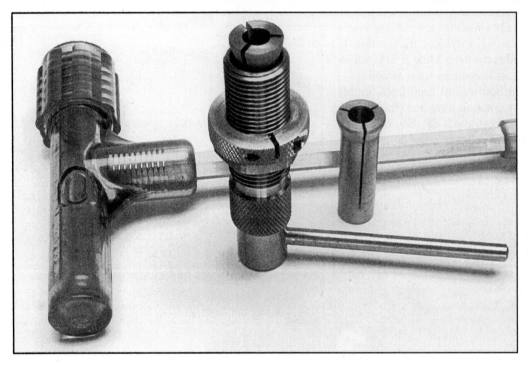

Bullet pullers come in two varieties: those that mount on the reloading press and those of the hammer-type kinetic variety *(left)*. The latter is perhaps gentler on bullets, but requires more energy on the part of the user.

an LCD readout if your eyes are having probems with fine lines. Cheap ones are made of plastic and not to be trusted for fine work. A steel one with a dial goes for $55 and up, if you fancy such names as Brown and Sharpe.

Bullet pullers are there for the same reason they put erasers on pencils. Everybody, sooner or later, puts together some loads that won't fly for one reason or another and they need to be taken apart. The two basic types are the one that screws into the die holding hole on your press and the kinetic type that looks like a hammer. The press-mounted type is easy to use but tend to cut up bullets, making them unshootable. The hammer model features a hollow plastic head into which the cartridge is fitted. A wad of cotton or

tissue can be used to cushion the bottom of the chamber where the bullet is caught. With this addition, even very soft lead-alloy bullets may be retrieved undamaged. The principle behind this tool is that the energy transferred to the bullet in the case inside the hollow head causes the bullet to slide out after whacking a convenient board, as though hammering a nail. Around $20.

CASE CLEANING EQUIPMENT

Do shiny-bright cases shoot bullets straighter than tarnished "grotty-looking" ones? Case cleaning is something like car washing — you either believe in it or don't. The real advantage of shiny-clean cases is that small cracks and flaws

The Lee Load-All II and MEC 600 Jr. Mark V are good machines to work with, if you are just starting out. The production rate is fast enough to satisfy most shooters unless they are heavily into competition trap or skeet shooting.

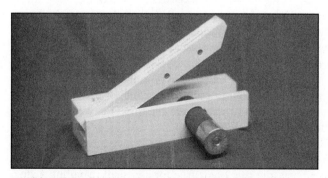

Hornady's Stack 'N' Pack makes boxing shotshells easier and is a good example of an inexpensive accessory that's well worth the money.

are more easily seen on shiny surfaces. If smokeless powder is used, most cases stay pretty clean unless they receive a lot of handling with sweaty fingers or fire a number of low-pressure loads that fail to expand the case fully and coat it with soot. Most cases will shine up in the sizing process, unless you only neck-size, and a polishing with a cloth before you put the finished cartridge into the box will generally keep them bright for a long time.

After much use and especially after using black or Pyrodex powder in them, brass cases will take on the look of a dirty penny. Since both black and Pyrodex leave corrosive deposits (sulfurous acid) they should be washed out soon after shooting. There are two basic case-cleaning methods – chemical and mechanical. Chemical cleaning involves washing the cases in a bath of an acid-based cleaner. The cleaner is sold as a concentrate to be mixed with water in a plastic, glass or stainless-steel container. The cases are given a wash then thoroughly rinsed. If the mixture is too strong or the cases are left in too long these cleaners will begin etching the metal. While tarnish and dirt are removed, the cases are not shiny, but a dull yellow color. A polish is achieved by some means of buffing. Liquid cleaners are effective and require no special equipment.

Precision Reloading's D-Loader does for shotshells what a bullet puller does for metallic cartridges. The case, however, cannot be saved, only the contents.

Mechanical polishers are motorized tumblers and vibrators with containers into which the cases are dumped along with a cleaning "media" composed of ground walnut shells or corn cobs. Liquid polish additives are also available to speed the process. The cases are tumbled or vibrated for an hour or more and come out with a high shine. They must be separated from the cleaning media and the media must be cleaned and replaced every so often. Prices for vibrators start around $100. Tumblers are more expensive $300.-$500. Tumblers have the advantage of being able to use either wet or dry cleaning media.

SHOTSHELL RELOADING

While shotshells can be reloaded with simple hand tools and RCBS does offer a shotshell reloading die set for use in its "O" frame presses, most shotshell reloading is done on press-type machines that are similar to the turret, multi-station and semi-automated (progressive) loader designs used for metallic-cartridges. Shotshells do not require the kind of precision alignment of bullets with cases that is needed for metallic cartridges, thus with a decline in a need for high precision, speed can be achieved. Precision is, of course, required in sizing, wad column seating and powder charging although shot shells work at far lower pressures than rifles and accuracy is a matter of density of pattern of a column of pellets. This not to say that one can take a cavalier attitude when loading shotshells. A shotgun can be blown up with an overload as easily as any other gun and with similarly disastrous results.

BASIC EQUIPMENT

If all you reload are shotshells your needs for a bench and storage are far less than for metallic cartridges. The stresses involved in sizing and reloading shotshells are far less than those in making rifle cartridges. While a bench of some sort is needed it does not have to be as large or robust. Shotshell presses do have to be firmly mounted. Overhead space is more of a consideration because many of these machines stand two feet high — more if you elect to attach hoppers to feed empty shells and/or wads.

Storage space is more of a concern if you are setting up for shotshell reloading since the components are very bulky and you have more of them. Wads and shot are sold in bulk, which means finding a place to store bread-loaf size bags of shot (25 lbs.) and grocery-bag-size bags of plastic shot cups now used in place of the old felt or paper wads. Shotshells, loaded or empty, are bulky, requiring four to five times the space needed for an equivalent amount of handgun ammunition. Shelves or cupboards are a good idea to have close to your bench.

ECONOMY VERSUS SPEED

The same rule holds true for shotshell reloading as for rifle and pistol ammunition manufacturing. Machines that turn out more ammunition faster cost more money.

Because the process is simpler for loading shotshells than it is for metallic cartridges, making ammunition goes faster. With most machines all the necessary dies, the powder charger, and the shot charger are contained in the press. With everything close together, and a need to do no more than pull an operating handle and move a shell from one station to the next, even a basic machine like the Lee Load-All II will turn out 100 rounds per hour at around $100. This is a pretty good investment. Lee offers update kits to convert older presses and conversion kits to load other gauges. Hornady offers a similar single-stage press and offers a conversion to progressive loader status via a kit. The basic press is about $200. Add on $275 worth of accessories and you have a progressive. The MEC 600 Jr. Mark V, while a single-stage machine, is set up for speed and will double the Lee's output. The price, not surprisingly, is a little over $200.

PROGRESSIVE LOADERS

Progressive machines are very popular with shotshell reloaders because of their output. Shotgun shooting, unlike rifle or handgun shooting, generally involves a lot of gun handling. Targets are close in the hunting field but appear only briefly. Practice for hunting as well as just plain fun is on the skeet or trap range. Developing the reflexes to become a good scattergunner requires practice, which means a larger consumption of ammunition than for most rifle or handgun work.

Progressive machines start at around $500 and machines of this general level will turn out between 300 to 400 rounds per hour. RCBS has its Grand progressive at a little under $1000. This one will do both 12 and 20 ga shells. Top of the line progressives like the Hollywood Automatic weigh 100 lbs. and can crank out an astonishing 1800 rounds per hour, if you have the muscle to keep pulling that long. Few individuals will invest at this level, when a MEC 8567 Grabber at $525 will turn out 500 finished shells an hour. These numbers are production time, of course, and don't include the time spent loading hoppers, canisters and tubes with shotcups, primers, shot and powder. Progressive machines, because of their complexity, are more subject to problems than more simple loaders. They require more cleaning and care as well to keep them running smoothly.

ACCESSORIES

Unlike rifle and pistol presses, where you must buy separate die sets, shotshell reloaders come equipped with a set to load the gauge you prefer. Extra sets, of course, may be purchased, but six sets would load everything from 410 to 10 gauge. A great many machines come with conversion kits to upgrade performance, handle more gauges or steel shot, which has its own requirements. There are dies to do six-fold, eight-fold or roll crimps. Most of the accessories for shotshell reloading are therefore "add ons" to the basic press. There are, however, several separate items that are necessary and useful. The precision scale for weighing pow-

```
CARTRIDGE_____Overall length_____

Case, make _____Times reloaded_____

Primer, make, type_____

Powder_____ Charge_____

Bullet, make, type , weight_____

For gun_____

Sight setting_____ Range Zero_____

Velocity, Chronographed_____ est_____

Date Loaded_____

Remarks_____

_____
```

A simple reloading data form can be created on a computer and reduced to stick-on labels for cartridge boxes, and/or kept in notebook form for ready reference. Accurate records are essential.

der and in this case shot is a must to work up and check loads. The same dial or digital caliper is also invaluable for checking case lengths and diameters. MEC makes a very handy metal plate gauge, cut with a dozen holes. This "ring gauge" allows a quick check on the diameters of all the standard U.S. made shotshells offering a "go" and "no go" gauge for each. Hornady's "Stack 'N' Pack" and MEC's "E-Z PACK" are nifty racks for packing shotshells ready to be dropped into standard boxes. The answer to the bullet puller is the Precision Reloading "D-LOADER" which allows the reclamation of shot, powder primers and wads from bad reloads. It also trims 10 and 12 gauge "TUFF-type" wads to length. It is a cutter tool, however, and will not save the shell itself.

ORGANIZATION

Getting all your stuff organized is a key to success in reloading. Tools too close together or too far apart for convenient reach slow your work and wear out your temper. Here again, one of the best ways to get started is to see how other reloaders set things up. If possible, try their equipment to get a feel for the process. Smooth operation stems from having the right tools in the right place and components where they can be easily handled and stored. The right way is the one that works best for you. Generally speaking, sizer lubricators are mounted on the front of the bench. They do not need to be particularly close to the loading press since bullet sizing and lubricating is generally done as an operation separate from the actual loading process. By the same token the case trimmer, if bench mounted, need not be very near the press since this operation is generally done separately, prior to loading. The press is really the center of your operation and should have clear space around it to place boxes or stacks of primers, bullets, cases and cans

of powder. You may want to try mounting tools with "C" clamps to start so a change in position to a final location and bolting down only has to be done once, as you develop a plan for working. Storage for the above should be close to avoid walks across the room with spilling along the way. A comfortable chair is a real asset since you will be spending many, hopefully happy and productive, hours there.

RECORD KEEPING

The importance of record keeping cannot be overemphasized. Your record book or file of what you load and how it shoots will keep you up on what you have tried, how well it worked and, depending on your analysis and commentary, will serve as a guide to further experimentation. Without accurate records you have to rely on that poorest of devices — memory. The type of data storage and method you choose are, again, whatever works best. A pocket tape recorder can be carried to the range and notes and comments spoken for writing down later. Some people prefer data forms as they require the least work. I have gotten along with a vest-pocket notebook for a number of years, but also have a tape machine, since writing takes time away from shooting. The only problem is that tape storage is linear and a page can be scanned at a glance.

Record keeping includes the box in which you keep your finished ammunition. Unmarked boxes equal "mystery" loads. When working up a load you should mark the box indicating primer type, primer make, powder type, charge, bullet weight, alloy, lubricant and exact size. You can write on the box or use stick-on notes. Less data may be needed once you have found a load you wish to produce on a regular basis. Here again, though, care must be taken to mark clearly high-pressure "hot" loads if you have both strong and weak-action guns of the same caliber.

You've made the decision to reload, you've collected all the necessary components, set up a safe workspace with the proper tools, and done the research. It's time to get started.

Rifle Cartridge Reloading

"BEGIN AT THE BEGINNING," the King said, very gravely, "and go on till you come to the end: then stop." This is about the only sensible advice from Lewis Carroll's King of Wonderland. Beginnings are at times a little fuzzy and there are small, but necessary side trips to be made along the way. This chapter will try follow the King's directive while getting in the necessary small bits.

The beginner is going to start off with once-fired, or better, new cases to work up a load. Once a load is tested and found to be satisfactory then quantity production can begin and some of the preliminary steps can be omitted.

CASE INSPECTION

Even new and first-fired cases should be checked over for defects. Any with splits or serious defects in the case mouth that are not ironed out in the resizing die should be discarded.

Cases should be segregated by maker as determined by the head stamp. Even though they are the same caliber, cases of different manufacture have slight differences in wall thickness, and vent size. Mixing brands will alter velocities and pressures and will open up shot-group sizes.

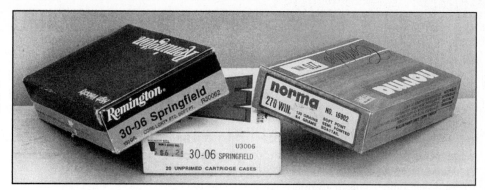

Empty cases should go back in the original box after firing so various brands and calibers don't get mixed.

FULL-LENGTH RESIZING

This is not necessary for new cases but must be done for fired cases. If these will later be used in only one rifle, further resizing can be limited to neck resizing only, unless heavy loads are used. To resize a case it must first be given a coating of case lubricant to allow it to work easily in the sizing die. Sizing lubricant is a special oil or grease made for this purpose. It is best applied by saturating a clean, rubber-stamp inking pad with lubricant, then rolling the case over it, lightly coating the outside of the case. Too much lubricant on the outside of the case will cause dents in the walls which will flatten out on firing, but will stress the metal. On bottleneck cases the inside on the neck should be lubricated with a dry graphite, or similar non-oil, case-neck lubricant. Oil will run into the powder and ruin it. Neck lubricating keeps the neck from stretching unduly in the die. A light coating of lubricant is all that is needed. My own preference for case lube is Imperial Die-Sizing Wax. This is used primarily for reshaping cases from one caliber to another, but is clean, can be applied easily with the fingers and only the barest coating is needed. Die wax rarely causes case dents. A minute amount on the case mouth does a good job of inside-neck lubricating. The prepared case is inserted in the shell holder, the operating lever is pulled, running the case completely into the die, assuming the die is properly adjusted. Properly adjusted? Read the manual.

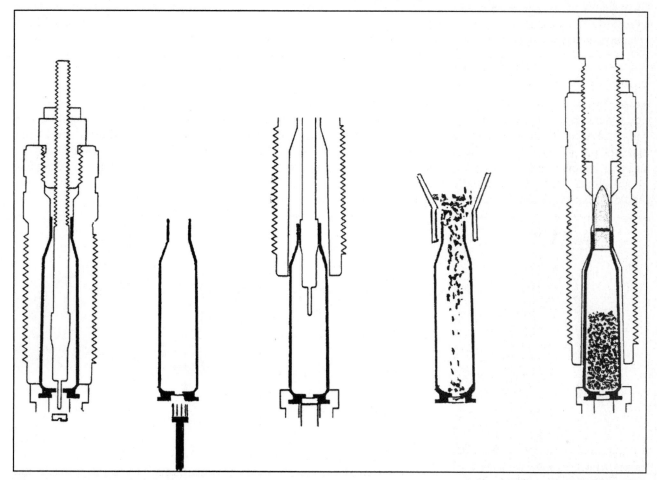

The basic steps in rifle reloading include, left to right, resizing and decapping, primer pocket cleaning, inside neck expanding (done in the upstroke of the decapping process), priming, powder charging and bullet seating.

DECAPPING

The die should be adjusted so the decapping pin removes the old primer, which will drop out at the end of the insertion stroke. The resizing/decapping process should require a medium amount of force. If a lot of force is required to get the case in the die you have not used enough lubricant.

INSIDE NECK EXPANDING

The decapping pin is mounted in a rod with an expansion ball on it that stretches the case mouth large enough to accept a new bullet. This operation is completed on the up or primer-removal stroke of the operating handle.

INSPECTION, GAUGING AND TRIMMING

The case is now removed from the shell holder for inspection. The case mouth should be smooth and perfectly round. "Trim to length" say the books because a too-long case will enter the throat of the barrel and raise pressures as the bullet is swaged down then expands as it goes through this hourglass waist you have created, before it enters the rifling. A quick check with a case-length gauge or measurement with your caliper tells you if the case is too long. Sometimes even new ones are. If the case is too long it goes in the trimmer, which is adjusted to cut the case to exact length. After trimming, the outside burr is removed and the inside is chamfered slightly to give the bullet a smooth start. Do not cut a knife edge on the case mouth. This trimming/chamfering operation needs to be done only when cases get too long.

PRIMING

If the case is a fired one, the primer-pocket should be scraped free of ash with a screwdriver or cleaning tool. The case is now ready for priming. Place a primer in the priming punch sleeve. This comes up, in most cases, through the center of the shell holder. Place the case in the shell holder and pull the operating handle to press the case onto the primer punch. This will seat it in the case. Enough force should be applied to seat the primer fully, but not crush or flatten it. Difficulty in seating may be experienced if you are using crimped military brass. If so, this crimp must be removed before proceeding. After priming, the case should be checked to see that the primer is fully in the pocket. This is done by placing a steel straight-edge ruler across the case while holding it to the light to see if the primer sticks up above the case head. It should not. A high primer gives poor ignition or may not fire at all as the firing pin simply drives it into the pocket. The primed, inspected case now goes into the loading block.

CASE MOUTH EXPANSION

This step applies only to straight-walled cases being loaded with cast, lead-alloy bullets, and uses the second die in a three-die rifle set. Three-die sets do not expand the case mouth in the decapping stage. The case is placed in the shell holder and run into this die, which has a stepped or tapered expander plug which opens the case mouth for insertion of a soft, cast bullet. This mouth expansion is generally done before powder charging, to avoid handling cases full of powder and spilling them.

POWDER CHARGING

The case is now ready for charging. When working up a load, always start with the beginning load listed in the data manuals. Increases in powder charges should be made by no more than half (.5) a grain at a time. Load at least ten (10) test cartridges before going to a heavier charge. Powder charges are weighed precisely on a powder scale for working up loads. The easiest method is to pour a half cup or so of powder into a small container (I use a glass custard dish) and dip it into the scale pan with a small spoon. Plastic spoons are lighter and allow you to tap out the powder in small amounts most easily. This is the slowest part of the operation, and the most critical. The scale should be properly set up and checked for adjustment. Once the charge is weighed, the powder funnel goes on the case and the powder is poured in, with no spills of course.

Too much lubricant will make dents in cases. These will flatten out on firing, but this works and weakens the brass.

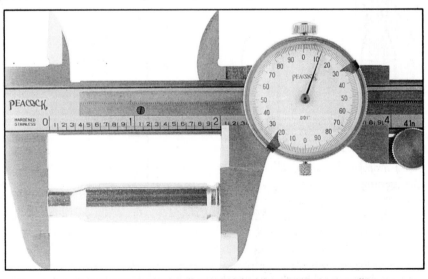

Case length should be checked after sizing and neck expanding.

Powder dippers can be purchased or homemade to pick up a fairly accurate charge of a particular type of powder. All dipped loads should be checked regularly on a powder scale.

Powder measures work well for reduced loads, but should not be used for maximum loads, particularly of fast-burning powders.

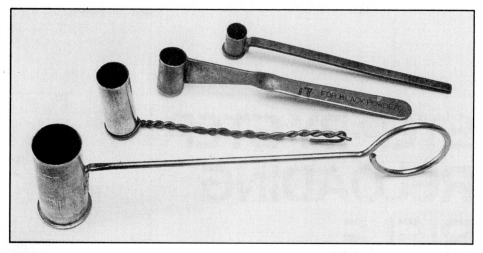

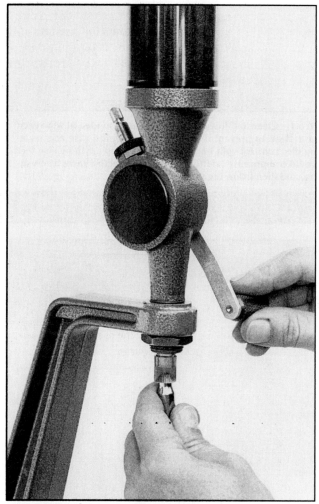

The reloader's powder funnel is especially designed to fit over the case mouth and deliver powder without spills. One size fits nearly all commonly reloaded cases.

USE OF A POWDER MEASURE

Mechanical powder measures should never be used to work up loads, but they're useful in making production loads. Precision depends to a great degree on consistency of pulling and returning the operating handle. After a powder measure is adjusted, check its accuracy, and yours, by dropping every fifth load into the scale pan for weighing. Accurate loads are within a tolerance of +/ - one tenth (.1) of a grain. Always check cases loaded with a powder measure in the loading block. It is very easy to pull the handle twice on the same case.

BULLET SEATING

This is the final step in the loading operation. Cases are placed in the shell holder. The bullet is placed in the case mouth as straight as possible, and the case is gently levered into the bullet-seating die. Proper die adjustment is nec-

The funnel is moved from case to case until every one in the loading block is filled. Make it a habit to check the powder level in all the cases in the loading block, examining them under good light, even though you are sure you did not double charge any of them. If the powder level in any case looks suspiciously high, weigh it again. The balance may be sticking on your scale or you may have accidentally shifted a weight – you'd be surprised at what can happen.

(Text continued on page 127)

STEP-BY-STEP RELOADING RIFLE CARTRIDGES

(Photos courtesy of RCBS/ATK)

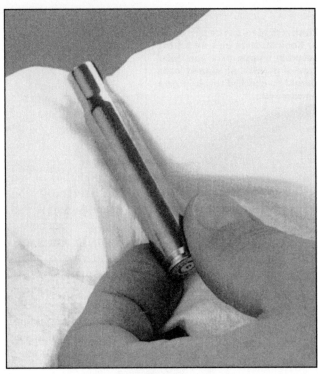

Step 1 - Clean and Inspect: It's always a good idea to wipe each case clean to prevent dirt from scratching the case and resizing die. Look for split necks, case cracks and anything else that would compromise safety. Destroy any defective cases by crushing, and then throw them away.

Step 4 - Adjusting the Sizer Die: With a shellholder installed in the ram, and the ram all the way up, thread the sizer die into the press until it touches the shellholder. Raise the press handle a little and turn the die in another 1/8- to 1/4-turn, then set the die lock ring.

Step 5 - Case Resizing: Insert an empty case into the shellholder and gently lower the press handle all the way to the bottom, running the case into the sizing die. Doing so will resize the case to factory dimensions and knock out the fired primer. Raising the press handle will lower the case and expand the case mouth to the proper dimension to hold the new bullet.

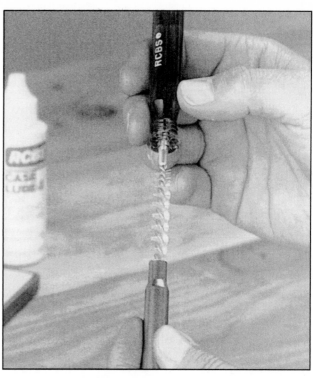

Step 2 - Lubricate the Cases: To prevent the case from sticking in the sizing die, it must be lubricated only with sizing die lube. With a bit of lube on the pad, roll a number of cases over it a few times to lightly coat the case body.

Step 3 - Case Neck Lubrication: Use a case neck brush to clean and lubricate the inside of the case neck. This will reduce resizing effort and neck stretching. Only a small amount of lube should be applied to the brush.

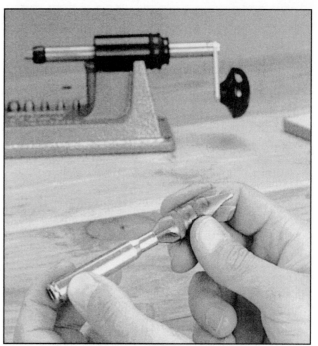

Step 6 - Case Trimming: Cartridge cases tend to stretch after a few firings, so they must be trimmed back to allow proper chambering and for safety reasons. Reloading data manuals will give the proper trim and maximum case lengths.

Step 7 - Chamfer and Deburr: After trimming, the case mouth will have a slight burr, and the sharp edge of the mouth needs to be smoothed. A twist of a simple hand tool removes the burr with one end and chamfers the case mouth with the other end for easy insertion of the new bullet.

Step 8 - Case Mouth Expansion: This step applies only to straight-wall cases and is done in a separate step. Install the expander die in the press, insert a case in the shellholder and run the case up into the die. This die should be adjusted so the case mouth is belled or flared just enough to accept a new bullet.

Step 9 - Priming (A): Place a fresh primer, anvil side up, into the cup of the primer arm and insert a case into the shellholder.

Step 12 - Powder Charging (A): Look up the load in your loading manual to see exactly how much and what powder you need. It's a good idea to weigh each charge for safety and consistency.

Step 13 - Powder Charging (B): After weighing the charge, use a funnel to pour it into the case without spilling.

Step 10 - Priming (B): Lower the press handle and push the primer arm all the way into the slot in the ram.

Step 11 - Priming (C): Gently and slowly raise the press handle. This lowers the case onto the priming arm, seating the fresh primer. Check each case to be sure the primer is fully seated.

Step 14 - Powder Charging (C): Another method of charging is to use the powder measure. It dispenses a precise, uniform charge with each crank of the handle, thereby speeding up the process. Use the reloading scale to adjust the powder measure until it throws several identical charges. Then, weigh about every ten charges to recheck the weight.

Step 15 - Bullet Seating (A): Thread the seater die into the press a few turns. With a case in the shellholder, lower the press handle, running the case all the way up into the die. Turn the die further in until it stops. While using the headstamp on top of the die as a reference, back the die out one full turn and lock it in place with the lock ring.

Step 16 - Bullet Seating (B): Now, unscrew the seater plug enough to keep the bullet from being seated **too deeply.**

Step 17 - Bullet Seating (C): With the handle up, insert a primed and charged case in the shellholder, and hold a bullet over the case mouth with one hand while you lower the press handle with the other, easing the bullet and case up into the die. This will seat the bullet. Measure the loaded round to see if the bullet is seated deeply enough.

Step 18 - Bullet Seating (D): If the bullet **needs to be seated** deeper into the case, turn the seater plug **down a little and run** the case back up into the die. Make **small adjustments and keep** trying and measuring until you get the **proper cartridge overall** length. Once the proper setting is reached, **tighten the seater** plug lock ring.

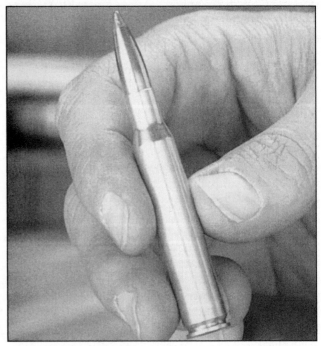

Step 19 - The Loaded Round: After wiping off any sizing lube, the first loaded cartridge is ready to be fired

(Text continued from page 121)

Seating dies have a crimping shoulder in them to crimp some hunting bullets. Never crimp bullets that do not have a crimping cannelure in them. (Courtesy Speer)

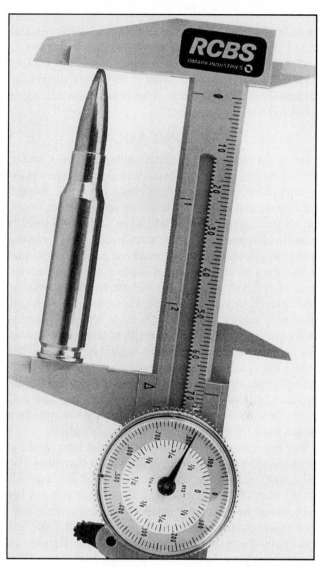

Finished cartridges should be checked to see they do not exceed overall length. If they do, the seater stem in the die can be adjusted to seat the bullets deeper.

essary not to exceed the maximum overall length of the cartridge as listed in the loading manual. An overly long cartridge will press the bullet into the rifling and raise pressures! The easiest way to avoid this problem is to make up a dummy cartridge. After the die is screwed in to the press, you will want to adjust it so the case enters freely its full length. Gradually ease the cartridge in the die and check to see it does not pass the crimping shoulder, which turns over the case mouth. The next adjustment is to the stem of the bullet seater, which gradually drives the bullet deeper into the case. When the correct overall length is reached, tighten the seater adjustment. Keep the dummy for easy readjustment, after loading longer or shorter bullets. You may want to make a dummy for every different-length bullet you load to facilitate easy readjustment. Once the die is adjusted, bullet seating is simply a matter of repetition.

Most dies have a built-in crimping shoulder to turn the case mouth over into a cannelure (groove) in the bullet. This is necessary for high-powered ammunition, particularly if it is jarred by recoil while being fed through tubular magazines and even some box magazines. Crimping keeps the

bullets from being forced back into the case under such circumstances. Military ammunition which will be fed through autoloaders and machine guns is always crimped, as is much commercial ammunition. Crimping degrades accuracy and should never be attempted on bullets that do not have a crimping cannelure in them. Hunting ammunition used in tubular magazines may have to be crimped.

"Easy does it" is the rule for all steps. Ramming, jerking or otherwise forcing leads to damaged cases, mashed bullets, flattened primers and broken decapping pins.

The final, final step is to wipe off any case lubricant that may be on the case and inspect the finished cartridge with a final check for overall length. Oil left on cases will cause excessive back-thrust and batter your gun. If all dies are properly adjusted and firmly in place, there should be no difference from one cartridge to the next. Place the loaded rounds in a cartridge box and mark them accordingly.

Clean-up is always a good idea. Powder should always be returned to the original container, even from a powder measure. Powder in open containers will lose volatiles and absorb moisture. Primers can absorb moisture and magnum and standard primers can be confused if not put back in their respective containers. Most of all there is always the chance of confusion regarding what powder you were using when you start the next time.

SELECTING A LOAD

Many people start with factory duplication loads, which, if you have already been shooting them, is a convenient place to start without varying any component. Generally, though, the best accuracy in your rifle will be something you work up on your own. This may take some doing even though many loading manuals list "accuracy loads." If you read the fine print you will see this applies to one particular test rifle. If yours is a different make, this one may not shoot best for you, but it is perhaps the best powder/bullet combination to start with. Loading data is presented as starting loads and maximum loads with a middle ground in between. It is generally in this middle ground where the most accurate loading will be found. Rarely is the hottest, highest pressure load the straightest shooter. Maximum loads, especially with jacketed bullets, shorten both case and barrel life. By working for accuracy, you start by getting a clear idea of just how well your rifle will shoot. With this as a starting point, you then have a standard by which other loads can be judged.

For the most part, you will probably not have need for more than three or four different loadings, if that many. For 30 caliber rifles and up, about three different loadings will do for most of the uses you will make of your gun. On the bottom end are short-range practice loads. These are usually cast bullets driven at modest velocities of around 1200-1500 fps. These offer good, cheap recreation and training without the expense, wear, noise and recoil of full-bore loads. They can be used for small game and varmint hunting at distanc-es under 100 yards with reasonable accuracy. Varmint loads with light bullets are practical in many 30 caliber rifles that will produce good accuracy and a flat trajectory. Hunting loads are the most common for the thirties unless you have a match rifle. For a hunting rifle, used primarily for hunting as opposed to competition, you would do best to work up the most accurate load you can from the selection of hunting bullets available.

WORKING UP A LOAD

Working up a load means not merely careful loading of ammunition, but targeting it and keeping records of the results. It also involves case inspection, looking for any signs of excessive headspace or pressures. I use a simple notebook for records. I list these under the name of the rifle and its caliber. Individual loads are listed under the bullet, indicating whether it is cast or jacketed, the weight, diameter and lubrication type. Next the powder type and charge is listed. Following this is a notation on the make of case and primer and type. Finally, there's a section for "remarks." This includes a summary of the performance of this particular load, especially its accuracy. Ten-shot groups are the accuracy test standard, although it has been demonstrated that seven-shot groups work just as well. Other remarks include the test range, the temperature, wind direction and velocity and light conditions. Also noted are any indications of pressure problems. These are underlined as a warning for future reference.

LOADING FOR AUTOLOADERS

Since WWII, autoloaders in all calibers and types have become very popular, owing mainly to the change-over by nearly all of the world's governments to this type of rifle for their respective militaries. While all autoloaders rely on the force of the explosion in the cartridge to function the action

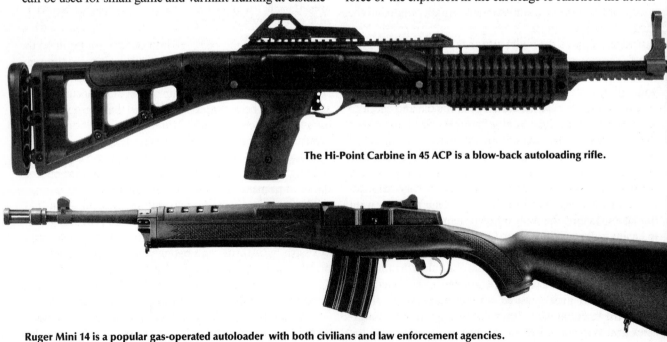

The Hi-Point Carbine in 45 ACP is a blow-back autoloading rifle.

Ruger Mini 14 is a popular gas-operated autoloader with both civilians and law enforcement agencies.

— ejecting the empty case, cocking the rifle and chambering a fresh round – there are a number of differences in the ways various actions operate and these features have a marked effect on how ammunition must be reloaded for them.

There are three basic types of autoloading actions: "straight blow-back", with a variant known as "delayed blow-back"; "recoil operated"; and "gas operated."

Blow-back actions are the oldest and most simple. They function by having the bolt held in contact with the barrel by a spring, thus the two are not locked together. When the gun fires, the bullet is driven down the barrel while the case is driven against the bolt face. The weight of the bolt and force of the recoil spring(s) and the internal pressure swelling the case against the chamber wall keep the case from moving backward until the bullet has exited the muzzle. Somewhere around this point, as chamber pressure begins to drop, the case begins to be "blown back" against the bolt, the inertial force given the bolt causing it to move rearward, cocking the rifle and ejecting the fired case. Tension in the compressed recoil spring then sends the bolt forward, stripping a fresh cartridge from the magazine and chambering it. This system works well with low-powered cartridges and is used in all 22 Long Rifle semiautos. It was used in only a relatively few center-fire rifles –namely in such U.S. made rifles as the obsolete Winchester 1905, 1907 and 1910 autoloading rifles and the Marlin and other carbines in 9mm and 45 ACP. See the handgun section on reloading these two cartridges.

The blow-back system is limited to straight-walled cases because a bottle neck case would likely have its neck pulled off or have gas come rushing around it as soon as the pressure seal was broken. Because of the necessity of equalling the forces of the forward-moving bullet with the proper amount of bolt weight and spring pressure, the limitations of the system are obvious. To fire a cartridge the equivalent of the 30-06, such a system would need a bolt that would weight several pounds and a very robust recoil spring. Thus, blow-back autoloaders are limited to cartridges developing little better than handgun velocities and pressures. The Winchester 351 and 401 rifles featured heavy bolts and recoil springs.

Not surprisingly, reloads for such guns must be kept very close to factory specifications. Lower-pressure loads will not function the action and high-pressure loads, even though the barrels can handle them, increase the velocity of the recoiling parts, battering them and causing serious damage to the rifle. Cast-bullet loads, both plain and gas-checked, work well if they are heavily crimped to provide proper burning of the powder. Slow-burning powders generally do not perform well in these rifles as they do not generate enough speed in the rearward motion of the bolt to make the action function reliably.

Recoil-operated actions represent an improvement over the blow-back in terms of the type and pressure of cartridge they can handle. In this system, the recoil of the rifle drives the operation. Recoil-operated systems keep the bolt and barrel locked together through part of the firing cycle using the barrel to add inertia. As the bullet travels forward, the barrel and bolt recoil as a unit. At about the midpoint of the operation, after the bullet has exited the barrel, the bolt unlocks and continues travelling backward, ejecting the empty case and cocking the hammer while the barrel moves forward to its original position. The bolt then strips a fresh round from the magazine chambering it as it comes forward.

This system was used in the Models 8 and 81 Remington in 25, 30, 32 and 35 Remington calibers and in the Johnson military and sporting autoloaders in 30-06, and the original Browning autoloading shotgun. The downside of this system is the amount of recoil experienced by the shooter, which is considerable, although the Johnson with its "delayed recoil" variant is on a par with the M-1. Because of the wearing action of the moving barrel, accuracy degrades over time. For this reason these rifles have become obsolete, though a number are still around, with refurbished Johnsons being sold by Miltech. Both blow-back and recoil-operated autoloaders have fairly generous chambers and require full-length case resizing. Not too surprisingly they are also rather rough on cases. Here again, the best functioning is with loadings close to factory specifications. Battering of internal parts will result from loads generating high pressures and high velocities!

Cast-bullet loads which operate at lower pressures than jacketed ones may develop higher velocities with lighter bullets and thus deliver higher energy levels to the recoiling parts, battering them. The best way to work up handloads for these two actions is to do so slowly, checking recoiling parts for any evidence of battering. The best loads are ones that will reliably cycle the action and no more.

Gas-operated rifles are by far the best, and most medium to high powered rifles made today use this system. The gas operated system features a locked bolt and non-moving barrel, much like the accurate and reliable bolt-action. They can thus fire very powerful cartridges. At some point on the barrel, forward of the chamber, a tiny hole is drilled through the barrel, tapping off a small amount of gas after the bullet passes that point. The gas is trapped in a small cylinder with a piston, much like that in an engine. The piston drives a rod which operates a camming lock on the bolt, which opens it after the bullet has exited the barrel. In some variants the gas is directed to the surface of the cam lock to unlock the bolt. As the bolt is driven back, the case is ejected and the hammer or striker is cocked and a spring drives the bolt forward stripping a fresh round from the magazine and chambering it. Most of today's high-powered autoloaders are gas operated. The advantages are a minimum of moving parts and an action that is comparatively gentle on cases.

The placement and size of the gas port is critical to reliable functioning because the amount and pressure of gas to be tapped must be enough to operate the rifle, but not so much as to cause damage through battering. Needless to say, the amount and type of powder used are also critical to this autoloader's functioning. Gas-operated autoloaders are therefore very ammunition sensitive and will work best with loadings duplicating factory or original military specifications. Cast bullets, generally, do not work well in gas-operated autoloaders. Relatively fast-burning powders such as IMR 4227 are about the only ones that will operate these actions reliably with cast bullets. Any cast bullets used in autoloading rifles are best cast of hard alloy, since soft-alloy bullets are often nicked and dented as they pass through the magazine and the rough handling they receive in the loading process, as they are slammed up feed ramps, will often cause them to catch and stick on something and jam the action. Because of the generous chamber proportions required to operate them reliably, cases fired in autoloaders almost always have to be full-length resized.

Ball powders tend to leave more fouling than some of the cleaner-burning flake powders. The performance of ball powders in terms of reliable functioning is good, so long as the gas port, piston and/or cam face is kept clean. For best functioning, the powders used in reloading should be close to those used in factory loadings. Cleaning of the gas system is necessary for reliable functioning. Cast bullets with reduced loads will not work. Generally the only cast-bullet loads that do work are those that are near the maximum pressure level. While these may operate the action reliably, they may often not deliver very good accuracy, and the accurate load may not operate the action. Reduced loads will not work reliably in any autoloader, with cartridges often getting jammed on the way out and chewed up in the process. Therefore, the range of loading options for autoloaders of any stripe is rather limited. There will usually be only a relative few loadings that will produce good accuracy and reliable functioning. Ammunition prepared for autoloaders should be given extra care to see that all tolerances are kept close to factory specifications. Exceeding overall length will jam rifles. Cases

too short and bullets too deep can have the same effect. In short, ammunition preparation for successful shooting of these guns requires extra care for best results.

TESTING AMMUNITION

Accuracy is, or should be, your first concern. An accuracy test can consist of nothing more than plunking a few cans at an unknown distance, but this won't tell you very much. The only meaningful test is firing from a solid rest at a known distance. This generally means getting to a target range with permanent bench installations, or setting up your own range if you live in a rural area or have access to a rural area with enough space and a safe backstop. The best kind of shooting bench is a permanent one, with solid legs at least 4"X 4" sunk below the frost line (4' in some areas) and anchored in concrete. The legs should be well braced. A light frame is built to true the top before the tops of the posts are cut. A heavy, solid top, 2" or more thick, prevents wobble and vibration. Few people have the place to construct such a bench and if they can find a shooting area must make do with what they can bring in.

Portable shooting benches can be home made or you can buy one of several on the market. The type that has a built-in seat is my recommendation, since with these, the weight of the shooter serves to hold the bench down. The top either has an attached forend rest for the rifle, or you can use a sand-bag rest on an adjustable base. These are better than simple sand bags which are softer and not shaped to fit a rifle. About the lowest level of support for reliable testing is a metal bipod or a crossed-stick "shooting sticks" (wooden bipod) rest for the rifle and a solid backrest against a tree or building to assure steady aim. With these measures, human error is, hopefully, reduced.

Testing should be done on a day with good light, no wind and moderate temperatures — 68 degrees F or higher. Calm

Testing ammunition should be done with a solid rest, firing at a known distance to determine accuracy.

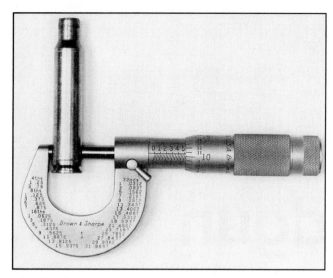

Checking a case for expansion beyond that produced by a factory load (along with stiff extraction) will give you the first indication of excessive pressures. It is a timely warning to tone things down.

conditions are generally found in the early morning or after 4PM. As indicated earlier, the place to start is with a test of factory ammunition for comparison. Really fine accuracy cannot be obtained without a telescopic sight, since this lets you see exactly where you are aiming. A spotting telescope of 20X or more gives you a clear view of a distant target. A distance of 100 yards is good enough to get a fair idea of the long range possibilities of your rifle and ammunition, though 200 yards is better. Most shooters use the standard of the "magic" inch at 100 yards as a benchmark by which all rifles are judged. Few hunting rifles will group this well, most will run groups of 2" to 3", all other things being equal. Factory ammunition groups are really the best for "head to head" purposes. Shoot seven to ten shot groups, taking your time to squeeze off the shots. If you intend to shoot cast bullets, be sure to clean the rifle of all copper fouling before shooting lead-alloy bullets, since they will strip lead on the copper fouling.

Shooting into turf will give you an idea of the ricochet potential of your ammunition if this is critical. You can usually hear the results if the bullets are not ricochet proof. For testing on game or varmint animals, there is not much in the way of practical substitutes for the real item. Ballistic gelatin is the standard by which determinations are made for bullet behavior in soft tissue. It is difficult to prepare and must be calibrated and used at the proper temperature.

Fortunately my fellow International Wound Ballistics Association member — Gus Coty Jr. – came up with a system that offers many of the useful outcomes of gelatin testing without the difficulty and mess.

Coty's reasonable substitute is half-gallon, paper, juice cartons filled with water, packed as closely as possible, in a row. For higher powered bullets, ten or more feet of cartons may be needed. Because bullets at times take a curving path, you may need three rows of cartons. By measuring the amount

of carton penetration at the distance you wish to shoot, gelatin penetration using ammunition of a disruptive sort can be calculated by dividing water-carton penetration by 1.5. This is with the caveat that exaggerated gelatin penetration figures will be achieved by high sectional-density, minimally-disruptive projectiles such as arrows, steel flechettes and so on. The lower the sectional density and the more disruptive a bullet's shape, the lower the impact speed at which carton penetration ÷ 1.5 will reliably equal gelatin penetration figures. The system works well for expanding ammunition at normal velocities below 3000 f.s.. Water-carton testing, therefore, yields a fair estimate of penetration and good evidence of expansion and fragmentation in tissue. This is at the sacrifice of any information regarding cavitation or fragment morphology.

Water-carton testing is thus a practical method of determining how well a particular type of ammunition behaves in your rifle at a range you choose. The results will serve to guide your decisions for choosing shots at a particular game animal or varmint.

A hollow-point round or soft-point round, for instance, is performing in the same manner as a solid if it fails to expand, thus such failure limits its effective range for varmint hunting. By the same token a HP round that fragments into many small pieces is not what you want for pot hunting, as it will be destructive of edible meat. The most effective killing round is one that provides good expansion without undo fragmentation and sufficient penetration to reach vital organs.

Packed wet snow is a fairly good tissue simulant and if there is enough of it, you can find your bullet somewhere along a long snow loaf. High-velocity pointed bullets are almost impossible to recover, but lower velocity cast bullets can usually be stopped within 20' to 30' of packed snow. These will generally be in almost pristine condition. This will give you a good opportunity to study your bullets for evidence of gas-cutting and of how well they take the rifling. Large or double sets of rifling marks on the front of a bullet indicates skidding or jumping the rifling — the bullet going straight for a fraction of an inch before taking the rifling and turning, as it should. Rifling marks that are higher on one side than the other indicate the bullet was not straight in the case, or the chamber of the gun is biased. Poor alignment of this sort, if there to a marked degree, degrades accuracy. Grease grooves that are heavily compressed and lack of lubricant will explain one cause of leading — not enough groove space or an inefficient lubricant. Alloys that are too soft will be evident in bullets that are overly compressed. Bullet recovery is for the seriously interested and those wanting answers to questions beginning with the word "why."

A final warning is to always check your cases after firing, particularly when you are testing loads that are on the high side of the pressure curve. Once you are there in the field, there is a great temptation to keep shooting. If there are signs of high pressure or excessive headspace, stop shooting. Don't risk your eyesight and rifle.

12

Even though
your favorite
handgun digests
all types of factory
ammo, you can
probably squeeze
out a little more
performance--and
save money, too.

Handgun Cartridge Reloading

LOADING HANDGUN AMMUNITION is perhaps a little easier than loading rifle cases, but the same level of care and attention must be given the task if good results are to be obtained. The place to begin is with once-fired, or better, new cases to work up a load. Once a load is tested and found to be satisfactory then quantity production can begin and some of the preliminary steps can be omitted.

Handguns come in three basic classes — revolvers, autoloaders (automatics) and single-shot, silhouette pistols. Each has its own characteristics and will be discussed accordingly. For all, there is the same general approach to loading for them, with special exceptions which will be given separate attention.

Good accuracy comes from consistency in the quality of your reloads as much as it does from the gun.

CASE INSPECTION

Even new and first-fired cases should be checked over for defects. Any with splits or serious defects in the case mouth that are not ironed out in the resizing die should be discarded.

Cases should be segregated by maker as determined by the head stamp. Even though they are the same caliber, cases of different manufacture have slight differences in wall thickness, and vent (flash-hole) size. Mixing brands will alter velocities and pressures and will open up shot-group size.

FULL-LENGTH RESIZING

This is not necessary for new cases, but must be done for fired cases. Handguns tend to have larger chambers than rifles so this is necessary. To resize a case it must first be given a coating of case lubricant to allow it to work easily in the sizing die. Sizing lubricant is a special oil or grease made for this purpose. It is best applied by saturating a clean, rubber-stamp inking pad with lubricant, then rolling the case over it, lightly coating the outside of the case. Too much lubricant on the outside of the case will cause dents in the walls which will flatten out on firing, but will stress the metal. On bottleneck cases the inside of the neck should be lubricated with a dry graphite, or similar non-oil, case-neck lubricant. Oil will run into the powder and ruin it. Neck lubricating keeps the neck from stretching unduly in the die. A light coating of lubricant is all that is needed. My own preference for case lube is Imperial Die-Sizing Wax. This is used primarily for reshaping cases from one caliber to another, but is clean, can be applied easily with the fingers and only the

barest coating in needed. Die wax rarely causes case dents. A minute amount on the case mouth does a good job of inside-neck lubricating. The prepared case is inserted in the shell holder, the operating lever is pulled, running the case completely into the die assuming the die is properly adjusted. Properly adjusted? Read the manual.

DECAPPING

The die should be adjusted so the decapping pin removes the old primer, which will drop out at the end of the insertion stroke. The resizing/decapping process should require a medium amount of force. If a lot of force is required to get the case in the die, you have not used enough lubricant.

INSPECTION GAUGING AND TRIMMING

The case is now removed from the shell holder for inspection. The case mouth should be smooth and perfectly round. "Trim to length" say the books, because a too-long case will enter the throat of the barrel and raise pressures as the bullet is swaged down then expands as it goes through this hour-glass waist you have created, before it enters the rifling. A quick check with a case-length gauge or measurement with your caliper tells you if the case is too long. Sometimes even new ones are. If the case is too long it goes in the trimmer, which is adjusted to cut the case to exact length. After trimming, the outside burr is removed and the inside is chamfered to give the bullet a smooth start if you are loading lead or even jacketed ammunition. This trimming/chamfering operation only needs to be done when cases get too long. Do not cut a knife edge on the case mouth, simply remove the burr. Cases that are too short cause problems in auto-loaders using rimless straight-walled cases such as the 45 ACP. (More on this later.)

INSIDE NECK EXPANDING

For bottleneck cartridges, the decapping pin is mounted in a rod with an expansion ball on it that stretches the case mouth large enough to accept a new bullet. This operation is completed on the up or removal stroke of the operating handle.

CASE-MOUTH EXPANDING

For straight-walled cases being loaded with cast, lead-alloy bullets, this step uses the second die in a three-die pistol set. Three-die sets do not expand the case mouth in the decapping stage. The case is placed in the shell holder and run into this expansion die which has a stepped or tapered expander plug which opens the case mouth for insertion of a soft, cast bullet. This mouth expansion is done before powder charging, to avoid handling cases full of powder and spilling them.

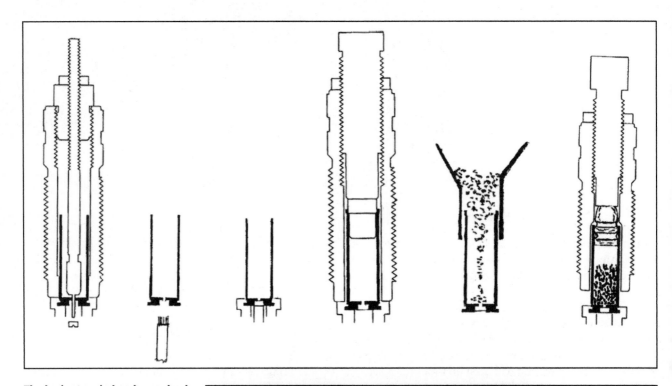

The basic steps in handgun reloading include (left to right): resizing and decapping, primer pocket cleaning, priming, case expanding, powder charging and bullet seating. Primer pockets should be cleaned after decapping. Note that primer-seating is done on the down stroke of the loading press lever.

Finished ammunition should be measured to see that the cartridge does not exceed the maximum overall length specified in the loading manual.

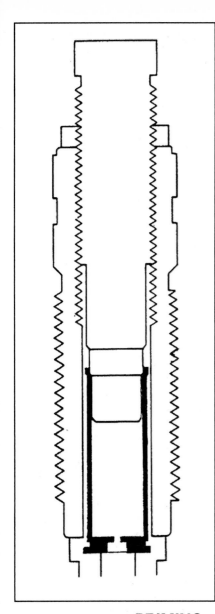

Powder charging through a funnel, with a weighed charge, is how you work up a load, with cases in a loading block.

Case-mouth expanding, or belling, prepares the case to accept a soft, lead-alloy bullet.

PRIMING

If the case is a fired one, the primer-pocket should be scraped free of ash with a screwdriver or cleaning tool. The case is now ready for priming. Place a primer in the priming punch sleeve. This comes up, in most cases, through the center of the shell holder. Place the case in the shell holder and pull the operating handle to press the case onto the primer punch. This will seat it in the case. Enough force should be applied to seat the primer fully, but not crush or flatten it. Difficulty in seating may be experienced if you are using crimped military brass. If so, this crimp must be removed before proceeding. After priming, the case should be checked to see that the primer is fully in the pocket. This is done by placing a steel straight-edge ruler across the case while holding it to the light to see if the primer sticks up above the case head. It should not. A high primer gives poor ignition or may not fire at all as the firing pin simply drives it into the pocket. The primed, inspected case now goes into the loading block.

POWDER CHARGING

The case is now ready for charging. When working up a load, always start with the beginning load listed in the data manuals. Increases in powder charges should be made by no more than half (.5) of a grain at a time and less than this for hot, fast burning powders. Load at least ten (10) test cartridges before going to a heavier charge. Powder charges are weighed precisely on a powder scale for working up loads. The easiest method is to pour a half cup or so of powder into a small container (I use a glass custard dish) and dip it into the scale pan with a small spoon. Plastic spoons are lighter and allow you to tap out the powder in small amounts most easily. This is the slowest part of the operation, and the most critical. The scale should be properly set up and checked for adjustment. Once the charge is weighed, the powder funnel goes on the case and the powder is poured in, with no spills of course.

The funnel is moved from case to case until every one in the loading block is filled. Make it a habit to check the powder level in all the cases in the loading block, examining them under good light, even though you are sure you did not double charge any of them. If the powder level in any case looks suspiciously high, weigh it again. The balance may be sticking on your scale or you may have accidentally shifted a weight. You'd be surprised at what can happen. Mistakes with pistol powders are more critical than with slower-burning rifle powders. They are more powerful. A little too much Bullseye can go a long way in wrecking your gun.

USE OF A POWDER MEASURE

Mechanical powder measures should never be used to work up loads, but are useful in making production loads. Precision depends to a great degree on consistency of pulling and returning the operating handle. After a powder measure is adjusted, check its accuracy, and yours, by dropping every fifth load into the scale pan for weighing. Accurate loads are within a tolerance of +/- one tenth (.1) of a grain. Always check cases loaded with a powder measure in the loading block. It is very easy to pull the handle twice on the same case. Since many, but not all, loads for handguns are nearly full-case loads a double charge will run over or fill the case to the point where a bullet can't be seated, but don't bet on it.

BULLET SEATING

This is the final step in the loading operation. Cases are placed in the shell holder. The bullet is placed in the case mouth as straight as possible, and the case is gently levered into the bullet-seating die. Proper die adjustment is necessary not to exceed the maximum overall length of the cartridge as listed in the loading manual. An overly long cartridge can press the bullet into the rifling and raise pressures in autoloaders, or jam them. In revolvers, they will jam the cylinder. The easiest way to avoid this problem is to make up a dummy cartridge. After the die is screwed into the press, you will want to adjust it so the case enters freely its full length. Gradually ease the cartridge in the die and check to see it does not pass the crimping shoulder, which turns over the case mouth. The next adjustment is to the stem of the bullet seater, which gradually drives the bullet deeper into the case.

Semi-wadcutter bullets are among the best cast revolver bullets in terms of both accuracy and killing power, which makes them suitable for both target shooting and hunting.

When the correct overall length is reached, tighten the seater adjustment. Keep the dummy for easy readjustment, after loading longer or shorter bullets. You may want to make a dummy for every different-length bullet you load to facilitate easy readjustment. Once the die is adjusted, bullet seating is simply a matter of repetition.

Most dies have a built-in crimping shoulder to turn the case mouth over into a cannelure (groove) in the bullet. This is necessary for high-powered rifle ammunition, particularly if it is jarred by recoil while being fed through tubular magazines and even some box magazines. Crimping is necessary on nearly all handgun bullets. Magnum handgun cases require heavy crimping to keep bullets from being jarred loose by recoil. No rimless automatic cartridge such as the .45 ACP should be crimped since it headspaces on the case mouth and a crimp will allow the case to enter too deeply and erratic ignition will result.

"Easy does it is" the rule for all steps. Ramming and jerking leads to damaged cases, mashed bullets, flattened primers and broken decapping pins.

The final, final step is to wipe off any case lubricant that may be on the case and inspect the finished cartridge with a final check for overall length. Oil left on cases will cause excessive back-thrust and batter your gun. If all dies are properly adjusted and firmly in place, there should be no difference from one cartridge to the next. Place the loaded rounds in a cartridge box and mark them accordingly.

Clean-up is always a good idea. Powder should always be returned to the original container, even from a powder measure. Powder in open containers will lose volatiles and absorb moisture. Primers can absorb moisture and magnum and standard primers can be confused if not put back in their respective containers. Most of all there is always the chance of confusion regarding what powder you were using when you start the next time.

SELECTING A LOAD

Many people start with factory duplication loads, which, if you have already been shooting them, is a convenient place to start without varying any component. Generally, though, the best accuracy in your handgun will be something you work up on your own. This may take some doing even though many loading manuals list "accuracy loads." If you read the fine print you will see this applies to one particular test gun. If yours is a different make, this one may not shoot best for you, but it is perhaps the best powder/bullet combination to start with. Loading data is presented as starting loads and maximum loads with a middle ground in between. It is generally in this middle ground where the most accurate loading will be found. Rarely is the hottest, highest pressure load the straightest shooter. Maximum loads, especially with jacketed bullets, shorten both case and barrel life. By working for accuracy, you start by getting a clear idea of just how well your handgun will shoot. With this as a starting point, you then have a standard by which other loads can be judged.

For the most part, you will probably not have need for more than three or four different loadings, if that many. On the bottom end are short-range practice loads. These are usually cast bullets driven at modest velocities of around 550-750 fps. These offer good, cheap recreation and training without the expense, wear, noise and recoil of full-bore loads. They can be used for short range target shooting where noise may be a problem. Hunting loads are really for handguns of the 38 Special class and up. These are near maximum pressure and velocity loadings with jacketed expanding bullets. You would do best to work up the most accurate load you can from the selection of hunting bullets available.

WORKING UP A LOAD

Working up a load means not merely careful loading of ammunition, but targeting it and keeping records of the results. It also involves case inspection, looking for any signs of excessive headspace or pressures. I use a simple notebook for records. I list these under the name of the gun and its caliber. Individual loads are listed under the bullet, indicating whether it is cast or jacketed, the weight, diameter and lubrication type. Next the powder type and charge are listed. Following this is a notation on the make of case and primer and type. Finally, is a section for "remarks." This includes a summary of the performance of this particular load, especially its accuracy. Ten-shot groups are the accuracy test standard, although it has been demonstrated that seven-shot groups work just as well. Other remarks include the test range, the temperature, wind direction and velocity and light conditions. Also noted are any indications of pressure problems. These are underlined as a warning for future reference.

LOADING FOR AUTOLOADERS

Since the 1980's autoloaders in all calibers and types have become very popular, owing mainly to the change-over by nearly all of this country's police departments to this type of handgun for police work. While all autoloaders rely on the force of the explosion in the cartridge to function the action – ejecting the empty case, cocking the pistol and chambering a fresh round – there are a number of differences in the ways various actions operate and these features have a marked effect on how ammunition must be reloaded for them.

There are three basic types of autoloading actions, "straight blow-back", with a variant known as "delayed blow-back, "recoil operated" and "gas operated."

Blow-back actions are the most simple. They function by having the slide held in contact with the barrel by a spring, thus the two are not locked together. When the gun fires, the bullet is driven down the barrel while the case is driven against the face of the slide. The weight of the slide, the force of the recoil spring(s) and the internal pressure swelling the case against the chamber wall keep the case from moving backward until the bullet has exited the muzzle. Somewhere around this point, as chamber pressure begins to drop, the case begins to be "blown back" against the slide, the inertial force given the slide causing it to move rearward, cocking the

pistol and ejecting the fired case. Tension in the compressed recoil spring then sends the slide forward, stripping a fresh cartridge from the magazine and chambering it. This system works well with low-powered handgun cartridges and is used in all 22 long rifle, 25 ACP, 32 ACP, 380 ACP autoloaders and the 9mm Makarov autoloading pistol. The system is limited to straight-walled, semi-rimmed cases because a bottle neck case would likely have its neck pulled off or have gas come rushing around it as soon as the pressure seal was broken. Because of the necessity of equalling the forces of the forward-moving bullet with the proper amount of slide weight and spring pressure, the limitations of the system are obvious. Thus, blow-back autoloaders are limited to cartridges developing low velocities and pressures.

Not surprisingly, reloads for such guns must be kept very close to factory specifications. Lower-pressure loads will not operate the action and high-pressure loads, even though the barrels can handle them, increases the velocity of the recoiling parts, battering them, causing serious damage to the handgun. Cast-bullet loads work well if they are crimped to provide proper burning of the powder. Slow-burning powders will not generate enough speed in the rearward motion of the slide to operate the action reliably. Taper-crimping as opposed to roll or "turn over" crimping is recommended for best functioning.

Recoil-operated actions represent an improvement over the blow-back in terms of the type and pressure of cartridge they can handle. In this system, the recoil of the pistol drives the operation. Recoil operated systems are generally designed to keep the slide or bolt and barrel locked together through part of the firing cycle. Some use a toggle-link system as in the Luger, or a roller lock as in the Czech M52 to delay, mechanically, the opening of the breech until the bullet has exited the barrel. As the bullet travels forward, the barrel and slide recoil as a unit. At about the midpoint of the operation, after the bullet has exited the barrel, the action unlocks and the slide continues travelling backward, ejecting the empty case and cocking the hammer while the barrel moves forward to its original position. The slide then strips a fresh round from the magazine chambering it as it comes forward.

This system is used in virtually all the high-powered autoloading pistols using the 9mm Luger (Parabellum) cartridge, 38 Super Auto, 45 ACP and similar cartridges adopted to military and police use. Battering of internal parts will result from loads generating excessive pressures and velocities!

Cast-bullet loads which operate at lower pressures than jacketed ones may develop higher velocities and thus deliver higher energy levels to the recoiling parts, battering them. The best way to work up handloads for autoloaders is to do so slowly, checking recoiling parts for any evidence of battering. The best loads are ones that will reliably cycle the action and no more.

(Text continued on page 142)

STEP-BY-STEP RELOADING HANDGUN CARTRIDGES

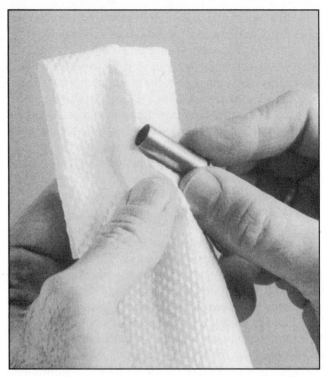

Step 1 - Clean and Inspect: It's a good idea to wipe cases clean before beginning to reload them. This also allows you to inspect them for any split necks, cracks, etc. Discard those that are damaged.

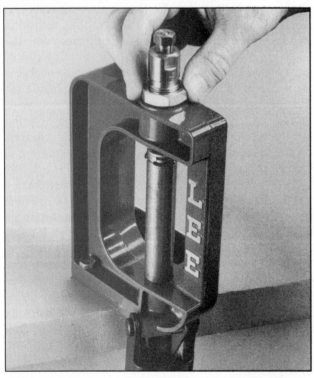

Step 4 - Adjusting the Sizer Die: Raise the ram to the top of its travel and screw the sizing die in until it just touches the shellholder. Now, slightly lower the ram and screw in the die an additional 1/4-turn. Tighten the lock nut.

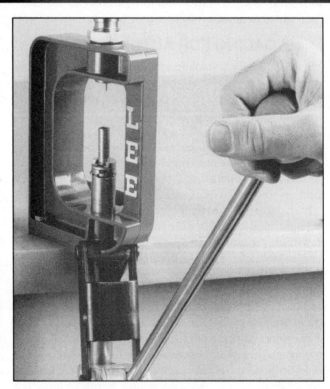

Step 5 - Case Resizing: Place a lubed case in the shellholder and raise the ram, guiding the case as it enters the sizing die. This step also knocks out the fired primer. Raise the press handle and remove the case.

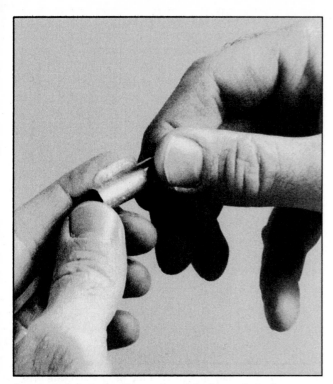

Step 2 - Lubricate the Cases: Case lube is needed when not using a carbide resizing die. Spread just a light film on each case with the fingers.

Step 3 - Installing the Shellholder: Choose the proper shellholder for the round you are loading. They usually come with the die sets. Raise the ram slightly to snap the shellholder into place with a twisting motion. Position it with the open side out to the left.

Step 6 - Chamfer and Deburr: To ease bullet entry, lightly chamfer the mouth of the case by inserting the pointed end of the chamfering/deburring tool into the case mouth and gently twisting it.

Step 7 - Case Mouth Expansion: After installing and properly adjusting the expander die, insert a case and run it into the die to bell the case mouth for easy insertion of a new bullet. Adjust the die just enough to allow easy bullet entry.

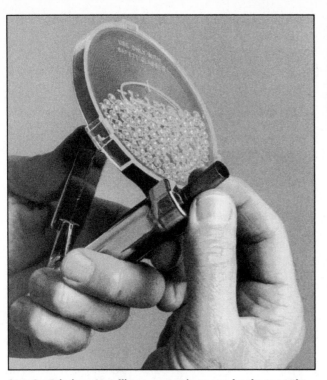

Step 8 - Priming: Installing a new primer can be done on the press or with a hand-held Auto Prime tool. After filling the primer tray, slip a deprimed case into the shellholder and press the lever to push a primer into the primer pocket. Follow the instructions that come with each tool.

Step 9 - Powder Charging (A): Find the proper and safe load for your cartridge in a loading manual or from another reliable source, then weigh each charge on your powder scale. This is the safest method, although a bit slow, and is best for accuracy and maximum loads.

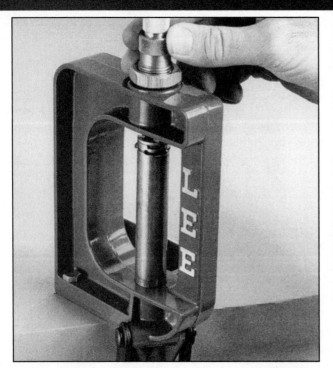

Step 12 - Bullet Seating (A): To install the bullet-seating die, place a case in the shellholder and raise the ram to the top of the stroke. Screw in the seater die until you feel it touch the case mouth. If no crimp is desired, back the die out 1/2-turn. If you want a crimp, turn it in 1/4-turn.

Step 13 - Bullet Seating (B): The knurled adjusting screw controls the bullet seating depth. Usually, seating to the same depth as a factory round works well. If you want a crimp, be sure the bullet cannelure is almost completely inside the case mouth. Screw the die in just enough to apply a good crimp. A little trial and error work is needed here.

Step 10 - Powder Charging (B): Lee's expander die allows the powder charge to be dumped from the scale pan into the primed case through the die. Cases can also be set into a loading block for powder charging.

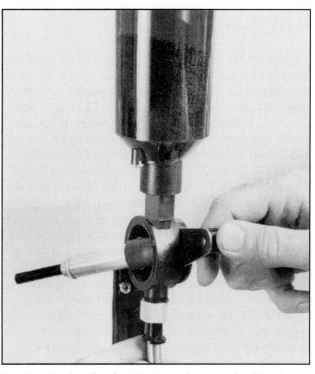

Step 11 - Powder Charging (C): Once the proper load has been found, you can dispense powder directly into the case with the powder measure. It will throw a precise, uniform charge with each turn of the handle. Check-weigh every fifth or tenth charge to be sure it is correct.

Step 14 - Bullet Seating (C): To seat a bullet, place one in the case mouth and guide it into the seating die as straight as possible. If the bullet needs to be deeper, screw in the seater plug a little bit and run the case back into the die. It may take a few tries to get the exact depth required.

Step 15 - The Loaded Round: That's all there is to loading a handgun cartridge. A final wipe with a clean cloth and the ammunition is ready to be fired. Don't forget to mark the ammo box with your load data so you can repeat the load.

(Text continued from page 137)

Generally the only cast-bullet loads that do work are those that are near the maximum pressure level. While these may operate the action reliably, they may often not deliver very good accuracy, and the accurate load may not operate the action. Reduced loads will not work reliably in any autoloader, with cartridges often getting jammed on the way out and chewed up in the process. Therefore, the range of loading options for autoloaders of any stripe is rather limited. There will usually be only a relative few loadings that will produce good accuracy and reliable functioning. Ammunition prepared for autoloaders should be given extra care to see that all tolerances are kept close to factory specifications. Exceeding overall length will jam actions. Cases too short and bullets seated too deep can have the same effect. In short, ammunition preparation for successful shooting of these guns requires extra care for best results.

Full-length resizing is almost always necessary with cartridges used in autoloaders since the chambers are on the large size to permit reliable feeding even when they are dirty with fouling.

Gas-operated autoloading pistols are uncommon and limited to expensive models that fire very powerful magnum cartridges that enter the lower region of rifle velocities. The gas-operated system features a locked bolt and non-moving barrel, much like gas-operated rifles, and are based on scaled-down rife actions. They can thus fire very powerful cartridges. At some point on the barrel, forward of the chamber, a tiny hole is drilled through the barrel, tapping off a small amount of gas, after the bullet passes that point. The gas is trapped in a small cylinder with a piston, much like that in an engine. The piston drives a rod which operates a camming lock on the bolt, which opens it after the bullet has exited the barrel. In some variants the gas is directed to the surface of the cam lock to unlock the bolt. As the bolt is driven back, the case is ejected and the hammer or striker is cocked and a spring drives the bolt forward stripping a fresh round from the magazine and chambering it.

The placement of the gas port is critical to reliable functioning because the amount and pressure of gas to be tapped must be enough to operate the pistol, but not so much as to cause damage through battering. Needless to say, the amount and type of powder used are also critical to this autoloader's functioning. Gas-operated autoloaders are very ammunition sensitive and will work best with loadings duplicating factory specifications. Cast bullets, generally, do not work well in gas-operated autoloaders. Fast-burning powders such as IMR 4227, Herco, Unique, 2400, H110 and AA1680 are about the only ones that will function gas-operated actions reliably.

Any cast bullets used in autoloading pistols are best cast of hard alloy. Soft-alloy bullets are often nicked and dented by the rough handling they receive in the loading process, as they are slammed up feed ramps. This will often cause them to catch and stick on something and jam the action.

Feed-ramp polishing may often be necessary when using cast loads with any autoloader to avoid jams. Magazine lips that are bent or sprung are a frequent cause of jamming in autoloading pistols and should be checked for wear or damage if this problem occurs.

LOADING FOR REVOLVERS

Modern revolvers are all of the solid frame type. The few exceptions are replicas of 19th century top-break and open-top revolvers and those old models that are still around that use this system. These guns are of a weaker design than the solid frame type and should be used only with low-pressure "starting loads" listed in the manuals, and then only if they are in good, tight condition.

Unlike the autoloader, with its box magazine and single-chambered barrel, the revolver features a cylinder with multiple chambers. The mechanism in a revolver turns these chambers, via a "hand" or "pawl" that aligns each with the barrel. The relationship between this rotation and the firing cycle is referred to as "timing." In revolvers where the timing is off because of wear and battering by too many heavy loads, this alignment between the chamber and the barrel is less than perfect, and poor accuracy, even badly shaved bullets, is the result. To an extent this can be corrected by a competent gunsmith. The alignment, however, is never really perfect which is one reason why revolvers rarely shoot as straight as autoloaders. The revolver has a second problem — the gap between the cylinder and the barrel. The bullet must jump this gap before entering the forcing cone at the rear of the barrel. There has been much written about gas loss in the process, but the final analysis is that it isn't that much in terms of lowering bullet performance. The jump is most detrimental to accuracy because of the aforementioned alignment problems and the fact that in making this jump, the bullet gains a fair amount of speed before it hits the rifling and may evidence "skid" marks as it moves straight for a fraction of an inch before beginning to turn.

The throat of the revolver cylinder guides, but does not really support, the bullet since it is larger than the bore diameter. Sizing revolver bullets is therefore something of a guessing game. The best course of action is to stick with factory diameters to start with and base your success on reloading with factory ammunition as the standard and then start experimenting after slugging your bore. The hardness of cast revolver bullets can have a decided effect on their accuracy. A fairly hard alloy (Lyman #2) generally works best, but softer alloys may be necessary to achieve proper upset to avoid leading in some revolvers. Leading can be a serious problem in some guns and these may require a hollow base bullet to obturate in the cylinder throat to avoid hot gas blowing by and melting the surface of the bullet. Before going to a hollow-base mould it is best to experiment with different lubricants and alloys to see if changes in these will eliminate the problem. Different styles of bullets with larger, deeper lubricant grooves to hold more lubricant may be

The Colt Gold Cup National Match in 45 ACP is a fine example of a recoil-operated auto-loading pistol.

The 380 ACP SIG-Super Model P230 is a typical small-frame blowback autoloading pistol.

The Desert Eagle from IMI, (imported by Magnum Research) is probably the most powerful autoloader around and the only one currentvly made that uses a gas-operated recoil system.

the answer. Failing that, buy some commercially-made hollow base bullets or factory loads with hollow-base bullets (if available) before getting another mould. Gas checks and wax wads may come to the rescue in some cases as will half-jacketed bullets which eliminate leading entirely, although they will wear the barrel faster.

Because they are loaded manually, revolvers work well with cast bullets both plain and gas-checked. Owing to the vibration they receive with each discharge, revolver cartridges should be crimped to keep the bullets from being shaken out of their cases.

Sizing depends on the size of the chamber and pressure of the load, but in most instances, revolver cases should be full-length resized for ease in loading the gun.

One major advantage of revolvers over autoloaders is their ability to handle low-pressure/low-velocity loadings. These will afford you economical practice with minimal wear and tear on your revolver. For the same reason (manual operation) revolvers can take a far greater range of bullets in terms of weight and length. Bullets with a long bearing surface generally align better and produce the best accuracy. While revolvers will function only with fast-burning pistol powders the range of loading possibilities surpasses that of the autoloader.

METALLIC SILHOUETTE PISTOLS

These handguns are a relatively recent arrival on the shooting scene and their use is primarily for long-range target shooting and varmint hunting. They are, for the most part, based on rifle actions cut down to handgun size. They chamber rifle cartridges and powerfully-loaded handgun cartridges. Because of their solidly built actions and longer barrels (10"- 16") they generate velocities and pressures in the rifle class. These guns might best be called "hand rifles." Owing to their light weight, most cannot use maximum rifle loadings and even with more modest pressures and velocities the muzzle blast and recoil is formidable. Most loading manuals contain special loading data for these guns. To use any of these loadings in a standard revolver or autoloader would wreck it in short order. Loading procedures for metallic silhouette guns follow rifle instructions. One of the more popular of these guns is the Thompson/Center Contender. The Contender is a single-shot design with a barrel that is easily removed. This allows the use of a number of barrels each in a different caliber. Contenders can thus shoot anything from the 22 Long Rifle on up to the 45-70. which, if you want to get a real "kick" out of handgun shooting, will certainly deliver the goods.

TESTING AMMUNITION

Accuracy is, or should be, your first concern. An accuracy test can consist of nothing more than plunking a few cans at an unknown distance, but this won't tell you very much. The only meaningful test is firing from a solid rest at a known distance. With handguns a test range doesn't really need much more than 50 yards, since this is about the maximum accurate range of most of them and 50 to 75 feet to is the standard distance. Accuracy testing requires a solid bench installation with a sand bag or adjustable rest. If you live in a rural area or have access to a range with benches you are set. The best practical shooting bench outside of a range is a portable model that can be home made or you can buy one of several on the market. The type that has a built-in seat is my recommendation, since with these, the weight of the shooter serves to hold the bench down. The top either has an attached forend rest for a rifle which may

Although made of modern steel, this top-break replica of the S&W Schofield revolver by Navy Arms probably should not be fired with maximum-pressure loads.

The **Thompson/Center Contender** (left) and **Magnum Research Lone Eagle** (above) represent the ultimate in handgun power, range, recoil and noise in calibers such as 45-70, 30-06 and 444 Marlin.

or may not be handy. A flat-top bench where you can use a sand-bag or adjustable rest will always work.

Testing should be done on a day with good light, no wind and moderate temperatures — 68 degrees F or higher. Calm conditions are generally found in the early morning or after 4PM. As indicated earlier, the place to start is to shoot some factory ammunition for comparison. A distance of 50 yards is good enough to get a fair idea of the long-range possibilities of your handgun and ammunition if you plan to use it for hunting. Only the more powerful calibers — 357 Magnum and up — have much use in the hunting field.

For most handguns a 2" to 3" group at 50' is about as good as you will get. Fine target guns will shoot under an inch at this range. Metallic silhouette guns are judged and tested more by rife standards. Factory ammunition groups are really the best for "head to head" purposes. Shoot seven to ten-shot groups, taking your time to squeeze off the shots. If you intend to shoot both cast and jacketed bullets, be sure to clean the barrel of all copper fouling before shooting lead-alloy bullets, since they will strip lead on the copper fouling.

Shooting into turf will give you an idea of the ricochet potential of your ammunition if this is critical. You can usually hear the results if the bullets are not ricochet proof. Most handgun bullets ricochet very readily, even hollow-points. For testing on game or varmint animals, there is not much in the way of practical substitutes for the real item. Ballistic gelatin is the standard by which such determinations are made, but it is difficult to prepare and must be calibrated and used at the proper temperature.

One tissue substitute of a cheap and easy sort is newspaper, soaked overnight to get it fully saturated. The wet paper is then put in a cardboard carton for shooting into. This is far heavier and more resistant than muscle tissue, but will give you an idea of bullet behavior. Probably closest to muscle tissue are paper milk or juice cartons filled with water. These can be lined up giving you an idea of expansion from the holes left behind. Fired bullets can usually be recovered. For details see the bullet-testing section in the rifle chapter.

Packed wet snow is a fairly good tissue simulant and if there is enough of it, you can find your bullet somewhere along a long snow loaf. High-velocity bullets are more difficult to recover, but lower velocity cast bullets can usually be stopped within 5' to 10' of packed snow. These will generally be in almost pristine condition. This will give you a good opportunity to study your cast bullets for evidence of gas-cutting and of how well they take the rifling, Large or double sets of rifling marks on the front of a bullet indicates skidding or jumping the rifling – the bullet going straight for a fraction of an inch before taking the rifling and turning, as it should. Rifling marks that are higher on one side than the other indicate the bullet was not straight in the case or were fired in a revolver with the cylinder slightly out of alignment. Grease grooves that are heavily compressed and lack lubricant will explain one cause of leading — not enough groove space and an inefficient lubricant or overly soft alloy. Bullet recovery is for the seriously interested and those wanting answers to questions beginning with the word "why."

A final warning is to always check your cases after firing, particularly when you are testing loads that are on the high side of the pressure curve. Once you are there in the field, there is a great temptation to keep shooting. If there are signs of high pressure or excessive headspace, stop shooting. Don't risk your eyesight and handgun.

Creating homemade scattergun fodder is not the same as metallic cartridge reloading. It requires different tools, components and knowledge.

Shotshell Ammunition Reloading

OF THE THREE basic types of ammunition, shotgun ammunition is perhaps the easiest to load, once you get the hang of it. Nevertheless, the same level of care and attention must be given the task if good results are to be obtained. The place to begin is with once-fired or, better, new cases to work up a load. Once a load is tested and found to be satisfactory then quantity production can begin.

MODERN AND OBSOLETE SHOTSHELLS

Modern shotshell cases are made of plastic for the most part, with a metal head. although the traditional paper shell is still offered by a few manufacturers.. All-plastic shells come and go and are reloadable until the heads get chewed up. Since shotshells operate at far lower pressures than rifle and most handgun ammunition, they are less robust in construction. Shotshells come in six sizes or gauges. The smallest is the 410, which is actually .410" in diameter or 410 caliber. The larger sizes are listed by gauge – an old system that determined a "gauge size" by the number of lead balls of that diameter to weigh a pound. The next size up is 28 gauge, then 20 gauge, 16 gauge, 12 gauge and finally 10 gauge. In the bad old days of market hunting, the now obsolete 8 gauge, 4 gauge and even 3 gauge guns

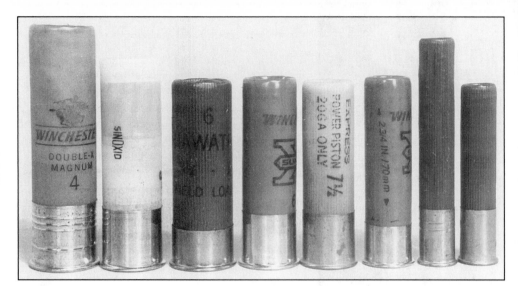

Modern shotshells, from left: 10-gauge 3-1/2-inch magnum, 12-gauge 3-inch, 12-gauge 2-3/4-inch, 16-gauge 2-3/4-inch, 20-gauge 2-3/4-inch, 28-gauge 2-3/4-inch, and .410 bore 3- and 2-1/2-inch.

Obsolete shotshells L. To R. 10 gauge 2-7/8". This one is for older guns. NEVER put a 3" shell in an old 2 7/8" gun! 12 gauge brass shell, early 12 gauge rolled crimp plastic shell, original 12 gauge high-brass shell, 12 gauge rolled-crimp paper shell.

Table 1. SHOTSHELL LENGTH

Ammo	Shell Length (ins.)
10 GAUGE	2-7/8" (obsolete) and 3-1/2"
12 GAUGE	2-3/4", 3" and 3-1/2"
16 GAUGE	2-9/16" (obsolete) and 2-3/4"
20 GAUGE	2-3/4" and 3"
28 GAUGE	2-3/4"
410 BORE	2 -/2" and 3"

TABLE 2. SHOTGUN CHOKE DENSITY

CHOKE DESIGNATION AMERICAN (EUROPEAN)	PELLET PERCENTAGE, 30" CIRCLE RANGE, 40 YARDS
Cylinder	40%
Skeet	45%
Improved cylinder (1/4 choke)	50%
Skeet No. 2 (3/8 choke)	55%
Modified	60%
Improved Modified (3/4 choke)	65%
Full Choke	70%
Extra Full	75%

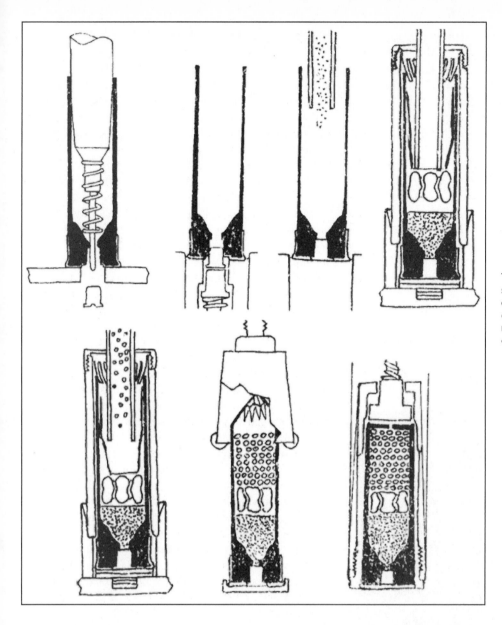

There are seven steps in shot-shell reloading: resizing and decapping, priming, powder charging, wad seating, shot metering, crimp starting and crimp finishing.

were used; the latter two were mounted like small cannons on boats for taking waterfowl.

As there are old guns still around and those of foreign extraction you may encounter odd gauges such as 14, 24, and 32. Ammunition is not generally available, but some custom makers are fabricating all sorts of interesting things including pinfire shells. Check the internet; it's full of surprises.

Early shells were made entirely of brass. Though "obsolete," new-made shells of brass, aluminum, zinc and steel are around. Loading these requires roll type crimping or a glue based crimp. Those with Berdan primers are reloadable only with the proper primers and decapping equipment. All-metal shells are not well adapted to autoloaders. Dealing with the above is "advanced" reloading.

At one time 9mm shotshells were made by Winchester along with a single barreled gun for shooting rats and the like. These are still loaded by Fiocchi and Bernadelli makes a semi-auto shotgun to shoot them. It is called a "garden gun" and is for short range pest shooting. As these are rim-fire, they are not reloadable.

Modern shotshells, in addition to the standard six gauges, are available in different lengths. Since 1933, 410 shotguns have been almost universally available to take the 3" shell which is ballistically superior to the old 2 1/2" shell. One exception is the Winchester 9410 lever gun. The 3" shell should NEVER be loaded in a gun chambered for the 2 1/2" shell. This rule applies to ALL gauges. To do so will result in serious pressure jumps which can wreck your gun and your face. The shorter-length shell can always be used in the longer chamber, but never the reverse. The big problem with this potential mismatching of length is that the longer shells will chamber in guns intended for the shorter-length load. This is because shotgun chambers are made long, allowing space for the opening up of the crimp in the case mouth. A 3 1/2" 10 gauge shell measures 3" unfired and 3 1/2" fired, ditto the 3 1/2" 12 gauge magnum. If you have an old gun or one of foreign make which is not marked on the barrel regarding the length of shell it is chambered for, take it to a competent gunsmith for examination.

Foreign shotguns may be chambered for shells of different lengths. Old guns should be regarded with suspicion unless the shell-length is clearly marked or can otherwise be identified. If length is the only problem, modern shells may be cut back to the proper length. Old guns should also be regarded as suspect if they cannot be identified as being safe for use with modern smokeless powder. Guns with "Damascus" barrels – identifiable by the "tiger stripe" pattern etched into the metal – are positively dangerous to shoot with any smokeless load. Because of weakening through internal corrosion over the years, loads with black powder or its substitutes should be approached with caution. If you elect to "re-proof" such a gun, secure it to an old tire and fire it from a distance from behind a suitable barrier. In the black powder era, three proof loads were tested for a gun to pass. Here again, we are in the world of "advanced" reloading.

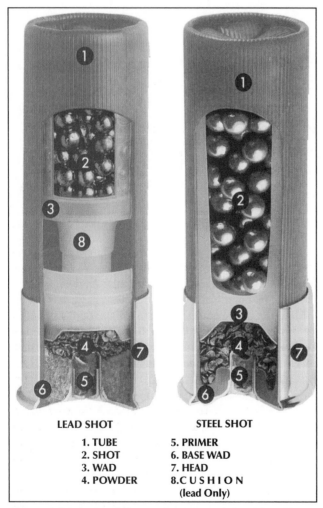

LEAD SHOT   **STEEL SHOT**

1. TUBE   5. PRIMER
2. SHOT   6. BASE WAD
3. WAD   7. HEAD
4. POWDER   8. C U S H I O N
                   (lead Only)

There are important differences between steel and lead shotshell components. Always use the proper components.

CASE INSPECTION AND STORAGE

As with rifle and handgun cartridges, shotshells should be inspected for defects. Those that are badly worn around the mouth, have splits in the case walls or heads, or leaks around the primers should be discarded. Paper shotshells are perhaps the most vulnerable of all. The bodies absorb moisture which can also enter the seam around the primer. Moisture-swollen shells will not chamber. Before buying, if the shells can't be tested, try chambering the more suspect ones, or check them with a ring gauge. Study exteriors for bleaching or water discoloration. Modern plastic shells don't have this problem, but in an economy move many are no longer made with brass heads. The steel heads are given a thin brass plate which will corrode quickly. The steel beneath will corrode even more quickly if exposed to pollutants. Old plastic shells that have been crimped for a long time tend to hold that crimp and reload poorly unless ironed out with a warming tool made for this purpose or a piece of metal rod or pipe the proper diameter heated in boiling water.

Shot shells come in a wide array of colors. There is a good reason for this – so you won't mix them up. Successful reloading depends on fitting all the components together correctly within the shell. There is a considerable difference in the inside capacities of various shells owing to the thickness of the base wad at the head of the shell. Matching loads to the particular brand and type of shell is critical to successful reloading. If the shotcup/wad is not used with the matching shell, it may be too long or too short for the shell to crimp properly. Therefore, different companies make their shells of certain colors to identify the make and further color code these shells by gauge so they are not mixed up. A 20 gauge shell accidentally dropped in a 12 gauge gun barrel will stop about where the choke is. If a 12 gauge shell is then fired, about six inches of the barrel is blown off. This has happened and that is why all modern American-made 20 gauge shells are some shade of yellow and all 12 gauge ones are other colors. Winchester uses red for all its shells except 20 gauge. Most Remington shells are green, 20 gauge excepted. Federal shells, including their paper-tube 12 gauge shell, are maroon, with the exception of the 10 gauge which is brown. The all-plastic Activ 12 gauge shell, which has no brass on it, but an internal steel reinforcing washer, is red. Fiocchi shells, from Italy, may be purple, blue, red, orange or brown. Within the various makes you will find shells with different base wads which thus require different shot cups. That is why critical inspection and storage are needed. If you are in doubt, you will want to consult a good shotshell reloading manual, such as the one put out by Lyman, which has a great many of these shells pictured in color, life size. If in doubt about the proper shot cup, sacrifice a shell by cutting it down the middle and comparing the sectioned shell with these illustrations. The height of the brass on the outside of the head may or may not indicate a base wad of a different height, but don't count on it. "Never mix components" is a good rule to follow.

SHOTSHELL PRIMERS

Shotshell primers, while they are all the same size, do have different burning characteristics. This will radically affect pressures. The substitution of one primer for another can raise pressures as much as 2000 psi with all other components being equal. This is why when working up loads, no substitution should be made for any component listed in a loading manual. If you have several brands of primers on hand, do not have more than one box open at a time so they don't get mixed up. Primers should be seated flush with the case head. High primers can be detonated accidentally in certain guns with disastrous results. Decapping live primers is not a good idea. Either snap them in the gun or discard the shell.

SHOTSHELL WADS

Old-style brass and paper shotshells used cylinder-shaped wads of cardboard, felt and similar fibers to serve as spacers between the powder and the charge of shot. This system was used for over a hundred years. It had a serious drawback — the wads did not obturate the shell or the bore of the gun very well and hot powder gas leaked around their edges and melted and otherwise distorted the pellets in the shot charge. Things improved in the 1940's with the addition of a cup wad over the powder to act as a gas seal. In the early 1960's a further improvement was made with a plastic wrap being placed around the shot charge to keep it from being distorted by direct contact with the barrel. Modern shotshells contain a single plastic wad with a cup-shaped base that goes over the powder and expands to obturate the bore. Above this is a cushioning section that compresses on firing to start the shot charge off more gently. At the top is a cup that holds the charge of shot. The sides are cut into several "petals" which open as soon as the wad exits the barrel. Unlike in the "old days" when loads were assembled by adding card or fiber wads of varying thickness to get the contents of the shell to stack up to the proper height for proper crimping of the case mouth, modern wads with shotcups are designed to hold a certain amount of shot; thus low volume wads with shallow shotcups are used for light field and target loads, while high-volume wads are used for heavy loads for water-fowl shooting. Attempting to over or underload these cups gives poor results when you crimp them. Components should be properly matched to the shells for which they are intended and not used in other shells. There are some instances of crossovers of components, but not for the beginner.

SIZES AND TYPES OF SHOT

Most shotgun shot is made of lead hardened with antimony. So-called "premium" shot is made of a harder alloy to keep it from deforming in the firing process. This is a good investment since deformed shot makes open or irregular patterns. This in turn means missed or crippled game. Sometimes hard shot is given a copper plating to make it

Shotcup/wads are designed for particular loads in particular shells. These wads hold 7/8 oz of No. 7, 7½, 8 or 9 shot. They are intended for use in the compression formed plastic shells and are for target shooting.

look attractive. Whether this makes it shoot any better or not depends on your powers of imagination.

Steel shot was introduced in the 1970's after the U.S. Fish and Wildlife Service concluded that bottom-feeding waterfowl were succumbing to lead poisoning from lead ingested and broken down in the bird's gizzards. USFWS placed a ban on lead shot for water-fowl hunting, and thus steel shot was born. Steel shot has a number of drawbacks, the least of which is its light weight. Thus, larger size shot must be loaded in greater volume to get the same weight equivalent as the old lead-shot loads. While the hardness of the shot makes it less subject to deformation than lead shot, it also means that steel shot will ruin a standard shotgun barrel and should never be fired in one. To do so will likely put a ring in the barrel and destroy the choke. Steel shot must be used in special hard-steel barrels. This generally means a barrel stamped: "For Steel Shot."

Bismuth-tin shot is more expensive than lead and not as heavy, but is heavier than steel. It has the advantage of being usable in standard shotgun barrels without harming them. The U.S. Fish and Wildlife Service has approved the use of bismuth-tin shot. The most recent innovation is tungsten-iron shot which will offer a claimed density 94% that of lead and the non-distorting quality of steel. It must be used in barrels intended for steel shot. Tungsten shot, as a reloading component, may likely replace steel. The cost is in the same price range as bismuth shot. There is shot made of an alloy of tungsten, nickel and iron which according to advertising claims is heavier than lead. This hardly seems possible since all these elements are lighter than lead.

SHOTSHELL LOADING EQUIPMENT

When it comes to loading shotshells, the basic steps are alike. However, the machines you will use to do this have different systems and the sequence of steps will vary from one machine to another. As was pointed out in the chapter on loading equipment, shotshell loading is done on a single machine with a lot of attachments while rifle and handgun ammunition is assembled using two or three bench-mounted tools with a number of attachments and several hand tools. Because of their relative complexity, shotshell reloading machines come with manuals that are (hopefully) clearly written and illustrated which show you how to load shotshells on that machine. If you buy a used machine, be sure that the proper manual is with it and that it has all the necessary component parts. Failing this, write the company or see if you can download one from the internet. The last option is to find someone who knows what he is doing to show you how to operate that particular machine. It is dangerous to attempt to load ammunition on a machine you don't know

how to operate on a "I think I can figure this out" basis. Obsolete machines that may not have all their parts and manual are no bargain. Manufacturers such as Texan and Herters are out of business and spare parts, manuals and factory support are out of the question.

If you have never done any shotshell reloading it is probably best not to start with a progressive loader. These machines are the most complicated to use and observing all the steps while determining whether or not they are being done correctly is difficult. Thus, the beginner would do best starting with a basic single-stage loader such as the Lee Load-All II or MEC 600 Jr. Mark V. Unlike rifle and handgun loading where the manuals offer suggestions for "working up" loads to find an accurate one, shotshell loads are pretty much cut-and-dried. The manual that comes with the loader will instruct you on the use of the powder and shot bushings to be inserted in the charge bar of the

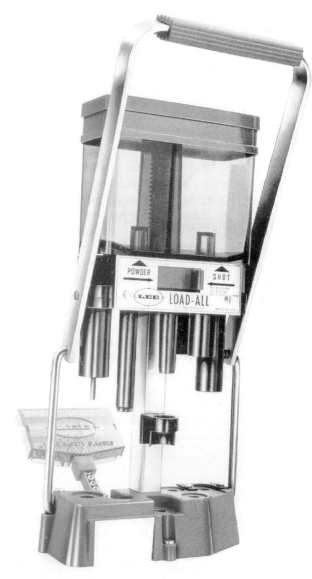

The Lee Load-All II is an excellent entry-level shotshell loader at an affordable price. It can turn out an average of 100 rounds per hour, and loads lead or steel shot.

Shotshell primers are load specific. Always use the type best suited to the load you are using.

Various crimp styles. L. To R: Old style rolled crimp on a paper shell with top wad. Rolled crimp is necessary for making slug loads. Six-fold crimp and eight-fold crimp.

machine. These must be matched to the proper type of powder and weight and size of shot. They will dispense preset amounts of powder and shot. MAKE SURE YOU MATCH THESE BUSHINGS AND POWDERS CORRECTLY! Read the manual.

PELLET COUNT COMPARISON			
Shot Size	12-Ga. 1⁷/₈ ozs. Lead pellets	Shot Size	12-Ga. 1³/₈ ozs. Steel pellets
6	422	4	263
4	253	2	172
2	163	BB	99
BB	94	T	71

SHOT SIZES			
Shot Size	Diameter (Ins.)	No. of Pellets/Oz. Lead	Steel
9	.08	585	—
8¹/₂	.085	—	—
8	.09	411	—
7¹/₂	.095	350	—
6	.11	225	316
5	.12	170	246
4	.13	135	191
3	.14	109	153
2	.15	87	125
1	.16	72	103
B	.17	59	84
BB	.18	50	72
BBB	.19	43	61
T	.20	36	52
F	.22	37	40

CASE INSPECTION

Even new and first-fired cases should be checked over for defects. Any with splits or serious defects in the case mouth or body or splits in the metal head should be discarded.

Cases should be segregated by maker as determined not only by the head stamp, but by the base wad configuration. Because they wear out sooner than rifle or handgun cases, and because worn cases give different velocities as the case mouths become softer, shotshells should be carefully identified by their intended loading as well as by maker and identified by the number of times they have been reloaded. This means careful handling when shooting so you don't mix them up and afterwards, boxing or bagging them accordingly.

MATERIALS/EQUIPMENT PRE-CHECK

Make sure that your wads match the shells you are about to load. Select the proper primers, powder and proper size shot for your loads. Check that you have the correct bushing and shot bar in place for that combination of powder and shot, or have made the proper adjustments on the bar for those types that have adjustable openings. Fill the canisters on the machine. Lay out no more than 100 primers on the bench.

CASE RESIZING AND DECAPPING

With machines such as the Lee, decapping and primer seating are done on the same location. With the MEC, primer seating is a separate step. Place the shell under the sizing die, or slip it into the die body and pull the handle to the bottom of the stroke. This resizes and decaps the shell.

(Text continued on page 154)

STEP-BY-STEP RELOADING SHOTSHELL CARTRIDGES

(Photos courtesy Lee Precision, Inc.)

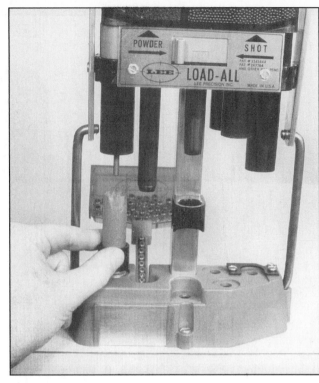

Step 1 - Sizing: Sort your hulls by brand and type, and discard the defective ones. Slip the sizing die, grooved end up, over the shell. Place the shell in Station 1 and pull down the handle. This full-length resizes and deprimes the shell.

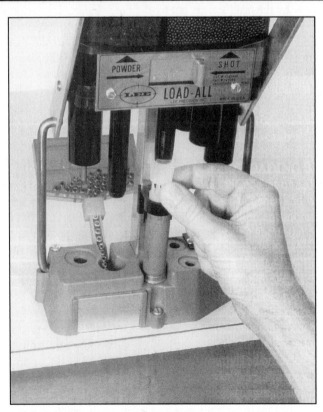

Step 4 - Inserting the Wad: Raise the handle, insert the proper wad and lower the press handle until it stops.

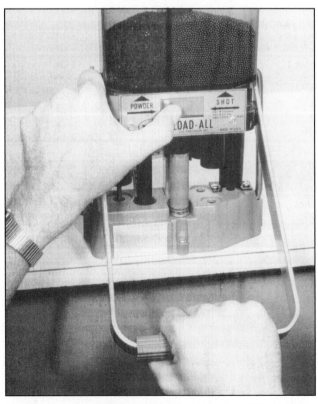

Step 5 - Shot Charging: Now slide the charge bar all the way to the left to add the shot. Raise the press handle.

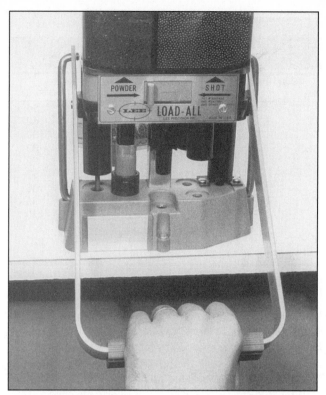

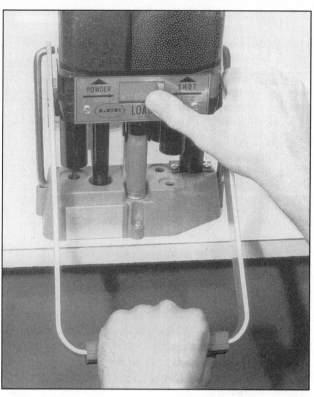

Step 2 - Priming: Place a primer in the priming pocket at Station 2. Move the shell onto Station 2 and pull down the handle. The sizing die will automatically be pushed off the shell at this station. Remove it completely.

Step 3 - Powder Charging: Slip the shell into the wad guide at Station 3, lower the handle and slide the charge bar to the right to add the powder.

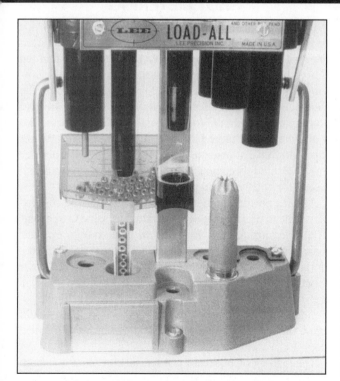

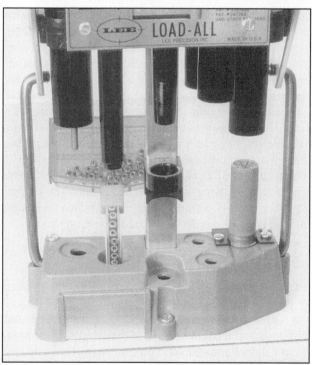

Step 6 - Crimp Start: Place the shell under the proper crimp starter, keeping an inward fold of the shell toward the front for proper alignment with the segmented starter. Pull the press handle down all the way, holding it there for about two seconds to set the plastic.

Step 7 - Final Crimp: Immediately move the shell into the shell-holder at Station 5, and pull the press handle down to complete the crimp. That completes the loading cycle, giving you a ready-to-shoot shotshell.

(Text continued from page 151)

LEAD VERSUS STEEL PELLET WEIGHT			
—Lead Pellet—		—Steel Pellet—	
Size	Wgt. Grs.	Size	Wgt. Grs.
BBB	10.4	F(TTT)	11.0
BB	8.8	TT	9.6
BB	8.8	T	8.3
B	7.3	BBB	7.1
1	6.1	BB	6.1
2	5.0	B	5.0
3	4.1	1	4.3
4	3.2	2	3.5
5	2.6	3	2.9
5	2.6	4	2.3
6	1.9	5	1.8
7¹/₂	1.3	6	1.4

STEEL VERSUS LEAD PELLET COUNT			
—Steel Pellet—		—Lead Pellet—	
Size	No. Per oz.	Size	No. Per oz.
F(TTT)	39	T	34
TT	46	BBB	42
T	52	BB	50
BBB	62	B	60
BB	72	1	72
B	87	2	87
1	103	3	106
2	125	4	135
3	154	5	170
4	192	6	225
5	243	6	225
6	317	7	299

PRIMING

A new primer is next placed on the primer-seating station and the handle is pulled down to bring the shell down on to the primer and seat it. This stroke must be firm, but not overly hard, in order to seat the primer flush with the shell head. Primers should be checked with a straight-edge to see that the primer is not high.

POWDER CHARGING

The case is next moved to the station below the powder container. Depending on the exact configuration of the machine you are using, the handle is pulled, bringing the case into contact with the powder/shot tube dispenser. The charge bar is then pushed across the bottom of the powder container (usually to the full left position) and the powder charge is metered into the case. IMPORTANT: This step should be verified by checking at least ten (10) charges on a powder scale. If you do not use a scale you have no idea whether your charges are close or even in the ballpark. If the machine is not delivering the proper amount of powder within a tolerance of five percent (5%) of the listed charge, you may have to try another larger or smaller bushing in the charge bar, or the bushing may be clogged if the powder is not dry and free-flowing. This step should be done at the beginning of each loading session and if/when you change to a different lot of powder. Once it is determined the charge bar is dispensing powder as it should, move on to the next step.

WAD/SHOTCUP SEATING

This step may be done at the same station as powder charging or the shell may have to be moved to a new station. The wad is placed on the wad guide. The handle is pulled fully down and the wad is seated on the powder. Some powders are more sensitive to wad pressure than others and will yield higher or lower velocities and pressures depending on their degree of compression. Red Dot is one of the more sensitive ones. The better machines have a pressure gauge on them. Note this and the wad seating height to determine that your wads are seated uniformly. If a wad goes far too deep, you have less than a full powder charge or no charge and you will have to recheck your charging operations. Care should be taken that the base cup on the wad is not caught and nicked or tipped by folds in the case mouth and descends straight on to the powder. If the seating pressure is too high you may have too much powder or an incorrect wad for that charge or a wad not properly matched to that case. Wad seating pressure should be at least 20 lbs. Finally, check to see that the petals of the shotcup are in full contact with the case walls so they will not interfere with shot metering.

SHOT METERING

Depending on your machine, the shell may or may not be moved to another station for shot metering. Whatever, the shell is raised to the powder/shot charging tube and the charge bar is generally moved to the right across the bottom of the shot canister and the charge is dropped into the shell. It is important to have the proper shot bar for the load you are making. MEC tools (at least the older ones) have a different shot charge bar for each weight of shot. Other machines have adjustable shot bars or bars with powder insert bushings. Lee and Hornady machines have bushing inserts for both shot and powder.

As with powder charging, shot charges must be checked on a scale to be sure they are accurate. The same five percent (5%) tolerance applies. Run several shot charges on your scale to verify that your machine is behaving properly. Occasionally a shot charge will jam or only partially feed. Thus a visual inspection of each shell you load should be made. If the shotcup is not full, return the shell to the charging position and give the charging tube a tap or two. This should cause the remainder to drop and you can move to the next step.

The loading of buckshot is a special consideration, since shot this large cannot be metered through the machine. Buckshot is loaded by pellet count, not by weight, and the shot have to be counted and hand-fed into the shotcup. More importantly, buckshot must be nested in layers in the cup or they will not fit properly. Some of these loads call for "buffering" with a finely ground plastic material. This should be added with each layer and the case tapped with the finger to settle it into the cup until it is level with the top layer of shot. Needless to say, buckshot loads are best assembled on a single stage press rather than on a progressive.

CRIMP STARTING

Shotshells have two forms of fold crimping — six-fold and eight-fold. The crimp starter should be matched to the fold pattern of the shells you are reloading. NEVER use a six-fold crimp starter on an eight-fold shell and vice-versa. The crimp starter is adjustable and can be raised and lowered to vary the amount of crimp start. When working with various brands of shells, a certain amount of experimentation is needed to get the proper amount of crimp start. Rem-

ington and Federal seem to require a little less start than Winchester shells. If your finished shells show indentations in the crimped end of the shell, the crimp starter is set too deeply and will have to be backed off a bit.

FINAL CRIMP

The shell is placed on the final crimp station. The handle is pulled down until it bottoms. Hold the handle is this position for a couple of seconds to give the crimp a firm set then raise the handle. If the crimp is not firmly closed this step may be repeated. Crimp depth should duplicate the original factory load. This die is adjustable and may need some tinkering to get it to accommodate the make of case you are using. Overall length of the finished shell is critical to feeding through magazines so die adjustment must be kept to a minimum. If the problem is the center of the shell being too high or too low, you can experiment with changing the wad

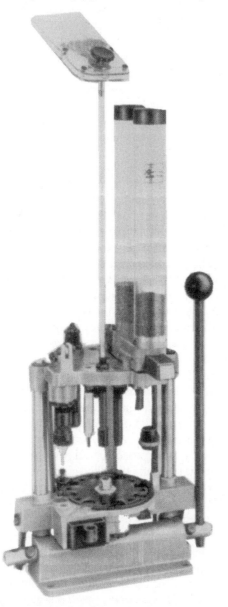

Hornady 366 machines produce a finely rounded crimp locked tightly in place, good for high production.

The MEC 600 Jr. Mark V can turn out 200 rounds per hour. It is available in 28 through 10 gauge.

for a longer or shorter one or adding or subtracting shot. Adding shot should be done with caution and not done with a maximum load. A 20 gauge card wad can be added to the bottom of the 12 gauge cup to act as a filler if needed. This should be done before the wad is seated. A supply of 1/8"and 1/16" card wads is a handy item to stock.

The MEC 600 Jr. Mark V, among other machines, has a feature to put a slight taper on the case mouth to facilitate feeding in repeating guns. Some of the more expensive machines such as the Hornady 366 Auto and Apex machines have a third crimping feature, that rounds the front of the shell and locks in the crimp with a slightly raised ring around the edge of the crimped end. This insures the crimp will not open through jarring as it is fed through an autoloading action.

FINAL INSPECTION

Since shotshells are made of plastic or paper and thus softer than brass cartridges, it is always necessary to do a final size check before boxing them. Any case with a poor crimp that cannot be repaired in the approved manner should be junked. The same goes for one that has cracked or split in the reloading process. MEC's ring gauge is a handy item for a quick size check with a "go — no go" hole for each standard size shell.

AMMUNITION TESTING

Since shotguns deliver a pattern of shot which is determined primarily by the choke of the barrel, testing mainly depends on duplicating factory performance. Light loads will obviously put fewer shot in the standard 30" circle at 40 yards than heavier loads. To check the patterning of your gun you need a 40 yard range and a large piece of paper at least one square yard in size. Aim at the center. Draw a 30 inch circle around the most dense area and count the holes. Various loading manuals will give you a shot count per ounce of shot so you can figure the percentage or you can make an actual count. Beyond this there are some other observations you can make. One is to see where the greatest area of density lies. It should be in the center of your point of aim and not biased to the side. The shot pattern should be more or less even within the circle. Some guns have a tendency to produce a very dense center with an uneven disbursal of shot at the edge of the circle. This may mean missed clays or crippled game. To check the efficacy of your pattern cut a clay target size circle (4 5/16" or 108mm) out of a piece of plastic and move it around the pattern. Areas with fewer than three pellets in them are in the doubtful zone in terms of an assured kill on most birds.

GOOD AND BAD LOADS

Good loads are the ones that do what you want them to do and often the bad load is one that does not. This may be because it is inappropriate to the situation — too small shot, too light a load, not enough pattern density. These problems are rooted mainly in the ignorance of the shooter and in taking shots that he should not attempt and then blaming the gun or the ammunition. There are, however, a few false notions and a similar number of home truths that should be addressed.

Larger-bore guns kick more than smaller-bore ones with the same loading. This is nonsense. The recoil is determined by the weight of the shot charge and the velocity. The difference in experienced recoil will only be affected by the weight of the gun and a heavy gun will absorb more recoil than a light one. *Larger- bore guns hit harder.* Not true. The velocity of all shotgun loads is virtually the same — in the 1200-1500 fps velocity. A #6 pellet from a 410 is flying as fast and hitting as hard as one moving at the same velocity from a 10 gauge even though the 410 makes less noise.

The same-weight load from a 20 gauge and a 12 gauge are equally effective. This tends not to be the case. Longer shot columns tend to result in greater compression-distortion of the pellets at the back of the load and thus produce more fliers and consequently a less dense pattern. This probably is what led to the notion of larger bore guns "hitting harder."

Harder shot hits harder. Not really, but hard and extra-hard shot, because of its being less distorted and having a smaller percentage of distorted shot in a given charge, delivers more shot to the central pattern with fewer fliers. Heavy loads, particularly in the 410 and 20 gauge 3" shells and the 12 gauge 3 1/2" magnum with their longer shot column, are most effective with hard shot.

Certain powders do not perform well at sub-freezing temperatures. This seems to be true, according to the Fackler brothers at Ballistic Products, who ran tests on powder performance and concluded that Blue Dot gave significantly lower velocities at low temperatures, much more so than other powders, although all velocities will be lower in cold conditions when the air is more dense.

High-velocity shotshell loads have some fans who believe that by pumping the velocity up to 1500 fps there is something to be gained by getting the shot to the target faster. More pressure and more recoil top these gains unless the shot charge is reduced. At the velocity top-end, patterns get pretty ragged. Around 1400 fps, however, patterns hold well and at ranges of 25 to thirty yards are quite lethal. Unfortunately this added lethality is at the price of tearing up what is shot to a greater extent than with more modest velocities. This is a plus in the varmint-shooting area, not so good for pot hunting. Do these loads really "reach out there and get 'em?" Not really, since pellets are very poor performers in the aerodynamic sense and the initial gain in velocity is soon shed and at 45+ yards are not going to perform much differently than the standard factory loading. If the velocity is achieved at a reduction in the amount of shot, things are a little worse because of a lower-density pattern.

The main advantage of such hot loadings would appear to be in trap and skeet shooting where the targets are at relatively close range. Hard hitting assures more breakage and higher velocities cut lead calculation in this game of hitting them fast and hard.

14

Reloading involves a number of processes before the trigger is tripped, but once the powder starts burning, it's all about ballistics.

Ballistics: The Basics

"SEND THAT GUN down to ballistics," is a throw-away line from dozens of forgettable TV cop shows. This notion of ballistics being what police crime labs do is ingrained in the minds of an astonishing number of people.

James Hamby, then Director of the Indianapolis/Marion County Crime Lab, recalled giving a lengthy and detailed explanation in court of the work of a firearms examiner and of the discipline known as "firearms examination," which involves matching crime and test bullets and cartridges to particular guns. The old judge looked hard and uncomprehendingly at Hamby and said: "Yeah, but what about ballistics?" It took Hamby a while to explain that ballistics was only a small fraction of criminal investigation involving firearms.

Calvin Goddard -- the father of the field of Firearms Examination and investigation -- later admitted that he rued the day he came up with the term "forensic ballistics," a hastily conceived name for the emerging science of firearms examination which, unfortunately, stuck in the public mind. As of this day there is only one police organization in the country that still refers to its firearms section as "The Ballistics Lab" – the NYPD – which, it might be added, embraces change with the enthusiasm of the Vatican.

Ballistics – real ballistics – is the scientific investigation of the behavior of projectiles in flight. The name is derived from an ancient Roman siege machine called a ballista -- a kind of king-size crossbow which launched spears, rocks and whatnot. The field of ballistics, in the modern sense, deals primarily with projectiles fired from guns and is further divided into three subsections: interior ballistics, exterior ballistics and terminal ballistics. Ballistics spreads over a number of scientific fields encompassing physics (including Newton's laws of motion), mechanics, dynamic forces, aerodynamics and the forces of air. It links up with chemistry, mathematics (including calculus), meteorology, metallurgy and medicine.

INTERIOR BALLISTICS

Interior ballistics deals with everything that happens from the beginning of the firing sequence to the point where the projectile exits the barrel of the gun. The first serious use of guns was at the Battle of Crécy, in 1346, in which the English forces employed small cannons against the French. This event initiated the consideration of problems of interior ballistics– questions of pressure and velocity and pressure and gun failure – discussed in chapter 3. It led to the investigation of propellants and ignition systems and considerations of gun barrel material and manufacture which eventually led to the creation of the field of metallurgy. The basic questions were: How much pressure can be generated in a gun barrel and have it hold together and how fast will a projectile be ejected? Rodman in the U.S. and Nobel in Great Britain developed the first reasonably reliable systems of pressure measurement.

Beyond the problem of establishing safe means of measuring internal pressures are considerations of increasing velocity without increasing pressure proportionally. There is the assessment of the best materials for making these projectiles, their shape, weight, strength and design, to see that they do not come apart in flight and either expand or penetrate or do some desired combination of both on reaching the target. There is the matter of material for gun barrels, the problems of barrel strength and wear. Suddenly the field of economics raises its dismal head as cost is pitted against longevity and efficiency.

Since a gun is an internal-combustion, pressure-driven engine it depends on gases from burning gun powder to overcome the inertia of the projectile. Considerable pressure builds up (up to 6000 psi in some instances) before the inertial force of the weight of the projectile is overcome and it starts to move. The action of swaging the projectile into the rifling causes pressure to increase to the point where the peak pressure is reached. Once the swaged projectile is in motion, pressure begins to drop as the speed of the projectile picks up and the space behind it increases in volume. When the projectile is out of the barrel, pressure drops rapidly to that of the surrounding atmosphere. Propellant materials are a major concern under the rubric of interior ballistics. These include priming materials that will burn in

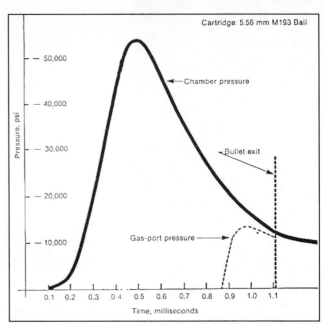

Since no one can see into the barrel of a gun when it's fired, we have only instrumental information telling us what happened.

such a way as to provide the best possible ignition, propellants that will produce a pressure curve best suited to a particular length of barrel, and both to be of material that will work reliably under a variety of temperature conditions and will not change their burning characteristics over time.

EXTERIOR BALLISTICS

Exterior ballistics is concerned with hitting the target with accuracy, which means achieving consistency of bullet behavior. It encompasses the study of everything that affects a bullet's flight from the moment it exits the barrel until it reaches the target. The line between interior ballistics and exterior ballistics is blurred since, from the start, the bullet is pushing air within the gun barrel and for a short distance the muzzle blast continues the acceleration process, often causing the bullet to yaw a bit in flight until rotation stabilizes it and it "goes to sleep," as riflemen say. Things happening within the gun barrel have a great deal to do with how a projectile will behave once it has exited that barrel.

Ballistics as a science had its beginning with the publication of Nicholas Tartaglia's treatise on the flight of projectiles, published in 1537. Tartaglia was the first to calculate trajectories and to theorize that maximum range was achieved at an exit angle of 45 degrees. He was wrong in this, but correct in assuming that all trajectories were curved.

The velocity of a projectile was first measured, in 1741, by Benjamin Robins, inventor of the ballistic pendulum, who fired projectiles of known weight into the weight of a pendulum, also of known weight, and measured the distance of the swing. Robbins was the first investigator to come up with a system for reasonably accurate velocity measurement to 1700 fps. Using the same pendulum, Hutton in England was the first to note that air resistance had a considerable influence on reducing velocity and that projectiles lost velocity in direct proportion to their speed – that the higher the

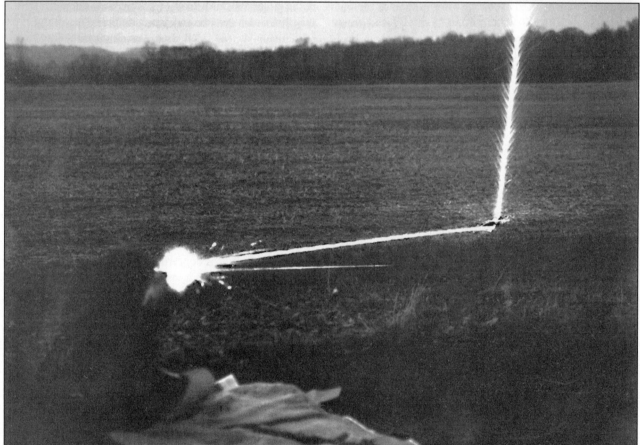

Ricochets are an aspect of exterior ballistics. Reconstructing such events is part of the work of the firearms examiner.

initial velocity, the more rapid the decline in velocity.

By the 1840's the ballistic pendulum became obsolete with Wheatstone's proposal to measure bullet flight through time as it passed through screens breaking electrical contacts. The Le Boulengé chronograph using such a system was in use in the 1860's to the 1930's when the first all-electronic machines using photoelectric screens were perfected.

The trajectory of a bullet is the curved path it takes from the gun muzzle to the target. The basic force affecting this curve (for small arms) is gravitation. Temperature, which affects air density, is a second factor. In a vacuum, the trajectory of a bullet would be affected only by gravity and it would thus describe a flight path that would be parabolic with the angle of decent being the same as the angle of ascent. Air resistance, however, reduces velocity and thus produces a much steeper angle of descent. As the bullet is slowed by this force and its forward velocity declines, the force of gravity predominates and the path of the bullet becomes less horizontal and more vertical.

The ballistic coefficient is a major factor in the calculation of the trajectory of a bullet. This figure is derived from the weight, diameter and form of a projectile. Form is the degree of streamlining based on an ideal shape with a needle nose tapering back to a rounded body and then to a tapered base. Bullets of this "boattail" design have a high ballistic coefficient and will fly much farther than a flat-nosed "wadcutter," which is nearly a perfect cylinder.

Air temperature will have a marked effect on bullet trajectory. Hot air is less dense because the molecules are farther apart and will offer less resistance than cold air wherein they are closer together. A rifle zeroed on a summer day at a temperature of 80 degrees will shoot low on a winter day with the temperature at 10 degrees. Moving air (wind) serves to accelerate or decelerate the forward motion of the bullet to a degree and will affect where it strikes. Head-winds will decelerate velocity and lower the point of impact. Tailwinds will accelerate velocity and raise the point of impact, all other things being equal.

No one knows who discovered that spin-stabilizing projectiles made a tremendous increase in their accuracy and permitted the development of highly efficient aerodynamic designs that would fly farther, lose velocity less quickly and retain more energy than a round ball. Arms with barrels containing helical grooves (rifling) first appeared in the late 1500's. While spin-stabilized projectiles fly far straighter than round balls, the rotation is affected by the air around the bullet, and to a degree irregularities on the bullet's surface, caused primarily by the rifling. This led to the notion (in dispute) of the bullet's working against the air causing it to roll or "drift" in flight in the direction it is spinning. Lt. Col. A.R. Buffington U.S.A. developed a sight for the Springfield rifle, in 1883, that contained an automatic compensation feature for this rotational drift.

Cross-winds will have a decided effect on the lateral displacement of a bullet. The greatest displacement is when the wind is blowing at a right angle to the bullet's flight path. Wind velocity affects drift in proportion to the speed of the wind. Bullet velocity also affects the amount of drift with the greatest degree of drift occurring when the bullet is moving at or slightly above the speed of sound. Above and below this point, wind drift is somewhat less. A bullet traveling above the speed of sound sets up a shock wave which indicates a loss of kinetic energy caused by "drag." The degree of drag is dependent on bullet diameter, velocity, air density, and the drag coefficient, which is figured from such factors as projectile shape, air density, yaw and Mach number -- the ratio of the projectile velocity to the speed of sound.

Other factors affecting lateral displacement are ricochets and deflections. Ricochets are the result of bullets striking hard ground, ice, pavement or water at a shallow angle.

When this occurs the bullet nearly always loses its rotational stability and tumbles in flight. Even when striking water, which most consider an easily penetrated substance, bullets will ricochet if they strike below a "critical angle of entry" -- 5.75 degrees. Bullets striking water at angles above 2 degrees will lose their rotational stability.

Deflection might be termed a lateral ricochet. For many years there have been questions raised regarding "brush busting" -- the ability of a bullet to hit a small branch and keep going (more or less) straight to the target. Debate over this issue had been fueled by stories of stellar performances by particular bullets which had penetrated small branches, often cutting them off in the process, then felled a game animal some distance away. There were perhaps a greater number of stories of the opposite happening, where a bullet clipped a twig and went spinning out of control, missing a large target entirely. This author's investigation into deflections found support for both claims. The critical factors were the angle of contact of the bullet and the branch and whether the bullet was damaged by the branch. If the bullet struck the branch dead center and was undamaged it continued on a relatively straight path. If it was damaged it lost stability. If it struck to one side of dead center it would deflect and usually lose stability and tumble. The greatest degree of deflection was at the point where half the bullet was in contact with the branch. The degree of deflection decreased as the point of contact moved closer to dead center or toward the edge resulting in a slight grazing of the branch.

TERMINAL BALLISTICS

Terminal ballistics involves everything that happens to a bullet from the moment it reaches the target to the point where all motion ceases. The term means different things to different people. For the target shooter, punching the paper or knocking over the metal silhouette is all that matters. The large-game hunter is concerned with the ability of a bullet to both penetrate into a vital area of a game animal, and expand, creating a large wound channel and quick incapacitation. The varmint hunter wants quick expansion on relatively thin skinned animals to create a large wound cavity and instant death. The small game hunter needs something between these two extremes -- bullets that will expand, killing quickly, but not causing the kind of disruption encountered in the varmint bullet that destroys a great deal of edible meat. For military ends, terminal ballistics includes penetrating concrete, building materials and armor plate and starting fires in fuel tanks.

WOUND BALLISTICS

Wound ballistics is a subset of terminal ballistics and is concerned with the medical aspects of gunshot wounds, including wound trauma incapacitation and treatment of gunshot wounds.

Improvements in terminal ballistics have not been as fast as those in interior and exterior ballistics and have come about with the development of high speed cinematogra-

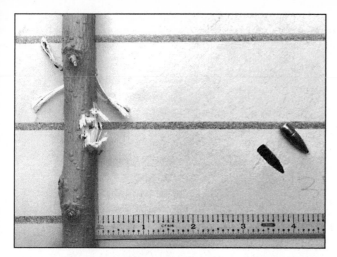

Bullet deflection from brush is of interest to hunters and forensic examiners alike. Where a bullet strikes on a branch radically affects where it winds up.

A great deal has been written regarding the role of velocity, that is to say high velocity, in the area of terminal and wound ballistics. According to Dr. Martin Fackler -- the leading wound ballistics expert in the country – bullet lethality is an easily understood concept. Lethality is determined by answering two questions: How big is the hole it produces? How deep is this hole? Bigger and deeper holes are more likely to intersect with vital organs, cause greater loss of blood, and result in death.

What about high velocity? In the 1960's, reports of horrendous wounds created by the M-16 rifles and to a lesser degree AK-47 rifles used in Vietnam began pouring in. The wounding effects, while genuine, were presented by an ignorant press as being wholly an artifact of high velocity. As often happens, misinformation and half truths become pillars of public opinion as they receive amplification by politicians and other public figures through the media, without scrutiny from the researcher. In the case of the velocity/lethality controversy, there is some truth to the wounding effects of hydrostatic or hydraulic shock of a high velocity bullet when it contacts an area of a body such as the liver or cranial vault. Liver tissue has poor elasticity and brain tissue behaves like a semi fluid in a sealed container. Anyone who has seen the effect of a 3000 fps bullet on a closed container of water has a good idea of the pressure-wave effect it produces. BUT this does not apply to other types of tissue with

phy and high speed radiography. Development of ballistic gelatin as a tissue substitute has been a particular aid to improved terminal ballistics. In the last twenty years, even the past five years, considerable advancements have been made in developing bullets which will produce "controlled expansion" that allows them to penetrate while expanding at a rate that will not result in breakup or in overexpansion and inadequate penetration.

Terminal ballistics of bullet behavior/performance in muscle tissue is studied in ballistic gelatin by the medical professional, but can be replicated to a good degree in water-filled cartons and dividing penetration by 1.5. Bullet upset/fragmentation is about the same.

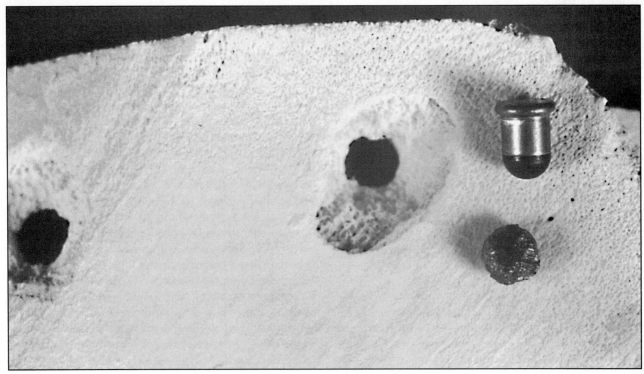

Using fresh bone samples, in this case beef shoulder blade of human-skull thickness, demonstrates the ability of a 22 BB Cap to pass through.

a higher degree of elasticity. While a large, instantaneous cavity is created, the resultant tissue damage of a permanent sort is minimal, not extending far beyond the path of the bullet.

In the case of extreme hyper-velocity impacts -- 3500-4000+ fps – both the bullet and target behave in the manner of fluids regardless of the material they are made of. This allows a 48 grain copper-jacketed bullet with an exposed lead point to knock a hole through a half inch of steel armor plate. At less than these velocities, the softer bullet would simply splatter on the surface of the harder material.

Bullet design had more to do with terminal/wound ballistics than other factors. For the first 400 years of their existence, bullets were made of lead. The creation of the jacketed bullet in the late 19th century came as a result of smokeless powder and the quest for flat trajectories. While this was achieved, the lethality of these small (30 caliber), round-nose bullets was far less than with large, soft, lead bullets of the 45-70 class. In their efforts to achieve still flatter trajectories, the Germans hit upon the discovery that their "spitzer" (pointed bullet), in addition to possessing less drag than the round-nose bullet, created a more severe wound. This design, with its long tapering point, had a heavy end and a light end and when the bullet lost stability by striking a body, the heavy rear would flip over the front, causing the bullet to make a larger hole -- often exiting base first as it tumbled. Soon, nearly everyone was using the spitzer bullet. The flip-over was improved by the British, who filled the pointed end with aluminum and the rear with lead. Later, the Russians simply left an air cavity in the front.

The Vietnam era saw the latest improvement in the spitzer bullet that gave it much the same effect as an expanding type. By the simple expedient of increasing velocity as in the case of the 7.62 X 39mm AK-47 bullet and the .223 (5.56 X 45mm) M-16 bullet, greater instability on impact was achieved. The 55 grain M-16 bullet with a muzzle velocity of over 3000 fps would often break in half at the cannelure in the middle and the two halves would shred in the body creating a more massive wound. Even more deadly was the 7.62 X 51mm (.308) NATO bullet made by the West German government which featured a very thin steel jacket, fifty percent thinner than the U.S. version, which would shred in a body causing, an even more massive wound by virtue of its greater size and weight. Velocity was critical to achieving these effects, but it did not cause them. Once velocity dropped below 2500 fps, lethality decreased to handgun level with equivalent-caliber jacketed bullets.

Bullets design for hunting bullets did not have to work under the constraints placed on nations by the Hague and Geneva conventions that attempted to create "rules" of warfare. Hunting bullets are intended for killing, as opposed to creating casualties in war, thus they can be made of a more lethal design, i.e. to expand in a controlled manner at predetermined velocities. Have we gone about as far as we can go along this line of development? In terms of bullet design, we probably have. In terms of making firearms capable of handling more powerful ammunition, making this ammunition more reliable and accurate and making both more compact, however, there are still some worlds to be conquered.

15
ABC's of
Reloading

No single book can supply all of the available knowledge on the subject of reloading, so here's where you can find whatever you want or need to know.

Sources and Resources

THE MOST DIRECT route to current information on reloading tools, accessories, supplies and reloading data is ask the manufacturers themselves, who are more than eager to provide any information you want. The major manufacturers in the reloading industry supply the bulk of tools, accessories and components, although there are many, many more companies, mail-order houses and retailers who offer their own catalogs, data books and the like. For openers, the following list of major suppliers will get you off to a fast start:

ACCURATE POWDER
Western Powders, Inc.
PO Box 158-Top of Yellowstone Hill
Miles City, MT 59301
(406) 234-0422
www.accuratepowder.com

ALLIANT POWDER
P.O. Box 6 Rt. 114
Radford, VA 24143-0096
(540) 639-8503
www.alliantpowder.com

BARNES BULLETS, INC.
P.O. Box 215
American Fork, UT 84003
(800) 574-9200
www.barnesbullets.com

CCI SPEER
P.O. Box 856
Lewiston, ID 83501
(866) 286-7436
www.cci-ammunition.com
www.speer-bullets.com

CLYMER MFG. CO.
1645 West Hamlin Road
Rochester Hills, MI 48309-3312
(248) 853-5555
www.clymertool.com
Guns tools, including reamers and headspace gauges

DILLON PRECISION PRODUCTS, INC.
8009 E. Dillon's Way
Scottsdale, AZ 85260
(602) 948-8009
www.dillonprecision.com
Reloading Equipment, Accessories and Components

FEDERAL CARTRIDGE COMPANY
900 Ehlen Drive
Anoka, MN 55303-7503
(800) 322-2342
www.federalpremium.com

HODGDON POWDER COMPANY, INC.
6231 Robinson
Shawnee Mission, KS 66202
(913) 362-9455
www.hodgdon.com

HORNADY MANUFACTURING
P.O. Box 1848
Grand Island, NE 68802
(308) 382-1390
www.hornady.com
Rifle & Handgun Bullets, Reloading Tools & Accessories

IMR POWDER COMPANY
(Now a part of Hodgdon Powder Co.
Contact Hodgdon for Information)

KALTRON-PETTIBONE
1241 Ellis Street
Bensenville, IL 60106
(630) 350 1116
www.kaltron.com
Importer of Vihtavuori Smokeless Powders and Lapua
ammunition and components

LEE PRECISION INC.
4275 Highway U
Hartford, WI 53027
(262) 673-3075
www.leeprecision.com
Reloading tools and accessories

LYMAN PRODUCTS CORPORATION
475 Smith Street
Middletown, CT 06457
(800) 225-9626
www.lymanproducts.com
Case Cleaning and Preparation Systems, Reloading Tools,
Bullet Casting, Black Powder Products

MEC (MAYVILLE ENGINEERING CO.)
715 South Street
Mayville, WI 53050
(920) 387-4500
www.mecreloaders.com
Reloading Tools and Accessories

MidwayUSA
5875 W. Van Horn Tavern Rd.
Columbia, MO 65203
(800) 243-3220
www.midwayusa.com
Major manufacturer, mail order and online provider of
shooting and reloading products.

MTM MOLDED PRODUCTS
3370 Obco Court
Dayton, OH 45414
(937) 890-7461
www.mtmcase-gard.com
(937) 890-1747 fax
Ammo cases & reloading supplies

NOSLER, INC.
P.O. Box 671
Bend, OR 97709
(800) 285-3701
www.nosler.com
Rifle, Handgun and Muzzleloading Bullets

PACIFIC TOOL & GAUGE
598 Avenue C
PO Box 2549
White City, OR 97503
(541) 826-5808
www.pacifictoolandgauge.com

PRECISION RELOADING, INC.
124 South Main Street
Mitchell, SD
(800) 223-0900
Technical Support & Customer Service
(860) 684-5680
e-mail address: info@precisionreloading.com
Shotgun, Rifle & Pistol Reloading Equipment, Components &
Supplies, Lead, Bismuth & Steel Shot Reloading Components
www.precisionreloading.com

RCBS
605 Oro Dam Blvd.
Oroville, CA 95965
(800) 533-5000
www.rcbs.com
Reloading Tools and Accessories

RAMSHOT POWDERS
Western Powders, Inc.
PO Box 158-Top of Yellowstone Hill
Miles City, MT 59301
(406) 234-0422
www.ramshot.com

REDDING RELOADING EQUIPMENT
1089 Starr Road
Cortland, NY 13045
(607) 753-3331
www.redding-reloading.com
Reloading tools, dies and accessories

REMINGTON ARMS CO., INC.
870 Remington Drive
Madison, NC 27025-0700
(800) 243-9700
Reloading Components

SIERRA BULLETS
1400 West Henry St.
Sedalia, MO 65301
(800) 223-8799 for Technical Information
(888) 223-3006
www.sierrabullets.com

STARLINE, INC.
1300 West Henry Street
Sedalia, MO 65301
(800) 280-6660
www.starlinebrass.com

SWIFT BULLET COMPANY
1001 Swift Ave. P.O. Box 27
Quinter, KS 67752
(785) 754-3959
www.swiftbullets.com

WINCHESTER SMOKELESS PROPELLANT
Hodgdon Powder Co.
6231 Robinson
Shawnee Mission KS 66202
913-362-9455
www.wwpowder.com
Ammunition and Components

KRAUSE PUBLICATIONS
700 E. State Street
Iola, WI 54990-0001
(715) 445-2214
www.krause.com
Special publications for the shooter and reloader including
Handloader's Digest.

Handloader Magazine
2625 Stearman Road-Suite A
Prescott, AZ 86301
(800) 899-7810
www.riflemagazine.com
Wolfe Publishing A Prescott, Arizona 8630
Call Us Toll-Free 1.800.899.7810Company 2625

National Shooting Sports Foundation
Flintlock Ridge Office Center
11 Mile Hill Road
Newtown, CT 06470-2359
(203) 426-1320
www.nssf.org

SAAMI
Sporting Arms and Ammunition Manufacturers' Institute
Flintlock Ridge Office Center
11 Mile Hill Road,
Newtown, CT 06470-2359
www.saami.org

A SELECTIVE BIBLIOGRAPHY

This chapter might be subtitled "Advanced Reloading Or Where Do I Go From Here?" Anybody who has bought this book and read it may likely have an interest in learning that goes beyond his own, necessarily limited, experience. Publication in the firearms field must be at an all-time high if one is to judge by the glorious book displays encountered at such gun shows as the one put on by the Ohio Gun Collectors Association. The plethora of new books, beautifully bound and exhaustively illustrated, present a challenge both exhilarating and daunting. Exhilarating because there is getting to be a separate book devoted to about every make and model of gun you ever heard of (and plenty you haven't), daunting because these volumes carry price tags that start at about $35 and go up to $75+ a copy. Unfortunately, few public libraries have any gun book collections to speak of, but interlibrary loan is worth a try. If you want to do in-depth reading you have to build your own library. There are those who ask to borrow gun books, but I refuse to discuss what happened to the last person who failed to return one of mine and have no knowledge regarding the disposition of the body.

The bibliography and source references that follow are a gleaning of some 40+ years of study and experience. It is both spotty and idiosyncratic, but contains those books and sources I have found to be worth the money and\or effort to locate.

BALLISTICS

The Bullet's Flight From Powder to Target, by Dr. Franklin W. Mann, MD. orig pub 1909, various reprints. This is the first real book on modern ballistics. Even today some 100 years after it was first published, this book contains useful information regarding bullet behavior under an astonishing number of conditions. Mann was more of a tinkerer than a scientist, but was one of those dedicated souls who set out in pursuit of that eternal quest of getting all the bullets in one hole. His experiments were often predicated on the notion of: I wonder what would happen if...? The good doctor had enough money to buy a lot of rifles and replacement barrels. His work with cast, lead-alloy bullets is probably second to none. His book probably raises as many questions as it answers. The second volume would probably have provided these answers had the manuscript not been destroyed shortly after his death.

Understanding Firearm Ballistics, 6th Ed., by Robert A. Rinker, Mulberry House, P.O. Box 575, Corydon IN 47112, 2005, 432 pp Pap. $24.95 In spite of the occasional sentence that isn't a sentence this book does a good job of explaining the scientific aspects of ballistics from the basic to the advanced level while keeping the math to a minimum and the explanations clear. A good glossary of ballistic terms is included. If you want to know about ballistics this is the best single source I have encountered.

Bullet Penetration, by Duncan McPherson, Ballistic Publications, Box 772, El Segundo, CA, 90245. 1994 303 pp. $39.95. This book deals exclusively with terminal ballistics with handgun ammunition. Anyone interested in "stopping power," "shocking power" and all that should forget anything you ever read on the subject except perhaps Julian Hatcher. McPherson, an engineer and one of the charter members of the International Wound Ballistics Association, has analyzed and scrutinized everyone's work in this area before conducting his very-thorough research. The result has cleared away a number of cherished myths regarding bullet performance and the measurement of same. Though technical in nature, this work is very accessible to those without a mathematics background.

Rifle Accuracy Facts, by Harold R. Vaughn, Precision Shooting, Inc., 1998. $34.95. This work has been justly described as the successor to Mann's *The Bullet's Flight*. The question Vaughn chose to address is: Why do some rifles shoot so much better than others? Vaughn, a WWII veteran, flew 100 combat missions in the Pacific. After the war he completed a Master of Science degree at the University of Colorado. He worked in aerodynamics, eventually becoming Supervisor of Aero ballistics at the SANDIA National Laboratory where he pioneered the use of computers in projectile design. Vaughn, like Hatcher, was a renaissance man with a wide range of interests including big game hunting and rifle shooting. While Mann, Sharpe, and Hatcher were aware of the qualities of accurate rifles, the experts of their day relied on trial and error methods to achieve these ends.

What makes this work so valuable is that Vaughn had the advantage of state-of-the-art scientific test and evaluation equipment to analyze pressure, barrel harmonics, throat design, throat erosion, barrel-receiver joint motion, effects of muzzle blast, gyroscopic stability, of bullets etc., etc. This made it possible (for the first time) to answer all those questions of WHY? Here are solid principles on which to base improvements in accuracy and explain the causes of inaccuracy.

RELOADING, GENERAL

Complete Guide to Handloading, by Philip B. Sharpe. Originally published by Funk & Wagnalls, reprint avail from Wolf Publishing Co, Prescott, AZ 727 pp, illus $60.00. Last updated in 1953, this massive work is dated, but contains a wealth of historical data on powder and cartridge evolution as well as the evolution of handloading. Anybody interested in the hows and whys of ammunition development will find this a treasure. Sharpe's book contains data on experiments of all sorts, many of which have a habit of turning up in contemporary magazine articles as "new" ideas and possibilities. Sharpe was a good experimenter and stands as one of the best known early experts in the field.

Principles and Practice of Loading Ammunition, by Earl Naramore, Small Arms Technical Publishing Company (Samworth), Georgetown SC, 1954 952 pp. One reprint by Stackpole Books. This last of the Samworth books is now out of print, but (hopefully) someone will reprint it again. Naramore gets into the "science" of reloading, but does so in layman's terms which makes this book very readable. His emphasis is on what happens to powder, primers, bullets, barrels and actions when guns are fired. His examination of all the forces at work and what they do is expressed in terms of how to deal with them in the reloading process. This is probably the best book when it comes to answering those "why" and "what if" questions. Naramore (after Mann) is about the only author-experimenter who conducted extensive examinations of fired bullets, collected in pristine condition, and observed and deduced a good bit of information therefrom. Few writers expend this kind of time and effort on their work these days.

Handbook for Shooters and Reloaders, by Parker O. Ackley,(2 vols) 14th printing, paper, Plaza Publishing, Salt Lake City, Utah 1962, 1102 pp $25.00. Ackley was one of the greats in the experimentation and development field of small arms and ammunition. A gun maker and shooter who was also a good writer, Ackley put the better part of a lifetime of experience into these two books which contain articles answering all sorts of questions regarding gun failures, pressure, headspace, wildcat cartridges, killing power, reduced loads, calculating recoil, bullet energy, loading data etc., etc.

Hatcher's Notebook, by Julian S. Hatcher 3rd ed., 2nd printing, Stackpole books, Harrisburg, PA 1996 640 pp $29.95. Julian Hatcher can be considered one of the fathers of modern firearms writing and co-founder of the field of forensic firearms examination. Hatcher was a technical editor of the *American Rifleman* and held posts as a shooter, coach and military expert that would fill an entire page. This volume is a collection of many of his best articles on military rifles, their development, autoloading and automatic systems, recoil, headspace, triggers, barrel obstructions, military rifle strengths and weaknesses, range, velocity, recoil, etc., etc. This is an excellent companion to the Ackley volumes.

RELOADING: DATA MANUALS

Many of the powder, bullet and equipment manufacturers publish loading data for use with their products. If you are looking for that ultimate load one of these manuals is where you are likely to find it.

Lyman Reloading Handbook 49 Ed., edited by Thomas Griffin, 464 pp Lyman Products Corp Middletown CT 2009 27.98; *Lyman Shotshell Reloading Handbook, 5th Ed.*, ed by Thomas Griffin, 230 pp $25.98 *Lyman Pistol and Revolver Reloading Handbook 3rd Ed*. ed by Thomas Griffin, 272 pp, soft covers,$23.98 Lyman Products Corp Middletown CN 2009. These are often discounted by dealers. The Lyman manuals -- one of the country's oldest also carry a full catalog of Lyman equipment. A catalog is free.

Hodgdon Annual Manual. This includes the latest data on Hodgdon, IMR, and Winchester rifle and pistol data. 170 pp, InterMedia Outdoors Inc., New York, NY $12.99

Hornady Handbook of Cartridge Loading, 8th Ed. Hornady Mfg Co., Grand Island NB, 2010, 1000 pp $40.00 One of the largest collections of loads between covers. The ballistic information for the complete line of Hornady bullets with updates is now on the Hornady website, www.hornady.com . This can be found under the Ballistics Calculator.

Norma Reloading Manual by Kenneth Axelsson et al, 432 pp, Norma Precision AB, Amotfors, Sweden 2004. Includes nearly all the loads for Norma powders. See their website for updates. This volume contains lots of additional information on cartridge and powder manufacture.

Sierra Rifle & Pistol Manual, 5th Ed. by Bob Hayden et al, 1150 pp, Sierra Bullets, L.L.C. Sedalia, MO, 2003, $28.95 Top of the line in data, filled with useful ballistic information on twist rates, barrel wear, articles on long-range shooting, hunting and reloading tools. Three-ring binder format allows the user to insert his own pages of notes where he wishes them.

Nosler Reloading Guide Number 6, ed by Justin Moore, Chevalier Advertising, Inc., Lake Oswego OR, 2007, 827 pp. $24.95. A solid guide for reloading rifle and pistol ammunition . Articles on hunting and reloading. This is keyed to Nosler bullets and contains useful information on the use of these unique bullets. A must for Nosler bullet shooters.

Speer Reloading Manual Number 14 , ed by Allan Jones, ATK/SPEER Inc., Lewiston ID, Third Printing 2009, 1149 pp. $35.95. One of my personal favorites for its excellent photos (some of which were borrowed for this volume) and clear explanations of the forces and stresses in operation in firearms. Complete loading data for the Speer line of bullets, with a wide variety of powders. The compact size and fine organization of this book makes it easy to use.

Cartridges of the World, by Frank C. Barnes, Layne Simpson, Ed. 12th ed., Gun Digest Books, Iola WI, 2009, 568 pp., pap, $32.99 for reloader or cartridge collector this the first source to reach for when it comes to figuring out what might go in a particular, often a peculiar gun, and be fired safely. Filled with load data on foreign, obsolete, military and experimental, wildcat cartridges this book is kept up to date as new cartridges come along and others become obsolete. This makes it a bargain compared to those one-edition, collector's-item books that cost $80 to $100 on the rare book shelf.

Handloader's Guide, Ashley Halsey Jr. Ed., Last published as Handloading by William C. Davis, NRA Publications Washington, DC 1992, 400 pp., pap, published at $15.95 out of Print. The earlier edition edited by Ashley Halsey Jr. was a grab bag of useful and interesting articles on reloading, "how I did it " pieces and included some material never published in the NRA magazines.

RELOADING: SPECIAL ISSUES

Cast Bullets (third printing 1982) by E.H. Harrison, NRA Publications Washington, DC 1982, 144 pp., paper, out of Print. Probably one of the best books on bullet casting. It covers alloys, mould care and handling and includes a lot of problem-solving pieces of great value when it comes to getting moulds, cast bullets and various alloys to perform the way they should. Hopefully, someone will reprint this.

Lyman Cast Bullet Handbook 4th Ed. ed by Thomas Griffin, Lyman Products Corp Middletown CT 2010, 416 pp., pap, 25.98 Excellent book on cast bullet making and shooting. Over 5000 cast bullets are covered with trajectory and wind-drift data.

The Paper Jacket, (Formerly *The Practical Paper Patched Bullet*,) by Paul Matthews, pap, Wolfe Publishing Co., Inc. Prescott, AZ 1991 75 pp., pap, $13.50. If you are interested in making and shooting paper-patched bullets this is the book you need.

Loading Cartridges for the Original 45-70 Springfield Rifle and Carbine, Third Ed., Revised and Expanded. by J.S. and Pat Wolf., Wolf's Western Traders, Lacombe, LA 2003, 182 pp, Spiral bound, $29.95. www.the45-70book.com . This book is an absolute must if you are going to load for one of these guns, because everybody else's data regarding bullets is wrong. Wolf researched the Frankford Arsenal's records and shot his way through several hundred pounds of lead discovering how to make these old guns shoot. The data is very likely to be valuable in working up loads for similar deep-groove rifles from the 1870-1890 era.

The Home Guide to Cartridge Conversions by George C. Nonte, Jr. The Gun Room Press Highland Park, NJ 1976, 404 pp $24.95. Detailed instructions on how to make centerfire cartridges for foreign and obsolete rifles and handguns from commonly-available cartridges. How to fabricate ammunition for those war souvenirs you never thought you could shoot-- chamber casting, fire forming, the works. Not for beginners.

BOOK RESOURCES

Finding gun books, especially the out of print ones is a difficult job and the costs are often high. There are two basic approaches to finding these. The first involves time. This method takes you to used-book stores where you ask where the gun books are. After you get a dumb look in response to this question you explain using simple words and appropriate gestures to get across what you're looking for. They will direct you to the bottom of the back where you will paw through a load of junk and occasionally find a treasure for $1.98. The second method is to bite the bullet (a non-lead one of course) and negotiate with the book dealers at gun shows (who know the price of everything) and pay the going rate. Now and then a bargain can be found.

A third variant is the easiest way. Send your want list to the following:

John Vallee (Outdoor books) P.O. Box 544 West Hempstead, NY 11552 Vallee is good at finding out of print and otherwise hard to find books in the firearms area.

The Rutgers Book Center, 127 Raritan Ave., Highland Park NJ 08904. They have about 7000 current titles and 5000 out-of-print books. R.B.S. also has a publishing adjunct, The Gun Room Press with about 40 current titles.

FREE MATERIAL

Most powder companies publish pamphlet-size loading guides for their products. These are short guides with basic reloading data are put out by Alliant, for their powders, Hodgdon for their powders and for IMR, Winchester, and VithaVuori powders. Western does the same Accurate and Ramshot powders. They are free and can sometimes be found at the larger gun shops and sporting goods stores. They can also be obtained by writing the company. These are a good source to start and a collection of them will give you a good amount of data to get started. These guides are about 50 to 60 pages long and contain data only, no articles or tips. These will likely become fewer as more of this data is available over the internet and postage rates increase. If you're not computer equipped and on the internet life will become more difficult.

THE INTERNET

The internet is a vast storehouse of information, misinformation, crappola, and outright lies. The trick is to sort them out. Virtually all the powder companies, bullet companies, and reloading component companies have websites. Many of these offer downloadable versions of reloading guides, product lists and user information. This is the best source to find information on new products as the material is frequently updated. A regular check for recall information is a good practice.

As mentioned in the safety section, loading data from individuals -- blogs, chat-room recommendations, etc., should be treated as anecdotal information -- no pressure testing and so on. If such claims are made, consider the source of this pressure information. Is this source "bonded" by anyone? Look for better than: "Shot real good, didn't blow up my gun" (yet.)

Two good out-of-print book sources are **bookfinder.com** and **bookfinder4u.com**. **Amazon.com** is good but prices tend to be higher.

WEB DIRECTORY
AMMUNITION AND COMPONENTS

A-Square Co.: **www.asquarecompany.com**
3-D Ammunition: **www.3dammo.com**
Accurate Arms Co. Inc: **www.accuratepowder.com**
ADCO/Nobel Sport Powder: **www.adcosales.com**
Aguila Ammunition: **www.aguilaammo.com**
Alexander Arms: **www.alexanderarms.com**
Alliant Powder: **www.alliantpowder.com**
American Ammunition: **www.a-merc.com**
American Derringer Co.: **www.amderringer.com**
American Pioneer Powder: **www.americanpioneerpowder.com**
Ammo Depot: **www.ammodepot.com**
Arizona Ammunition, Inc.: **www.arizonaammunition.com**
Ballistic Products, Inc.: **www.ballisticproducts.com**
Barnaul Cartridge Plant: **www.ab.ru/~stanok**
Barnes Bullets: **www.barnesbullets.com**
Baschieri & Pellagri: **www.baschieri-pellagri.com**
Beartooth Bullets: **www.beartoothbullets.com**
Bell Brass: **www.bellbrass.com**

Berger Bullets, Ltd.: www.bergerbullets.com
Berry's Mfg., Inc.: www.berrysmfg.com
Big Bore Bullets of Alaska: www.awloo.com/bbb/index.htm
Big Bore Express: www.powerbeltbullets.com
Bismuth Cartridge Co.: www.bismuth-notox.com
Black Dawge Cartridge: www.blackdawgecartridge.com
Black Hills Ammunition, Inc.: www.black-hills.com
BlackHorn209: www.blackhorn209.com
Brenneke of America Ltd.: www.brennekeusa.com
Buffalo Arms: www.buffaloarms.com
Calhoon, James, Bullets: www.jamescalhoon.com
Cartuchos Saga: www.saga.es
Cast Performance Bullet: www.castperformance.com
CCI: www.cci-ammunition.com
Centurion Ordnance: www.aguilaammo.com
Century International Arms: www.centuryarms.com
Cheaper Than Dirt: www.cheaperthandirt.com
Cheddite France: www.cheddite.com
Claybuster Wads: www.claybusterwads.com
Clean Shot Powder: www.cleanshot.com
Cole Distributing: www.cole-distributing.com
Combined Tactical Systems: www.less-lethal.com
Cor-Bon/Glaser: www.cor-bon.com
Cowboy Bullets: www.cowboybullets.com
Defense Technology Corp.: www.defense-technology.com
Denver Bullet Co.: denbullets@aol.com
Dillon Precision: www.dillonprecision.com
Dionisi Cartridge: www.dionisi.com
DKT, Inc.: www.dktinc.com
Down Range Mfg.: www.downrangemfg.com
Dynamit Nobel RWS Inc.: www.dnrws.com
Elephant/Swiss Black Powder: www.elephantblackpowder.com
Eley Ammunition: www.eleyusa.com
Eley Hawk Ltd.: www.eleyhawk.com
Environ-Metal: www.hevishot.com
Estate Cartridge: www.estatecartridge.com
Extreme Shock Munitions: www.extremeshockusa.net
Federal Cartridge Co.: www.federalpremium.com
Fiocchi of America: www.fiocchiusa.com
Fowler Bullets: www.benchrest.com/fowler
Gamebore Cartridge: www.gamebore.com
Garrett Cartridges: www.garrettcartridges.com
Gentner Bullets: www.benchrest.com/gentner/
Glaser Safety Slug, Inc.: www.corbon.com
GOEX Inc.: www.goexpowder.com
GPA: www.cartouchegpa.com
Graf & Sons: www.grafs.com
Hastings: www.hastingsammunition.com
Hawk Bullets: www.hawkbullets.com
Hevi.Shot: www.hevishot.com
Hi-Tech Ammunition: www.iidbs.com/hitech
Hodgdon Powder: www.hodgdon.com
Hornady: www.hornady.com
Hull Cartridge: www.hullcartridge.com
Huntington Reloading Products: www.huntingtons.com
Impact Bullets: www.impactbullets.com
IMR Smokeless Powders: www.imrpowder.com
International Cartridge Corp: www.iccammo.com
Israel Military Industries: www.imisammo.co.il
ITD Enterprise: www.itdenterpriseinc.com
Kent Cartridge America: www.kentgamebore.com
Knight Bullets: www.benchrest.com/knight/
Kynoch Ammunition: www.kynochammunition.com
Lapua: www.lapua.com
Lawrence Brand Shot: www.metalico.com
Lazzeroni Arms Co.: www.lazzeroni.com
Leadheads Bullets: www.proshootpro.com

Lightfield Ammunition Corp: www.lightfieldslugs.com
Lomont Precision Bullets: www.klomont.com/kent
Lost River Ballistic Technologies, Inc.: www.lostriverballistic.com
Lyman: www.lymanproducts.com
Magkor Industries: www.magkor.com
Magnum Muzzleloading Products: www.mmpsabots.com
Magnus Bullets: www.magnusbullets.com
MagSafe Ammunition: www.realpages.com/magsafeammo
Magtech: www.magtechammunition.com
Masterclass Bullet Co.: www.mastercast.com
Meister Bullets: www.meisterbullets.com
Midway USA: www.midwayusa.com
Miltex, Inc.: www.miltexusa.com
Mitchell Mfg. Co.: www.mitchellsales.com
MK Ballistic Systems: www.mkballistics.com
Mullins Ammunition: www.mullinsammunition.com
National Bullet Co.: www.nationalbullet.com
Navy Arms: www.navyarms.com
Nobel Sport: www.nobelsportammo.com
Norma: www.norma.cc
North Fork Technologies: www.northforkbullets.com
Nosler Bullets, Inc.: www.nosler.com
Old Western Scrounger: www.ows-ammunition.com
Oregon Trail/Trueshot Bullets: www.trueshotbullets.com
Pattern Control: www.patterncontrol.com
PMC: www.pmcammo.com
Polywad: www.polywad.com
PowerBelt Bullets: www.powerbeltbullets.com
PR Bullets: www.prbullet.com
Precision Ammunition: www.precisionammo.com
Precision Reloading: www.precisionreloading.com
Pro Load Ammunition: www.proload.com
Quality Cartridge: www.qual-cart.com
Rainier Ballistics: www.rainierballistics.com
Ram Shot Powder: www.ramshot.com
Reloading Specialties Inc.: www.reloadingspecialties.com
Remington: www.remington.com
Rio Ammo: www.rioammo.com
Rocky Mountain Cartridge: www.rockymountaincartridge.com
RUAG Ammotec: www.ruag.com
Samco Global Arms: www.samcoglobal.com
Schuetzen Powder: www.schuetzenpowder.com
Sellier & Bellot USA Inc.: www.sb-usa.com
Shilen: www.shilen.com
Sierra: www.sierrabullets.com
Simunition: www.simunition.com
SinterFire, Inc.: www.sinterfire.com
Speer Bullets: www.speer-bullets.com
Sporting Supplies Int'l Inc.: www.ssiintl.com
Starline: www.starlinebrass.com
Swift Bullets Co.: www.swiftbullet.com
Ten-X Ammunition: www.tenxammo.com
Top Brass: www.top-brass.com
Triton Cartridge: www.a-merc.com
Trueshot Bullets: www.trueshotbullets.com
Tru-Tracer: www.trutracer.com
Ultramax Ammunition: www.ultramaxammunition.com
Vihtavuori Lapua: www.vihtavuori-lapua.com
Weatherby: www.weatherby.com
West Coast Bullets: www.westcoastbullet.com
Western Powders Inc.: www.westernpowders.com
Widener's Reloading & Shooters Supply: www.wideners.com
Winchester Ammunition: www.winchester.com
Windjammer Tournament Wads: www.windjammer-wads.com
Wolf Ammunition: www.wolfammo.com
Woodleigh Bullets: www.woodleighbullets.com.au
Zanders Sporting Goods: www.gzanders.com

CASES, SAFES, GUN LOCKS, AND CABINETS

Ace Case Co.: www.acecase.com
AG English Sales Co.: www.agenglish.com
All Americas' Outdoors: www.innernet.net/gunsafe
Alpine Cases: www.alpinecases.com
Aluma Sport by Dee Zee: www.deezee.com
American Security Products: www.amsecusa.com
Americase: www.americase.com
Assault Systems: www.elitesurvival.com
Avery Outdoors, Inc.: www.averyoutdoors.com
Bear Track Cases: www.beartrackcases.com
Boyt Harness Co.: www.boytharness.com
Bulldog Gun Safe Co.: www.gardall.com
Cannon Safe Co.: www.cannonsafe.com
CCL Security Products: www.cclsecurity.com
Concept Development Corp.: www.saf-t-blok.com
Doskocil Mfg. Co.: www.doskocilmfg.com
Fort Knox Safes: www.ftknox.com
Franzen Security Products: www.securecase.com
Frontier Safe Co.: www.frontiersafe.com
Granite Security Products: www.granitesafe.com
Gunlocker Phoenix USA Inc.: www.gunlocker.com
GunVault: www.gunvault.com
Hakuba USA Inc.: www.hakubausa.com
Heritage Safe Co.: www.heritagesafecompany.com
Hide-A-Gun: www.hide-a-gun.com
Homak Safes: www.homak.com
Hunter Company: www.huntercompany.com
Kalispel Case Line: www.kalispelcaseline.com
Knouff & Knouff, Inc.: www.kkair.com
Knoxx Industries: www.knoxx, com
Kolpin Mfg. Co.: www.kolpin.com
Liberty Safe & Security: www.libertysafe.com
New Innovative Products: www.starlightcases
Noble Security Systems Inc.: www.noble.co.ll
Phoenix USA Inc.: www.gunlocker.com
Plano Molding Co.: www.planomolding.com
Rhino Gun Cases: www.rhinoguns.com
Rhino Safe: www.rhinosafe.com
Rotary Gun Racks: www.gun-racks.com
Safe Tech, Inc.: www.safrgun.com
Saf-T-Hammer: www.saf-t-hammer.com
Saf-T-Lok Corp.: www.saf-t-lok.com
San Angelo All-Aluminum Products Inc.:
    sasptuld@x.netcom.com
Securecase: www.securecase.com
Shot Lock Corp.: www.shotlock.com
Smart Lock Technology Inc.: www.smartlock.com
Sportsmans Steel Safe Co.: www.sportsmansteelsafes.com
Stack-On Products Co.: www.stack-on.com
Starlight Cases: www.starlightcases.com
Sun Welding: www.sunwelding.com
Technoframes: www.technoframes.com
T.Z. Case Int'l: www.tzcase.com
Versatile Rack Co.: www.versatilegunrack.com
V-Line Industries: www.vlineind.com
Winchester Safes: www.fireking.com
Ziegel Engineering: www.ziegeleng.com
Zonetti Armor: www.zonettiarmor.com

CHRONOGRAPHS AND BALLISTIC SOFTWARE

Barnes Ballistic Program: www.barnesbullets.com
Ballisticard Systems: www.ballisticards.com
Competition Electronics: www.competitionelectronics.com
Competitive Edge Dynamics: www.cedhk.com
Hodgdon Shotshell Program: www.hodgdon.com
Lee Shooter Program: www.leeprecision.com

Load From A Disk: www.loadammo.com
Oehler Research Inc.: www.oehler-research.com
PACT: www.pact.com
ProChrony: www.competitionelectronics.com
Quickload: www.neconos.com
RCBS Load: www.rcbs.com
Shooting Chrony Inc.: www.shootingchrony.com
Sierra Infinity Ballistics Program: www.sierrabullets.com

CLEANING PRODUCTS

Accupro: www.accupro.com
Ballistol USA: www.ballistol.com
Battenfeld Technologies: www.battenfeldtechnologies.com
Birchwood Casey: www.birchwoodcasey.com
Blue Wonder: www.bluewonder.com
Bore Tech: www.boretech.com
Break-Free, Inc.: www.break-free.com
Bruno Shooters Supply: www.brunoshooters.com
Butch's Bore Shine: www.lymanproducts.com
C.J. Weapons Accessories: www.cjweapons, com
Clenzoil: www.clenzoil.com
Corrosion Technologies: www.corrosionx.com
Dewey Mfg.: www.deweyrods.com
DuraCoat: www.lauerweaponry.com
Eezox Inc.: www.xmission.com
G 96: www.g96.com
Gunslick Gun Care: www.gunslick.com
Gunzilla: www.topduckproducts.com
Hollands Shooters Supply: www.hollandgun.com
Hoppes: www.hoppes.com
Hydrosorbent Products: www.dehumidify.com
Inhibitor VCI Products: www.theinhibitor.com
Iosso Products: www.iosso.com
KG Industries: www.kgcoatings.com
Kleen-Bore Inc.: www.kleen-bore.com
L&R Mfg.: www.lrultrasonics.com
Lyman: www.lymanproducts.com
Mil-Comm Products: www.mil-comm.com
Militec-1: www.militec-1.com
Mpro7 Gun Care: www.mp7.com
Old West Snake Oil: www.oldwestsnakeoil.com
Otis Technology, Inc.: www.otisgun.com
Outers: www.outers-guncare.com
Ox-Yoke Originals Inc.: www.oxyoke.com
Parker-Hale Ltd.: www.parker-hale.com
Prolix Lubricant: www.prolixlubricant.com
ProShot Products: www.proshotproducts.com
ProTec Lubricants: www.proteclubricants.com
Rusteprufe Labs: www.rusteprufe.com
Sagebrush Products: www.sagebrushproducts.com
Sentry Solutions Ltd.: www.sentrysolutions.com
Sharp Shoot R Precision Products: www.sharpshootr.com
Shooters Choice Gun Care: www.shooters-choice.com
Silencio: www.silencio.com
Slip 2000: www.slip2000.com
Stony Point Products: www.uncle-mikes.com
Tetra Gun: www.tetraproducts.com
The TM Solution: thetmsolution@comcast.net
Top Duck Products: www.topduckproducts.com
Ultra Bore Coat: www.ultracoatingsinc.com
World's Fastest Gun Bore Cleaner: www.michaels-oregon.com

FIREARM MANUFACTURERS AND IMPORTERS

A-Square: www.asquarecompany.com
Accuracy Int'l North America: www.accuracyinternational.org
Accuracy Rifle Systems: www.mini-14.net
Ace Custom 45's: www.acecustom45.com
Advanced Weapons Technology: www.AWT-Zastava.com

AIM: www.aimsurplus.com
AirForce Airguns: www.airforceairguns.com
Air Gun, Inc.: www.airrifle-china.com
Airguns of Arizona: www.airgunsofarizona.com
Airgun Express: www.airgunexpress.com
Alchemy Arms: www.alchemyltd.com
Alexander Arms: www.alexanderarms.com
American Derringer Corp.: www.amderringer.com
American Spirit Arms Corp.: www.gunkits.com
American Tactical Imports: www.americantactical.us
American Western Arms: www.awaguns.com
Anics Corp.: www.anics.com
Anschutz: www.anschutz-sporters.com
Answer Products Co.: www.answerrifles.com
AR-7 Industries, LLC: www.ar-7.com
Ares Defense Systems: www.aresdefense.com
Armalite: www.armalite.com
Armi Sport: www.armisport.com
Armory USA: www.globaltraders.com
Armsco: www.armsco.net
Armscorp USA Inc.: www.armscorpusa.com
Arnold Arms: www.arnoldarms.com
Arsenal Inc.: www.arsenalinc.com
Arthur Brown Co.: www.eabco.com
Atlanta Cutlery Corp.: www.atlantacutlery.com
Auction Arms: www.auctionarms.com
Autauga Arms, Inc.: www.autaugaarms.com
Auto-Ordnance Corp.: www.tommygun.com
AWA Int'l: www.awaguns.com
Axtell Rifle Co.: www.riflesmith.com
AyA: www.aya-fineguns.com
Baikal: www.baikalinc.ru/eng/
Ballard Rifles, LLC: www.ballardrifles.com
Barrett Firearms Mfg.: www.barrettrifles.com
Beeman Precision Airguns: www.beeman.com
Benelli USA Corp.: www.benelliusa.com
Benjamin Sheridan: www.crosman.com
Beretta U.S.A. Corp.: www.berettausa.com
Bernardelli: www.bernardelli.com
Bersa: www.bersa-llama.com
Bill Hanus Birdguns: www.billhanusbirdguns.com
Blaser Jagdwaffen Gmbh: www.blaser.de
Bleiker: www.bleiker.ch
Bluegrass Armory: www.bluegrassarmory.com
Bond Arms: www.bondarms.com
Borden's Rifles, Inc.: www.bordensrifles.com
Boss & Co.: www.bossguns.co.uk
Bowen Classic Arms: www.bowenclassicarms.com
Briley Mfg: www.briley.com
BRNO Arms: www.zbrojovka.com
Brown, David McKay: www.mckaybrown.com
Brown, Ed Products: www.brownprecision.com
Browning: www.browning.com
BRP Corp.: www.brpguns.com
BSA Guns: www.bsaguns.com
BUL Ltd.: www.bultransmark.com
Bushmaster Firearms/Quality Parts: www.bushmaster.com
BWE Firearms: www.bwefirearms.com
Caesar Guerini USA: www.gueriniusa.com
Cape Outfitters: www.doublegun.com
Carbon 15: www.professional-ordnance.com
Caspian Arms, Ltd.: www.caspianarmsltd.8m.com
Casull Arms Corp.: www.casullarms.com
Calvary Arms: www.calvaryarms.com
CDNN Investments, Inc.: www.cdnninvestments.com
Century Arms: www.centuryarms.com
Chadick's Ltd.: www.chadicks-ltd.com

Champlin Firearms: www.champlinarms.com
Chapuis Arms: www.doubleguns.com/chapuis.htm
Charles Daly: www.charlesdaly.com
Charter Arms: www.charterfirearms.com
CheyTac USA: www.cheytac.com
Christensen Arms: www.christensenarms.com
Cimarron Firearms Co.: www.cimarron-firearms.com
Clark Custom Guns: www.clarkcustomguns.com
Cobra Enterprises: www.cobrapistols.com
Cogswell & Harrison: www.cogswell.co.uk/home.htm
Colt's Mfg Co.: www.colt.com
Compasseco, Inc.: www.compasseco.com
Connecticut Valley Arms: www.cva.com
Cooper Firearms: www.cooperfirearms.com
Corner Shot: www.cornershot.com
CPA Rifles: www.singleshotrifles.com
Crosman: www.crosman.com
Crossfire, LLC: www.crossfirelle.com
C.Sharp Arms Co.: www.csharparms.com
CVA: www.cva.com
Czechpoint Int'l: www.czechpoint-usa.com
CZ USA: www.cz-usa.com
Daisy Mfg Co.: www.daisy.com
Dakota Arms Inc.: www.dakotaarms.com
Dan Wesson Firearms: www.danwessonfirearms.com
Davis Industries: www.davisindguns.com
Detonics USA: www.detonicsusa.com
Diana: www.diana-airguns.de
Dixie Gun Works: www.dixiegunworks.com
Dlask Arms Corp.: www.dlask.com
D.P.M.S., Inc.: www.dpmsinc.com
D.S.Arms, Inc.: www.dsarms.com
Dumoulin: www.dumoulin-herstal.com
Dynamit Noble: www.dnrws.com
EAA Corp.: www.eaacorp.com
Eagle Imports, Inc.: www.bersa-llama.com
Ed Brown Products: www.edbrown.com
EDM Arms: www.edmarms.com
E.M.F. Co.: www.emf-company.com
Enterprise Arms: www.enterprise.com
E R Shaw: www.ershawbarrels.com
European American Armory Corp.: www.eaacorp.com
Evans, William: www.williamevans.com
Excel Arms: www.excelarms.com
Fabarm: www.fabarm.com
FAC-Guns-N-Stuff: www.gunsnstuff.com
Falcon Pneumatic Systems: www.falcon-airguns.com
Fausti Stefano: www.faustistefanoarms.com
Firestorm: www.firestorm-sgs.com
Flodman Guns: www.flodman.com
FN Herstal: www.fnherstal.com
FNH USA: www.fnhusa.com
Franchi: www.franchiusa.com
Freedom Arms: www.freedomarms.com
Galazan: www.connecticutshotgun.com
Gambo Renato: www.renatogamba.it
Gamo: www.gamo.com
Gary Reeder Custom Guns: www.reeder-customguns.com
Gazelle Arms: www.gazellearms.com
German Sport Guns: www.germansportguns.com
Gibbs Rifle Company: www.gibbsrifle.com
Glock: www.glock.com
Griffin & Howe: www.griffinhowe.com
Grizzly Big Boar Rifle: www.largrizzly.com
GSI Inc.: www.gsifirearms.com
Guerini: www.gueriniusa.com
Gunbroker.Com: www.gunbroker.com

Hammerli: www.carl-walther.com
Hatfield Gun Co.: www.hatfield-usa.com
Hatsan Arms Co.: www.hatsan.com.tr
Heckler and Koch: www.hk-usa.com
Henry Repeating Arms Co.: www.henryrepeating.com
Heritage Mfg.: www.heritagemfg.com
Heym: www.heym-waffenfabrik.de
High Standard Mfg.: www.highstandard.com
Hi-Point Firearms: www.hi-pointfirearms.com
Holland & Holland: www.hollandandholland.com
H&R 1871 Firearms: www.hr1871.com
H-S Precision: www.hsprecision.com
Hunters Lodge Corp.: www.hunterslodge.com
IAR Inc.: www.iar-arms.com
Imperial Miniature Armory: www.1800miniature.com
Interarms: www.interarms.com
International Military Antiques, Inc.: www.ima-usa.com
Inter Ordnance: www.interordnance.com
Intrac Arms International LLC: www.hsarms.com
Israel Arms: www.israelarms.com
Iver Johnson Arms: www.iverjohnsonarms.com
Izhevsky Mekhanichesky Zavod: www.baikalinc.ru
James River Mfg.: www.jamesriverarmory.com
Jarrett Rifles, Inc.: www.jarrettrifles.com
J&G Sales, Ltd.: www.jgsales.com
Johannsen Express Rifle: www.johannsen-jagd.de
Jonathan Arthur Ciener: www.22lrconversions.com
JP Enterprises, Inc.: www.jprifles.com
Kahr Arms/Auto-Ordnance: www.kahr.com
K.B.I.: www.kbi-inc.com
Kel-Tec CNC Ind., Inc.: www.kel-tec.com
Kifaru: www.kifaru.net
Kimber: www.kimberamerica.com
Knight's Armament Co.: www.knightsarmco.com
Knight Rifles: www.knightrifles.com
Korth: www.korthwaffen.de
Krebs Custom Guns: www.krebscustom.com
Krieghoff Int'l: www.krieghoff.com
KY Imports, Inc.: www.kyimports.com
K-VAR: www.k-var.com
L.A.R Mfg: www.largrizzly.com
Lazzeroni Arms Co.: www.lazzeroni.com
Legacy Sports International: www.legacysports.com
Les Baer Custom, Inc.: www.lesbaer.com
Lewis Machine & Tool Co.: www.lewismachine.net
Linebaugh Custom Sixguns: www.sixgunner.com/linebaugh
Ljutic: www.ljuticgun.com
Llama: www.bersa-llama.com
Lone Star Rifle Co.: www.lonestarrifle.com
LRB Arms: www.lrbarms.com
LWRC Int'l: www.lwrifles.com
Magnum Research: www.magnumresearch.com
Majestic Arms: www.majesticarms.com
Markesbery Muzzleloaders: www.markesbery.com
Marksman Products: www.marksman.com
Marlin: www.marlinfirearms.com
Mauser: www.mauser.com
McMillan Bros Rifle Co.: www.mcfamily.com
MDM: www.mdm-muzzleloaders.com
Meacham Rifles: www.meachamrifles.com
Merkel: www.hk-usa.com
Miller Arms: www.millerarms.com
Miltech: www.miltecharms.com
Miltex, Inc.: www.miltexusa.com
Mitchell's Mausers: www.mitchellsales.com
MK Ballistic Systems: www.mkballistics.com
M-Mag: www.mmag.com

Montana Rifle Co.: www.montanarifleman.com
Mossberg: www.mossberg.com
Navy Arms: www.navyarms.com
Nesika: www.nesika.com
New England Arms Corp.: www.newenglandarms.com
New England Custom Gun Svc, Ltd.:
    www.newenglandcustomgun.com
New England Firearms: www.hr1871.com
New Ultra Light Arms: www.newultralight.com
Nighthawk Custom: www.nighthawkcustom.com
North American Arms: www.northamericanarms.com
Nosler Bullets, Inc.: www.nosler.com
Nowlin Mfg. Inc.: www.nowlinguns.com
O.F. Mossberg & Sons: www.mossberg.com
Ohio Ordnance Works: www.ohioordnanceworks.com
Olympic Arms: www.olyarms.com
Panther Arms: www.dpmsinc.com
Para-USA: www.para-usa.com
Pedersoli Davide & Co.: www.davide-pedersoli.com
Perazzi: www.perazzi.com
Pietta: www.pietta.it
PKP Knife-Pistol: www.sanjuanenterprise.com
Power Custom: www.powercustom.com
Professional Arms: www.professional-arms.com
PTR 91, Inc.: www.ptr91.com
Purdey & Sons: www.purdey.com
Remington: www.remington.com
Republic Arms Inc.: www.republicarmsinc.com
Rhineland Arms, Inc.: www.rhinelandarms.com
Rigby: www.johnrigbyandco.com
Rizzini USA: www.rizziniusa.com
Robar Companies, Inc.: www.robarguns.com
Robinson Armament Co.: www.robarm.com
Rock River Arms, Inc.: www.rockriverarms.com
Rogue Rifle Co. Inc.: www.chipmunkrifle.com
Rohrbaugh Firearms: www.rohrbaughfirearms.com
Rossi Arms: www.rossiusa.com
RPM: www.rpmxlpistols.com
Russian American Armory: www.raacfirearms.com
RUAG Ammotec: www.ruag.com
Sabatti SPA: www.sabatti.com
Sabre Defense Industries: www.sabredefense.com
Saco Defense: www.sacoinc.com
Safari Arms: www.olyarms.com
Sako: www.berettausa.com
Samco Global Arms Inc.: www.samcoglobal.com
Sarco Inc.: www.sarcoinc.com
Savage Arms Inc.: www.savagearms.com
Scattergun Technologies Inc.: www.wilsoncombat.com
Searcy Enterprises: www.searcyent.com
Shiloh Rifle Mfg.: www.shilohrifle.com
SIGARMS, Inc.: www.sigarms.com
Simpson Ltd.: www.simpsonltd.com
SKB Shotguns: www.skbshotguns.com
Smith & Wesson: www.smith-wesson.com
SOG International, Inc.: soginc@go-concepts.com
Sphinx System: www.sphinxarms.com
Springfield Armory: www.springfield-armory.com
SSK Industries: www.sskindustries.com
Stag Arms: www.stagarms.com
Steyr Arms, Inc.: www.steyrarms.com
Stoeger Industries: www.stoegerindustries.com
Strayer-Voigt Inc.: www.sviguns.com
Sturm, Ruger & Company: www.ruger-firearms.com
Tactical Rifles: www.tacticalrifles.com
Tactical Solutions: www.tacticalsol.com
Tar-Hunt Slug Guns, Inc.: www.tar-hunt.com

Taser Int'l: www.taser.com
Taurus: www.taurususa.com
Taylor's & Co., Inc.: www.taylorsfirearms.com
Tennessee Guns: www.tennesseeguns.com
TG Int'l: www.tnguns.com
The 1877 Sharps Co.: www.1877sharps.com
Thompson Center Arms: www.tcarms.com
Tikka: www.berettausa.com
TNW, Inc.: www.tnwfirearms.com
Traditions: www.traditionsfirearms.com
Tristar Sporting Arms: www.tristarsportingarms.com
Uberti: www.ubertireplicas.com
Ultralite 50: www.ultralite50.com
Ultra Light Arms: www.newultralight.com
Umarex: www.umarex.com
U.S. Firearms Mfg. Co.: www.usfirearms.com
Valkyrie Arms: www.valkyriearms.com
Vektor Arms: www.vektorarms.com
Verney-Carron: www.verney-carron.com
Volquartsen Custom Ltd.: www.volquartsen.com
Vulcan Armament: www.vulcanarmament.com
Walther USA: www.waltheramerica.com
Weatherby: www.weatherby.com
Webley and Scott Ltd.: www.webley.co.uk
Westley Richards: www.westleyrichards.com
Widley: www.widleyguns.com
Wild West Guns: www.wildwestguns.com
William Larkin Moore & Co.: www.doublegun.com
Wilson Combat: www.wilsoncombat.com
Winchester Rifles and Shotguns: www.winchesterguns.com

MISCELLANEOUS SHOOTING PRODUCTS

10X Products Group: www.10Xwear.com
Aero Peltor: www.aearo.com
American Body Armor: www.americanbodyarmor.com
Armor Holdings Products: www.armorholdings.com
Battenfeld Technologies: www.battenfeldtechnologies.com
Beamhit: www.beamhit.com
Beartooth: www.beartoothproducts.com
Bodyguard by S&W: www.yourbodyguard.com
Burnham Brothers: www.burnhambrothers.com
Collectors Armory: www.collectorsarmory.com
Dalloz Safety: www.cdalloz.com
Deben Group Industries Inc.: www.deben.com
Decot Hy-Wyd Sport Glasses: www.sportyglasses.com
E.A.R., Inc.: www.earinc.com
First Choice Armor: www.firstchoicearmor.com
Gunstands: www.gunstands.com
Howard Leight Hearing Protectors: www.howardleight.com
Hunters Specialities: www.hunterspec.com
Johnny Stewart Wildlife Calls: www.hunterspec.com
Merit Corporation: www.meritcorporation.com
Michaels of Oregon: www.michaels-oregon.com
MPI Outdoors: www.mpioutdoors.com
MTM Case-Gard: www.mtmcase-gard.com
North Safety Products: www.northsafety-brea.com
Plano Molding: www.planomolding.com
Pro-Ears: www.pro-ears.com
Second Chance Body Armor Inc.: www.secondchance.com
Silencio: www.silencio.com
Smart Lock Technologies: www.smartlock.com
Surefire: www.surefire.com
Taser Int'l: www.taser.com
Walker's Game Ear Inc.: www.walkersgameear.com

MUZZLELOADING FIREARMS AND PRODUCTS

American Pioneer Powder: www.americanpioneerpowder.com

Armi Sport: www.armisport.com
Barnes Bullets: www.barnesbullets, com
Black Powder Products: www.bpiguns.com
Buckeye Barrels: www.buckeyebarrels.com
Cabin Creek Muzzleloading: www.cabincreek.net
CVA: www.cva.com
Caywood Gunmakers: www.caywoodguns.com
Davide Perdsoli & co.: www.davide-pedersoli.com
Dixie Gun Works, Inc.: www.dixiegun.com
Elephant/Swiss Black Powder:
    www.elephantblackpowder.com
Goex Black Powder: www.goexpowder.com
Green Mountain Rifle Barrel Co.: www.gmriflebarrel.com
Gunstocks Plus: www.gunstocksplus.com
Harvester Bullets: www.harvesterbullets.com
Hornady: www.hornady.com
Jedediah Starr Trading Co.: www.jedediah-starr.com
Jim Chambers Flintlocks: www.flintlocks.com
Kahnke Gunworks: www.powderandbow.com/kahnke/
Knight Rifles: www.knightrifles.com
Knob Mountain Muzzleloading:
    www.knobmountainmuzzleloading.com
The leatherman: www.blackpowderbags.com
Log Cabin Shop: www.logcabinshop.com
L&R Lock Co.: www.lr-rpl.com
Lyman: www.lymanproducts.com
Magkor Industries: www.magkor.com
MDM Muzzleloaders: www.mdm-muzzleloaders.com
Middlesex Village Trading: www.middlesexvillagetrading.com
Millennium Designed Muzzleloaders:
    www.mdm-muzzleloaders.com
MSM, Inc.: www.msmfg.com
Muzzleloader Builders Supply:
    www.muzzleloadersbuilderssupply.com
Muzzleload Magnum Products: www.mmpsabots.com
Muzzleloading Technologies, Inc.: www.mtimuzzleloading.com
Navy Arms: www.navyarms.com
Northwest Trade Guns: www.northstarwest.com
Nosler, Inc.: www.nosler.com
October Country Muzzleloading: www.oct-country.com
Ox-Yoke Originals Inc.: www.oxyoke.com
Pacific Rifle Co.: pacificrifle@aol.com
Palmetto Arms: www.palmetto.it
Pietta: www.pietta.it
Powerbelt Bullets: www.powerbeltbullets.com
PR Bullets: www.prbullets.com
Precision Rifle Dead Center Bullets: www.prbullet.com
R.E. Davis CVo.: www.redaviscompany.com
Remington: www.remington.com
Rightnour Mfg. Co. Inc.: www.rmcsports.com
The Rifle Shop: trshoppe@aol.com
Savage Arms, Inc.: www.savagearms.com
Schuetzen Powder: www.schuetzenpowder.com
TDC: www.tdcmfg.com
Tennessee Valley Muzzleloading: www.avsia.com/tvm
Thompson Center Arms: www.tcarms.com
Tiger Hunt Stocks: www.gunstockwood.com
Track of the Wolf: www.trackofthewolf.com
Traditions Performance Muzzleloading:
    www.traditionsfirearms.com
Vernon C. Davis & Co.: www.stonewallcreekoutfitters.com

PUBLICATIONS, VIDEOS, AND CDS

Arms and Military Press: www.skennerton.com
A&J Arms Booksellers: www.ajarmsbooksellers.com
American Cop: www.americancopmagazine.com
American Firearms Industry: www.amfire.com

American Handgunner: www.americanhandgunner.com
American Hunter: www.nrapublications.org
American Pioneer Video: www.americanpioneervideo.com
American Rifleman: www.nrapublications.org
American Shooting Magazine: www.americanshooting.com
Backwoodsman: www.backwoodsmanmag.com
Black Powder Cartridge News: www.blackpowderspg.com
Blue Book Publications: www.bluebookinc.com
Combat Handguns: www.combathandguns.com
Concealed Carry: www.uscca.us
Cornell Publications: www.cornellpubs.com
Countrywide Press: www.countrysport.com
DBI Books/Krause Publications: www.krause.com
Fouling Shot: www.castbulletassoc.org
George Shumway Publisher: www.shumwaypublisher.com
Gun List: www.gunlist.com
Gun Video: www.gunvideo.com
GUNS Magazine: www.gunsmagazine.com
Guns & Ammo: www.gunsandammomag.com
Gun Week: www.gunweek.com
Gun World: www.gunworld.com
Harris Publications: www.harrispublications.com
Heritage Gun Books: www.gunbooks.com
Krause Publications: www.krause.com
Law and Order: www.hendonpub.com
Man at Arms: www.manatarmsbooks.com
Muzzleloader: www.muzzleloadermag.com
Paladin Press: www.paladin-press.com
Precision Shooting: www.precisionshooting.com
Ray Riling Arms Books: www.rayrilingarmsbooks.com
Rifle and Handloader Magazines: www.riflemagazine.com
Safari Press Inc.: www.safaripress.com
Scurlock Publishing: www.muzzleloadingmag.com
Shoot! Magazine: www.shootmagazine.com
Shooting Illustrated: www.nrapublications.org
Shooting Industry: www.shootingindustry.com
Shooting Sports Retailer: www.shootingsportsretailer.com
Shooting Sports USA: www.nrapublications.org
Shotgun News: www.shotgunnews.com
Shotgun Report: www.shotgunreport.com
Shotgun Sports Magazine: www.shotgun-sports.com
Single Shot Rifle Journal: www.assra.com
Small Arms Review: www.smallarmsreview.com
Small Caliber News: www.smallcaliber.com
Sporting Clays Web Edition: www.sportingclays.net
Sports Afield: www.sportsafield.comm
Sportsmen on Film: www.sportsmenonfilm.com
SWAT Magazine: www.swatmag.com
The Single Shot Exchange Magazine:
    singleshot@earthlink.net
The Sixgunner: www.sskindustries.com
Varmint Hunter: www.varminthunter.org
VSP Publications: www.gunbooks.com

RELOADING TOOLS

Antimony Man: www.theantimonyman.com
Ballisti-Cast Mfg.: www.ballisti-cast.com
Battenfeld Technologies: www.battenfeldtechnologies.com
Bruno Shooters Supply: www.brunoshooters.com
Buffalo Arms: www.buffaloarms.com
CabineTree: www.castingstuff.com
Camdex, Inc.: www.camdexloader.com
CH/4D Custom Die: www.ch4d.com
Colorado Shooters Supply: www.hochmoulds.com
Corbin Mfg & Supply Co.: www.corbins.com
Dillon Precision: www.dillonprecision.com
Forster Precision Products: www.forsterproducts.com

GSI International, Inc.: www.gsiinternational.com
Hanned Line: www.hanned.com
Harrell's Precision: www.harrellsprec.com
Holland's Shooting Supplies: www.hollandgun.com
Hornady: www.hornady.com
Huntington Reloading Products: www.huntingtons.com
J & J Products Co.: www.jandjproducts.com
Lead Bullet Technology: www.lbtmoulds.com
Lee Precision, Inc.: www.leeprecision.com
Littleton Shotmaker: www.leadshotmaker.com
Load Data: www.loaddata.com
Lyman: www.lymanproducts.com
Magma Engineering: www.magmaengr.com
Mayville Engineering Co. (MEC): www.mecreloaders.com
Midway: www.midwayusa.com
Moly-Bore: www.molybore.com
Montana Bullet Works: www.montanabulletworks.com
MTM Case-Guard: www.mtmcase-guard.com
NECO: www.neconos.com
NEI: www.neihandtools.com
Neil Jones Custom Products: www.neiljones.com
Ponsness/Warren: www.reloaders.com
Quinetics Corp.: www.quineticscorp.com
Ranger Products:
    www.pages.prodigy.com/rangerproducts.home.htm
Rapine Bullet Mold Mfg Co.: www.bulletmoulds.com
RCBS: www.rcbs.com
Redding Reloading Equipment: www.redding-reloading.com
Russ Haydon's Shooting Supplies: www.shooters-supply.com
Sinclair Int'l Inc.: www.sinclairintl.com
Stoney Point Products Inc: www.stoneypoint.com
Thompson Bullet Lube Co.: www.thompsonbulletlube.com
Vickerman Seating Die: www.castingstuff.com
Wilson (L.E. Wilson): www.lewilson.com

RESTS: BENCH, PORTABLE, ATTACHABLE

Battenfeld Technolgies: www.battenfeldtechnologies.com
Bench Master: www.bench-master.com
B-Square: www.b-square.com
Bullshooter: www.bullshooterssightingin.com
Desert Mountain Mfg.: www.benchmasterusa.com
Harris Engineering Inc.: www.harrisbipods
Kramer Designs: www.snipepod.com
L Thomas Rifle Support: www.ltsupport.com
Level-Lok: www.levellok.com
Midway: www.midwayusa.com
Predator Sniper Styx: www.predatorsniperstyx.com
Ransom International: www.ransom-intl.com
Rotary Gun Racks: www.gun-racks.com
R.W. Hart: www.rwhart.com
Sinclair Intl, Inc.: www.sinclairintl.com
Stoney Point Products: www.uncle-mikes.com
Target Shooting: www.targetshooting.com
Varmint Masters: www.varmintmasters.com
Versa-Pod: www.versa-pod.com

SHOOTING ORGANIZATIONS, SCHOOLS AND RANGES

Amateur Trapshooting Assoc.: www.shootata.com
American Custom Gunmakers Guild: www.acgg.org
American Gunsmithing Institute: www.americangunsmith.com
American Pistolsmiths Guild: www.americanpistol.com
American Shooting Sports Council: www.assc.com
American Single Shot Rifle Assoc.: www.assra.com
Antique Shooting Tool Collector's Assoc.:
    www.oldshootingtools.org
Assoc. of Firearm & Tool Mark Examiners: www.afte.org

BATF: www.atf.ustreas.gov
Blackwater Lodge and Training Center:
   www.blackwaterlodge.com
Boone and Crockett Club: www.boone-crockett.org
Buckmasters, Ltd.: www.buckmasters.com
Cast Bullet Assoc.: www.castbulletassoc.org
Citizens Committee for the Right to Keep & Bear Arms:
   www.ccrkba.org
Civilian Marksmanship Program: www.odcmp.com
Colorado School of Trades: www.gunsmith-school.com
Cylinder & Slide Pistolsmithing Schools:
   www.cylinder-slide.com
Ducks Unlimited: www.ducks.org
4-H Shooting Sports Program: www.4-hshootingsports.org
Fifty Caliber Institute: www.fiftycal.org
Fifty Caliber Shooters Assoc.: www.fcsa.org
Firearms Coalition: www.nealknox.com
Front Sight Firearms Training Institute: www.frontsight.com
German Gun Collectors Assoc.: www.germanguns.com
Gun Clubs: www.associatedgunclubs.org
Gun Owners' Action League: www.goal.org
Gun Owners of America: www.gunowners.org
Gun Trade Asssoc. Ltd.: www.brucepub.com/gta
Gunsite Training Center, Inc.: www.gunsite.com
Handgun Hunters International: www.sskindustries.com
Hunting and Shooting Sports Heritage Fund:
   www.huntandshoot.org
I.C.E. Traing: www.icetraining.com
International Defense Pistol Assoc.: www.idpa.com
International Handgun Metallic Silhouette Assoc.:
   www.ihmsa.org
International Hunter Education Assoc.: www.ihea.com
Int'l Law Enforcement Educators and Trainers Assoc.:
   www.ileeta.com
International Single Shot Assoc.: www.issa-schuetzen.org
Jews for the Preservation of Firearms Ownership: www.jpfo.org
Mule Deer Foundation: www.muledeer.org
Muzzle Loaders Assoc. of Great Britain: www.mlagb.com
National 4-H Shooting Sports: www.4-hshootingsports.org
National Association of Sporting Goods Wholesalers:
   www.nasgw.org
National Benchrest Shooters Assoc.: www.benchrest.com
National Muzzle Loading Rifle Assoc.: www.nmlra.org
National Reloading Manufacturers Assoc:
   www.reload-nrma.com
National Rifle Assoc.: www.nra.org
National Rifle Assoc. ILA: www.nraila.org
National Shooting Sports Foundation: www.nssf.org
National Skeet Shooters Association: www.nssa-nsca.com
National Sporting Clays Assoc.: www.nssa-nsca.com
National Wild Turkey Federation: www.nwtf.com
NICS/FBI: www.fbi.gov
North American Hunting Club: www.huntingclub.com
Order of Edwardian Gunners (Vintagers): www.vintagers.org
Outdoor Industry Foundation:
   www.outdoorindustryfoundation.org
Pennsylvania Gunsmith School: www.pagunsmith.com
Piedmont Community College: www.piedmontcc.edu
Quail Unlimited: www.qu.org
Remington Society of America: www.remingtonsociety.com
Right To Keep and Bear Arms: www.rkba.org
Rocky Mountain Elk Foundation: www.rmef.org
SAAMI: www.saami.org
Safari Club International: www.scifirstforhunters.org
Scholastic Clay Target Program: www.nssf.org/sctp
Second Amendment Foundation: www.saf.org
Second Amendment Sisters: www.2asisters.org
Shooting Ranges Int'l: www.shootingranges.com

Sig Sauer Academy: www.sigsauer.com
Single Action Shooting Society: www.sassnet.com
Students for Second Amendment: www.sf2a.org
Suarez Training: www.warriortalk.com
S&W Academy and Nat'l Firearms Trng. Center:
   www.sw-academy.com
Tactical Defense Institute: www.tdiohio.com
Tactical Life: www.tactical-life.com
Ted Nugent United Sportsmen of America: www.tnugent.com
Thunder Ranch: www.thunderranchinc.com
Trapshooters Homepage: www.trapshooters.com
Trinidad State Junior College: www.trinidadstate.edu
U.S. Concealed Carry Association: www.uscca.us
U.S. Int'l Clay Target Assoc.: www.usicta.com
United States Fish and Wildlife Service: www.fws.gov
U.S. Practical Shooting Assoc.: www.uspsa.org
USA Shooting: www.usashooting.com
Varmint Hunters Assoc.: www.varminthunter.org
U.S. Sportsmen's Alliance: www.ussportsmen.org
Winchester Arms Collectors Assoc.:
   www.winchestercollector.com
Women Hunters: www.womanhunters.com
Women's Shooting Sports Foundation: www.wssf.org

MAJOR SHOOTING WEBSITES AND LINKS

24 Hour Campfire: www.24hourcampfire.com
Alphabetic Index of Links: www.gunsgunsguns.com
Auction Arms: www.auctionarms.com
Benchrest Central: www.benchrest.com
Big Game Hunt: www.biggamehunt.net
Bullseye Pistol: www.bullseyepistol.com
Firearms History: www.researchpress.co.uk/firearms
Glock Talk: www.glocktalk.com
Gun Broker Auctions: www.gunbroker.com
Gun Industry: www.gunindustry.com
Gun Blast: www.gunblast.com
Gun Boards: www.gunboards.com
GunsAmerica.com: www.gunsamerica.com
Guns Unified Nationally Endorsing Dignity: www.guned.com
Gun Shop Finder: www.gunshopfinder.com
GUNS and Hunting: www.gunsandhunting.com
Hunt and Shoot (NSSF): www.huntandshoot.org
Keep and Bear Arms: www.keepandbeararms.com
Leverguns: www.leverguns.com
Load Swap: www.loadswap.com
Outdoor Press Room: www.outdoorpressroom.com
Real Guns: www.realguns.com
Ruger Forum: www.rugerforum.com
SavageShooters: www.savageshooters.com
Shooters Forum: www.shootersforum.com
Shotgun Sports Resource Guide: www.shotgunsports.com
Sixgunner: www.sixgunner.com
Sniper's Hide: www.snipershide.com
Sportsman's Web: www.sportsmansweb.com
Surplus Rifles: www.surplusrifle.com
Tactical-Life: www.tactical-life.com
Wing Shoooting USA: www.wingshootingusa.org

Introduction to the Gun Digest® Reloading Archives

WELCOME TO THE 9th Edition of *ABCs of Reloading*!

In this edition, we proudly present you with what we feel are the best – the most enduring – reloading articles ever printedin Gun Digest. Founded in 1944, Gun Digest was meant to be a one-time-only publication, but it was so successful that it continued on to the present day as the world's biggest and best firearms annual.

Gun Digest first took notice of the reloading hobby in its 1947-1948 edition, devoting a few pages to ammunition and a basic primer on reloading. The distinction of having the very first piece dealing specifically with reloading to appear in Gun Digest falls to Lt. Col. E. Naramore, for his 1948 piece titled, simply, "Reloading Ammunition." In 1952, Gun Digest presented a brief treatise on bullet casting by the great Col. Townsend Whelen, dean of American gunwriters. Then, for some unknown reason, Gun Digest Editor John T. Amber didn't feature reloading pieces in Gun Digest to any appreciable extent until the 1958 edition, choosing instead to deal with the subject in the book's catalog section. Happily, in the 1958 edition, Amber reversed his position and began running full-length articles on reloading, many of which you can read in the following pages.

In selecting the articles that follow, w have tried to avoid pieces that are hopelessly outdated. For example, Gun Digest over the years presented many cutting-edge pieces on chronographs – cutting-edge in their day, that is. Modern digital technology has rendered chronographs from the 1960s and 1970s obsolete, though we can tell you from personal experience that many are still in use.

Likewise, we have avoided articles that emphasized contemporary reloading products such as the Winchester AA shotshell wad and plastic hulls. Big news then, of course, but today, not so much.

A caveat: Some of these articles, such as Smokeless Loads for Double Rifles, from the 1975 edition, contain reloading data that was accurate when the article was first published. Over the years, powder formulations may have changed – so no reloading data in these pages should be used to create reloads! The information presented here is not to be used for reloading cartridges, and neither the author, the editor, nor the publisher accept any responsibility for any consequences arising from the use of any data contained herein. To repeat: THE INFORMATION PRESENTED HERE IS NOT TO BE USED FOR RELOADING CARTRIDGES, AND NEITHER THE AUTHOR, THE EDITOR, NOR THE PUBLISHER ACCEPT ANY RESPONSIBILITY FOR ANY CONSEQUENCES ARISING FROM THE USE OF ANY DATA CONTAINED HEREIN.

Here, then, are the pieces we have selected for your enjoyment, edification, and education:

1947-1948 Gun Digest, Reloading Ammunition, by Lt. Col. E. Naramore
1949-1950 Gun Digest, Ammunition Guide, by Maurice H. Decker
1952 Gun Digest, Casting Lead Alloy Bullets, by Col. Townsend Whelen
1958 Gun Digest, Special Bullet Sizing Dies, by E. J. Krava
1959 Gun Digest, Practical Pressures, by John Maynard
1959 Gun Digest, Early Loading Tools, by Richard H. Chamberlain
1961 Gun Digest, Better Handloads, by Kent Bellah
1962 Gun Digest, New Brass for Old, by George C. Nonte
1966 Gun Digest, Case Neck Variations, by Norman E. Johnson
1969 Gun Digest, Handloading Philosophy, by Don Martin
1970 Gun Digest, Shot Loads for Revolvers, by Edward Dams
1973 Gun Digest, Pressures and the Revolver, by William M. Caldwell
1973 Gun Digest, Square Shot and Little Flying Saucers, by Roger Barlow
1975 Gun Digest, Smokeless Loads for Double Rifles, by Ray Marriage and Dick Vogt
1976 Gun Digest, The Lyman Story, by Mason Williams
1978 Gun Digest, Double Bullets! by V. R. Gaertner
1980 Gun Digest, Compact Loading Bench, by William F. Greif
1980 Gun Digest, Shooting Lead Bullets, by Ron Wozny

If you would like to own a complete set of Gun Digest –every page of ever yedition from 1944 to 2009 – go to:
http://www.krausebooks.com/product/gun-digest-1944-2009-3-dvd-set/cd-dvd-downloads
It's a tremendous bargain, and one that has never before been offered to the general public.

Now sit back and enjoy the best reloading pieces from the Gun Digest Archives!

The Editor
July, 2010

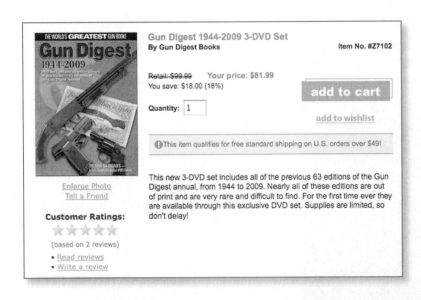

Reloading Ammunition

No one is better qualified to write on this subject — one in which he has been interested for 35 years and on which he has written two books and many articles. Was given a reserve commission as 1st Lieutenant of Ordnance in 1924 and was retired for service-incurred physical disability in 1945 after extensive World War II experience in top ordnance positions at various arsenals and proving grounds.

by LT. COL. E. NARAMORE

THE LAST SHOT had been fired from the loop-holed shutters of the frontier cabin, the Indians had withdrawn from a costly attack and inside the sturdy log structure, half filled with acrid powder smoke, there was a new kind of activity. Bullet moulds, cans of powder and tools made their appearance; women ran new, shining bullets from a kettle of lead at one end of the great fireplace while others seated new primers, measured powder charges and pushed new bullets into the fired cartridge cases that, through the day's fighting, had been picked from the floor lest they be stepped on and damaged. For, in those days, cartridges were scarce and expensive things — even more so then than in the past few years.

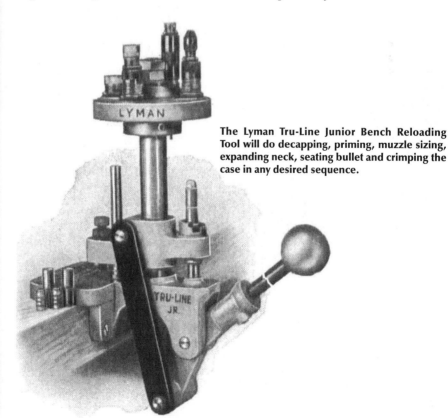

The Lyman Tru-Line Junior Bench Reloading Tool will do decapping, priming, muzzle sizing, expanding neck, seating bullet and crimping the case in any desired sequence.

From a common frontier occurrence of some eighty years ago to the present time, only two things have changed materially: (1) our fire arms are now used mostly for sport and recreation, and (2) you will have a devil of a job to get your mother, wife or sweetheart to reload your ammunition for you.

The basic reason for reloading is, without doubt, economy. The fired cartridge case, shell, hull or whatever you wish to call it is the most expensive part of a cartridge, the only part that is not lost or consumed and, to all intent and purposes, is just as good and serviceable after it is fired as it was when new. By performing carefully and intelligently a few simple operations, such as replacing the fired primer with a new one, putting in a charge of powder and seating a new bullet, it is returned to its original state at a considerable saving over its original cost. The resulting ammunition not only will be as accurate and effective as the factory product, but possibly even more so.

This may sound strange to the uninitiated, but two guns of the same make, model and caliber, and made at the same time, will not be exactly alike in all respects. There must be some small allowances or tolerance in producing the cutting tools used in manufacturing them, and there must be a further allowable tolerance in machining the parts. The same is true of ammunition, for cartridge cases and bullets of all makes must be small enough so they will work properly in the smallest chambers and barrels made by any manufacturer. When a cartridge is fired, the high internal pressure developed in it causes the case to expand so that it fits the chamber perfectly and to a degree of accuracy that could hardly be obtained by any other method. The selection of bullets of a diameter suitable for the individual barrel also permits a more accurate fit than might be found in run-of-the-mill ammunition. Then, the proper powder charge to give the best accuracy the particular gun is capable of makes for a tailor-made combination fitted to one particular arm. This does not mean that ammunition cannot be reloaded so it will be interchangeable in all arms of the same caliber, for it is as easy to do it one way as the other.

Another advantage derived from reloading lies in the versatility that can be imparted to a firearm. Take, for example, a high power rifle. Its ammunition can be loaded to duplicate the power of factory ammunition, it can be loaded with light lead alloy bullets and light charges of fast burning powder or anything in between the two and thus be suitable for anything from indoor target work or short range, small game shooting, and shooting requiring high striking velocities or long ranges. Ammunition reloaded for revolvers is usually reloaded at about the level of the charges and velocities found in factory ammunition. It is, of course, perfectly feasible to use bullets and charges much lighter than those used in the commercial product for short range, indoor practice or other special purposes.

Automatic pistols require reloads that approximately duplicate factory bullet weights, powder charges and pressures to insure the proper functioning of such arms. This also holds true for semi-automatic or self-loading rifles.

Now to get a little more specific about the components necessary for reloading ammunition.

Primers

All ammunition manufacturers designate the various primers made for sale to reloaders by a series of numbers, but primers fall roughly into five classes: large size for rifle

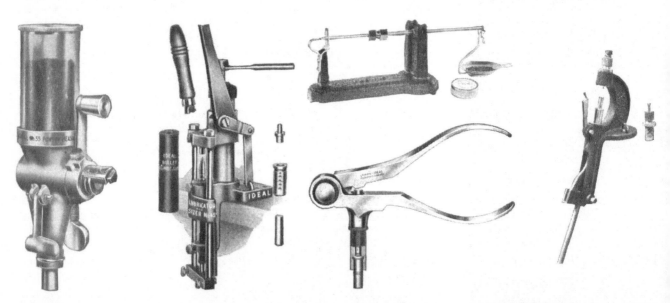

Left Illustration — Lyman No. 55 Powder Measure. The transparent plastic powder chamber enables operator to see powder level at all times. 2nd from Left — Lyman No. 45 Lubricator and Sizer. Has steel grease tube and rachet type handle that accurately regulates grease pressure. Employes same sizing dies used in the No. 1 Lubricator and Sizer.

Top Illustration (Center) — Pacific Powder and Bullet Scales, sensitive to less than 1/10 of a grain; capacity 242 grains. Bottom Illustration (Center) — Ideal No. 310 tong-type tool, with new priming chamber, for both rimmed and rimless cartridges. Depth of primer seating is adjustable. Right Illustration — Pacific Standard Reloading Tool, one of those greatly favored by reloading fans.

cartridges, large size for pistol and revolver cartridges, small size for rifle, small size for pistol or revolver, and a special size made only by the Frankford Arsenal for Cal. .45 Gov't. automatic cartridges of its own manufacture. These primers may only be purchased by N.R.A. members, through the Director of Civilian Marksmanship, *and are only suited to the one cartridge mentioned.* Commercial cartridges for the .45 Automatic pistol take the large commercial pistol primers. Any of the commercial primers are ordinarily obtainable through ammunition dealers and sporting goods stores.

The sizes of these primers have long been standardized and primers of one make will fit the primer pockets in cases of other makes taking that particular size. However, it is generally advisable to use primers of the same make as the cases they are to be used in.

While the diameters of the large and small primers are the same whether they are for rifle or pistol cartridges, their potency is not. Rifle primers are made to ignite relatively large charges of coarse grained powders, while pistol primers are designed to properly ignite small volumes of finer and faster burning powders. For this reason, the use of pistol primers in rifle cases and vice versa is not advisable. More detailed information on the different primers, their numbers and the range of cartridges to which each is best suited may be found in any book on reloading. The reader is advised to read one or another of these books whether he ever intends to reload any ammunition or not, for its perusal will greatly enhance his knowledge and understanding of the arms he uses.

Bullets

Any type and caliber of bullet used in factory ammunition can normally be purchased for reloading. The one exception is bullets for automatic pistol cartridges which, for some reason, the manufacturers will not sell separately. As all ammunition has the type and weight of the bullets with which it is loaded printed on the box, no one should have any difficulty in properly specifying such bullets when ordering them. Factory bullets are the ones to get where it is desired to reload rifle cartridges that duplicate or approximately duplicate factory cartridges in power and velocity. Jacketed bullets of one type or another must be used for such loads as the high pressure and intense heat developed by full charges of high velocity rifle powders is ruinous to lead alloy bullets, which are suitable only for reduced loads.

Which brings us to the subject of how to get lots of bullets for practice purposes — cheap. The answer is to cast the bullets yourself. The equipment required need not be expensive and the casting operation is not arduous. If homemade bullets are not overloaded and are used at velocities for which they are suited, they will give excellent accuracy.

Practically all manufacturers of reloading tools either make or supply bullet moulds, obtainable through your sporting goods dealer, to cover the entire range of metallic ammunition. There is such a wide and varied assortment that it is often difficult for the beginner to decide just which

to buy, but a pretty safe rule is to select one that approximates the weight and shape of the factory bullet. However, there is another way. Find a shooter who reloads his own ammunition and casts his own bullets. All you have to do after you find him is to ask what bullet he thinks you should use in your thu'ty-thu'ty Winchester — from there on you will only have to listen. All the boys who reload and cast bullets are brothers under the skin — including the blisters. Any of them will help you out.

These cast bullets fall into two classifications: plain base and gas-check. The former are of a form where the base band is the same size as the rest of the cylindrical portion, while gas-check bullets have a heel of reduced diameter at the base onto which a copper or gilding metal cup is fitted. The latter type is for use in rifles at somewhat higher velocities than plain base bullets will stand; the gas-check or copper cup serves to protect the bullet base from melting from the heat of the heavier charges, but these bullets will *not* stand high velocities — around 1800 f. s. to 2000 f. s. (in some cases) is about their limit. For higher velocities, jacketed bullets should be used.

Cast bullets cannot be used as they come from the mould. The grooves in them must be filled with a wax lubricant and they must be sized and trued up to the proper diameter. Lubricant can be rubbed into the grooves or the bullets may be stood on their bases in a shallow pan of melted lubricant and cut out after the lubricant has hardened. All that is necessary for this is a fired cartridge case with the head cut off or drilled out to permit the bullets to be forced up through it when passed over them. Both methods serve well enough but are messy. A cleaner, more desirable and more efficient method is to get one or the other of the little lubricating and sizing machines that are available. These permit bullets to be sized and grease forced into their grooves at one fell swoop. Where the lubrication is done separately, the sizing must be done later with a special die or chamber, either in the form of a separate tool or for use in connection with the basic reloading tool.

Powder

This is the one component where ignorance and carelessness can get the reloader into trouble. A plain, honest mistake will do the trick just as well for there are a variety of smokeless powders available for reloading purposes and each kind has characteristics that impose definite limitations on how it may be used.

Smokeless powder, when burned in the open air, burns at about the same rate of speed as a piece of untreated celluloid, to which it is closely related chemically. When burned in a confined space such as the chamber of a gun, and with the front end of the chamber plugged by a bullet that offers considerable inertia and resistance to being moved and forced through the barrel, its burning rate is tremendously accelerated. The main factors that govern this burning rate are: the chemical characteristics of the particular powder, the size of the grains and their thickness, the relation of the volume of the powder charge to the volume of the chamber, the resistance to movement offered by the bullet, and the heat and duration of the flame from the primer.

The burning rates of different powders vary considerably but all of them burn so fast that their differences are only measureable in hundred thousandths of a second.

This does not mean that it is dangerous to reload ammunition but it does mean that you should seek advice as to the proper powder to use, either from experienced reloaders or from books on reloading, preferably both. From the few factors given, the reader will be able to understand how the wrong kind of powder, too much of the right kind, too heavy or too hard a bullet or one that is too large for the barrel and, to a lesser extent, the wrong kind of primer, can cause unsatisfactory performance of ammunition varying from failure to drive the bullet out of the barrel up to spoiling a nice gun and possibly injuring the shooter as well.

Lest the reader, be frightened at such statements, let us draw an analogy by comparing the reloading of a cartridge with the preparation of a druggist's prescription. Suppose you needed a prescription requiring the use of strychnine. If you had the ingredients, balances and graduates and the prescription in a form that was clearly understandable to you, you could make up that prescription just as a druggist without taking up the study of pharmacology and do so with perfect safety, while to attempt such a thing without the prescription would be disastrous.

While minor errors in the loading of a cartridge would never produce results remotely comparable with an error in the quantity of strychnine, the same basic principle holds. The data on the bullet, powder and weight of charge and the primer to use in reloading any cartridge can be regarded as a prescription and one that is very simple to follow. If you follow it, or even come reasonably close thereto, you will have good ammunition. But if you go at it "b'guess and b' gawd," you can hardly expect satisfactory results.

A word of caution about taking advice from other reloaders. There are a few who delight in stuffing all the powder they can into a case in an endeavor to convert a revolver into a rifle or a rifle into a cannon. While the use of overloads may have some justification from an experimental point of view, their general use only can be condemned. Every firearm has its limitations as to the pressures it will withstand and still give satisfactory service over a long period of time. This limit is known as the maximum rated or maximum permissible pressure. It is set somewhat below the ultimate strength of the arm so as to provide a margin of safety for the protection of the shooter, and this margin of safety should never be deliberately encroached upon. *Do not use combinations of loads that exceed the maximum rated pressure for any arm.* To do so is to deliberately create a dangerous condition; the slight increase in muzzle velocity obtained is not at all in proportion to the considerable increase in pressure and strain on the gun.

Tools

Now we have arrived at a point where we have some hypothetical fired cases, primers, powder and bullets. What are we going to do with them? Obviously we need some tools to put them together.

A small dipper of a volume that cannot exceed the prescribed limit of the charge will do quite well as a powder measure, though the most desirable equipment is one or another of the mechanical powder measures made for the purpose, a scale or a balance. In selecting the former, be sure it will do what you want for some of these are intended for loading rifle ammunition only and will not measure small charges of pistol powders well.

If you prefer the slower but slightly more accurate method of weighing charges, select a scale or balance sensible to 1/10 grain. Cheap scales for photographic work have a sensibility of about ¼ grain and while such a variation is not of much consequence in a charge weighing 40 grs. or more, it is not fine enough for light pistol charges.

Reloading tools or presses are no more than a series of dies or chambers suitable for performing the operations of poking out fired primers, seating new ones, resizing the case necks to hold bullets tightly and crimping the cases onto the bullets in some instances, while seating the bullet to the proper depth. Some of the heavier presses, when equipped with the proper dies, are capable of completely resizing cases to their original dimensions. Most of the basic tools can be provided with dies for any calibers of cartridges. The tool or press proper is only a mechanical pusher. It is the dies that do the business.

All of these many different makes of tools have their particular design features and talking points, but from the cheapest to the most expensive they will all reload excellent ammunition if used *intelligently* — that is the key to obtaining good ammunition. Tools are only a means of accomplishing a result, so before selecting a reloading tool, decide just what you want to do and consider the factors involved in reloading for your particular gun. Then study the advertising literature and pick one that will do these things. Beyond that you can let the appearance of the tool, its special features and your pocketbook be your guide.

If you should succumb to the, yen to reload your own ammunition, you will have embarked on a productive pastime that is an interesting hobby in itself. You may find yourself on your hands and knees in the half light of sundown, groping in the grass for the last fired cartridge case. You may have a furtive look in your eye and a feeling of committing grand larceny in your heart when you "poach" on someone else's firing point, but you will derive greater pleasure from firearms and a greater return on your investment, you will be a safer person to be around when handling guns, and you will be a better shot. These, to my mind, are the real advantages of reloading ammunition rather than the pennies saved.

Maurice Decker was a well-known gunwriter during the post-WWII "golden years" of the shooting sports. Here he gives a 101-level course on ammunition.

The Ammunition Guide

by **MAURICE H. DECKER**

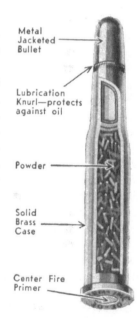

Metal Jacketed Bullet

Lubrication Knurl—protects against oil

Powder

Solid Brass Case

Center Fire Primer

THE LOAD YOU choose for your gun is vitally important because it determines the killing power and range of the weapon and also, to a large extent, its accuracy. Ammunition can be a complicated subject, too, since different loads are often made for the same caliber and distinguished from each other by such names as "High Power", "High Speed", "Low Power", "Short" and "Long". In addition there are the distinctions of "Soft Point", "Metal Cased" and "Hollow Point" bullets and shot charges loaded in shells of varying length. Different weight bullets are available for the same rifle in many instances, and ammunition containing pellets of a dozen sizes can be had for the same gauge shotgun.

The common 22 rim fire cartridge is made in five sizes and in at least four different types; furthermore, it is by no means unusual to find twenty different loads in 12 gauge alone on the shelves of an ammunition store. So much complexity can be and often is confusing, especially when we remember all loads have their legitimate uses at certain times. A good understanding of ammunition and its details is, therefore, important and the following is offered to clear up any doubt or confusion in the mind of the gunner and help him pick the kind most suitable for his shooting.

Nomenclature

A more or less standard nomenclature has been evolved to designate the different loads, calibers and bores from each other and this should be strictly followed when ammunition is described or ordered so all parties concerned will know exactly what is meant. This is important from both the angles of efficiency and safety, since load names may closely resemble one another and be distinguished by only a decimal figure. (Editor's Note: Gun and ammunition manufacturers have recently eliminated the use of decimals in designating cartridge calibers.) Consider for instance the 300 Savage. It is larger than the 30-30, yet less powerful than the 300 Magnum and 30-06, and although all are fired from what we call a 30 caliber barrel, none fit a rifle chambered for the others.

The most common and simple cartridge nomenclature consists of two figures giving the diameter of barrel bore or its bullet in hundredths of an inch. Examples are the 22 and 32 rim fire, the 25 and 32 center fire pistol loads. Recently, however, it has become more popular to use three digits in place of two for expressing caliber as illustrated by such rifles as the 257, 270 and 351. Now the digits express caliber in thousandths of an inch and mean that instead of being a 25, the load is 257, a helpful and necessary distinction because of the many 25 caliber cartridges which are made in different *sizes* and *powers*, yet carry bullets of similar *diameter*.

When two or three digits are not sufficient to clearly identify caliber, descriptive words may be added like 303 *Savage*, 303 *British*, 22 *Long Rifle* and 22 *Special*. Other names have also been attached to caliber figures which do not refer to manufacturer or designer of gun load but which carry publicity or advertising appeal. Examples of these names are 22 *Hornet*, 218 *Bee* and 220 *Swift*.

In Black powder days it was customary to label metallic ammunition with two or three sets of figures. The first designated bore, the second the number of grains of black powder in the load and the third indicated bullet weight in grains. Thus 32-20 means a 32 caliber cartridge using 20 grains of black powder. The term 45-90-300 refers to a 45 caliber load holding 90 grains of black powder and a 300-grain bullet.

It is interesting to note that when the very first smokeless powder loads appeared, the two-figure nomenclature was retained for them. Thus we have the 30-30 and 30-40. Obviously the second digit in each of these examples is misleading because the 30-30 is not loaded with 30 grains of smokeless today and neither does the regular load of the 30-40 contain 40 grains.

Sometimes the second figure in a cartridge's name refers to something different than the powder charge. Example is the 30-06. The "06" means the model year, 1906 to be exact. Another example is the 250-3000. Here the second figure means velocity, as the 87-grain bullet of this load carries a muzzle speed of 3000 feet per second.

Continental Europe mainly uses the millimeter system for identifying cartridges. Popular names are the 6.5m/m, 7m/m, 8m/m and 9m/m. When more than one cartridge is made in the same bore diameter, a second figure is added which indicates the length of the cartridge case. Thus "8×57m/m" means an 8m/m load whose case measures 57m/m long.

Shotgun bores are with one exception designated by the dimension of gauge. The exception is the 410 whose barrel is bored approximately 41/100 of an inch, making it a 410 caliber. Its actual gauge, however, is 67½. Gauge is determined by the number of round lead balls which fit the bore and weigh one pound. Thus a lead ball which fits the bore of a 12 gauge barrel weighs 1/12 of a pound. Similarly it would take 16 of the balls which fit the 16 gauge gun to weigh one pound.

Ammunition Safety

Gunner Safety. The shooter should be absolutely sure the ammunition he fires exactly fits his gun. Do not experiment with different off-sizes like shooting 30-06 loads in a 303 rifle, etc. Use only fresh, correctly loaded ammunition. Discard very old cartridges with corroded bullets and aged, obsolete military loads.

Bystander Safety. The shooter must always make sure his shots cannot cause damage or injury in the background beyond his target. This is especially important when firing in settled districts. Even the bullets of small, low power calibers carry surprising distances when the immediate target is missed. Maximum *harmful* range of the 22 rim fire long rifle bullet for example is easily 1,500 yards.

The dangerous zone of high power and military bullets like the 30-06 will run as far as 5,400 to 6,000 yards. The bullet from a 45 auto pistol can inflict injuries at 1,500 yards and that of the comparatively low power 32-20 could, when fired at a sufficient angle, carry one mile into the background. The dangerous zone of shotgun pellets varies from 175 yards for small bird and skeet shot up to 375 yards in the case of duck and goose sizes.

Generally speaking, the extreme high speed loads are more safe to shoot in settled country than slower moving bullets because they break up more readily upon impact against ground or rock. The slower projectiles are apt to glance or ricochet when they hit a solid substance and fly off at an angle, thus constituting a menace for considerable range.

Performance of Rifle Ammunition

The three principal factors in rifle ammunition performance are accuracy, trajectory or bullet path, and killing power. When selecting ammunition, appraise and consider each with respect to the size and kind of game you hunt or the class of target marksmanship in which you plan to compete.

Accuracy. Should always be sufficient to insure hits in the vital area of the game hunted. Small targets require finer accuracy than large ones, for while the vital area of big game might equal a space 8 inches in diameter, that of small animals may be only as wide as 1½ or 2 inches. It is easy to understand now why ammunition which makes 6-inch groups can perform ably on moose and elk but fail badly if used for woodchucks or coyotes. A good rule is to select ammunition sufficiently accurate to make groups of five or eight shots that are no wider than the vital area of the game you hunt.

Special types of ammunition in certain calibers are produced expressly for target shooting and should always be chosen by the marksman. The 22 rim fire is an excellent example. Each manufacturer has his own special brand of this ammunition loaded with close limits of tolerance and with special attention to uniformity. Such ammunition sells at extra cost but is well worth it to those who shoot in competitive matches. Since the performance of target rifles can vary with different brands of ammunition, marksmen usually test all available kinds and then stick to that making the closest groups in their individual weapon.

Trajectory. This is important because a fairly flat: bullet path permits you to make hits at different ranges without much danger of missing and without having to estimate the range and adjust sights to match. This advantage is very helpful to hunters who fire only a relatively few rounds each season and have fewer opportunities to lie-come well acquainted with the performance of their rifles at different ranges. High velocity and light bullets permit a flatter trajectory or bullet path. Low velocities and heavier bullets give a more curved flight.

In general the bullet of big game ammunition should not rise or curve higher than 2½ to 3 inches above your line of sight at any point in the bullet's flight to the target. In small game and vermin ammunition, the bullet should not rise higher than 1 to 1½, inches for best results. This much curve in either case will hardly cause direct misses when game is shot at closer range than the distance for which your sights are zeroed.

Power. Striking or killing power is also of vital import. It is very unsatisfactory, as well as unsportsmanlike, to hit game and then lose it because of inferior powered ammunition. Deer have, on occasions, been killed with a 22 rim fire bullet but no thinking sportsman would start out on a deer hunt with a caliber so definitely lacking sufficient power. A workable definition of "sufficient power" is the amount that will kill cleanly the game hunted with one shot whenever the bullet is rightly directed and aimed.

The hunter may not always be able to aim correctly and place his bullet in the vital part of the game's body. Therefore, because bullets will occasionally miss the exact point which must be struck for a clean kill, we compensate for these times by choosing ammunition having some extra margin of power. Then the poorly directed ball has a better chance of proving fatal. In most instances hunters find it better to be *over* rather than *under gunned.*

Factors exist, of course, which limit the power of the ammunition you can effectively use. Too much power will result in too much spoiled game meat, though this need not be considered when shooting species in the vermin, or varmint, class. Again, excess power may result in heavy rifle recoil. While some shooters are apparently insensible to hard gun kick, others are badly disturbed by it and are unable to aim and fire accurately under its punishment. Obviously no one should use ammunition which produces enough recoil to spoil his marksmanship by making him flinch. Both velocity and bullet weight influence recoil. When different bullets are available in one caliber of ammunition, the hunter can sometimes reduce gun kick by using the lighter weight projectile.

Still another important angle in killing power is the range at which most of your game is struck. You seldom shoot it at or very near the gun's muzzle. For this reason ballistic figures of ammunition velocity and energy taken at the muzzle do not indicate the true killing power of the load at the range you most often use it Ballistic figures for 100 and 200 yards are more revealing since some loads lose speed and power more rapidly in flight than others.

The power of rifle ammunition should also be appraised with an eye to future use. If you are shopping for a deer caliber now, consider if you might not also want to hunt elk and moose in the near future. Unless you plan on a second caliber then, pick one now with sufficient power for all.

The following table shows how much popular rifle cartridges kick in foot-pounds and can be used to help arrive at a practical and workable compromise between the two factors of recoil and power. To better understand the significance of the figures, remember that the recoil of a 12 gauge shotgun using heavy loads is approximately 26 to 28 ft. lbs. This comparison isn't exactly accurate because rifles have a sharper recoil than shotguns, but it is reliable enough to be employed when making a caliber choice.

Foot-Pound Rifle Recoil Table		
250-3000	87 grain bullet	4.47 ft. lbs.
250-3000	100 grain bullet	6.27 ft. lbs.
257	100 grain bullet	7.00 ft. lbs.
270 Winchester	130 grain bullet	14.30 ft. lbs.
30-30	170 grain bullet	9.00 ft. lbs.
30-40	220 grain bullet	11.50 ft. lbs.
30-06	150 grain bullet	13.00 ft. lbs.
30-06	180 grain bullet	17.50 ft. lbs.
30-06	220 grain bullet	19.00 ft. lbs.
300 Magnum	220 grain bullet	27.20 ft. lbs.
348 Winchester	200 grain bullet	22.60 ft. lbs.
375 Magnum	300 grain bullet	33.60 ft. lbs.
405 Winchester	300 grain bullet	12.00 ft. lbs.

Note: Since heavier rifles have less recoil than lighter ones, and since the foregoing figures refer to standard models, recoil will be slightly reduced when a scope and mounts are added to the gun.

Although individual shooters differ materially in their ability to withstand recoil, in the main these conditions will prevail. Almost anybody physically able to hunt can handle with comfort rifles whose recoil runs no more than 6 or 7 pounds. Many, too, can absorb as much as 15 to 18 ft. lbs. of recoil without having the accuracy of their shots impaired. Fewer people, however, can manage calibers with a recoil of 25 pounds and over. Practice is a big aid in mastering recoil and practice firing with the big guns should be done rather frequently. A rubber recoil pad also helps, both because of its softness and its additional weight; one should be installed on rifles that kick enough to make their owners flinch.

Sectional Density. Although bullet penetration is largely controlled by the construction of its point, another factor, sectional density, exerts a certain influence. The term refers to the ratio of a bullet's length to its diameter. Long, small caliber projectiles have a good sectional density, short, big bullets a poorer one. A 150-grain bullet in 27 caliber, for example, has a sectional density superior to the same weight in 30 caliber and will, consequently, possess more stability in flight and exert a deeper penetration in animal tissue when other factors are similar. The longer bullet of any particular cartridge is, therefore, best in most instances to hunt large, tough-meated animals demanding the maximum penetration for clean, sportsman-like kills.

Rim Fire & Center Fire Rifle Ammunition

These two broad divisions of metallic ammunition indicate the location of the priming (igniting) mixture in the head of the cartridge case. Rim fire ammunition carries this priming mixture in the rim of the case, which is pinched between firing pin and face of barrel chamber to produce the pressure that fires the mixture, which in turn ignites the powder in the load. Center fire ammunition carries a separate primer pressed into an opening at the center of the cartridge case's head. This primer is supplied with a tiny "anvil" against which the firing pin of the rifle forces the priming mixture and explodes it.

Whereas rim fire ammunition was formerly made in a large variety of calibers from 22 to 58, all are now obsolete, or nearly so, except the 22 sizes. The rim type of primer is cheaper to produce and, in this caliber, perfectly reliable. Modern 22 rim fire ammunition is truly a marvel of production. It is very accurate, uniform, reliable and inexpensive. No other load delivers so much value for its cost as the 22 long rifle. Little wonder that American shooters use such huge quantities, firing more of it annually than any other size.

A factor limiting the power of rim fire cartridges is the case. This must be made of soft metal so it is easily indented by the firing pin. With heavy loading, such soft cases would expand and "freeze" to the sides of the chamber, making extraction difficult or impossible. They would also be likely to rupture and blow open near the head if loaded too heavily. Obviously rim fire ammunition cannot be used in a center fire rifle and *vice versa* (without changing the firing pin). Neither can the rim fire cases be reloaded.

Necked-Down Cartridge Cases. Some of our highest speed loads were developed by using necked-down cartridge cases from older calibers. For instance, the 22 Hornet is a modernized 22 W.C.F. The 220 Swift is loaded in a 6MM Lee Navy cartridge case trimmed shorter and necked to smaller size. The 218 Bee carries a re-sized 25-20 Repeater case while the 219 Zipper employs a 25-35 case reduced at the reck and shortened. The 257 is loaded in a re-formed 7MM case, the 270 in a 30-06 case with reduced neck diameter.

Variations in Ammunition Power

Some calibers of ammunition are loaded with only one type of powder and in one degree of power. Others are, or have been, produced in several degrees of performance and some understanding of each type is necessary in order to choose and use the best kind for your shooting.

Low Power Ammunition. Originally such sizes as the 25-20, 32-20, 32-40, 45-70, etc., contained black powder only and were regarded as regular powder, or Low Power, loads. When smokeless powder appeared, users of these older calibers naturally wanted to benefit by its advantage of cleanliness, so much black powder ammunition was also supplied with smokeless and jacketed bullets to eliminate the caked barrel fouling that otherwise prevailed. These smokeless loads gave the same ballistics as black powder and were named Low Power Smokeless for that reason. They could and can be used in the same guns, including revolvers, and for the same purposes as the original black powder cartridges.

High Velocity Ammunition. When such high power loads as the 30-30 and 30-40 demonstrated the advantages of increased velocity and flatter bullet path, some of the black powder ammunition was loaded with improved types of smokeless to give it greater bullet speed. These loads were named High Power or High Velocity to distinguish them from the smokeless Low Power kind. Among the sizes made in High Power form are the 25-20. 32-20, 32-40, 38-40, 38-55, 44-40, 45-70 and 45-90. These High Power cartridges developed more velocity and energy and were more powerful than either Black Powder Regular Power or Smokeless Low Power loads. They carried the same weight of bullet, however, as these others. Because of its greater killing power and flatter trajectory, High Power ammunition proved best for killing game. In some instances it was not quite as finely accurate but the accuracy was still good enough for hunting at moderate ranges. This High Power, or "H. V." as it has also been called, should when available be used only in rifles of good condition with reasonably clean bores and tight breeches.

CAUTION. Do not use the center fire High Velocity or High Speed (described next) ammunition in revolvers, in the Winchester model 1873 rifle or in the single shot 45-70 Springfield army rifle.

High Speed Ammunition. Still a third type of smokeless powder loading has been given some of the older ammunition. Called High Speed to distinguish it from the other kinds, it develops a still higher velocity than the High Power but obtains the extra speed by using a lighter bullet. Whereas High Velocity ammunition carried standard weight balls. High Speed loads fire projectiles both shorter and lighter. For example the standard weight of the 25-20 Low Power and High Velocity bullet is 86 grains, but a 60-grain bullet is used in 25-20 High Speed ammunition.

High Speed loading is not confined to black powder calibers alone. Modern smokeless loads like the 270, 30-30, and 32 Special have also been given increased velocity by the use of lighter bullets. The High Speed 30-30 bullet only weighs 150 grains compared to the regular weight of 170. Although High Speed loads give a flatter trajectory, they are in most instances inferior in striking power on medium and large sizes of game. The High Speed loads also may not hold up as well in long range accuracy as regular ammunition. Their best function is to kill what is popularly known as vermin (crows, coyotes, woodchucks, etc.) at short to moderate range. Do not use 30-30 or 32 Special High Speed cartridges for deer. The regular ammunition with 170-grain projectile kills more quickly and humanely. The faster, lighter High Speed bullets sometimes fail to penetrate tough game deeply enough to produce a quickly fatal wound.

Variations in Rifle Bullets

Weight. Shooters are sometimes confused by the number of different weight bullets furnished for the same cartridge and hardly know which to choose. The 30-06, for instance, is commercially loaded with half a dozen different projectiles. Details on specific uses of heavy and light bullets will be found in the Compendium of Calibers to follow. In general, however, the lightest, speediest balls usually work best on small game and vermin. Medium weight bullets moving at high speed are suitable for game taken at long range, and long, heavy bullets giving extreme penetration and good brush-cutting power should be selected for tough, hard-to-kill species taken at both moderately long range and in the woods.

Lead Bullets. Lead bullets are suitable only for rather low velocities, being too soft to stand the heat and strain of greater speeds. Given enough weight and diameter, lead bullets kill well. Such cartridges as the 38-55, 40-82 and 45-70 gave splendid results on American big game. Their large, heavy bullets penetrated deeply and when an animal was not knocked off its feet, it was generally wounded too badly to travel far and, moreover, left a good blood trail for easy pursuit. Lead bullets are cheap and their use in the popular 22 rim fire ammunition contributes largely to its reasonable cost. The present use of lead bullets is largely confined to rim fire and low power center fire rifle ammunition and to revolver cartridges. In other types, better results are usually obtained with some form of jacketed projectile.

Jacketed Bullets. When manufacturers discovered lead bullets wouldn't follow the rifling in a gun barrel at high speed and would also melt at the base before the intense heat of high power charges, they developed the jacketed bullet consisting of a lead core sheathed in a cover or jacket of some copper alloy to provide strength and resistance. The alloy of bullet jackets or cases is compounded to reduce friction and to prevent a residue of metallic fouling in the bore.

Metal Cased Bullets. Jacketed bullets are made in several forms. The metal or full cased type has its point completely covered by the regular alloy jacket. It seldom will expand when striking flesh but usually passes through the game animal and makes a hole the size of its regular caliber. The killing power of such ammunition is consequently small and it is not advised for hunting.

Metal cased bullets are specified for military use by international warfare rules. They are also sometimes used for long range target shooting in high power rifles and are then built with a sharp, or Spitzer, point and a boat-tail base. This streamlining reduces air resistance at the bullet's point and air drag at its base and materially increases the velocity over that of regular type bullets.

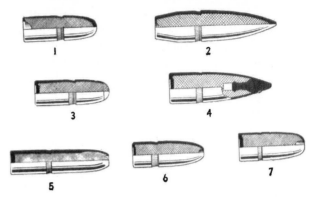

TYPES OF RIFLE BULLETS (Remington). 1. Metal cased 30 Remington. 160 gr. "Core-Lokt," round nose. Also comes in flat nose and pointed Spitzer types. 2. Pointed, Taper Heel (Boat-tail) 30-06, 172 gr. "Core-Lola" bullet. The pointed Spitzer type (without boat-tail) is in this same classification. 3. "Kleanbore" Soft Point 30-30 Win., 170 gr. 4. Bronze Pointed Expanding 300 Savage, 150 gr. "Kleanbore" bullet with lead core, metal jacket and bronze point. 5. "Core-Lokt" Mushroom (or Controlled Expansion) bullet. A 30-06, 220 gr., expands to over 60 caliber. 6. 257 Roberts, 87 gr. "Hi-Speed" Mushroom with lead core. metal jacket, hollow point. Used primarily for vermin us bullet has tendency to explode before penetrating vitals of large game. 7. 35 Remington. 200 gr. Express Mushroom with hollow point. Used for North American big game as the bullet is relatively heavy in weight.

Occasionally a shooter with a supply of military or target full cased ammunition will attempt to convert it over for hunting use by (1) drilling a small hole in the bullet's point, or (2) by splitting the bullet nose with two hack saw cuts made at right angles to each other, or (3) by filing the bullet's nose (point) off square until the soft lead core is exposed. Properly done these alterations will cause a full cased bullet to expand and inflict a more serious wound on game. Unskillfully y performed, these alterations are ineffective and dangerous. The drilled, sawed or filed bullet may fly into small pieces at impact and produce only a shallow wound. Or the lead core may be blown out through the jacket's weakened end and leave the jacket wedged in the barrel. The next shot put through the rifle then ruins it and probably injures the gunner.

Soft Point Bullets. Regular factory made expanding bullets should be used on game. An exception occurs when the trapper or hunter wishes to take small animals without much bullet damage to their pelts, in which case metal cased bullets can be tried. The regular soft nose bullet is one popular kind of expanding projectile. In it the lead core is left uncovered by the jacket at the; forward end. This exposed lead rolls back when it strikes, splitting or spreading the jacket until the bullet is as much as twice its original diameter. Such projectiles cause more serious wounds and better bleeding. The amount of lead exposed at the point must be adjusted in ratio to diameter and weight of the ball, its speed and also to the toughness of the game hunted. Too much exposure may make the bullet fly into small pieces and cause only surface wounds. Too little may make it act like a full metal cased ball and penetrate without any expansion in size.

Controlled Expansion Bullets. These represent the newest development in jacketed expanding ammunition to hunt big game. They are especially designed to expand uniformly and well (good expansion means to double its normal size), penetrate deeply and at the same time stay together in one solid piece. Various features like additional thinner jackets, notched jackets and belted or knurled jackets are employed to assure this good performance.

The "Silvertip" bullet, for instance, is provided with a second, thinner jacket which protects the sensitive tip, prevents it being battered in the shooter's pocket or gun and blocks any too-rapid expansion or disintegration while the bullet is penetrating an animal's tough hide and outer muscles and bones. The outside regular jacket is knurled to hold the three separate parts of this bullet securely together as it expands.

The "Core-lokt" and "Inner Belted" bullets (these two brands are essentially alike in form) use notched jacket edges to give uniform expansion and varying thicknesses of jacket material to produce immediate yet controlled expansion and to hold lead core and jacket in one piece.

When a choice between regular soft point bullets and controlled expansion bullets is possible, the latter are especially recommended for hunting our larger and harder to kill species of big game.

Hollow Point Bullets. Other jacketed bullets have hollow points proportioned in size and depth to give the desired amount of expansion and penetration. A hollow point high speed bullet can be practically explosive when it strikes animal tissue and cause extreme nervous shock as well as a very bad (if rather shallow) wound. Hollow point ammunition is often employed for vermin and tender meated game like deer. Lead bullets are also made with hollow points, the 22 rim fire sizes being especially successful for making clean kills on very small targets.

Notes on Bullet Shock. Years ago we tested the shocking and expanding ability of 22 rim fire bullets by shooting them into cakes of laundry soap. Those experiments conclusively proved the superior killing power of hollow point projectiles over those with solid noses, but could not accurately indicate actual bullet performance on game. Today laboratory materials have been so highly perfected experiments are possible that duplicate the effect bullets exert on real flesh.

Present tests are made with blocks of special gelatin, whose density closely resembles that of animal tissue and are recorded by high-speed photographic apparatus capable of stopping bullets dead in their tracks at any point along their flight. In addition to proving the superior shocking power of expanding projectiles, the resulting photos have shown that contrary to common belief, the greatest shock to a struck target occurs after the bullet had penetrated through it and passed some distance beyond.

Formerly we thought bullet shock was greatest *upon* initial impact. Photos of pierced gelatin blocks now show that material to be at its maximum extent of disruption *after* the ball reaches a point one foot beyond. This disruption is due to what ballistic men call hydraulic shock, the result of energy and motion being imparted to body fluids and tissues by the pressure of the bullet. Such shock is in direct proportion to projectile velocity, the most speedy calibers causing a greater destruction. This explains why high speed loads are so successful in killing the various species of vermin and pests and why a paunch shot made with one will sometimes result in the quick death of game like deer.

Shot Loaded Metallic Ammunition. A few rifle and handgun cartridges are loaded with light charges of small shot to make these arms project the scattered pattern of shotguns. The number of pellets in these loads is very small, which results in short effective range, small or thinly scattered patterns and low killing power. Such shot cartridges should be used only to break small fragile targets at close range and to kill very small pests such as sparrows. Shooting them at larger game and at long range will result in deplorable waste and suffering when the targets are wounded and crippled.

Guide to Rifle Calibers

The following summary of rifle ammunition [many now obsolete, alas — Editor] offers some of the outstanding points of popular loads with suggestions for their use. When a load is recommended for vermin, that word includes such non-game species as woodchucks, badgers, crows, harmful hawks, foxes, bob-cats, ground squirrels, jackrabbits, coyotes and small wolves. When the term "small vermin" is used, the two latter animals are excluded.

Deer load takes in small hear and antelope as well. Timber or brush shooting ranges are calculated at from 40 to 125 yards. Moderate range means up to 200 yards, and long range any distance over 200. Recommendations for the use of any load or caliber are subject to special laws which have been or may he enacted by any state or province to regulate the use and power of hunting arms.

Note: Alt cartridge illustrations on the following pages are actual size.

22 BB (Bullet Breech) Cap. Reputed to be the first load produced in 22 rim fire caliber. It's very weak with low velocity and poor accuracy. The round bullet weighs from 18 to 20 grains. Not recommended for game but permits cheap, short distance target practice. Will not work through the magazine of repeaters and may badly lead the bore.

22 Conical Ball (CB). More accurate and powerful than the Cap but still advised only for short range practice and the very smallest of live targets. Bullet weighs 29 grains. This load can be worked through the magazine of some repeaters. Its only advantage is lower price; whenever practical, the 22 Short should be chosen for minimum power in 22 caliber.

22 Short. Accurate range up to 50 yards with its best performance within 25. The standard shooting gallery load for which special purpose ammunition with splashless bullets are made. Use of the 22 Short on live targets should for humane reasons be restricted to killing sparrows, rats and ground squirrels and furbearers caught in traps. Best results are had in rifles chambered for this size cartridge alone since its bullet requires a different twist of rifling than that of the 22 Long Rifle — 1. turn in 20 or 22 inches compared to 1 turn in 16 or 17. Extensive use of shorts in the long rifle chamber will eventually corrode its sides and give extraction trouble.

22 Long. Not as accurate or useful as either the short or long rifle size and not recommended when these others can be obtained.

22 Long Rifle. Easily the best of the 22 rim fire line, standard for small bore target shooting. While it lacks power to kill woodchucks cleanly at their average hunting range, it has enough striking force for squirrels and similar species when the high speed load carrying hollow point bullet is employed. Game shots should be limited to under 100 yards, at which distance the 22 Long Rifle load has suffered a 40% loss of its initial energy. Use high speed ammunition for most hunting, regular power loads for practice shooting and very small live targets and the special precision rounds for match shooting.

22 Special or 22 W.R.F. More powerful than the 22 Long Rifle but slightly less accurate. Less popular, too; ammunition is restricted to a few lightweight rifles. Seventy-five yards marks its accuracy limit for squirrel size targets. Although the writer has killed wild turkey with this load, it is not recommended for such large game. Will usually be found lacking in energy for killing woodchucks cleanly ouside their holes. Use high speed loading with hollow point bullets for game.

25 Rim Fire. Years ago this ammunition in short and long size was very popular with small game hunters and trappers. At one time shooters had hopes the 25 rim fire would be modernized with more accuracy and power. These hopes were not realized, however, and a lack of rifles chambered for the ammunition has helped put it in a near-obsolete classification.

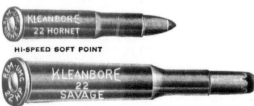

HIGH POWER "CORE-LOKT" SOFT POINT—70 GRAINS

22 Hornet. A very successful center fire small bore load

sufficiently accurate for small game and target work at 150 to 200 yards. Excellent for woodchucks at moderate ranges. When fired from heavy barrels, makes machine-rest groups of 1 inch at 100 yards, 2½ inches at 200. Its best performance occurs up to 150 yards; over this distance the 45-gr. Hornet bullet is susceptible to strong cross winds. Has the advantage of being used in high grade bolt rifles in heavier than average weights if desired. This ammunition is comparatively safe for farming districts as its speedy bullet usually breaks up on impact.

218 Bee. Another small bore, high speed load designed for small game and pest shooting. Has the advantage of being used in lever action rifles, making it popular with shooters who do not prefer the bolt breech. Carries more velocity than the Hornet, but not considered as finely accurate (100-yard groups shot with the Bee may measure about 2½ inches); suitable for small targets up to 125 yards, sometimes farther.

SOFT POINT

220 Swift. One of the fastest loads produced commercially with the enormous velocity of 4,140 ft. sec. Although the light bullet loses velocity substantially as the range lengthens, it provides a very flat trajectory up to 300 yards, at which range it is credited with being able to make 6-inch groups. A fine load for all sizes of vermin but not recommended for big game. Bullets explode on hitting almost any substance and are safer in settled areas than many older calibers. Has the drawback of giving comparatively shorter barrel life due to its high speed and intensity.

HI-SPEED MUSH.

25-20. This ammunition has been popular for farm and ranch use to shoot small game and small vermin and to butcher cattle. Lately has lost some ground to the newer Hornet and Bee. The 60-grain High Speed bullet of the 25-20 is advised for pests and vermin but will destroy much meat if used on small game. Most effective range is up to 125-150 yards. Any 25-20 load is too powerful for squirrels and grouse. The low pressure ammunition is sometimes employed for wild turkey. All loadings are very accurate.

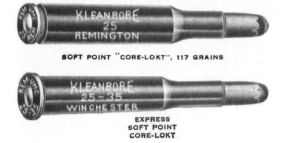

SOFT POINT "CORE-LOKT", 117 GRAINS

EXPRESS
SOFT POINT
CORE-LOKT

25-35 and 25 Remington. These highly accurate rimmed and rimless cartridges have similar ballistics and their 117-grain bullets are quite suitable for killing vermin and medium sized game. Best results are had when you limit their use to short and medium range. The 25-35 and 25 Remington have sometimes been named as the medium power loads we should use for deer and antelope. They are excellent, too, for vermin but are not recommended for game larger than whitetails. Having a very mild recoil, are suited for use by women and youngsters.

"CORE-LOKT" SOFT POINT – 100 GRAINS

250 Savage (250-3000). One of our first high speed, small bore calibers that has successfully endured the tests of time and usage. Very accurate up to moderately long ranges. Try both 87 and 100-grain ammunition for vermin since in some rifles the heavier bullet gives closer groups at maximum range. Use 100-grain size only for killing deer because its better sectional density shows deeper penetration and glances less from twigs of trees and brush. This ammunition is handled both by lever and bolt action rifles of good quality. The mild recoil is enjoyed by shooters of light weight and build. Not recommended for game larger or harder to kill than deer and black bear.

HI-SPEED
MUSHROOM
CORE-LOKT

257 Roberts. In the particular of performance, can be regarded as a stepped-up 250-3000. To date bullets of two different weights are available in factory ammunition. The 100-grain size may be chosen for vermin, the 117-grain size for larger targets. While the 257 has killed most species of American big game at moderate range, its most successful functions are hunting deer and antelope both in timber and on the plains and for shooting vermin. The recoil is mild and accuracy very good up to 300 yards. Because of its high velocities, the 257 delivers a slightly shorter barrel life than the 250-3000.

HI-SPEED SOFT POINT

270 Winchester. Fires a heavier series of high speed bullets than the 257 and is likewise very accurate at both short and long range. One of our best calibers for all American big game with possible exceptions of big bear, elk and moose at very long range. Excellent with above exceptions for plains and mountain hunting. Produces about 20% less recoil than the 30-06. Shoot the 130-grain ball for any long distance hunting and choose the 150-grain size for bigger animals hunted in timber or where ranges do not exceed 200 yards. The 130-grain bullet is probably most useful for all-purpose shooting.

SOFT POINT "CORE-LOKT", 150 GRAINS

SOFT POINT "CORE-LOKT", 170 GRAINS

30-30 and 30 Remington. These loads possess similar ballistics and are very popular for hunting deer and black bear in timber and brushy cover where long ranges are seldom encountered. The bullets are stable and have good penetration. Shoot the 170-grain size for deer, the lighter ball for vermin. When hunting deer, bullets should be accurately placed for minimum loss in wounded animals. Not advised for regular hunting of species larger than deer or for maximum shooting distances. Extreme danger range of this ammunition is between 1,300 and 1,400 yards. Bullets are still capable of causing injury or death to hunters after traveling this far.

SOFT POINT "CORE-LOKT", 220 GRAINS

30-40 Krag. Once the service ammunition of our army (in the Krag-Jorgenson rifle), the 30-40, or 30 Army as it is also called, is excellent for big game. It performs ably on deer with either 180 or 220-grain bullets and has a noticeable advantage in killing power and long range accuracy over the 30-30 and similar so-called "deer" calibers. The 180-grain bullet is better for extreme distances. Use the 220-grain size for hunting the bigger species in timbered cover. The 30-40 would probably be used more widely if more rifles were available to shoot it. In hands of a careful marksman will account for any game found in North America.

BRONZE POINT

SOFT POINT "CORE-LOKT", 180 GRAINS

300 Savage. With 180-grain bullet this ammunition shows ballistics similar to those of the 30-40. this heavier bullet should be used whenever game larger than deer is hunted. The lighter 150-grain weight ball is suggested for vermin and deer and for long range shots at any target. Being handled by a popular lever action rifle, the 300 is much used by left-handed hunters and others who do not prefer the bolt breech.

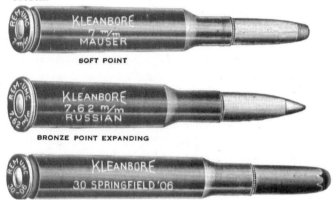

SOFT POINT

BRONZE POINT EXPANDING

SOFT POINT "CORE-LOKT", 220 GRAINS

30-06. One of our very best all-round big game calibers. Supplied with bullets light enough for vermin -and heavy enough for moose, elk and large bear. The 110 (when available) and 150-grain loads are usually employed to kill vermin. The 150-grain bullet can be selected for deer although the 30-06 is rather powerful for this species. Hunters who expect to encounter both deer and larger targets like moose and elk on the same hunt carry ammunition with 180-grain bullets. This size is also the best for very long distance shooting. The 220-grain bullet load is splendid for big bear, moose and elk taken in timber or muskeg cover. Watch your background when shooting the 30-06 and similar long range ammunition in settled country. The danger zone can extend for as many as 3½ miles and a missed shot could cause deplorable damage.

EXPRESS MUSH. 220 GRS.

300 H. & H. Magnum. Because of its superior velocity, this is a better killer of tough big game at long range than either 270 or 30-06. The 300 shows almost as much velocity at 300 yards with its 220-grain bullet as the 30-06 does at 200 yards with a 180-grain ball. The 300 has a heavier recoil, however, and not every rifleman can handle it effectively. When he can, the 300 is splendid for greater than average ranges since its 180 and 220-grain bullets retain enough velocity to expand properly at 300 and 400 yards, and moreover are very accurate. In case any reader is tempted to regard the 300 Magnum as the most desirable caliber because of its bal-

listic rating, bear in mind that kills on big game at 300 and 400 yards are rather rare, especially with hunters who shoot only a few days each year and are not completely trained to consistently hit moving targets 1,000 feet and more away. The 300 is especially effective for quartering or rear-on shots we must occasionally make with escaping game; its bullets have the power to range on through flesh and bone until they reach a vital place like heart or lungs.

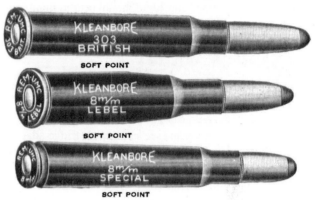

SOFT POINT

SOFT POINT

SOFT POINT

8m/m. Because of the numerous Mauser rifles brought back by service men there is a good demand for this ammunition. Used in well made rifles it is very accurate; fired from weapons assembled with miscellaneous or junk parts, the accuracy is often bad. The 8m/m has somewhat less velocity and striking energy than the 30-06. Shooters must be careful not to confuse the 8MM and the 30-06 because of their general similarity in size. An 8MM load can be forced in some 30-06 rifle chambers but, when fired, the over-size bullet invariably wrecks the gun.

32-20. Similar to the 25-20 and formerly popular on farms and ranches. Too powerful for squirrels but will kill woodchucks at short to moderate range. The 25-20 is better for such shooting, however, and is recommended

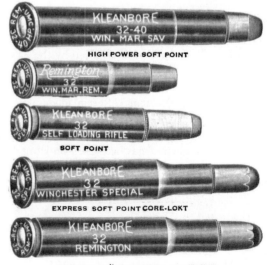

HIGH POWER SOFT POINT

SOFT POINT

EXPRESS SOFT POINT CORE-LOKT

SOFT POINT "CORE-LOKT". 170 GRAINS

32 Special and 32 Remington. These loads are so similar in performance to the 30-30 and 30 Remington it actually makes no difference which of the four you choose for hunting. The same remarks as to performance and use apply to all.

33 Winchester. This cartridge has the same bullet weight, velocity and energy as the 35 Remington and is recommended for the same uses. At one time it was very popular with western and northern hunters because of its good performance on big game and also because of the excellent rifle action (1886) in which it was used. Caliber 33 rifles are no longer made but owners of the model 1886 in such old style sizes as the 38-56, 40-82 and 15-90 should bear in mind they can have such guns re-barreled for the 33 load and benefit by its superior velocity and flatter bullet path.

HI-SPEED SOFT POINT

348 Winchester. This is an excellent new cartridge adapted to an improved model 1886 rifle which for years was the most popular big game gun in service. Since the model 1895 Winchester has been discontinued, the 348 is our most powerful lever action arm. Three different bullets are available. The 150 and 200-grain sizes are suggested for deer. The 200-grain ball is probably the best one for all long range shooting and the tremendous power of the 250-grain bullet should always be employed on our largest, toughest game in marsh or timber cover. Has a bit more recoil than the 30-06 and a recoil pad is advised for 348 rifles used by most hunters. This caliber is not as suitable for extreme long range as the 270 or 30-06.

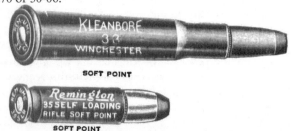

SOFT POINT

SOFT POINT

35 Remington. Ballistics of this ammunition resemble those of the 33 Winchester (now replaced by the 348). Its superiority in killing power over the 30-30 is easily discovered by experience and a 35 should be tried for brush hunting by those who find a 30-30 or 32 Special inadequate. One of the best loads we have for shooting through brush without bullet deflection. The 35 is more effective when used at medium range. Although it has been used on game larger than deer, is not recommended for moose and elk unless ranges are moderate.

METAL CASED

351 Winchester. A low velocity load used in the model 1907 self-loading Winchester rifle. Best suited for fast, short-range shots at deer and small bear in wooded country. Has only half as much ballistic energy at 100 yards as the 30-40. In recent years has been promoted for police and law enforcement service.

SOFT POINT "CORE-LOKT", 200 GRAINS

375 H. & H. Magnum. A load similar to but larger and more powerful than the 300 Magnum. Carries bigger, heavier bullets at greater velocities than any other standard American factory loaded ammunition. Has tremendous shocking power and excellent penetration. Suitable for the biggest, toughest species of American game at all practical ranges. Sufficiently powerful for much African hunting, particularly on antelope and lions. Has a heavy recoil and strong muzzle blast and should be used in rifles with 25-inch (or longer) barrels weighing 9½ to 10 lbs. More skill obviously is needed to handle these big Magnum loads with the accuracy required to utilize their long range potentialities. Magnum ammunition is not recommended to those easily disturbed by recoil.

SOFT POINT

HIGH POWER SOFT POINT

SOFT POINT

SOFT POINT

401 Winchester. Previously removed from the active production list, this short range, big bore cartridge is again available. Similar in power to the 35 Remington and best suited for woods hunting where ranges do not exceed 150 yards. Under these conditions the 401 has ample shocking power for deer and black bear, and in the hands of a careful marksman will account for moose. The big caliber bullet usually leaves a plain blood trail that makes it easier to follow wounded animals.

405 Winchester. Another big, powerful cartridge recently reinstated on loading schedules. Once the highest power caliber produced regularly in this country, the 405 has seen much service in game fields of North America and Africa. Hits hard enough to hunt any big game found on this continent. Too heavy for deer but the right medicine for moose and big bear taken at moderate ranges.

Handgun Ammunition

In some instances handgun cartridges with different names will fit and shoot satisfactorily in the same caliber arm. A list of these follows, arranged so those loads which do interchange are grouped together.

22 Rim Fire Short, Long and Long Rifle.

These three sizes can be used in the same gun, except in those cheap, light handguns which are safe only with, or are chambered only for, the 22 Short. Automatic pistols in 22 caliber handle long rifle cartridges only.

32 S. & W., 32 S. & W. Long, 32 Colt New Police.

Warning. Do not use cartridges containing bullets in 32 revolvers built to shoot blanks only. Again do not fire 32 Longs and Colt New Police ammunition in cheap, light-weight revolvers designed for the 32 Short alone.

38 S. & W., 38 Colt New Police.

These loads do not fit revolvers chambered for the other 38 loads listed next.

38 Colt Short, 38 Colt Long, 38 S. & W. Special, 38 Colt Special, 38-44 S. & W. Special.

Note that while revolvers made with the extra long chamber for the 357 Magnum load will also fire all of the cartridges listed in this group, revolvers chambered for them alone *will not handle the 357 ammunition and no attempt should be made to alter them so they do.*

44 Special, 44 S. & W. Russian.

The 44 Special is the most accurate and most powerful of these two and should be used whenever possible.

Types of Revolver and Pistol Bullets

When both metal cased and soft point bullets are supplied for any revolver or pistol ammunition, select the latter type when it will be used for self protection or home protection purposes. While soft point bullets flying at the low velocities developed by handguns do not always expand well or expand at all, any small upset is a decided advantage to the shooter and the soft point type will give just as good performance as the metal cased even if does not expand on impact. Lead bullets have even better shocking ability and should be chosen for the purposes named above when available.

Police and law enforcement officers should consider the special bullets loaded in 38 Special and 45 Auto ammunition which are built expressly for riot duty or to give maximum penetration through metal, such as automobile bodies, etc.

Rifle Loads Used in Handguns

These include the 22 rim fire, 32-20, 38–40 and 44-40 sizes. The 22 long rifle is the most popular one. It shows splen-

did accuracy when fired from either revolver or pistol and is widely used for target shooting, practice marksmanship and hunting very small game at close range. Shooters who want to learn handgun technique often start with a 22 rim fire weapon because the ammunition is cheap and has no recoil.

The larger center fire cartridges named above are not as popular now as in earlier times when shooters appreciated the convenience of being able to fire the same ammunition in both revolver and rifle and when such arms as the 38–40 and 44-40 Winchester and Marlin repeaters were in common service. Because of the handgun's shorter barrel and because of its chamber (in case of the revolver), rifle loads show a loss in velocity of from 12% to 25% (depending on caliber) from the velocities they develop in the longer weapons. Rifle loads, too, are a bit less accurate when fired in handguns, the 32-20, 38–40 and 44-40 particularly so. These losses, of course, are not serious when the purposes of the handgun are correctly understood.

Caution. In no case should High Velocity, High Power or High Speed 32-20; 38–40 or 44-40 ammunition be used in revolvers. This ammunition is manufactured for safe use in rifles only. High Speed 22 Rim Fire loads are safe in handguns fitted with the recessed type of chamber or cylinder

Guide to Handgun Calibers

25 Auto. This small bore load is adapted to pocket and vest pocket size auto pistols. Because of its small bore and light bullet, is not recommended for serious offensive or defensive purposes when the shooter can carry a larger weapon.

32 S. & W. Short & Long. A multitude of small pocket revolvers have been chambered for this ammunition. The S. & W. Long (or Colt New Police) should be chosen for all revolvers built strongly enough to handle it, as the Short is quite inferior in both accuracy and range. Some very light, cheap revolvers may be unsafe with any but the Short size. Due to its small noise and recoil, the Long is sometimes used by beginners in learning handgun marksmanship and for outdoor practice on inanimate targets.

32 Auto. This clean shooting, semi-rimmed ammunition is similar in power to the 32 S. & W. but handicapped for outdoor practice shooting because it is fired only in pistols with short barrels. Recommended when a lightweight, short pocket weapon only can be carried.

32 Colt Short & Long. A totally different breed of load that does not fit Smith & Wesson and later Colt model revolvers. Was designed for early Colt pocket guns and the Marlin 1892 rifle (when fitted with center fire firing pin). Accuracy is low compared to present standards.

38 S. & W. A great many pocket revolvers are chambered for this ammunition which in the writer's opinion is the very minimum (in power) one should carry for self-defense purposes. Develops more power than the 32 pocket gun loads and less recoil than other 38 calibers. Not advised for target or outdoor practice.

38 Auto. Developed to meet the demand for a pistol more

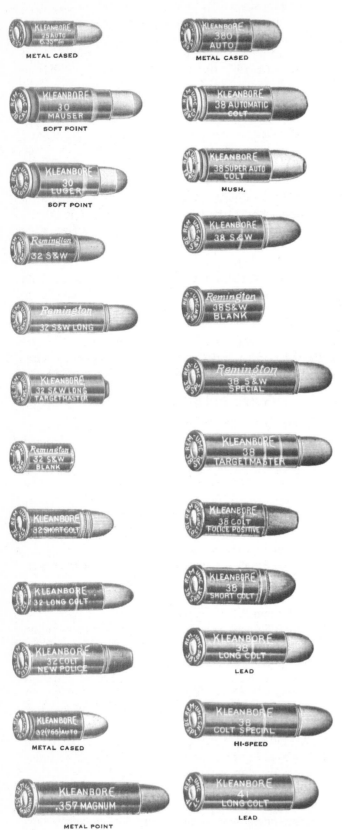

powerful than the 32 and without the recoil and weight of the regular 38 Auto. Has proved quite satisfactory as such. Do not use 380 ammunition in regular 38 pistols.

38 Colt Short & Long. Have fallen into disuse because the 38 Special is superior in both accuracy and power. Shooters who formerly chose the 38 Short for economical practice now find the 38 Special Mid-Range cartridge just as low in cost and much cleaner to fire.

38 S. & W. Special & Colt Special. In the writer's opinion one of our most useful sizes for all-purpose shooting. Excellent for self-defense and home protection, very accurate and widely used in target matches. Also the standard with city police departments. The special 200-grain bullet load designed for law enforcement use gives tremendous power and penetration.

38 Super Automatic. Develops more striking energy than the 45 pistol and the most powerful ammunition used in American made self-loading handguns. Excellent for any service that demands high velocity and long range.

357 Magnum. The most powerful handgun ammunition produced in this country. Widely used by police officers because of its tremendous penetration. In tests one' shot has wrecked a running automobile engine. The bullet will range clear through a sedan body shot from the rear to reach occupants in the front seat. If any hunter plans to shoot big game with a handgun (a practice the writer does not advise), this is the load to choose. The 357 cartridge is longer than the 38 Special and should be used only in revolvers chambered expressly for it. The owner of a 357 handgun, however, can fire any of the 38 Special and 38 Colt loads in it.

44 S. & W. Special. An outgrowth of the old 44 S. & W. Russian which in turn was developed from the original S. & W. The 44 Special is very accurate with its cartridge case made especially long to efficiently burn its powerful charge of powder. While popular for target match work, the great shocking power of this ammunition also makes it suitable for defensive and offensive purposes.

45 Colt. One of the most famous and most powerful loads ever produced for a revolver. The large, heavy bullet develops enormous shocking power and is accurate enough for ordinary handgun uses. Has a heavy recoil and is scarcely suitable for beginners.

45 Auto. Our military service load and the largest caliber ammunition fired from an automatic pistol. Is replacing the 45 revolver among heavy gun toters because its milder recoil makes accuracy easier. Recommended for any purpose where fire power and shocking energy are both required.

Types of Shotgun Loads

Broadly speaking there are three kinds of shotgun ammunition: high power, regular power and special target loads designed for trapshooting and skeet. High power loads usually contain maximum quantities of powder: 4¾ drams in 10 gauge, 4 or 4¼ drams in the 3-inch 12, 3¾ drams in the regular 12, 3 or 3¼ drams in the 16, and 2¾ drams in the

TYPES OF PISTOL BULLETS (Remington). 1. Lead 38 S. & W. Special, 158 gr. 2. "Sharp Shoulder" 38 S. & W. Special, 146 gr. Designed for target shooting. Also supplied in 32 S. & W. Long. 3. 30 Luger Soft Point, 93 gr. Metal case and lead core with exposed nose. 4. Mushroom 38 Super Automatic Colt, 130 gr. Used, as a hunting bullet at close range for use in side arms. 5. Metal Point 38 S. & W. Special, 158 gr. Lead core with metal jacket over nose. Gives better penetration than lead type. 6. Metal Cased 45 Colt Automatic, 230 gr. Gives deep penetration. 7. Metal Penetrating 38 S. & W. Special, 110 gr., "Hi-Way Master." Made of zinc. In 45 Auto, bullet has zinc core and metal jacket.

20. Regular power loads will carry 4¼ drams in 10 bore, 2¾ to 3¼ in 12 gauge, 2½ to 2¾ drams in the 16 and 2¼ or 2½ drams in the 20.

Shooters are cautioned that shotgun shells do not always contain exactly 2¾ or 3¾ or any of the other quantities named above. Actually they may hold a less amount of some special powder which is loaded by grains rather than by drams but of which enough is used to develop the same velocity as the quoted amount of the older "loaded by bulk" types gave. *Dram equivalent* is shown in ammunition catalogs mainly for the convenience of shooters in appraising and comparing the power and scope of the load. This fact is noted to prevent any misunderstanding by shooters who might decide to hand load their own shot shells.

Figures which indicate the components contained in shotgun ammunition are found both on the ammunition box and on the top wad of the round. The legend "3-1-6" on this top wad means "3 drams of bulk powder (or its equivalent if powder is the "dense" type loaded by weight) and 1 ounce of number 6 shot.

High Power Shotgun Ammunition. Should be used for difficult hunting conditions and hard to kill game taken at medium to long range (ducks, geese, foxes, etc.); when hunting with a 410, shoot high power (3-inch) loads only, because this small gun needs every possible advantage to avoid unsportsmanlike wounding and crippling of birds and animals. Choose high power ammunition for the 20 bore except when pursuing small birds and rabbits in open cover. In thick cover, 20 gauge high power loads are best for rabbits because they cut through brush more ably. High power loads are especially desirable when you hunt pheasants with 16 or 20 and should also be tried any time regular ammunition fails to give the expected percent of clean kills.

Since high power ammunition develops maximum pressures, it should be fired only in well made shotguns of good condition. Do not use it in cheap, lightweight models and especially foreign guns with short chambers and thin barrels or in any gun fitted with twist or Damascus barrels.

Low Power Shotgun Ammunition. Giving less recoil and muzzle blast, this ammunition is more comfortable to shoot and, moreover, develops all the power in 12, 16 and 20 bore guns that is needed for the less hard to kill species. There is seldom any real advantage gained by shooting high power loads in these three gauges for quail, grouse, snipe, ptarmigan, doves and rabbits unless the brush is very dense and unless the shooting range exceeds 38 to 40 yards. Because of its economy, low power ammunition is suitable for any gauge when firing at composition targets or other practice material.

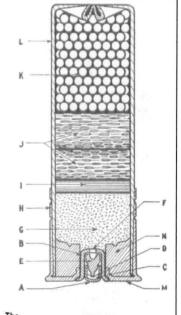

REMINGTON SHOTSHELL COMPONENTS

A	Primer Cup
B	Battery Cup
C	Primer Composition
D	Paper Disc
E	Primer Anvil
F	Flash Hole
G	Powder Charge
H-M	Brass Head
I	Over-powder Wad
J	Filler Wads
K	Shot Charge
L	Paper Body
N	Base Wad

BATTERY CUP AND PRIMER. The primer cup (a), made of brass and copper plated for identification, is enclosed in a reinforcing cup known as a battery cup (b), made of copper plated steel or brass. Within the primer cup is placed the correct amount of priming mixture (c) pressed to a definite density. This is covered with a paper foiling disc (d). The anvil (e) is placed in the cup in such a way that it insures compression of the mixture when the primer cup is hit by the firing pin, thus causing the priming mixture to explode. The explosion is carried to the powder charge through a small hole (f) in the battery cup.

Scatter Ammunition. A special type of regular power load designed to spread or scatter its short charge out in wide patterns at close range when fired from full choked barrels. This ammunition permits the hunter to use his choked duck gun with fair effectiveness on upland game taken at moderate yardage. While the patterns of these loads are rather irregular and uneven, their width or spread is almost twice as much at 20 yards as those from a normal shell put through the same choked muzzle which gives an undeniable and often valuable advantage to the hunter. Besides, the wider, thinner pattern of this ammunition reduces the mangling of game taken fairly close. It is sold under such trade names as "Brush", "Thicket", "Spreader" and "Scatter".

Target Shotgun Ammunition. This ammunition will be marked "Trap" or "Skeet" as the case may be and should always be chosen for competitive match shooting because its manufacturers have expended much time and expense in perfecting it in the matters of range, power and uniformity. Trap loads are also suitable for hunting many species of upland game and coots. Skeet loads, containing number 9 pellets, can often be employed advantageously to hunt small birds like rail and jacksnipe.

Ammunition Shell Length. Although modern American made shotguns have been well standardized in the matter of chamber length, variations are found in early models and in imported guns. For instance, 12 gauge shotguns have been made with chambers ranging from 2½ to 3 inches and 12 gauge loads can be purchased in 2⅝, 2¾ and 3-inch cases. These conditions make it imperative to match ammunition correctly with your gun. While no harm (other than a slight thinning out of the shot pattern) results when shells are shorter than a gun's chamber, a definitely dangerous condition exists when they are longer. Under no circumstances should 3-inch loads be used in a standard 2¾-inch chamber. It would be equally disastrous to fire 2¾-inch shells in a 2½-inch chamber. The 3-inch 410 loads should not be used in 410 guns chambered for the shorter, older shell. A safe rule is: *be sure your ammunition is the same length or shorter (never longer) than the chamber of your gun.*

High & Low Brass Shell Bases. Some shotgun ammunition is loaded in shells with a low brass band around the head of the shell, other types carry a brass band almost twice as wide or high. This difference carries no significance in the points of safety or strength. The wide band supplies no needed reinforcement, in fact the writer has fired shot shells without any brass covering whatever about the paper shell head and with entire safety. The real significance of the wide brass band is appearance. It is used almost exclusively on higher priced high power and special target loads to distinguish them from the ordinary kind.

Shot Composition

Formerly shooters had a choice of using either "Soft" or "Drop" shot made of pure lead, or "Chilled" shot cast from lead hardened by a small proportion of tin or other metal. At present shotgun ammunition is loaded with shot

especially prepared to give the best results in the shooting for which the load is intended. No choice need be expressed when selecting and buying regular type of loads.

An option of shot composition, however, is available since at least one factory supplies special shells containing "Copper-plated" pellets. These have a thin copper plating over the surface which hardens them without a substantial reduction of weight which can occur when alloys of tin and lead are used. This hardening helps the pellets stay round and true during their passage through the gun. Because they may be squeezed less out of shape by powder pressure and the resistance of cone and choke, plated pellets may fly a little farther and straighter. Deformed shot obviously can't hold velocity or their direction as well as perfectly round ones. Gunners who seek every possible advantage in long range and handicap shooting should test this special ammunition. The writer, however, doubts if plated shot gives enough improvement over the regular kind to make its choice important for ordinary shotgun work.

Shot Sizes

Buckshot. These big, heavy pellets are loaded in shotgun ammunition for use in killing big game and for police, guard and riot duties. They should be employed mainly for law enforcement purposes and perhaps to hunt rather small animals at short range where their very open pattern may offer some advantages in hitting. Buckshot, on the other hand, are very poor killers of deer and larger animals. They lack the penetration necessary for clean, instant kills and spread out so far apart that few if any pellets are liable to hit the target. It is not at all uncommon to have a load of 16 buckshot spread over a space five feet wide at 50 yards.

Rifled Slugs. Much more effective on big game and should be chosen when the shotgun is used to hunt deer and black bear. Only the larger gauge guns like the 16 and 12 should be used. While the 20 bore slug delivers a fair amount of striking force, it is hardly adequate to put deer down in their tracks at 50 yards. The 410 slug load is especially ineffective at any range.

The biggest fault of slug loads are their poor accuracy. Only a skilled marksman or a lucky one can be sure of hitting the vital part of a deer-sized target at average timber hunting range. Because of the irregular grouping of the slugs and the difficulty of aiming a shotgun with rifle precision, slugs are recommended only for distances up to about 180 feet. Shooters compelled by law circumstances to hunt big game with the shotgun should do plenty of practice work with this ammunition beforehand and familiarize themselves with its performance. Contrary to the belief of many, neither factory loaded buckshot or slug ammunition will injure full choked barrels.

No. BB. Use these, coarse shot in 12 and 10 gauge shotguns for hunting big geese at long range. Suitable, too, for foxes and coyotes shot in thick cover. Not for 16 and 20 bores because their loads will not contain enough BB pellets to make a killing pattern.

No. 2. The standard shot size for small geese taken at all ranges and big geese and foxes shot at moderate range. Has the advantage over BB of giving more dense, better filled patterns. Too coarse in size for shotguns smaller than 12 gauge. As with buckshot and slugs, BB and No. 2 will not injure a full choked barrel.

No. 4. Strictly a long range pellet for waterfowl and the bigger species of upland game. It is the largest pellet you should shoot in 16 gauge guns if you want effective patterns. Too coarse for the 20. If a regular 12 gauge will kill ducks at 60 yards, number 4 is the load to use.

No. 5. This size holds a truer course in stiff wind and cuts brush better than the very popular number 6. Fives are good for long range in 10, 12 and 16 bores. Rabbit hunters sometimes use No. 5 because fewer pellets hit the animal and accordingly drag fewer bunches of fur into the meat.

No. 6. One of the most popular and useful sizes made. It performs well on ducks, pheasants, prairie chickens, rabbits and squirrels. Six is the largest size practical for 28 ga. and 410 bore shotguns. If game or range requires bigger shot, use a bigger gun.

No. 7. Not as widely used as other near-size numbers. Hunters sometimes try sevens when they think the 6 pellet gives too thin a pattern and when size 7½ lacks penetration. Sevens will kill coots, small ducks, rabbits, crows and partridges. Will break composition targets well and at present is loaded mainly in trapshooting ammunition.

No. 7½ The original and standard pellet for trap-shooting and useful to the upland game hunter when different species may be encountered. Use 7½ for grouse, coots, quail, partridge and also to kill crippled ducks swimming in the water.

No. 8. A popular load for grouse and quail but not always available in small stores. Consequently hunters shoot the well distributed 7½ shot loads instead. Number 8 will kill rabbits if one is sighted when you have a quail shell in your gun.

No. 9. The standard pellet for skeet. Good for woodcock and jacksnipe but too small for grouse and quail, especially for the range at which most second shots at a covey must be taken. Nines will bring grouse and quail down but too many such birds are winged only and may go unrecovered.

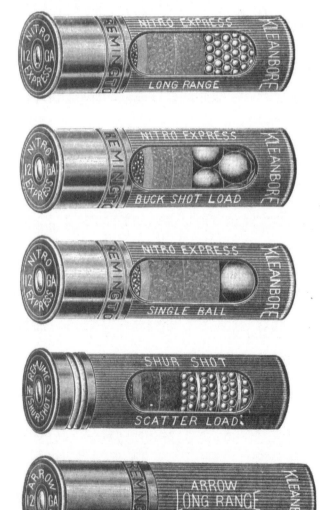

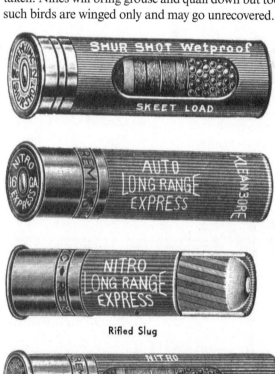

Rifled Slug

12 Gauge 3" Magnum

RIFLE BALLISTICS OF WINCHESTER CENTER FIRE CARTRIDGES

CARTRIDGE	BULLET Type	BULLET Wt.-Grs.	VELOCITY Muzzle	VELOCITY 100 Yds.	ENERGY Muzzle	ENERGY 100 Yds.	TRAJECTORY IN INCHES 100 Yds. Hgt. at 50 Yds.	200 Yds. Hgt. at 100 Yds.	300 Yds. Hgt. at 150 Yds.
218 Bee, Super Speed	H.P.	46	2,860	2,260	835	520	0.8	3.5	10.5
219 Zipper, Super Speed	H.P.	56	3,050	2,530	1,155	795	0.6	2.5	8.0
22 Hornet, Super Speed	S.P.	45	2,650	2,080	700	430	0.8	4.0	12.5
22 Hornet, Super Speed	H.P.	46	2,650	2,090	715	445	0.8	4.0	12.5
22 Savage, Super Speed	Ptd. S.P.	70	2,780	2,480	1,200	955	0.6	3.0	7.0
220 Swift, Super Speed	Ptd. S.P.	48	4,140	3,490	1,825	1,300	0.3	1.5	3.5
25-20 Winchester	Lead	86	1,450	1,190	400	270	2.6	11.5	31.5
25-20 Winchester	F.P.	86	1,450	1,190	400	270	2.6	11.5	31.5
25-20 Winchester	S.P.	86	1,450	1,190	400	270	2.6	11.5	31.5
25-20 Win., W.H.V. Super Speed	H.P.	60	2,210	1,700	650	385	1.1	6.0	18.5
25 Remington	S.P.	117	2,300	2,020	1,375	1,060	0.9	4.5	11.0
25-35 Winchester, Super Speed	F.P.	117	2,280	1,970	1,350	1,010	1.0	4.5	12.0
25-35 Winchester Super Speed	S.P	117	2,280	1,970	1,350	1,010	1.0	4.5	12.0
250 Savage, Super Speed	Ptd. S.P.	87	3,000	2,710	1,740	1,420	0.5	2.5	6.0
250 Savage, Silvertip Super Speed	Exp.	100	2,790	2,550	1,730	1,445	0.6	2.5	6.5
257 Roberts, Super Speed	H.P.	100	2,900	2,530	1,870	1,420	0.6	2.5	7.0
257 Roberts, Silvertip Super Speed	Exp.	100	2,860	2,610	1,815	1,515	0.6	2.5	6.5
270 Winchester, Super Speed	S.P.	100	3,540	3,210	2,785	2,290	0.4	1.5	4.5
270 W'chester, Silvertip Super Sp'd	Exp.	130	3,120	2,880	2,810	2,395	0.5	2.0	5.0
270 Winchester, Super Speed	H.P.	130	3,140	2,820	2,850	2,295	0.5	2.0	5.5
270 Winchester, Super Speed	S.P.	150	2,770	2,490	2,560	2,065	0.6	3.0	7.0
7 x 57 mm Mauser Super Speed	S.P.	175	2,460	2,220	2,350	1,915	0.8	3.5	9.0
7.62 mm Russian	H.C.P.	145	2,810	2,570	2,545	2,130	0.6	2.5	6.5
30-30 Winchester Super Speed	F.P.	170	2,200	1,930	1,830	1,405	1.0	4.5	12.0
30-30 Winchester, Super Speed	S.P.	170	2,200	1,930	1,830	1,405	1.0	4.5	12.0
30-30 Winchester, Super Speed	H.P.	150	2,380	2,060	1,890	1,415	0.9	4.0	11.0
30-30 W'ch'ter Silvertip, Sup. Sp'd.	Exp.	170	2,200	1,930	1,830	1,405	1.0	4.5	12.0
30 Rem. Silvertip, Super Speed	Exp	170	2,200	1,930	1,830	1,405	1.0	4.5	12.0
30 Rem., Super Speed	S.P.	170	2,200	1,930	1,830	1,405	1.0	4.5	12.0
30-40 Krag, Super Speed	H.P.	180	2,480	2,210	2,460	1,955	0.8	3.5	9.0
30-40 Krag, Super Speed	S.P.	180	2,480	2,210	2,460	1,955	0.8	3.5	9.0
30-40 Krag, Silvertip, Super Sp'd	Exp.	180	2,460	2,250	2,420	2,020	0.7	3.5	8.0
30-40 Krag, Silvertip, Super Sp'd	Exp.	220	2,190	1,980	2,345	1,915	1.0	4.5	11.0
30-06 Springfield, Super Speed	S.P.	220	2,410	2,190	2,840	2,345	0.8	3.5	9.0
30-06 Springfield Super Speed	S.P.	180	2,710	2,420	2,940	2,340	0.7	3.0	7.5
30-06 Sp'gfield, Silvertip Sup. Sp'd.	Exp.	180	2,690	2,500	2,895	2,500	0.6	3.0	7.0
30-06 Sp'gfield Silvertip Sup. Sp'd.	Exp.	220	2,410	2,190	2,840	2,345	0.8	3.5	9.0
30 06 Springfield, Super Speed	H.P.	180	2,710	2,420	2,940	2,340	0.7	3.0	7.5
30-06 Springfield, Wimbledon Cup	F.P.	180	2,690	2,500	2,895	2,500	0.6	3.0	7.0
30-06 Springfield	F.P.	150	2,800	2,560	2,610	2,185	0.6	2.6	6.6
30-06 Springfield, Super Speed	H.P.	150	2,980	2,650	2,960	2,340	0.6	2.5	6.5
300 Savage, Super Speed	H.P.	150	2,680	2,380	2,390	1,890	0.7	3.0	8.0
300 Savage, Super Speed	S.P.	180	2,380	2,140	2,265	1,830	0.8	4.0	10.0
300 Savage, Silvertip, Super Sp'd	Exp.	180	2,380	2,140	2,265	1,830	0.8	4.0	10.0
300 H. and H Magnum, Silvertip, Super Speed	Exp.	180	2,900	2,700	3,365	2,920	0.5	2.5	6.0
300 H. and H. Magnum Silvertip, Super Speed	Exp.	220	2,610	2,380	3,330	2,770	0.7	3.0	7.5
300 H. and H. Magnum, Match	F.P.	180	2,900	2,700	3,365	2,920	0.5	2.5	6.0
303 British, Super Speed	S.P.	215	2,160	1,940	2,230	1,795	1.0	4.5	11.5
303 Savage, Super Speed	S.P.	190	1,960	1,740	1,620	1,280	1.3	6.0	14.5
303 Savage, Silvertip, Super Sp'd	Exp.	190	1,960	1,740	1,620	1,280	1.3	6.0	14.5
8 x 57 mm Mauser, Super Speed	S.P	170	2,530	2,210	2,415	1,845	0.8	3.5	9.0
32 Winchester Self Loading	S.P.	165	1,390	1,190	710	520	2.6	12.5	31.0
32 Remington Super Speed	S.P.	170	2,200	1,910	1,830	1,380	1.0	5.0	13.0
32 Remington Silvertip, Super Sp'd.	Exp.	170	2,200	1,910	1,830	1,380	1.0	5.0	13.0
32-20 Winchester	Lead	100	1,280	1,060	365	250	3.1	15.0	40.5
32-20 Winchester	F.P.	100	1,280	1,060	365	250	3.1	15.0	40.5
32-20 Winchester	S.P.	100	1,280	1,060	365	250	3.1	15.0	40.5
32-20 W'chester W.H.V. Super Sp'd Not adapted to Pistol or Model 73 Winchester Rifle	H.P.	80	2,050	1,520	745	410	1.4	7.5	23.0
32 W'chester Special, Super Speed	S.P.	170	2,260	1,960	1,930	1,450	1.0	4.5	12.0
32 Win. Spec. Silvertip Sup Sp'd	Exp.	170	2,260	1,960	1,930	1,450	1.0	4.5	12.0
32-40 Winchester	S.P	165	1,440	1,230	760	555	2.6	12.0	28.0
33 Winchester	S.P.	200	2,180	1,870	2,110	1,555	1.1	5.0	13.5
348 W'chester Silvertip, Sup. Sp'd	Exp.	250	2,320	2,050	2,980	2,330	0.9	4.2	10.8
348 Winchester Super Speed	S.P.	200	2,520	2,160	2,820	2,075	0.8	4.0	10.0
348 Winchester, Super Speed	S.P.	150	2,880	2,380	2,765	1,890	0.6	3.0	8.5
35 Winchester	S.P.	250	2,160	1,910	2,590	2,025	1.1	5.0	12.0
35 Winchester Self-Loading	S.P.	180	1,390	1,170	775	545	2.5	13.0	31.0

RIFLE BALLISTICS OF WINCHESTER CENTER FIRE CARTRIDGES (Continued)

CARTRIDGE	BULLET Type	BULLET Wt.-Grs.	VELOCITY Muzzle	VELOCITY 100 Yds.	ENERGY Muzzle	ENERGY 100 Yds.	TRAJECTORY IN INCHES 100 Yds. Hgt. at 50 Yds.	200 Yds. Hgt. at 100 Yds.	300 Yds. Hgt. at 150 Yds.
351 Winchester Self Loading	F.P.	180	1,850	1,560	1,370	975	1.5	7.5	19.0
351 Winchester Self Loading	S.P.	180	1,850	1,560	1,370	975	1.5	7.5	19.0
35 Remington Super Speed	S.P.	200	2,180	1,870	2,110	1,555	1.0	5.0	13.0
35 Remington Silvertip, Sup. Sp'd.	Exp.	200	2,180	1,870	2,110	1,555	1.0	5.0	13.0
375 H. and H Magnum, Silvertip, Super Speed	Exp.	300	2,540	2,290	4,300	3,495	0.7	3.5	8.5
375 H. and H Magnum, Sup. Sp'd.	F.P.	300	2,580	2,300	4,435	3,525	0.7	3.5	8.5
375 H and H Magnum. Sup. Sp'd.	S.P.	270	2,720	2,460	4,440	3,630	0.7	3.0	7.0
32-40 Winchester	S.P.	180	1,310	1,090	685	475	3.2	15.5	37.5
38-55 Winchester	S.P.	255	1,320	1,150	985	750	3.0	13.5	32.5
401 Winchester Self Loading	S.P.	200	2,140	1,750	2,035	1,360	1.1	5.5	16.5
405 Winchester	S.P.	300	2,220	1,940	3,285	2,510	1.0	4.5	12.0
44-40 Winchester	S.P.	200	1,980	1,430	1,395	730	1.6	8.0	25.5
45-70 Government	S.P.	405	1,310	1,160	1,545	1,210	2.8	14.0	32.5

RIFLE BALLISTICS OF WINCHESTER RIM FIRE CARTRIDGES

CARTRIDGE	BULLET Type	BULLET Wt.-Grs.	VELOCITY Muz.	VELOCITY 100 Yds.	ENERGY Muz.	ENERGY 100 Yds
B.B. Caps	Lead Gr.	18	780	570	24	13
C. B. Caps	Lead Gr.	29	720	605	33	24
Leader 22 Short, Staynless	Lead Gr.	29	1,015	850	66	46
Spatterpruf 22 Short, 500 in carton	Lead Gr.	26	995	....	....	....
Spatterpruf 22 Short, Wax-coated, 500 in carton	K.K.	26	995	....	....	....
Spatterpruf 22 Short, 50 in carton	Lead Gr.	26	995	....	....	....
Super Speed 22 Short, Kopperklad, Wax-coated	K.K.	29	1,125	920	81	54
Super Speed 22 Short, Kopperklad, Hollow Pt., Wax-coated	K.K., H.P.	27	1,155	920	80	51
Super Speed 22 Long, Kopperklad, Wax Coated	K.K.	29	1,240	965	99	60
Leader 22 Long Rifle, Staynless	Lead Gr.	40	1,145	975	116	84
Smokeless EZXS 22 Long Rifle	Lead Gr.	40	1,145	975	116	84
Super Speed 22 Long Rifle, Kopperklad, Wax-coated	K.K.	40	1,335	1,045	158	97
Super Speed 22 L.R., Kopperklad Hollow Ponit, Wax-coated	K.K., H.P.	37	1,365	1,040	149	86
Super Speed 22 W.R.F., Kopperklad (inside lubricated)	K.K.	45	1,450	1,110	210	123
22 Auto, Kopperklad (inside lubricated)	K.K.	45	1,055	930	111	86
32 Long, Staynless	Lead Gr.	90	945	850	178	144

K.K. = Lead, Kopperklad H.P. = Hollow Point

REVOLVER BALLISTICS OF WINCHESTER RIM FIRE CARTRIDGES

When Fired in Revolver with 6-inch Barrel. All these Cartridges are Winchester Staynless (Smokeless Powder)

CARTRIDGE	Bullet Wt.	Muz. Vel.	Muz. Energy	CARTRIDGE	Bullet Wt.	Muz. Vel.	Muz. Energy
Super Speed 22 Short	29	1,035	69	Super Speed 22 Long Rifle	40	1,160	120
Leader 22 Short	29	925	55	Leader 22 Long Rifle	40	980	85
Super Speed 22 Long	29	1,075	75	Super Speed 22 W.R.F.	45	1,170	137

PISTOL & REVOLVER BALLISTICS OF WINCHESTER CENTER FIRE CARTRIDGES

CARTRIDGE	BULLET Type	BULLET Wt. Grs.	MUZZLE VELOCITY Ft. Per Sec.	MUZZLE ENERGY Ft. Lbs.	PENETRATION 7/8" Pine Boards At 15 Ft.	BARREL LENGTH Inches
25 Automatic	F.P.	50	820	75	3	2
30 Mauser (7.63 mm)	F.P.	86	1,420	385	11	5½
30 Luger (7.65 mm)	F.P.	93	1,250	323	11	4½
32 Automatic	F.P.	71	980	152	5	4
32 Colt New Police	Lead	98	795	138	3	4
32 Smith and Wesson	Lead	85	720	98	3	3
32 S. and W. Long	Lead	98	795	138	4	4
9 mm Luger (Parabellum)	F.P.	115	1,190	362	10	4
357 Magnum, Super Speed	Lead	158	1,450	690	12½	8⅜
38 Automatic	F.P.	130	1,070	331	9	4½
38 Automatic, Super Speed	F.P.	130	1,300	488	10	5
38 Smith and Wesson	Lead	145	745	179	4	4
38 Smith and Wesson	Lead	200	630	176	5	4
38 Colt New Police	Lead	150	695	161	4	4
38 Special	Lead	150	870	264	7	6
38 Special	Lead	200	745	247	7½	6
38 Special	M.P.	158	870	266	8	6
38 Special, Flat Pt.	Lead	158	870	266	6½	6
38 Special Match	Lead	158	870	266	7	6
38 Special Mid-Range Match	Lead	148	770	193	....	6
38 Special, Super Speed	Lead	158	1,115	436	7½	5
38 Special Metal Piercing, Super Speed	Metal Pierc.	150	1,175	460	11	5
380 Automatic	F.P.	95	970	199	5½	3¾
44 S. and W. Russian	Lead	246	770	324	7½	6½
44 S. and W. Special	Lead	246	770	324	7½	6½
45 Colt	Lead	255	870	429	6	5½
45 Automatic Rim	Lead	230	820	343	6	5½
45 Automatic Rim	F.P.	230	820	343	6	5½
45 Automatic Match	F.P.	230	750	288	....	5
45 Automatic	F.P.	230	860	378	6	5

Rifle Sighting Tables

(Reprinted through the courtesy of Winchester Repeating Arms Co.)

TO HELP THE shooter to quickly adapt his holding to various ranges, Winchester has developed the following tables showing the approximate actual positions of the bullets at the ranges given. These are based on the rim fire rifle being zeroed at 50 yards and the center fire rifle at 100 yards —in many cases 200 yards also. These figures show the distance in inches above or below the line of sight. In the center fire tables, positions above the line of sight are indicated by a plus sign, those below by a minus sign. It must be understood, of course, that due to wind conditions and other factors there are bound to be variations in the flight of bullets, which cannot be avoided. Therefore these figures in all cases must be read as indicating approximate positions. The rifles used in determining these ballistics had standard length barrels. This new presentation has been developed because it makes it simpler and quicker for the shooter to adapt his holding to any range. Note: these are revised (1948) figures which supersede all previous tables printed in *The Gun Digest*.

RANGE TABLE FOR WINCHESTER CENTER FIRE CARTRIDGES

(Note: The following tables are generally representative of all similar standard ammunition of factory loading.)

CARTRIDGE	BULLET Wt. Grs.	Type	Path of Bullet Above or Below Line of Sight in Inches 50 Yds.	100 Yds.	200 Yds.	300 Yds.	400 Yds.	500 Yds.
218 Bee. Super Speed	46	H.P.	+0.7	0	—6.0	—26.5		
219 Zipper, Super Speed	56	H.P.	+0.6	+3.5	—4.5	—19.0		
22 Hornet, Super Speed	45	S.P.	+0.8	+2.5	—7.5	—13.5	—32.0	
22 Hornet, Super Speed	46	H.P.	+0.8	+4.0	—6.5	—22.5		
22 Savage, Super Speed	70	Ptd. S.P.	+0.6	+3.5	—4.5	—17.0		
220 Swift, Super Speed	48	Ptd. S.P.	+0.3	+1.5	—2.5	—11.0	—24.0	—50.5
25-20 Winchester	86	Lead	+2.6	0	—18.5	—76.0		
25-20 Winchester	86	F.P.	+2.6	0	—18.5	—76.0		
25-20 Winchester	86	S.P.	+2.6	0	—18.5	—76.0		
25-20 Win. W.H.V., Super Speed	60	H.P.	+1.2	0	—11.0	—48.0		
25 Remington	117	S.P.	+0.9	0	—6.5	—26.0		
25-35 Winchester, Super Speed	117	S.P.	+1.0	0	—7.5	—29.5		
25-35 Winchester, Super Speed	117	S.P.	+1.0	0	—7.5	—29.5		
250 Savage, Super Speed	87	Ptd. S.P.	+0.5	0	—3.5	—14.5		
250 Savage, Silvertip, Super Speed	100	Exp.	+0.6	+2.5	0	—9.0		
257 Roberts, Super Speed	100	H.P.	+0.6	+2.5	0	—16.0		
257 Roberts, Silvertip Super Speed	100	Exp.	+0.6	+2.5	0	—10.0		
270 Winchester, Super Speed	100	Exp.	+0.4	+2.5	0	—17.5		
270 Winchester Silvertip, Super Speed	130	Exp.	+0.5	+1.5	0	—10.5	—27.5	—47.0
270 Winchester, Super Speed	130	H.P.	+0.5	+2.0	0	—12.5	—23.0	—46.0
270 Winchester, Super Speed	150	S.P.	+0.6	+2.0	0	—13.0	—30.0	—54.5
7 x 57 mm Mauser, Super Speed	175	S.P.	+0.8	+3.5	0	—18.0	—44.0	—86.5
7.62 mm Russian	145	H.C.P.	+0.6	+3.5	0	—14.0		
30-30 Winchester, Super Speed	170	F.P.	+1.0	0	—7.5	—28.0		
30-30 Winchester, Super Speed	170	S.P.	+1.0	0	—7.5	—28.0		
30-30 Winchester, Super Speed	150	H.P.	+0.9	0	—7.5	—26.0		
30-30 Winchester, Silvertip, Super Sp'd.	170	Exp.	+1.0	0	—7.5	—28.0		
30 Remington, Silvertip, Super Speed	170	Exp.	+1.1	0	—7.5	—29.5		
30 Remington, Super Speed	170	Exp.	+1.1	0	—7.5	—22.5		
30-40 Krag, Super Speed	180	S.P.	+0.8	+3.5	0	—14.0	—55.0	—108.0
30-40 Krag, Super Speed	180	Exp.	+0.8	+3.5	0	—22.5	—42.5	—108.0
30-40 Krag. Silvertip Super Speed	220	Exp.	+1.0	+3.0	0	—19.5	—46.0	—92.5
30-40 Krag, Silvertip, Super Speed	220	S.P.	+0.8	+3.0	0	—16.5	—35.0	—87.0
30-06 Springfield, Super Speed	180	S.P.	+0.8	+3.0	0	—16.5	—52.0	—127.5
30-06 Springfield, Super Speed	180	S.P.	+0.7	+4.5	0	—9.5	—36.5	—102.5
30-06 Springfield, Silvertip, Super Sp'd.	220	Exp.	+0.6	+3.0	0	—9.5	—44.5	—88.5
30-06 Springfield, Silvertip, Super Sp'd.	180	H.P.	+0.8	+5.5	0	—13.5	—38.0	—76.0
30-06 Springfield, Super Speed	150	F.P.	+0.7	+3.5	0	—16.5	—28.0	—71.5
30-06 Springfield, Wimbledon Cup.	180	F.P.	+0.6	+4.5	0	—15.5		—59.0
30-06 Springfield	150	H.P.	+0.6	+4.5	0	—15.5		
300 Savage, Super Speed	150	S.P.	+0.6	+4.0	0	—15.5	—52.0	—102.5
300 Savage, Super Speed	150	Exp.	+0.7	+4.0	0	—9.5	—36.5	—87.0
300 Savage, Silvertip, Sup. Sp.	150	Exp.	+0.9	0	—7.5	—28.5		
300 H.&H. Magnum, Silvertip, Sup. Sp.	180	Exp.	+0.9	0	—7.5	—24.0		
300 H.&H. Magnum Match	180	F.P.	+0.5	0	—4.5	—69.5		—130.0
303 British, Super Speed	215	S.P.	+1.0	+7.0	0	—35.0	—58.0	
303 Savage, Super Speed	190	S.P.	+1.5	0	—28.5	—24.0		
303 Savage, Silvertip, Super Speed	190	Exp	+0.8	0	—7.5	—35.0		
8 x 57 mm Mauser, Super Speed	170	S.P.	+0.8	+5.5	0	—23.0		
32 Winchester Self-Loading	165	S.P.	+2.6	0	—21.0	—74.0		—116.0

RANGE TABLE FOR WINCHESTER CENTER FIRE CARTRIDGES (Continued)

CARTRIDGE	BULLET Wt. Grs.	Type	Path of Bullet Above or Below Line of Sight in Inches 50 Yds.	100 Yds.	200 Yds.	300 Yds.	400 Yds.	500 Yds.
32 Remington, Super Speed	170	S.P.	+1.0	0	—7.5	—32.5		
32 Remington, Silvertip, Super Speed	170	Exp.	+1.0	0	—7.5	—32.5		
32-20 Winchester	100	Lead	+3.1	0	—24.5	—98.0		
32-20 Winchester	100	F.P.	+3.1	0	—24.5	—98.0		
32-20 Winchester	100	S.P.	+3.1	0	—24.5	—98.0		
32-20 Winchester W.H.V., Super Speed	83	H.P.	+1.3	0	—13.5	—59.0		
32 Winchester Special, Super Speed	170	S.P.	+1.0	0	—7.5	—28.5		
32 Winchester Spec., Silvertip, Super Sp.	170	Exp.	+1.0	0	—7.5	—28.5		
32-40 Winchester	165	S.P.	+2.6	0	—19.5	—66.0		
33 Winchester	200	S.P.	+1.1	0	—8.0	—32.5		
348 Winchester. Silvertip. Super Speed.	250	Exp.	+0.9	0	—6.5	—26.5	—66.5	—132.0
348 Winchester Super Speed	200	S.P.	+0.8	+4.0	0	—17.0	—52.0	—114.0
348 Winchester Super Speed	150	S.P.	+0.6	+4.0	0	—16.0	—73.0	—147.5
35 Winchester Self-loading	250	S.P.	+1.1	0	—14.5	—58.5	—129.5	
35 Winchester Self-loading	180	F.P.	+2.5	0	—22.0	—70.0	—143.0	
351 Winchester Self-loading	180	S.P.	+1.0	0	—12.5	—75.0		
351 Winchester Self-loading	180	F.P.	+1.1	0	—11.5	—45.5		
35 Remington, Super Speed	200	S.P.	+0.7	+8.5	0	—27.0	—58.0	—128.0
35 Remington, Silvertip, Super Speed	200	Exp.	+0.7	+8.5	0	—32.0		
375 H.&H. Magnum, Silvertip, Sup. Sp'd	300	Exp.	+0.7	+5.5	0	—21.0	—49.0	—94.5
375 H.&H. Magnum Super Speed	300	S.P.	+0.7	+5.5	0	—17.5	—49.0	—94.5
375 H.&H. Magnum Super Speed	270	S.P.	+0.7	+4.5	0	—10.5	—41.5	—82.5
38-40 Winchester	180	S.P.	+3.3	0	—26.0	—90.5	—32.0	—70.5
38-55 Winchester	255	S.P.	+3.0	0	—22.0	—76.0		
401 Winchester, Self-loading	200	S.P.	+1.2	0	—9.5	—41.0		
405 Winchester	300	S.P.	+1.0	0	—7.0	—31.0		
44-40 Winchester	200	S.P.	+3.3	0	—31.0	—91.0		
45-70 Government	405	S.P.	+2.8	0	—21.0	—76.0		

RANGE TABLE FOR WINCHESTER RIM FIRE CARTRIDGES

CARTRIDGE	BULLET Wt.-Grs.	Type	DROP OF BULLET Zero at 50 Yards 100 Yds.	150 Yds.	200 Yds.
Leader 22 Short, Stainless	29	Lead Gr.	—9.5	—31.0	—67.0
22 Short, Super Speed, Wax-coated	29	K.K.	—7.0	—31.5	—68.0
22 Short, Super Speed, Wax-coated	27	K.K., H.P.	—7.0	—24.5	—54.0
22 Long, Super Speed, Wax coated	29	K.K.	—5.5	—24.5	—60.0
Leader 22 Long Rifle, Stainless	40	Lead Gr.	—7.5	—29.0	—60.0
Smokeless EZXS 22 Long Rifle Staynless	40	Lead Gr.	—5.0	—29.0	—50.5
22 Long Rifle, Super Speed, Wax-coated	37	K.K.	—5.0	—24.0	—50.5
22 Long Rifle, Super Speed, Wax-coated	40	K.K., H.P.	—5.0	—24.0	—46.0
22 W.R.F. Super Speed (inside lubricated)	45	K.K.	—5.0	—22.5	
22 Automatic (inside lubricated)	45	K.K.	—8.0	—22.5	
32 Long, Stainless	89	Lead Gr.	—8.5		

K.K. = Lead, Kopperklad   H.P. = Hollow Point   S.P. = Soft Point   F.P. = Full Patch

HOW FAST FOR HOW LONG?

A bullet leaves the muzzle of a rifle at a certain speed, but how fast is it traveling when it gets where it's going? This is a question which has puzzled many shooters for long time. The Remington Arms Company has recently compiled a table of "remaining velocities" for the 22 caliber cartridges which provides the answers to such questions. Here is what they have to say in explanation:

"Sound travels at the rate of approximately 1090 feet per second, which is considerably less than the speed at which a Remington 22 long rifle Hi-Speed hollow-point bullet leaves the muzzle of a rifle. The muzzle velocity of this bullet is 1365 feet per second, which is approximately 930 miles per hour. Air resistance immediately retards the bullet; at 50 yards it is traveling at the rate of only 1155 feet per second, or about 790 miles per hour. At 100 yards it is still zipping along at 1040 feet per second, a 710-miles-per-hour clip. When it passes the 200 yards mark its speed has diminished to 900 feet per second, which, at the rate of 610 miles per hour, is still faster than a limping walk.

"The new table will allow you easily to figure out the speed of various 22 cartridges at various distances. An object traveling 88 feet per second is going at the rate of a mile a minute. Divide any of the remaining velocities shown in the table by 88 and multiply the result by 60 and you have the rate of speed in miles per hour the bullet is traveling at that point."

Complicated electrical recording machines were used in determining the figures contained in the table. In explaining the project, Dr. C.S. Cummings, Remington's supervisor of ballistics standardization, said:

"The experiments on the basis of which these tables were computed involved the very precise measurement of bullet velocities at a number of points. These measurements were made by shooting electrically charged bullets through a number of coils and recording the instant of passage of the bullet through each coil by means of an oscillograph and camera with moving film. The time interval standard was a 50,000 cycle quartz crystal oscillator. The resultant measurements were accurate to about two-tenths of a foot per second. From the basic data, tables were constructed by means of which remaining velocities, times of flight, bullet drop, wind drift and other trajectory information can be computed for various bullets, providing the *ballistic coefficient* is known. Ballistic coefficient is based on the weight of the bullet, its shape and its sectional density.

"Since the same ammunition would give slightly different results when fired in different guns (due to differences in chambers and bore dimensions), the figures have been rounded off to the nearest five feet per second."

REMAINING VELOCITIES — REMINGTON CAL.22 RIM FIRE CARTRIDGES

Distances form Muzzle in Ft	Short Hi-Speed Ball	Short Hi-Speed Hollow Pt	Long Rifle Std. Vel. Ball	Long Rifle Hi-Speed Ball	Long Rifle Hi-Speed Hollow Pt.
0	1125	1155	1145	1335	1365
30	1095	1120	1120	1295	1315
50	1075	1095	1105	1265	1285
60	1070	1085	1100	1255	1270
75	1055	1075	1090	1235	1250
90	1045	1060	1080	1215	1230
120	1025	1035	1060	1180	1190
150	1005	1015	1045	1150	1155
180	985	995	1030	1125	1125
210	970	975	1015	1100	1100
225	960	965	1005	1090	1090
240	955	955	1000	1080	1075
270	935	940	985	1065	1040
300	920	920	975	1045	1040
375	...	...	945	1010	1000
450	...	...	915	975	965
525	...	...	885	945	930
600	...	...	860	915	900

WESTERN-WINCHESTER SIMPLIFIED TRAJECTORY CHART

MUZZLE POINT < Iron Sights >

Yards from muzzle: 50 100 150 200 250 300 350 400 450

* OPE — Open Point Expanding
ST — Silvertip
SP — Soft Point

270 Win. 130 gr. *OPE →

3. 30-06 Sprg. 180 gr. ST (also 257 Roberts, 100 gr.; 300 Sav., 150 gr.) →

2. 348 Win. 150 gr. SP (also 257 Roberts, 117 gr.; 30-40 Krag, 180 gr.; 300 Sav., 180 gr.) →

1. 30-30 Win. 170 gr. ST (also 32 Win. Sp., 165 and 170 gr.; 303 British, 215 gr.) →

GRID — EACH LINE REPRESENTS ONE INCH

MUZZLE POINT A
1. DRAW SIGHTING IN LINE
2. MEASURE DISTANCE BETWEEN C AND D
3. COMPARE MEASUREMENT WITH GRID AT RIGHT
GRID / RULER

One of the secrets of successful hunting is the ability to know how much to hold over or under your target when game appears at any range other than that for which your rifle is sighted in.

For example, if you are shooting deer with a Model 94, sighted in at 100 yards, and are using a 30-30 with a 170-grain bullet, you should hold over three inches if your game appears at 150 yards. At 200 yards, you should hold over nine inches.

Hunters can easily teach themselves to aim more effectively by familiarizing themselves with the trajectories of the more popular cartridges. A little practice with a ruler and this new simplified trajectory chart will pay out in the hunting field.

It is approximately accurate for use at the ranges covered by the curves as shown for rifles equipped with iron sights.

Here is how to use the chart with the example given above:

1. With a ruler draw a "sight-in-line" from the "Muzzle Point" dot (A) of your cartridge (30-30, 170-grain) through the distance (B) at which you are sighted in (100 yards) on the trajectory curve of that cartridge, and extend it well beyond the distance (150 yards) for which you want to find the amount by which you should hold over.

2. At the 150-yard point (C) on the trajectory curve, draw a line upward which is perpendicular to the "sighting-in" line and intersects it at D.

3. With a ruler measure the distance from C to D. Then compare the distance shown on the ruler with the Grid at the right which will show in inches how much to hold over.

To determine how much to hold under when shooting at distances shorter than those at which you are sighted in, measure the distance of the trajectory curve above the sighting line.

VELOCITIES OF STANDARD LOADS
(Western Cartridge)
(Mean Velocity over 40 Yards)

Gauge	Shell Length	Dram Equiv.	Wt. Shot	Size Shot	Velocity Ft./Sec.
12	2¾"	3	1⅛ oz.	8	855
	2¾"	2	1¼ "	7½	850
	2¾"	Super-X	1¼ "	6	975
	2¾"	Magnum	1⅝ "	4	1005
16	2 9/16"	2¾	1⅛ "	8	845
	2 9/16"	Super-X	1⅛ "	6	925
	2¾"	Magnum	1⅛ "	8	955
20	2¾"	2½	1 "	8	840
	2¾"	Super-X	1 "	6	900

VELOCITIES OF SKEET LOADS (Western Cartridge)
(Mean Velocity over 40 Yards)

Gauge	Shell Length	Dram Equiv.	Wt. Shot	Size Shot	Velocity Ft./Sec.
12	2¾"	3	1⅛ oz.	9	920
16	2¾"	2½	1 "	9	920
20	2¾"	2¼	⅞ "	9	920
28	2¾"	2¼	¾ "	9	920
410	2½"	—	½ "	9	920
410	3"	—	¾ "	9	880

Velocity for any given dram equivalent varies with the size of shot, the smaller size have lower velocities.

SCIENCE SHOWS SHOT STRING IN FLIGHT

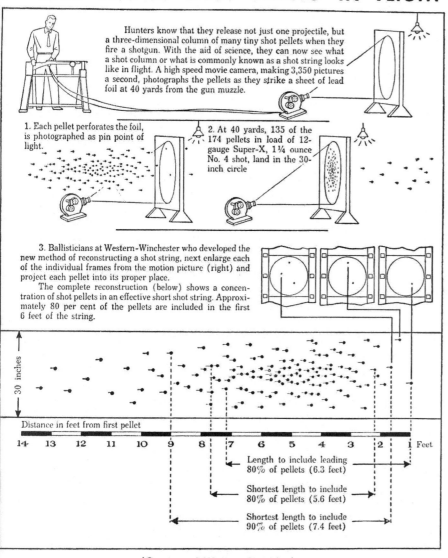

Hunters know that they release not just one projectile, but a three-dimensional column of many tiny shot pellets when they fire a shotgun. With the aid of science, they can now see what a shot column or what is commonly known as a shot string looks like in flight. A high speed movie camera, making 3,350 pictures a second, photographs the pellets as they strike a sheet of lead foil at 40 yards from the gun muzzle.

1. Each pellet perforates the foil, is photographed as pin point of light.

2. At 40 yards, 135 of the 174 pellets in load of 12-gauge Super-X, 1¼ ounce No. 4 shot, land in the 30-inch circle

3. Ballisticians at Western-Winchester who developed the new method of reconstructing a shot string, next enlarge each of the individual frames from the motion picture (right) and project each pellet into its proper place.

The complete reconstruction (below) shows a concentration of shot pellets in an effective short shot string. Approximately 80 per cent of the pellets are included in the first 6 feet of the string.

Distance in feet from first pellet

14 13 12 11 10 9 8 7 6 5 4 3 2 1 Feet

Length to include leading 80% of pellets (6.3 feet)

Shortest length to include 80% of pellets (5.6 feet)

Shortest length to include 90% of pellets (7.4 feet)

(Courtesy of Western Cartridge)

Diagram of a bullet's flight shown in conjunction with a rifle so aimed that the bullet will reach its objective. A indicates the line of sight, B is the trajectory of the bullet, C the point where the bullet crosses the line of sight shortly after emerging from the rifle's muzzle, and D the point of impact coinciding with the point of aim.

STANDARD SHOT CHART

No.	12	11	10	9
Dia. in Inches	.05	.06	.07	.08
No. Pellets to the ounce	2385	1380	870	585

No.	8	7½	7	6
Dia. in Inches	.09	.095	.10	.12
No. Pellets to the ounce	410	350	300	225

No.	5	4	2 Air Rifle	BB
Dia. in Inches	.12	.13	.15 .175	.18
No. Pellets to the ounce	170	135	90 55	50

No.	4 Buck	3 Buck	1 Buck	0 Buck	00 Buck
Dia. in Inches	.24	.25	.30	.32	.33
No. Pellets to Pound	340	300	175	145	135

SHOT SHELL PATTERNS
(Western Cartridges)

Choke	Percentage of Shot in 30" Circle at 40 Yards
Full	65% to 75%
Improved Modified	55% to 65%
Modified	45% to 55%
Improved Cylinder	35% to 45%
Cylinder	25% to 35%

The size of the circle in which the above percentages of shot will be distributed at ranges greater or less than 40 yards will be approximately in proportion to the ratio of the two ranges.

The "grand old man" of precision shooting explains bullet casting.

Casting Lead Alloy Bullets

by COL. TOWNSEND WHELEN

IN BLACK POWDER Days (prior to about 1896) all bullets were made of lead, usually slightly hardened with a small percentage of tin or antimony to prevent their leading the bore. They were formed with grooves around their cylindrical bearing surfaces, and these grooves were filled with grease or wax to lubricate them and thus further prevent their leading the bore of the rifle. Lead bullets are still used almost universally (except for military purposes) in revolver cartridges, but in centerfire factory loaded rifle cartridges they have been almost entirely replaced by metal cased or jacketed bullets.

There are two reasons for this: (1) Because the demand has been for greater velocity, meaning larger powder charges that generate hotter gas which melts the bases of lead bullets while they are traveling through the bore. Given extremely high velocity, lead bullets may strip in the rifling. (2) It is difficult to prevent a certain amount of deformation of the soft bullets during manufacture, shipping, and use. Metal cased bullets stand up much better under handling and are not deformed so much when they jump from the case through the throat of the chamber into the rifling. They are more accurate for this reason.

However, lead alloy bullets still present many advantages to the handloader, perhaps the chief being economy. Metal cased bullets must still be bought from their manufacturer through retail dealers and cost from $2.00 to $6.00 per hundred depending on weight and caliber. But if the hand-loader has the necessary mould and accessories (which are not expensive) he can easily make his own lead alloy bullets for the cost of the lead alone, which brings their cost down to only a small fraction of metal cased bullets. It is just beginning to be possible for handloaders to make their metal cased bullets also, but while these are cheaper, the economy is not as great as with lead bullets.

Lead alloy bullets are still very useful and in many cases highly desirable in rifles, while in revolvers they are a necessity. In rifles they can be used for target practice at short and mid ranges for both economy and to lessen the wear on rifle barrels, and for use on target ranges where the higher velocity metal cased bullet loads might be unsafe. They are also useful for reduced loads for small game shooting and for indoor gallery practice. The heavier lead alloy bullets may also be satisfactory for large game. In addition, of course, there are many of the old black powder rifles still in use, and for these lead bullets are a necessity.

Alloy for Lead Bullets

Lead bullets are usually alloyed with a small amount of tin or antimony or both to make them slightly harder so that they will not lead the bore. The amount of tin or antimony used is designed by proportionate weight. Thus an alloy composed of ten pounds of lead to one pound of tin was called a 1 to 10 tin and lead alloy, or a 10% tin alloy. In black powder days most of the bullets used in centerfire rifles were alloyed 1 to 16 or 1 to 20 tin and lead. Generally speaking, the quicker the twist of rifling the greater the proportion of tin used to make the bullet harder. Schuetzen riflemen using 32–40 and 38–55 black powder rifles experimented a lot with various tempers of bullets to get one that caused the most perfect bullet upset in the bore and thus gave the best accuracy.

Today it has been found that generally for lead alloy bullets, either plain base or gas check, for use in modern high velocity rifles having quick twists of rifling, the best alloy is a 1 to 10 tin and lead alloy, or an alloy of 90 parts by weight of lead, 5 parts of tin, and 5 parts of antimony. This 90-5-5 alloy is often called the Ideal Alloy, or Ideal Bullet Metal No. 2, because it was originally developed in conjunction with Ideal reloading tools by the Lyman Gun Sight Corporation. This corporation continues to sell Ideal Bullet Metal No. 2 (90-5-5) in six-pound ingots to handloaders, and it is very convenient for those handloaders who mould their own bullets. This Ideal Bullet Metal No. 2 may be used as a basis for making softer alloys according to the following table:

1 tin to 10 lead equivalent to No. 2 Metal
1 tin to 15 lead equivalent to 2 parts No. 2 Metal to 1 part lead
1 tin to 20 lead equivalent to 1 part No. 2 Metal to 1 part lead
1 tin to 25 lead equivalent to 2 parts No. 2 Metal to 3 parts lead
1 tin to 30 lead equivalent to 1 part No. 2 Metal to 2 parts lead
1 tin to 40 lead equivalent to 1 part No. 2 Metal to 3 parts lead

Bullets for revolvers should not be softer than 1 part of tin to 40 parts of lead, and alloys as hard as 1 to 10 may be used. Often quite a little experimenting is necessary with alloys in preparing revolver bullets to get just the right alloy for an individual revolver that gives fine accuracy but does not lead the bore. But with smokeless powders and the rifles of today, the 1 to 10 tin and lead alloy or the Ideal Bullet Metal No. 2 seems to work excellently in almost all powder loads that are proper for lead bullets. The reason for using antimony is that it has a higher melting point than tin, and accordingly alloys with antimony are not so liable to suffer from powder gases melting the bases of bullets, and consequently slightly larger powder charges can be used with this alloy.

When — for economy — cable sheathing, storage battery plates, plumber solder, or type metal is used for lead, it is almost impossible to accurately determine the hardness of the alloy unless one has a lead tester such as that made by the Potter Engineering Company, which tests the hardness of a slab or ingot of lead by forcing a small steel ball into the lead in much the same manner as Brinell hardness is measured. Then if the metal is not of the required hardness, other kinds of metal can be added to make it right.

The following tools and accessories will be required for casting bullets:

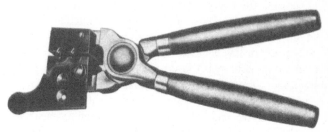

Lyman Ideal Double Cavity Bullet Mould

Bullet mould	Blanket or cushion
Lead melting pot	Cloth to cover blanket
Special dipper or ladle	Old tin pan
Lubricant	Cotton gloves
Furnace	Chair
Wooden mallet	Bench or boxes

The bullet mould for the particular bullet you wish is purchased from makers of reloading tools. The principal bullet mould makers are Lyman Gun Sight Corporation, Belding & Mull, Modern Bond Corporation, Hensley & Gibbs, and Cramer Bullet Mould Co.

The cast-iron melting pot, also procurable from reloading tool makers, should hold not less than three pounds of molten metal; or about 15 pounds for quantity casting. Most electric furnaces have the melting pot built in them.

The dipper or ladle for casting with bullet moulds that have one or two cavities should be of the type furnished by reloading tool makers with a spout that fits the pouring hole in the mould. The ordinary plumber's lead dipper will not be satisfactory. But for casting in a multiple cavity mould a ladle of the plumber type with ordinary pouring lip is necessary.

If the home or workshop is supplied with gas, then an ordinary Bunsen burner is very satisfactory as a furnace. One of the larger gasoline single burner furnaces such as the Coleman can also be used. Where electricity is available, one of the special electric furnaces furnished by some makers of loading tools is very convenient.

A cushion or a blanket folded to several thicknesses is needed to let the bullets drop onto as they fall from the mould so they will not be deformed. A piece of cotton cloth to cover the blanket to keep the hot bullets from scorching it is desirable.

The most convenient mallet is a stick or billet of hard wood, about 2 × 2 × 12 inches, with one end rounded for hand grasp. The old tin pan is to dump the hot dross into as it is skimmed off the molten lead from time to time. The bullet lubricant or wax is to flux the lead and to lubricate the joint of the mould.

Arrangement of Materials

As the job of bullet casting is going to take two hours or more, and should not be interrupted, it is well to have everything comfortable and convenient before starting. It is much easier and less tiring if you can rest your elbows on your knees as you cast. Therefore have a sturdy kitchen chair to sit on, and perhaps a cushion on it. Arrange the furnace on a level box or low bench so that the top of the melting pot comes on a level with your knees, and the near edge of the pot about a foot in front of the knees. Cover your lap, knees, and lower legs with a heavy apron or piece of canvas to keep off any possible lead splatter. To the left of the furnace have another box on top of which you place the folded blanket, with the top of the blanket several inches below the lop of the melting pot. To the right of the melting pot have a third bench, top about on a level with the top of the pot. This is for the tin pan to receive the dross, to rest the wooden mallet on between casts, for extra metal, etc.

Take off your coat and tie, for you are going to sweat before it is over. Wear the cheap cotton gloves to protect your hands. Have plenty of ventilation in the room.

Casting Bullets

Weigh out the proper proportions of lead, tin and/or antimony. You will mould better bullets if you work with from three to ten pounds of metal in the pot — easier to dip from and that amount of lead holds an evener temperature. The metal will melt quicker if you place only several pounds of lead in the pot at first, and when that is melted, add the remainder gradually. Keep the dipper or ladle in the molten lead constantly except when filling the mould.

The mould must be very hot, almost as hot as the lead, to cast good bullets. Therefore, to save time, prop the mould up with its cavity block touching the outside of the pot so that it receives some of the heat that comes up around the pot while the lead is melting.

When the alloyed lead is all melted, add a ¾" ball of beeswax, tallow, or bullet lubricant, and stir the metal well with the dipper. The lubricant will begin to smoke and then ignite; if it does not ignite, touch it off with a match. This fluxing helps to mix the metals in the alloy together and causes any impurities or dross to rise to the surface, when it should be skimmed off with the dipper and dumped into the tin pan, leaving the surface of the molten metal bright and mirror-like as it always must be while casting bullets. Fluxing, thorough stirring, and removing the dross may be necessary every fifteen minutes or so while casting, but never skim off dross without first fluxing with the lubricant.

Now fill the dipper about two-thirds full of metal. Hold the mould, top to the right, over the pot; connect the nozzle of the dipper with the pouring hole in the mould, then turn the mould and dipper upright. The lead will then flow from the dipper into the mould, and the weight of lead in the body

Saeco Electric Furnace

of the dipper will cause the lead to completely fill the cavity in the mould. Keeping the mould upright, turn the dipper over, leaving a little puddle of liquid lead in the opening of the pouring hole of the mould, and return the dipper to the metal in the pot. The temperature of the lead and the mould should be such that it takes four or five seconds for the sprue — the puddle of lead in the pouring hole — to solidify.

Then take the mallet in the right hand and cut off the sprue by striking the sprue cutter on the mould sharply so that the little piece of sprue falls into the melting pot. Hold the mould over the blanket, open it, and let the bullet drop out onto the blanket. If the bullet does not drop from the mould of its own accord, tap the mould with the mallet at the mould hinge to jar it out. Never strike the mould with anything metal.

A new mould will not cast good bullets until it has become oxidized, nor will any mould cast well until it has become very hot. Practically always you will have to cast ten to thirty bullets before the mould comes to the right temperature to cast good bullets that completely fill the mould with all their grooves, bases and points perfectly formed. The bullets should be perfect, bright, and shiny. If they have a frosted appearance, it indicates that the metal and mould are too hot. Turn down the gas or current slightly on the furnace. The mould may also be cooled by dipping it for a few seconds into hot water, but only when its cavity is filled with a bullet. With a lead and tin alloy the metal should be at about 600 degrees F., but with an alloy containing antimony the temperature should be higher, about 750 degrees F.

When three or four imperfect bullets have accumulated on the blanket, pick them up with your gloved hand and drop them back into the pot again. Never drop imperfect bullets from the mould into the pot because lead might splash up onto the inside surface of the mould, and adhering there keep the mould from closing completely. If this happens, lift the flake off carefully with a sharp knife.

Never dip from the surface of the metal. Insert the dipper down into the bottom of the pot, turn its cavity up, and bring it to the surface. This stirs the metal at each dip and keeps the alloy properly mixed (the lighter metal — tin and antimony — tends to rise to the top of the molten mass).

Finally you are beginning to cast good bullets, and aside from occasionally fluxing and skimming off the dross you should be able to cast good bullets right along. As they begin to accumulate on the blanket, push them to one side so that you will always have a free spot for the bullets to fall on, and thus no bullet will strike another as it falls.

When you are through casting, turn off the furnace and let the bullets on the blankets cool a bit. Then carefully pick each bullet up in turn and set it base down in a pasteboard box to be conveyed to the loading bench for sizing and lubricating. Never tumble bullets or pour them into a box, or handle them in any way that might dent or damage them, particularly that might dull the edges of their bases, as all such injuries will make them inaccurate.

When the mould has cooled so that it can be handled, wipe it off with an oily rag and pack it away. When about to use that mould again, wipe it off inside and out with gasoline and then wipe all the gasoline off with a dry rag. When the metal remaining in the pot has solidified and cooled, scratch the alloy on its surface so that you can identify it afterwards and dump the remaining ingot out of the pot.

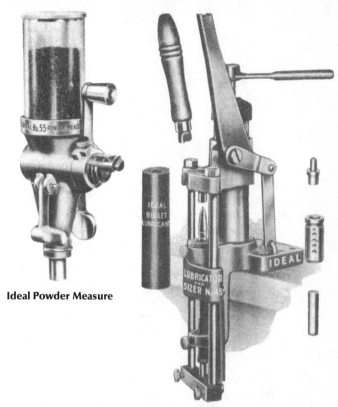

Ideal Powder Measure

Ideal Lubricator and Sizer

Quantity Casting

The above technique will work with bullet moulds having one or two cavities. For casting in large quantities, an armory or multiple cavity mould that casts four to ten bullets at a time is used. These moulds are heavy and tiresome, require considerable skill in their use, and do not pay for themselves unless thousands of bullets have to be cast for police or club use. When using them a large electric furnace with a large lead capacity is desirable. The sprue cutter on these multiple cavity moulds has a deep channel connecting the pouring holes of each cavity. An open ladle is used and the lead is run into the channel until all the cavities are filled, taking care to hold the mould level. Proper lubrication of the joint of the mould is necessary. Probably the best lubricant to stand the heat is Alemite Pyro Lubricant, which may be ordered through any Alemite dealer.

Antimony Alloys

There is no difficulty in alloying lead and tin. Just keep the mixture stirred by always dipping from the bottom of the pot. Antimony has a higher melting point than lead. To alloy it with lead, weigh out the proper quantity of the antimony and break it up very fine by pounding with a hammer. Melt the lead and raise it to a red heat, then add the antimony and cover the surface of the metal in the pot with powdered charcoal. Let the metal remain at this heat for a few minutes. Stir occasionally and when the antimony is completely melted, flux with lubricant and skim off the charcoal and dross, then lower the heat slightly to bring the metal to proper casting temperature. With a mixture high in antimony keep the metal hotter and stir more often, and never skim without fluxing and stirring, because the light antimony has a decided tendency to float on top of the lead.

Other Suggestions

After casting for some time the mould may become too hot, and the bullet may not have set, even though the metal in the sprue hole has solidified. Long and heavy bullets require more time to solidify and set than lighter ones. Also if the mould is too hot, the bullets may not have time to shrink much and they may stick and not drop from the mould so readily. The cure for all this is simply to give more time after pouring before you open the mould. Also stop when the mould gets too hot and dip it in warm water, taking care however that there are bullets in the cavities. Do not tighten the cut-off plate screws on the mould so that they bind. The cut-off plate must be left free to swing with its own weight. Use great care never to injure or scratch the cavities or to dull their edges. Never use a metal brush on a mould cavity or face. If a new mould refuses to close completely, it may be that the dowel pins bind a little. Close the mould, gripping the handles tightly, and strike the mould a smart tap on the side with the wooden mallet, which practically always overcomes this difficulty.

Question: How in thunder did our ancestors ever cast good bullets over a camp fire? *Answer*: They cast only round balls, and they trued them up afterwards with a jack-knife!

(Reprinted from *Why Not Load Your Own?*, by courtesy of The Combat Forces Press, Washington, D. C.)

A home-made
approach to
precision shooting.

Special Bullet Sizing Dies

by E. J. KRAVA

FREQUENTLY A HANDLOADER with a tight barrel will wish he had jacketed bullets a bit smaller than standard available. Such was the case with a 35 caliber rifle of mine; the barrel insisted on a .3565" diameter bullet but all I could find in the desired weight "miked" a full .3585". Because pressures for my pet load ran around maximum, I didn't care to boost them higher by making the burning powder gas squeeze that extra .002" diameter thru the barrel.

Unable to obtain the correct size bullet, I made a special sizing die for the Pacific loading press and sized the bullets to .3565". (Other presses may be used by altering the various dimensions.) Results were all I'd hoped for, and I've used the same scheme since with other bullets, both jacketed and cast lead. .311" jacketed and cast bullets have been sized to .308" for the Springfield, and with the Magnum revolver sizing the bullet to .357" eliminated some leading and accuracy was improved. Bullets for the Magnum came out of my regular Ideal Lubricator and Sizer at .3585" and then were run thru a home made sizing die to come out .357".

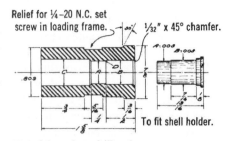

Relief for ¼–20 N.C. set screw in loading frame.   1/32" x 45° chamfer.

To fit shell holder.

Material: carbon drill rod.
A: diameter of finish-sized bullet (polished).
B: .001" over unsized bullet (polished).
C: approx. 1/32" over size of A (drilled).
D: Shoulder rounded by polishing

Making the Tools

Desiring to make the sizing die as simply as possible, the ⅞"-14 thread that is standard on most dies was left off. Instead, the die is made to slip

Two sets of dies and punches. Left punch is relieved for pointed bullets. Note set screw marks in groove on left die.

Bullets I have sized in dies. Top row shows jacketed bullets as bought and the cast type after regular lubricating and sizing. Below, same bullets after being run thru special sizing dies.

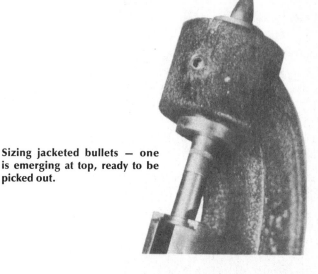

Sizing jacketed bullets — one is emerging at top, ready to be picked out.

Determine the base diameters for the bullet punch by measuring a cartridge head that fits your shell holder. It will then slip into the shell holder the same as a case does.

Sizing Bullets

Operation: apply a thin film of good grease to a jacketed bullet and insert it point first into the die. Bring the punch up and force the bullet thru the sizing step A and into the top relief C. Next, insert and size another bullet, which will lift the first one high enough to be picked out of the die with your fingers. Even soft nose spitzer bullets will not be damaged for the. bullet in the relief step is loose and free. If your die is well polished the bullet jacket will be smooth and shiny where it was resized.

For lead bullets, size and lubricate them in the conventional manner and then run them thru the die *base first*. This will prevent any lead extruding on the base end, which adversely affects accuracy. Flat nose bullets may use the punch described above, but round or pointed bullets require a cavity in the punch for the bullet nose. This can easily be machined in the lathe. Gas check bullets are run thru the same as jacketed bullets, nose first.

These special sizing dies tailor your bullets to each particular barrel — some barrels vary considerably and if you find yours is on the tight side for the bullets you are using, you can cut down pressure and probably improve accuracy by this method. I've found best accuracy resulted with jacketed bullets of from .001" under groove diameter to exact groove diameter size. For cast lead bullets, best results were obtained with bullets of groove diameter to hot more than .001" over.

Groove diameter can be checked by driving a pure lead un-sized bullet thru the barrel and "miking" the largest diameter; this corresponds to the groove diameter in your barrel. Use a hardwood block to start the bullet and carefully tap it into the barrel with a small brass punch. Then push it all the way thru with a polished steel rod of almost bore size.

inside the threads in the tool head. Held in place by a shoulder, against which the thrust is exerted, the die is locked by an Allen set screw.

Carbon drill rod was used, and the parts were not hardened. Drill rod is extremely tough and will stand considerable wear in its soft state, eliminating the lapping or internal grinding necessary after heat treating.

Parts are machined in a lathe and the hole sizes should be reamed or bored carefully. Diameter C can be drilled; it is only a relief for the bullet after it goes thru the sizing step A. Diameter A and B must be concentric and B should be not over .001" larger than your bullet, before it is run thru this special die. Diameter B lines up the bullet for correct entry into the sizing chamber A. The best way to reach diameter A correctly is to ream it to .001" smaller than the desired finish size of your bullet. Then polish lightly with fine emery cloth. Install the die in the loading press, run a bullet thru it and measure the reduced size with a micrometer. It will probably be undersize, but by careful polishing in the lathe, and measuring a bullet that has been run thru the die, the correct size can be obtained. Finish polishing with a piece of crocus cloth. Use care when polishing so that shoulder D becomes only *slightly* rounded. Don't try to blend it in — definite but rounded shoulder is needed.

Drill and tap the top part of the loading press for a ¼" -20 thread. Use a No. 7 or a ¹³⁄₆₄" drill and position it about the center up and down. To find the position of the groove in the sizing die, the easiest way is to slip it into place with the shoulder against the bottom of the loading frame and tighten the set screw. The mark of the set screw can be readily seen, and a ¹⁄₆₄" deep groove is lathe-cut at this point. This groove prevents any burr from making the removal of the die difficult.

An expert explains
what goes on inside
that brass case.

Practical Pressures

by JOHN MAYNARD

EVER STOP TO think, my shooting friend, that when you fire a modern rifle there stands between you and the blasting destruction of gas at many thousand pounds pressure, just a little brass? Just a brass bottle, corked at one end by a bullet and at the other, the end nearest your's eye, with the little metal cap called a primer? A bottle of a soft metal weighing a half-ounce or less? Skating on thin ice, isn't it?

But before, all fear and trembling, you hang your musket over the door, before you sell your handloading equipment for junk and solemnly swear to shoot no more, consider. Remember that the little brass bottle is supported by barrels of good metal and actions, or breechings of more or less gas-proof design, and that accidents resulting from powder pressures gone wild are few and far between. Among people of common sense that is. You're safer shooting than driving the family sedan down Main Street — after all, who knows what the other driver is going to do?

Not that there aren't common misconceptions about the pressures generated by contemporary nitro powders. To begin with, pressures are usually — and most solemnly — quoted in terms of pounds per square inch. When they are quoted, that is, it being the habit of our ammunition and powder makers to maintain dark silence on such matters. But in any event they might well be quoted as *frurs* or *milliframmises,* since there is grave doubt that the index numbers arrived at by today's pressure-measuring methods actually are pounds per square inch.

Whatever is measured, the methods employed in setting up loading machines to blend powder, primer mix, case capacity and bullet type into a cartridge combination delivering the velocity and pressure specified for a factory load, are hardly accurate. Even less so are the methods (so rarely used) in checking out wildcat developments. For many years laboratories have employed the crusher gauge system; for pistol or shotgun loads they measure the amount of squeeze given a lead

Reading primers for pressure is much like reading tea leaves — only a highly-trained reloader, one who considers all the other factors that affect primer appearance, can guess pressures by primer flattening and cratering. The 257 case at the right, for example, was fired with a high-pressure load that (in this rifle) would flatten and crater one brand of primer, but showed only gentle pressures with another. The two 300 H & H case heads demonstrate the effect of firing pin size and spring strength on apparent cratering. That at bottom was fired in a 300 Weather by Magnum, with 76 grs. of 4350 and 180-gr. bullet, but a weak firing pin spring. The center round shows *less* cratering with a charge 3 grs. heavier; same bullet, same case capacity, but a properly strong firing pin spring.

pill by powder-gas pressure, for the hotter rifle loads using copper pills in cylindrical form. The squeeze given these pills — which may be only a matter of .0865 in. in the case of a full-pressure rifle load — is translated into "pounds per square inch" via a tarage table, standardized to a given lot of pills.

Sounds simple and reasonable. But, the pressure barrel and chamber must be held to most precise dimensions — which is hardly the case with either custom or factory rifle barrels — and a pressure gun will hold those dimensions for only a limited number of "shots." The hole in the chamber and the piston in that hole, against which the powder gases thrust to squeeze the crusher pill between piston and the anvil or outer arbor of the pressure gun, must be fitted to micro-perfect dimensions. The pressure gun operator must be precisely trained and something of a human robot to duplicate the conditions of each test firing. Temperature, minute variations in size or metallurgy of the crusher pills, relative amounts of piston lubrication — these and many more factors make pressure-taking a kind of informed guess-work.

For the safe loading of factory ammunition it is accurate enough, since machine-production cartridges are ordinarily loaded well within the safe performance limits of a given cart ridge case and the kind of action in which it is likely to be fired. Shot-shells, of treated paper and thin brass heads, need be subjected only to something between 8000 and 12000 lbs. of pressure to give all the speed scatter-gun pellets can handle. Until recently revolver and pistol cartridges needed to operate only somewhere between 15000 and 25000 lbs. — until the 357 Magnum and more recently the 44 Magnum came along, that is. When smokeless powder charges for black powder cartridges and guns became standard it was no trick to get all the speed needed with pressures under 35000 p.s.i.; and it has been no great problem to produce commercial loads for obsolescent military bolt actions, like the single-lug Krag and those assorted Mauser- and Mannlicher-based European jobs that would stay in one piece only so long as the boiler readings are kept well under 45000. The great majority of today's commercial loads produce their advertised bullet speeds with heads of steam — thanks to modern powders — that stay well under the strength

Testing the pressure of a centerfire metallic cartridge at Winchester's ammunition development laboratories. The operator is about to place the copper crusher cylinder between piston and anvil attached to test barrel.

limits of either brass cases or of the actions enclosing them. It is only when the tarage chart gives off figures in the mid fifty-thousands for mean pressures — and remember that a *mean* pressure of 54000 lbs. may mean *maximums* of 58000 or more — that we begin to skate near the ragged edge of brass strength. It is not only practice in pressure-reading but improvements in case design that make the fifty-thousand-plus level possible for cartridges like the 270, the heavy-headed 220 Swift, some of the belted magnums.

Time-Pressure Study

More complex laboratory equipment employing oscilloscopes and Piezo strain gauges (the latter based on the fact that squeeze on certain types of crystal markedly affects its ability to pass electric current) permits even more precise reading of the pressures or frurs or milliframmises that are built up when powder burns behind a bullet. And, more important, it permits studies of the time-pressure curve which is the real measure of what happens inside the cartridge when it goes off. The "pressure" or whatever it is does not stay at 50000 lbs., for example, from the moment the primer is sparked by the striker until the bullet leaves the gun muzzle. It builds up from zero to fifty thousand and then falls off to nothing again in a matter of milliseconds. Since obviously a fast peak and a fast fall-off will develop less velocity than a pressure generation which holds up near its peak, even if that peak is lower, it is clear that time-pressure study holds the real secret of efficient cartridge loadings, far more so than concern with peak pressure, which is all the crusher cylinder can measure or reveal.

But so far as the handloader is concerned, even though he cuts close to the heart of this time-pressure matter when he discovers that with slow-burning 4831 he can get bullet speeds impossible (from a given cartridge, the 270 for example), with 4064, all this is academic. He does not know what pressures are generated inside his handloads — not unless he can pony up for expensive test programs at the H. P. White Laboratories or can work some polite blackmail at Remington or Winchester. If his pet loads are wildcats the bill from White's will be a bigger one, and no manner of squeeze will work at New Haven or Bridgeport. But he doesn't need to know exactly what the pressure or the index number of milliframmises is — so long as his loads work at pressures apparently safe in his rifle.

The gimmick is in that word "apparently." We do not amble down the road at sixty per, blithely disregarding the signs that say S-Curve, Slow, and Stop. Not for long we don't. The pressure-warning signs to reloaders are only a bit less obvious, well within the mental limitations of anybody with common sense enough to drive a car safely.

The first reaction — or it ought to be — of any beginning reloader is to buy himself a small library of loading handbooks. His next, in all too many unfortunate cases, is to disregard all the information therein save the powder charge and bullet weight data, and even all of that save the maximums listed. Now the works published by the Messrs. Lyman, Speer, Herter, and Belding & Mull are good books, in most cases prepared only after considerable study and testing of loads. Speer's handbooks, for example, are definitely not collections of load dope from haphazard sources, but include only combinations that have been fired against the one Potter chronograph, with every care taken to record only loads which seemed OK in respect to primer appearance, extraction ease, and lack of cartridge head expansion. Yet in the Speer booklets, as in the others, the injunction is repeated that the loads cited were right *only for the rifle and*

job lot of brass tested, that maximum loads are not to be used until lighter charges have been fired without indication of excessive pressures. Neither the handbook people nor your favorite gun editor nor the helpful handloading buddy down the block can be held responsible for the changes in the loading recipe you'll inevitably make, variations which may turn your stew explosive. Beginner or "expert," you must work by a trial-and-error process in which plenty of trials but mighty few errors are permitted; and in which less than few will occur if you read the signs.

Pointers on Pressure

Time was when primers were the basis of informed pressure guesses, items like the famous FA-70 cap, for example, showing progressive changes of shape as loads were increased. But reading primers today is strictly a crystal ball operation. The Federal 210 primer, relatively mild and with an outer cup made very consistent in thickness and hardness, will — all other things being equal — as loads and pressures are increased show a steadily greater flattening at its edges, build up fairly regularly to the point where it is completely flat. Its center will become extruded back around the firing point like a little volcanic crater, with the flat surfaces carrying the reverse imprint of any odd tool marks or pits the gunbuilder left in the face of your bolt. At that point you've arrived at that "Danger — Thin Ice" sign. But try this with Winchester 120 or Remington 9'/2 primers, especially the latter, which seem to be mildly armor-plated, and you can be led off down the lane, brother. These are hot enough in primer compound and pellet size so that they can almost flatten themselves — and will continue to look much the same up to the point you finally go overboard.

Primer extrusion, or "cratering" as we usually call it, is a complete bust as a real indication of pressure. An undersized firing pin or an oversized firing pin hole will produce a crater where there is not nor ever was volcanic danger. A weak firing pin spring will do the same thing. One of my rifles is a 300 Weatherby built on an Enfield action, extensively reworked and speed-locked. That is, the firing pin assembly was rebuilt to give a shorter, faster fall. As part of this job the spring was shortened. With the original spring, 76 grs. of Du Pont 4350 and any 180-gr. bullet made the primers look like Fujiyama in miniature; yet no other evidence of pressure extremes appeared. The firing pin spring was switched to a stiffer one. Then 79 grs. of powder could be burned with only the faintest

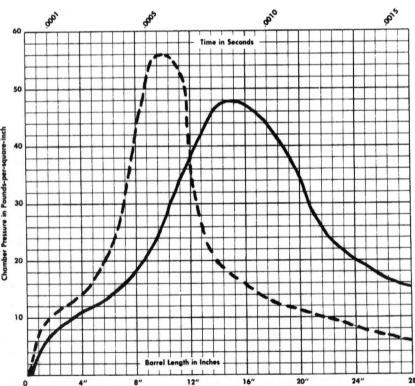

Time-Pressure Curves for Centerfire Rifle Cartridges

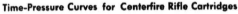

Fast peak pressure and a fast drop (dotted curve) will develop less velocity than pressures that remain near their peak (solid curve), even though that peak is lower. Time: pressure study is the key to better, safer, more efficient cartridge loading.

beginnings of a Fujiyama sensible to the fingertip.

Flattening is likewise (by itself) an unreliable sign of too much steam. Shoot a minimum cartridge in a maximum chamber, or size your brass a hair too far down at the shoulder so that you create a condition of slightly excessive headspace, and you'll get flat primers with the greatest of ease. Reason? The firing pin impact knocks the case forward into the chamber; the primer's own explosion pops it back out of the primer pocket flat against the bolt face; the stretch of the cartridge case under full powder pressures pushes the head of the case back over the primer. Presto, a flat primer.

The appearance of the primer, therefore, has meaning only in a relative sense. If your Remington 9½ primed recipe, properly sized as to its case, shows more decidedly smeared or cratered primer cups than a Remington factory round, it probably was fired at a higher pressure. Same would apply for an all-Winchester comparison. And that's about all you can tell, though when primers begin to look at all odd it's time to look and listen, usually to stop.

But the primer situation gives you clear signs when you've already gone too far. If there's a soot-dark ring around the primer cup, your homebrewed round is firing at pressures so high as to force gas between the tight-fitting primer and its pocket. The whole head of the cartridge is being expanded, pooshed out. The next step beyond a leaky primer is a blown primer, one that drops out or is blasted out because the head expansion has so enlarged the primer pocket that our brass bottle is coming unstoppered at both ends. And powder gases flaring back through a flash hole, perhaps bringing with them odd bits of primer metal, have punch enough to damage an action or to squirt back into your shooting eye. This is desirable only if you crave to pose for Hathaway shirt advertising.

It's obvious enough that you're in serious trouble if you have to pound a rifle bolt up through the last half of its lift, where it starts the camming action that starts the cartridge out, the primary extraction. But the real indication of

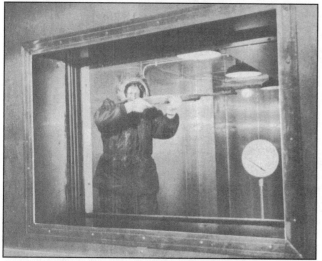

Test firing the Model 88 Winchester in the cold room at New Haven, the thermometer reading — 40 degrees! Breech pressures are down at these temperatures, too.

abnormal pressure showed up *long before* you had to do any bolt handle pounding. Do you remember that with charges one to three grains lighter you noted it took a definite effort to lift the bolt, enough extra effort so it would have been difficult to function the rifle at the shoulder? Remember those cases that came out with the head-stamping showing a high polish part way round the head? Those are the first danger signs, the ones you should have read.

Sticky cases, difficult extraction, these are just other symptoms of the same illness which becomes full-blown — and that is no pun — with the blown primer and the burst case head, the illness of excessive case expansion which is usually the result of too darned much pressure.

Signaling Brass

Cartridge brass is drawn with a distinct taper from the near-solid head end to the thin case mouth. It is expected to expand forward, to seal off gases that might escape backward along the chamber wall, and normally its thinner sections shrink back rapidly so that we can extract the round to try another shot at the deer. The thicker butt end of the case expands less or not at all. Pick up a once-fired factory case of our most commonly reloaded type, the rimless. Note that up to about a quarter-inch above the extractor groove it is smooth, shiny. Then there's a little hump, discernible to your touch or against the light, and forward of that point the brass is rougher, carries evidence of the tool mark roughnesses normal inside your chamber. That line around the case represents the point to which normal loads will expand the brass as it thickens toward the head.

If we reload that case with a hotter combination, the higher pressures will expand the thicker sections of the brass, pushing that expansion line closer and closer to the cartridge head. The noticeable hump becomes more noticeable. That this progressive movement of the expansion line is the basis of the best scheme we have for pressure estimation, the method set forth by Naramore in his tome, *Principles and Practice of Loading Ammunition** is only incidental. Few are such fanatical precisionists as to follow Naramore's scheme, though probably more of us should. The point is that as we push this line downward with repeated high-pressure loadings we are expanding progressively thicker brass, squashing it out into the chamber to the point where it won't extract at all, because the head end of the case won't shrink back as does the thin mouth and neck section. The ultimate end of excessive head-end expansion is a complete burst or a flowered primer pocket, in either event disaster.

So it would seem to be a simple matter of watching that expansion line, or of miking case heads after each use (.001" of expansion at belt or rim means you're really overstoking the boiler) or of watching for stiffness of bolt-handle lift. And indeed it is, save for the rare conditions of softheaded brass, which can occur in cases of any make, or badly pitted chambers, which leave obvious bind marks on the fired cases anyway.

* *Published by Samworth (Georgetown, S.C., 1954)*

Two of the surest signs that we are loading to pressures foolishly close to the edge of safety show up only late in the game. One comes in the form of cases that get "tired" after repeated loadings, are over-worked to the point where they won't reeham-ber without a complete full-length sizing or the primer slips into its pocket with suspicious ease. Another is growth of cases, a brass flowage into the neck section, a phenomenon less often noted in the sharp-shouldered wildcats than it is in easy-shouldered — and usually heavily loaded — items like the 270, 220 Swift, 257, and 243. The original cases for one of my 222 bench rifles were reloaded at least sixty times apiece without significant change of dimension — with ¾-throttle accuracy loads, 21-4198-50 grain bullets. Brass for a 25-caliber wildcat, however, always foolishly loaded right up to the limit, was good for only four or five shots before it had to be trimmed and full length sized to chamber.

So regardless of what the actual pressures or millifram-mises may read on any gauge, we can assume that the good-shooting load (and remember that high pressures are usually highly variable and productive of inaccuracy) which does not stretch case necks or expand primer pockets or case heads, which produces brass that extracts and resizes easily, is strictly copacetic for your own rifle.

Of Variables

Which is, of course, no guarantee that the same recipe will be proper, or even safe, in Joe Blow's rifle. One of my pet 270's will digest 51.5 grs. of 4320 powder with 130-gr. bullets; another, using the same primers, bullets, same make of brass, produces sticky, butt-sprung cases with 49.5 grs. The difference is in the rifles, obviously; and let it here be said that a prime cause of pressure variation is the dimensional variation inside chambers and barrels even of factory-made rifles presumably made to "standard" specifications. The variations among wildcats or custom jobs made with non-standard reamers can produce even wilder results. A friend's 6mm wildcat will interchange brass with one of mine chambered by the same gunsmith, but he must cut his loads 1½ to 2 grs. below mine when using heavy bullets. Reason? His barrel is short-throated for use with 85-gr. spitzers; mine has a deep throat intended for long-shanked bullets.

Chambers cut with minimum room for case neck expansion, less than .002", will give the same extra-pressure effects as cartridge brass that is unduly thick or overlong in the neck section, either because it was made that way or has "grown" through repeated high-pressure loadings. Early custom chambers were made with minimal neck expansion room until experimenters like Niedner found their velocity aims were defeated by pressures peaking too rapidly, but among today's handloaders it is more often the swollen neck situation that produces trouble. A dentist friend of mine once showed up with a horrified expression, powder specks in his right cheek, and the 220 Swift case he'd finally worked out of the jammed action of his Model 70. The entire head of the case was pressure-bloomed, with a great gaping hole instead of a primer pocket. The load, 38.5 grs. of 4064, he'd been using with the same 55-gr. bullets for two seasons of wood-chucking. Why the sudden pressure jump? He'd also been using the same brass over and over again. Case necks had lengthened and thickened until they were jammed into the chamber, simply could not open up to let loose of the bullet until pressures had jumped sky-high, to 75000 p.s.i. or so. He did not lose an eye because he habitually wore shooting glasses, but what he saved in doctor bills promptly went into case trimming and gauging equipment.

It is no secret that cases of various makes vary widely in wall and head thickness and so in the amount of powder they can burn safely. Weather-by, for example, now cites as maximums, in his present Norma-made brass, loads several grains under the charges possible for his cartridges when Weatherby shooters were fire-forming Western and Remington cases. Of the two lots of cases used in my wife's 7×57mm, one will handle only 43 grs. of my lot of 4895 surplus powder, with 130-gr. Speer bullets; the other will digest 45 grs. with no more evidence of pressure stiffness. To short-cut the process of starting from scratch in working up loads for a new batch of brass, accomplished loaders check rela-

Test firing and zeroing the Winchester 458 African at the New Haven ballistic laboratories.

HAND LOAD DATA SHEET

GUN	CALIBER	BULLET	WEIGHT	POWDER	AMOUNT	PRIMER	NO.	DATE	LOAD

POWDER: Kind.. Amount..
   Measure Setting.. Scale Data..
   Lot No.. Purch. from............................ Date..............

BULLET: Make.. Wt............................ Type..............
   Point.................... Base.................... Dia.................... Length.............
   Cast By.................... Alloy.................... Lead.................... Tin.................... Ant..........
   Mould.................... Gas Ck.................... Lub.................... S: Dpth..........
   Lot No.. Purch. from............................ Date..............

CASE: Make........................ Orig. Cal.................... Case Length..........
   Neck Size.................... Die.................... Exp. Dia.................... Length O. A..........
   Size F. L.................... Die.................... New.................... Used.................... Formed..........
   Lot No.. Purch. from............................ Date..............

PRIMER: Make.. No............................
   Lot No.. Purch. from............................ Date..............

RECOMMENDED by.. Pressure....................
   Velocity Muzzle.................... 100 yds.................... 200 yds.................... 300 yds.
   Energy ft. lbs.—Muzzle.................... 100 yds.................... 200 yds.................... 300 yds.
   Mid-Range Trajectory.................... 100 yds.................... 200 yds.................... 300 yds.

REMARKS:

HERTER'S, INC., Waseca, Minn., U.S.A., World's Largest Manufacturers of Quality Reloading Supplies.

It's easy, too easy, to load cartridges today, then forget just what combination of powder, primer, bullet, etc. went into them. The careful reloader keeps a detailed record of his handloads.

tive capacities by careful weighing of the water each set of cases will hold, and adjusting loads downward as indicated. But what few shooters realize is the variation in the capacity of cases by the same maker but from different lots. Since the war, for example, 22 Hornet brass has — from all loading plants — changed in wall thickness; and there is a marked difference between very early and most recent 222 Remington cases, enough to make unwise any casual interchange of max charges without knowing the vintage of the brass.

The reloader gets one big break in that canister powders from DuPont and Hercules differ only minutely from lot to lot in the amount of fire and fury they contain. Save for fool-headed super-pressure experiments, he who handloads can figure that 55 grs. of DuPont 4350, all else being equal, is the same whether from Lot 50 or Lot 68. And the surplus powders coming through in present shipments are far more alike, one batch to the next, then they were five years back. But primers are still an unknown quantity, Mr. Winchester being under no obligation to use, forever, and amen, the same mix in his 120 primer, for example. Personally, I have never — and we'll pause here to knock on wood - pushed a load off the deep end by switching from one brand or lot of primer to another; but since there's enough variation in ignition or brisance characteristics among the various "large rifle" (.210") primer mixes to change pressures by 5% or more, that's always a possibility if primer changes aren't accompanied by careful load re-build-up when you're working with the hotter items. And variation in flash hole size (particularly likely with the punched-out flash holes common to U.S. made brass), though easily gauged with the butt ends of a set of machinists drills, can really upset the pressure applecart. The normal flash hole in 30-06 commercial cases is .080" or close to it. The Hercules Powder people drilled a few out to .101", found that pressures jumped between 15% and 20% up over the red line.

Bullets and Bullets

Only the cagiest of reloaders can predict the effect on pressure of the forward stopper in our brass bottle, the bullet. And even assuming said bullet is of standard diameter for its caliber, dead on the nose at .224" or .257" or .308", for example, there is still no reason to believe that a bullet of 180 grs., Make X, will not stopper that bottle far more tightly than the same weight of slug of Make Y. With half a dozen major outfits, aside from the big loading plants, turning out reloader-pills by millions, home bullet-swaging equipment churning out more, handloaders now use an infinite variety of projectiles on which there is not and can not be reliable dope on their pressure-creating characteristics.

It takes no pressure gun, however, to discover that bullets make a difference. Cores come both hard and soft, pure lead, antimony-alloyed or work-hardened. Jackets not only vary in thickness from one make to another but, even more importantly, in hardness, resistance to the engraving action of the lands at just that point where the time-pressure curve is hitting its peak as the bullet starts up the bore. One batch of B&A-swaged 50-gr. .224" pills, for example, popped three primers of the first ten rounds fired in a 222 Remington rifle, with a load that had, in perfect propriety, shot hundreds of Sierra, Speer, and Hornady bullets of the same weight and diameter. It should have been no surprise that the solid-based bullet Ackley once made in 30 caliber and others should give sticky cases when fired over the charge proper with Fred Barnes soft copper-jacketed slugs, or that the original Nosler game bullets, with their extra-stiff design and reinforcing partition midway of the shank should run pressures up until Nosler began to turn off a relief band midway of the bearing surface. But with projectiles of the normal core-plus-jacket construction we have no such obvious signs of pressure-inducing stiffness and have to proceed cautiously, dropping loads when we switch from one bullet make to another. Bud Waite of the NRA once conducted pressure experiments that indicated stiffer pressures resulted from the use of one certain 30 caliber bullet made by Speer — but that hardly proves the pudding for other Speer bullets or the other makes in other calibers.

Extreme pressures may be the bugaboo of the reloader, yet it is only by permitting unwatched variations in rifle, case, or components to push pressures to the busting point that the reloader can get into trouble. But we wouldn't get anywhere without that head of steam. The vaunted efficiency of modern rifles and cartridges is about ninety per cent the combined result of increased pressure, increases made permissible by better brass and better case head design, and increased pressure held near its peak for a longer period of time, a longer shove against the bullet base made possible by more smoothly burning powders. We work calmly at 55000 p.s.i. today where 35000 was tops yesterday. We can't do without pressure; but the smart reloader is he who does without too much of it.

Tools for handload-
ing metallic car-
tridges go 'way back
to the 1870's. Here
are just a few of the
great variety offered
in an earlier day.

Early Loading Tools

by RICHARD H. CHAMBERLAIN

THE CIVIL WAR gave great impetus to firearms experimentation. While the war
was fought primarily with muzzleloading weapons, breechloaders appeared in
great profusion and self contained cartridges began to come into use. These were,
for the most part, copper rimfire cartridges and thus could not be reloaded. But
by the late 1860's and early 1870's, centerfire cartridges of brass were being produced, since the soft rimfire cases were not well suited to heavy charges of powder - and it was loads of more power that the frontiersmen wanted. Two of the
most important of these powerful centerfires were the 44-77-2¼" necked Sharps
and Remington and the 50-70-1¾" straight Government cartridges. These had
removable primers which could be replaced with new ones after firing. Pouring
in the powder charge and seating a new bullet completed the cartridge. Reloading
had the same appeal then as now. It reduced the cost of shooting and also made
possible a variety of loads from short range or "gallery" loads, as they were then
called, to very heavy long range target loads, which called for so much powder
the bullet could hardly be seated in the case mouth. There was another important
advantage. In a time when transportation was slow and expensive and when a
hunter might be far from a source of supply it was a distinct advantage to be able
to reload his ammunition. Most of the serious buffalo "runners" and other market hunters were reloaders.

With the great interest there is in handloading today, a brief look at the reloading equipment of the past might be of interest. Perhaps the most significant fact
about the early days of reloading was that loading tools were furnished by each of
the individual arms companies rather than by specific loading tool manufacturers, as is the case now. (The gunmakers today look on handloading with disfavor
— a blind, irrational opposition, but that's another story.) The principle exceptions were the famous Ideal Manufacturing Company which began in the middle

A pair of rare H. M. Pope "Universal Bullet Moulds,"
so called because the mould blocks could be readily
interchanged. Sprue cutters operate automatically.

A New Loader
SCHOYEN & PETERSON,

Patentee's and Manufacturers.

Offered ca. 1905, this powder measure dropped two charges — one the priming load from the smaller glass jar, the other jar metering a main charge, usually black powder. The price was $5.00.

1880's and the Bridgeport Gun Implement Company.

Shotgun shell loading tools were produced in large quantities but do not display the great ingenuity nor variety seen in those made for rifle and pistol cartridges. Loading tools were furnished at one time or another by Winchester, Remington, Marlin, Savage, Sharps, Maynard, Whitney, Smith and Wesson, F. Wesson, Colt and others. Often these items bear no company name and can be difficult to identify. This is especially true of bullet moulds. The tools and moulds chosen for illustration

here are some of the less frequently encountered ones.

In loading cartridges for single shot rifles no case mouth crimp was needed, in fact it was usually undesirable, especially when paper patched bullets were used. For such use, as well as for the type of accurate target shooting in which the bullet is seated directly into the rifling rather than into the case, (A) was produced by the Ideal Manufacturing Company. It was known as a re- and decapper. Primers were pushed out with the plug and pin on the end of one handle and new ones seated with the capping part of the tool. Both the case holding die (the half-cylinder seen near joint) and the decapping plug were interchangeable with others of different sizes permitting other caliber cases to be handled. Later styles had a full circle die to hold the cases for capping.

The Bridgeport Gun Implement Company is best known for its shot-shell loading sets, but many rifle and handgun cartridge loading tools and bullet moulds were also made. This re-and decapper (B) of theirs was for Berdan primers.* When the small handle is moved downward a tiny chisel cuts into the primer; then the large handles are opened, pulling out the primer. Berdan primed cases do not have a central flash hole and have to be extracted by a chisel of some sort. Many early tools have these chisels, and so do modern

---

*Col. Hiram Berdan, a U.S. Officer who distinguished himself in the Civil War as the leader of "Berdan's Sharpshooters," invented the primer type that bears his name. Until recently, Berdan primers were used exclusively in Europe, while Boxer-type primers, developed by the English Col. Boxer, are used in all U.S. made ammunition.

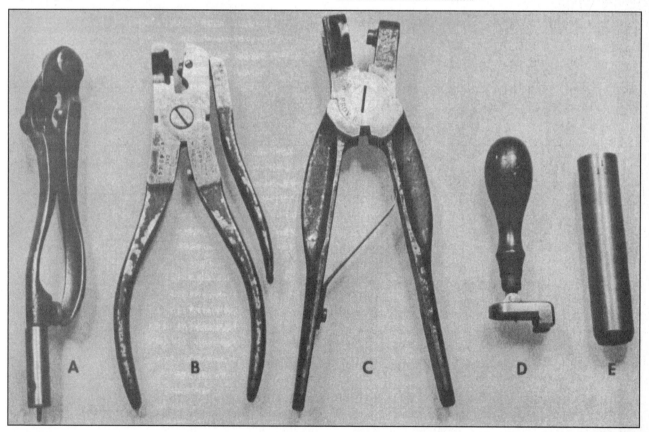

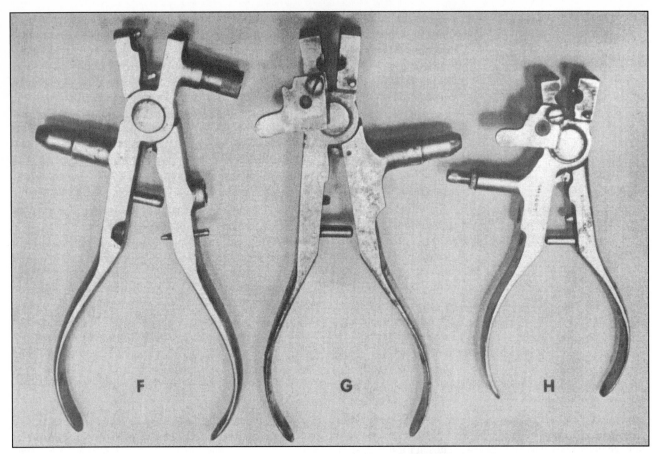

European-made re- and decappers. It was common practice on many of the early tools to paint all or part of each tool. Gold, red, and black are the most frequently seen colors. Tool (B) is marked ".42 .43 .44," indicating that it was for these large centerfire rifle cartridges; the 42 Russian, 43 Spanish, and 44 Sharps, all of which have about the same head size.

(C) is a Providence Tool Company recapping device for use with their Peabody-Martini rifle cartridges. It has a return spring to open the jaws. A decapper and bullet seater were made with similar handles. The tool is painted black.

The unusually thick rimmed 1873 Maynard cartridges were decapped with this (D) Hadley's Device patented March 26, 1878. The wooden handle actuated the chisel.

The simplest of bullet seaters is this Sharps product (E). It is one piece, with one end open to receive powder-filled cartridge case and bullet, the other end closed except for a small vent. Its purpose was simply to seat the bullet firmly and accurately in place on the powder. The only marking is "45 420 2-1/10," indicating the Sharps version of the 45–70 Government cartridge loaded with their 420-gr. paper patched bullet and 2-1/10" case.

The Ideal "nutcracker" tools are probably the commonest of all the old loading tools. They were made in many styles, but the three shown here are far less common than most.

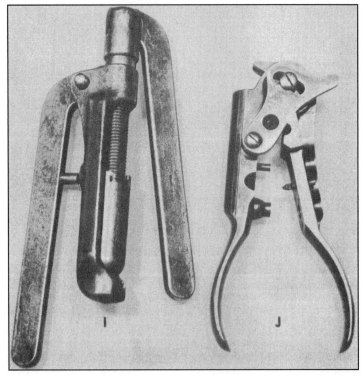

(F) is the #5 or armory tool made for the 45–70 Government cartridge. Note that the bullet sizer is the reverse of those usually seen. The capper is at the tip of the jaws near the adjustable case-mouth sizer.

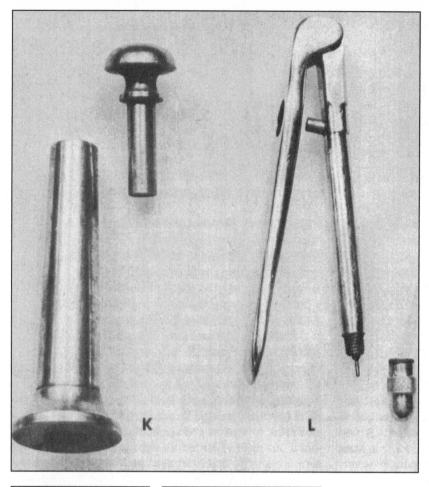

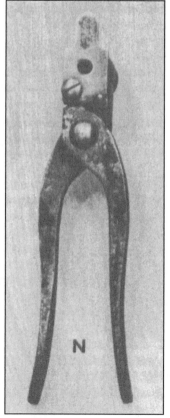

Tool (G) was made by Ideal for the J. Stevens Arms and Tool Company especially for the Stevens line of "everlasting" cartridges used in their tipup and other rifles. The one shown here is for the 38-35 Stevens everlasting cartridge and the mould cutoff plate is marked "For Stevens Arms Co., Chicopee Falls, Mass." The cutoff plate is on the opposite end of the mould from that on other Ideal combination tools except #6, thus making the tool seem reversed. Stevens designated it the Ideal #6-A.

The Ideal #2 tool (H) was designed specifically for Smith and Wesson cartridges. Its distinguishing feature is that the bullet seating chamber is adjustable for bullet seating only. In other single-adjustable chambers the adjustment is to regulate the crimp. This tool is for the 38–44 S.&W. Target cartridge. It could load full or gallery loads. In the latter, a round ball was seated well below the case mouth on top of a light powder charge. This cartridge differs from the modern 38–44, which is a heavy loading of the 38 Special.

Winchester made tools from 1874 until well into the 20th century. They were produced in many models but most were of the nutcracker type. However, they made three different tools which would full-length resize the case at the same time as the bullet was being seated and crimped into place. The most common is the 1894 tool, less common is the 1891, and least common is this 1888 tool (I) in 38–56 WCF caliber. One handle operates the capper, the other revolves, forcing the sizing die over the cartridge. The die had to be removed in order to cap. Such tools were somewhat slow — but they were adequately fast for their purpose, the loading of small batches of hunting ammunition. A real advantage was that the fully resized cases would not stick in the rifle chamber thus putting the gun temporarily out of use.

The workmanship on the 1881 Marlin tool (J) is outstanding. The finish is a beautiful blue. All of those seen by the writer are numbered with what might be a serial number. The bullet mould is on the handle side of the hinge. What appears to be a bullet sizer is really a wad cutter. There is a Berdan decapper. The assembled cartridge is placed in a chamber in one handle. When the handles are *opened* the cartridge is forced into the chamber, thus seating the bullet and crimping the case mouth.

Marlin sold many special tools for their famous Ballard single shot rifles. Item (K) was referred to as a "ball seater." The plunger pushed the bullet, then called a "ball" as a holdover from muzzleloading days, down on the powder but did not crimp the case. These tools are marked with only

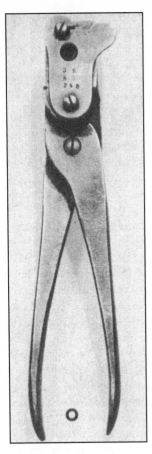

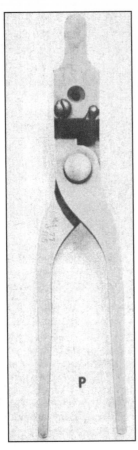

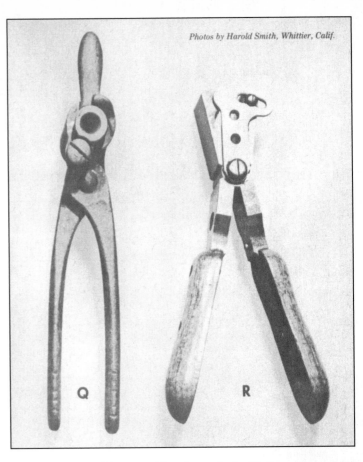

Photos by Harold Smith, Whittier, Calif.

the caliber and it may appear on the top of the plunger or on the underside of the base. The seater here is for the 40–65 Ballard everlasting cartridge cases. The everlasting cases were of extra heavy metal. Some would interchange with the regular cartridges of the day, but others were special cases with thick mouths, and none could be crimped. They could be reloaded almost indefinitely.

The next two items were also designed for the Ballard. (L) is a re- and decapper. A cover on the end of one handle screws on to protect the de-capping pin. In operation it is similar to (A). This and the ball seater were nickel plated.

Moulds

The Ballard mould (M) is for the 38 caliber 255-gr. paper patched bullet. It is marked "M F A Co 38–255P." Patched or grooved bullets could also be store bought, which was especially convenient if the shooter wished to avoid the tedious patching operation.

(N) was made by the Bridgeport Gun Implement Company for the 44 WCF bullet. It is painted black.

Mould (O) is by Remington. The caliber marking may be found on the cutoff plate as shown here or at other locations. This particular mould is unusual in that the full cartridge designation is given, "38-40-245," which is a special Remington number not to be confused with the 38–40 WCF and Colt cartridge. The finish is blue.

(P) may be a Winchester mould. It is almost identical to the iron moulds made by Winchester but the two principle

parts are of brass and is only marked with the caliber, which is "44–77 395." Most of these moulds have tiny matching numbers on the plate, plate screw, and mould proper, which may be assembly numbers.

Most of the moulds like (Q) are lightly marked "U M C Co." The caliber is heavily stamped on the bottom. This specimen is 45–70 Marlin caliber.

Smith and Wesson sold reloading sets of which (R) is the main piece. It has fine walnut handles and is beautifully made. In addition to being the bullet mould it is a capper. Usually these cast one regular bullet and one round one for short range work.

These tools are only a small sample. There were many others, most of them reasonably effective in the days of black powder, and still capable of loading well if properly used. Though some of these may look rather primitive, it is interesting to realize that some of the most accurate shooting ever done was made with ammunition loaded by such tools. They seem to reflect the wonderful enthusiasm of their time; the heyday of civilian shooting, both on the target and in the field.

ABC's of Reloading

Close attention to many details and the correct use of quality equipment makes for better, more accurate ammo — here are important tips for

Better Handloads

by KENT BELLAH

DO YOU WANT more fun at less cost, and more zest and zing in life? A doctor says handloading may be better than the elixirs of old, or the vitamins of today. Loading is fun. It's safe and simple. Home brewed fodder assembled with T.L.C. (Tender Loving Care) is superior to factory stuff. You can load $100 worth for as little as $10 by following simple directions. Handbooks by Speer, makers of the fine Speer bullets, and by Lyman, makers of a variety of accessories, are a "must." The RCBS catalog has detailed instructions and good tips. This article carries tips for precision loads to help tighten your groups.

Primer Control

Sloppy priming opens groups, even if your ammo fires okay. If brittle compounds are crushed, incomplete detonation causes poor ignition. Some lads seat primers like driving nails. Seat 'em easy, slightly below the case head face. Compression, however, if controlled, increases sensitivity, if the compound is not crushed. Check for "high" primers by setting cases on a surface plate to see if they wobble, or use the mirror from your wife's purse. Reseat high primers in shells, but play it doubly safe by pulling bullets from loads beforehand!

A round with a long primer may discharge when chambered in a rifle and the bolt hits the primer. In revolvers, the cylinder may not turn. They cushion the firing pin blow, causing slow ignition or a misfire. They are worse than crushed primers. Primer stops that seat in relation to the rim thickness have no value, as rims vary too much. The best type of stop is on the RCBS big A-2 press. It seats to an adjustable depth in relation to the head face. You can "seat by feel" in tools without this type stop.

Some primers, like the excellent CCI, are designed for loading with the type of tools most of us use. The compound is not too brittle for adequate compression. The seating depth is not critical, but .003" to .008" low (from the head face) is correct. A flat face punch is best, but a round face will work. Remington primers are seated .002" low. W-W makes are seated .003" to .008" low, using a punch that fits the crown.

Handicapped craftsmen take pride in casting at Accuracy Bullet Co., using SAECO furnaces. A week's production would last the average shooter a lifetime.

A few primers may have a cocked anvil, or other defects, easily detected with a magnifying glass. The No. .3 Magni-Focuser, made by Edroy Products, 480 Lexington Ave., New York 17, gives 3-dimensional viewing, far superior to a single lens. With matched lenses and a headband, it's worn with or without eye glasses; it's tops for all component inspection and many other uses.

Primers should not be handled with soiled hands. This can be avoided with a Fitz Flipper. This clever gadget is made by the people who make Fitz handgun grips, powder funnels, cartridge boxes, etc. Empty 100 or 200 primers in the Flipper, shake it a second, and they will all be face down, ready for fast optical inspection, or feeding to a primer arm without fumbling. If you use an auto primer feed, reverse the Flipper. All primers are then face up, so you can load tubes in less than half the usual time.

Cartridge Cases

Factory brass-inspection is not 100% perfect. Some lots are better than others. Common faults are variations in the length, neck, vents and capacity, faults that merely open groups. Once in a blue moon an invisible defect, like a soft head, or an internal flaw, is found in the first firing. With moderate loads, these seldom harm a gun. I check out all new hulls. New cases mixed with old ones of the same lot will usually have a different center of impact.

I never use old, brittle, or much-fired brass, especially with hot loads. It's like running old, worn tires at high speeds, and it ain't etiquette in higher gun society.

Necks harden from cold-working in a die. They stretch and thicken with firing, and the brass structure changes. They require trimming and neck turning (or inside reaming) for accuracy and safety.

I like to start with new, unprimed shells of the same lot. I check them in a combination length-and-head-space gauge quickly, and again after firing. Forster and Wilson make these. Webs and vents are inspected before priming. Sorting shells by weight has some value, but variations are often in the heads. Filling each case with water, then weighing them, while tedious, is a sure check. I use a Forster Case Trimmer, discarding hulls with a visible variation in mouth-wall thickness after trimming, and before de-burring. Bench resters "mike" neck walls as a uniformity test. The final test is firing. If you get flyers, separate those hulls to test with the next loading.

Bullets

Good rifle bullets are made by Norma, Speer, Nosler, Sisk, Sierra, Hornady, and others. Nearly all shoot well with the right amount and type of powder in a good rifle of suitable twist. Selecting the proper bullet for your rifle calls for some experimenting — try several types, weights and makes. Soft pills at high-V give fast expansion or blowup for medium game or varmints, hard ones penetrate deep, with little shock or expansion. Nosler Partition bullets at high speed allow fast expansion of the soft nose, while the body holds together for deep penetration. They have excellent accuracy. For target use in 30 caliber, try Sierra's new 168-grain H.P. boat-tail — you'll be pleased!

For top precision rifle shooting, such as the bench resters are doing, you can make your own bullets. Biehler & Astels, Bahler and others furnish bullet making dies, while jackets, lead wire, etc., are supplied by many.

Division Lead Wire, of Summit, Ill., are now marketing (through your jobber or dealer) lead wire in 25-lb. packages, cut to 14" lengths — a handy and convenient arrangement.

Speer Products Co., Lewiston, Idaho, also offer lead wire packages, these in 10-lb. units holding 12" lengths, at $6.20 a box, and 38 or 44 half-jackets at $10.25-$12.25 per thousand — cost of 160-gr. 38 complete bullets works out to about 2½¢ each. Low enough, but you can buy Speer's 38 jacketed bullets ready-made at $3.25-$3.50 per 100 — and excellent bullets they are. Caliber 44 half-jackets run $4-$4.25 per 100, HP or solid nose.

Handgun power depends even more on the bullet material and design, due to comparatively low velocity. I think Harvey Jugular half-jacketed bullets are the greatest advance in efficiency since the 45 Colt was born in 1873. Jim Harvey originated them and their forerunner, the zinc-washer-base Prot-X-bores. Both types use a pure, soft lead body. Harvey also originated dies for home swaging his bullets in 1951. You can save money by home swaging, but I don't believe there is any accuracy advantage over the factory pills.

Jugulars have been widely imitated by people who still think in terms of cast alloys or jacketed 45 ACP pills. Jugulars are not kissin' kin to either, and they deliver more shock than any other handgun bullet. Large big game is out of the handgun class, but for game larger than about 500 pounds, a round nose or alloy core bullet would be better than a Jugular, so greater penetration would reach the vitals. Compare any other bullet with Jugulars in the field, and you'll see what I mean by more shock. Mason Williams, Stanfordville, N.Y., is the licensed manufacturer and distributor of

Left to right: flat primer correctly seated; round primer deformed by flat punch; primer marked by round punch because case not in alignment in shell holder; "long" primer shows bolt-face imprint; expanded packet indicates excess pressure and/or a soft head; protruding primer, after firing, may mean excess headspace.

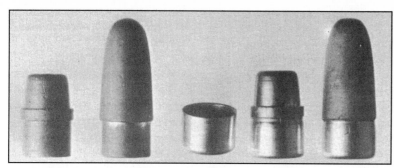

Cast "Jugular" handgun and rifle cores with half jacket. Right, finished bullets with jackets canne lured on for precision accuracy.

both Harvey designs. See Williams' article, elsewhere in this issue of the GUN DIGEST, on swaged and jacketed handgun bullets.

Dies — Bullet and Loading

In 1957, Jim Harvey suggested RCBS make a 4-die set, to permit seating Harvey bullets in one operation and crimp in another. These aid uniformity and reduce lead shaving with *any* bullet, and are especially good with soft lead types that deform in seating with regular dies. If you have one of the excellent 3-die sets made by RCBS or C-H, add the extra crimper. Then adjust the seater so it does not start to crimp.

I don't recommend a 2-die set for straight wall cases. If you have these, add an expander and crimper, thus allowing today's approved separate operations of sizing; expanding; seating, then crimping. Or, after sizing, tap a bearing ball on the case mouth to slightly bell it. Adjust your seater to seat without crimping for a batch of loads. Then adjust to crimp without seating. This long way around makes quality ammo.

Quality dies of proper dimensions are important. I use a tungsten carbide die for faster, easier handgun case-sizing without lube. It does beautiful work, burnishes cases, doesn't scratch, and will outwear a dozen ordinary dies. I use it to decap and size in one operation, with the expander replaced with a smaller size. For example, a 38 expander is in my 44 die. The regular expander plug is in another die for the second operation. I use a separate seater and crimper.

After Harvey (Lakeville Arms, Lakeville, Conn.) started selling handgun bullet-swaging dies, Bahler, Hollywood, Lachmiller, and others appeared. One bullet maker, Shooters Accessory Supply, offers handgun bullet-making dies at an amazingly low price — $9.00, even including enough lead and jackets to make 50 bullets! Perhaps even more surprisingly, in view of this very low price, these dies make darn good bullets. Ted Smith, S.A.S. owner, has sold over 600 sets of these.

C-H has just announced another low cost bullet making outfit — a "C" type press plus a set of 1"–18 thread dies in 38, 44 or 45 caliber, solid- or hollow point, sells for $29.95. The press, of course, while similar to C-H's Model "C" loading tool, will not handle 7/8–14 cartridge dies. Extra bullet making die sets cost $14-$16.50, and a lead wire cutter is priced at $7.50.

Lachmiller Engineering Co. also has announced inexpensive bullet-making dies in revolver calibers at $14.95 a set.

Lakeville is the only supplier of dies for Prot-X-bore bullets, and moulds to cast them. They give excellent accuracy at slightly lower velocity than Jugulars. Lakeville is the only supplier of moulds for casting Jugular cores. Cast Jugulars are good, but are less dense and uniform than slugs swaged under pressure.

Notes and Tips

Precision loading means uniformity in every component and operation, with charges in the best burning range of the right powder. Cast pills, popular because they are so cheap, are best sorted for uniformity by weighing, after inspection. Put under-weights back in the pot. Light but perfectly filled out bullets may indicate an internal defect, such as an air pocket, slag, a tin- or antimony rich alloy, etc. This throws a bullet out of balance, a major cause of flyers. Weight variation is less serious in big bores. For example, a 44 won't notice two grains nearly as much as a 22 caliber.

The most important thing is where the weight loss is. If you file three grains of metal from a bullet-base edge, accuracy will be poor. Drill that much metal from the nose with a Forster hollow pointer and the bullet is still in balance, will stay in your groups. Naked cast pills that are too soft or driven too fast may be erratic.

Good scales are important. Those with a notched beam and attached weights are more convenient, and Redding makes a good low-priced one. Of the seven Webster models, the low-cost RW-1 is an excellent buy. Their RWC reads in 1/20th grain, which you can about halve for delicate weighing. Both have large clear figures and wide, deep notches that help eliminate the human error, which is more important than 1/10th-grain accuracy. Webster originated the hydraulic scale-damper and all their models have this feature, plus self-aligning bearings and adjustable sensitivity. Their Fun-

Left to right: first firing generally shows any brass defects, like this one near the head; other shell sized in wrong die, or one not adjusted; last three: headspace is altered when shoulders stretch (right) from cases sized without necessary bit of die lube. Use only a trace of lube, though, and not oil.

nel Attachment, which fits all models, is handy as a third hand to speed weighing charges. Their AR-5 is a precision balance, using separate weights. It's more expensive, and slower to use than scales, but is a fine piece of equipment.

Recent trial of the new mahogany-cased Ohaus scale was disappointing. The 0 to 10-gr. bar was bent on arrival, and could not be installed after straightening, the screw holes for it being too short on centers by about Hi-inch.

Quality in general was not high, many parts being stampings, and not too well-made.

Accuracy Bullet Co. (40 Willard St., San Francisco 18, Calif.) make good cast bullets for dealers. One-armed owner G. E. Murphy deserves high praise because he employs handicapped people, workers who obviously take pride in their bullets. Their best high-V pills are "Copper Coated" to eliminate gas checks. A good 357 bullet is their Hensley & Gibbs No. 51, using 6% antimony and 2% tin, plated with .008" copper over .005" nickel. Their new 44's, H&G No. 521-S and the heavy Keith design are both good, using 9% antimony and 2% tin. A good target 38 is their H&G No. 50 B-B, using 3% antimony and 2% tin. They group as tight as Remington Targetmas-ters, using 2.7 grains Bullseye and CCI primers.

Home-mixed antimony or ternary alloys are very difficult to make. (Lads who have done it for 20 years may have shot non-uniform bullets for 20 years!) Antimony alloys are best for naked or gas check pills at high-V, and perhaps for any velocity. It's best to use a good commercial mix for any alloy except tin and lead. For high-V, use gas-checked castings rather than naked alloy.

One good commercial mix (I'm not familiar with all) is Illinois Bullet Alloy No. 7, supplied dealers by Division Lead Co., Summit, Ill. They also have other good lead products, chilled shot, etc. They list IBA No. 7 (Brinell 18) for up to 1,250 fps naked, or 1,500 fps gas-checked. I've revved it up much faster in rifles, holding accuracy without leading. So much depends on your particular gun and load that a max velocity cannot be set for an alloy. Your best test is in your gun. If IBA is not sold locally you can order by mail. One dealer is Gil Hebard Guns, Knoxville, Ill. Gil offers an excellent hand-gunners' 50¢ catalog with much handloading and shooting data for hand-gunners.

Some bullets or loads shoot better in one gun than another. A friend tried my favorite Swift load in his custom rifle.

You can make a max-length case gauge from sheet metal. Or use an inexpensive caliper. This one cost $1.49.

It's a 55-grain Sisk Express pill, 37 grains 4064, and CCI primers. His groups were the largest I've seen with this load. He worked charges down and up, changed bullet makes and powder, even glass-bedded the stock, and groups were still lousy. Then he tried a 50-grain Sisk Lovell, 39 grains 4064, and CCI primers. Groups screwed down pronto! Then, in my custom F.N.-Apex Swift, not sensitive to loads, his Lovell pill (made for lower velocity), shot groups twice as large as the Sisk Express, throwing a comet tail of melted nose-lead. Anyway, the semi-melted Lovell at 4,100 fps, twisting at over 200,000 revolutions per minute, will certainly damage a varmint beyond repair!

If you assemble some crummy ammo, a collet type bullet puller such as made by Forster and RCBS is best to salvage bullets. Inertia type pullers often loosen cores in the jackets, so salvage bullets by this method make erratic groups.

A good alloy for routine plinking is a 1: 16 tin-lead mix for handguns, or 1:10 for handguns or rifles. Weigh both metals. Melt the lead, add the tin, flux well, and keep the pot stirred. Use the lowest temperature that makes perfect bullets, around 750°. SAECO's thermostat furnace maintains uniform temperature. Their Lubri-Sizer is excellent also. Oversize castings run in a rickety sizer, with rough dies out of alignment, result in poor bullets. Final size should be near groove diameter. Writers who advise up to .003" over groove are living in the black powder "daze." The object then was to drive an oversize slug down the bore to increase pressure and form a gas seal. Smokeless powder has plenty of whoosh. There is no need to use the bore for a sizing die, even with a sloppy throat.

It takes good cast handgun loads to equal factory target-fodder. The average load is far inferior, being assembled as quickly and cheaply as possible. If you are loading just to hear a "Pop!," try the "Dollar Dandy" cap pistol. But the best bullets, carefully loaded and revved up, will exceed standard and high-V factory loads in accuracy and efficiency. 2400 is the best fuel for top velocity. Jugular charges can not be used with cast pills. Fast powders like Bullseye are not for hot loads, and excessive charges of it may damage a gun. Use slower powders for higher power.

Coated powders meter well, except the largest tubular types. Charges are less critical than with sticky pistol pow-

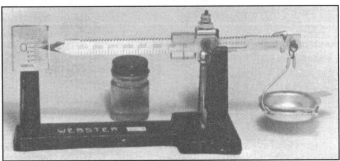

Good scales have large figures and large notches, accurately calibrated, to reduce the chance for error. Webster models have an adjustment for sensitivity, with self-aligning bearings.

Forster Outside Neck Turner insures concentric walls for tighter groups, helps start bullet down the bore in alignment. Uniformity is better than with inside reaming.

Shack got an F. N. rifle with a hot tube. He stocked up with 300 cases of one lot, and enough powder, primers and bullets of identical lots to load 3,000 rounds, his estimate of the potential barrel life. His loads will be uniform as long as the bore holds accuracy. Then he will trade or rebarrel the piece. This is better than buying components in small lots and testing each batch for uniformity. This isn't for deer hunters who hope to clobber bucks at 150 yards, but it's a real good tip for lads who want to squeeze the ultimate in accuracy out of a fine rifle.

der. If your measure and technique holds slow rifle-powder to, say, 1 grain, loads in the best burning range may hold accuracy, but be erratic in the high or low pressure range. The same 1-grain variation in a 2.5 grain Bullseye charge (which isn't uncommon) will give squib loads, and otherwise crummy ammo.

If your measure and/or technique isn't good, weigh all charges, or get a good measure and learn to use it. Clean and dry the drum, bearing surfaces and charge cavity. Throw and weigh 100 charges. Double the average variation, and keep all thrown charges of this load at least this much below max. Always use the same operating technique. With RCBS and SAECO measures I bump the handle lightly, twice at the top and once at the bottom. I keep the powder pressure uniform by putting an aluminum funnel in the top of the hopper, and keep it filled with powder. Before starting a batch, I throw about six charges to settle the powder before charging for keeps. Keep your measure clean and oil-free, using graphite for a lube, if necessary.

Loading Tools

Loading equipment does not have to be expensive, but it must be good. The press must hold the die and shell holder in alignment. Some troubles are not in faulty equipment. I have about 2,000-odd 38 hulls with rims too large for a standard shell holder. As this is a fine lot of brass, I had a shell holder made to fit. I also have about 1,000 each of two other makes in good lots. Different bullets are used in each, which gives positive identification, and they are easily sorted by make if they get mixed up after firing. When too many split necks start showing up, I'll discard each lot and start over with new brass. W-W makes often have larger rims than Remington brass. Monroe Thomas, a precision loader, recently found a lot of 222 cases that pulled out of a standard shell holder. Another make worked perfectly. Check-out your equipment before blaming the maker. If it is faulty, a reputable firm will make a prompt adjustment.

Light "C" type presses are okay for light duty routine loading, but they do spring a bit with heavy sizing. The strongest presses have an "O" frame. The one-hole "H" frames are strong also. A quality press is not expensive and is a good investment.

Take a tip from my shooting buddy, Kenneth Shackelford.

If your rifle groups are not better than factory fodder, work loads down, or up (if you load below max), than change powder, then bullets. Gunsmiths can often tighten groups by bedding production guns. You can speed weighing charges with Ted Smith's "Little Dripper" or his nicer "Electric Dripper," that puts precision loads on a semi-production basis. It "drips" complete handgun charges without a measure.

Some items in some makes of equipment will be faulty. The better makes are better than ever before, with few faults. A trouble in loading 44 Magnum ammo is due to the Sporting Arms and Ammunition Manufacturers' Institute max specifications of .432" bullet diameter. Heavy recoil with our correct .429" bullets causes bullet creep if loaded with "standard" dies. Some of the better die makers, at least RCBS and C-H, have revised their specifications for dies in this caliber. W-W mouth lacquers this case with "Lucalastic," made by John Lucas Co., Philadelphia. It works, but I prefer correct dimension dies without any mouth lacquer, and bullets tightly crimped. If you experience bullet creep with hot loads, try sizing cases without expanding. If this doesn't correct it, you'll have to reduce the load and crimp tighter, or purchase new dies.

Keep 'em Safe

A safe rule is to cut top published charges 10% or so for one round, then work up in steps, stopping at the usual signs of pressure: harder extraction, cratered primers (sometimes), gas leakage, loosened primer pockets, etc. Duplex loads (using a small amount of fast powder for an "igniter") are dangerous. Current powders over-lap in speed, and modern primers give excellent ignition. It's foolish to start with hot loads without working up, though beginners may be too cautious. "Pressure" is not a dirty word, unless it is out of control. It makes bullets perform like a circus pony in this jet age. With too little you are back in black powder days. You'll get best accuracy long before primers blow, or a rifle action locks. Let's load for precision and performance, and have more fun then ever before!

Fully detailed instructions on making cases for obsolete or hard-to-find calibers

New Brass For Old

by Capt. GEORGE C. NONTE, Jr.

ALL OVER THE U.S., their voices now still from long disuse, lie countless thousands of fine old rifles, mostly of pre-1900 vintage — the disappearance from the shelves of one caliber after another spelled their doom.

Most of the loads for the old '76, '86 and '95 Winchesters have been dropped. The revered Sharps and Ballards, too, are without fodder except in 32–40, 38–55 and 45–70, — those three, let's hope, will be with us for many years to come.

These venerable relics of our Nation's formative frontier days hang silent on the walls, perhaps never again to belch forth those fragrantly pungent clouds of spark-shot white smoke as they did when a new nation was being carved from the wilderness. They can be rescued, though, for few indeed are the obsolete American calibers for which it is not possible to make up a supply of cases from currently available brass. The informed handloader, using the correct basic case, can make up just about anything he needs. Many present-day cartridges, simply logical developments of earlier loads, retain many characteristics and dimensions of the old timers. The 45–70, for instance, is identical except for length and bullet diameter to a dozen or more of yesterday's discontinued numbers. Similar situations exist with respect to other cases — that old workhorse, the 30-06, can be used to form more current and obsolete metric calibers than you can shake a ramrod at.

Now let's get down to cases — no pun intended — on what you can do to make Great-Gran'pappy's old buffalo gun bellow again.

Little more than what is already to be found in the average handloader's shop

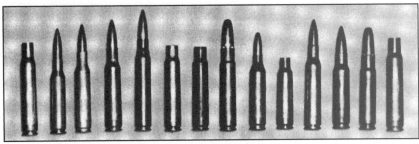

Many different cases, all formed from 30-06 brass. Left to right: 30-06, 6.5×52 Carcano, 6.5×55, 7×57, 7×64, 7.7×58 Jap., 8×57, 9×57, 243, 250 Sav., 256 Newton, 308, 358 Win., 30-06.

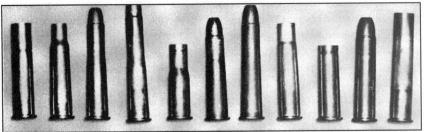

Various formed cases, none yet fire-formed. Left to right: 45–70; 33 Win., 38–56, 38–70 Win., 40–50 Sharps, 40–60 Win,, 40–82 Win., 45 Danish Rem., 45–60 Win. and 45–90 (redrawn out), all made from 45–70 cases.

will be required for most forming jobs. Perfectly good, safe cases can be (and have been) turned out with nothing more than a hand type sizing die, a file and a good bench vise. For speed, efficiency and comfort, though, these tools will be helpful.

Loading press
Full length sizing dies
Case trimmer
Lubricant (for dies and cases)
Assorted sizing dies (for use as intermediate stages)
Lathe (for those few times when that nasty phrase "Turn down rim" appears)
Peace and quiet

With the exception of tong tools and a few light-duty presses, all presses currently made will do a good job of case forming. The operator must do his part, though. Presses can't think. Presses with the greater mechanical advantages will, of course, make the job easier. The RCBS Model A-2 is ideally suited to this sort of thing and I have used one for years. The Super Turret that Hollywood Gun Shop makes is also excellent. Case forming does place more of a stress and strain on tools than does normal reloading.

Selection of the correct basic case for forming to the desired caliber requires particular care — most importantly, see that the head and rim dimensions are as close as possible to those of the case to be formed. The head of a case receives the least support during firing and therefore is most likely to let go if all is not well. If you must use a case a few thousandths large at this point, it can be reduced by swaging, which we'll get to later. Conversely, a case somewhat small at the head (no more than .015" smaller) may be used, fire-forming it with a light load to expand it before using full charge loads. Remember — only a few thousandths of an inch of soft brass stands between your face and white hot gas at a pressure of many thousands of pounds!

Normally, only rimmed basic cases may be used to form rimmed types, and rimless basics for like variants. There are, however, a couple of exceptions to the rule — a rimmed case may have its rim turned off flush with the head, a new extraction groove cut, and we have a rimless case. Many 9mm Luger cases, made in this fashion from 38 Special brass, were used by the writer back in 1948; they were satisfactory with light loads, and that is the type of load cases so-formed should be limited to.

Conversely, a rimless case can be reduced in diameter ahead of the extraction groove while the rim proper is left full diameter. Depending on the amount of reduction, it will be converted to a semi-rimmed or rimmed case. Thousands of 6.5mm. Japanese cases have been made up this way from 30-06 and 300 Savage brass.

The case alterations just described are extreme, last ditch resorts, to be used only when there is no other way to get what you need. Such work should never be attempted on anything but late-manufacture, solid head cases. The earlier folded-head and balloon-head cases simply do not have enough metal in this critical area to stand the strain (fig. 1).

To make certain your cases are sufficiently strong after such a job, section the first few before going further — clamp the formed case horizontally in your vise, then use hacksaw and file to cut it down to the midpoint. You can then easily see just how much brass is left and determine whether it will hold.

Case condition is also quite important. Odds and ends picked up on the range or donated by well-meaning friends should be viewed with suspicion. There is no way of knowing how many times they were fired, or with what. Mercuric primers, repeated firings or excessive pressures may have damaged them — such damage may not be evident until firing, and then it is too late. Be safe. Stick to cases that you know are new or once-fired with sensible loads. Any sign whatsoever of leaks, splits or cracks is ample reason for rejection. Throw 'em away.

So, tools and the right basic cases at hand, we'll proceed with what we have to do to make what we want from what we got. One or more of the following operations will be necessary in any forming job. A few of the more advanced jobs will require all of them but such undertakings should be held in abeyance until considerable experience has been gained. Making 9.3×72R cases from 30-06 brass, for instance, would try the patience of the best.

Resizing This will be familiar to anyone with a bit of loading experience, but a few points are worth additional emphasis. Lubrication is vital. Those of you who have wrestled a stuck case know how the lack of a bit of lubricant can louse things up. Forming cases works them much more than normal full length sizing, thus they're more likely to stick in the die if not adequately lubricated. Any of the prepared lubricants furnished by the loading tool makers are excellent. Anhydrous lanolin from the corner drugstore is equally good. Apply a thin even coat with your fingers or a cloth, but do it *sparingly*. Any excess will be trapped at the junction of neck and shoulder as the case is forced home in the die. Since it can't be compressed, it deforms the case, making "oil dents." Minor dents do no harm, other than to make a sloppy looking job, but the larger ones can split or crack the brass (fig. 2c). Incidentally, if you lack any other lubricant, moisten the fingers and rub them over a cake of toilet soap and apply the soap in a very thin film over the case. It works fine. Don't use light household or machine oils — they lack the film strength necessary for this kind of work.

When full length dies are used, adjust them as recommended by the makers. Make certain that the force required to press the case into the die does not push the die away from the shell holder. With a case in the die and the holder at the top of its stroke, holder and die must make firm contact. If they do not, the case is not fully sized. Screw your die in until cases go all the way in and the holder bumps right up against the die mouth.

In some instances, it may be desirable to use intermediate stage dies. Less effort is required to form 7×57mm cases from 30-06 brass if the shoulder is first pushed back to about the correct position by running the case into a 308 Winchester die. The case will then go into the 7mm full length die much easier. Two easy operations rather than one harder one. Some jobs make the use of intermediate dies a necessity rather than a convenience, as in forming 30 and 35 Newton cases from Norma cylindrical magnum brass. Attempts to run the basic case directly into the full length die will result in crumpled cases like that shown in fig. 2a. Adjustment of intermediate dies is by trial and error until the desired results are obtained. One can, however, record the distances between shell holder top and die mouth after the correct setting has been obtained. This will enable you to get it right the first try, next time.

Occasionally it will be possible to form a case without using the die of that particular caliber. 6.5×55mm Mauser-Krag cases can be made up this way. First size 30-06 brass full length in a 7×57mm die, then trim to 2.156". Now run the case into a 250–3000 or 22–250 die until the bolt will close on it with just the faintest trace of drag. Next, expand the neck to hold .264" bullets and fire-form with a light load. This method is of particular value when the number of cases to be made up does not justify the cost of a new set of dies.

Trimming Most basic cases will not be of the correct length and will require trimming — from a few thousandths to upwards of a half-inch may have to be removed. When only a small amount is to be cut, any of the commercial trimmers will do a fine job. They're all slow, though, and a better method is required if you have lots of brass to remove or many cases to process. Forster-Appelt makes a fine tool for this purpose. It consists of a spot facing tool and pilot of the correct diameter to be chucked in a drill press. It is used with a collet type case holder (like those used in their bench type trimmer) that is bolted to the press table. Once set up for the correct case length, any amount of brass can be trimmed from a case with one smooth stroke of the handle. With a little practice, several hundred cases per hour can be trimmed with ease.

Large amounts of brass can be removed with a copper tubing cutter, though the burr and crimp left will have to be removed before a bullet can be seated. Run the case over an expander plug of the correct diameter, then chamfer the mouth with a knife or the Wilson chamfer tool. A couple of strokes with a fine cut mill file will remove any feather edge that remains.

Generally, final trimming should be done after neck expan-

sion and sizing are completed. These operations tend to drag one side of the neck down a bit, leaving the case mouth out of square. The finished case length should be a thousandth or so less than specified. This will allow it to stretch during subsequent firing, obviating the need to trim again after only a few firings. Don't, however, cut them too short if you want to crimp them in a standard seating die. Strike a happy medium; short enough to stretch, long enough to crimp. Remember that a good solid crimp is essential to proper magazine functioning in many of the older arms.

Neck Expansion Many jobs will require that the neck of the basic case be opened up to accept bigger bullets. When this increase is slight, it may be done during resizing by having the correct diameter expanding plug in place. Some plugs have a sharp shoulder that will shave brass or even crumple necks when much expansion takes place. These should be ground to a smooth taper and polished, then no further trouble will be encountered. Tapered plugs are available in some calibers and are well worth the nominal extra cost. Such a plug will open 30-06 necks up to take .357" bullets in one pass with no trouble at all.

When a really great amount of neck increase is required, such as opening up 30–40 necks to take .403" bullets (for the straight Sharps cases), it should be done as a separate operation. Several stages may be required to avoid splitting the necks. The RCBS expander die, ideal for this purpose, fits the press frame, and is bored out to accept a large variety of cases. Expander rods, in a wide range of diameters, are threaded into this die from the top. If in doubt about the amount of expansion that a case will stand without splitting, go up by .020" steps. The amount that can safely be done in one pass will vary from one lot of brass to another. Some arsenal 30-06's will stand as much as .060" to .075" at one pass without splitting or crumpling.

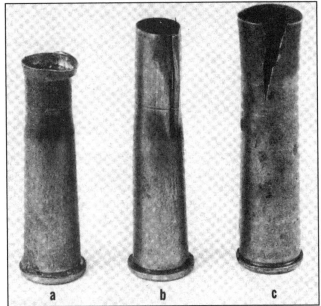

Fig. 2 — a) 40–60, crumpled by using too blunt an expanding plug, b) 45–70, folded in sizing to 38–56, probably through trapped air or oil, c) 348, split from excessive expansion in one step.

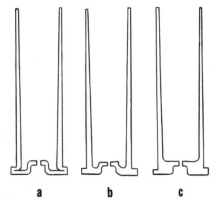

Fig. 1 — a) Folded head type. Entire head formed from one single fold of the case metal. b) Balloon head type. Relatively thin web, protruding primer pocket. c) Solid head, modern type. Heavy, thick web, head full depth of primer pocket.

a   b   c

Fire-forming Body and shoulder dimensions of a basic case may be less than required, even though other dimensions are OK. The only easy and practical way to correct this is to go ahead with other forming operations, then fire the case in the correct chamber for which it is intended. This is known as fire-forming. The expanding powder gases expand the soft brass case walls until they are stopped by the chamber walls, thus the case is reshaped to fit the chamber to perfection. Except where only a small amount of expansion is to take place, *light loads must be used.* The reduced capacity of the undersize case and the added resistance to the powder gases make this necessary.

An example of full load fire-forming is found in making 8.15×46R cases from 32–40 brass. The 32 is a straight taper case while the 8.15 has a very slight bottleneck. Only a few thousandths expansion is required to produce the new shoulder. Here a full charge load may be safely used. Thirteen grains of Hercules 2400 powder behind a 150- to 180-grain cast bullet will produce perfectly formed cases every time.

An alternative to the use of bulleted loads for forming is the filler load. It consists of a light charge of fast burning pistol powder such as Bullseye behind a case full of granular filler such as corn meal or cream of wheat. Powder and filler should be separated by a thin wad. A quarter sheet of bathroom tissue works well for this. IPCO grease wads will prevent spillage during handling, but if not available, just stick the case mouth into a stick of bullet lube or soap, give it a twist and pull it out, leaving a plug of grease or soap in the neck. Such loads, happily, require no range facilities for

firing. Nothing but dust-like filler emerges from the muzzle, its energy dissipated within a very short distance — perfectly safe to use in your basement.

It is possible, however, to develop dangerous pressures with filler loads unless caution is observed. Since no published data is available, start with a charge of Bullseye that fills approximately 10% of the case volume. Work up from this until satisfactory expansion is obtained. Be alert for any signs of excessive pressure and back off from the load that caused them immediately. Thick, heavy cases may not always blow out completely with this type of load. If not, don't worry about it. They will be so close to final shape that the first firing with a full charge will finish the job in fine order. A filler load may also be substituted for other operations, such as neck expansion. 30-06 cases may be fire-formed directly to 35 and 400 Whelen without any preliminary expansion, with 15 grains of Bullseye plus corn meal. This also produces a nice square neck and mouth, not always possible with mechanical expansion.

Turning Rim & Head On occasion, one will be forced to use a basic case that has a rim too great in thickness and/or diameter. This is easily corrected in a lathe. Set the case up in a tapered collet or chuck and turn the rim to desired thickness and diameter. Always remove the excess metal from the *front* of the rim, not from the rear face where the headstamp appears. The latter course will reduce the depth of the primer, allowing it to protrude. A premature firing could result from the use of such a case. Of course, the pocket could be deepened with a drill or end mill, but why add another operation to the job? Also, deepening the pocket will reduce web thickness, possibly to the danger point. Do it the safe and easy way, from the front.

A tool bit ground to the shape shown in fig. 3 can be used to reduce both diameter and thickness in one pass. While dimensions do vary from case to case, the tool shown will produce a serviceable rim in nearly all cases. Just make sure it is set up to give the correct thickness, thus headspacing the new case correctly. Using this tool, it's relatively simple to reduce 30–40 rims to form the rimmed Mauser 57mm series. If only a few cases are to be made up, the job can be done with a safe-edge file, but it's a lot of work.

Cases may be reduced a slight amount just ahead of the extraction groove. This is practical only in thick walled, solid head modern cases (fig. 1c). The older folded and balloon head type simply do not have any metal to spare at this critical point. Any reduction here is achieved at the expense of wall thickness and strength. Go easy on this sort of thing and section the first few you make up, as described earlier.

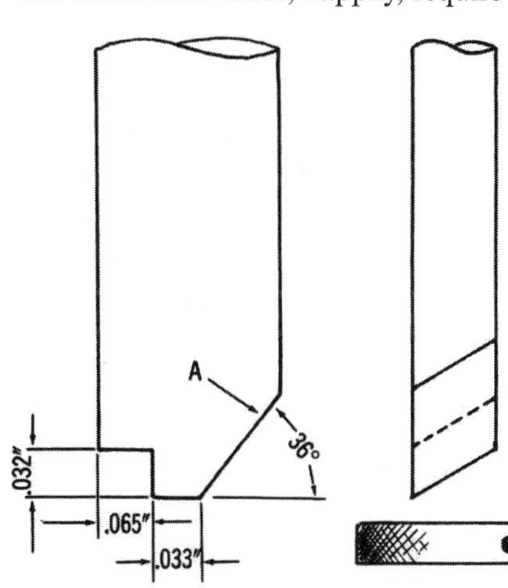

Fig. 3 — Tool for reshaping case rims and extraction grooves (not to scale). See text for details and use.

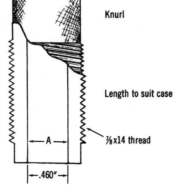

Fig. 4 — Swaging die for reducing 30-06 head to .460" (or other diameter needed). Inside needs exact dimensions only up to about point A. Above that point, inside could be larger and, if so made, rimless cases could be pushed out through top of die, provided rim was turned beforehand to .460" (in this example). Pushrod could be thicker (almost diameter of case head) thus obviating possible case damage via smaller inside-use rod. (Not to scale.)

Standard lock ring

Knurl

Length to suit case

⅞x14 thread

A

.460"

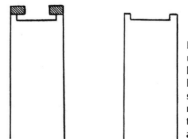

Fig. 5 — Shell holder for use with swaging dies in loading press. Standard holder (left). Cut away shaded portion until recess is equal in depth to rim thickness. Right, altered holder.

This, too, can be done with a file if you have no lathe at hand.

Some turning may be required on rimless cases, usually when the head diameter has been reduced by swaging or other means and the extraction groove must be deepened or recut. This can be done with the same tool bit shown in fig. 3. It is shaped to reproduce approximately the groove of the 30-06 case. While not all cases have exactly this same groove, they are close enough to it that a new groove of this shape will function quite well. The extended angle (A) will also permit the same tool to be used for turning the reduced head type of case. It will carry the forward slope of the groove on out to the edge of the head.

Swaging Cases may be reduced at the head as much as .040" by using dies of the proper diameter. Considerable power is needed so a hydraulic or arbor press is a convenient item to have. Lacking either, a heavy bench vise or the more substantial loading presses will do the job. Simple dies (fig. 4) can be made up for this job. The drawing shows a threaded die for use in a loading press but no threads are needed for use in a vise or other type press. The interior should be reamed and lapped to size, then hardened. If more than .005" reduction is desired, a set of dies, each one of .005" reduction, will be needed, unless you have a very powerful press. For use in a loading press, the standard shell holder should be faced off as shown in fig. 5 — case rims won't stand the strain of pulling them out of this type of die. A rod is inserted in the top of the die and the case is driven or pressed out. Care must be used or the head will be deformed and the primer pocket distorted. A smooth even push is best.

If you have neither the facilities nor the inclination to make up these dies, RCBS will be happy to sell you a set of "Base Forming" dies which do a very fine job. The price is about $20.00, as of this writing.

Resizing dies for almost any caliber, however odd-ball, may also be had from RCBS — send them a chamber cast and/or several fully fire-formed cases.

Swaging 30-06 case heads will enable one to make up 6.5mm Japanese, 6.5mm Carcano, 6mm Lee-Navy, 7.35 Terni and numerous other hard-to-find calibers. Even the long 9.3×72R can be made up by combining swaging with redrawing to get the length required. The writer has used many 45–90 cases drawn from 45–70 brass by Robert Pomeroy of Waterbury, Conn. He does a good job and the cases have held up well, even when loaded heavily with 53 grains of 4895 behind a 405-grain bullet.

Redrawing This is mechanically simple but the equipment required is beyond the means of the average loader. Precision made dies and punches are used, just as in original case manufacture. It is a quite advanced job, requiring complete machine shop and heat treating services.

For simple annealing, stand a case (without primer) in a half-inch of water, heat neck and shoulder area with propane or other torch quickly to dull red, then knock case over into water and allow to cool. Water keeps the critical head area from softening.

Most such redrawing may soon be a thing of the past now — Nonte-Taylor Ammunition, 1112 Buena Vista, Decatur, Ill., are importing new basic cases from which a great many obsolete calibers can be formed. These are virgin brass, properly made to accept standard .210" large rifle primers and are 3¼" long. The necks are annealed farther down than is normal practice, thus may be trimmed to shorter lengths without further annealing before necking down as desired. Cylindrical in form, they have only just enough taper to facilitate entry into sizing dies. Three types are available, and details of the many cases they will form will be found in the Basic Case Table. These straight cases will be about $22.50 per 100, prepaid. For a small extra cost you can get them already formed into any caliber on the list, or loaded as well.

Using some procedures already covered, let's take up a couple of typical forming jobs and see just how much work is involved. The first, quite simple, will produce nice shiny new brass for that 40–60 Winchester '76 you've been wanting to shoot. If new cases are used, the result will, be more durable than any of the original cases you might find around these days.

While the 40–60 case head is almost identical to that of the readily available 45–70, the latter is 2.10" long as opposed to the 1.88" of the 40–60. Run the 45–70 case into a 40–60 full length sizing die, removing the expander rod if need be, to allow the longer case to go all the way in. If a hand type die is used, support the neck end on a large nut or a piece of metal tube. This will allow the excess case length to protrude from the die without crumpling against your vise. After sizing, trim to 1.87" and chamfer the mouth lightly to aid bullet seating. Now run the case over the expander plug, if necessary, to bring the neck to correct inside diameter. All done, and you've made a new 40–60 case at least equal in quality to the original factory product and, by your own efforts, returned to service a fine old vintage rifle.

The second example — the 45–75 Winchester — is a bit more complicated, but still well within the capabilities of the average loader. The only large rimmed case that comes reasonably close to it, the 348 Winchester, is a bit small at the head and rim, but its heavy construction will easily stand the strain of expansion at this point. The rim is still large enough for the extractor to get a good bite. The 348 is 2.40" long compared to 1.88" for the 45–75, so it will do nicely for length when trimmed. First expand the neck to accept .457" bullets. This is best done in two stages, to about .400" first, then up to .457". Now size the new case full length in a 45–75 die, then trim to 1.879" or a wee bit less. Now your new case needs only a small amount of fire-forming to fill the 45–75 chamber fully — 25 grains of 4759 behind a 300-grain cast bullet will do the trick, and you've got a case that will probably last twice as long as any originals you might find.

The foregoing examples show what can be done without much trouble or equipment. For your convenience we show a chart that will let you quickly select the proper basic case for a number of forming jobs, without comparing and measuring several dozen specimens just to get one job done. The chart is by no means complete, but does list the cases most in demand today. Because of space limitations, we have printed a very comprehensive list separately — this gives all forming data needed, just as the chart shown here does, and will be mailed to you on request if you will send a stamped, self-addressed No. 10 envelope to Case Forming, Box 9060, Chicago 90, Ill.

Whichever centerfire metallic rifle case you need, there's probably a solution. A little thought and research, the use of our table, a few tools, and you'll have that old buffalo buster a-bellering again.

Case Interchangeability Chart U.S., British and Metric

The case listed for forming to a particular caliber is not necessarily the only one usable. Basic cases were chosen for their availability as well as suitability. For example, it is obvious that 8×57mm brass can easily be reformed into 7×57mm and 9×57mm cases. Nevertheless the 30-06 is listed as the basic case for the simple reason that it is more readily found than 8×57mm.

SBO, meaning "seat bullet out," will be seen in the forming instructions. This is necessary when the basic case used will not finish out to the full length of the case being formed. In magazine weapons the bullet must be seated far enough out for an overall length that will function correctly through the magazine. To do so, seat the bullet progressively deeper into an unloaded case, trying it in the weapon until proper functioning of the magazine and feed mechanism is obtained. Now record this dimension for future use. In single shot arms bullets should be so seated that they lack about 1/16" of touching the rifling. Seat a bullet progressively until it just touches the lands, then turn the seating stem down 1/16". Many single shot shooters, the bench resters among 'em, feel that this seating depth gives the best accuracy.

Dimensional data in this chart comes from many sources. Much of it is from personal measurement and examination of the cartridges and weapons concerned, some from standard reference works. The rest comes from friends and associates who, handy with micrometer and caliper, check new specimens for their collections. These sources are considered reliable but not infallible. In some instances only one or two specimens of a particular caliber were measured. In others, references were relied on in their entirety. In view of this, dimensions of your cases-cartridges may not fully coincide with the data given here. This does not mean that your cases are wrong or that my figures are wrong. Both are probably within the rather generous tolerances allowed in years gone by in the manufacture of the old timers. Should any cases formed in accordance with these instructions fail to chamber correctly in your gun, or if you are seeking a case not on our chart, write to me — we'll try to work out something that will do the job for you.

BASIC CASE TABLE

No. 1 Case	No. 2 Case	No. 3 Case
8x58R Krag	32-40 Rem-Hep.	43 Egyptian
33 Win.	35 Win.	40-90 Bullard
38-56 Win.	375-303	40-110 Win.
38-70 Win.	375 Flanged NE 2½"	45-75 Win.
40-50 Sharps BN	375-370	45 Peabody Martini
40-60 Win.	38-40 Rem-Hep.	45-125 Win.
40-60 Marlin	38-45 Bullard	50-50 Maynard 82
40-65 Win.	38-50 Rem-Hep.	50-70 Maynard 82
40-70 Sharps BN	38-72 Win.	50-100 Maynard 82
40-70 Win.	40-40 Maynard 82	50 Carbine
40-75 Bullard	40-50 Sharps St.	50-70 Gov't.
40-82 Win.	40-45 Rem.	50-90 Sharps
40-90 Sharps BN	40-65 Sharps St.	50-95 Win.
44-60 Maynard 82	40-60 Maynard 82	50-100 Win.
44-70 Maynard 82	40-70 Maynard 82	50-110 Win.
44-100 Maynard 82	40-70 Sharps St.	50-140 Win.
45-60 Win.	40-72 Win.	50-3¼" Sharps
45-82 Win.	405 Win.	Any other case of the same head size up to 3¼"
45-85 Marlin	38 Win. Exp. 3¼"	
45-85 Win.	40-90 Sharps 3¼"	
45-75 Sharps	Any other case with 30-40 head size up to 3¼"	
45-90 Win.		
45-100 Sharps		
45-3¼" Sharps		
Any other case with 45-70 head size up to 3¼"		

Abbreviations and Footnotes to Case Interchangeability Chart

1 Most large caliber Newton chambers accept the belt of the 300 Magnum without alteration. If yours won't, turn or file the belt down until it enters the chamber freely. Do *not* reduce rim diameter. You can now size the case full length, trim it and finish up by fire-forming.

2 The smaller British belted cases can be formed from 30-06 brass by swaging a belt on the latter. In a block of steel about 2½" long, drill and ream a .448"–.450" hole full length. Counter-bore both ends to .470", to a depth of .220". Lightly chamfer the bottom of one counterbore, but leave the bottom of the other clean and sharp. Press your 30-06 case into the chamferred end first, then into the other. Be sure the case goes all the way in so that case head is flush with the face of the die. This produces a belt .470" in diameter and .220" long. Sizing this belted '06 full length in the proper die and trimming to length will give you the small belted British series.

3 Reduce the '06 neck in a 250–3000 or similar die, then trim it to 2.40". Now size progressively deeper in a 22–250 die until the bolt will close on it. Ream the neck, expand to hold .227" bullets and trim to the length shown. To last more than a couple of firings, these cases must be annealed at the neck and shoulder. After annealing, fire-form and the job is finished.

4 Turn or file the belt down to the head diameter shown. Now reduce the rim to the diameter shown, deepening the extractor groove if necessary to give the extractor a good bite. Size full length and trim. Fire-form if necessary.

5 To make a .512" (or less) diameter case from the belted magnums, first turn the belt down flush with the body. Swage the case to required diameter as outlined in the text under "swaging." The rim must now be turned to the diameter given and the extractor groove deepened at the same time. When all this is done, size full length and trim to length.

6 Cases for low pressure calibers may be formed by sweating an extension on to an existing case of the correct head dimensions. For the 9.3×72R, expand the neck of a 30-30 case up to an outside diameter of about .358–.360" and tin the first quarter-inch thoroughly. Now cut the head off a 38 Special case and tin a corresponding length of it on the inside. Press this extension over the 30-30 neck. Stand this composite case in a half-inch of water and apply enough heat to flow the solder. When cool, clean off excess solder and trim to length. Sizing full length will finish the job. Examine such built-up cases carefully after each firing to see that the joint is holding. Keep loads moderate and pressures low.

BSA — Birmingham Small Arms
BN — Bottleneck
BP — Black powder
BPE — Black Powder Express
DEG — Deepen extractor groove
EL — Extra Long
EN — Expand neck
Exp — Express
Extr — Extractor
FF — Fire-form
Fl — Flanged
G&H — Griffin & Howe
HP — High-Power
Mann — Mannlicher
M-S — Mannlicher-Schoenauer
Mau — Mauser
May — Maynard
NE — Nitro Express
Nor — Norwegian
NS — Neck Size
NTE — Nonte-Taylor Enterprises
(a) NTE case No. 1 may be used by sizing and trimming.
(b) NTE case No. 2 may be used by sizing and trimming.
(c) NTE case No. 3 may be used by sizing and trimming.
R — Ream neck
Rem — Remington
Rem-Hep — Remington-Hepburn
Russ — Russian
S — Size
Sav — Savage
SBO — Seat bullet out
SFL — Size full length
Shps — Sharps
Sht — Short
SL — Self Loading
SS — Single shot
St — Straight
T — Trim
WCF — Winchester Center Fire
Win — Winchester
WR — Westley Richards

Old case	Head dia.	Rim dia.	Length	Bullet dia.	New case	Head dia.	Rim dia.	Length	Forming data
U.S. CALIBERS									
6mm Lee-Navy	.443	.440	2.36	.243	30-06	.466	.469	2.494	Swage head to .440, recut extr. groove, SFL, T, R.
25-36 Marlin	.417	.500	2.12	.256	30-30 Win.	.418	.497	2.044	SFL, T.
25 Rem.	.417	.419	2.05	.256	30 Rem.	.418	.417	2.05	SFL, T.
256 Newton	.468	.468	2.457	.264	30-06	.466	.469	2.494	SFL, T.
30-30 Wesson	.380	.442	1.66	.306	357 Mag.	.375	.432	1.28	NS for .306 bullets, SBO, FF.
30 Newton	.525	.520	2.497	.308	300 Mag.	.512	.532	2.850	See footnote I.
32 Ideal	.350	.404	1.75	—	32-20 Win.	.353	.405	1.40	SBO, FF.
32-40 Rem-Hep.	.455	.534	2.110	.307	30-40 Krag	.457	.545	2.314	SFL, T to 2.109, (b).
32-40 Bullard	.450	.508	1.84	—	30-40 Krag	.457	.545	2.314	Turn rim to .508, SFL, T to 1.839, (b).
33 Win.	.505	.608	2.105	.338	45-70	.501	.602	2.10	SFL, T to 2.104, (a).
33 Newton	.522	.520	2.495	.333	300 Mag.	.512	.532	2.850	See footnote I, then EN for .333 bullets.
351 Win. SL	.380	.410	1.38	.352	357 Mag.	.375	.432	1.28	Turn rim to .410, DEG, SBO.
35 Rem. Auto.	.435	.454	1.920	.359	30-06	.466	.469	2.494	Swage head to .453, SFL, T to 1.919.
35 Newton	.520	.525	2.495	.357	300 Mag.	.512	.532	2.850	See footnote I, then EN for .357 bullets.
38-40 Rem-Hep.	.454	.537	1.772	.372	30-40 Krag	.457	.545	2.314	EN for .372 bullets, T to 1.771, SFL, FF, (b).
38-40 Ballard	.421	.504	1.807	.396	30-30 Win.	.418	.497	2.044	EN for .396 bullets, T to 1.806, FF.
38-56 Win.	.501	.603	2.11	.376	45-70	.501	.602	2.10	SFL.
38-72 Win.	.460	.519	2.57	.375	9.3x74R	.465	.524	2.925	SFL, T to 2.569, (b).
40-50 Shps. St.	.451	.551	1.855	.401	30-40 Krag	.457	.545	2.314	EN for .401 bullets, T to 1.854, FF, (b).
40-60 Win.	.503	.618	1.87	.408	45-70	.501	.602	2.10	SFL, T to 1.869, (a).
40-65 Win.	.500	.601	2.10	.403	45-70	.501	.602	2.10	SFL, (a).
40-82 Win.	.508	.610	2.390	.408	45-70	.501	.602	2.10	SFL in 40-65 Win. die, SBO, FF, (a).
40-85 Ballard	.478	.556	2.93	.403	9.3x74R	.465	.524	2.925	EN for .40 bullets, FF, (b).
40-90 Shps. St.	.477	.540	3.25	.403	9.3x74R	.465	.524	2.925	EN for .403 bullets, SBO, FF, (b).
40-110 Win. Exp.	.544	.651	3.25	—	450-400-3¼	.542	.618	3.25	SFL.
44-90 Shps. 2⅝	.517	.633	2.626	.443	45-90 Win.	.504	.603	2.395	SFL, SBO, FF, (a).
45-90 Win.	.504	.603	2.395	.454	45-70	.501	.602	2.10	SBO, (a).
45-120 Shps.	.506	.610	2.875	.454	45-90 Win.	.504	.603	2.395	SBO far as possible, (a).
45-100 Ballard	.498	.487	2.812	.454	45-90 Win.	.504	.603	2.395	Swage head to .498, SBO, (a).
45-3¼ Shps.	.505	.601	3.25	.454	45-3¼ Nitro	.544	.612	3.25	Swage head to .505, SFL, (a).
45-125 Win.	.533	.601	3.246	.456	45-3¼ Nitro	.544	.612	3.25	Use as is, rim may need reduction, (c).
50-70 Gov't.	.563	.660	1.75	.510	348 Win.	.546	.605	2.40	EN for .510 bullets, T to 1.749, FF, (c).
50-95 Win.	.562	.628	1.913	.499	348 Win.	.546	.605	2.40	EN for .499 bullets, T to 1.912, FF, (c).
50-100 Win.	.552	.602	2.407	.499	348 Win.	.546	.605	2.40	EN by FF in chamber with filler load, SBO, (c).
BRITISH CALIBERS									
240 Apex	.448	.467	2.49	.245	30-06	.466	.469	2.494	See footnote 2, then SFL, T to 2.49.
350-7mm Rigby	.470	.528	2.490	.280	9.3x74R	.465	.524	2.925	T to 2.489, SFL in 7x57 die until breech closes, FF.
303 British	.452	.528	2.209	.311	30-40 Krag	.457	.545	2.314	SFL, T to 2.208.
310 Cadet	.354	.407	1.075	.316	32-20 Win.	.353	.405	1.315	SFL, T to 1.074.
333 R'less NE	.540	.542	2.450	.333	348 Win.	.546	.605	2.40	Turn rim to .542, cut new extr. groove, SFL.
450-400 2⅜ B.P. Exp.	.548	.615	2.37	.406	348 Win.	.546	.605	2.40	En for .406 bullets, SFL, T to 2.369, FF, (c).
416 Rigby	.589	.589	2.90	.416	.378 Wea.	.584	.606	2.92	Turn belt to .589, SFL, DEG, EN for .416 bullets.
577-450	.668	.746	2.335	.454	577 NE 3″	.660	.739	3.00	SFL, T to 2.334.
500-465 NE	.572	.646	3.23	.468	500 NE 3″	.571	.641	2.99	SFL, SBO, (c).
470 NE	.571	.650	3.28	.468	500 NE 3″	.571	.641	2.99	SFL, SBO, (c).
METRIC CALIBERS									
5.6x61 VomHofe	.476	.479	2.40	.227	30-06	.466	.469	2.494	See footnote 3.
6.5x50 Jap.	.451	.474	1.968	.263	30-06	.466	.469	2.494	Swage head to .451, SFL, T to 1.967, R.
6.5x55 Mau.	.476	.476	2.157	.263	30-06	.466	.469	2.494	SFL, T to 2.156, R.
6.5x68	.520	.509	2.661	.265	300 Mag.	.512	.532	2.850	See footnote 4.
280 Halger Mag.	.529	.554	2.598	.283	300 Mag.	.512	.532	2.850	SFL in 280 Ross die, T to 2.587, FF.
7.5x53.5 Swiss	.496	.496	2.177	.304	7.62 Russ.	.485	.564	2.107	Turn off rim, cut new extr. groove, SFL, FF.
7.62 Lahti	.480	.481	1.375	.310	7.62 Russ.	.485	.564	2.107	Turn off rim, cut new extr. groove, SFL, T to 1.374.
7.7x58 Jap.	.472	.473	2.271	.300	30-06	.466	.469	2.494	SFL, T to 2.270, FF.
7.92 Kurz	.470	.470	1.299	.318	30-06	.466	.469	2.494	SFL, T to 1.298, R.
7.92x60.8 Nor.	.488	.469	2.396	.322	300 Mag.	.512	.532	2.850	See footnote 5, then SFL, T to 2.395.
8x51R Lebel	.541	.627	1.99	.327	348 Win.	.546	.605	2.40	SFL, T to 1.989.
8x57 Mau.	.467	.470	2.237	.323	30-06	.466	.469	2.494	SFL, T to 2.236.
8x60S	.470	.460	2.338	.323	30-06	.466	.469	2.494	SFL, T to 2.337.
8x68S	.522	.510	2.657	.323	300 Mag.	.512	.532	2.850	Turn belt to .522, DEG, turn rim to .510, SFL T to 2.656.
8x72R	.429	.483	2.838	.324	9.3x72R	.427	.481	2.835	SFL.
8.15x46R	.421	.506	1.815	.316	30-30 Win.	.418	.497	2.044	SFL, T to 1.814.
9.3x62	.467	.466	2.480	.366	30-06	.466	.469	2.494	T to 2.479, EN for .366 bullets, FF.
9.3x72R	.427	.481	2.835	.369	30-30 Win.	.418	.497	2.044	See footnote 6, then SFL.
10.75x68	.492	.488	2.67	.424	375 Mag.	.512	.532	2.850	See footnote 5, then SFL, T to 2.669, FF.
11.2x72 Schuler	.536	.467	2.815	.439	300 Mag. Norma spec. case	.512	.532	2.850	T to 2.815, NS for .439 bullets until breech will close, FF.

To get those half-minute of angle groups coming, the utmost consistency of components becomes mandatory. You can easily build — or buy — the case gauge described.

Case Neck Variations... And Their Effect On Accuracy

by **NORMAN E. JOHNSON**

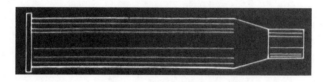

IF WE WANT the utmost accuracy in our shooting — at the bench or not — we cannot afford to overlook any aids to our handloading or any new methods of improving our performance. The winning bench rest shooters are well aware of this, as a glance at their scores clearly demonstrates.

Shouts of praise were heard when the minute-of-angle rifle appeared on the scene. Then came the half-minute bench rifle, and we've even excelled its performance. Now the half-minute average groups are no longer winning top honors in tight bench rest competition. Granted, a rifle capable of shooting half-inch groups at 100 yards is a fine rifle indeed, but it is just such rifles that are forcing the handloader to be even more selective in his choice of ammunition components in order to bring out the highest accuracy of these fine arms.

The bullet, seated to the correct depth, must have the correct weight and shape for the twist of the rifle's bore. It must be the correct diameter for the rifle it will be used in if it is to perform well. The precise amount of the best suited powder must be ignited by primers having uniform flash consistency. Many riflemen, however, fail to select carefully the one remaining link to fine accuracy: the cartridge case itself.

The proper selection of this all-important component can make a great deal of difference in the accuracy your rifle will deliver. Flash holes must be of uniform size and the case must be checked for capacity variation. One can get a rough idea of this by simply filling the case with powder or water, or even by weighing each case.

Now there remains still another factor, probably the most important phase of case selection. This is the degree of variation in the individual case neck-wall thicknes. Not only, note, the variation in the thickness of the cartridge case neck-metal from one to another case, but the variation as measured around the neck of *each* case. No matter the type of shooting you do — varmint, bench rest or big game hunting — accuracy will improve if you select your cartridge cases properly.

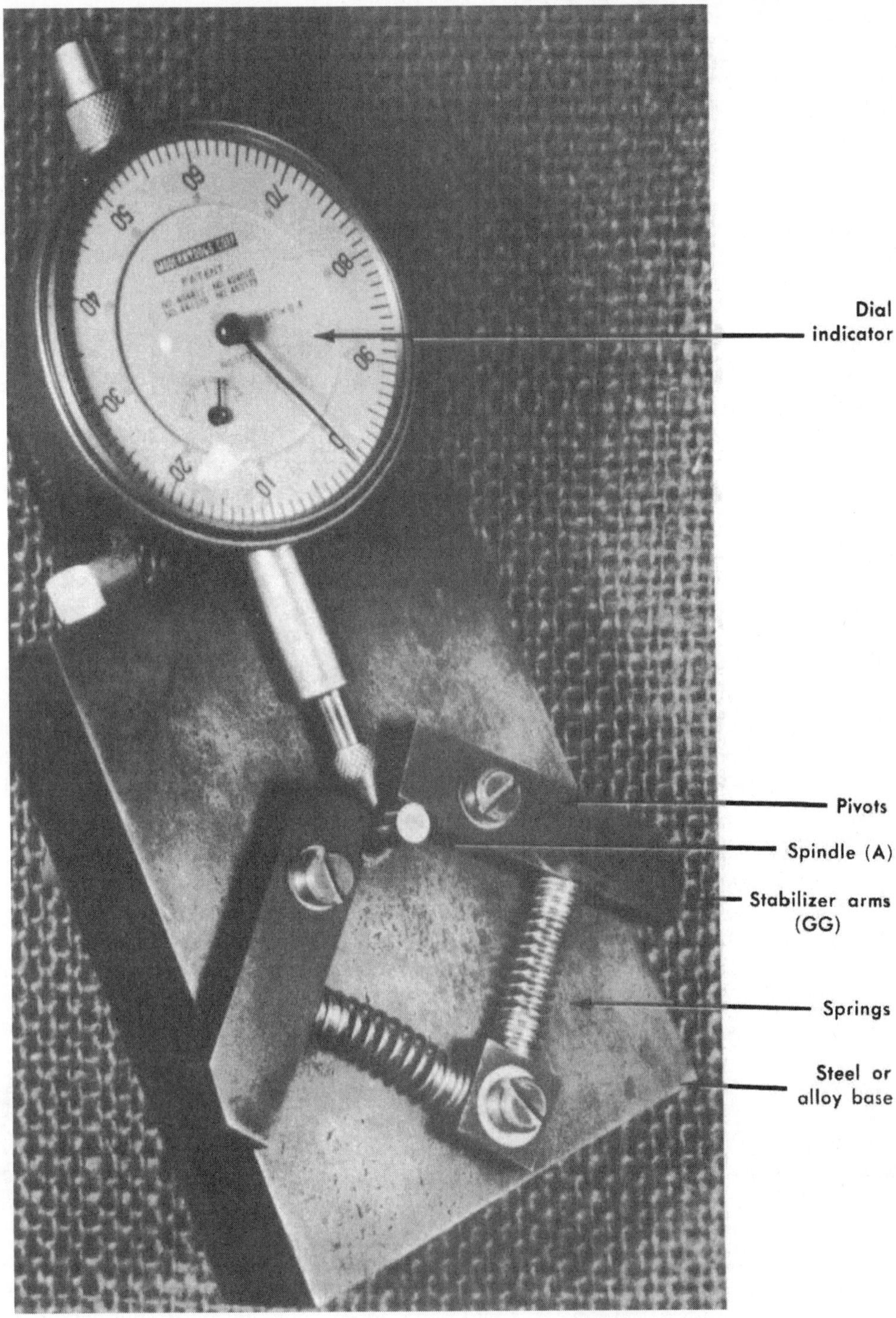

Dial indicator

Pivots

Spindle (A)

Stabilizer arms (GG)

Springs

Steel or alloy base

Dial indicator case-neck gauge. To operate, open spring-loaded stabilizer arms (GG), drop case mouth down over spindle (A) and release arms; now the case is pressed tightly against spindle and dial indicator gives a true reading of wall thickness at that point on the case. Rotate case to read gross variation and, for finer determination, rotate case and release at intervals of maximum difference. Then read DI for a greater degree of accuracy.

Some cases, we found, varied as much as .008" from one side of the neck to another, yet this same case might have the exact volumetric capacity as others; it may even weigh the same, but you can bet it won't have the same point of impact in any fired group at the target. Let's see why — here is a bullet held in a cartridge neck not of uniform wall thickness. When this bullet is fired the ogive engages the lands at a slight angle, the bullet being pushed slightly to one side. Our recent tests have demonstrated to us that the accuracy loss due to neck-wall variations to be by no means negligible.

Table of Neck Wall Variations and Related Accuracy

Max. Variation	MOA *	Remarks
.00025"	.250=.500	Bench rest matches
.0005"	.500=.625	Bench shooting
.0015"	.750=1.00	Varmint rifles
.0025"	1.00=1.50	Varmint rifles
.008"	2.00=4.00	Hunting rifles †

* MOA=minute of angle

† This accuracy level permits shooting cartridges from the factory boxes.

Our test groups revealed a definite accuracy imperfection in every instance where we selected uniform brass as our control, firing groups using this brass against brass from the same lot known to have neck-wall thickness variations. I have designed an instrument which will measure neck-wall thickness variations in a matter of seconds, to within .00025" or closer. Experiments with this tool bear out our belief that case-neck variations have a decided effect on accuracy in all types of rifles and shooting. The same tool also proved that no brass cartridge cases made and sold commercially today are acceptable for fine accuracy as they come from the box. We have rejected as high as 20% of some lots of brass, and neck-wall variations of from .001" to as much as .009" are not uncommon. To date I have not found one manufacturer of brass immune from this.

Two rifles of known accuracy potential, both of which have fired consistently fine averages, were selected for our group tests: (A) a M70 Winchester target rifle in cal. 243, the load being 39½ grs. 4064, the 75-gr. Sierra HP bullet, Federal 210 primer. (B) M40X Remington target rifle in 222, the load 22 grs. 3031, Remington 6½ primer, Speer 52-gr. bullet. Both rifles will average about ½ minute of angle; the .243 shoots about a ⅝" average, while the 40X .222 will average ⅜".

tAll cases were selected from the same lot of brass, and ample rejects were found for our control group. Cases which measured within .0005" were accepted as good for the .243; those measuring beyond that, up to variations of .002" to .006", were fired as poor brass.

Using the 243 load described, we averaged .979" for the good brass, and 1.948" for the poor stuff, firing 300 rounds to get these figures. Admittedly, from this lot of brass, the very poorest cases were fired against the best cases from the same lot; an assortment of brass that could very well have been yours!

In shooting the 40X Remington 222 target rifle we again selected the best brass and the poorest, but all from the same lot. While differences weren't as easy to find in this Remington brass, we did locate enough cases, varying from .002" to .004", to shoot against the good brass. The asymmetrical necks gave an average of .812" compared to a .367" for the brass which varied by no more than .00025"! 200 loads were fired in this test.

With this article you'll find a table giving acceptable neck-wall variations, a guide which will indicate roughly the size of the groups you can expect from brass with the neck dimensions listed. Since case-neck length, bullet length and seating depth can be made to somewhat correct this condition, our table is only a provisional starting point for you to work from.

The tool we present for measuring case necks is simple and easy to operate. A neck can be measured in seconds by opening the spring-loaded neck stabilizer arms and placing a case neck on the upright spindle. The caption gives full details.

The best time to measure the case neck is right after it has been resized, and with the sizing lubricant removed. Normally a trace of lubricant remains, which makes the measuring operation easier. A fired case usually contains enough soot to interfere with good measurement, while new cases from the box are normally deformed slightly at the neck, irregularities often existing in this area that make for poor measurements.

To obtain average neck-wall thickness set the DI on zero before placing case in position, then read dimensions. Now if you double this reading and add it to the bullet diameter you will have the loaded case-neck diameter before you load your bullet. If the neck has thickened from repeated-firings it can be reamed at this time. As an example, the 243 factory cartridge neck diameter is .276". If our cases show a neck wall thickness of .017", that times two equals .034" Which, added to .243", gives us .277", a case-neck diameter very likely to clamp down on our bullet when chambered in the rifle. True, the case neck can be miked after the round is loaded, but that would be too late; the bullet will have to be pulled to correct this situation.

The picture of our neck measuring instrument shows its construction isn't complicated; anyone handy with shop tools could make one easily. To begin, obtain a flat aluminum or other metal block about 3"×3½"×2" thick. Drill a hole in the center to take the spindle, which should be a tight, pressed fit. The spindle should be about .220" in diameter and should extend out of the block about one inch. The two spring-loaded stabilizer arms hold the case neck firmly against the spindle at an angle, thus the neck is held truly vertical, and if moved will return to that position. Any suitable dial gauge can be used for this measuring instrument, preferably one with a dial that can be set to zero. Mount it so that the contact point touches the spindle about ¼" above the block. The contacting surfaces of each arm may be polished to eliminate friction, and their pivot points should be located about as shown. The spring must be strong enough to hold the case neck firmly against the upright spindle.

This briefly comprises the makeup and operation of this instrument; if you construct one, we hope it will add as much to your shooting enjoyment and precision as it has to ours.

NOTE: The author has decided to make his neck-wall gauge available to interested shooters. The tool will be $26.50, complete with a special dial indicator. Write to Plum City Ballistic Range, Plum City, Wise.

An effective and forceful essay on the basic tenets of handloading. Don't miss this.

Handloading Philosophy

by DON MARTIN

IT MIGHT APPEAR to an unthinking person that handloading ammunition is only a matter of exact knowledge of cases, bullets, gunpowders and primers and the mechanical process of uniting them into a shootable cartridge. This information the operator must have, but he needs other mental equipment as well. The flour of technical knowhow, alone, will not produce a satisfactory handloading biscuit. It also requires the salt of common sense, the milk of caution and the baking powder of philosophy to make it edible.

This article is dedicated to such philosophical propositions as:

Ignorant, uninformed handloading is not to be tolerated.

Careless, slipshod handloading is equally intolerable.

Only the best handloads possible are good enough.

Nothing that reduces the possibility of error or accident is to be neglected.

Time spent getting the best is time well spent.

If Johnny can't read understandingly, or won't, he should not hand-load. Black powder handloading of 80 years ago was comparatively simple and foolproof. It was just a matter of filling the case to a point where the seated bullet would slightly compress the charge. There was no chance of making a mistake in the choice of powders. There was but one choice. Today there are at least 30 different types of smokeless powder available to the handloader, no two exactly alike. The spread between the fastest-burning pistol powder and the slowest rifle powder is incredible. All of these propellants have two characteristics in common; they are safe and satisfactory if the correct charge is loaded in the right cartridge case, but every last one of them can be plenty obstreperous otherwise.

All handloaders owe it to themselves, their eyes, fingers and heirs to read Phil Sharpe's book *Complete Guide to Handloading* and Earl Naramore's great work,

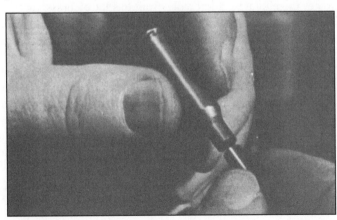

Use a bullet to check the neck-wall thickness of a fired case. If it slips into the case easily, all is well. Otherwise, neck reaming may be necessary to prevent excessive pressure from developing.

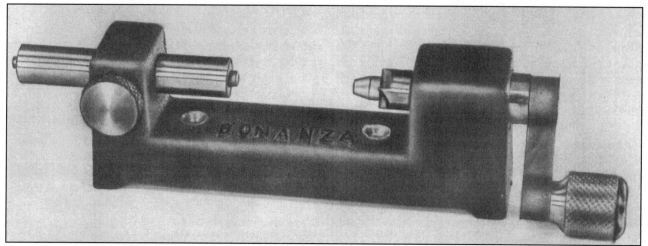

Cases which have stretched beyond their proper length may be quickly trimmed to size by using a case trimmer. The Bonanza tool holds the case centered between the primer pocket and case mouth.

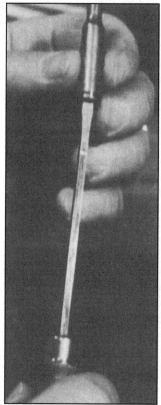

There are many tools available to clean the primer pocket of residue. The author prefers a screwdriver with a blunted blade.

Principles and Practice of Reloading Ammunition. Sharpe's volume is slightly out of date but is comprehensive. They should also peruse the latest Speer, Hornady. Hodgdon and Lyman handbooks and keep them in the shop for reference. All give exact loading data. The Handloader's Digest has all the latest dope on tools, gadgets, and components, plus many informative articles, and is well worth its cost. Certainly no one should attempt handloading without first charging himself with the basic rules of the game.

Here are the operations necessary to reload a rifle cartridge properly.

1 — Check inside neck diameter.
2 — Lubricate cases.
3 — Resize cases.
4 — Check case length and condition.
5 — Lightly chamfer all new or trimmed cases.
6 — Lubricate inside of neck.
7 — Expand neck and decap.
8 — Clean primer pockets.
9 — Seat primers.
10 — Charge cases with powder.
11 — Seat bullets.
12 — Remove all grease from loaded cases.

Cases must be processed in the foregoing sequence and all of these jobs completed before the next one is started. It is very much to the hand-loader's advantage to establish a fixed routine. It not only speeds up the work but insures against omitting an essential step. We'll try to explain, as briefly as possible, each one of these steps in the evolution of an empty case to a loaded round.

1. Pressure is required to insure full ignition of smokeless powder. That is obtained by bullet inertia, by seating it friction tight in the neck and, if necessary, by a crimp. Chamber throats are made large enough to allow the case neck to expand and permit the bullet to move forward into the barrel as soon as this pressure is built up. Resizing cases causes brass to flow forward. Sometimes it results in a thickened neck, preventing the expansion-release of the bullet and building up excess pressure in the chamber. There must be enough resistance to produce full ignition but not enough to retard its release.

A bullet makes a good neck-thickness gauge. If it will slip into a fired case all is well; if the bullet will not go into the case neck, the neck has thickened, and that case must not be used until the excess metal has been removed with an inside or outside neck reamer. Neck thickening is an irregular process and only a small percentage of cases are likely to check out tight, but such cases must not be used without reaming. However, note, sometimes the bullet refuses to enter the neck because of the old crimp. If the bullet will slip in after the muzzle has been lightly chamfered the neck is OK.

2. Lubricating cases for resizing. Work in as much case lubricant as possible in a soft rag 7 or 8 inches square. Work the cases in the rag until every square micro-millimeter of the surface has a *light* coat of lubricant. While doing this wipe off all the powder smut and dust. It is abrasive and will wear and some times scratch the highly polished resizing die. It will also contribute to the possibility of a stuck case. There are some alleged shortcuts to this job. Don't fall for them.

While lubricating cases in this way, it is easy to inspect them for defects at the same time. Watch for split necks, breaks in case walls and signs of incipient head separation.

3. Resizing cases. Remove the de-capping pin and neck-expanding plug from the resizing die and see if they will fit in the bullet seating die. If so leave them there. Resize in one separate operation, with *nothing* in the top of the resizing die. There are two excellent reasons for doing it this way: One is that if a case should .stick, it can easily be driven out with a punch, first removing the die from the press, of course. The other is that neck-expanding plugs and decapping pins are, as far as I can see, universally mounted on soft steel rods, readily bent if the decapping pin fails to center. The operator can easily feel anything wrong when de-capping in the loose bullet seating die, thus preventing damage to the rod. If he decaps in the resizing die, case friction will completely mask any trouble in the primer area.

4. The matter of case length is a trifle more complicated than it appears at first glance. Speer, Hornady, and Lyman handbooks give outside dimensions of cartridge cases. In the matter of length this data is *maximum*. New cases will always be shorter, usually 8 or 10 thousandths of an inch (.008"— .010"). The case length gauge should be set at such a figure or taken from an unfired case. Here's why: If the mouth of the case is pushed past the chamber, on into the barrel throat, it will be squeezed down on the bullet, raising pressures in exactly the same manner as an overthick neck does.

Rifle bullets are supplied with and without crimping cannelures. Ordinarily a jacketed bullet does not need to be crimped if seated with a snug friction grip unless the car-

Seating primers to the same depth assures good ignition. The Zenith primer mike will show seating depth irregularities of less than .001".

Consistent ignition depends on primer flash holes being nearly the same size. Herter's flash hole gauge is made specifically for this use. Wire gauge drills of proper size may also be chosen for this job.

tridge is to be used in a tubular magazine. However, there have been a number of hard-kicking magnum rifle cartridges, with short necks, put on the market recently where there may not be enough friction to hold bullets against the sharp recoil of a light gun. This should be watched. The old 30-06 has approximately 50% more inside neck area than the much more powerful 7mm Remington Magnum.

All high-power rifle cases should be run through a "No-go" length gauge, after they have been resized, to be sure they are not going to jump pressures by being too long. A case trimmer is an essential tool for the full-charge reloader.

Recently a gun magazine published an account of a chap who reloaded, with full charges, some 30-06 cases 50 times. It was specifically stated that he did not need to use a neck reamer or case trimmer during his 50-load run. I found it hard to accept. I mentioned it to three old time handloaders. Their reaction was vociferous and profane. (Regardless of veracity, error or misprint, it was a thoroughly mischievous story and should not have been published.) Pay no attention to such statements. Check high-power rifle cases for inside neck diameter and length every time they are reloaded. Nothing takes the place of being absolutely sure.

5. All new cases, and all cases being reloaded for the first time, and all cases that have been in the case length trimmer should have the mouth lightly chamfered. It is good insurance against crumpled cases. Chamfering tools, handling both inside and outside of the case neck, are cheap; get one.

6. It is good practice, if not absolutely necessary, to lubricate the inside of cases before neck expanding. They can be dipped in a quarter inch of powdered graphite, molybdenum disulphide, mica or with a lightly oiled rag on a stick. Be stingy with the lubricant. Very little is needed. An excess can seep down into the powder, causing misfires or hangfires.

7. Now we are ready to pick up the *bullet seating die* carrying the decapping pin and inside neck-expanding plug. The expanding plug will have passed the neck before the recapping pin arrives at the base of the case. The operator will feel the pin contact the spent primer. It should slip out with a modicum of pressure. Remember any tool with enough leverage to full length resize a rifle case has a great deal more push than decapping requires. If there is resistance it may be from one of three causes; crimped primers, not centering the flash hole, or too large a de-capping pin. (I once had to make a special small decapping pin for some 220 Swift cases.) With a little care there need be no bent or broken pins or rods.

(If your seating die won't accept the decapping rod-expander, separate decap rods are available, as in the Simmons tool, which decaps and primes as well, and may be had with one or several different caliber heads. Neck expansion must still be considered, especially if your sizing die squeezes the neck down considerably. One solution is to have a die tailored for your chamber-case neck dimensions, in which instance no expansion is needed; the "custom" die brings the neck down just enough to accept the bullet without undue seating force, yet with adequate neck tension.

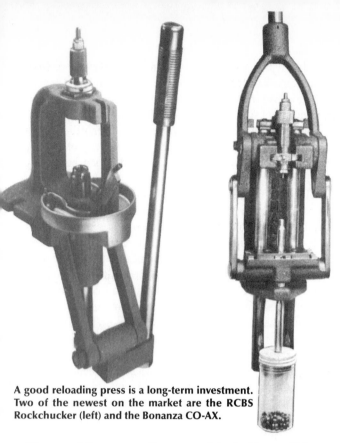

A good reloading press is a long-term investment. Two of the newest on the market are the RCBS Rockchucker (left) and the Bonanza CO-AX.

If none of these suggestions appeal, looks like you'll have to decap and expand in the sizing die! ED.)

8. Exploding primers leave a brittle deposit in the bottom of primer pockets. This deposit should be removed so the primer, in each reloading operation will be seated exactly as in a new and unused case. A small screw driver, with all the edges blunted will do the job perfectly. Primers are retained in the primer pocket by frcton fit and the depth measurement is exacting. Any kind of a polishing job is to be avoided.

9. Repriming offers no difficulties. Place the required number of primers in a small, shallow dish. Be sure the case to be primed is exactly positioned in the case holder. Put a primer, open end up, on the primer punch. Push the punch under the case. Lower the case on the punch gently. It requires no great effort. If the primer does not slip into the pocket readily something is wrong. The case may be not exactly positioned or it may be the wrong-sized primer. Find out the trouble. Too much pressure on a primer may crush it. Be sure no primers are lost. A careless heel can easily explode one. Primer magazines are not recommended to small-time handloaders and most certainly not to beginners. Careless or inexperienced handloading can set off the whole bunch. High intensity primers have appeared on the market. They are not needed with standard pistol powders but may offer an advantage with 2400 powder in magnum handgun cases. In rifle ammunition their use should be restricted to such slow-burning propellants as 4831 and possibly 4350, H570, H870 and 5010. They may over-ignite faster powders, raise pressures.

Don't stand in front of *any* priming tool, nor put your hand or head in front of the case mouth when priming.

Should a primer accidentally explode, it could cause a nasty burn — shooting or safety glasses would be another worthwhile precaution.

10. Smokeless powder should not be measured by bulk in near-max charges. It must be measured by weight. A powder measure can only be adjusted to throw a previously-ascertained weight of powder. It cannot be set any other way. It must be exact. "Near enough" *is not* near enough where full charges are concerned. Nothing can be guessed at or taken for granted in the management of smokeless powder. A powder scale weighing to 1/10-grain is a prime necessity for the handloader. In fact he can't get along without it. A mechanical powder measure is almost as essential. Weighing each separate charge is truly a slow business. Set the measure by the scale — exactly. Weigh the first 10 charges to give the measure a chance to settle down. After that, weigh every 5th or 10th charge as a check. Or set the scale for a slightly low charge and use a powder trickier to bring the scale in balance.

Place the primed cases to be charged in a cigar- or cardboard box on the right. The loading block should be on the left, with the powder measure and scales in the center. Pick up a case with the right hand, charge it with powder and set it upright in the block on the left. Always follow this routine. It is not just a cranky notion. It was described long ago by a great handloader to minimize the possibility of getting two charges of powder in one case. (Seating the bullet right after charging the case also helps to prevent double-charging pistol cases.) The loading block is a necessity. Anyone with a brace and bit can make one or they can be purchased for a dollar or two. The best one I have was handmade by a gunsmith and given to me as a Christmas present. Eddie knew just what I wanted.

When the block is filled or all of the cases charged, examine each one, individually, under a strong light. If there is any variation apparent, weigh it out. Take no chances.

11. The only troublesome thing about seating bullets is in getting the seating die correctly adjusted. With the case holder in place and the ram as far up as it will go, screw the seating die body down as far as it will go, then back it up two full turns. The last movement is to get the crimping shoulder if any) out of the way. Now back the bullet seater stem up and out of the way. If there is a properly loaded cartridge available, use it for a gauge. Run it up in the die and screw the bullet seater down to contact. Now place a charged case and bullet in the tool. Close the handle slowly until the bullet slips in the neck. Open the tool for a look. Keep on doing the same until the bullet is seated exactly right. It may require some further adjustment of the seating screw. If only a friction seating is desired, that is all there is to it.

If the bullet is to be crimped-in here's what to do. Following the foregoing outline, seat the bullet so the case mouth is positioned exactly over the center of the crimping cannelure. Back out the seating screw. Rotate the die down, little by little, until the crimping shoulder in the die is reached. Test each adjustment as you go, looking carefully at the

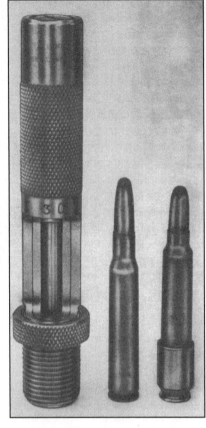

Keeping the bullet concentric with the case is easily accomplished using a benchrest seating die. This one is made by Vickerman, and is the type preferred by many shooters who demand highest accuracy.

case mouth. At this point the adjustments cannot be too fine. Don't get impatient. Probably no two dies will produce exactly the same crimp effect, and the length of the cases has just as much to do with the final result as the die. All must be exactly the same in over-all length. Once a crimp has been obtained, lock the die tightly in place.

Some crimping grooves are deep and some shallow. If the case is not exactly positioned there will be either no crimp or the neck will be crumpled. It is much easier to crimp cast lead bullets in handgun cartridges since they are soft enough to give way under the crimping shoulder. There is no such safety valve in jacketed bullets. The crimp setting has to be *exactly* right. Once this has been established, screw the bullet seater stem down to just contact the bullet.

12. Wipe all lubricant from the loaded cases. Slick cases increase back thrust in the chamber. Wipe out all grease from barrels and chambers before shooting. It has the same effect.

Always complete each operation before starting the next one. Set up a routine. Stick to it. It is the only way to get high quality handloaded ammunition.

Care in Handloading

Handloading ammunition isn't dangerous if it is done with commonsense care and precaution.

Volatile liquids such as gasoline or cleaning fluid, which can be set off by a spark of static electricity, are more dangerous than gunpowder. So are many acids, disinfectants and bug poisons which no one takes very seriously. The family car is a thousand times more likely to kill or injure than a set of reloading tools.

With 35 years of handloading and reading gun magazines behind me, I know of only one fatal shop accident. That involved a chain cigarette smoker who didn't die of lung cancer. He blew himself up. The vast majority of mishaps that can be blamed on handloading happen because of loading mistakes.

The rules that follow may sound unnecessarily fussy but please remember that all so-called accidents are caused by carelessness, ignorance, in-advertance or absentmindedness.

1 — No smoking in the shop when gunpowder is present.

2 — Buy gunpowder in the original sealed package. Don't buy a coffee can of bulk powder from anyone. This is no condemnation of any powder. They're all perfectly safe if the purchaser *knows* what he is getting. Anytime, and for any reason, if he does not positively *know*, he isn't safe.

3 — Do not use giveaway powder. It may not have been generosity that inspired the gift.

4 — Keep gunpowders in the original screwtop tin cans. Don't use glass jars; they can break and strew powder all over.

5 — If enough room can be spared, an excellent magazine is an old refrigerator or deep freeze box. They are heavily insulated, thus prevent quick temperature changes. A tight box in a cool basement is good, and it is a wise precaution to keep it locked.

6 — Never have but one can of powder on the workbench at a time — the one you are using. Loading accidents can easily occur from using the wrong powder or getting two types of powder mixed up in the powder measure. Again: overlook no precaution against absentmindedness and in-advertance. Many handloading accidents are set up when the case is being charged with powder. It may be an overcharge, a double charge, mixed powder or the wrong powder. Take every possible precaution against such errors.

7 — When a loading job is finished, clean up the powder measure thoroughly. Remove *all* the powder from it. Suppose you're loading Bullseye and switch to 2400. Enough Bullseye could remain in the measure to detonate the first load of 2400.

Most handbooks give a maximum load and one well under it. Start at the bottom and work up one grain or less at a time. If heavy or excess pressure is noted drop back two grains and stay there — primer pocket looseness, difficult case extraction, case-head expansion, etc. Any time there is a change of cases, bullets or primers, in a maximum load, drop back some 5%-6%.

A few last words. Don't chase the super-load will-o-the-wisp. Load everything 4, 5 or 6 percent under book maximum. The bear, moose or deer you shoot will never know the difference.

Don't shoot other peoples hand-loads. They may have been afraid to shoot them themselves.

Don't pass your own handloads around. A civil liability exists if there is an accident.

26
ABC's of Reloading

Handloaded shot-shells are easier to prepare than many suppose — here's how to make 'em for 45 Colt, 44 and 357 Magnum, 38 Special.

Shot Loads For Revolvers

by EDWARD DAMS

IN A PINCH, a shotshell cartridge in your revolver is a very handy item to have. Hearing the rattle of a snake, if your side arm is loaded with shot-shells, you can feel confident of knocking it off with the utmost dispatch. Because of its wide and successful use against snakes, the handgun shot-shell cartridge is usually called a "snake load."

There are other useful applications, however. They may be used for shooting pests or very small birds and game for the pot. In aerial target practice, where a bullet's range might be dangerous, shot loads may be used to build the shooter's skill and confidence.

The idea is not new. Flintlock pistols are said to have been loaded with shot, scrap metal, small gravel or rock salt. At one time Peters Cartridge Co. manufactured 45 ACP shot cartridges for use in the Thompson submachine gun. Such cartridges were to be fired over the heads of rioters or a mob — the noise and small shot falling would encourage the crowd to disperse in haste. These rounds could be used in the 1917 Colt or S&W Army revolvers if half-moon clips were provided. They could also be fired from the 1911 Colt automatic, but had to be singly loaded as their over-all length was too great to permit their use in the magazine.

Until some years ago, too, shot loads were factory made in 44-40, 44 Russian, 45 Colt and other calibers. The 44 Marble Game-Getter shot load, made for Marble's over-under pistol-carbine, was a highly popular shell for years.

Before they became unlawful, smoothbore revolvers were made by a few gunsmiths. Some of the barrels had chokes machined into them and good patterns — a 20" circle at 20 yards — were not unusual. These smoothbore revolvers could, of course, also fire bulleted rounds safely and fairly accurately, but beyond 40 yards or so the bullets would keyhole.

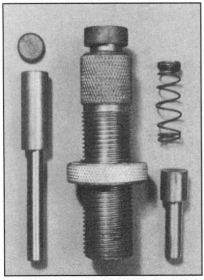

Component parts of the SAS die. At left are the parts needed to seat wads; right, those used to hold wad and shot in place while cartridge is being crimped; both sets fit die body in the center.

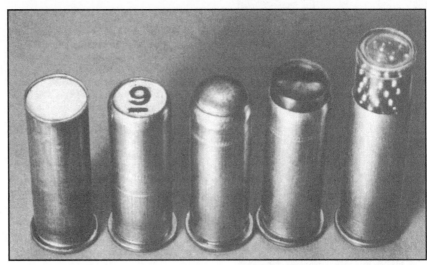

Five ways to finish shot cartridges. From left: top wad held in place with water-glass; top wad crimped in place; gas check for top wad; Hodgdon plastic half-jacket allows more shot; Shot Cap carries the largest shot weight of these shown.

Three sizes of Shot Caps now available; 44 Mag., 38 Spec.-357 Mag. and 45 Long Colt. Note small cup in the base, which should be in contact with the powder for best results.

Wad Specifications

A good wad must possess a number of desirable qualities. Most importantly, it must form a good gas seal between powder and shot, not only while it is in the case, but as it pushes the shot out the cylinder and down the bore. The wad should be able to hold the powder under pressure so that good and consistent ignition results. At the same time, it should lubricate the bore to reduce the possibility of leading — a big job for a thin wad less than one-half inch in diameter.

Most of these problems have been solved by shotgunners, and we'd be foolish if we didn't avail ourselves of what they have learned. The best thing, then, is to use the same wads.

The Alcan Co., probably the best-known manufacturer of conventional wads, graciously contributed a quantity of wads in their "Special Sizes" (see catalog section) for use in our tests. Before the advent of these products it was necessary to use a Lyman Kake Kutter of appropriate caliber, using it to punch wads from old felt hats and chip board. The special Alcan wads are a great convenience and time saver.

Anyone who has ever loaded a shot-shell knows the procedure: powder, nitro card, felt wad, shot and over/shot card. That's exactly how I began, using 357 Magnum brass. First, I made up a dummy round with one .070" nitro card, ¼" felt wad and shot, but less primer and powder. There was room for only 71 grains of shot, so that idea was scrapped. My next move was to try the same thing using a .135" nitro card only — ah, much better — now the case held 123 grains of shot with room for an over/shot card.

Shotshells generally produce less pressure than a bulleted round, so since 3 grains of Bullseye is a suggested starting load for the 357 Magnum with lead bullets, that charge was assumed safe with less weight in front of it. Six cases were sized, primed and their mouths belled, just as you would prepare any handgun cases, using the usual metallic cartridge

Today, according to law, we must have a rifled barrel on the revolver. This complicates the efficient loading of shotshells, but we can produce acceptable loads which will more than discourage a snake at reasonably short range.

Let us consider what we have to work with — shot, powder and wads. Powder and lead don't pose any problem, but those wads take up a lot of space. Then, too, the lead being loose shot, the charge will have to be contained within the cartridge. Solid bullets will often project 50% or more from the case mouth.

The problem is logically resolved if we use the longer cartridge cases. 45 Long Colt, 44 and 357 Magnum cases were chosen for this reason. We'll also cover the popular 38 Special in connection with a new device that makes it as efficient for our purpose as the 357 Magnum.

dies. The cases were charged with powder, the .135"
nitro card seated with a new pencil and 123 grains
of shot poured in, then topped off by an over/shot
card. All went wonderfully well.

Retracting the seating stem from the crimp die, I
attempted to crimp the newly-made shot cartridge.
What a mess! The crimp could not be made heavy enough
to hold the card without multiple manipulations of die and
press handle — even then it wasn't really strong enough to
hold the shot against the heavy recoil of a magnum bulleted load fired from the same cylinder.
This problem was easily solved by using water
glass (sodium silicate, obtainable from your
drug store). The top wad was "glued" in place
with this stuff, and allowed to dry overnight.

Firing these first loads was a disappointment. The water
glass wasn't hard enough and, even though the crimp held
on a few cartridges, the 30" wide roll of wrapping paper
used as a target showed the pattern to be inconsistent. Back
to the drawing board!

Two dozen rounds were made and allowed to dry thoroughly. Meanwhile, I wrote to Ted Smith of SAS for one of
his shotshell pistol dies I'd seen advertised. The die arrived
just about the time that an opportunity arose to do some
shooting. In haste, two dozen more rounds were assembled
using Ted's die and what a charmed day that was. Components just about flew together.

Some people have a knack for solving others' problems,
and Ted Smith is one of those people. The die he sent convinced me that I'd want others in 44 Magnum and 45 Long
Colt for the work that lay ahead. Ted's die comprises one die
body, two punches, a spring, a rubber pad and a screw top
for each caliber. The long punch is used to seat the wads with
the rubber pad between it and the screw cap. When wads
have all been seated firmly upon the powder the long punch
and pad are exchanged for the short punch and spring. The
die is turned down until it touches the case, then given an
extra ¾-turn to form a crimp that rivals the factory product,
while the short punch and spring hold the wad and shot in
place. Fast and simple, if only the cartridges work — they
looked highly professional.

357 Magnum Loads

Back at the range, I was surprised to find that both groups
of cartridges performed about the same. The ones made with
the SAS die were just a bit more consistent, if a bit spread
out. At 20 feet, the shot charge covered the 30" paper. The
question now was how to tighten up the pattern and close
up the holes. There were 5 or 6 places where a snake could
slip by unscathed.

Since patterns were just about the same, and the SAS die
made loading so easy, I took the path of least resistance and
made up a couple dozen more rounds. These were in groups
of 6 with the powder charge changed by increments of 2/10-
gr. each. When these were fired the result was unusual. The
best load in the 6" barreled Python test gun was 3.4 grains

These two guns, a S&W Combat
Magnum and Colt Python, used
in developing 357 Magnum loads
gave different patterns; probably
because of differences in bore,
cylinder gap and barrel length.

of Bullseye. The load either side of it (3.2 and 3.6 grains)
spread wider. A few more rounds were loaded at 3.3, 3.4 and
3.5 grains. The 3.5 grain load proved best, showing no holes
that a snake's head could slip through!

Demonstrating the nice 20" pattern at 20 feet to a friend
one day made everything look wrong again. That 20" circle
spread out over the 30" paper like fly-specs. I couldn't believe
it, not until it was realized that it wasn't the Python being
fired, but a 357 S&W Combat Magnum with a 4" barrel.
This is not to imply that the Colt is better; it's just different.
Working up a load for the Smith, I got the best patterns with
3.2 grains of Bulls-eye, about the same spread and density
as before. Number 9 chilled shot was used in all tests.

44 Magnum-45 Colt Loads

Having achieved success with the 357 Magnum, the same
procedure was followed in working up loads for the big 44
and the 45 Colt. Progress was swift, success almost instantaneous. The best load, using a 7½" barrel Super Dakota
single action 44 Magnum for a test gun, worked out at 5
grains of Bullseye, .135" nitro card and 165 grains of shot.
For the 45 Long Colt, with a Colt S.A. with 5½" barrel, the
best load was 4.5 grains Bullseye, .135" nitro card and 172
grains of shot produced very tight, evenly spaced patterns at
20 feet, usually less than the 20" circle drawn.

This story could end right here, but being a dyed-in-the-
wool hand-loader, I hated to see those nice new felt wads
sitting on the shelf. Both the 44 Magnum and 45 Long Colt
were throwing quite a charge of shot, so even if some pellets
were sacrificed in favor of a felt wad, I reasoned there would
still be enough left to do in a snake. Then, too I had a can

of Hodgdon's new Grey B powder that hadn't been opened — no loading dope was available for anything that I shoot often. Teaming up these components did effect the desired result, and a few surprises, too.

Starting with the 44 Super Dakota, a load of 5.8 grains of Grey B, .70" nitro card, and a ¼" felt wad still left room for 144 grains of shot and an over/shot card. The surprise was that the group tightened up even more — showing about a 16" circle — and the pellets were more evenly spaced. Muzzle blast sounded more like a shotgun and less like a pistol, making this load easier on the ears.

The 45 Long Colt gave best results with only 5.3 grains of Grey B, using the same combination of wads, and the average load held 147 grains of shot. For some reason the barrel of this old timer (it has a three digit serial number on the frame) showed traces of lead in the bore but a Speer half-jacket reduced this problem to some extent. It is common knowledge among shotshell pistol cartridge loaders that a gas-check or a half-jacket works well as a shot cup, but I didn't find that out until after I began to brag a bit.

Here is another way to cut down on the lead which gets scraped off the shot by the rifling: Before placing the over/shot card, spray the shot in the cartridge with Dry Gun Lube, a product of Nutec Inc., P.O. Box 1187, Wilmington, Del. 19899. This lube has fine particles of Teflon suspended in a vehicle and is dispensed from a spray can making it convenient to use for coating the loaded shot. Just a quick spray cut the leading to darn near nothing. In retracing my steps with the other loads, the same result was always shown.

Shot Caps

A new approach to the shotshell revolver cartridge problem of poor patterns and not enough shot is the Remco Shot Cap. These are caliber size plastic tubes, sealed at both ends, and containing a pre-measured quantity of #9 shot. This makes the loading of shot cartridges easy — you prepare the cases as usual using the loading data supplied. The shot doesn't touch the bore and you gain about 30% in shot-charge weight. Shot Caps are packed 50 to a box, are available for 38 Special and 357 Magnum at present, and sell for $4.95 per box postpaid from Rem-

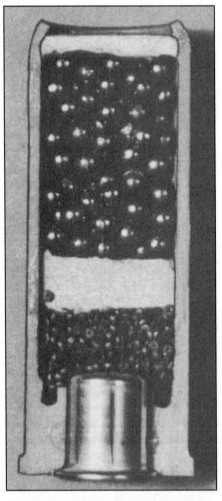

Alcan's 45 Long Colt shot cartridge in cutaway view. Shot shell primer is used to ignite the 3.5-gr. charge of a special single-base powder. The .135" O/P wad and 142½-gr. charge of No. 9 shot is similar to the load we worked out.

co, 1404 Whitesboro St., Utica, N.Y. 13502. Other sizes to come are 44 Magnum, 45 Colt and 45 ACP at $5.95 a box.

The Shot Caps are very easy to assemble and less critical of the powder charge used. Patterns were as good or better than any that I was able to build from loose components and, in the 38 Special, more shot is thrown than is possible out of the 357 case when loaded with loose shot. The Remco shot cap contains 145 grains of #9 shot — the best I could cram into the 357 case was 129 grains, using two of Hodgdon's plastic half-jackets, one over the powder and the other over the shot. If you only intend to shoot shot cartridges occasionally or would rather not bother to work up a load for aerial practice, the Shot Caps may be for you. However, if any amount of shooting is anticipated 10¢ a round may be considered a bit expensive.

These plastic tubes of shot are loaded just as you would load a bullet. No wads are necessary and the shot projectile is seated easily with the thumb. The cartridge is inserted in the seating die of the press, and the bullet seating die adjusted to seat the shot capsule to slightly less than the cylinder length of your gun while giving the case mouth a slight crimp at the same time. Don't use the SAS die for crimping as it will crush the capsule.

Rocking Chair Reloading

For those who want only a few 45 LC shotshell cartridges for a hunting trip, there's another alternative. Al-can makes 45 Long Colt plastic cartridges, for one time use only; they carry a shotgun type primer have a fast-burning single base powder which I can't recognize, and carry a healthy charge of #9 shot. They're packed 50 to the box and sell for $5.15. They can also be used in your shotgun with a brass adapter available from Alcan for a dollar (specify gauge).

A number of custom reloaders make up shot cartridges, and perhaps one near you might be willing to make them for your revolver. Their names and addresses will be found in the Directory section of this book, or write to Howie's Shooters' Supplies, Pine Plains N.Y. 12567 or Montana Custom Handload, 408 S. Bozeman Ave., Bozeman, Mont. 59715.

The author's invention of a system for taking gas pressures in a revolver-which had never been feasible before-revealed truly new data on gas losses, pressures and loading techniques. An outstanding development, probably the most important one of our time.

Pressures and the Revolver

by WM. M.CALDWELL
Photos by Elmer Imthern

AS A MEMBER of the ballistic team of Speer, Incorporated, the Lewiston, Idaho, bullet-making firm, it is my pleasure to work with guns and ammunition daily. In July of 1970 the Number 8 manual was at last a reality. During the development of the much-increased revolver data section for this manual, I often wondered just how much energy was lost through the gap between barrel and cylinder. No other firearm, of course, develops pressures in the same way a revolver does. Complicated though their innards may be, the utter simplicity and reliability of their function has led most of us to forgive them for their velocity losses.

About this time Speer was all geared up to start loading 38 Special and 357 Magnum ammunition. Since daily testing of this ammunition was to be part of my job, I was more than ever concerned about the effects of the revolver gap. The ammunition market is very competitive these days, and the average buyer is quite knowledgeable about the products offered him. Efforts to soup up the old 38 Special were being shot down by split forcing cones and velocities that had a way of getting lost when fired in a revolver. With these problems in mind, new testing tools were ordered.

The new lab equipment arrived, the oscilloscope very impressive with its little TV screen looking like a piece of green graph paper. The pressure barrels were tapped for a peanut-size gadget called a quartz crystal transducer. (See fig. 2.) It looked like a spark plug from my little boy's toy car. Out of place though it seemed, the development of this transducer was to lead up to the most significant advance in revolver ammunition since the days of Sam Colt. Transducers use a quartz crystal which emits an electrical pulse when pressure is applied to it. These crystals are very carefully cut so that the electrical pulse is of a known value. This pulse, or electron, is carried by way of a coaxial cable to a charge amplifier which changes the electrons to volts. The volts are then viewed on the oscilloscope screen in the form of a pressure curve.

Crusher or Transducer

The use of lead and copper crushers has long been the standard for pressure taking in the ammunition industry. There is much discussion going on these days over which is best-the crusher or transducer-and only a saint could have the patience

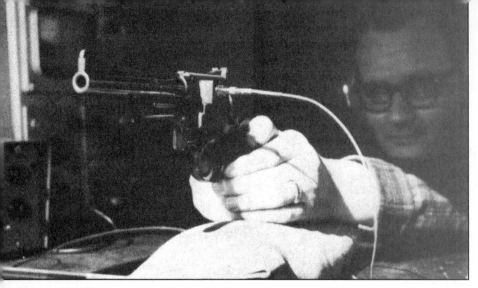

Fig. 1 — Author using 357 Magnum pressure revolver. Pressures are carried by the coaxial cable from the revolver to the charge amplifier and oscilloscope in background.

Fig. 2 — A "solid" pressure barrel herewith transducer fitted.

to keep from swearing when trying to correlate between the two.

As an example, let's assume that a given lot of 38 Special ammunition is giving crusher pressures of 16,000 psi. This same ammunition would then give about 20,000 psi in the pressure revolver. I have come to expect a difference of from 15 to 20 percent between the crusher system and the transducer-equipped revolver.

While it may be possible to install a crusher system on a revolver, it would be clumsy and slow at best. I doubt if the short time duration of revolver pressures would allow much change in the crusher cylinder. An added benefit of using the transducer for taking pressures and displaying the pressure curve on the oscilloscope screen is that time may also be taken. So far, time is the only key I've found for correlating between the two methods.

Table 1 — Pressure Time

Revolver vs. Solid Barrel
(both barrels 6")

Load #1

357 Magnum, Speer 158-gr. JSP Bulletin, 15.0 gr. 2400

| | | Pressures at | | |
	Peak	100 Microseconds	200 Microseconds	300 Microseconds
Solid Barrel	31,412 psi	23,020 psi	14,914 psi	9,682 psi
Revolver	33,558	22,338	9,996	5,100

Load #2

357 Magnum, Speer 158-gr. JSP Bullet, 9.0 gr. Unique

| | | Pressures at | | |
	Peak	100 Microseconds	200 Microseconds	300 Microseconds
Solid Barrel	31,221 psi	17,685 psi	9,979 psi	5,829 psi
Revolver	33,201	14,943	5,967	2,907

These two popular 357 Magnum loads were used to illustrate pressure vs. time in both revolvers and solid barrels. Note that while in both loads the pressure was highest in the revolver at the peak, at 300 microseconds the pressure is only about half as much in the revolver. This then explains the velocity loss in revolvers.

Fig. 3 — A Smith & Wesson K-38 with its two interchangeable cylinders, yoke and transducer.

Fig. 4 — A loaded round in the pressure cylinder, ready for testing.

Table 2
Effect of Bullet Diameter on Pressure

Load #1

357 Magnum, Speer 125-gr. JSP Bullet, dia. .357", 19.5 gr. 2400

	Average Pressure
Solid barrel	36,152 psi
Revolver	39,168

Load #2

357 Magnum, Speer 125-gr. JSP Bulletin, dia. .355", 19.5 gr. 2400

	Average Pressure
Solid barrel	35,270 psi
Revolver	33,860

Note here that the .357" diameter bullet raised pressures in the revolver by 3,000 psi. The .355" diameter bullet in Load #2 lowered pressures in the revolver by 1,500 psi. The difference between the two revolver loads is a big 5,000 psi.

The smaller bullet has an extra .002" to upset. This gives it time to cross the gap with less distortion and pressure.

Velocity loss with the smaller diameter bullet? 50 fps.

Table 3
Modern Lightweight Bullets

357 Magnum, 15.0 gr. SR-4756, Primer - CCI 500, Bullet · 110-gr. JHP, dia. .3555"

	Average Pressure
Solid barrel	38,334 psi
Revolver	33,048

Table 4
Effects of Alloy with Cast Bullets

Alloy	Wgt./grs.	Dia./inch
1-200	154	.3585
1-24	154	.3585
1-16	154	.3590
1-10	149	.3595
Type metal	140	.3595

The above bullets were cast in the same mould and sized in the same sizer. The difference in weight and diameter was caused by the alloy used.

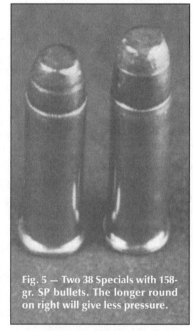

Fig. 5 — Two 38 Specials with 158-gr. SP bullets. The longer round on right will give less pressure.

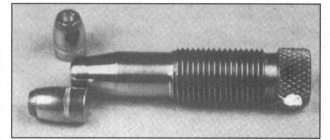

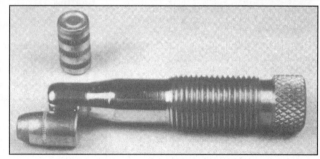

Figs. 6 and 7 — Expanders for light bullets (below left) on those seated out should have short shank of smaller diameter • Both lead and jacketed bullets that require deep seating need expander of adequate length and diameter.

After several months of pawing through pages of pressure data taken in solid (no gap) barrels by both methods, I wanted to know, more than ever, what really happened in a revolver. About this time, remembering just how small a transducer was, I began dreaming of ways to install one on a revolver. I talked to boss Ray Speer, who felt that since no one had tried taking pressure in a revolver before, we might well have another Speer "first."

The machine shop crew was supplied with a Smith & Wesson Model 27 chambered for the 357 Magnum. Like our solid test barrel it too had a barrel length of 6 inches. Within a week the original 6-shot cylinder was replaced by a single-shot cylinder which used the original yoke to swing out for normal loading and unloading. (See figs. 3 and 4.) On its left side it was tapped for the transducer. Finally, after all the years the revolver had been in use, it was at last given its own pressure system. The replacement cylinder came from the heat treatment with a soft blue finish. When the small stainless steel transducer was installed in its side it sat there shining like the eyes of a new bride. With the impatience of a groom I headed for the laboratory to try the new test gun.

High psi, Low fps

I'll never forget how disappointed I was when I tried my new invention and found that pressures were higher. Here I was, trying to find what the psi loss was for a long list of powders, and not getting the expected loss. I thought of placing a second transducer on the other side of the gap in search of a way to measure the pressure "loss" in revolvers. Because of the gap, revolvers had always lost velocity. So why not pressure? For a long time we had known about base upset or the slugging-up of bullets in revolvers, as some refer to it. Sure, we knew that, but who could have guessed that

Table 5

Pressure Changes with Cast Bullets

Load #1

38 Special, 2.7 gr. Bullseye

Bullet Alloy	Average Pressure, Solid Barrel	Average Pressure, Revolver
1-200	7,064 psi	8,568 psi
1-24	7,064	10,710
1-16	7,904	10,506
1-10	8,052	12,138
Type metal	6,916	12,138

Load #2

38 Special, 5.0 gr. Unique

Bullet Alloy	Average Pressure, Solid Barrel	Average Pressure, Revolver
1-200	12,745 psi	18,258 psi
1-24	13,783	19,482
1-16	13,239	21,012
1-10	13,289	20,400
Type metal	11,609	20,400

The bullets used in the above test are the same as the ones shown in Table 4. As may be seen, alloy is important.

Table 6

Pressure Changes Related to Seating Depth with Light Bullets

Load #1

38 Special, Speer 125-gr. JSP Bullet, dia. .356". Loaded to over-all length of 1.450", 6.5 gr. Unique.

	Average Pressure
Solid barrel	18,300 psi
Revolver	19,400

Load #2

38 Special, Speer 125-gr. JSP Bullet, dia. .356". Loaded to over-all length of 1.550", 7.5 gr. Unique.

	Average Pressure
Solid barrel	17,500 psi
Revolver	16,300

Table 7

Pressure Changes Related to Seating Depth with Heavy Bullets

Load #1

38 Special, Speer 158-gr. JSP Bullet, dia. .356". Loaded to over-all length of 1.450", 5.0 gr. Unique.

	Average Pressure
Solid barrel	15,500 psi
Revolver	16,500

Load #2

38 Special, Speer 158-gr. JSP Bullet, dia. .356". Loaded to over-all length of 1.550", 6.0 gr. Unique.

	Average Pressure
Solid barrel	17,000 psi
Revolver	16,000

Load #2 used a bullet cannelured especially for the 38 Special. This allowed a loaded length longer by .100" and one more grain of powder!

While the velocity of the two loads is the same, Load #2 gave 3,000 psi less pressure in the revolver!

In this test Load #2 again used bullets cannelured especially for the 38 Special and again one more grain of powder.

While pressures were about the same in the revolver. Load #2 this time gave 50 fps more velocity.

this unavoidable aspect could cause higher pressures. Throat diameters in revolvers will often vary as much as .002" between the 6 holes of a single cylinder. In a 357 Magnum these 6 exit holes could be from .358" to .360". In any firearm the *base* of the projectile always starts to move *first*. In the revolver, with its oversize throats, the moving base upsets even *more*. Next, another feature common only to the revolver is a funnel-shaped forcing cone leading into the barrel proper-again, a place for the bullet base to upset further. The best way to realize all this is to remove the barrel from a revolver and fire a cartridge from the cylinder only. Upon recovery note that the base of the bullet, not the point, is very much upset or expanded.

At the moment of peak pressure, we now learned, there is no gap! The much enlarged bullet has it filled. It takes an average of an extra 3,000 to 4,000 psi to swage the bullet back down to groove size. As soon as the bullet clears the gap, the powder gases then escape very rapidly, thus we get a lower velocity from our revolvers. The pressure lasts only half as long in revolvers as in solid barrels of the same length with most powders. (See Table 1.)

Variables are the things that cause people in this business many sleepless nights. The gap in revolvers will vary from .006" to .015". Even in quality revolvers I've seen some which would measure .006" on one side and .013" on the other. Barrel groove diameter for the 38 Special and 357 Magnum comes in "standard" sizes from .355" to .358". The groove diameter of the two solid test barrels used in this report is .3567". The groove diameters of the revolver barrels used in this same report are .357" for the 38 Special and .3572" for the 357 Magnum.

By realizing that these variables do exist, it is possible to use some of them to our advantage to reduce pressures. The three most important dimensions of revolver bullets which we may vary are weight, length and, most important, diameter. We have always reduced our powder charges as the bullet weight was increased, so nothing new here.

Bullet Diameters

Bullet diameter, however, is the most important dimension related to pressure in revolvers. A change in diameter makes things happen fast. A charge of 2.9 grains of Bullseye with the popular 148-gr. hollow-base wadcutter of .358" diameter in the 38 Special gives a pressure of 9,000 psi in the solid test barrel. The same load in the new pressure revolver gives 13,000 psi. Again using 2.9 grains of Bulls-eye and the 148-gr. wadcutter of .3565" diameter, the pressure is the same in both guns but the velocity is less than the velocity of the .358" diameter bullet. (See effect of diameter with jacketed bullets in Tables 2 and 3.) The 357 Magnum, operating at higher pressures, is just as quick to detect a diameter difference in the tougher jacketed bullets as is the 38 Special with its slowest load and lead bullets. (See fig. 5.)

Bullet length becomes a factor as the weight and diameter are increased. If the seating depth is deep then more time is required for the longer bullet to cross the gap, allowing more time for base upset.

Modern lightweight bullets take advantage of all these variables to gain velocity with acceptable pressures. This again is illustrated with the 110-gr. bullets used in Table 3. The 357 Magnum is limited to one seating depth-*deep*! In the 38 Special, should one choose to use jacketed bullets cannelured (crimp grooved) for the 357 Magnum, the resulting load would not only be quite short over-all but it would result in higher pressures if the load were not reduced. However, with bullets cannelured especially for the 38 Special it is possible to reduce pressures with all bullet weights. (See fig. 6 and Tables 6 and 7.) Why? Because this bullet has only a short jump to clear the gap and doesn't have time to upset and raise pressures.

Only a few years ago the available handgun bullets were of relatively large diameter. In the 38 Special and 357 Magnum, cast bullets were .358" to .359" at least, and the few jacketed bullets to be had were at least .357". The expander plug which came with a set of dies was, and unless otherwise specified still is, .3565" to .357". Most of these bullets were of semi-wadcutter, wadcutter, or round-nose design with crimp grooves near the point so the expanders were not only large but quite long.

Expander Diameters

Nowadays, especially, the guy who loads the 38 Special and 357 Magnum needs two or

three expanders. An expander of about .354" to .355" with a very short shank is necessary for short, lightweight bullets of the new smaller diameters or the heavier ones to be seated out with only a short portion of the bullet inside the case. (See fig. 7.) The workhorse among expanders for the 38 Special and 357 Magnum is still the one of medium shank length in a diameter of .3565". Wadcutters, especially the hollow-base types, need an expander of at least .358", with a shank about as long as the bullet to prevent a partial closure of the hollow base upon seating.

———°By reducing bullet weight, length, and diameter it is possible to produce revolver loads which give velocity with acceptable pressures.

Cast bullets have been around longer than the revolver. The more knowledgeable have known for many moons that different alloys will produce bullets of different diameter and weight from the same mould. (See Table 4.) Table 5 illustrates the pressure differences for each lot of these cast bullets in both solid barrels and revolvers. The very ordinary loads of 2.7 grains of Bullseye and 5.0 rains of Unique were used. As may be seen from the tables, if you cast your own bullets you should try to use as near the same alloy for each lot of bullets as possible.

It has been my experience that most of the revolvers in the Speer lab gave the best accuracy with the smaller diameter bullets. It is my belief that, as the larger bullets are swaged up and down in the forcing cone, their jackets and cores are loosened and the bullet is no longer one solid unit. The smaller bullet of .355", say, crosses the gap with much less change, resulting in a more concentric projectile in flight — hence better accuracy.

Cannelure Problems

It seems there is always one fly around to fall into the soup. The fly this time is that few jacketed bullets are available cannelured especially for the 38 Special. Most sporting goods dealers' shelves are already full of items designed to catch the sportman's eye. To carry bullets for both the 38 Special and the 357 Magnum would mean twice the inventory and shelf space. It is easier to carry bullets for the 357 Magnum which may be used in the 38 Special also, even though the resulting load is not all that it could be. The low-pressure loads developed by seating the bullets out in the 38 Special should not be used with some ball powders. The slower-burning ball powders burn best at higher than 38 Special pressures with bullets seated out to maximum over-all length. When these powders do not ignite and burn properly, squib loads will often result.

It's not always that something which starts out in disappointment ends in pleasure, as happened in the case with the pressure revolver. By finding the bullet dimensions which contribute to high pressures in revolvers, and making the necessary changes, it is now possible to load revolver ammunition at lower working pressures. The fact that the same ammunition improved accuracy and did not give large pressure and velocity changes in different guns was indeed a nice bonus.

The revolver has been with us for a long time. I still find it hard to believe that it has kept its secrets from us until after man was on the moon. Yet we have our space-age technicians to thank for giving us the transducer. Revolvers usually last a long time. If through this Speer research your revolver lasts even longer, then our efforts were not in vain.

Here are two highly unusual-not to say unique - forms of shot that few American gunners have ever heard of. Highly effective at the shorter upland ranges, too, they're not all that hard to make at home- at least until some alert outfit starts importing the FN Dispersante cubes.

Square Shot & Little Flying Saucers

by Roger Barlow

CONTRARY TO WHAT that heading strongly suggests, Barlow, has not, repeat *not*, been hitting the bottle to excess nor has he taken up the smoking of illegal forms of flora. He has, in all truth, only been shooting test patterns and killing quail, grouse, rabbits and pheasants using shot that is even more square than Lawrence Welk-and with other shot looking very much as though it hailed from another world than ours.

These unusual, even unbelievable, shot pellets were merely some of the oddities encountered in a thorough investigation of what exists in the field of "spreader," "scatter" or "brush" loads.

As a good example of the Perverseness of Things in General, consider that no sooner did birdshooters obtain those long sought-after dense patterns (through the invention of choke boring) than some of them decided they needed, on occasion, some way of opening up those tight patterns! So someone coined the phrase about "… eating your cake and having it too."

Extreme close-up look at the roughly shaped cube shot loaded by FN in their superb Dispersante shells. (Round shot is #8)

Left to right-FN *Dispersante* shotshell with cube shot. Next, W-W's brush load with X-shaped cardboard divider in the shot charge. Then the R-P scatter load with two O-S type wads in the shot charge. On the far right are Italian style disc shot made by the author. These proved to be excellent pellets for homemade spreader loads.

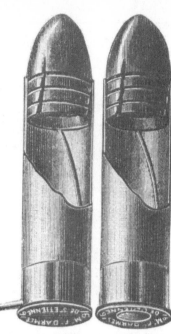

A French sporting goods catalog of 1902 listed these pinfire and centerfire rifled cartridges for use in modern smoothbores. Although the case is shown loaded with a bullet it is like those loaded with shot. To receive any spin the bullet must have been seated much deeper.

Comparison of pellets used in various scatter loads. At left are 3 of the FN cube shot (same weight as a #7 round shot)-note the bit of "tail" left on one from its fabrication; this must help it steer a suitable erratic course! The 2 round shot are #8s from a Winchester brush load. On the right are some disc shot by the author made by flattening #8 shot to varying degrees.

Or was it, "Wanting your choke and cylinder patterns, too?" This apparent contradiction has actually been achieved-in several different ways. Even before choke boring arrived, shooters knew they could control the pattern density of their muzzleloaders to some extent by varying the powder charge. With a normal shot charge and a light powder load they got more dense, even patterns. With a lighter shot load and a heavy charge of powder the pattern would be more open. Loading thinner than normal wadding over the powder and a thicker than normal wad over the shot was also said to produce a thinner and broader pattern. (And an undesirably irregular one, I suspect.)

I can't tell you who actually came up with the first genuine "spreader" shotshell but W. W. Greener in *The Gun**, published in the 1880s, shows one which produced an open pattern from the placement of two thin over-shot wads within the shot charge. This 90-odd year old scatter load is almost identical to the modern Remington-Peters type except that

*London, 1881.

the Greener load used a very thick final O-S wad. Winchester-Western "brush" loads spread their # 8 shot in a thin, broad pattern by means of a cardboard X-shaped divider in the shot charge, and they close the case with a folded crimp.

Both of these U.S.-made spreader shells give something approaching improved cylinder patterns from most modified and even full choke barrels, with the distribution of shot being surprisingly even-considering all that cardboard mixed up in the shot charge; yet on occasion there are patterns with sizeable gaps.

The FN *Dispersante* shotshells, from Belgium, achieve their dispersion effect through purely aerodynamic means-with square or cube shot of about # 7 size which have a very erratic flight pattern. These shells provide a somewhat more rapid opening up of the pattern at close range, as well as a more consistently even distribution of the shot, than can be managed with round shot plus those in-the — charge wads.

The Italian scatter loads carry little *disco volante* or flying saucer type pellets, securing a rapid and extensive opening of the pattern through the erratic paths traveled by these unusually shaped pellets. Although I didn't have the opportunity of shooting patterns with factory loads of this type, my own handloads made up with #8 and #6 shot-which I flattened myself in my basement flying saucer factory-performed reasonably well, although not as consistently as did the FN cube shot.

I'm amazed that Winchester-Western and Remington-Peters stick to the card-in — the-shot system, as it must be rather complicated to load these shells; with the cube or disc shot, loading would be a straightforward machine process, easy *and* economical.

I'm also surprised that someone here in the U.S. hasn't either imported or manufactured cube or disc shot. Surely it would be a very simple mechanical operation to take square lead wire of the correct dimension and just chop off "pel-

Even a 1-oz. load of #6s in an IC barrel is going to put too many shot into a pheasant at close range. Waiting until that bird reached the nearby trees would have more than likely meant losing him. The answer-as with much upland game hunting-a cylinder bore or a spreader load!

Here's where a quail hunter needs a scatter load, even if he is using an IC barrell When those birds blast out of this hedgerow they'll be out of sight before they've been airborne 25 yards-so they'll have to be dropped at not much beyond 15-18 yards. This can be done with a light, fast handling gun, but the broadest possible pattern is needed as below.

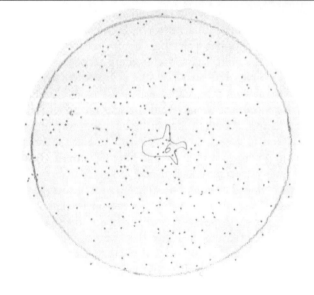

lets" at a great rate, or to flatten commercial round shot by passing them between rollers.

Considering the vast number of over-choked guns used for rabbit and upland bird hunting, there *should* be a substantial market for such products. I did say, "should be," for I suspect there really isn't a great demand for spreader loads, largely because so few people know about them or fully understand their usefulness.

Even an improved cylinder barrel throws a somewhat overly dense pattern for many shots at quail and woodcock and could definitely benefit from the use of brush loads in such situations. Certainly modified and full choke barrels are far too destructive of game when used at 20-30 yards, but would kill without mutilating one's birds if turned into improved cylinder barrels through the use of spreader loads.

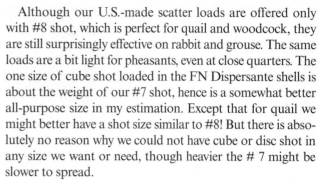

Although our U.S.-made scatter loads are offered only with #8 shot, which is perfect for quail and woodcock, they are still surprisingly effective on rabbit and grouse. The same loads are a bit light for pheasants, even at close quarters. The one size of cube shot loaded in the FN Dispersante shells is about the weight of our #7 shot, hence is a somewhat better all-purpose size in my estimation. Except that for quail we might better have a shot size similar to #8! But there is absolutely no reason why we could not have cube or disc shot in any size we want or need, though heavier the # 7 might be slower to spread.

While spreader loads (of any type) can provide a heavily-choked gun with a good 20-30 yard "quail pattern," unfortunately they cannot endow an overlong, heavy and slow handling "duck" gun with the lively feel a genuine upland game gun should have. Of course there are a great many guns in use for rabbit, quail, grouse, woodcock and pheasants which do have fair "upland" handling characteristics, though they may be a bit too tightly choked for much of this sort of shooting. A spreader load in the first barrel will do much to make these guns more efficient for this work.

In fact, with a double, choked IC and modified (or full), one might well use a spreader load in the more heavily choked barrel-and fire this one first; the IC pattern would usually be just right (with regular shot loads) for the second shot, or for the second bird, under upland conditions. This would be one of the few times a selective single trigger would

Quailburgers on the wing! Thai's sure to be the result of that shot if one of those birds is well centered-regardless of how that gun is choked (unless it's completely UNchoked) and perfectly illustrates the situation which calls for the first shot to be some sort of a spreader load.

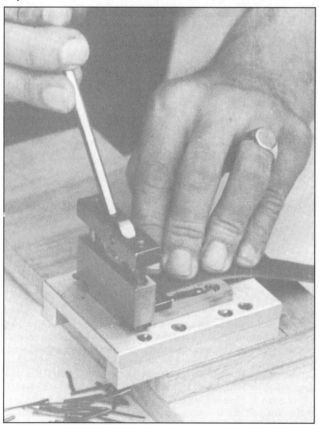

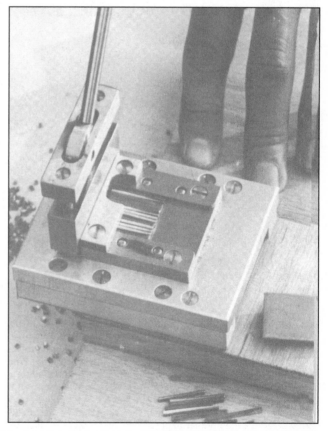

Left-Using David Baker's cutting device, first, strips are cut from a 2-inch wide roll of soft lead. A ledge behind the cutting blade acts as a stop, thereby measuring equal width strips which are then fed through the machine lengthwise (right), to produce 13 cube shot at each stroke.

serve some genuinely useful purpose.

What about the man with a modified or full choke pump or autoloader? How is he to take advantage of a spreader load for that first shot at close-in, heavy-cover birds? Well, it's not all that complicated or difficult to stuff a scatter load in the chamber and normal loads in the magazine, is it, then reload the same way after a shot or shots have been fired.

This situation does indeed illustrate the shortcomings of the repeating scattergun, which serves well enough, when all the shooting is at targets roughly the same distance away; but it is seen to be vastly inferior to the double, which provides the shooter with an instant choice of pattern (through choke and/or load) to effectively meet widely varying field requirements. The first shot may have to be made at 20 yards, the next one might have to be taken at nearer 35 or 40 yards. *One* choke and one *pattern* in a multi-

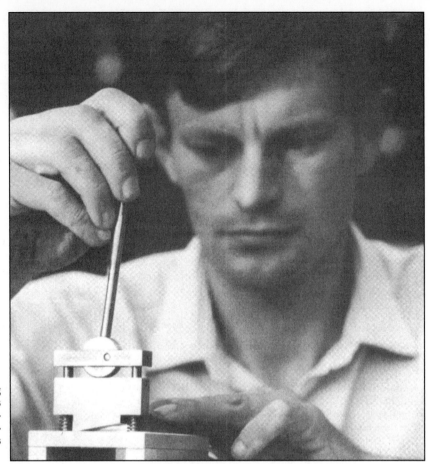

David Baker, the author's English shooting friend and associate in investigating various aspects of the sport, demonstrates his version of a cutting device for making exceptionally precise cube shot. The cam provides a powerful central push on the blade.

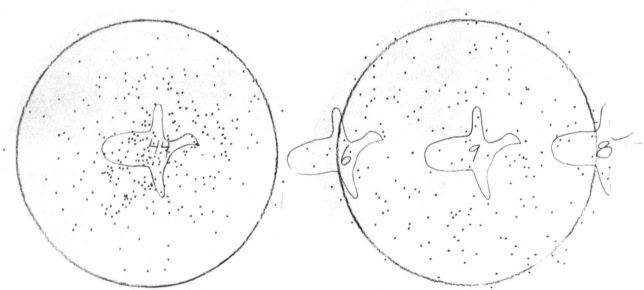

Left — One of the most noted shooting authorities once wrote that the most useful, all-round choke is the modified or half-choke, and that in his experience a modified 12 bore with 1¼ ors. of #6 shot will grass a pheasant to about 45 yards, yet will not shoot him to pieces at 20–25 yards. The above pattern, made with a modified barrel using 1¼ ozs. of #6 shot, pretty clearly shows that a bird centered by this charge at 25 (not even 20) yards isn't going to be worth bringing home! Reducing that shot charge to 1⅛ ozs. of #6 shot will reduce the number of pellets in a pheasant at 25 yards to somewhere between 20 and 30, which is still too many. Even a light 1-oz. load is going to put more than 3 times the necessary number of shot into a 25 yard pheasant, while still handicapping the shooter with a narrow spread of pattern a modified barrel gives. In a modified or full choke barrel at under 30 yards a spreader load of some type is certainly called for-unless you're such a great shot that you can count on hitting those birds with just the thin edge of those tight patterns! Right-Same modified choke barrel but this time shooting FN *Dispersante* cube shot. A pheasant size target will receive sufficient pellets for a kill out to 30 yards; and even at 20 yards will not be excessively damaged. Equally important is the fact that there is a wide and even distribution of pellets over a greater area, making a kill more likely even though one's hold is not perfect. This pattern would also be very effective for grouse or rabbit.

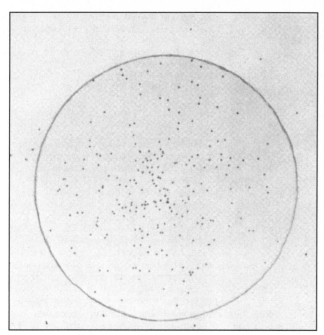

Even a true cylinder barrel delivers a high concentration of shot in the center of a small pattern area at close range. Yet there are occasions when rabbits and even pheasants must be taken at 12–20 yards.

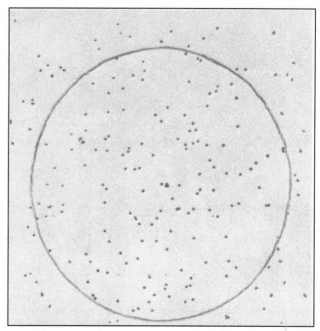

The same shot load fired in the lightly rifled spreader barrel of a Bretton O-U shows remarkably even dispersion of the pellets over a usefully wide area, makes a superb pattern for any necessary close shooting.

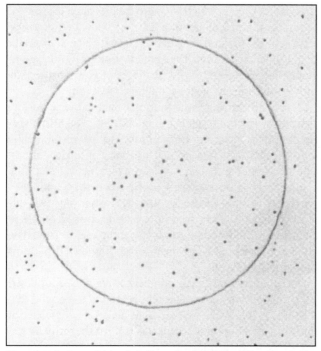

Use of a shot cup type of shell made very little difference to the pattern thrown by the French rifled barrel. But this pattern shows that this rapid means of obtaining wide shot dispersion is still effective with #6 shot for large birds and rabbits out to beyond 20 yards.

shot scattergun is just about as satisfactory an approach to the practical needs of the upland game hunter as would be just *one* gear in an automobile. It is mighty rare, indeed, when I want 2 or 3 quick consecutive cylinder patterns or the same number of consecutive half- or full-choke ones!

This is one of the main reasons so many upland game shooters much prefer doubles. Sure, they're more expensive, but they're the only really satisfactory way for us to be certain of having the most suitable pattern for whatever circumstances must be dealt with when our game flushes.

I guess it would be a fair assumption to claim that pumps and autoloaders can benefit even more from using scatter loads than will doubles.

Just as we are far too much in the habit of buying our shotguns too tightly choked for the use to which we put most of them, so do we tend to value most of those shells which, we are told, will deliver "better" patterns. Better for what? Better at what range? For smashing clay targets? For duck and geese at 50 yards or more? Or for quail, rabbits and woodcock at 18-25 yards?

Our modern shells, with more effective wads and plastic shot protector cups, do deliver patterns having a more uniform distribution of the shot charge and in which slow moving, badly deformed pellets are virtually eliminated. Yet the value of these "advantages" of our latest shotshells (those slightly tighter and more dense patterns) are vastly over emphasized as far as rabbit and upland game hunters are concerned. Most upland game is killed at well under 30 yards, if not under 25, where pattern regularity is far less a matter for concern than it is out beyond 35 yards.

Slower moving, deformed pellets may arrive at the 40 yard target (clay or feathered) too late, too far off course and with far too little remaining energy to be of any use; but at 20-30 yards these deformed pellets are very little behind the main body of the shot charge, are not too far off course to be of use and they still have sufficient striking energy for effective penetration. It is entirely possible that our modern shot protector shells, which deliver those usefully more dense

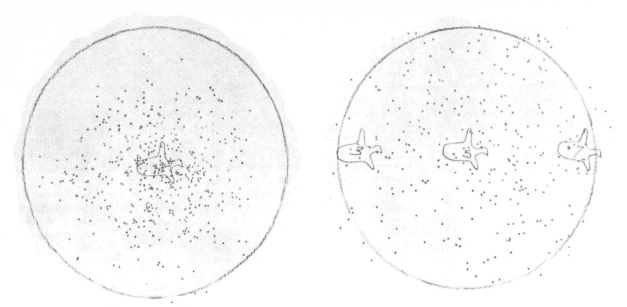

Left — The popular modified choke with the equally popular load of 1⅛ -oz. of #8 shot is often used on small upland game-with the above results at average range on a quail size target. Right — What is wanted is something like the pattern shot by a 100-year — old cylinder bore Purdey.

patterns for Skeet, trap and waterfowl shooters, may very well be unnecessarily "good" for the needs of the upland game shoter who takes his game at relatively close range and wants enough of it left for eating purposes. This would be even more true for the man using a gun made a few years ago, one choked in relation to the shotshells of that period. (Today some chokes are bored with a couple of points less constriction to compensate for the new type of shells.)

As far as the matter of the deformed shot being able to effectively penetrate a game bird is concerned, consider those spreader loads of cube or disc shot which are made up of nothing but "deformed" shot of the most distorted shapes imaginable-yet in many situations are fully as effective as any load of perfect, undeformed round shot. Certainly the penetration of the "imperfect" square or disc shot is more than adequate at the 18-30 yard range at which most upland game is killed.

In France many rabbit and bird hunters find a very broad pattern (wider even than true cylinder) so useful that often they have one barrel of a double gun bored cylinder and then, to further spread the shot charge, *rifle* it with broad, slow-twist, shallow grooves! Such a barrel, shooting any ordinary shotshell, produces a wide and non-mutilating pattern useful for taking game as close-in as 12 yards and effective out to around 25 yards. With the second barrel choked IC or modified, such a gun has an effective operating range of from about 12 to 45 yards-what more could any upland game hunter want?

As I have one of these rifled or *canon raye* barrels on a light and fast handling Bretton O-U, I can vouch for this range of performance. The accompanying patterns were shot with this gun.

The French shooter has long shown an interest in wide patterns. In 1898 M. Galand, a Parisian gunmaker, patented and began manufacturing a rifled shotshell. His paper case apparently had a metal liner with prominent rifling of fairly rapid twist (1 in 12) which is said to have resulted in a spread of no less than 50 inches at a little over 20 yards. Another version of the Galand shell had rifling with a twist of about 1 in 25, which reduced the spread of the shot charge to around 35 inches at 22 yards-the degree of gun choke apparently not having much effect, one way or the other.

(A similar cartridge was the somewhat earlier Courtier, also deeply rifled internally but intended for use with a special ball or slug having deep grooves to match the rifling to insure that it would not "strip" but would get a useful amount of spin in that short distance of contact.)

Ingenious as were those Galand rifled shotshells, they eventually fell into disuse for various reasons; one was difficult extraction. They could not have been inexpensive to manufacture and were undoubtedly more costly than some other solutions to the problem of getting broad patterns from a choked barrel.

Under no circumstances can the scattergun be considered a long range arm and we should stop trying to pretend that it is. It is precisely its "scatter" that makes it so effective at short range. We should accept this fact for the virtue that it is and take full advantage of it.

Give thought, then, to buying or making a box or two of "scatter loads" for your next upland game hunt, unless you're already shooting with a true cylinder barrel-that's what is needed at close range; and it doesn't matter whether you come by it by the way your barrel is bored or the way your shells are loaded!

The modern American one-gun shooter who needs, or thinks he needs, a heavily choked gun for some of his huvnting, should certainly get better acquainted with some of today's short range scatter loads. It's like having a spare cylinder or improved cylinder barrel in your pocket-and for free!

As for handloading these specialized shotshells, it requires no more skill or knowledge than does the making of the normal types.

Let us start with the simplest of all spreader loads-the Remington-Peters type. No special equipment or components are required-unless the over-shot card wads are now considered to be something out of the ordinary.

Powder and wads suitable for the desired shot charge (1 – 1⅛ oz. 12 ga., 1 oz. 16 ga., ⅞-1 oz. 20 ga.) are inserted into the primed case and seated with the appropriate pressure. However, as the shot charge must be divided into three fairly equal portions it requires special handling. I use the charge bar and drop tube of my favorite Honey Bair press to first put each metered charge into (what else?) a whisky "shot cup." I then pour from this into a clear plastic vial which has a mark on its side indicating exactly one-third of the selected shot load. This first third of the shot is poured into a case already charged with powder and wadding and a thin over-shot card seated on top of it; the second third of the shot load is added plus another O-S card. Finally, the case is closed with either a roll or folded crimp-depending upon the amount of case available for this purpose.

The Winchester-Western type of scatter load is faster and easier to load as the shot charge can be dropped directly into the case once the X divider has been inserted. Cutting these cardboard X dividers is a job best delegated to a youngster eager to be helpful. I close these shells with a normal folded crimp, same as the factory W-W loads.

Disc shot tends to jam in the charge bars of all the loading presses I've tried and, as true-weight charges won't be thrown anyway, I weigh each charge after scooping the *plomb disco* out of a bowl with an old fashioned shot measure. So far I've made all my disc shot by simply flattening round shot with a hammer blow. To somewhat accelerate this rather slow process I ground a slight depression in my anvil where at least half a dozen pellets can be placed without rolling away before being flattened.

The degree of flattening will, of course, vary somewhat no matter how carefully one gauges the hammer blows; but for all practical purposes this doesn't really matter, especially if maximum dispersion is desired.

However, if greater uniformity of flattening is wanted, just drill small holes for the appropriate size shot in a thin sheet of hard steel having a thickness equal to what you want the flattened shot to measure. A slight chamfering of the hole edges would facilitate their filling by merely spilling and rolling the shot across the plate. Once the holes are filled the shot can be quickly and uniformly flattened by striking with a large diameter hammer. Round shot could also be quickly turned into disc shot by passing it between a pair of adjustable steel rollers but such a device (somewhat on the lines of an old fashioned clothes wringer) would not be easy to build in a home workshop.

Another way of making *plomb disco* (perhaps the easiest of all) is to take lead wire of a suitable diameter and simply cut off discs with a paper cutter! A number of lengths of wire can be laid side by side so as to produce a dozen pellets at each stroke of the cutting blade.

Although square or cube shot isn't capable of quite as rapid dispersion or of such wide patterns as disc shot, nevertheless it gives adequately rapid spread of the shot charge along with the most uniform and dependable patterns of all spreader loads; it should be considered by any handloader planning to brew some shotshells of this type.

Here the only problem is obtaining the shot itself, but until some enterprising organization imports it from FN, or makes it here, we'll have to make our own. Again, because lack of uniformity in size, shape or symmetry is more of an advantage than otherwise, some fairly crude procedures are entirely permissible.

First, get some soft sheet lead, about .085"-.090" thick, from a local plumber and then simply cut narrow strips from this with a paper cutter. Next, pass a number of these strips under the cutting blade again and off come your very own square shot! Just *how* square they are depends entirely upon how carefully you work but slightly rectangular and irregular shot will spread, penetrate and kill birds and rabbits just as well as will perfect examples.

This sort of soft lead cube shot will also jam in most charge bars so I generally drop the thrown charges onto a scale and adjust accordingly. Although FN closes their cube-shot cases with a frangible cork O-S wad and a roll crimp I prefer to use the more conveniently made folded crimp, for the pattern spread is not noticeably affected either way.

Making your own scatter loads, especially when you use home-made disc or cube shot, adds spice and novelty to this activity, as well as providing some highly useful shells not usually obtainable at your local gunshop. Such shells will not only put more game in your bag in many situations but will also confound your less enterprising shooting companions. They'll never believe you're killing birds with square shot or little flying saucers-until after they have paid off an ill-considered bet you've cleverly suckered them into.

29
ABC's of Reloading

A detailed and comprehensive report on the methods and advantages of substituting smokeless powder for Cordite or black powder propellants in yesteryear's big bore rifles.

Smokeless Loads for Double Rifles

by RAY MARRIAGE and DICK VOGT
— as told to Bert Popowski.

DOUBLE RIFLES EXISTED in the 18th century, perhaps earlier, but exact knowledge about the proper rate of twist for rifled barrels was then unknown, and the complicated art of properly "regulating" the barrels had yet to be mastered. The earliest double rifles were effective only at very short ranges and on large game targets. Even some of the earliest "best quality" percussion doubles — several of which we've worked with extensively — gave trouble. Each barrel shot to a different point of impact, thus good accuracy from them was impossible at any range beyond 40 yards.

Building double rifles presents unique problems. How such rifles *should not* be built, and the reasons therefore, is probably as good a way as any to indicate what double rifle construction requires to provide satisfactory accuracy.

Let's imagine a double rifle built with barrel bores exactly parallel to each other. The barrels would then lie to either side of the center of balance of the rifle. When the right barrel was fired it would have a tendency to whip somewhat to the right and the left barrel would whip to the left when fired. The heavier the charge-bullet load, which would produce a correspondingly greater recoil, the greater would be this sidewise whip or vibration.

In short, as each barrel was fired, it would tend to rebound away from the inert mass of the unfired barrel. This effect would be somewhat similar to resting a rifle barrel directly against a vertical support, such as a tree trunk for instance, or some other obstacle to its natural vibration. Even when simply shouldered and held in the hands in the offhand position the net result would be widely separated points-of-impact of bullets from the two parallel barrels. The shooter of such an improperly built rifle would have to know where each barrel hit and compensate by holding off accordingly from true line-of-sight.

A secondary effect has to do with the velocity of the projectiles. The slower its velocity the longer the projectile would remain in the barrel and the more it would be thrown to right or left, ordinarily, depending on which barrel was first fired.

This problem can be solved only by spacing the barrel axes farther apart at the breech than at the muzzle, so they have a definite convergence from rear to front. As noted above, the greater the amount of recoil and the lower the velocity of the bullets the greater will be the amount of convergence required to compensate for this sidewise whip or vibration. Thus an 8-bore rifle will always be found to have considerably more convergence than a more modern caliber, such as a 303 or a 240. However, even in a rifle of small caliber, light recoil and high velocity, some convergence of the barrels is required. Such inaccuracy could cost a hunter his life were he after big, tough and dangerous game.

Experienced doubles gunmakers doubtless learn to make an educated guess as to the amount of convergence required when building a given rifle. But the final adjustment can only be done by the "try" man, who continues to test-fire the rifle, adjusting the regulating wedges and resoldering the barrels together until the accuracy qualities of the rifle are acceptable. Such work requires considerable time and skilled experience, which explains why double rifles are vastly more costly than any other type of firearms. Additionally, while these rifles are not usually intended for use with high-intensity cartridges, they all do operate at higher pressures than other double-barreled firearms — such as ordinary shotguns, for example. Consequently, very careful fitting of all parts is absolutely essential.

Such care in manufacture explains why double rifles made by the better gunsmiths of 70 to 80 years ago are usually found to be sound and tight, even after extensive hard use. Some of these older rifles have been reproofed for modern Cordite loads. This practice is not desirable in that it merely gives the shooter reasonable assurance that modern loads will not destroy his gun. Further, guns which were originally regulated for bullets of specific weight, driven by specified charges of black powder, would print properly with modern factory ammunition only by the sheerest accident or unless used with those factory loads designated "Nitro for Black Powder" arms. However, continued use of such heavier modern loads, even if they did group well, might eventually crack the rifle frames.

Fact and Fiction About Double Rifles

Much misinformation has been passed on as gospel fact about the large English double rifles. Repetition, by word of mouth and also in print, has given these comments the aura of "basic facts." Some years ago the bar-stool set magnified the recoil of these rifles to truly heroic proportions. Men who had never fired anything more potent than a 270 or a 30-06 became "instant experts" in describing the massive, even crippling recoil of such doubles as the 470 Nitro or anything similar. Broken shoulders or collar bones, said these oracles, were frequently suffered. Such reports, of course, are pure hog-wash.

The fact is that rifles as potent as the 458 Winchester, which corresponds to the English 450×3¼-inch Nitro Express, can be fired from bench rest without undue discomfort — given a rifle of adequate weight. Neither should be fired from the prone position for obvious reasons; first, the butt rests directly on the unprotected collarbone and, second, the shooter's body cannot give with the recoil. The really big ones, from the 577 on up, can be fired from any position from which the shooter's body is entirely free to move with the recoil.

(Just in passing let me mention that Ray Marriage regularly shoots an 8-bore double from a sitting position. Ray weighs 120 pounds as he steps from the shower but enjoys shooting this rifle. Loaded with 20 grains of 4759, 350 grains of FG and a 1,330-gr. bullet, this powerhouse always rolls him over from a sitting position. But there is no bruising, no fractures or any other recoil damage.)

For the average man, standing is the best position for shooting the big doubles. It's quite permissible to use a rest, such as the side of a tree, providing one hand is between the rifle and the object used to steady the gun. Direct contact between the rifle and the support will cause interference with the recoil cycle and will usually alter the point of bullet impact. Standing, while resting the fore-end over a bedroll on the hood of a car is a good steady position when testing a rifle or ammunition for accuracy — but again, rest the fore-end in the palm. However, adequate protection must be given to the hood of the vehicle. The first shot fired from an 8-bore in that position, Ray told me, scorched the paint so badly that a repaint job was needed. So much for recoil. The best way to tolerate it is by learning to roll with it.

Load Development

Another misleading belief deals with the supposed inflexibility of the doubles in regard to the ammunition which can be successfully used in them. Each rifle, it's true, was built

British loading tools — at upper left an 8-gauge brass-case Paradox cartridge, with various bullets below. The tool at the center is a 1 2-bore re- and decapper, to its right a crimper and a bullet sizer. The pliers-like tool puts circular indents into 8-bore Paradox brass cases. The mould casts the 8-gauge hollow-point bullets seen near the mould.

to shoot properly with a given load and many of the better doubles are clearly marked to indicate that load. In such cases the assembling of suitable loads is greatly simplified.

It is only when a rifle is not marked with its intended ammo requirements that the shooter is faced with a problem. A 450, for example, might have been originally regulated for a given charge of powder and a bullet ranging from lighter than 300 grains up to one heavier than 500 grains. Considerable experimenting might then be required before an accurate load for that particular double was found.

However, the search for a suitable load need not be all guesstimation. A very valuable reference book is *Cartridges of the World*, authored by Frank C. Barnes and edited by John T. Amber. This cites the original loadings offered by the English manufacturers so the handloader can start by duplicating the black-powder loads or testing equivalent loadings of suitable smokeless powders. The main thing is to start with a load which may be assumed to be safe to fire and then alter such loadings as indicated hereinafter to make the rifle group its shots properly from both barrels.

If the bullet chosen is much too light or too heavy it may not be possible to develop a load which groups properly with it. For instance, the first experimental load may print to the right of the point of aim from the right barrel, and to the left with the left barrel. In nearly all cases the cure for this is to increase the powder charge, assuming that this can be done without producing excessive chamber pressures. This increased powder charge will slightly increase the recoil and thus increase the amount of sidewise whip and might be assumed to make the barrels shoot even more to right and left than with the original lighter load. However, the increase in velocity and thus the decrease in the time the bul-

let remains in the bore, will nearly always more than offset the effect of increased recoil whip.

On the other hand, if the barrels crossfire — the left delivering to the right of the point of aim and the right to the left of that point — it will nearly always be found that the powder charges should be reduced, thereby leaving the bullet within the bore for a longer period of time while it is exposed to a corrective sidewise whip. Conversely, if the powder charge is left constant and the bullet weight is changed, substitution of a lighter bullet will result in higher velocity. This will have the same effect as increasing the powder charge. Because of different weights of rifles and other individual peculiarities, it is conceivable that reverse effects could be encountered. To date, however, this situation has not been found by Marriage in working with any of many test rifles.

Using the above technique it is occasionally possible to develop reduced loads which will shoot very accurately from some big-bore doubles Since shooting about 20 full-power loads is about all any big-bore devotee wants to handle during any given day, such reduced loads provide considerably more shooting. Such practice is invaluable in prepping for a foreign big game safari or simply for the plain pleasure of handloading for and shooting a handsome and accurate specimen of double rifle craftsmanship. Admittedly, too, there's a certain amount of pride and prestige involved in being able to hand a visitor such a rifle and invite him to try a few shots. Reduced loads permit him to enjoy this without suffering the rather impressive recoil of fullpower loads.1

Marriage who formerly operated Montana Custom Handloads,* made a project of developing reduced loads for the 577/3-inch Nitro Express. He found that three different rifles of this caliber shot very well with 588-gr. cast bullets ahead of from 56 to 62 grains of 2400 powder — the exact charge for top accuracy depending on the individual rifles. Inasmuch as 577 factory bullets cost 30¢ apiece the saving on such cast bullets for extensive test shooting was significant. These reduced loads had a muzzle velocity of about 1730 feet per second compared to around 1950 fps for full-power loads — and were just as accurate as any full-power factory loads.

Handloading of such English cartridges offers another valuable advantage which should not be overlooked. American powders are much cooler burning than English Cordite and their proper use may be expected to substantially prolong barrel life. One look through the bores of a double which has been extensively and exclusively used with Cordite loads by a professional hunter is often abundant reason for the wise handload-er to eschew Cordite forever. Finally, since Cordite is not available for reloading, this automatically forces the use of less erosive American smokeless powders.

Tools and Components

Gathering specific information on the components, tools and services for handloading for double rifles is often frustrating. Therefore, hereafter, the names of various firms will

Ray Marriage was forced out of business by the Gun Control Act of 1968, as were others who had been furnishing cartridges and components by mail.

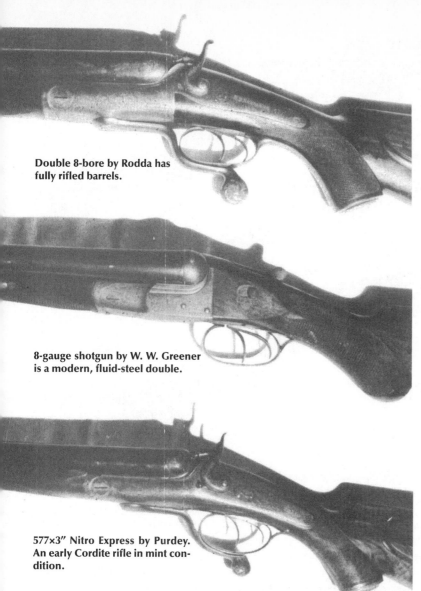

Double 8-bore by Rodda has fully rifled barrels.

8-gauge shotgun by W. W. Greener is a modern, fluid-steel double.

577×3″ Nitro Express by Purdey. An early Cordite rifle in mint condition.

of powder, such as 140 grains of 4831 in the 577/3-inch Nitro Express. The seating of Berdan primers is accomplished exactly as with our conventional Boxer primers. It is most easily done by the use of the RCBS Precision Priming Device. The extraction of fired Berdan primers is more complicated but should not be regarded as serious since it simply adds one additional step to conventional loading procedures.

If possible, a European three-legged re- and decapper should be obtained but they are often difficult to find. A simple Berdan decapper is manufactured in the United States by Lachmiller Engineering Co. The lip of this tool should be carefully ground to fit the radius of the cartridge case head on which it is to be used, but many are used "as is." With care it is also possible to drill a very small hole through the fired primer, toward the edge, after which the primer may be removed with a suitable pick or awl. Whichever method is used, the beginner should have little trouble after a bit of practice, during which he may damage a few primer pockets or anvils in getting this experience!

The hydraulic method of removing Berdan primers should be avoided completely. This is done by filling the case with water, then a slip-fit plug is inserted into the mouth of the case and given a sharp rap to drive the fired primer from its pocket by hydraulic pressure. There are several serious disadvantages to this method. A plug which properly fits a case fired in one chamber will not necessarily fit a case from the rifle's other chamber. It is sometimes desirable to deprime a case which has been resized but not fired and here a plug of still another size would have to be used. This hydraulic method is messy, subjects the walls of the cartridge case to heavy pressure and can cause bulging. Any other method is superior to this one.

For black-powder loads, or for small quantities of smokeless in small cases, it is better to use less powerful primers than the *hot* Ky-noch. Oregon Ammunition Service offers RWS 1786 Berdan shotshell primers which are fine for rifle cartridges and Godfrey Reloading Supply sells RWS 1784 rifle primers, which also work well. Although the hard tough brass of Kynoch primers makes them more difficult to seat and extract — compared to RWS primers — this should not be the sole factor in deciding which primer is best for specific purposes in double rifle loads.

Over-powder wads should be used in all except bottleneck cases. Any competent machinist can make a custom wad-cutter at small cost to cut wads from cork-gasket material, and plumber's supply houses often have a variety of gasket cutters. It is just as cheap and far more convenient to use either .135- or .200-inch card wads made for use in shotshells. The Alcan Company manufactures 32-gauge wads

be mentioned in connection with certain products which might be difficult to locate. Other firms may offer equivalent services or products, but those subsequently named are known to be reliable and their full addresses are listed at the conclusion of this article.

For factory-loaded ammunition for any currently existing caliber write to Oregon Ammunition Service. This firm also stocks empty unprimed cartridge cases, bullets and Berdan primers. From this large stock it is often possible to select and alter an available cartridge case to work just fine for an obsolete caliber. RCBS offers suitable loading dies and shell holders. RCBS has dies for many foreign calibers and will make every effort to help with any specific reloading problems.

Lyman offers a fantastic range of bullet moulds. If they don't have a mould suitable for your purpose they'll make a special custom mould for $100. A bit expensive, but it isn't too much to pay for a lifetime of shooting pleasure.

The most potent Berdan caps available are Kynoch primers, available from Oregon Ammunition Service. Their use is indicated where it is necessary to ignite a very large charge

Three more double rifles from the Maynard Buehler collection. From the top — W. & J. Jeffery 600 Nitro Express; 475 No. 2 by Halliday of London and another Jeffery, this one a 400 Nitro Express.

which are perfect for use in caliber 500 cases and their 24-gauge wads are ideal for the 577. They save punching out your own wads one at a time.

It is almost impossible to seat properly fitted wads in bottleneck cases, except with full-case black powder loads, though you can try attaching card, greased fiber or other wads to the base of the bullet with grease or a mild adhesive. But it occasionally works very well to fill the over-powder space in them with a pinch of Nylon or Dacron fiber. Such fiber filler material, plus an excellent bullet lubricant, is available from Javelina Products, Inc.

In black-powder loads the over-powder wads offer some protection to the bases of bullets, similar to that provided by metallic gas-checks. To a degree these also act as bore conditioners, wiping out the residue of each shot. In smokeless loads the over-powder wad holds the powder in a uniform position within the cases, thus promoting more uniform ignition. When the load is fired this wad is often fragmented, leaving the muzzle in small pieces. For this reason it is also wise to seat a similar wad at the base of the bullet, to act as gas-check and bore conditioner. When using cast bullets an added refinement is to pour a very thin layer of melted bullet lubricant over this uppermost wad.

Clean burning loads are essential in double rifles, for a single particle of unburned powder, lodged under the extractor or in a couple of other places, may put the rifle out of commission until it is located and removed. If a load isn't burning cleanly more and tighter wadding is generally indicated. Other solutions may require heavier bullets or a faster burn-

ing powder. Usually the larger calibers are the ones found to be most difficult to match with suitable loads.

In the 12-bore rifle, using Alcan brass cases with all excess space in the case filled with 10-gauge wads, it was found that 3031 powder burned cleanly only when used with bullets heavier than 800 grains. For bullets weighing under 800 grains it was found necessary to use faster powders. A heavy charge of 3031 was tried with 900-grain bullets but this load did not print properly and was used only as a proof load.

It should be here noted that *experimenting with large calibers, heavy bullets and fast powders is a highly dangerous pastime!* The development of good smokeless loads for the 12-bore proved to be so time-consuming, and presented so many problems, that the idea of working up similar loads for the 10- and 8-bores was abandoned. Some risk of damage to the rifles and injury to the shooter would have been involved. One cannot, nowadays, merely go to the nearest hardware store and buy a new set of 8-bore rifle barrels!

Cast vs. Jacketed Bullets

In casting bullets it should be remembered that changing the alloy of the bullet metal will not only change the hardness but will also change the weight of the finished bullets. In large bullets this change in weight can easily become significant. For instance, when using Lyman mould 585213-S to cast .585-inch bullets they were found to vary from 585- to 605-grains, depending on the type of alloy used. This bullet is a most useful one since it can be used in both black-powder and smokeless powder rifles. To lubricate this bul-

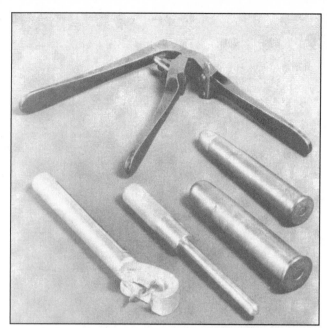

At top is the once-common, and usually German-made, 3-legged tool for de- and recapping Berdan primers. Below is the type of Berdan primer decapper marketed by Lachmiller Engineering, these offered ordinarily only for 8mm Mauser cases and similar case-head sizes. The cartridges seen are a 577-500 (above) and the 600x3″ Express.

let it is best to purchase a .580-inch size-and-lube die — the largest die of this kind supplied by Lyman — and hone out the upper portion of the die so that the .585-inch bullet is lu-bricated but not sized.

Some writers claim that jacketed bullets will cause rapid and noticeable barrel wear in older rifles, whose barrel steel is softer than that which is now used. As a result only cast bullets were used in barrels known to be made of mild steel. Extensive correspondence with two major bullet-making firms indicates considerable doubt about such barrel wear and that further research is needed in this field. Both manufacturers have conducted reasonably extensive tests and have concluded that jacketed bullets do not cause abnormal barrel wear *unless steel-jacketed bullets are used. They believe that gas-cutting is the basic cause of all barrel wear.* Thus if jacketed bullets are large enough to completely fill the barrel grooves, are given sufficient velocity to slightly upset the bases, and if slightly over-sized gas-sealing wads are used, then perhaps the use of jacketed bullets is not nearly as harmful as has been previously believed.

Reloaders curious about the muzzle velocities of their handloads can get excellent chronographs from Oehler Research, Avtron, B-Square, and others. See our Directory of the Arms Trade pages at the back of this book.

Repairs or alterations of double rifles are occasionally required. The sleeving or reboring of doubles should be avoided whenever possible.

As of mid-1971, Westley Richards was still rebarreling doubles from $600-$800 with six-months delivery, which will amply take care of most such jobs. Rechambering to

an available case while leaving the barrels as they are does not usually affect a rifle's shooting characteristics. Snapp's Gun Shop does such rechambering, including lengthening the 2¾ -inch chambers of 577 rifles to 3-inch capacity. Another highly desirable conversion offered by this shop is re-chambering 8-bore shotguns or rifles to accept industrial paper and plastic cases. These cases are inexpensive, readily available and the alteration is so slight that all other types of 8-gauge cases can still be used. Fine gunsmithing of double rifles is done by Iver Henriksen and by Purcell's Gun Shop. The latter firm can also re-regulate double rifles if such adjustment is needed.

All loads shown in our Table have been fired in double rifles by R. C. Vogt, Ray Marriage or both. Mr. Vogt has extensive notes, compiled over many years, on load and rifle performance. He was enormously helpful in loaning rifles for testing, test-firing experimental loads and supplying data and comments thereon.

Nearly all of the loads listed were chronographed, except in the few cases where they were found to print the same as with factory ammunition. All of them gave good accuracy in the rifles in which they were tested, but for best accuracy in other rifles, slight variations of these loads should be tried. While these suggested loads were definitely safe to fire in the test]rifles, that does not positively establish they would be equally safe to use in *all* rifles.

All of the test rifles were in excellent condition and none had Damascus barrels. However, quite a few double rifles were built with twist barrels and most of these are upwards of 80 years old. If the owners of such elderly rifles insist on using them the ammunition should be restricted to black powder loads — and even then they're not really safe.

Nitro Load Table

1. 6.5×53R (256 Mannlicher) 160-gr. jacketed bullet, muzzle velocity (MV) 2350, muzzle energy (ME) 1960.

2. 333 Flanged Nitro Express 300-gr. bullet, MV 2150, ME 3090.

3. 400/350 Nitro Express 310-gr. bullet, MV 2000, ME 2752.

4. 400/360 Nitro Express 286-gr. Norma 9.3 bullet, MV 2132.

5. 360 Nitro Express 300-gr. bullet.

6. 360 #2 Nitro Express 300-gr. bullet.

7. 9.3×74R 286-gr. bullet, MV 2360.

8. 375 Flanged Nitro Express 270-gr. bullet, MV 1975, ME 2340.

9. 450/400/3¼ Nitro Express 400-gr. bullet, MV 2150, ME 4110.

10. 450 3¼ Nitro Express, One wad, case filled with Wheatina, 500-gr. bullet, MV 1930.

11. 450/3¼ Nitro for Black 300-gr. Hornady S.J. bullet. One wad, case filled with Wheatina.

12. 450/3¼ Nitro for Black 300-gr. Hornady S.J. bullet. One wad, case filled with Wheatina.

Five big bore rifles from the collection of Maynard P. Buehler, scope mount maker of Orinda, California. From the top — a 4-bore double by R. Hughes & Son, London. Next, a double-barreled 4-bore by Holland and Holland, London. Third down, an 8-gauge single by Manton, London. Fourth, a W. W. Greener 8-bore double and, last, a 600 Nitro Express 3-inch from W. J, Jeffery.

13. * 450/3¼ Nitro for Black. 350-gr. cast bullet, MV 1550.

14. * 450/3¼ Nitro for Black. 400-gr. cast bullet, MV 1500.

15. 500/450 #1 Nitro for Black. One wad, case full of Wheatina, 300-gr. bullet.

16. 500/3 Nitro for Black. One OP wad, another wad at base of bullet; Lyman #509133, 428-gr. cast hollow-point bullet, MV 1600.

17. 500/3 Nitro for Black. One wad, fill case with Wheatina, 440-gr. bullet.

18. 500/3 Nitro Express One wad, fill case with Wheatina, 570-gr. bullet.

19.† 577/500 #2 Nitro for Black. One wad, fill case with Wheatina, 440-gr. bullet.

20. 577/3 Nitro Express One wad, 750-gr. factory bullet, MV 1962.

21. 577/3 Nitro Express One wad, 750-gr. factory bullet, MV 1950.

22. ** 577/3 Nitro Express One OP wad, another at bullet base with a thin layer of melted bullet lube atop; Lyman bullet #585213-S, solid-base version weighing 588 grains when cast from type metal, MV 1735.

23. 577/3 Nitro for Black. One OP wad, case filled with Wheatina, 580-gr. cast bullet.

24. 577/3 Nitro for Black. One OP wad, another .220" thick at bullet base with thin layer of melted bullet lube atop. Lyman bullet #585213-S, cast from medium alloy, weight 600 grains, MV 1690.

25. 12-bore Westley Richards Explora 574-gr. bullet.

26. 12-bore Rigby Paradox two .135" card wads, two ³/₈" felt wads, .735" 580-gr. round ball in paper or plastic cases, MV 1250.

27. 12-bore Turner full double rifle Alcan 2¾" brass cases, case full of 10-gauge wads, 860-gr. cast bullet, MV 1200.

The following firms offer reloading components, equipment, custom loads or gunsmithing for double rifles:

Custom gunsmithing

Iver Henriksen, 1211 S. Second St., Missoula, Mont. 59801

Purcell's Gun Shop, 915 Main St., Boise, Idaho 83702

Bullet moulds, reloading tools, lubes, etc.

Lyman Gun Sight Corp., Middlefield, Conn. 06455
RCBS, Inc., P.O. Box 1919, Oroville, Calif. 95965
Ohaus, 29 Hanover Rd., Florham Park, N.J. 07932
Javelina Products, Box 337, San Bernardino, Calif. 92402

Rechambering

Snapp's Gunshop, 6911 E. Washington Rd., Clare, Mich. 48617

Alcan wads, RWS Berdan primers, etc.

Godfrey Reloading Supply, R.R. 1, Box 688, Brighton, Ill. 62012

Components, English and other foreign factory ammo.

Oregon Ammunition Service, P.O. Box 19341, Portland, Ore. 97219

James Tillinghast, Box 568, Marlow, N.H. 03456

Berdan decapping tools

Lachmiller Co., Box 97, Parkesburg, Pa. 19365

Reboring or rebarreling of double rifles

Westley Richards & Co., Ltd., Grange Road, Bournbrook, Birmingham 29, England

For reliable information and enjoyable reading these books are highly recommended:

Cartridges of the World by F. C. Barnes, edited by J. T. Amber.

African Rifles and Cartridges by John Taylor.

The Gun and Its Development by W. W. Greener.

Cartridge Conversions by George C. Nonte.

English Guns and Rifles by J. N. George.

Finally, if an early Kynoch catalog can be located, especially one printed between World Wars I and II, prior to the discontinuation of so many cartridges, this will prove to be a highly valuable reference. These catalogs list the powder charges used, the weights of bullets and their style, the velocities and energies for various ranges and the breech pressures generated by all loadings listed. Unfortunately these catalogs are scarce and quite difficult to find.

---

* Loads 13 and 14 may have powder charge safely increased to 39 grains in quest for most accurate load.

† Some shooters may prefer to use Nylon or Da-cron filler. In some cases this will be as satisfactory as Wheatina or other cereal filler. Also be reminded that 32-gauge shotshell wads are perfect for use in all 50-cal. rifles, 24-gauge wads in 577 rifles.

** Developed as a reduced load for Cordite rifles. Testing in several rifles showed that best accuracy and proper grouping required 56 to 62 grains of 2400. In several rifles tested this load was more accurate than the full-power Cordite loads.

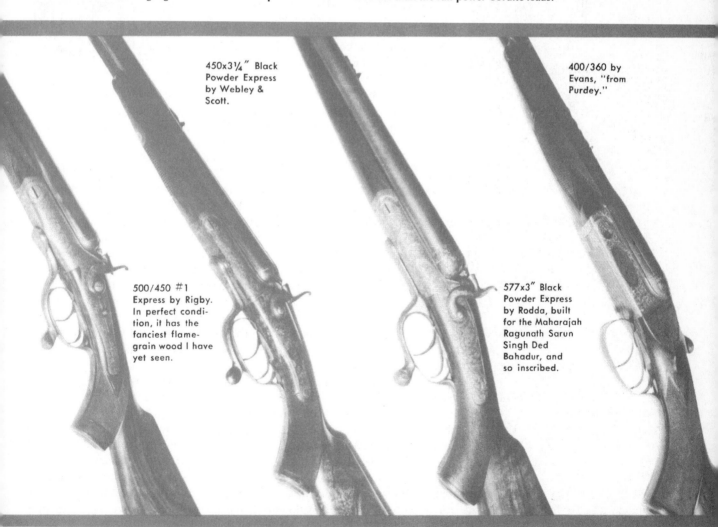

450x3¼" Black Powder Express by Webley & Scott.

400/360 by Evans, "from Purdey."

500/450 #1 Express by Rigby. In perfect condition, it has the fanciest flame-grain wood I have yet seen.

577x3" Black Powder Express by Rodda, built for the Maharajah Ragunath Sarun Singh Ded Bahadur, and so inscribed.

Now nearing its centennial celebration year, the famous old company looks forward with confidence to another century of service to shooters everywhere.

The Lyman Story

This massive and heavy tool is an **Ideal Armory Press**, made about 1900or so for military use essentially. Automatic primer feeding and ejection of the sized and recapped case are speed features.

by **MASON WILLIAMS**

ABOUT 1876, A young man named William Lyman became dissatisfied with the coarse, open V-type sights commonly used in those days. An ardent sportsman and knowledgeable about firearms, he'd learned their shortcomings through personal hunting experience. The more he used them the more he became convinced that the V-sight was an unsatisfactory way of aiming a rifle, and that something considerably better was needed.

A few years earlier, Civil War Sharpshooters had used Vernier rear sights attached to the upper grip of their rifles, enabling them to shoot accurately at long distances. From that time on target shooters had turned almost exclusively to these Vernier sights for precision shooting, but Lyman knew that these high, delicate sights would not stand up under hunting abuse, nor did the tiny opening usually found in the sight disc permit enough light to come through for field use. In other words, they were impractical for hunting, and he decided to improve them. He wanted an adjustable, strong rear sight close to his eye, and he wanted to be able to throw the rifle up to his shoulder and instantly "get on-target." With this in mind, he made his way to the Metropolitan Washing Machine Company, one of the Lyman businesses located on the Lyman Farm in Middlefield, Conn.

There, at the age of 24, he founded the Lyman Gun Sight Company, for that same year he was granted a patent covering a tang peep or aperture sight. Before long, he took over a room in the plant to produce sights for sale to the public.

In those days, front sight beads were round-faced. The tiny gold or ivory bead, mounted near the muzzle was, under ideal light conditions, quite practical. However, on those days when sunlight streamed from the sky at all angles, glancing off the round bead to distort and alter the true sight picture, these rounds beads left a lot to be desired. William Lyman developed a front sight with a flat face that gave minimal light distortion, remaining sharp and clear under virtually all shooting conditions. He appreciated the advantages of gold and ivory and he kept them. This combination of a practical rear sight and a clearly distinguishable front sight was a revolutionary combination that had a terrific impact upon the shooting public, so much so that his correspondence was filled with testimonial letters. Today,

Lyman 48 micrometer-click receiver sight at left is of long-slide type for extreme long range shooting. The 48 Lyman at right is of later type, its short slide offering ample adjustment for usual ranges.

it is difficult to appreciate the effect the new Lyman sights had on the shooting world of the 1890s, when shooting was a big time sport, comparable to today's baseball and football. These sights were enthusiastically accepted not only by the average American hunter, but by the professional shooters who put on demonstrations and entered contests where thousands of dollars could be won or lost in an afternoon.

Lyman's 48 Sight

At the turn of the century, the U.S. Army was searching for a rifle to replace the 30-40 Krag. The development and acceptance of the Model 1903 Springfield rifle opened up an entirely new field for the Lyman firm. Lyman had been making rear sights for various hunting rifles, the Model 47 with adjustable windage being in widespread use. The Model 47 was a modified Model 1A with fine windage adjustment built into the top of the sight stem. In addition, Lyman Nos. 21, 35 and 38 sights, while fully adjustable, were not strong enough nor were their adjustments positive enough for use on a high power, high velocity rifle like the Springfield. They had been more than adequate on the Winchester Model 86s and 95s, and on other comparable rifles, but they did not measure up to the re-requirements for the Springfield. After years of experimenting that included modifications based on voluminous correspondence with a young army lieutenant named Townsend Whelen, Lyman brought out the Model 48 receiver sight in 1910. This new sight was so well designed that it became highly popular overnight. In the July 6, 1911 issues of *Arms and the Man,* Lieutenant Whelen wrote a glowing report on the Lyman 48. Even today, it stands as the sight against which all others are measured. They are today, as then, hand-fitted and hand-assembled by a few old employees. Today, Lyman sights are so universally recognized and used that the company continues to be the leader in the field, producing more metallic sights than all other sight manufacturers combined.

Early Tools

Back in the days when William Lyman was a young man, John Barlow, a hunter, outdoorsman, and a machinist, was conducting experiments in improving the crude tools then used for the reloading of metallic ammunition and shot-

shells. His simple, easy-to-use tools caught on rapidly and soon became well known to all shooters. He founded the Ideal Manufacturing Company in 1884 and, some-time in the next few years, he put together the first *Ideal Hand Book.* The exact publication date is not known but it carries testimonial letters dated 1891. The growth of the Ideal Company can be seen in the *No. 12 Hand Book,* which lists some 8 variations of the famous "tong tool." Models 1, 2, 4, 6 and 8 had moulds in the ends. These tools are so simple to use that a man can sit on a log in the wilderness and reload his fired cartridges — and many have done just that. Surprisingly enough, sales of this tool, in its modern form, have increased substantially in recent years. Gone is the old iron-and-steel frame, replaced by a lightweight alloy to reduce weight, but it's otherwise basically unchanged from the original 1884 Barlow design.

Other items listed in the No. 12 Hand Book, which came out about 1900, are bullet resizers, shotshell crimpers, shotshell pocket loaders, case resizers, "Star" crimpers for shot-shells, and the Universal Powder Measures Models 1, 2, 3 and 4. Ideal also offered the Model 1899 loading machine, which would reload shot-shells in 10, 12, 14, 16 and 20 gauge.

The Ideal Perfection Mould, made for both grease-grooved and paper-patched bullet-casting, had an adjustable plug that allowed the shooter to alter bullet weight. The regular Ideal moulds were conventional, single-cavity types that covered just about every form, weight and caliber of bullet then in use.

Sometime around 1908 to 1910, Marlin Firearms bought out Ideal and the ensuing issues of the Ideal Hand Book, commencing with No. 20, carried the Marlin name at the bottom of the front cover. In 1924 Phinias Talcott bought the company from Marlin, but a few months later turned round and sold it to Lyman in October of 1925. Lyman has continued to publish the *Ideal Hand Books,* and has manufactured tools ever since.

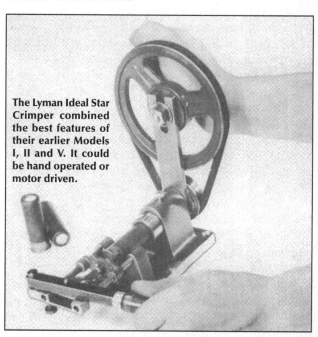

The Lyman Ideal Star Crimper combined the best features of their earlier Models I, II and V. It could be hand operated or motor driven.

Lyman tang sights. At center is a standard No. 1 type; left, an early micrometer elevation style, and at right a lever-locking No. 1A.

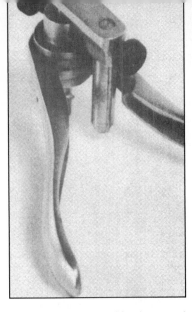

The tool shown here is a case indenter. The case is placed on the central spindle and the handles closed to let the small pin (at left) form a dimple or depression in the case neck or wall, at one or more of 4 places. Two thumbscrews allow vertical adjustment of the

Lyman Scopes

In 1928, Lyman bought the Winchester and Stevens lines of rifle scopes, thus giving Lyman another entirely new but related market and a greatly increased sales potential. However, Lyman never manufactured its own lenses, preferring to buy them, made to their specifications, from specialists in that field. The first Lyman scope offered was the 5-A (a duplicate of the Winchester 5-A) that made its debut on February 6, 1929. The 438 was Lyman's first design, appearing March 5, 1930. The Lyman 3x Stag big game scope went on the market May 18, 1933, but it was a complete flop. To offset this, the first Lyman Targetspot match rifle scope left the factory August 16, 1933 and, like the Model 48 micrometer sight, proceeded to make history — and it still is a top choice among target shooters. Then came a series of scopes for 22 rimfirerifles, and on April 1, 1937, Lyman introduced the Super-targetspot scope and, later in the same year, the Junior Targetspot. Then came the first really practical and modern big-game, high-power-rifle scope to appear on the American market — the Lyman Alaskan. This was followed, in 1948, by the Challenger, the Wolverine in 1953 and finally the original All American in 1954. On December 8, 1961, Lyman shipped the first Perma-Center All-American rifle scopes that remain leaders in the Lyman line today.

Cutts Comps

In the middle of the depression, in 1932, Charles Lyman had enough faith in America's recovery and in the growth of trap and Skeet shooting to buy rights to the Cutts Compensator, a recoil-absorbing, interchangeable choke tube device. This had been designed originally by Colonel Cutts for use on cannons and rifles. It proved to be one of Lyman's most profitable investments. It soon sold in large numbers, with Lyman also installing it on shotguns — as accredited gunsmiths later did also — and that installation department continues busy today.

Then, some years ago, economic and other problems arose to plague the Lymans, and a decision was made that a new approach to the changing times, plus the need for modern financing methods and better sales promotion was in order. The Lymans had always operated a close-knit family business, but despite an increasing flow of orders, new products and planning were needed if Lyman was to retain its share of business and gain new markets. No longer could the Lymans pitch in — as they did during depression years — and work for nothing to pull the company out of trouble. No longer could they continue to confine their thinking solely to Middlefield and the family organization.

Because of all this the Lymans ordered a survey of the entire organization — it took a year to complete — then brought in as president the man who ran the survey. Roland Van Name.

For 10 years Van Name guided Lyman through the intricacies of modern-day financial and business problems, bringing in several capable executives who aided in improving Lyman's public image, as the modern cant has it.

In September of 1969, Van Name retired and, at the same time, control and management of the Lyman company was turned over to the Leisure Group, an organization with headquarters in Los Angeles, California. This holding company controls many widely diversified businesses, among them lawn mower and camping trailer manufacturing. Lyman has been placed in a division that includes High Standard — gunmakers — and Sierra Bullets. Ken Wright, now Operations Manager for Lyman, is understandably reticent about future plans at this stage, but he did say that there will be much new product development in the immediate future. Plans are being redrawn for a new plant. Lyman's Research and Development section will be substantially expanded — more people, more chronographs, more pressure guns are planned. A new backstop has already been bulldozed for the R&D section.

There will be a few changes that may disconcert some old Lyman customers, at least. In the past Lyman stocked over 900 cast lead bullet mould styles, some for such oddball calibers as the 23, only a few of which were ever sold, yet the moulds remain in stock. Lyman plans to reduce stock moulds to around 600, these to be available through normal channels. The others will go into a special order group, available at a premium price directly from Lyman. In the meantime those in doubt about a mould's availability can write to Lyman at Middlefield, Conn.

Peace officers are confronted daily with threats to their lives from wounded felons, still capable of dealing out death. The heart of the problem is not killing power, but stopping power, the ability to put the gunman down and out of the fight. Dual bullets may well be the solution.

Double Bullets!

by V. R. GAERTNER

HANDGUNS ARE VITAL to society and to the general public primarily as defensive arms. These firearms must meet tough requirements, including speed of firing from the holster, dependability, convenient size and weight for carrying (concealed or in view), sufficient firepower, good accuracy, and more.

Present models offer these qualities in great variety. Even so, reports persist that the mainstays of our defensive handguns — the .36" (true caliber) revolvers and the 9mm semi-autos — too often fail to protect law enforcement officers and others in life-and-death situations.

A True Experience

The experience of a shooting friend, then a patrolman, started my thinking on this problem. He was driving a patrol car in a high-crime section of our metropolitan area. Answering a routine stolen credit card complaint at a supermarket, he found himself in a gun battle with an armed thug. The man snapped two or three wild shots at him before the officer could return the fire without hitting busy shoppers.

As these pedestrians scattered, my friend fired two carefully aimed shots from his Smith and Wesson 357 Magnum. The man shot again, then fled down an alley, and the officer thought he had missed. Following his attacker cautiously and expecting to be fired on at each step, he found the man dying of two wounds, one in the neck and the other through the chest. The ex-con had been wanted on other charges in a nearby jurisdiction.

Firing the Ruger Security-Six with a high-performance double-bullet handload. Note the light trace made by a pen-light taped to the author's wrist; it shows the typical initial backward thrust of recoil, followed by the upward motion as the wrist flexes. Taken at night by open-shutter flash, followed by firing.

Two 357 jacketed bullets, cut and ready for loading. The Sierra 150-gr. JHC (left) is less suitable for heaviest magnum DB loads; its cannelure is not as deep as that on the Hornady 158-gr. JHP (right), but either is excellent for milder 38 Special use.

The patrolman in this case is an expert competitive pistol shot and he handles a 44 Magnum with about the same ease and accuracy as a 22. He considered himself lucky to be alive, and his answer to the "weakness" of the 357 was to carry a 44 stuffed with high-performance loads. Soon after this incident, however, he moved up to chief in a suburban department, and he has not been forced to use the 44 on an attacker.

Few officers have the 44 option and many are limited to 38 Specials, but this problem — a felon physically capable of dealing out death after sustaining serious wounds — confronts law officers and other defensive shooters again and again, especially with the 36s in both Special and Magnum persuasions.

The heart of the problem is not killing power, which the duty calibers have, but stopping power, meaning simply the ability to put a felon down and out of the fight without necessarily dealing him a fatal wound. That distinction is easily seen with the 22 Long Rifle, a so-called pipsqueak cartridge which has little stopping power, although it kills efficiently enough by virtue of the tiny holes it drills into vital organs.

Stopping Power

Stopping power (SP) has been studied most extensively by military experts. Foremost among them was Gen. Julian S. Hatcher and a service team. They finally decided from animal tests that SP could be calculated by a mathematical equation which may be put into these words:

Stopping Power equals Momentum times Sectional Area times Shape Factor

Now momentum depends only on velocity and mass: momentum equals mass times velocity. Mass is proportional to weight; mass equals weight divided by g, the gravitational constant. Energy, on the other hand, equals mass times velocity squared divided by 2, thus energy depends more on velocity, while SP is proportional to both velocity and mass. In practical terms, lighter bullets develop more energy since they can be driven at higher velocities, while heavier bullets at lower speeds have higher momentum and higher SP.

In terms of calibers, the 357 develops more energy than a 44 Special or a 45 ACP, but the old-fashioned pair would be rated better stoppers, or at least as good, and this seems to agree with experience.

Table 1
Defensive Handgun Cartridges

Caliber	Bullet/grs.	MV	ME	Recoil	RSP*
38 Special	158	855	256	3.3	100
357 Magnum	158	1550	845	6.3	193
44 Special	246	755	311	4.0	193
45 ACP	230	850	370	4.3	207
41 Magnum	210 JSP	1500	1050	12.5	371
44 Magnum	240	1470	1150	16.3	457

*Relative Stopping Power, based on an arbitrary value of 100 for the 38 Special.
MV = Muzzle velocity in feet per second.
ME = Muzzle energy in foot pounds.
Recoil is given in foot pounds.

The following table lists factory loadings for the standard defensive calibers; the velocities are the data obtained from solid test barrels and are higher than those obtainable from revolvers or semi-autos, especially for the magnums, but they are close enough for general comparisons.

The Relative Stopping Powers (RSP) were calculated using the Hatcher equation and then restated by assigning the 38 Special result an arbitrary value of 100, adjusting the others on that basis. Most authorities accept this scale as agreeing with experience in actual duty or hunting conditions. The 38 Specials (and also the 9mm Luger) are considered inadequate in stopping power, only the large bores being good to excellent. This is where we stand on stopping power. Can we improve this situation, considering the Hatcher equation and its implications with no preconceived ideas?

The Double-Bullet Concept

Let's consider the factors in the Hatcher equation to determine what is needed to increase stopping power, ignoring for the moment the practicality of possible changes. If we increase any of the factors, we soup up SP proportionally. To increase momentum, we must push up either bullet mass or velocity or both. But the present loadings give the heaviest bullets at the highest speeds which can be handled by these calibers at standard operating pressures.

The shape factor is highest for wadcutter designs with flat noses or hollow points, already available in high-performance ammo.

Finally, the sectional area is constant for a given caliber, or so it seems at first thought. However, there is a way of *doubling the sectional area*, in addition to possible benefits of bullet expansion. Simply use *double bullets*, that is, load two bullets, one on top of the other, which separate upon leav-

Left — Hornady 357 JHP and finished double bullets ready for loading. Below — Sierra 240-gr. 44 JHP has been sawed and deburred. Especially suitable for DB handloads, its deep cannelure permits hard crimping necessary to hold the front half securely under heavy 44 Magnum recoil.

ing the muzzle and strike the target at two points. I began to wonder whether this was a practical possibility.

Preliminary Trials

Double bulleting is not entirely new, having been tried in military rifle cartridges to increase effective firepower. However, the results apparently did not meet tough service criteria. Defensive shooting is another ball game, and no effort had been made to apply the concept to modern defensive handgunning, as far as I know.

Some months ago I started to experiment with double-bullet handloads (DBs) in medium and large calibers. I had no idea of what to expect, but I began with the idea of proving that it couldn't work.

In trying to be my own devil's advocate, I chose the 44 Magnum for the early work, because it is a caliber I've handloaded and hunted with for years. If the concept proved successful it should succeed as well in lesser loadings.

Working cautiously up to the charges developed for hunting dangerous game with my old, scoped Herter 44, I was pleasantly surprised to discover that nothing terrible happened when a cleaved JHP hunting bullet over heavy charges of 2400 or H110 powders was fired. The very strong Contender 44 single shot pistol was used in these early firings, but this was an unnecessary caution. DBs actually develop less pressure than the same loads made up with the original single bullet.

Any of several bullets of different weights and types could be "doubled" in the same way. A quick trial of the idea in the 357 Contender looked equally promising.

I began to measure performance seriously. Velocities were normal in revolvers and could be pushed to high-performance levels. But what about grouping and accuracy of such mutilated, light bullets?

Further testing was encouraging. First, half-bullets were not hopelessly inaccurate. Even at 25 yards, longer than the usual combat or defensive ranges, jacketed types usually

placed at least one projectile in the 9 or 10 ring of a standard target, and the other half was a 7, 8, 9, or 10. The spread per shot for the best loads was 3–6 inches and the group sizes were 4–8 inches at 25 yards. That seemed to qualify the loads for combat and defensive use, since many a G.I. 45 will not shoot tighter.

At this stage, the work was broadened to cover other calibers, leading to some negative conclusions. First, the front half-bullet must be crimped heavily to keep it in the case under recoil. This eliminated semi-auto calibers, because they headspace on the case mouth, not feasible with a heavy crimp. Even leaving out such old standards as the 9mm Parabellum, 38 Super, 45 ACP and the like, the concept still looked good for revolver cases headspacing on the rims.

Cast bullets were eliminated, because a heavy crimp deforms them and they tend to lead the bore at high velocities, raising pressures. Finally, only the heaviest bullets in each caliber are suitable for doubling, since half-bullets are lighter than even the shortest bullets regularly used in each caliber. This fact has far-reaching consequences which we need to consider later, some favorable and some not so good. One positive fact is that short bullets are very stable in flight, necessary for accuracy and dependability.

At this point I tried to visualize just what was happening when a double-bullet load is fired. The front half, the original nose section with cannelure, is pushed down the barrel by the rear half, which in turn is driven by the pressure of the burning powder gases. The front half lacks a jacketed base, but it needs none. In fact, recovered fronts have light rifling marks, showing that they upset poorly, and some of them are marked unsymmetrically. Little wonder that they are less accurate than the rear sections, and that they expand less.

Rear half-bullets are more accurate, both because they upset better and because they have a jacketed base. It has been known for a long time that a perfectly symmetrical base is more important to accuracy than the shape of the nose. The soft, flat nose (cut surface) of the rear half-bullet is not the best shape for distance, but it strikes with great impact and expands better than a hollow point, adding to stopping power.

The rear section cannot move faster than the front half, but the rear is in the barrel longer and is given added push after the front leaves the muzzle. Contact between the two halves at this point is not uniformly distributed, so the rear jostles the front, which is deflected a bit off course, this producing a deflection of the rear half. These deflections cannot be in the same direction, and the paths of the halves diverge slightly.

This description of DBs may be a bit vague, but it will do for a working understanding.

Double-Bullet Handloading

Having satisfied myself that the DB idea would work, I developed uniform methods of handloading. The following procedure has given consistent, safe handloads in the 4 defensive revolver calibers. I consider my own loads entirely safe in any modern revolver in excellent condition, but they should not be tackled by a beginning handloader. An advanced worker should be able to work up loads for his guns, watching for pressure signs, but not exceeding the top charges listed. I disclaim any responsibility for the results of others, as does the publisher of this book. This said, here is the procedure I used.

1 Bullet selection and cutting. The bullets listed in the Table have given me good results. Others may do a good job, but extra caution is suggested in adapting them.

Cutting is done with a hacksaw or a bandsaw. The latter is quickest and most convenient. To hold the bullet for cutting without denting it, a slightly undersized hole may be drilled in a piece of hardwood to grip the bullet firmly. This holder can be clamped in a vise or handheld for bandsaw use. Jacketed bullets have a thin gilding metal skin and a soft lead core, both of which are easily sawed. With a little trial and error, the two halves will weigh the same within a few grains. Burrs are filed or ground off. It is not necessary to smooth the sawed surfaces, as this roughness has no sizable effect on performance. Care should be taken to mate the original front and back halves for constant total weight. A lengthwise scratch on the jacket simplifies correct alignment of the halves during seating.

2 Case preparation. The case is resized and expanded as usual; the expander should be at least .002" smaller than the bullet diameter. Flare the casemouth well, to ease seating of the front half-bullet. New cases should be used for firmest bullet holding, if any serious use of the loads is planned.

Bandsawing 357 JHP bullets clamped in wood holder. The bullet holder is usable with a hacksaw, too.

Typical 10-yard groups from 357 Ruger Security-Six.

3 Powder charge. Accurate weights of the powders listed in Table 2 are used. I suggest starting 10% below the listed weights and working up in 0.5-gr. increments, watching closely for pressure signs. These are not the hottest possible charges in my guns, but they are "stout," as they say. I have designed these loads on the basis that defensive loadings should be heavy, but not to exceed normal operating pressures.

4 Seating and crimping. This is the key to reliable results. The two matched halves of a bullet are lined up, then the front is set aside, keeping the aligned position. The rear is seated with its nose about 1/16" below the casemouth. Then the front half is seated with most of the cannelure inside the mouth. Seating the front pushes the rear farther into the case.

A heavy roll crimp must be applied to hold the front half under recoil. The crimp should be no tighter than neces-

sary, or it will run up pressures. I apply a crimp which will just hold the front half-bullet to finger pressure. The bullet should not turn, tilt, or move in any way under as much force as I can manage to exert with the bare fingers. I use standard RCBS crimpers, which will secure even 44 Magnum DBs against recoil of the heaviest hunting loads without excessive pressures, but crimp must be kept uniform from round to round for consistent performance.

The final test of crimping is to load the gun with 5 double-bullet rounds, and one load made up with the original bullet over the same powder charge. Fire the latter load first and check the DBs for movement. If any front bullets loosened, the crimp is tightened gradually until none of the fronts move after several heavy firings. Watch carefully for pressure signs, and back off one grain or more if you see them. A tighter crimper could be obtained as a last resort.

Never seat a bullet deeper than indicated by the crimping cannelure, as this raises pressures. Bullets without cannelures are not suitable for DB work. Do not fire loads with canted front bullets, but cases may be reclaimed by pulling out the front half, then firing out the rear bullet. Increase mouth

Table 2

Load No.	Bullet/net wt./grs.	Powder/grs.[1]	MV[2]	ME	Spread[4]	10-yd. Data Group size[5]	RSP[3]
38 Special — Colt Official Police, 4" barrel							
1	Sierra 158 JSP/145	2400/11.5	934	270	2.4	4.5	200
2	Hornady 158 JHP/146	Unique/6.0	965	300	2.5	3.9	208
3	Sierra 150 JHP/139	Unique/6.5	979	309	1.8	4.2	201
357 Magnum — Ruger Security-Six, 6" barrel							
4	Sierra 158 JSP/145	H110/16	1209	471	1.5	2.8	276
5	Hornady 158 JHP/146	Unique/8.5	1312	554	0.9	1.8	302
6	Sierra 150 JSP/139	H110/17	1409	613	2.7	4.3	309
44 Special — See 44 Magnum							
7	Sierra 240 JHP/223	Unique/8.0	1006	500	2.4	4.3	466
44 Magnum — Herter SA, 6½" barrel							
8	Sierra 240 JHP/223	H110/25	1325	867	1.3	2.8	766

1 — Heavy loads with hard crimps. Approach cautiously, reducing charges initially at least 10% below those listed with the same bullets.
2 — Velocities by Model 10 chronograph at 5 feet from the muzzle. ME — Muzzle Energy in foot pounds.
3 — Relative to factory 38 Special 158-gr. bullet at 855 fps, corrected for total weight of double bullet and measured velocity, assuming no change in shape factor; see text.
4 — Spread per shot in inches.
5 — Group size for 4 shots in inches.

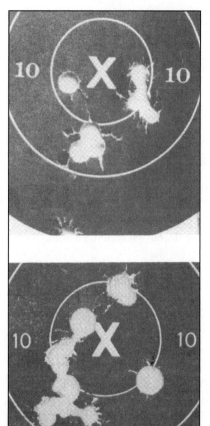

Left top — Tight 10-yd. 4-shot double-bullet group from the Ruger 357 Magnum, using the 158-gr. Hornady JHP. Below — High-performance 44 Magnum DB group. Sierra 240-gr. JHP, 4 shots at 10 yards, 25 grains of H1100. Herter revolver with 6½" barrel.

flare to ease seating of front halves.

The only near-miss I have had with DBs came when I fired a load from which the front bullet had been pulled. Unfortunately I had also neglected to charge any powder (even writers have lapses!). Normally a primer will shove a regular bullet just beyond the forcing cone, but in this case a "bullet" flew out of the barrel. I was suspicious and checked the barrel to find that the jacket had stuck at the forcing cone, and the core had continued merrily on its way. If a round had been fired behind the jacket, a ruined barrel might have resulted. Of course, the reason is clear: the jacket of the rear half is not held to the core by a swaged nose. If there is too little pressure to push the jacket along, the core is free to depart alone. A good general rule: if anything unusual is noted in firing a DB or any other load, check the gun thoroughly before firing again.

Crimping effects and the need for careful adjustment limits DB hand-loading, as noted, to advanced workers. Following these directions, I have never seen pressure signs or any other problems. Case expansion measurements showed that the loads are within normal pressures.

Double-bulleting is not a two-hour project even for an expert handloader, but two or three loading sessions and a couple of trips to the range should be enough for the able worker to develop a safe high-performance DB handload for his favorite handgun.

Handload Performance

Let's get down to the nitty-gritty — the numbers in Table 2. By caliber, the following comments are mainly for hand-loaders who wish to try them personally.

38 Special The first load is designed for longer barrels and is not great in a 4" tube. Load 2 is best for all-round consistency and accuracy; my fixed-sight Colt centered it right at factory point-of-aim at 10 yards. Load 2 will do the best job also in short barrels and does not have the heavier muzzle flash of load 1. Load 3 is a bit on the hot side, but is included to show the spread-tightening effect of hotter loads. Unfortunately it is less accurate and a few fliers show up. The Sierra and Hornady bullets can be interchanged in these loads.

357 Magnum Loads 4, 5, and 6 are not exceptionally hot but they should not be compared unfavorably with factory loads, which are listed in Table 1. Factory data are taken from solid test barrels, and actual results from revolvers are around 1300 fps (6" barrels) for 600 ft.-lbs. (not 1550 fps for 845 ft.-lbs.); quite a come-down, but still very substantial. Load 4 is for 6" or longer barrels, a good consistent performer. Load 5 is the best for most serious purposes, very consistent and accurate. Load 6 is for those who want a hotter, lighter bullet, at the cost of wider spread and some fliers. These two 158-gr. bullets are interchangeable.

44 Special A suitable gun in this caliber was not available to me for tests. Loads were made up in 44 Special cases and fired from the 44 Magnum guns, the data being reported for the 6½" Herter. Load 7 is a good load and should give smaller spreads and groups from 44 Special-chambered guns.

44 Magnum Load 8 is the ultimate in DBs. Although very few people carry the big magnum for defense against two-legged varmints, this would be my choice for a back-up stopper for handgun hunting. The load does not seem to pack the recoil of a regular full-house load. The same discounting should be made for factory 44 Magnum loads as for 357s–1470 fps dropping to around 1370 from actual revolvers. Test your crimp thoroughly to be certain that front bullets do not move before depending on handloads in a tight situation.

Stopping Powers

A glance at the Relative Stopping Powers in Table 2 will raise questions in the thinking shooter's mind. Do I seriously suggest that a 38 Special with a double bullet RSP of 200 or so can equal the regular 357 Magnum (193). If Gen. Hatcher's well-respected equation is correct, then I must conclude that the numbers do not lie. Of course, the equation was not designed for double bullets, but mathematically the numbers

Typical 38 Special double bullet grouping, 4 shots fired from a 4" barreled Colt Official Police at 10 yards.

Four double bullet shots from a 4" barreled Colt 38 Special, fired at 10 yards from a 2-hand crouching hold. The load — 11.5/2400/160 Sierra JSP, MV 934 fps. Widest shots are 4½" apart, with 7 holes well distributed around point of aim (X mark).

Table 3
Duxseal Wound Casts

Caliber	Load	A.V.	A.L.
38 Spcl.	158 lead/6.0 Unique[a]	16	4.5
38 Spcl.	2[b]	14	3.0
357 Mag.	Rem. 158 lead	29	4.4
357 Mag.	5[b]	26	3.0
44 Spcl.	250 lead/8.0 Unique[a]	16	7.3
44 Spcl.	7[b]	20	3.3
44 Mag.	Rem. 240 JSP	79	5.7
44 Mag.	8[b]		

Notes: [a]Handload, considered a normal duty load. [b]See Table 2 for DB loads. [c]Estimated, see text. A.V.—Average Volume per shot, ml. A.L.—Average Length, inches.

are unavoidable. Only tests on animals will determine the final answer, and of course, life-and-death fights.

Can we visualize the results in more understandable terms? Well, what is the effective caliber of a DB load? This is just the caliber corresponding to a single bullet with the same sectional area as a given DB. By calculating the sectional area of the bullet, doubling it, and calculating back to the caliber, we obtain the diameter of a single slug with this doubled area. For a 38 or 357 bullet (both .357") the sectional area is .1001 square inches, doubled it is .2002 sq. in., and the effective caliber of the DB is .507". In other words, the stopping power corresponds to .507 caliber. For .429" bullets the area is .1445 sq. in., doubled it is .2890 sq. in., and the effective caliber is 607. The stopping powers seem more reasonable when we think of them as 51- and 61 caliber equivalents.

Wounding Effects

To illustrate the differences between conventional loads and DBs, I used the Duxseal method. Johns-Manville's Duxseal is a plastic, resistant sealing composition which does not harden and retains any shape it is given. Forming it into crude cylinders about 5" in diameter and a foot or so long, then shooting handgun bullets into it produces a "wound" which can be preserved by simply pouring in a thin plaster slurry. The cast is easily cut out of the Duxseal. A series of such casts for typical defensive single- and double-bullet loads is shown in the illustration, and the following Table 3 lists cast volumes, including the bullet, corresponding to wound size and penetration. Shooting was done at about 5 yards.

It was necessary to estimate the 44 Magnum DB volume because the two bullets opened up fused, partially collapsed holes. The front bullet struck first, making a cavity which was then partly filled in as the rear bullet ploughed into the Duxseal. These results are somewhat misleading because the bullets expanded to different extents in this tough composition. But the pattern is clear. Single bullets penetrate 50–100% more deeply, and the total volumes of both loads are roughly equal, confirming greater stopping powers at short ranges. The most interesting result in these tests is that expansion of DBs is greater than conventional bullets and this is particularly true for the rear bullet. This promises decreased killing power at about the same total initial energies.

External Ballistics

At this stage of the work, the next question was obvious. If larger calibers give greater RSPs, why not push up handgun calibers to .50" or even .60"? The answer is that the ballistic losses of larger caliber bullets of reasonable weights are too great for general-purpose shooting. And the same losses will apply to DBs. The theory points out what we are giving up to get greater Stopping Power.

Apply the old saw, "You can't get something for nothing" to ballistics. The longer, heavier bullet of a given caliber carries better than the shorter, lighter slug. For bullets of equal weight, the smaller-caliber projectile has the greater range. Mathematically, this is expressed by the ballistic coefficient, C, which is calculated from remaining velocities at a series of ranges, using ballistic tables such as those derived from Ingalls (refer to "Hatcher's Notebook" for tables and their use).

For our purposes, the most interesting fact about C is its dependence on weight. According to the equation, $C = w/id^2$, C is proportional to weight, w, if i, the form factor, is unchanged, where d is the diameter, also unchanged. For a bullet with a known C, cutting it in two decreases C proportionally. Actually, taking the weight loss of sawing into account, C is corrected by a weight factor which is less than 0.5.

Take an example. The Hornady 158-gr. JHP is listed in the *Hornady Handbook II* with a ballistic coefficient of .162. The weight of each half-bullet is 73 grains. The C for the half-bullets is then .162 times 73/158 or .0748, approximately. Using the ballistic tables we can now find the remaining velocities for any range from the initial velocity and the ballistic equation: $C = X/(S_R — S_V)$, where X is the range in

Measuring velocities of 44 Magnum handloads from the Herter revolver with an Oehler Model 10 chronograph. The shooting bench is supported by two trees.

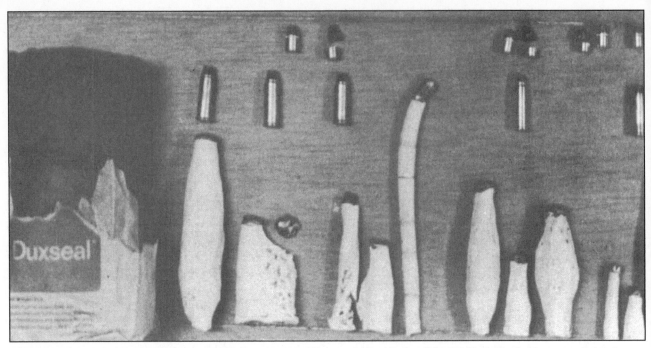

Duxseal plaster casts of "wounds," discussed in the text. Note shorter cavities produced by double-bullet loads, compared to longer, more deeply penetrating conventional-load channels. DBs cause larger entry holes, and expend more of their energy in surface damage and bullet expansion, evidencing greater stopping power and decreased killing power.

feet and S_r and S_v are tabulated functions at range X and initially (at the muzzle).

In the same way the Hornady 240-gr. JHP (C is .173) half-bullets have a C of about .0800, and so will other 240-gr. JHP bullets of similar shape. Some revealing estimates come out of calculations which follow logically from these Cs. Without going into the details here, DBs lose velocity about *twice* as fast as does the original bullet. For the 44 bullet at 25 yards, for example, this amounts to around 12% of the 1500 fps muzzle velocity for the DB against 6% for the original bullet. Translated to energy, that means about 12% for the full bullet and 23% loss for the DB. At longer ranges the loss is proportionally greater.

Gen. Hatcher also measured "woundingdistances," concluding that a projectile must have about 100 ft-lbs of energy to inflict a wound in animal flesh. Using the ballistic tables (and extrapolating the data), the wounding distance for a 240-gr. 44 bullet started at 1500 fps is more than 1100 yards, while the distance for DBs is somewhat over 300 yards, less than 30% of that for the full bullet.

These estimates are not very accurate, because the rear bullet has a flat full-caliber nose with a higher form factor, and the front bullet has a butchered base, but they are close enough to make the point that DBs are very inefficient ballistically. Their drops at any range are undoubtedly more than three times as great as standard bullets show, thus effective ranges before striking the ground (if fired horizontally) are less than a third of those of conventional bullets at the same muzzle velocities.

Both range and ricochet are reduced to less than a third of full-bullet figures. The same conclusions are valid for

36-caliber bullets, and these lighter projectiles start out at a big discount. More detailed calculations or actual, complex measurements cannot change these points much. By gaining stopping power, we lose ballistically. But this loss may seem to be a gain, if we consider the purposes and circumstances of defensive hand-gunning.

Thoughts on Defensive Shooting

A law officer, a guard, anyone who carries or keeps a handgun for defense must decide in advance the circumstances which justify using it. If his own life and those of his loved ones are threatened, most of us would not question the use of the most effective firepower available, but the situation will rarely be clear cut.

Do DB loads change this picture? I think they do, and for the better from this defender's viewpoint.

First, make no mistake about one thing — these loads are deadly at combat ranges. The Duxseal data demonstrate that loud and clear. DB shooting demands the same caution and fine judgment as the heaviest conventional ammunition. However, there are important differences which may well change our defensive options.

Life-and-death defense calls for speed first and accuracy second. The attacker grabs the initiative, but a defender does not go into action until an attacker threatens. No expert combat handgunner will let his opponent get the first shot — if he can help it. Accuracy is a great thing at medium to long ranges. But at point blank the first shooter has the edge. Here we must worry about the psychology of this deadly game.

Facing a man pointing a gun in your direction is enough

to rattle anyone. When he fires, few will not find their determination and coordination shaken. It needs a hard-nosed type indeed to take a bullet, even a "flesh" wound, then return fire effectively. What effects will double-bullet loads have on this shooters' psychology?

The DB shooter will know that he packs heavy stopping power, even with a much-maligned 38 Special. DBs deal out somewhat less recoil than the corresponding conventional loads, which should aid double-action smoothness, speed and accuracy. Mark up two positive psychological factors for DBs.

Killing power is rarely discussed by gun writers, because they don't want to sound bloodthirsty, I suppose. However, it must be considered here for completeness. In honesty, we must say that a trained combat shot always aims for the easiest, biggest target the body of his opponent presents, the chest. A hit there is likely to take the fight out of his assailant. If the aim is off slightly in any direction, a hit still has the probability of shaking up the attacker. Unfortunately, the chest is also a fatal area with conventional, deeply penetrating duty loads. Statistically, that has to mean that double-bulleting will reduce fatalities due to decreased penetration. This could be a strong argument in favor of DBs.

I think most of us do not welcome the thought of taking a human life, even to save our own, no matter how well justified we may feel in a given situation. The result has to be some hesitation to fire — at the very instant when speed is vital. The DB-equipped defender will believe that he is using ammunition which has a lowered fatality rate, and he may shoot faster when delay could be disastrous.

Double bullets should have a similar psychological effect to the empty rifle in the firing squad. Each member can believe that his was the empty rifle, and the DB shooter can hope that he has the chance of stopping his opponent without killing him. An important plus for DBs, especially for inexperienced or hesitant defensive shooters.

These are positive arguments for double bullets: greater stopping power, lower killing power, greater bystander safety, better psychological confidence, less hesitation to fire. But what about the negatives?

Lower penetration is a disadvantage if an officer has to shoot through an automobile or other obstacle. DBs would not be recommended for highway patrol work, or the like. One metropolitan police department has recently switched their ammunition to metal piercers, but the danger to innocent bystanders will soon cause a public outcry, it seems to me.

Poor DB carrying power is a possible disadvantage, but defensive shooting by definition is not a long-range proposition. Those 100-yard snap shots (no recoil, of course) look great on television, but very few experts would even attempt a handgun shot beyond 50–60 yards. At something like half of that distance, handgunning ceases to be truly defensive.

To my way of thinking, the potential advantages of DBs far outweigh the known disadvantages from the shooter's viewpoint. His main concern is surely to stop his attacker as quickly and positively as his firepower allows. A great deal of development and testing are needed before DB loads can be made available to police and others. Handloaders, however, can make and try them now.

Handgun hunting offers the toughest test for this new load. Having taken both black bear and wild boar with the 44 Magnum, I know that visions of a wounded, charging animal haunt the handgunner. In hunts for dangerous game, the use of DBs to back up hunting loads should yield hard answers about their stopping power.

Despite all that has been written about the power of the 44 Magnum, I know from personal experience that even the full-house 44 has none too much stopping power. My Colorado black bear, a 325-pounder, was shot at about 20 yards as he fought off a half-dozen slashing hounds. The 225-gr. Speer JHP slug knocked him back on his haunches, but he continued to take vicious swipes at the dogs. Three more shots, timed to miss the dodging pack, settled the matter. The first wound was probably fatal, but not instant poison.

My wild boar was also shot at bay at pretty close range, and before I could aim a second time, he disappeared in the brush. The dogs chased him under a rocky overhang on a muddy, slippery hillside. He showed no sign of injury, although we later found that the first slug had entered just behind the heart/lung area. I wrapped myself around a tree to hang on to the slope and put in the heart shot, aiming between two hounds as they dodged the 250-pound hog's short, vicious charges.

The point of describing these hunts is that heavy hunting loads in the most powerful of the handgun hunting calibers are not enough to down large, dangerous game instantly, even when shot placement is pretty good. Had these animals decided to head for me instead of concentrating on the hated dogs, I might have needed stoppers the worst way. DBs in the last two or three chambers should do a better job than hunting ammo in such a situation. Hunting is a striking, sporting use for DBs, but how about something closer to true defense?

Home protection is such a case, where stopping power is the prime consideration and decreased penetration is an important family safety factor. Handloaders who keep a handgun around for emergencies will want to work up the load carefully. Once it has been range-tested they can have confidence that it combines the most desirable characteristics for their purpose.

In summary, I believe the data and reasoning in this article justify a trial by the ammunition factories. Serious handloaders may speed that day along. The experimental work described here has been pleasurable to me, because handgunning and experimental hand-loading are favorite avocations. If this study proves helpful to the socially vital area of defensive handgunning, it will have been doubly rewarding.

Here's a movable, carefully-designed loading bench that; is easy to build and yet decorative in most areas. Complete plans, detailed instructions and a bill of materials are included. Grab a saw....

Compact Loading Bench

by **WM. F. GREIF**

THE LOT OF the reloader is a happy one these days. An almost limitless variety of presses, dies, gadgets and components are available to the cartridge stuffer, excepting only one basic necessity, the reloading bench itself!

Most handloaders would, I think, agree that something in modern monolithic, about 12 feet long, would just manage to fill their needs. Unfortunately, apartment dwellers like myself are apt to have unreasonable objections raised to our erecting a functionally attractive creation of 2×12s in the living room.

Having had to face this sad situation, I was told that if I built my little reloading center, it had damned well better be little *and* good looking, if I expected to keep it in any visible area of our home.

In laying out my plans, then, an attractive exterior, compact design and storage space were vital needs. The apartment-dwelling handloader has trouble right from the start finding enough storage space, and certainly esthetic reasons require concealment of equipment between working sessions. Weight and sturdiness were my next consideration. Weight that would keep the bench from jumping around could be attained in part by the storage of lead, bullets, cases, etc., and the use of fairly heavy structural components would also give me the sturdiness needed.

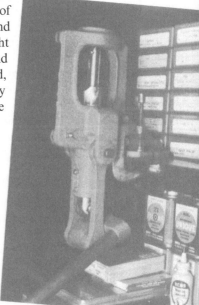

The inside shelves hold die sets, powder, etc. The RCBS press is stored inside vig C-clamps.

The completed compact loading bench, tools and components out, ready to go to work. Everything is handy, easily set up.

I decided on a basic closed box design, with interior shelving and a pegboard for the inside face of the door to give me maximum storage space. I also included a small cupboard on top, both for storage and to allow eyelevel placement of my powder scale. The work top was drilled with various holes so that all my presses, powder measures, etc., could be securely mounted on the top. While the counter as designed is more than strong enough, a masonite covering was added since the top is bound to become somewhat battered with the passage of time and a detachable one is easy to replace or to refinish.

Since I am not a journeyman cabinet maker by any means, my design was planned with emphasis on the simplest forms of construction, using basic hand tools and a minimum of power equipment. The average guy, given only a bit of skill and a few tools, can attack this project with confidence. Make no mistake, though, for my construction technique, while simple, is strong. Though I used butt or lap joints, with no mortising, everything is securely glued and screwed together. The heavy shelving also contributes mightily to the strength of the bench. The work top, made of two thicknesses of ply, totals a rigid 1½ inches thick, not counting the masonite.

Few Tools Needed

The plywood panel was cut on a table saw, but it could have been cut, as everything else was, with my sabre saw. I used an electric sander, which can be rented or, even better, borrowed from a friend. The only other power tool used was a ¼" electric drill.

Of course, if you have your lumber and masonite pre-cut and are willing to depend on elbow grease and a sanding block, the only power tool needed is the electric drill — all those screw holes make it a necessity. Incidentally, a great time and sweat saver is a little contoured spade bit made by Stanley. This marvelous gadget simultaneously cuts screwhole, shank relief hole and countersink! A bonus benefit is that each countersink is exactly the right depth. I did find that in tough ply, operations were greatly speeded by drilling a small pilot hole first.

As for finishes, I felt that a good stain varnish would be best for the interior, but the outside of the cabinet was something else. There would be so many screw heads pocking the bench surfaces that some sort of opaque finish would have to be used. Paint or lacquer wouldn't have suited our furnishings, so I used a self-adhesive, wood-grained vinyl. The one I chose, "Con-tact," is well known and nationally distributed. It comes in two widths, 18" and 27". Get the wider type to avoid seams. Con-tact comes in two or three different wood grains. I chose a dark walnut. The 5½ yards needed cost about $6.50.

Basic material is ¾" interior, A-D plywood. Flaws and knotholes on the D side can easily be handled with a little plastic wood. I chose plywood because of its superior strength and stiffness compared to plain lumber of like thickness. Elmer's glue was used on every joining surface and the basic box was tied together with 8×1½-" flat-head screws on 2" centers. (The cupboard top and the masonite work top were fastened with 8×1" screws; door construction and hinge used 6×5/8" wood screws.)

In the interest of economy, the bench was planned so that, with careful layout, all of the required pieces could be cut from one 4'×10' sheet of plywood. Since I planned on using a pegboard door interior, hollow door construction had to be used. For the door exterior, ¼" tempered masonite was used with 1/8" pegboard for the inside. The two panels were spaced ½" apart, using ½"×¾" stock for framing.

A door lock was added to discourage little noses from poking around where they shouldn't. For the top cabinet I used aluminum channel as sliding door guides, with 1/8" masonite doors. Be sure that you get the correct door height. The measurement I give is correct for the channel used, but yours may have different dimensions. Normally, the bottom channel will be ¼" deep and the top ½, to allow for door removal. Make sure your doors are 5/16" shorter than the maximum groove-to-groove measurement.

I wanted my unit to be movable so casters were indicated. I had some Fairbanks heavy duty 3" rubber wheel casters on hand, so I used them. Locking casters would be better, but those I had were sufficient for my purpose.

Because of the weight of the door when loaded with tools and other brie a brae, a piano hinge was used. Brass-plated steel is preferred to solid brass, both for its superior strength and much lower price. Piano hinge is only sold in 6" lengths, so you'll have to cut it to size and think up another project.

Standard cabinet knobs can be used for the doors, but for a distinctive touch I used 38 Spl. cases for the sliding cupboard doors and a 30-06 for the large door. Shotshell bases could also be used, say 12 gauge and 410, but no knobs are required, really. The doorlock key could serve well.

I designed the bench to be used while standing, or seated on a high stool. For those chores that take a bit of elbow grease, you can't beat getting off your butt and on to your feet.

Please note that I am 6' 2" tall and that you might want to

make some adjustment in bench height to suit your dimensions. Just leaving off the casters lowers the bench 3¾". I suggest setting up a mock work surface, at various heights, and decide for yourself.

Construction Notes

Now for the actual construction. Be extremely careful when laying out your cuts on the sheet of ply. There is little room for error, so check and recheck your layout before putting a saw to the panel and don't forget to allow for the saw cuts (kerfs) by adding the width of the teeth of your saw in figuring your layout. First, cut off the counter and top pieces, then cut the rest into the component pieces.

It's a good idea to pre-sand the bench parts, otherwise you'll find yourself scrunching into some pretty weird positions trying to finish those awkward spots.

Cut the rest of your material: Masonite, door framing, etc. In some cases, we'll cut and fit certain parts, but we won't install them permanently until we get to the final stage of applying the Con-tact. More on that later.

Assemble the sides and back with glue and screws, remembering that the back goes *between* the sides. Continue by putting in the shelves. The short (10") shelf was made shallower than the others to allow storage of my RCBS A2 press, which is held to the shelf with a "C" clamp. Spacing of the shelves is not critical. I spaced mine about 10" apart. Just remember to align the underside of the bottom shelf flush with the bottom of the bench as it will form part of the support for the casters.

To provide sufficient strength, the 8×1¼" screws should be spaced no more than 3" apart through the sides and back. Next, glue and screw the counter pieces together and attach to the bench proper. Lightly tack the cupboard top in place with a few brads, drill the attaching screw holes, then remove the cupboard top. Cut the door tracks to fit, but do not attach. Clamp the masonite

top to the counter and drill for the attaching screws. This is also the time to drill the top for the tool mounting holes. Plan carefully and use as few holes as possible.

Cut the masonite-pegboard doors and check for fit. Next, build the main door frame, with lock reinforcement. If it seems rather flimsy, don't worry. The door will get its rigidity from the masonite facings. Now fit the front and permanently attach it to the framing with the usual glue

Here's the pre-assembled loading bench, ready for the application of the Con-Tact vinyl covering material.

Bill of Materials

Quantity	Description
one	¾″×4′×10″ panel, interior A-D plywood
one	¼′×22 5/16″×41½″ tempered masonite door face
one	¼″×12″×24″ tempered masonite counter top
one	1/8″×22 5/16″×41½″ masonite pegboard
two	1/8″×71 5/16″×12″ tempered masonite — sliding doors
two	½″×¾″×21 9/16″ hardwood strips — door framing
two	½″×¾″×40¾″ hardwood strips — door framing
one	½″×¾″×6″ hardwood strip — lock support
one	½″×¾″×1½″ hardwood strip — door pull spacer
one	¾″×¾″×15″ hardwood strip — upper door stop strip
one	3/8″×¾″×24″ hardwood strip — lower door stop strip
four	Fairbanks Co. 21-3 heavy duty casters or Bassick SHB 13706 heavy d locking casters
one	set 1/8″ aluminum door channel — normally sold in 4′ lengths
one	1½″(open) 41″ long brass-plated steel piano hinge (sold in 6′ lengtl
one	cabinet lock & plate
three	brass or wood door pulls (or handmade; see text)
5½ yds.	Walnut Con-tact (27″ wide)′
one	C 8×1¼″ flathead wood screws — general work
2 dozen	8×1″ flathead wood screws — cupboard, work top
one	C 6×5/8″ flathead wood screws — door & hinge
4 dozen	6×¾″ flathead wood screws — door
4	6 1½″ flathead wood screws — door-framing
12	12×1½″ flathead wood screws — caster
4	12×¾″ flathead wood screws — caster
one	8-oz. Elmer's glue
one	8-oz. plastic wood or wood putty
one	qt. stain varnish
one	qt. shellac sandpaper, assorted

Compact Reloading Bench Materials

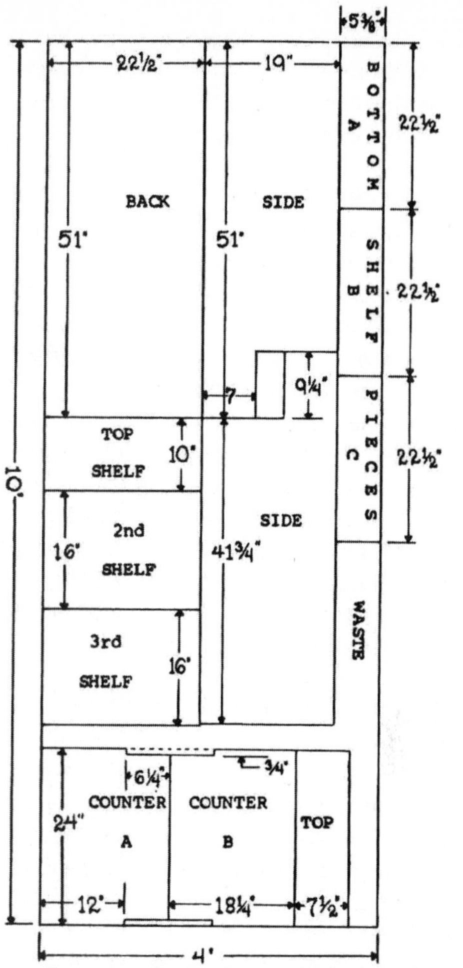
5⅜"
22½"
19"
BOTTOM A
SHELF B
PIECES C
WASTE
BACK
SIDE
51"
51"
22½"
22½"
22½"
TOP SHELF
10"
7
9¼"
2nd SHELF
16"
SIDE
41¾"
3rd SHELF
16"
10'
6¼"
¾"
COUNTER A
COUNTER B
TOP
24"
12"
18¼"
7½"
4'

Figure 1 — Cutting Pattern Scale .45" to 1'

Figure 2 — Door Details Scale .90" to 1' Door Door Frame

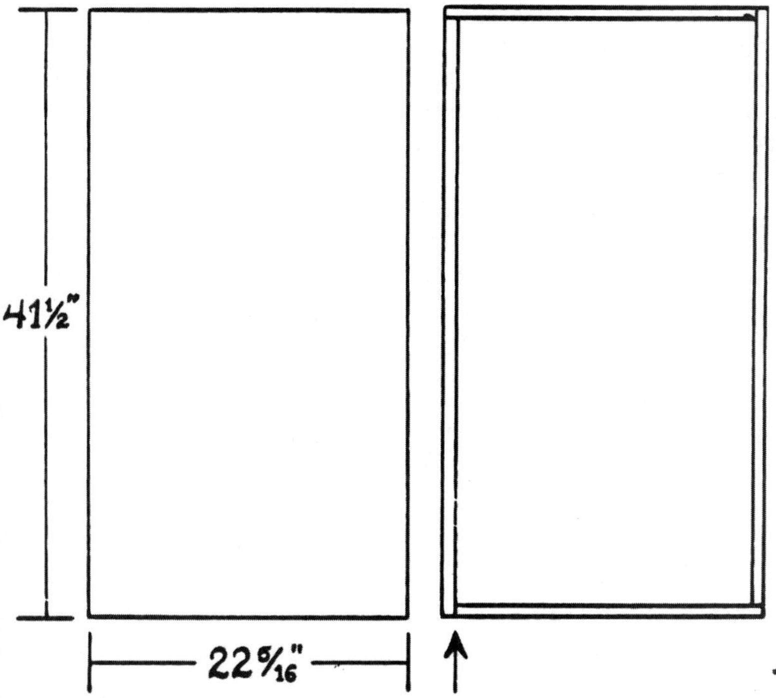
41½"
22 9/16"

Figure 1A — Bench Side Scale .75" to 1'

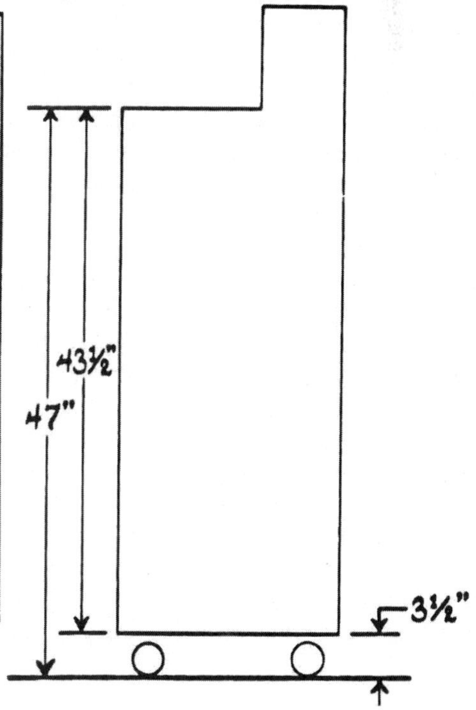
43½"
47"
3½"

and screws. Next, carefully position the wooden block that will act as the door knob spacer and reinforcement and nail and glue it to the inside of the door face. Now, temporarily attach the inside face and drill it and the frame for the mounting screws. Next, drill through the door sandwich for the door knob screw and for the lock cylinder, then remove the inner face. I placed the lock 16" from the top of the door to the center of the lock. The length of the door stop pieces in the bill of materials reflects this positioning, so if you decide to reposition the lock, be sure to alter the length of the two door stop pieces to match. Cut the piano hinge and fit it to the inside of the left wall so that the door can be opened to a full 180 degrees. Mark the bench and door and drill both for the hinge screws. With this done, fill all the screw holes, cracks, etc., with plastic wood or wood putty. Let it dry thoroughly, at least for 24 hours, before sanding. Then sand the entire bench. Be sure that all spots you filled are level and slightly chamfer all the outside edges.

With the construction and sanding completed, we have only to apply our finish.

Con-tact Vinyl Finish

Con-tact won't adhere to raw wood so all surfaces to be covered must receive a coat of shellac to seal them. For those surfaces not to be covered by Con-tact, brush on one (preferably two) coats of stain varnish. Let dry for several days so that the varnish and shellac are good and hard.

Before applying the Con-tact, read the directions printed on the backing material, and keep these hints in mind when you start using the stuff.

When cutting the material, allow enough extra for folding over the edges and, when actually laying the Con-tact, be sure that the surfaces to be covered are scrupulously clean. I found that tiny pieces of grit will stick out like a sore thumb. Work in a clean area and, when you are about to apply a piece of Con-tact, wipe the surface with a clean, lint-free cloth. If, despite your precautions you should miss some debris, the Con-tact can be carefully pulled up and relaid. Pull off the backing little by little, as you apply the covering, and press it down with a soft cloth to eliminate bubbles and avoid stretching.

Now we come to the reason for not completely assembling the bench during construction. By covering the various portions of the bench and *then* doing our final assembly, we hide and firmly fasten the edges of the Con-tact under the joints, hinges and so on.

First cover the cupboard top. Screw the upper aluminum track to it and set it aside. Now cover the front edge of the countertop. After that, cover the sides, working from the bottom up. On the side where the hinge will fasten, be sure that the Con-tact laps around a hair less than the width of the hinge. On the opposing side, carry the vinyl around on the inside so that its edge will be covered and secured by the door stop strips.

Cover the door, attach the pegboard-backing (which will seal down the edges of the Con-tact) and attach the hinge. An easy way to find the screwholes covered by the Con-tact is to press along the area with your fingers, making a depression at each hole and then pierce the spots with a pointed tool. Cover the small sliding doors, attach the knobs and you're ready to finish our assembly.

Attach the masonite work top and the lower sliding door track. Hang the main door and then attach the cupboard top. Use a razor blade to trim away the excess material over the screw holes. If you drilled your screw holes carefully, the screws will pull up flush, or very slightly below the surface. I used a ½" wadcutter to cut pieces of Con-tact to cover the screw heads, which gives a doweled effect.

Now coat the lock bolt edge with a marking medium such as chalk. Close and align the door so that it is flush with the front edge of the right wall and turn the lock so that the bolt will make a clear impression on the inside wall. Use your razor and cut away enough Con-tact to clear the bolt, then cut a recess in the side wall for it. With that done, attach the lock-plate.

The last items are the stop strips. Cover them with Con-tact, carefully measure the thickness of the door, then lightly tack the upper strip in place, the thickness of the door from the edge. Check the accuracy of the placement, then nail permanently in place. Follow the same procedure with the lower strip.

All that's left to do is to re-attach the casters, which I hope you removed when you were applying the covering to the sides.

As a finishing touch, I bought an unfinished bar stool and finished it to match, complete with a foam rubber, Naugahyde-covered seat.

The completed project has been a great success. It gives me a lot of bench in a very small space, (three square feet to be exact) yet it isn't an eyesore to the rest of the family.

So, if you've stuck with me this far, put your tool hooks on the door, load the cabinet with your reloading equipment and get to it!

33

ABC's of
Reloading

Full and detailed information on making any rifle — old or modern — perform well, whatever the caliber, with low-level, pleasant loads.

Shooting Lead Bullets

by RON WOZNY

FIRST OF ALL the author claims no supreme expertise, no magic formula for casting perfect bullets every time, or infallible loads that shoot perfectly. What I'm going to attempt is to show you how to develop a low velocity lead bullet load that will shoot well in *your* rifle or rifles.

I've had some 20 years of reading everything available, absorbing and discounting thousands of words of advice, and there have been countless hours of enjoyment in correlating information — loads, lubes and so on — at the range.

First of all, check your barrel's rate of twist. It could be too fast or too slow to stabilize your chosen bullet. Using a very, very tight patch on a cleaning rod, put a mark on the rod and push it into the barrel for a half-turn or a full turn. Now measure the distance from the mark to the muzzle. If you made a half-turn double it and you have your rate of twist. The full turn, of course, represents the total twist.

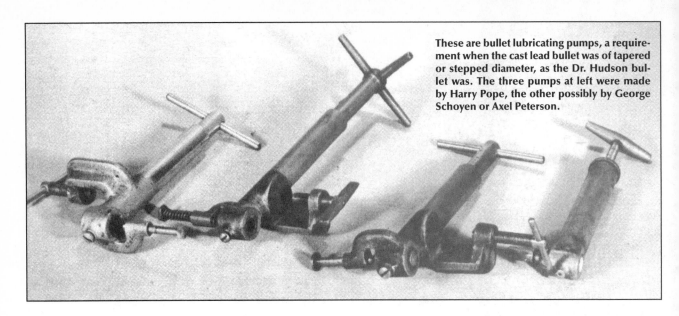

These are bullet lubricating pumps, a requirement when the cast lead bullet was of tapered or stepped diameter, as the Dr. Hudson bullet was. The three pumps at left were made by Harry Pope, the other possibly by George Schoyen or Axel Peterson.

At left is a modern recapping tool, no longer made and the only such device familiar to me that is adjustable for case-base variations — rotating the tool's head section cams the case upward against its shell holder, removing all play. At center an Ideal bullet sizer, a pivoted pin pushing the bullet through an exchangeable bushing. Last, the well-known H. M. Pope re- and decapper, its fixed head not interchangeable. Jerry Simmons' like tool has replaceable heads and most calibers are available.

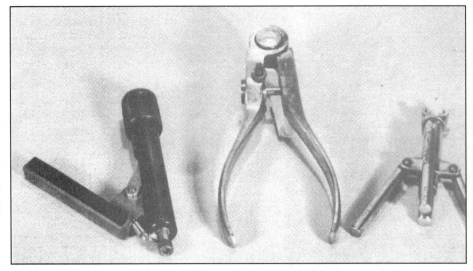

Elementary, huh? Don't laugh! I took out a new (to me) 38-50 Martini rifle by Toggenburger of Chicago and proceeded to shoot a nice round 4" or 5" group, with every bullet printing perfectly sideways! Why? I had neglected to measure the twist, which I'd assumed was a normal 16 or 18 inch, but which was, in fact, 26 inches. That rifle required a short, almost wadcutter form of bullet, a mould for which I obtained. After that it shot and still shoots inch groups when I do my part. So check your twist; if it's slow for the caliber use a shorter bullet, if faster use a longer projectile. For instance, in 30 caliber barrels 10 inches is fast (as in the 30-06) whereas 16 or 17 inches is slow as in the 30 carbine, the 32-20, etc. In 45 caliber barrels a 16" or 18" twist is fast, 22 to 24 inches about normal, and 26 to 28 is rather slow. Many of the old single shots and hunting rifles, those made for so-called "Express" cartridges, had a relatively slow twist; they used rather light bullets in order to get fairly high velocity from lead bullets and black powder. Please note that I write in generalities, because there is little agreement, even today, on what is "correct" twist. Each rifle of the older types under discussion will have to be approached carefully and thoughtfully to attain the best results.

Now to barrels. I've read and heard much hogwash from self-anointed experts, shooting "authorities" and manufacturers singing the praises of our modern precision production rifles. Most of this has related to fit, to bore and groove consistency, barrel finish and so on. After measuring several new beauties of mine I think we should go back to the handmade era. In the old days buyers of target rifles, at least, usually received a mould (and other tools) with the rifle, one that was made or selected to match its bore/groove dimensions.

I've found new barrels running from 0.001" to 0.0015" under factory specifications and to 0.002" and 0.003" over! That's precision? One close friend has a new single action revolver, made by a famous U.S. maker, that's a full 5 thousandths (0.005") over standard groove diameter. The poor beginner reading this may throw up his hands and say "Hoo boy, what now?" Well, it's really rather simple. We go back to the old days again, match the bullet to the barrel's groove diameter and twist, and with cast lead bullets we're in business, no matter what.

Now again you're going to say "How?" OK, take a soft lead slug somewhat over bore diameter and position it atop the muzzle. (A round ball or a soft lead revolver bullet works well.) Now, with an under-bore diameter wooden dowel tap the lead slug carefully down the barrel, stopping it about 1½ or 2 inches below the muzzle. Next insert a flat ended longer rod, ideally just under bore size, from the breech. Have a helper hold the breech rod against the slug, then tap the upper dowel with a mallet — gently — to upset (expand) the slug into the rifling grooves. Push the slug out the muzzle and catch it carefully. If you're checking a lever action or the like upset a tight slug and push it all the way through the breech. Carefully, though, as any loose spots or rough spots might upset your measurements and you might want to allow 0.0005" to 0.001" for imperfect fit for driving the slug the length of the barrel. Now, using a micrometer, measure the slug carefully and gently across the full groove diameter. The soft lead can be easily squeezed, resulting in a false reading. Usually this groove dimension is fairly close to normal, and buying the correct mould and sizing die should give you good results. By the way, many well worn and rough looking barrels will shoot well by using oversize bullets to fit the worn bore. A friend's 7mm Mauser is worn so badly he uses a 0.289" bullet for quite good results, whereas 0.284" is standard. It and an old Norwegian Krag of mine with a rough dark bore showed a marked improvement after shooting several hundred gas check linotype bullets. Their accuracy continues to improve also.

Moulds

Usually moulds available commercially deliver bullets enough oversize so that correct sizing to full groove diameter is possible. I find that a full groove diameter bullet is necessary for good accuracy when using plain base bullets. When using gas checks on 30-cal. bullets they may be sized .309" and I use as much as .311" oversize in .308"-.309" bores for good results. Remember we're discussing target loads at relatively low velocity with gas checked or plain-base bullets, so pressures are rarely a problem. However, each load, each bullet and rifle is quite individual, and good results are achieved by attention to detail, not guessed at or obtained from a reference book. Just take it easy, work up your load from below, starting 5% or 10% under any suggested maximum loading.

Watch your primers for flattening. If you see pressure signs your loads are too hot for good lead bullet results anyway. Many lead bullet shooters use pistol primers, which have relatively soft cups, and they show pressure signs very easily. My 32-20 Winchester High Wall, which likes 10.5 gr. of Dupont 4227, shows pressure signs at 11.5 and occasionally pops a primer if I'm using Remington

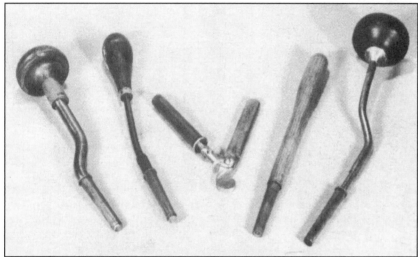

Five breech bullet starters, generally required to seat bullets with oversize base bands or having multi-diameters. The four long tools are early types, the center device is a lever type built to be used on Ballard actions. All use a cartridge case — its head drilled out — sliding on a metal shaft, to center and guide the bullet into the chamber.

Three old bullet moulds. At left a 19th century Ideal Perfection for grease-grooved bullets, but also offered for paper-patched (smooth) bullets. The leg in the foreground is a machine screw, used to propel and position an internal bullet-base section, which permits a wide variation in bullet length/weight. At center is a rare specimen, made and so-marked by the Remington Arms Co. In cal. 32- **40 B&M, this mould has double cutoffs for the sprues (top and bottom), the top cutoff plate unusually and commendably thick for better rigidity and heat holding. This mould came with a "Remington Schuetzen" rifle (a much-modified No. 3 or Hepburn action) and was probably made about 1888-1890. The third mould is a pre-1900 Winchester of conventional construction.**

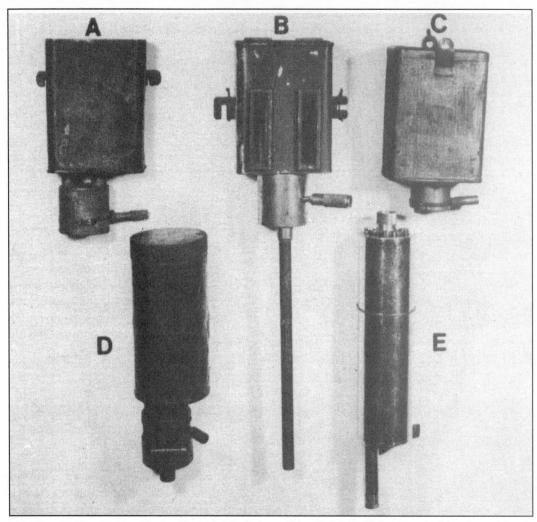

Early-day powder measure, but quite accurate and reliable then and now. All but one (E) are designed to throw two charges atone lever movement — a small priming charge, black or smokeless, and the main charge. Only C is not adjustable for charge weight or volume via the rotatable sections below the reservoir(s). Measures A, C and D have, literally, powder reservoirs made from commercial baking powder tins or canisters, these attached to brass (or brass and steel) discharge devices below. The measure B is a more refined version, the 2-window (glass of sturdy metal stock with two threaded caps atop for powder loading. The adjustable lever-handled unit is nickel-plated. The drop tube seen was a standard and removable fitting — measures A, C and D are shown without their drop tubes. Measure E is an early Ideal Mfg. Co. type, adjustable for charge weight via the short tube at bottom. In use this all-nickeled measure was turned end-for-end to position the charge, then turned again to discharge.

1½ pistol primers. When using rifle primers I went up to 14 grains with no pressure signs but no better results either. Pistol primers are used with such powders as 4227 and 4759 as a hot primer might flash through the light charge, moving the bullet before the main charge ignites.

Big Bores, Little Bullets

In my considered opinion more barrels are harmed or ruined by the use of undersized bullets than from the number of rounds shot. The hot powder gases squirting by a too-small bullet raise hell with a barrel, doing far worse damage than will a full sized bullet or an oversized one loaded lightly. This also applies to jacketed bullets. I'll probably get a lot of flack on that comment, but I'd bet most of the jacketed-bul-

let barrels that show early wear or shoot out quickly were oversized to start with or were fed bullets slightly undersized. It's possible to upset an undersized bullet with black powder or even a jacketed one in a loose barrel with hot smokeless loads. Think of all the articles you have read showing loads running over indicated maximum. Usually they're accompanied by "approach with caution" or "not recommended in your rifle," etc. I'm sure that if the barrel were measured it would be oversized or the chamber too big; the too-large chamber gives, in effect, a larger capacity case than would result otherwise. I have a 22-250 custom Mauser with a 28-inch barrel. When chronographed (using two instruments, an Oehler and a Potter) it averaged 4000 fps for 5 shots, using 36 grains of 4320 and a 52-gr. BT bullet. Impossible? No,

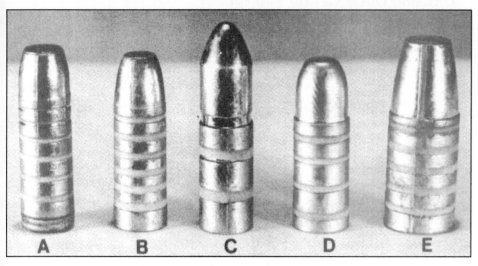

Lead bullets cast and processed by the author. All require pan lubrication. A is 175-gr. 30 cal. Pope-Gibson type cast in an old Hensley & Gibbs mould of linotype metal. The gaschecked base is 0.311" diameter, larger than rest of body. B is 170-gr. 30-cal. Pope style cast in Lyman 311403 mould of 30-1 lead-tin. This tapered bullet has 0.314" base. C is a Dr. Hudson 2-diameter 30-cal. bullet of 210 grains cast 30-1. D is 182 gr. 32-40 bullet from H&G mould, cast 10-1 from wheelweights. Body taper is 0.318"-0320". E is a 310-gr. bullet of 0.412", cast in a point-cut off mould and is tapered.

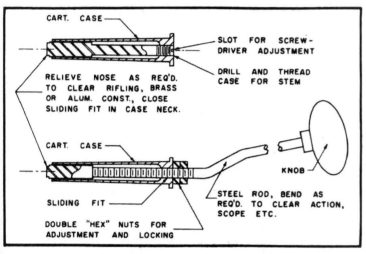

Here's how to make a breech bullet seater, the design and drawing by Dennis Hrusosky, a long-time shooter of schuetzen rifles — old and new.

just a tight and choked barrel by Adolph Pfeiffer, chamber and headspace right on by Paul Chan and everything else just right. In fact it just barely shows pressure signs, only marginal primer cratering, and it gives ½-minute accuracy — I won't argue! This is getting a long way from the subject but helps to show what precision loading can do.

Bullet Alloys

Now to bullet temper. Bullet weight and diameter will vary with the temper or alloy used. A large heavy bullet will shrink in cooling more than a small and light one, all else being equal. By adding more tin and/or antimony, or going to linotype or similar metal, your mould will cast larger bullets, which is to say they shrink less. How much? That depends on you, mould and metal temperature, the

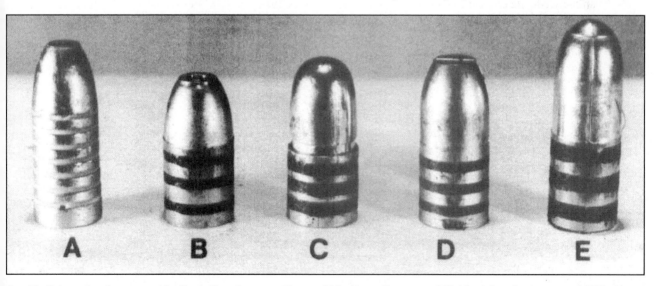

Lead bullets cast and processed by the author. A was cast in mould by Henry Beverage of 30-1 lead-tin mix, measures 0.439" at base (tapered) and weighs 392 grains. B is 333-gr. Gould hollow-point 45 ceil, bullet cast of 10-1 wheelweights and sized to 0.460" diameter. C is 375-gr. 45-cal. bullet cast in Lyman 457124 mould of 10-1 metal and sized to 0.460⊠. D weighs 383 grains, was cast 10-1 in Ohaus mould and sized to 0.460" for 45-cal. shooting. E is from old Winchester mould, weighs 471 grains and as cast measures 0.454⊠. It was sized as shown to 0.453", the mix 10-1 lead tin.

Groove Diameters and Rifling Twists
U.S. and Other Center Fire Rifles

Caliber and Cartridge	Make	Groove Diameter Inches		Twist of Rifling 1 turn in – inches
		Min.	Max.	
22 W.C.F.	Winchester	.224	.2245	16
22 Baby H.P.	Niedner	.223	.2235	16
22 Savage H.P.	Savage	.226	.2265	12
6mm Lee Navy	Winchester	.242	.244	7½
25 Stevens R.F.	All	.257	.2575	17
25-20 S&W C.F.	Winchester	.257	.2575	14
25-35 W.C.F.	Winchester	.257	.2575	8
25-36 Marlin	Marlin	.257	.2575	9
25 Rem. Auto	Remington	.257	.2575	10
25 Niedner, Spg. & Krag	Niedner	.2565	.2575	12
250-3000 Savage	Savage	.257	.258	14
6.5mm Mannlicher	Austrian	.263	.264	7½
256 Newton	Newton	.264	.265	10
270 W.C.F.	Winchester	.278	.2785	10
28-30 Stevens	Stevens	.285	.286	14
7mm Mauser	German	.2854	.2874	8.66
7mm Mauser	American	.2854	.2855	10
280 Ross	Ross	.289	.290	8.66
30-30 W.C.F.	Winchester	.308	.3085	12
30-30 Rem. Auto	Remington	.308	.3085	12
30 Krag	U.S. Govt.	.308	.310	10
30-06 Springfield	U.S. Govt.	.308	.309	10
300 Savage	Savage	.308	.309	10
30 Magnum	Griffin & Howe	.3083	.3085	14
32-20 W.C.F.	Winchester	.311	.3115	20
32 Ideal	Stevens	.323	.324	18
32-40 W., B. & M.	Winchester	.320	.3205	16
32 Win. Special	Winchester	.320	.3205	16
32 Rem. Auto	Remington	.319	.3195	14
8mm Mauser	German	.318	.326	9 to 10
303 British	English	.312	.314	10
303 Savage	Savage	.308	.309	10
32 Win. Self-Loading	Winchester	.321	.322	16
33 W.C.F.	Winchester	.338	.3385	12
35 Win. Self-Loading	Winchester	.351	.352	16
351 Win. Self-Loading	Winchester	.351	.352	16
35 Rem. Auto	Remington	.356	.3565	16
35 W.C.F.	Winchester	.358	.3585	12
35 Whelen	Griffin & Howe	.357	.3575	18
35 Newton	Newton	.359	.359	12
35 Magnum	Griffin & Howe	.357	.3575	18
375 Magnum	Hoffman	.375	.376	14
38-40 W.C.F.	Winchester	.400	.4005	36
38-40 W.C.F.	Remington	.400	.4005	20
38-55 W., B. & M.	Winchester	.379	.3795	18
38-56 W.C.F.	Winchester	.379	.3795	20
38-70-255 W.C.F.	Winchester	.379	.3795	24
38-72-275 W.C.F.	Winchester	.379	.3795	22
38-90 W.C.F.	Winchester	.379	.3795	26
40-50 Sharps Straight	Winchester	.403	.405	18
40-70 S.S. and Ballard	Winchester	.403	.405	20
40-70-330 Win.	Winchester	.403	.405	20
40-72-330 Win.	Winchester	.406	.407	22
40-82-260 Win.	Winchester	.403	.405	28
40-90 Sharps Straight, 3¼	Winchester	.403	.405	18
40-110 Win.	Winchester	.403	.405	28
40-60 Win.	Winchester	.403	.405	40
400 Whelen	Griffin & Howe	.4105	.4115	14
401 Win., S.L.	Winchester	.407	.408	14
404 Magnum	Hoffman	.423	.424	14
405 Winchester	Winchester	.413	.4135	14
43 Spanish	Winchester	.439	.440	20
44-40 W.C.F.	Winchester	.4285	.429	36
44 Henry R.F.	Winchester	.4285	.4295	36
45-60 W.C.F.	Winchester	.456	.458	20
45-70 Winchester	Winchester	.456	.458	20
45-70 U.S. Govt.	U.S. Govt.	.457	.458	22
45-70 W.C.F.	Winchester	.456	.458	20
45-90 W.C.F.	Winchester	.456	.458	32
45-125 W.C.F.	Winchester	.456	.458	36
45 Sharps, 3¼	Sharps	.458	.459	18
50 Sharps	Sharps	.509		
50-95 Winchester	Winchester	.512		60
50-110-450 Win.	Winchester	.512		54
50-70 Govt.	U.S. Govt.	.515		24 & 42
505 Magnum	Hoffman	.5045	.5055	16
58 Govt. M.L.	U.S. Govt.	.590		68

particular alloy in use. To further cloud the issue hard alloys seem to require a gas check in many cases or leading occurs. Why? Well, the harder the metal alloy the lower the melting (or freezing) temperature of the bullet. I know that's hard to believe, but it's true; pure lead is harder to melt than linotype and other hard mixes. In plain base bullets I vary my alloys from 10-1 lead and tin (speaking in general terms again for simplicity and ignoring the antimony) to 30-1 to reach a certain size, ease of loading, and results. Every time I've used pure linotype in plain base bullets I've had leading problems, but that doesn't mean it might not work for you in different circumstances. I also often find that bullets shot as cast (not sized) or sized less than 0.001', shoot much better than those sized down several thousandths. Moral — vary your bullet temper, within limits, so that you need to size as little as possible. Or pan lube and shoot bullets as cast, which is what many of our single shot shooters do.

Bullet Lubes

I'm going to touch on lubes with some hesitancy. First, because no one agrees on which is best, and also because I don't think one lube will work in every application. That's a hard fact well known to old time lead bullet shooters. True, an alox/beeswax lube comes closest to an all-round lube when used in a lubrisizer or grease pump. However, don't try to pan lube with it for re-heating seems to break it down, after which it leads heavily. In using lubrisizers with multi-grooved bullets I've had good success with Lyman and Green Bay lubes, my own and various others. However, I use alox and beeswax on all bullets with only one or two grease grooves, for it seems to do a better job in this application.

For pan lubing I use an American Single Shot Rifle Association formula developed by several shooters (Rupe Hill, Marve Manny, and Don Metzler), plus my own variations. It's somewhat complicated in that the waxes have to be special ordered, but it's the only lube (except Pope's) that can be re-used over and over in pan lubing. I pan lube by using muffin tins or pans of any convenient size or shape. Stand the bullets upright and pour in the melted lube. Let it cool completely and the bullets may be pressed out with the thumb, perfectly clean and ready to use. The Pope lube is not quite as good in hot weather; it must be kept out of the sun. The ASSRA lube is perfectly stable in hot or cold weather and gives excellent and uniform results. I spent several years arriving at these conclusions, via a hell of a lot of shooting, so I'll stick with my goop till someone proves theirs is better. Here it is:

9 oz. beef or mutton tallow (I use mutton).

2 oz. ozocerite.

1 oz. bayberry wax.

1 oz. Japan wax.

5 oz. yellow beeswax.

2 tablespoons steam cylinder oil.

Another good lube is the old Harry Pope lube:

6 oz. mutton tallow.

4 oz. bayberry wax.

2 oz. beeswax.

2 oz. steam cylinder oil.

2 teaspoons of colloidal graphite (may be omitted).

This is an excellent lube but must be kept out of the hot sun or not left overly long in a hot barrel.

These two lubes must be mixed and reheated for re-use, using a double boiler to prevent burning.

The waxes are available from:

Frank B. Ross Co., Inc., 6 Ash Street, Jersey City, NJ 07304.

Will Scientific Inc., P. O. Box 2003, Rochester, NY 14603.

A. C. Drury Co., 421 E. Illinois St., Chicago, IL 60611.

The tallows may be had from your butcher and rendered out in a large pan. Get the steam cylinder oil from a commercial lubricant supplier.

I've kept these tips general, hence any caliber can benefit. Here's an example:

A 32-40 Rifle

A 32-40 Winchester High Wall rifle I have was barreled by Adolph Niedner years ago, the barrel in excellent condition and the work first class. Yet that barrel gave me trouble in the beginning — leading, bullet selection, grouping. Then I discovered that its groove diameter ran 0.325"-0.326", well off standard dimensions, and the rate of twist one turn in 14". It shows a liking for fairly soft bullets, 30 parts lead and one part tin, and a charge of 13.5 grains of DuPont 4759 powder. The bullets used are the Pope tapered-diameter style or a Lyman Hudson-type, No. 319273. Either weighs about 180 grains as cast, and their bore diameters are held to 0.326" and 0.325" respectively.

Anything harder in temper drops the accuracy, and the barrel is fussy about the bullet lube used, preferring the Manny-Metzler type or Pope's formula. Other lubes tried produced light to severe leading.

This 32-40 Niedner shoots best when the bullet is breech-seated ahead of the case mouth 1/16, and a card — postcard thickness is about right usually — pushed down into the case to lie on the powder lightly.

Loading Tools

Breech-seating tools were made long ago by Lyman-Ideal, and they're offered today by Darr Rifle Co. and others. These consist usually of a steel rod holding a 32-40 (or other caliber) case drilled out at the head, the rod passing through the case and lock-screw adjustable to permit the bullet to be seated in the rifle's throat as desired. An offset arm, with a knobbed palm seat, completes the breech seater.

Other types of breech seaters are used — a hinged form was and is made, these operating via a short steel pin set into the receiver, on which the breech seater attaches for each seating operation.

Other rifles may well call for variations in chambering the cartridge, with or without the bullet seated in the case mouth. Experimentation is required — try seating the bullet shallowly in the case mouth, with or without a wad (card, thin cork, etc.) seated on the powder, then pushing the cartridge into the chamber and letting the breechblock seat the cartridge fully, if the action permits such camming action.

The barrel throat may be eroded enough to require seating the bullet farther out, to engage the lands, than the 1/16" 1 find most effective with my 32-40 Niedner. I have a 28-30 rifle which requires seating the bullet 5/16" ahead of the case! I've had no undue pressure signs or collapsed case walls — which can occur with such seating and light powder charges. The low gas pressure can get between the chamber walls and the case, pushing the case walls inward. However, I use two wads when shooting the 28-30 — a cork wad over the powder and a card at the case mouth.

Range Loading

Shooting of the kind implied here means doing the loading at the bench, not at home — and therefore the shooting box is usually a pretty hefty one.

Many such shooters use only one or two cases for a day's shooting, for several reasons, otherwise it might be supposed that a batch of cartridges could be processed at home. But often enough temperature and humidity call for a small alteration in the powder charge, or one might want to try out a "new" bullet, one of different composition or weight, one with more or fewer grease grooves, and so on. Using the one case over and over is feasible because the light powder charges generate low pressures that do not heavily expand the case in the chamber, thus no full length sizing is necessary, nor does the case mouth need squeezing down to hold the bullet tightly — breech seating obviates the need. Such cases, so used, can be fired hundreds of times!

As I've said, such shooting calls for several bench tools — a portable reand decapper is a necessity. The double-arm Pope style, as made by Jerry Simmons, is a popular one, its case-holding heads interchangeable for various calibers. These work quickly and efficiently without removing the fired case from the tool until the primer is seated. Simple rod and-base decappers are also used, in which instances such recappers as the Lee and Lyman can be used, either often modified by attaching primer magazines.

Loading at the shooting bench requires a powder measure, of course, but powder scales are seldom seen — if for no other reason than the difficulty of weighing charges in the open. The Lyman No. 5 is a popular measure, as are the Belding & Mull and the Redding. The last two, because of their slide-across measuring, work well with 4759 powder, a coarse grained type.

The long-discontinued Ideal No. 6 measure was a great favorite in the days when dual powder charges were thrown. It was, in fact, brought forth to meet such a need, following the success of such measures made by Pope, Schoyen and others.

These measures had two powder reservoirs, one of less capacity than the other — for the priming charge — and both adjustable for volume. Black powder, then as now, fouled the barrel and prevented accurate shooting unless removed, and the removal process was tedious and time-consuming. When smokeless powders were introduced — among them, later on, types intended to take the place of black powder — it was soon discovered that small charges of one or another of them, say 10% or so of the main charge of black powder, acted materially in keeping the rifle bores cleaner and permitted the firing of several shots without cleaning — sometimes of many shots.

The dual-charge measure followed that discovery and, in more recent years, the mode of loading was reversed — priming charges of black powder were used, in those same measures, to make ignition of some smokeless powders easier.

All in all lead shooting can be a lot of fun at a bargain price in these days of high component costs. It's about the only way of doing a lot of shooting at the expense of some of your leisure time, which could well be the enjoyable part. To top it off accuracy can be excellent and the wear and tear on your precious barrel is practically zero.

Have fun, and I hope your results are as pleasurable as mine.

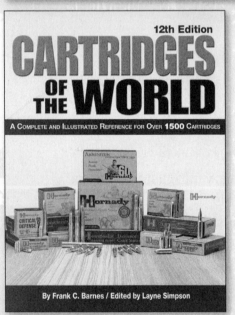